2024
California Bar Exam Total Preparation Book

www.CaliforniaBarTutors.com

About This Book

Scope

The purpose of this book is to help you pass the bar exam and become an attorney. Those looking for a legal practice guide, a pro-se handbook, or a philosophical discussion on jurisprudence will be disappointed. In order to pass the bar exam, you must know the rules of law that are tested, and that is what we aim to provide.

In this book, the lawyers, law professors, former bar graders, and retired judges who have contributed to this book have attempted to distil what you need to know into succinct rules of law that can be written in the exam. Consequently, a level of prior education is assumed on the part of the reader. If you did not have the opportunity to take the corresponding class during your legal education, we recommend that you first review a hornbook for that particular subject before committing the rules contained within this book to memory.

Ultimately, our goal at CBT is to help you. If you have any suggestions or feedback as to how we can help you more effectively, we want to hear from you. Please feel free to reach out to us at any time at **Admin@CaliforniaBarTutors.com**

Our Comprehensive Outlines

The legal issues and discussions contained under the umbrella of each legal subject are forever expanding. It is overwhelming to consider the testing possibilities for each individual subject. It would be quite possible to have a three-day exam that tests only one subject and still leave large areas untouched. Knowing what to include in an outline is a daunting proposition for bar takers and bar review companies alike.

Some companies take the "kitchen sink" approach where everything they can think of is included in their materials. The problem with this approach is that people only have a limited amount of cognitive capacity from which detailed recollection is possible. This results in large areas of law not being reviewed by the bar taker and the corresponding feeling of being overwhelmed and unprepared hampers bar exam performance.

At CBT, we consider the "kitchen sink" approach to be not only lazy, but also counterproductive. We believe it is important to consider whether a certain issue is testable before adding it to an outline. Additionally, we believe it is important to moderate the attention paid to a particular issue based on its testing frequency and propensity. As CBT's staff of lawyers, law professors, former bar graders, and retired judges will tell you, this intense study of the bar exam is not easy, but it's worth it!

As a result, following a review of the last 30 years of bar exams and recent testing trends, CBT's comprehensive outlines attempt to cover the testable areas of the bar exam in the requisite detail needed to pass the exam. We recommended that these outlines be the primary study material up until three weeks before the exam. At that time, we recommend that bar takers move on to the Primer outlines.

Our Primer Outlines

By the time the exam is just weeks away, you will have covered a great deal of material and you will hopefully have a solid understanding of the rules and their applications. Additionally, you will have a greater need for efficiency and succinctness in your study as you begin to quickly move from subject to subject in your final review. Primer outlines are designed to assist you in this endeavour.

By reducing the legal rules and concepts rules to their fundamental requirements, Primer outlines are designed to elicit the further understanding and detail that you have acquired over the course of your study. Use them for quick review and reference as you begin to work independently of your study aids and towards being exam-ready.

Our Issue Spotters

One of the main reasons people fail the bar exam is that they do not spot all of the relevant issues raised by a fact pattern. Most people rely on the assumption that their years of legal education will result in issues becoming apparent to them as they read through the facts. This is a passive issue spotting technique. Unfortunately, this only works for some of the issues and it leaves the bar taker in a position where he or she must do an outstanding job on the issues discussed in order to obtain a passing score.

At CBT, we recommend taking an active approach to issue spotting. Our recommended approach not only helps you spot more issues, but it reduces your stress along the way!

How does it work? It's quite simple. Start by reading the question twice to identify the subject(s) tested. Write out your checklists on your scratch paper and then begin to outline your answer. While outlining your answer, use the checklists to actively hunt for issues. Make a conscious determination whether each of the issues in your checklist are raised by the fact pattern – you'll be surprised how many additional issues you may have missed!

What is a checklist? A checklist is a list of each of the major issues / issue groups within each of the tested subjects. We have examples for you in this book, but we encourage bar takers to create their own based on their knowledge base. For instance, if you are someone who never forgets the elements required to form a valid contract, perhaps you will simply have "Valid Formation" on your contracts checklist. However, if you have a particular weakness (you frequently miss a certain issue in practice), make sure it's on your list!

Customize your checklists to fit you and then memorize them. Do not be afraid to use acronyms or other memory devices to help you recall each of the items on your checklists.

Preparation Tips

The bar exam is probably the most important exam you will undertake in your professional life. Here at CBT we understand exactly what is required of you in order to pass the bar. We have enlisted some of the top experts in law and education to provide the best possible experience, enabling you to pass with flying colors. To start you on your journey our experts have shared some of their 'top tips' for successful preparation for the bar exam:

Do Not Cram — Plan!

Start early, study often. It is a horrible cliché to say, "Rome was not built in a day", but it underscores what we all already know to be true: you cannot expect to accomplish something significant in a very short period of time.

How long will it take for you to learn enough of the legal rules and the correct essay approaches in order to pass the bar exam? It varies by person, but for everyone it takes times and patience. The good news is that you have been preparing since your first day of law school. Bar preparation is about refining your legal knowledge and learning the correct strategies to employ on the actual exam.

Whether you are preparing with CBT, by yourself, or with another company, CBT wants you to get started with your prep as soon as possible. Create a long-term plan that permits you to learn the information you need. Right now, you might only have time on your lunch break or on your commute, and the time period might be so short that you are tempted to skip it. Resist the temptation. Break up your bar exam review into chunks that are small and manageable, which is much better for learning and memory retention – not to mention reducing your stress levels!

Take every opportunity to study and do not worry about how much time you have. It all adds to your understanding and you will be surprised how much progress you will make. So do not put it off, grab some flash cards, an outline, or download a lecture and get going!

Memorization: The Power of Flash Cards

Flash cards are often the unsung heroes of bar exam preparation. They provide a quick, on the go review of the main legal rules and their exceptions. In addition, they help you avoid burnout by changing your study medium, and they're portable enough to allow you to change your study location.

Many bar takers just rely on the printed flash cards published by CBT and other companies. While commercial flash cards are a good first step, the best preparation involves homemade flash cards. If you're struggling to remember a particular rule nuance, make a flash card! Get an MBE question wrong because you did not understand the correct application of a rule – make a flash card! Keep missing a certain issue on your essays – make a flash card! Add your homemade flash cards to your commercial flash cards to help with your study. Once you're confident that you will not make the same mistake again, take the homemade flash card out of your review set. If you are still not sure about flash cards, give them a try for a week. You will be surprised how helpful they really are.

Learn More Than the Definition

Stuck trying to memorize a particular term? Try placing it more specifically within your realm of knowledge. For example, if you were trying to memorize the definition of the word *coffee*, you might find it difficult to verbatim remember "a beverage made by percolation, infusion, or decoction from the roasted and ground seeds of a coffee plant." But taking a second to recall how you have seen coffee made—or what your own coffee routine looks like—will make the technical definition stickier and therefore easier to recall.

Two Methods to Lock in Information

If you have mastered the quick memorization of your terms, take it to the next level with one of two methods: teaching others or applying the knowledge.

1. Have a partner, friend, or family member whom you can subject to legal terms? If so, try teaching them about the terms you have memorized. Studies have indicated that teaching others is the best way to retain information in the long run.

2. Prefer to work solo? You can gain tremendous benefit from thinking through *how* the content you are memorizing will be applied in the bar exam. Try taking a term you have memorized and thinking through what kinds of questions could be asked about it. This method has the added benefit of allowing you to more clearly connect and distinguish between terms.

Outlining

Whether you're looking at a specific case or a state statute, outlining is an immensely useful way to organize, synthesize, and retain information in preparation for the bar exam. In particular, creating your own outline of a key document enables you to truly internalize important information. Take a minute to read the information below and brush up on the fundamentals of outlining.

1. **Read the Document**
   Note the verb "read." Do not skim, do not browse. Take your time and truly read the document in front of you. Doing so permits you to grasp both the straightforward and the nuanced aspects of it, which in turn prepares you to recall the information as you sit for the bar.

2. **Name Key Points**
   As you begin your outline of the document, the first thing to write is a recapitulation of the key points, for this creates an easily referenced list with which you can later study. As you complete this task, push yourself beyond merely copying the key points directly from the document, as this will do little to aid your comprehension or memorization of the document. Instead, summarize and paraphrase the key points, for this facilitates your brain's internalization of them. While this method requires more work on the front end, it will pay off when you can more vividly and accurately recall the information down the road.

3. **Supplement**
   Fill out your outline by adding supplemental information beneath your key points. While this supplemental information may seem extraneous, it can actually be quite essential and is certainly worth your time. Imagine you are outlining the Declaration of Independence - while your key points over the actual content of the document are key, so too are the dates, names, influences, and consequences of the document.

   The two major types of supplemental information are *details* and *connections*.

- ***Details*** on an outline include all the information from the original document that is not essential. Dates, names, and important sub-points are all included here, and many are worthy of committing to your outline (and eventually, to your memory). In our example of the Declaration, you would certainly want to note that the document was written by Thomas Jefferson and adopted in 1776 (even though these facts are not the key points of the Declaration itself).

- ***Connections*** on an outline include information not taken directly from the original document; information such as influences, effects, or comparison may all be included on your outline as connections. Thinking through this extra information requires mental effort from you, as you must make these connections yourself, but the result is a holistic approach to the material that will boost your performance on the bar exam. To return one last time to the Declaration of Independence, think of the degree to which Enlightenment thinkers influenced the document; think also of the Declaration's role in the larger context of the American Revolution. Connections such as these are essential to a thorough understanding of a document.

4. **Review**
In the final few weeks leading to the bar exam, take a few minutes each day to look over the outlines you've created to ensure you are retaining the information you'll need. This will result in remembering key details that may have slipped your mind, and you'll also find that it promotes a broad view of the law itself.

Practice Makes Perfect!

It is understandable that bar takers put off writing practice essays because they do not feel that they know the law sufficiently well. The problem is, most bar takers will not truly feel confident that they know the subject matter until the week before the exam. That is far too late to start writing practice essays!

If you are a CBT client you have access to large library of previously administered bar exam questions, courtesy of the National Conference of Bar Examiners. We encourage you to jump in early; you are not going to run out of questions!

It is an adage we have all heard repeated numerous times throughout our lives, and it's no less true for the bar exam that it was for your first-grade spelling test. You have already put in countless hours studying for the bar, and you now can solidify what you have learned through completion of a few practice tests. Not only will these practice tests allow you to see how you actually perform on a comprehensive test of your legal knowledge; they are also an excellent opportunity to examine a larger picture of what you've studied and to identify the gaps in your personal knowledge. Outlined below are two types of practice exams: essay-based and multiple-choice.

Essay-Based Practice Exams

Tackling a practice essay may seem tedious, but it can easily make the difference between feeling prepared and feeling rushed on the actual examination. In particular, the ability to understand *how* you need to manage your time on the essay will be of great assistance, for after a few practice runs, you will comprehend how much time you should spend on the planning, execution, and revision of your essay.

There are three additional ways in which a practice essay will make you even more bar-ready:

1. **Synthesis**
   By writing a few practice essays, you will have a heightened understanding of how different legal issues can be grouped together. Such a broad awareness of legal issues can be difficult to study in isolation, which makes essay-writing the perfect way to think deeply about them in preparation for the bar.

2. **Application**
   By applying your knowledge of the facts within an essay, you will better understand the relationship between the facts and those issues they pertain to. Through this application, you will have a greater understanding of the facts and the issues themselves.

3. **Self-Check**
   Perhaps most importantly, a practice exam tests your ability to recite legal rules. After completing the practice essay, you'll have a sense of how well you actually know legal rules and which ones you need to brush up on before sitting for the real bar exam.

Multiple-Choice Practice Exams

In addition to practicing your essay-writing skills, you should also take time to complete at least one practice exam with multiple-choice questions. Doing so will strengthen your testing-taking stamina and improve your management of time.

One Wednesday in the future, you will sit down for six hours to complete two hundred multiple-choice questions. Love them or hate them, successfully completing the multistate portion of the bar exam is essential. Do not despair though, the answer is right there in front of you. The key to knowing which answers to select is practice!

It can be tempting to judge your progress and preparation by how many multiple-choice questions you complete per day or week. At CBT, we encourage you not to do that. Quantity is important, but not at the expense of quality.

At CBT we recommend that you answer questions in blocks of ten to twenty. Once you have answered the questions, carefully review your answer and the answer explanations – this is where the most effective learning takes place! Do not be tempted to breeze by a question that you got correct, make sure that you were correct for the right reason!

Squeeze in MBE review sessions where possible and you will be impressed by the quantity of MBEs you actually review. More importantly, you will have learned more effectively and used your time more efficiently! Also, varying your study from lectures to outline review, practice essays, flash cards, and MBEs, helps you avoid burnout and gets you closer to the finish line!

In addition, you will find three other intellectual benefits:

1. **Self-Correction**
   Incorrect answers (and their explanations) are often quite useful in learning or reviewing a subject. After you complete and grade your multiple-choice practice test, you will possess a clearer picture of what facts and terms you need to brush up on, which allows you to eliminate any misconceptions you have and consequently perform better on the actual exam.

2. **Comparison**
   As you apply what you have studied in law school to a multiple-choice practice exam, you will also have an opportunity to compare legal concepts via the answer choices. Through this process of comparing and contrasting answers, you will gain a more nuanced understanding of what each concept means and how it should be applied.

3. **Fact**
   These multiple-choice practice exams also allow you, the test taker, to better comprehend how legal issues arise. As you look over the facts that are presented in each portion of the test, you are strengthening your memory of them; this equips you with the knowledge of what to look for if you see those facts on the real bar exam.

In short, take a few practice exams before you sit for the bar. You will gain an understanding of what concepts and facts you should study in your final weeks of review, you will strengthen your understanding of the bar exam's format, and perhaps most importantly, you'll gain some peace of mind in the process.

Self-Care

When you are studying for the bar exam, you may be reluctant to take a break. You can not relax, you feel guilty, you feel as though you should be studying in every waking moment… you have even considered playing your bar lectures while you sleep to see if your subconscious is paying attention.
The problem is, you're training your brain for the hardest exam of your life and just like a marathon runner's legs, a brain needs time to recuperate and become stronger. Allow yourself to rest, allow yourself to have fun and to find distraction. If you've paced yourself correctly, there's no reason why you cannot keep your sanity while preparing to pass the bar.

At CBT, we recommend bar takers who are studying full time take two half-days and one full day off a week for themselves. You will not fail the bar exam because you took an afternoon off to go and watch a movie, but you will if you burn out! So be kind to yourself, take a break once in a while! In the meantime, here are some essential things to remember in order to perform at your best:

1. **Maintain Your Routine**
   In busy times of our lives, it is easy to cut out the things we are used to. Time asleep shortens, meals are eaten on the counter, and running shoes get left unused by the door. Decrease your stress and improve your mood by working a study routine into your life rather than the opposite. Make time for the things you value, whatever they may be.

2. **Sleep**
   Remember life as an undergraduate? The nights spent at the library or coffee shop, hammering out an essay or cramming for the next day's test? Those days are—and should remain—behind you. Get that full night of sleep and enjoy myriad benefits: improved cognition, retention, and alertness are just a few. It may be tempting to stay up and study just a few minutes more, but sleep deprivation, in the long run, provides more detriment than benefit.

3. **Eat Healthily**
   It can be tempting to call the neighborhood pizza joint and cross "cooking" off your evening's to-do list. However, the few extra minutes spent preparing a meal add nutrition and relaxation to your life, which will help propel you even further in your studies. Best of all, it is an easy way to make time for loved ones.

4. **Relieve Stress**
   How do you blow off steam? Sports? Painting? A phone call to your best friend?
   Reserve time at least twice a week to do something that relaxes you and you will feel the benefits of reduced cortisol (stress) levels, improved sleep, and a less-distracted mind.

The day of the Bar Exam!

You might not feel like it but:

1. Have a good breakfast and stay hydrated! Low blood sugar and dehydration can, amongst other things, lead to weakness, dizziness and confusion. Not a great condition to be in at anytime, but especially not the day of your bar exam.

2. Take a walk. Research, by Dr Chuck Hillman at the University of Illinois, has shown that walking for twenty minutes before an exam boosts brainpower.

3. Meditate. There is growing support for the benefits of meditation and not just for stressful situations such as exams. Perhaps a good idea to include this as part of your bar prep?

4. Prepare the night before. Yes, even decide what clothes you will wear! Being ready to leave on time without the stress of finding your ID or your lucky mascot will help keep you calm.

5. Allow extra time for travel. You might guess someone will want to dig up a road, or breakdown on the highway the day of your exam. Keep your stress levels to a minimum, do not get caught in a traffic hold-up!

After the Exam

Take a break and congratulate yourself. It was not easy to get into Law School, graduate and study for the bar. Not everyone could have achieved what you have done. Celebrate your achievement!

Good luck for the future from the CBT Team!

Exam Subject Matter Coverage

	MBE Tested	Essay Tested	CA Specific Rules Tested in Essay Section
Business Associations	No	**Yes**	**Yes**
Civil Procedure	**Yes**	**Yes**	**Yes**
Community Property	No	**Yes**	**Yes**
Constitutional Law	**Yes**	**Yes**	No
Contracts & UCC	**Yes**	**Yes**	No
Criminal Law	**Yes**	**Yes**	No
Criminal Procedure	**Yes**	**Yes**	No
Evidence	**Yes**	**Yes**	**Yes**
Professional Responsibility	No	**Yes**	**Yes**
Real Property	**Yes**	**Yes**	No
Torts	**Yes**	**Yes**	No
Trusts	No	**Yes**	**Yes**
Wills and Intestate Succession	No	**Yes**	**Yes**

Updates & Feedback

Our goal at CBT is to make bar study as simple for you as possible. If you think that there is something that we can do better, we want to hear from you! Reach out to us at:
Admin@CaliforniaBarTutors.com

If you would like to receive law updates and information on free book, flash card, essay grading, and tutoring giveaways, send an email to the above address with the subject "Signup" to be added to CBT's email list.

About CBT

Law schools may teach the law, but they do not prepare you for the bar exam. Many students hope that their commercial bar review course will provide them with that preparation. Until now, unless you were willing to spend $10,000 or more, you did not receive the individualized attention needed to be successful on the bar.

Other commercial bar review programs only provide the opportunity to submit three or four essays and two performance tests for critical review during the program. Furthermore, the feedback received is generally vague and provides no guidance for improvement. Quite simply, for most people this is insufficient. If you want more from your bar review company, please review what we have to offer.

At CBT we not only teach the law, we teach you how to apply the law, and be successful on the most difficult licensing exam in the country. To help you achieve your goal of becoming a licensed attorney, we have created a variety of products that include:

- Comprehensive Written Materials
- Essay and Performance Test Approaches
- Essay and Performance Test Review and Grading
- Individual Tutoring
- Online Lectures
- Practice Exams
- A Review Service for Repeat Takers
- Passer's Packages with Pass Guarantee

Let CBT help you reach your goals!

Total Preparation Book purchasers are eligible to receive a discount on CBT'S services. Go to CaliforniaBarTutors.com and fax or email a copy of your receipt to CBT to receive your discount code, while supplies last!

Don't Forget: Free Practice Exams

When you're ready to put your knowledge to work and practice answering exam standard questions, we're here to help you!

Email us at **admin@CaliforniaBarTutors.com** with **"Downloads"** in the subject line, and we'll send you a link to download a packet of practice essay questions and answers covering the bar exam tested subjects. We also include practice performance test questions and answers!

If you need more assistance with your preparation, just let us know.

Table of Contents

°*Topics discussed in the Remedies Primer are more fully explored within the respective substantive law outlines.*
**Agency & Partnerships and Corporations have been combined in the substantive outlines as "Business Associations".*

Comprehensive Outlines

BUSINESS ASSOCIATIONS

Table of Contents

I. CORPORATIONS

A. Formation

1. Statutory Requirements

a) Effect of Defective Incorporation

(1) Corporation Liability

The shareholders of a validly formed corporation will not be subject to personal liability for the corporation's debts. If corporate formation is defective, active shareholders and management may be personally liable for corporate debts.

b) De Facto and De Jure Corporations

(1) De Jure Corporations

When incorporators comply with all applicable statutory requirements and file the articles of incorporation with the state, they have successfully created a de jure corporation.

(2) De Facto Corporation

Even if a corporation does not file, or correctly file, the articles of incorporation, the law may still recognize it as a legal corporation with all the rights and powers of a corporation, a de jure corporation. A state may, however, challenge a de facto corporation's authority to act in a quo warranto proceeding.

Requirements: A de facto corporation only exists where:

i. There is an incorporation statute under which the entity could have been validly incorporated had the articles of incorporation been correctly filed;
ii. The corporation made a good-faith effort to comply with the incorporation statute; and
iii. The business is being conducted as a corporation.

Limitation: If a person acts on behalf of a corporation with knowledge that it is an invalid incorporation, that person is subject to individual liability.

c) Corporation by Estoppel

A corporation by estoppel refers to either a person who operates a business as if it were a corporation, or a person who deals with a business as if it were a corporation. It does not matter whether or not there was a good-faith effort to comply with an incorporation statue.

(a) A person who deals with a business that is not a de jure or a de facto corporation, as if it were a corporation, will be estopped (prohibited) from arguing that it is not a corporation in an attempt to get at the incorporator's assets.
(b) A person or entity that acts as a corporation will be estopped from arguing that it is not a corporation to deny liability as a corporation.
(c) Estoppel prevents parties from renouncing contracts, but it generally will not apply to a tort because tortious acts do not usually depend on knowledge of the existence of a corporation.

2. Actions by Promoter

Promoters are those who organize the corporation. Promoters may enter into contracts on behalf of the corporation.

a) Fiduciary Duty

A promoter owes a fiduciary duty to the corporation. The duty is to act in good faith and is accompanied by the obligations of confidence and trust. Thus, the promoter must make full disclosures.

(1) **Breach Arising from Sales to the Corporation**

A promoter may make profits by selling property to the corporation as long as he provides a full disclosure of all material facts. If a promoter does not disclose all material facts, he may be liable to the corporation for the profits.

(a) If the promoter discloses the transaction to an independent Board of Directors, which approves it, the promoter has met his duty of full disclosure and will not be liable to the corporation.

(b) The promoter must disclose material facts to those who are part of the initial financing scheme. This means that a promoter who buys all shares and later resells them is not liable for disgorgement of his profits.

(2) **Fraud**

Regardless of whether a promoter made a full disclosure, if the plaintiff can show he was damaged by the promoter's fraudulent misrepresentations or failure to disclose all material facts, the promoter will be liable.

b) **PRE-INCORPORATION AGREEMENTS**

(1) **Promoter's Liability**

If a promoter enters into a contract with a third party on behalf of a planned but not-yet-formed corporation, the promoter will be held personally liable on the contract.

(a) The promoter remains personally liable after the corporation is formed, even if the corporation adopts the contract and benefits from it.

(b) The promoter will only be released from personally liability where there is a novation – an express or implied agreement among parties to release the promoter from liability.

(2) **Exception – Agreement Expressly Relieves Promoter of Liability**

A promoter and a third party may expressly agree to relieve the promoter of liability. Under this arrangement, there is no contract; rather, it is merely a revocable offer to the proposed corporation and the promoter has no rights or liabilities under the agreement.

(3) **Promoter's Right to Reimbursement**

If a promoter is held personally liable on a pre-incorporation contract, the corporation may have to reimburse him to the extent that it benefitted.

(4) **Corporation's Liability**

If the promoter enters into a contract on behalf of an entity before incorporation, the corporation cannot be bound by the contract since the corporate entity did not exist before incorporation. If the corporation expressly or impliedly adopts or ratifies the contract, it will be bound.

c) **STOCK SUBSCRIPTIONS**

Under a strict definition, a "stock subscription" is a promise to purchase shares of stock in a yet-to-be formed corporation. However, agreements to buy stock after a corporation is formed are often called stock subscriptions.

(1) **Pre-Incorporation Subscriptions**

(a) Subscribers cannot cancel or revoke their subscriptions for six (6) months unless: (a) The subscription agreement provides otherwise; or (b) All subscribers consent to the revocation.

(b) Subscribers must remit payment upon the Board of Directors' demand, unless otherwise provided for in the agreement.

(c) A subscriber who fails to pay the promised amount may forfeit his subscription and lose any amounts that he has already paid, or he may have to sell his shares.

(2) **Post-Incorporation Subscriptions**

Post-incorporation subscriptions are revocable at any time before acceptance. California holds that such subscriptions are irrevocable.

(3) **Enforcement of Subscriptions**

(a) **Enforcement by Corporation**

An agreement can be enforced against a subscriber but not a bona fide purchaser transferee without notice.

(b) **Enforcement by Creditor**

If a corporation is insolvent, the subscriber's obligation is enforceable in equity.

(c) **Release of Subscription**

Subscriptions can be released only when shareholders and subscribers consent and there is no harm to creditors.

(4) **Valid Issuance of Stock Subscriptions**

(a) **Requirements for Valid Issuance**

Proper Authorization and Issuance: The Articles of Incorporation and the Board of Directors must authorize the issuance of stock.

Consideration: Adequate consideration must be paid for the stock.

i. Traditionally, a stock may be issued for money paid, labor done, or property acquired.
ii. Modern statutes allow a corporation to issue shares for whatever consideration the Board of Directors deems proper, whether tangible or intangible, provided it is a benefit to the corporation.

(b) **Amount**

Traditionally, a corporation must sell stock for par value or a stated value unless there was a good-faith decision by the Board of Directors that stock cannot be sold at par or stated value.

i. Under modern statutes, shares may be paid for with any tangible or intangible property, or a benefit to the corporation.
ii. Shares paid for and issued by any method of payment other than cash are considered paid in full.
iii. A shareholder who fails to pay the full amount agreed upon can be held liable for unpaid balance.

(c) **Inadequate Consideration**

Historically, bonus, watered, and discount stocks were not allowed. Modern laws allow such stocks as long as there is a good-faith determination.

Effect: The corporation can cancel the stock to the extent that the stock is watered but cannot recover money damages; the shareholders can enjoin; the creditors can recover damages; no cause of action against a bona fide purchaser without notice.

(d) **Preemptive Rights Issues**

Shareholders may have the right to purchase a proportionate number of shares of newly authorized stock before it is offered to outsiders. However, this is so only if it is provided for in the Articles of Incorporation.

(e) **Classification of Stock**

i. Preferred Stock: Preferred stockholders receive dividends before common stockholders; and they may have preference as to liquidation and be able to convert their shares into another class of stock.

ii. Treasury Shares: Treasury shares are those stocks that are issued and repurchased by the corporation.

iii. Outstanding Shares: Outstanding shares are stocks that are issued but not repurchased.

3. AMENDMENT TO ARTICLES OF INCORPORATION

A corporation can amend its Articles as long as the provision would have been lawful in the original Articles. Most changes require shareholder approval. "Housekeeping" amendments, such as changing names, etc., can be made without shareholder approval.

4. MERGER, SHARE EXCHANGE, AND CONVERSION

a) MERGER

A merger is a blending of one or more corporation(s) into another corporation. The latter corporation survives while the merging corporation ceases to exist once the merger is complete. Approval of shareholders is not required when:

(1) The Articles of Incorporation of the surviving corporation are the same as the Articles before the merger;

(2) The shareholders will retain the same number of shares with identical preferences, limitations, and rights;

(3) The voting power of the shares issued because of the merger does not amount to more than 20% of the outstanding shares before the merger; or

(4) The parent company owns at least 90% of the outstanding shares of the subsidiary with which it is merging.

b) SHARE EXCHANGE

A share exchange occurs where one corporation purchases all of the outstanding shares of one or more classes or series of another corporation. Only the shareholders of the corporation whose shares will be acquired need to approve a share exchange. A share exchange is not a fundamental corporate change for the acquiring corporation, so those shareholders do not need to approve.

c) CONVERSION

A conversion occurs when one business entity changes its form to another business entity, such as a corporation converting into an LLC. The procedure for approving a conversion is the same as approving a merger where the converting corporation is not the survivor.

B. CORPORATE POWERS

1. SHARE RE-PURCHASE

In a repurchase agreement, a corporation agrees to buy back shares at a shareholder's option. A shareholder may enforce the option if there are available funds.

a) REDEMPTION

A corporation may acquire outstanding shares pursuant to its Articles of Incorporation.

(1) If a corporation is or will become insolvent, it cannot repurchase or redeem shares. To do so is illegal.

(2) If only one class of stock is outstanding, the corporation cannot redeem those shares. Directors cannot discriminate between classes of stock.

(3) Redemptions are treated as dividends and are subject to the same limitations.

2. Gifts and Loans

a) Gifts

(1) Common Law: Under common law, all shareholders must approve of any gift of corporate property.

(2) Modernly, most states now permit corporate gifts, but limit their nature and object. Corporations may make gifts without shareholder approval if they are reasonable, approved by directors, made from profits, and made for charitable purposes.

b) Loans

(1) Corporations may lend money and invest and reinvest funds.

(2) This power may be limited by statute, or by the corporation's charter, bylaws, or resolution.

3. Asset Transfer

When a corporation sells, leases, or exchanges all or substantially all of a corporation's property outside of the regular course of business, it is considered a fundamental corporate change and the appropriate procedure must be followed. *See "Protection Against and Limitations on Fundamental Changes" below.*

4. Ultra Vires Acts

If the incorporators include a provision narrowly defining the corporation's business purpose in the corporation's articles of incorporation, the corporation may only act in accordance with the stated business purpose. Activities beyond the scope of a corporation's enumerated powers are said to be ultra vires.

a) Under early common law, any ultra vires action is void and unenforceable.

b) Under modern law, ultra vires acts are not automatically void, but are voidable. Thus, it is no longer an excuse or defense to invalidating a contract. An act or decision can only be questioned where:

(1) A shareholder sues the corporation to stop it from acting;

(2) The corporation sues an officer or director for damages resulting from an ultra vires act; and

(3) The state brings an action to dissolve a corporation for committing an ultra vires act.

C. Officers and Directors

1. Duties and Powers

a) Duties

Duties are determined by bylaws, the Board, or an officer authorized by the Board.

b) Powers

Ordinary rules of agency apply regarding actual and apparent authority.

(1) The corporation is not liable for a contract made by an officer without authority.

(2) The corporation may become bound by unauthorized actions taken by officers through ratification, adoption, or estoppel.

(3) The corporation is liable for actions by its officers that are within scope of their authority, even if the particular act in question was not specifically authorized.

2. Compensation

a) Directors are entitled to reasonable compensation if authorized by shareholder vote, by law, or by an independent Board of Directors, and reimbursement for corporate expenses.

b) Directors are responsible for managing the compensation of officers.

3. Indemnification

a) Mandatory Indemnification

Absent a provision stating otherwise, a director or officer who prevails in defending a proceeding against himself is entitled to indemnification from the corporation for reasonable expenses, including attorney fees, incurred in connection with the proceeding.

b) Discretionary Indemnification

If the director or officer is unsuccessful, a corporation has the discretion to indemnify the officer for reasonable expenses if: (i) the director acted in good-faith; and (ii) the director believed her conduct was in the best interests of the corporation (when within her official capacity), was not opposed to the best interests of the corporation (when not within official capacity), or was not unlawful (in criminal proceedings).

c) Exceptions

There is no discretion to indemnify when an officer is found liable to the corporation, or when an officer received an improper benefit.

d) Determination

The decision of whether to indemnify an officer is to be made by a disinterested majority of the Board of Directors, or if there is no majority, a majority of a disinterested committee, shareholders, or legal counsel.

(1) Officers and Directors

Officers may be indemnified to the same extent as directors.

(2) Court Order

A court order for indemnification can be made when appropriate.

4. Inspection Rights

a) Directors generally have greater inspection rights than shareholders.

b) Directors have a right to inspect all books, records, documents, facilities, and premises. Some states limit a director's right to inspect to purposes reasonably related to the director's position as a director. This right is almost absolute and cannot be restricted by the Articles or bylaws.

5. Meetings and Actions

a) Meetings

(1) Annual

Every corporation must hold an annual meeting. If it has been 15 months since the last meeting, a court may order one.

(2) Special

Either a Board of Directors or the holders of 10% of the shares entitled to vote may call a special meeting. The corporation's bylaws may also provide for special meetings.

(3) Written Notice

Written notice is required at least 10 days before a meeting and not more than 60 days. Notice can be expressly waived.

(4) Actions Taken at Meetings

(a) Failure to comply with formalities makes any action taken at a meeting void.

(b) Regular meetings do not require notice. Special meetings require reasonable written notice. Notice must be given at least 2 days in advance unless express waiver of attendance is given.

(c) Action can be taken without a meeting with unanimous written consent by all directors.

(d) A quorum of directors is required at meetings or as stated in the bylaws, but not less than one third of all directors.
(e) Unlike shareholder meetings, a withdrawing director can break a quorum.

(5) **Approval of Action**

A director has actual authority to bind the corporation where a directors' meeting was held after proper notice was given, a quorum was present, and a majority of the directors approved the action. A director also has actual authority where all directors consent in writing.

6. Fiduciary Obligations

a) Conflicts of Interest

(1) **Conflicting Interest Transactions**

The duty of loyalty requires a director to act in the corporation's best interest, not the director's own best interest. A director's duty of loyalty may be implicated by a conflict of interest with respect to a transaction if the director knows that he or a related person is either:

(a) A party to the transaction;
(b) Someone with a financial interest in, or closely linked to, the transaction, making the director's judgment susceptible to influence; or
(c) A director, partner, agent, or employee of another entity with whom the corporation is transacting business and the transaction is one that would normally be brought before the Board.

(2) **Upholding the Transaction**

Even if there is a conflict of interest, a transaction does not give rise to an award of damages if:

(a) A majority of directors approved of the transaction after all material facts were disclosed;
(b) The shareholders approved of the transaction, through casting a majority of the votes entitled to be cast, after material facts have been disclosed to the shareholders. The written notice for the meeting must describe the transaction at issue; or
(c) The transaction was fair to the corporation. Whether or not the transaction was fair is judged according to the circumstances present when the transaction was entered into.

(3) **Requirements**

Whether or not the interested director was present at the meeting is irrelevant. A quorum must be present and comprised of disinterested directors or shareholders.

(4) **Fairness**

In order to determine fairness, courts will look at the consideration provided, corporate need to enter into transaction, financial position of corporation, available alternatives, and waste.

(5) **Remedies**

Remedies include enjoining the transaction, setting aside the transaction, and awarding damages.

b) **Competition Against Corporation**

(1) **Competing Business**

Directors may engage in businesses or opportunities unrelated to the corporation's business; however, participating in a competing business creates a conflict of interest.

c) **Transactions Involving Corporation**

(1) Directors have a duty of care to the corporation and shareholders in making decisions in their capacities as fiduciaries. The duty of due care requires directors to make decisions: (i) in good faith; (ii) with the care that a reasonably prudent person in their position would; and (iii) in a manner they reasonably believe is in the best interests of the corporation.

(2) Officers must carry out their duties in good faith, with the same care as a reasonably prudent person in a similar position under similar circumstances. They must act in a manner they reasonably believe to be in the best interests of the corporation.

d) **Delegation of Authority**

(1) **Powers**

(a) Directors are responsible for managing the corporation's business affairs. These powers include:

1) Unfettered discretion in making management decisions (typically with a quorum present unless the bylaws state otherwise);
2) Selection, removal, and compensation of officers, agents, with or without cause;
3) Incurring debt;
4) Declaring dividends;
5) Filling vacancies on Boards by a majority vote;
6) Making and amending bylaws where a statute so provides or where shareholders grant the power to do so;
7) Delegating duties;
8) Buying and selling corporation property and stock; and
9) Delegating authority to officers or executive committees.

(2) Unless the articles or bylaws provide otherwise, the Board of Directors may create one or more committees made up of two or more members, who may also be members of the Board of Directors.

(a) While committees may act for the Board, the Board must supervise committees.

(b) The Board may also delegate its powers or duties, or portions of, to officers.

e) **Shareholder Relations**

The shareholders choose directors to manage the corporation. Therefore, the directors and the officers they appoint have a fiduciary relationship to shareholders that requires a duty of loyalty to the company and the exercise of reasonably good judgment in managing the corporation's affairs. Directors cannot usurp corporate opportunities, make personal use of the corporation's assets, or deal unfairly with the corporation's stock.

7. Director Liability

a) **Limitation of Personal Liability**

The Articles may limit or eliminate a director's personal liability for money damages to the corporation or shareholders for a breach of fiduciary duty through an action or omission. However, the articles may not limit or eliminate a director's liability if:

(1) He receives financial benefits to which he is not entitled;
(2) He intentionally inflicts harm on the corporation or its shareholders;
(3) He unlawfully makes corporate distributions; or
(4) He intentionally commits a crime.

8. De Facto Officers and Directors

a) A person who was not formally appointed as a director or officer, but performs the duties of the position, may be a de facto officer or director.

b) De facto officers and directors have the rights and obligations of a director and are liable for their acts.

9. Election, Resignation, and Removal

a) Directors

(1) Qualifications

Unless the corporation's Articles or bylaws state otherwise, directors do not need to be shareholders, nor do they need to reside in any particular state.

(2) Election

There need only be one director, unless the Articles or bylaws require additional directors. Directors are elected at shareholder meetings. If there are at least nine (9) directors, they may be divided into equal size classes and their terms staggered.

(3) Removal

The shareholders may remove the directors with or without cause, unless the Articles or bylaws state that they may only be removed for cause.

(a) If the directors are elected by a cumulative vote, a director cannot be removed if the number of votes cast against removal would be enough to elect him.

(b) If a director was elected by a voting group of shareholders, only that group of shareholders may participate in the vote.

b) Officers

(1) Election

The Board of Directors chooses officers to manage the corporation on a day-to-day basis (this is not required unless stated in the Articles).

(2) Resignation and Removal

An officer may resign at any time upon giving notice to the corporation, and the corporation may remove an officer with or without cause, regardless of any term in the Articles, bylaws, or other contract.

(a) If an officer's resignation or removal is considered a breach of contract under a governing agreement, the non-breaching party may have a right to damages. But officers do not have a right to remain in office.

10. Business Judgment Rule

a) Duty of Care

Directors have a duty of care to the corporation and the shareholders in making decisions in their capacities as fiduciaries. The duty of due care requires directors to make decisions: (i) in good faith; (ii) with the care that a reasonably prudent person in their position would; and (iii) in a manner they reasonably believe is in the best interests of the corporation.

b) **Business Judgment Rule**

Directors will not be liable for corporate decisions made in accordance with these standards even if they later turn out to be poor or erroneous. Under common law, this principle is referred to as the business judgment rule.

(1) **Burden on Challenger**

The party challenging the decision must prove the standard was not met.

(2) **Director May Rely on Reports, Etc.**

When making decisions, a director may rely on information, opinions, reports, or statements, if prepared or presented by:

(a) Corporate officers or employees who are believed to be reliable and competent;

(b) Legal counsel, accountants, or other persons, as to matters that are within the person's professional competence; or

(c) A committee of which the director is not a member, if the director reasonably believes the committee merits confidence.

11. **Obligations with Respect to Corporate Opportunities**

a) **Corporate Opportunity Doctrine**

A director's fiduciary duties prohibit him from taking advantage of a business opportunity that would benefit the corporation without first disclosing the opportunity to act.

(1) **Corporation Interest or Expectancy**

A director only violates his fiduciary duty if the opportunity is one in which the corporation would have an interest or expectancy. The closer the opportunity is to the corporation's line of business, the more likely a court will find it to be a corporation opportunity. The director must disclose all material facts.

(2) **Financial Ability**

The director cannot claim that the corporation could not have financially taken advantage of the opportunity in his defense. The director must still present the corporation with the opportunity so that it can decide it is an opportunity it can and wants to take advantage of.

(3) **Board Generally Decides**

Since the Board is generally responsible for decisions concerning the management of the corporation, the Board must decide whether to accept or reject an opportunity.

b) **Remedies**

If a director usurps the opportunity before giving the corporation an opportunity to act, the corporation can either recover the profits that the director made from the transaction or it may force the director to convey the opportunity to the corporation for whatever consideration the director paid.

D. Shareholders

1. **Rights**

a) **Meetings and Elections**

(1) **Attendance**

A quorum is required for any vote to be taken.

(a) A quorum requires a majority of the outstanding shares that are entitled to vote, unless the Articles or bylaws require a greater number.

(b) Once present, in California, shareholders leaving cannot break a quorum.

b) **Voting**

(1) The shareholders elect the directors and may remove them.

(2) Only the shareholders of record date can vote.

(3) The shareholders decide major decisions. Ordinary changes require the presence of a majority of shareholders, while fundamental changes require a majority of all outstanding shares.

(4) **Proxy Votes:** A proxy is a power of attorney to vote shares.

(a) **Duration**

An appointment of a proxy is valid for 11 months unless the appointment provides otherwise.

i. A shareholder may revoke an appointment of a proxy at any time. The shareholder revokes the proxy when he appears at a meeting to vote or appoints another proxy.

ii. A shareholder cannot revoke a proxy if the appointment states that it is irrevocable and grants the proxy an interest.

(b) **Solicitation of Proxies**

Common law proxies obtained by fraud are void.

Section 14(a) applies only to corporations with more than $10 million in assets and at least 500 shareholders.

i. Proxy statements must include all pertinent facts and be filed with the SEC and cannot contain material misstatements or omissions. Proxy solicitations that contain material misstatements or omissions are void.

ii. Management is required to provide a shareholder list or mail a dissident shareholder's proxy solicitation and must include a shareholder's proposal of up to 200 words in their own solicitation, unless a director's election is the only business to be conducted at the meeting or the proposal does not concern a proper subject of shareholder action.

Remedy for Violation: The SEC can get an injunction; a private plaintiff can enjoin voting of proxies, cancel election of directors, or receive money damages.

(c) **Closed Corporation Shareholder Agreements**

Closed Corporation Shareholder Agreements are valid if they are for a proper purpose.

i. **Pooling Agreements:** Rather than creating a trust, shareholders may enter into a written and signed agreement providing for the manner in which they will vote their shares. A court may grant specific performance unless the contract is not in the best interest of the corporation.

ii. **Voting Trust:** The shareholders may create a voting trust to combine their voting powers. A voting trust is a written agreement among shareholders under which all the parties transfer their shares to a trustee, who then votes in accordance with the agreement. A voting trust requires: (i) shareholders to transfer legal title to the trustee; (ii) a writing and filing with the corporation; (iii) open to inspection; and (iv) is no longer than 10 years in duration.

iii. **Stock Transfer Agreements:** Reasonable restrictions to keep stock from being freely transferred will be enforced.
The provisions of a stock transfer agreement bind a third-party purchaser if: (i) the restrictions are conspicuously noted on the certificate; and (ii) the third party knew of the restrictions at the time of purchase.

(d) **Straight and Cumulative Voting for Directors**

i. Straight Voting: One vote per share.

ii. Cumulative Voting: The number of shareholder's shares multiplied by the number of directors to be elected. This may be avoided by staggering terms for the directors (unless mandated by law) allowing a majority to remove the directors without cause and reducing the size of the Board.

iii. Class Voting: When an amendment to the Articles will affect only a particular class of stock, that class has the right to vote on the action even if the class otherwise does not have voting rights.

c) **INSPECTION**

(1) Shareholders have a right to inspect corporate books and records. This right, however, may be limited depending on the nature of the records sought and the purpose of the request.

(2) Generally, any shareholder may inspect the annual reports, minutes of shareholder meetings, bylaws, charter, and list of the shareholders.

(3) A group of shareholders (usually five or ten percent of outstanding stock) may inspect all books and records. Some states require that the shareholders show good cause.

d) **DIVIDENDS**

A corporation may make distributions in the form of dividends, through the redemption or repurchase of shares, or by distributing assets upon liquidation.

Rights to Distributions: Distributions are generally left to the discretion of the corporation. At least one class of stock must have the right to receive the corporation's net assets on dissolution.

Board's Discretion: Absent agreement or a provision in the Articles of Incorporation, the shareholders have no right to compel a distribution. Even if a corporation's Articles authorize distributions in certain circumstances, the decision of whether or not to declare a distribution is left solely with the directors, subject to solvency limitations and a shareholders' agreement or the Articles.

(1) **Solvency Requirements:** A corporation cannot make a distribution if, after giving it effect: (i) the corporation would not be able to pay its debts as they become due; or (ii) the corporation's total assets would be less than its total liabilities, plus the amount needed to satisfy the preferential rights of shareholders whose rights are superior to those receiving the distribution. The Articles may provide otherwise.

(2) **Restrictions in the Articles:** The Articles may infringe on the Board of Director's discretion and restrict its right to declare dividends when the corporation makes a certain amount of profit.

(3) **Share Dividends:** The above restrictions do not apply to a corporation's distribution of its own share to its shareholders, as these are not included in the formal definition of a distribution. But shares of another class may not be issued as dividends unless authorized by the Articles, a majority approves, and there are not outstanding shares of that class.

e) **PROTECTION AGAINST AND LIMITATIONS ON FUNDAMENTAL CHANGES**

Dissenting Shareholders: The shareholders who do dissent from a decision approving a fundamental change may exercise their right to have the corporation purchase their shares.

(1) Dissenting Shareholders must:

(a) Have been entitled to vote on the merger;

(b) Be the shareholders of the corporation being acquired;

(c) Be the shareholders entitled to vote on disposition of corporation property; or

(d) Be the shareholders whose rights will be materially and adversely affected by an amendment of the Articles.

(2) Procedure
   (a) The corporation must give the shareholders notice of the meeting at which to exercise dissenting rights.
   (b) Before a vote is taken, the dissenting shareholder must give written notice of his intent to demand payment for shares before a vote is taken.
   (c) The corporation must give dissenters notice within ten (10) days of approving the fundamental change and detail how to submit claims or requests for repurchase.
   (d) A shareholder must demand payment in accordance with terms of notice.
   (e) The corporation must pay amount estimated at fair value.
   (f) A notice of dissatisfaction must be filed within 30 days with the shareholder's own estimate of value and a payment demand for that amount.
   (g) If the corporation does not want to pay that amount, the corporation must file an action with the court within 60 days of receiving the demand to determine the fair value of the shares; otherwise, they must pay.

2. Derivative Actions

a) Direct Actions

A shareholder may bring a lawsuit, on her own behalf, against an officer or director for breach of fiduciary duty.

To determine whether the defendant breached a duty owed to the corporation or owed to a shareholder, ask:

(1) Who suffers the most immediate and direct damage?
(2) To whom did the defendant's duty run? In a shareholder action, any recovery will benefit the individual shareholder.

b) Derivative Actions

A shareholder may also bring a lawsuit against an officer or director on behalf of the corporation, asserting the corporation's rights rather than her own rights.

(1) The corporation, not the shareholder bringing the lawsuit, generally receives a recovery in a derivative action.
(2) Nevertheless, the shareholder is named as the defendant.

c) Standing

To bring a derivative proceeding, the shareholder must have been a shareholder at the time of the act or omission complained of, or have become a shareholder through a transfer from an individual who was a shareholder at that time. The shareholder must fairly and adequately represent the interests of the corporation.

d) Demand

Before filing an action, the shareholder must demand in writing the corporation take suitable action.

(1) The shareholder must wait 90 days from the date of demand before filing the action unless:
   (a) The shareholder bringing the action has been notified that the corporation rejects the demand; or
   (b) The corporation would suffer irreparable injury if the shareholder waits for the 90 days to pass.
(2) **Corporation's Best Interests**: If a majority of the directors, who have no personal interest in the controversy, find in good faith and after reasonable inquiry, that the suit is not in the corporation's best interests, they may petition the court to dismiss the action.

(a) **Burden of Proof:** If a corporation petitions for a dismissal, the shareholder bringing the suit must show that the corporation's decision was not made in good faith after reasonable inquiry.

(b) If a majority of the directors have a vested interest, the burden is placed on the corporation to show good faith after reasonable inquiry.

(3) **Discontinuance or Settlement:** The parties may discontinue or settle a derivative proceeding only with the approval of the court.

(4) **Payment of Expenses:** A court may order the corporation to pay the shareholder's reasonable expenses if the court finds that the corporation substantially benefitted from the action. On the other hand, if the court finds that the shareholder brought or maintained the action without reasonable cause or for an improper purpose, the shareholder may have to pay the corporation's reasonable expenses.

3. Fiduciary Obligations

Even though the shareholders are the owners of the corporation, they do not directly control or manage the corporation, except to elect the Board of Directors. However, controlling shareholders owe a duty of loyalty to the corporation and minority shareholders when engaging in transactions concerning the corporation.

4. Shareholder liability

Minority shareholders do not have a fiduciary duty to the corporation or fellow shareholders. Liability is generally limited to the liabilities discussed below for controlling shareholders, and for unpaid stock, a pierced corporate veil, or absence of a de facto corporation.

a) Controlling Shareholder

One exception is a controlling shareholder who has a fiduciary duty to the corporation and other shareholders, and cannot take any action to her benefit and detriment of other minority shareholders or to the corporation.

(1) Controlling shareholders must investigate a buyer in order to prevent looting and corporate raiding. If the controlling shareholder is found to have not investigated the buyer properly, that shareholder will be held liable.

(2) When a controlling shareholder sells a corporate asset, he must share any premium with minority shareholders.

(3) A controlling shareholder may not use her power to exploit corporate assets.

5. Restrictions on Share Transfer

The Articles or shareholder agreements may restrict the transfer of shares by the shareholders.

a) Preemptive rights

Under modern law, the shareholders do not have a preemptive right, or right of first refusal, to purchase new shares unless the Articles of Incorporation provide otherwise.

Even if the articles do provide the shareholders with a preemptive right, the right will not apply to shares that were issued for consideration other than cash (i.e., services) within 6 months after incorporation, and without voting rights but having a distribution preference.

b) Compulsory Buy-Out Provisions

One shareholder may compel the company or other shareholders to purchase his shares, in the event certain triggering events occur.

c) "SHOTGUN" CLAUSES

A dissatisfied shareholder can put an offer to the other shareholders to either buy all their shares or to sell his shares. The other shareholders then have the option to either buy out the dissatisfied shareholders or sell all their shares to him.

E. FEDERAL SECURITIES LAWS

1. RULE 10(B)(5)

Under Rule 10(b)(5) of the Securities Exchange Act, it is illegal for any person to use any means or instrumentality of interstate commerce to employ any scheme to defraud, make an untrue statement or material fact (or omit), or engage in any practice that operates as a fraud in connection with the purchase or sale of any security. A plaintiff bringing a claim under this section must prove:

a) FRAUDULENT CONDUCT

The plaintiff must show that the defendant engaged in some fraudulent conduct by making a material misstatement or omission of material fact.

b) MATERIALITY

A statement or omission is material if there is a substantial likelihood that a reasonable investor would have considered it important in making an investment decision.

c) SCIENTER

To be actionable under 10(b)(5), the conduct complained of must be undertaken with the intent to deceive, manipulate, or defraud. Recklessness as to truth also appears to be sufficient culpability.

d) IN CONNECTION WITH PURCHASE OR SALE BY PLAINTIFF

If the plaintiff is a private person, the plaintiff must connect the fraudulent conduct to the actual sale or purchase of a security. This excludes potential purchasers who do not buy and people who already own and refrain from selling.

(1) Non-Trading Defendants Can Be Liable

Non-trading defendants can be held liable where the plaintiff shows that misleading press releases were published and the plaintiff purchased or sold securities on the market on the basis of the press release.

e) IN INTERSTATE COMMERCE

The fraudulent conduct must involve the use of some means of interstate commerce for a federal court to have jurisdiction.

f) RELIANCE

A private plaintiff must prove that he relied on the defendant's fraudulent statement, omission, or conduct. Reliance will be presumed where an omission is material.

g) DAMAGES

A private plaintiff must show that the defendant's fraud caused the plaintiff's damages. Damages are limited to the difference between the price paid (or received) and the average share price in the 90 day period after corrective information is disseminated.

2. INSIDER TRADING

a) Rule 10(b)(5) also prohibits most instances of trading securities on the basis of material inside information (not disclosed to public). A person violates Rule 10(b)(5) if, by trading, he breaches a duty of trust and confidence owed to:

(1) The issuer;

(2) Shareholders of the issuer; or

(3) Another person who is the source of the material nonpublic information in the case of misappropriation.

b) **Who is liable?**

(1) **Insiders:** Anyone who breaches a duty not to use inside information for personal benefit can be held liable under 10(b)(5).

(2) Who is liable in a tipping interaction?

(a) If an insider gives a tip and shares inside information with someone else who then trades on the basis of that inside information, the tipper can be liable under Section 10(b)(5) if the tip was made for any improper purpose, such as in exchange for money, kickbacks, and reputational benefits.

(b) The person receiving and using the information given by the tipper can be held liable only if the tipper breached a duty and the person receiving and using the information knew that the tipper was breaching his duty.

(3) **Misappropriation:** Under the misappropriation doctrine, the government can prosecute a person under Section 10(b)(5) for trading on market information, thus breaching the duty of trust and confidence owed to the source of information; the duty need not be owed to the issuer or shareholders of the issuer.

3. SHORT SWING PROFITS – SECTION 16(B)

a) Section 16(b) requires a director, officer, or shareholder owning more than 10% of a class of the corporation's stock to surrender to the corporation any profit realized from the purchase and sale, or sale and purchase, of any equity security within a six-month period. This section applies to publicly-held corporations:

(1) With more than $10 million in assets and 500 or more shareholders; or

(2) Whose shares are traded on the National Stock Exchange.

b) **Strict Liability:** The purpose of Section 16(b) is to prevent unfair use of inside information and internal manipulation of price. This is accomplished by strict liability.

c) **Essay Approach:**

(1) Was the defendant an officer, director, or more than 10% shareholder?

(2) Did the defendant trade an equity security?

(3) Did a purchase and sale occur within a six-month period?

(4) What was the profit realized? The recoverable profit under Section 16(b) is determined by matching the highest sale price against the lowest purchase price for any six-month period. Thus, the profit can be either a gain or avoidance loss.

4. SALE OF CONTROLLING INTEREST

a) TENDER OFFERS

(1) Regulation of Bidder

If a bidder makes a public, open offer that would result in the bidder receiving more than 5% of a class of securities of the target corporation, the bidder must file a 14D schedule disclosing: (i) identities of the bidder and subject company; (ii) the source of funds used to finance the tender offer; (iii) past dealings with the target; (iv) its plans for the target; (v) the bidder's financial statements; and (vi) any arrangements made with target persons.

A tender offer is a widespread public offering to purchase a substantial percentage of the target's shares.

(2) Regulation of the Offer

A tender offer must be held open for at least 20 days and open to all members of class sought. Shareholders must be permitted to withdraw. If the tender offer is oversubscribed, it must be purchased on a prorated basis among shares deposited in the first ten (10) days; and if the offer price increases, the higher price must be paid to all shareholders.

(3) **Regulation of Target**

The target company's board of directors or management must make recommendations for acceptance or rejection of the tender offer or state why it cannot make a recommendation. Some states do not grant voting rights to all shares if a certain number of shares are purchased.

(4) **Anti-Fraud**

If the bidder makes any false or misleading statements, shareholders can sue for damages or the SEC may seek an injunction blocking the transaction.

F. DISREGARD OF THE CORPORATE ENTITY

1. COURTS

Can pierce the corporate veil and hold shareholders liable for corporate actions or debts in a number of circumstances:

a) FRAUD

A court may pierce the corporate veil if necessary to prevent shareholders from using the corporation to commit fraud or to avoid existing personal obligations.

b) UNDERCAPITALIZATION

If the corporation is not adequately capitalized, a court may pierce the corporate veil when the corporation is inadequately capitalized; i.e., when there are not enough assets to cover the corporation's possible liabilities.

c) ALTER EGO THEORY

If the corporation is merely an "alter ego" of the owner or another corporation, the corporate veil may be pierced.

Evidence that a corporation is an alter ego includes: (i) where shareholders utterly fail to observe formalities (as opposed to sloppy administration); (ii) treating the corporation's assets as their own; or (iii) operating the corporation solely on their own funds.

d) ENTERPRISE LIABILITY THEORY

When the same shareholders own stock of two corporations engaged in the same enterprise, a creditor of one corporation can reach the assets of the other.

e) DEEP ROCK DOCTRINE

Under the Deep Rock Doctrine, loans to a corporation by controlling shareholders may be subordinated to claims by outside creditors when the corporation is undercapitalized, or where there is bad-faith, fraud, or gross mismanagement.

2. WHO IS LIABLE?

When the corporate veil is pierced, the individuals who actively operated or managed the corporation will be jointly and severally liable as individuals.

3. TYPES OF LIABILITY

The corporate veil is more easily pierced in tort cases than in contract cases since a party entering into a contract with a corporation generally has had an opportunity to investigate the corporation.

4. WHO MAY PIERCE

Creditors may pierce the corporate veil.

G. Dissolution

1. Effect

a) Generally, a corporation exists perpetually; however, its existence can be terminated voluntarily or judicially.

b) A dissolved corporation still exists but it cannot carry out any activities other than those associated with winding up and liquidation.

c) After dissolution, the Board of Directors liquidates the assets and distributes the proceeds – first to creditors, then to the preferred shareholders, and finally to the common shareholders.

2. Voluntary and Involuntary Methods

a) Voluntary

Procedure:

(1) The Board of Directors adopts a resolution;
(2) The Board provides written notice to shareholders;
(3) The shareholders approve changes by a majority of votes that are entitled to be cast; and
(4) The corporation files the changes with the state.

b) Administrative

The state may seek dissolution for failure to pay fees, fines, file annual reports, or failure to maintain a registered agent.

c) Judicial

(1) Attorney General

The Attorney General may seek dissolution on the basis that the corporation fraudulently obtained its Articles of Incorporation, or is exceeding or abusing its authority.

(2) Action by Shareholders

Grounds include:

(a) The Board of Directors are deadlocked and irreparable injury to the corporation is threatened because of the deadlock;
(b) The directors have committed or will commit fraud, illegal or oppressive acts; or
(c) The directors have failed to elect one or more directors for two consecutive annual meetings; corporation assets are being wasted or used for non-corporation purposes.

(3) Creditors

Where a creditor's claim has been reduced to a judgment that is unsatisfied (or the corporation admits the claim is due and owing) and the corporation is insolvent.

H. Close Corporations

A close corporation is a corporation held by few persons, usually family members. Most states limit the number of stockholders.

1. Formation

a) Close corporations are formed in the same way as ordinary corporations, but the Articles of Incorporation must state that the corporation shall be considered a "close corporation." It usually must also impose restrictions on transfer of shares of stock.

b) A close corporation may be operated like a partnership with no Board of Directors or officers.

2. Rights and Liabilities

a) In a close corporation, the shareholders, directors, and officers are often the same individuals. Thus, there is generally no real independent Board of Directors. The shareholders of a close corporation may manage the corporation and override the directors.

b) If the shareholders manage the corporation, they may be liable for acts or omissions for which the corporate directors are usually liable. Actions by the directors may impute liability to the shareholders.

3. Creditors' Rights

A creditor may get a charging order to satisfy a shareholder's personal debt liability. With a charging order, the creditor is essentially able to participate in the management of the corporation and vote in favor of liquidating the debtor's interests.

4. Dissolution

a) A close corporation may be dissolved like any other corporation – voluntarily or judicially.

b) The shareholders in a close corporation may seek involuntary dissolution where it is necessary to protect the shareholders.

I. Professional Corporations

A professional corporation is like a corporation but is limited to certain professions. Each individual in a professional corporation is still liable for her own malpractice.

1. Formation

a) Professional corporations are created by state-licensed professions—lawyers, doctors, accountants, engineers, etc.

b) A professional corporation is organized under state laws and it must get approval from the state licensing board that regulates the relevant profession.

c) Identified by abbreviations – P.A. (Professional Association); P.C. (Professional Corporation); or S.C. (Service Corporation).

2. Operation

a) The shareholders must be actively engaged in the business, and not act as passive investors.

b) Many states require that the corporation be established only to provide professional services.

c) The corporation must operate in compliance with state laws that are enacted in conformity with tax requirements to gain tax advantages for activities that are traditionally attributed to partnerships or proprietorships.

3. Creditor Rights

A shareholder in a professional corporation cannot be sued for the corporation's business debts or for the careless acts of another shareholder. The shareholder can be sued for losses caused by the shareholder's own careless acts.

4. Dissolution

a) Professional corporations may be dissolved like any other corporation – voluntarily or judicially.

b) Most states require an agreement of dissolution to be filed with the Secretary of State.

II. PARTNERSHIPS AND UNINCORPORATED ASSOCIATIONS

A. Agency Principles

Agency is a legally binding relationship wherein the agent represents the principal in business dealings with third parties.

1. Formation of the Agency

Agency is a relationship created by the mutual consent of the principal and agent. Contractual formalities are not necessary to create an agency relationship.

a) Capacity

The principal must have the capacity to enter into a contract. An agent must have mental capacity but not contract capacity.

b) Disqualification

An agent risks disqualification for representing the principal as well as the third party or for not having a required license.

c) Formalities

(1) Consent

The consent of both the principal and the agent is required.

(2) Consideration

The agency relationship need not be supported by consideration.

(3) Writing

Generally, no writing is required. However, many states require a written agency agreement when the contractual agreement between the principal and the third party is within the Statute of Frauds, i.e., the acquisition of real property.

d) Modes of Creation

(1) Act of Parties

By agreement between the principal and agent (actual authority); by the principal holding out the agent as its agent (apparent authority); or the principal's approval of an act of its agent (ratification).

(2) Operation of Law

(a) Estoppel

An agency may be created through estoppel, if the third party relies on the principal's communication.

(b) Statute

State statutes may create agency relationships. This generally applies to real estate transactions.

2. Powers of the Agent

An agent is authorized to act for the principal. The terms of the contract provide the powers for which the agent is authorized to exercise on behalf of the principal.

When acting within her authority, the agent can bind the principal contractually. The authority to transact a principal's business usually carries with it the authority to contract in furtherance of that business.

3. Principal's Liability for Contracts and Torts of the Agent

a) Actual and Apparent Authority

To decide whether a principal will be bound on the agent's contract, it should first be determined whether the agent had actual authority. If he did not, determine whether apparent authority was present.

b) Actual Authority

Actual authority is that which the agent reasonably believed he possessed based on the principal's dealings with him. Such authority may be express or implied.

(1) Express Authority

Express authority is that which is actually described within the agency agreement.

(2) Implied Authority

(a) Implied authority is that which the agent reasonably believed he had as a result of the principal's actions. It includes authority:

1) Incidental to the principal's given express authority;
2) In line with the principal's customs, of which the agent knows;
3) Under a prior agreement;
4) Necessary in an emergency;
5) Necessary to delegate authority for ministerial acts when delegation is customary for the required performance;
6) Necessary to pay for and accept delivery of goods where the agent has the authority to purchase and accept goods;
7) Necessary to give general warranties as to fitness and quality, authorize covenants regarding land sales, collect payment, and deliver where the agent has the authority to sell; and
8) Necessary to manage investments in accordance with the prudent investor standard.

(3) Termination of Actual Authority

(a) Has the authority been terminated? Termination of actual authority may occur by:

(b) Lapse of specified or reasonable time;

(c) Occurrence of a specified event;

(d) Change in circumstances such as when the subject matter is destroyed, insolvency or a change in law or the business's status;

(e) The agent's breaching his fiduciary duty;

(f) One party's terminating authority (although such action may also constitute a breach);

(g) Operation of law – such as the death of the principal (unless the authority is irrevocable), or the loss of capacity of one of the parties.

(4) Irrevocable Agencies

An agency coupled with an interest or a power given as security may not be unilaterally terminated by the principal if the agency was given to protect the agent's (or a third party's) rights and the agency is supported by consideration, nor can such agencies be terminated by operation of law.

c) Apparent Authority

A principal directly or indirectly confers apparent authority on an agent when he holds another out as possessing certain authority, thereby inducing reasonable reliance by third parties. *(Look to what transpired between the principal and the third party to make the third party believe that the agent apparently had authority.)*

(1) Types of Apparent Authority

(a) Imposters

Where the principal negligently permits an imposter to be in a position appearing to have agency authority, the principal will be held liable for an imposter's actions when the principal negligently allows the person to be in a position in which he appears to have agency authority.

(b) **Lingering Apparent Authority**

Notice: When the principal terminates the agent's actual authority, the agent will still have apparent authority with third parties with whom the principal knows the agent dealt, until the third parties receive actual or constructive notice of termination.

Writing: When the principal terminates the agent's actual authority, but third parties rely on a written authority, the agent will still have apparent authority.

Death or Incompetency: An agent's authority ends when the principal dies or becomes incompetent. No notice to either the agent or third parties is necessary. There is a limited exception where a bank may honor transactions until it learns of the death or incompetence and has had a reasonable time to act.

(2) **Exceeding Actual Authority**

In certain situations, the principal may still be bound by an agent's acts even when he has exceeded his authority.

(a) **Prior Act**

The principal is bound by the agent's unauthorized acts when the principal has previously permitted the agent to exceed his authority, of which the third party is aware.

(b) **Position**

The principal is liable for the agent's acts within the scope of the agent's customary responsibilities.

(3) **Inherent Authority (Inherent Agency Power)**

A principal may be bound by an agent's act that is within the agent's inherent authority even though the agent had no actual authority to perform the particular acts.

(a) **Respondeat Superior**

Under the doctrine of respondeat superior, the principal is liable for the torts that an employee commits within the scope of employment.

(b) **Conduct Similar to that Authorized**

Where an agent exceeds his actual authority, but the agent's conduct is similar to authorized conduct, the principal will be held liable for the agent's acts.

d) **RATIFICATION**

When an agent purports to act on behalf of a principal and the principal subsequently validates the act, the principal is bound by the act.

(1) **Prerequisites**

To be bound by ratification, the principal must know (or should have known) all material facts, ratify the entire transaction, and have the capacity – competency, be of legal age – to ratify the act. No consideration is required.

(2) **Methods**

The act of the agent can be ratified by either the express or implied conduct of the principal, i.e., the acceptance of benefits, the principal's silence where there is a duty to disaffirm the act, or the principal filing a lawsuit based upon the transaction.

(3) **Effective**

Where performance is not illegal, a third party has not withdrawn, or there is no material change in the situation.

e) **LIABILITIES OF THE PARTIES**

(1) **Third Party v. Principal**

The principal is liable to a third party on a contract entered into by an agent with authority.

(2) **Third Party v. Agent**

The agent's liability depends on whether or not the principal was disclosed.

(a) **Disclosed Principal**

A disclosed principal is always liable. An agent is not liable. Exception: The parties intended that the agent be liable; the agent misrepresents the principal's contractual capacity or agent's authority.

(b) **Partially Disclosed/Undisclosed Principals**

If the principal is partially disclosed or undisclosed, the principal and the agent are liable.

(3) **Third Party Liability to Principal and Agent**

(a) **Principal Disclosed**

Only the principal, not the agent, may enforce the contract where the principal is disclosed.

(b) **Partially or Undisclosed**

Either the principal or the agent may enforce the contract where the principal is undisclosed or partially disclosed.

(c) **Not Enforceable**

Where there has been fraud, the contract is not enforceable.

f) **TORT LIABILITY – RESPONDEAT SUPERIOR**

The doctrine of Respondeat Superior imputes joint and several liability to the employer-principal for torts committed by the employee-agent within the scope of the employee's employment.

(1) **Employer-Employee Relationship**

(a) **Independent Contractor or Employee**

A principal is only liable for torts committed by agents who are employees, not for torts committed by independent contractors.

Right to Control: A principal cannot control the manner or method in which an independent contractor performs a job. A principal can exercise such control over an employee.

Factors to Consider: (i) the parties; (ii) whether the business is distinct; (iii) local customs; (iv) the level of skill required for the job; (v) whether the contractor is using his own tools or the facility's tools; (vi) time; and (vii) the basis for compensation.

(b) **Estoppel**

If the principal creates the appearance of an employer-employee relationship and a third party relies on it, that principal will be estopped from denying the existence of an employer-employee relationship.

(c) **Borrowed Employee**

Any liability is determined by who has the primary right to control the employee's actions.

(d) **Liability for Acts by Independent Contractors**

The principal will be liable where: (i) the work is inherently dangerous; (ii) the independent contractor delegates non-delegable duties; or (iii) the principal knowingly selected an incompetent independent contractor (if negligent, then negligence).

(2) **Scope of Employment**

Where there is an employer-employee relationship, the employer will be liable for the employee's torts if they were committed within the scope of employment.

(a) **Same General Nature of Job**

The activity need not be actually authorized, nor does a prohibition remove the activity from the scope of employment. If the nature of the conduct is similar or incidental to that which is authorized, the conduct is probably within the scope of employment. Criminal acts are never within the scope.

(b) **Frolic and Detour**

Was the frolic and detour within the time and place of authorized employment? A detour or small deviation is within the scope. When there is a major detour, proof of return is needed before liability resumes.

(c) **Intentional Torts**

Intentional torts are not within the scope of employment unless they are incidental to the employee's duties, such as where the use of force is authorized. The principal is liable for the agent's misrepresentations if the agent had actual, apparent, and/or inherent authority to make statements regarding the subject matter.

(d) **Ratification**

An employer may ratify the tortious acts of an employee if the employer has knowledge of all material facts.

4. Fiduciary Duties

The agent owes all express contractual duties to the principal, as well as the fiduciary duties of loyalty, obedience to any reasonable directives given by the principal, reasonable care under the circumstances, and the duty to disclose.

B. General Partnerships

When two or more persons carry on as co-owners of a business venture for profit, they are engaged in a partnership.

1. Formation

a) Agreement

To form a partnership, a writing is generally not required unless it falls within the purview of the Statute of Frauds. Intent to form a partnership is sufficient. The parties' intent may be implied from their conduct.

(1) **Sharing of Profits**

The sharing of profits raises a presumption of an existing partnership, unless the sharing of profits was meant to serve as a payment of debt, for services rendered, as rent payment, as an annuity or other retirement benefit, interest on a loan, or goodwill of a business. This can be rebutted.

(2) **Evidence Indicative of Partnership**

A court will likely find that a partnership existed where parties hold title to property in joint tenancy or tenancy in common, the parties have designated their relationship as a partnership, there is extensive activity among the parties, and they share gross returns or expenses.

b) **Capacity**

A partner may be anyone who is capable of entering into a binding contract. If the individual lacks the capacity to enter into a contract, he is only liable to the same extent as his contribution.

c) **Legal Purpose**

Individuals may not form a partnership to achieve an illegal purpose. Courts will not compel an accounting or settlement of a voided partnership's affairs.

d) **Consent**

No third party can become a partner without the express or implied consent of all existing partners.

2. **Partnership Assets**

a) **Titled Property**

Property is that of the partnership if: (i) the partnership holds title in its name; or (ii) one or more of the partners hold title in their name(s) and the instrument transferring title denotes the titleholder's capacity as a partner or the existence of a partnership.

b) **Presumed Partnership Property**

Property that is purchased with partnership funds is presumed to be partnership property, regardless of in whose name title is held.

c) **Presumed Separate Property**

Property is presumed to be separate property if: (i) the property is held in the name of one or more of the partners; (ii) the instrument transferring title does not indicate the person's capacity as a partner or mention the existence of a partnership; and (iii) partnership funds were not used to acquire the property. There is a rebuttable presumption that it is separate property even if it is used for partnership purposes.

d) **Approach**

Will it be titled in a partnership name or titled in a partner's name and listed as a partner? Will it be purchased with partnership funds?

e) **Untitled Property**

If there is no title, courts will look to: (i) the source of funds that were used to acquire the property; (ii) how the partnership uses the property; (iii) whether it was entered into the partnership's books as an asset; (iv) the relationship between the property and the business; and (v) whether partnership funds were used for the maintenance or improvement of the property.

f) **Rights of Partner**

If the partner is not a co-owner, he will have no transferable interest in the property. The partner can only use property for the benefit of the partnership.

3. **Powers of Partners to Bind the Partnership**

a) **Apparent Authority**

The act of any partner, for apparently carrying on in the ordinary course of the partnership business or business of the kind carried out by the partnership, binds the partnership unless: (i) the partner had no authority to act for the partnership; and (ii) the third party knew that the partner lacked authority.

As agents of the partnership, partners have the apparent authority to bind the partnership to any contract within the scope of the partnership business. Unless the partner has actual authority, the partnership will generally not be bound if the contract is outside the scope of the partnership business.

b) Actual Authority

If a partner has actual authority, a partnership will be bound by an act of the partner. Actual authority is the authority a partner reasonably believes she has based on the communications between the partnership and the partner.

4. Enforcement of Partnership Rights and Obligations

a) Partners' Rights

(1) Management

All partners have an equal right to participate in the management of the partnership unless the partnership agreement provides otherwise.

(2) Distributions

Partners have whatever rights are granted in the partnership agreement as to distribution of profits. If the agreement is silent, the partners share equally in profits and losses.

(3) Remuneration

Except for the winding up of the partnership business, partners have no right to remuneration for their services to the partnership.

(4) Indemnification

A partner has the right to be indemnified by fellow partners for expenses incurred on behalf of the partnership.

(5) Contribution

A partner has a right to contribution from fellow partners where the partner has paid more than his share of partnership liability.

(6) Inspection

A partner has the right to inspect and/or copy the partnership's financial records.

5. Lawsuits

Generally, a partner may sue his partnership and the partnership may sue a partner in an action at law or in equity.

6. Partner Relationship

a) Obligations

Generally, each partner:

(1) Has the right and duty to help manage the partnership;
(2) Must contribute to the partnership fund;
(3) Must work only on behalf of the partnership;
(4) Must observe any limitations adopted by a majority of the partners;
(5) Has a duty to inform the partnership of all matters relevant to the partnership;
(6) Has a duty to produce and receive complete information on all aspects of the partnership's business; and
(7) Has a duty to maintain the confidentiality of partnership information.

The partnership agreement may provide for additional obligations.

b) Fiduciary Obligations

(1) Each partner is an agent for the other partners. Therefore, he owes the others a fiduciary duty of care similar to that of a principal–agent relationship.

(2) Partner must act in good faith for the benefit of the corporation.

7. Dissolution and Dissociation

a) Dissolution

The dissolution of a partnership generally requires that the partnership business be wound up.

(1) Events Causing Dissolution

(i) the notification of the intent to withdraw; (ii) the expiration of a term; (iii) the consent of all the partners to dissolve; (iv) the happening of an agreed-upon event; or (v) a judicial decree that the economic purpose of the partnership has been frustrated, is no longer practicable or lawful, or cannot be performed pursuant to the partnership agreement.

(2) Partner's Power to Bind Partnership After Dissolution

A partner's power to bind the partnership after dissolution occurs can be bound by the act of any partner appropriate for winding up, as well as for any other act with a party with whom partner dealt that did not have knowledge of the dissolution. Particular liability can be limited by filing notice with the state (all parties deemed to have knowledge after 90 days).

(3) Partnership Continues After Dissolution

A partnership continues even after dissolution until the business is wound up and can be waived and reinstated by a unanimous vote.

(4) Distribution of Assets

Upon dissolution, the partnership's assets are liquidated and the partnership's liabilities are paid first to creditors and then to the other partners. A partner who paid more than her fair share is entitled to contribution.

b) Dissociation

A dissociated partner is any partner ceasing to be associated in the carrying on of the partnership business.

(1) Events of Dissociation

(i) notice of the partner's express will to withdraw; (ii) the happening of an agreed-upon event; (iii) a partner's expulsion by agreement, vote, or judicial decree; (iv) a partner's bankruptcy; (v) the death/incapacity of a partner; (vi) the appointment of a receiver; or (vii) the termination of a business entity that is a partner.

(2) Dissociated Partner's Power to Bind Partnership

If, within two (2) years, an ex-partner performs an act that would have bound the partnership and the other party reasonably believes that he is still a partner and the other party did not have notice of dissociation, the partnership is bound.

(3) Dissociated Partner's Liability

An ex-partner is liable for a former partner's acts if the other party reasonably believed the person was still a partner and the other party did not have notice of the partner's dissociation. Liability lasts for two (2) years after leaving, although it can be cut short by filing a notice of dissociation with the Secretary of State.

8. Personal Liability of Partners for Partnership Obligations

a) Purported Partners

(1) Liability of Person Held Out as Partner

When a person, by word or conduct, represents herself as a partner, or consents to being represented by another as a partner, she will be liable to third parties who extend credit to the partnership in reliance on the representation. If a person who is not a partner is merely held out as a partner, she does not have a duty to deny it and will not be held liable as a partner.

(2) **Liability of Person Who Holds Another Out as Partner**

When a person holds another out as a partner, that person is an agent who is bound by third parties. If there is a partnership, only partners who have knowledge will be bound.

b) **LIABILITY OF PARTNERSHIP**

(1) **Civil**

The partnership is liable for all contracts entered into by a partner within the scope of partnership business or outside of the scope but with valid authority. The partnership is liable for all torts committed by a partner or partnership employee within the ordinary course of partnership business.

(a) **Joint and Several Liability**

A partner is liable for all obligations of the partnership, whether in tort or in contract. A partner is entitled to indemnification, or for contribution when he pays more than his fair share. A judgment is not personally binding on a partner unless served.

(b) **Incoming Partner**

An incoming partner is not liable for obligations incurred by the partnership before the person became a partner.

(c) **Outgoing Partner**

An outgoing partner remains liable for obligations incurred while he was a partner unless there has been a release or novation.

(2) **Criminal**

Partners will not be criminally liable for the crimes of other partners unless he participated in the commission of the crime.

C. LIMITED PARTNERSHIPS

A limited partnership is comprised of one or more general partners and one or more limited partners. The liability for a limited partner for partnership debts is generally limited to the capital that he contributes to the partnership.

1. FORMATION

a) **CERTIFICATE OF LIMITED PARTNERSHIP**

The certificate must be signed by all of the partners setting forth the name of the partnership, the identity and address of the agent for service of process, and of each general partner, and the latest date upon which the partnership is to dissolve must be filed with the Secretary of State.

b) **RECORDS OFFICE**

A limited partnership must maintain an office with records of the certificate, partnership agreements, tax returns for the last three (3) years, and the amount of each partner's contribution and special rights.

c) **AGENT**

A limited partnership must maintain – in the state – an agent for service of legal process.

***Exam Tip*:** A limited partnership is a statutory creation and therefore if one partner tells another that he can have limited liability, it is not valid unless paperwork is filed with the Secretary of State. Until that time, full liability attaches.

d) **NAME OF PARTNERSHIP**

The name of a partnership may not contain the name of a limited partner unless it is also the name of a general partner. It must contain the words "Limited Partnership" and cannot be deceptive or similar to another limited partnership.

e) **ADDITION OF A PARTNER**

Adding a partner is governed by the partnership agreement. If it is silent, written consent of all partners is required.

f) **NATURE OF CONTRIBUTION**

It can be cash, property, or services rendered. A limited partner's promise to pay is not enforceable unless it is in writing. If a partner gets his contribution back, for one (1) year, it can be used to satisfy partnership debts. If it is a wrongful return, the entire amount can be liable for six (6) years.

2. **PARTNERSHIP ASSETS**

a) Partnership assets are those assets that are owned by the partnership as such, as opposed to assets used by the partnership but owned by one of the partners.
b) Even where one partner purchases an asset, it may be a partnership asset if all partners so intend. If the partnership purchases property with partnership assets, courts will presume it is an asset of the partnership.
c) Individual partners may not sell or assign partnership property without consent of all partners.

3. **GENERAL PARTNERS' RIGHTS AND LIABILITIES**

a) General partners have the right: (i) to share in profits and losses pursuant to a partnership agreement or in proportion to contribution *(cf: regular partnerships where the share is equal)*; (ii) to assign their interest, but the assignee is not entitled to exercise the rights of a partner; (iii) to transact business with the partnership (lend it money); (iv) to withdraw; and (v) to apply for dissolution.
b) General partners have all the rights that a partner in a regular partnership would have with regard to management.
c) General partners are subject to all of the liabilities of a partner in a regular partnership, including personal liability for partnership obligations.

4. **LIMITED PARTNERS' RIGHTS AND LIABILITIES**

a) Limited partners have the right to share in profits and losses pursuant to partnership agreement or in proportion to contribution *(cf: regular partnerships where the share is equal)*; to assign their interest, but the assignee is not entitled to exercise the rights of a partner; to transact business with the partnership (lend it money); to withdraw; and to apply for dissolution.
b) Limited partners have the right to: (i) vote on specific matters, but not to participate in control of the business; (ii) obtain partnership information (inspect books); (iii) bring a derivative action if the general partners refuse to do so or an attempt would be futile.
c) A limited partner is not liable for partnership obligations beyond their contributions. Exceptions: Where the limited partner: (i) is also a general partner; (ii) participates in control of the business and person dealing with partnership reasonably believes the limited partner is a general partner; and (iii) knowingly permits her name to be used improperly.
d) One who believes she is a limited partner, but is a general partner, can avoid general partner liability if, upon discovering the mistake, she files with the Secretary of State a

certificate of amendment or withdraws from participation by filing a certificate of withdrawal. However, she will be liable as a general partner to any third party who actually and in good-faith believed she was a general partner and the transaction occurred before the correction or withdrawal.

5. Fiduciary Obligations

a) Because limited partners are not usually involved in managing the business, they typically do not owe fiduciary duties to the limited partnership. However, limited partners who manage the business may owe the associated fiduciary duties.
b) General partners owe the same fiduciary duties to limited partners that partners owe to each other in a general partnership.

6. Dissolution and Disassociation

Dissolution may take place by: (i) occurrence of time stated in certificate of limited partnership; (ii) occurrence of event/time provided in partnership agreement; (iii) written consent of all parties; (iv) withdrawal of a general partner unless otherwise provided for in the agreement or by consent of all partners; or (v) judicial dissolution.

D. Joint Ventures

1. A joint venture is formed when two or more individuals or companies are engaged in a single business enterprise but have not formed a partnership or corporation. A joint venture is based on a single business transaction, not an ongoing relationship.
2. A joint venture is formed by a contract or an agreement.
3. A joint venture terminates upon a time or event specified in the contract, accomplishment of purpose, death of a member, or court order.

III. LIMITED LIABILITY COMPANIES ("LLC")

A. Nature of the Entity

LLCs are hybrid organizations that offer pass-through taxation, offer their owners limited liability similar to that of the shareholders of a corporation, and can be run like a corporation or a partnership.

B. Formation

An LLC is formed by filing the Articles of Organization with the Secretary of State.

1. Contents

A statement that the entity is an LLC, the name of the LLC, the address of the registered office, the name of the registered agent for service of process, and the names of all the members.

C. Management

Management of the LLC is presumed to be by all of the members, but the Articles may provide otherwise. If by a member, a majority vote is required to approve most decisions, and each member is an agent of the LLC.

D. Financial Rights and Obligations of Members

1. Internal Allocation of Financial Interests

Members share profits and losses equally unless otherwise agreed.

2. Member Contributions

Members must adequately fund the LLC so that it can meet its foreseeable expenses and liabilities.

3. Liability of Members for LLC Obligations

The members are not personally liable for the LLC's obligations.

4. Creditors' Rights

A personal creditor of a member may:

a) Get a court order requiring the LLC to pay the creditor from the LLC;
b) Foreclose on the owner's LLC ownership interest; or
c) Ask a court to dissolve the LLC.

E. Management

1. Members and Manager

a) Member-Managed LLC

In most LLCs, the members participate in the management of the business.

b) Manager-Managed LLC

Members may designate one or more members or outsiders to manage the LLC.

2. Liability of Managers and Officers

A member may be personally liable if she:

a) Personally guarantees a loan or debt and the LLC defaults;
b) Intentionally does something fraudulent, illegal, or reckless that harms the LLC or another person; or
c) Fails to treat the LLC as a legal entity separate from her personal affairs.

3. Indemnification

LLCs can agree, and some states require, that an LLC reimburse and indemnify members and managers for payments and liabilities incurred in the ordinary conduct of business.

4. Failure to Comply with Organization Formalities

If managers and owners do not treat the LLC as a separate business, a court may decide they are personally liable.

F. Fiduciary Obligations of Managers, Managing Members, and Members

1. Members of a manager-managed LLC owe fiduciary duties of loyalty and care to the company and its other members. However, members may reasonably restrict or eliminate fiduciary duties.
2. Managers of a manager-managed LLC also owe fiduciary duties of loyalty and care to the company and other members.

G. Dissolution

Dissociation (death, incompetency, etc.) of an LLC member generally causes dissolution.

IV. LIMITED LIABILITY PARTNERSHIP ("LLP")

A. Nature of the Entity

Much like an LLC, an LLP provides pass-through taxation and personal liability protection from business debts and liabilities. Unlike an LLC, where members are not protected from the liability created by other members, LLP members are shielded from the liability created by other members.

B. Formation Requirements

1. Voting

The terms and conditions by which a partnership becomes an LLP must be approved by whatever vote is required to amend the partnership agreement. If the agreement is silent, all partners must approve the creation of the LLP.

2. Filing

To become an LLP, a statement of qualification must be filed with the Secretary of State. It must be executed by at least two (2) partners and contain such information as: (i) the name and address of the partnership; (ii) a statement that the partnership elects to become an LLP; and (iii) the preferred effective date.

3. Name

The name of the partnership must end with the words "Registered Limited Liability Partnership," or the letters "LLP."

C. Financial Rights and Obligations of Partners

1. Agreements For Partner Compensation and Profit Sharing

The partnership agreement dictates individual partner compensation and additional profit sharing.

2. Distributions to Partners

The partnership agreement specifies when financial distributions are to be made to the partners and under what circumstances.

3. Indemnification and Loss-Sharing Provisions

Indemnification and loss-sharing provisions may provide for indemnification and contributions for a partner's negligent acts.

D. Liability of Partners

A partner in an LLP is not personally liable for the obligations of the partnership. However, a partner remains personally liable for his wrongful acts.

1. Creditors' Rights

a) Creditors can pierce the protection from a limited liability corporation to hold a partner individually liable.

b) An individual's liability depends on the scope of the state's statute. Many states only provide protection for intentional torts, not negligence or incompetence. Some states extend protection for contractual claims.

2. Extent of Liability

Partners will not be personally liable for professional malpractice against another partner.

3. Indemnification

Some states hold that a negligent partner is not entitled to indemnification or contribution for his negligent acts.

E. Fiduciary Obligations

Partners owe fiduciary duties of loyalty and care to the LLP and other partners.

F. Dissolution

Like in a partnership, an LLP may be voluntarily or judicially dissolved. It must file Articles of Dissolution or a Certificate of Cancellation with the Secretary of State. It also must notify creditors and anyone else who has an interest in the LLP first.

CIVIL PROCEDURE

Table of Contents

Overview

Whether the plaintiff has a meritorious claim or that the defendant has a good and valid defense, is only part of the legal process.

A party pursuing a claim or a party defending a claim needs to be aware of the rules of civil procedure applicable in the jurisdiction in which the action is brought not only to ensure the proceedings are adequately and effectively dealt with but also to ensure that a breach of the rules does not result in some penalty being imposed. The rules of civil procedure have an underlying logical basis and apply throughout the proceedings to which they relate, from the issue and service of proceedings through to final judgment and enforcement.

It is important, of course, that a claim is brought within the jurisdiction of the court in which the proceedings are issued and, once commenced, the rules are observed and applied at the relevant stage of the proceedings.

California Jurisdiction – Court / Trial Court

The California State Constitution vests judicial power in the State Courts comprising:

(a) The Supreme Court of California. The SCC is the highest court in California and its decisions are binding on all other courts in California. It has power to review decisions of the State Courts of Appeal and has original jurisdiction in proceedings for mandamus, certiorari and prohibition in civil proceedings and habeas corpus in criminal proceedings.

(b) Courts of Appeal. The CofA has appellate jurisdiction in cases where Superior Courts have original jurisdiction.

(c) Superior Courts. The SC has civil jurisdiction over all civil cases and also criminal trial jurisdiction over all criminal cases.

Following constitutional amendments, the California Superior Court has jurisdiction in all matters that previously fell under the jurisdiction of either the superior court or municipal court. However, jurisdictional differences between the superior/municipal court remain relevant in the context of certain trial procedures including, for example:

-The size of the jury
-For purposes of the court for appellate review

An action may be classified as a "limited civil case" or "unlimited civil case". A limited civil case is one where the amount in controversy does not exceed $25,000, and an unlimited civil case is one where the claim is for more than $25,000, or is a claim designated by statute as unlimited regardless of the amount in controversy. See California Code of Civil Procedure (CCP) §§ 85 and 86.

NOTE: Although provisions of the CCP apply generally, there are some provisions that apply only to limited civil cases, including:

(i) § 92 – Limitation on pleadings;
(ii) §§ 94, 95 – Limitations on discovery;
(iii) § 98 – Admitting "affidavits or declarations under penalty of perjury" in lieu of direct testimony;
(iv) § 92 – The option to serve questionnaires with the complaint.

CCP § 85 defines "amount in controversy" as "the amount of the demand, or the recovery sought, or the value of the property, or the amount of the lien, that is in controversy in the action, exclusive of attorney's fees, interests and costs."

NOTE: 1. If a single plaintiff alleges multiple causes of action against a single defendant, the amount in controversy is the aggregate of all the claims.

2. If the good-faith demand identifies the claim as an unlimited civil case, but the amount recovered by the judgment is within a limited civil case, the court is not required to reclassify the action, but may refuse to award costs to the plaintiff.

I. JURISDICTION OVER PERSONS AND PROPERTY

A. In Personal Jurisdiction

In personam or personal jurisdiction, refers to the ability of the court having subject matter jurisdiction to exercise power over a particular defendant or item of property. Under the Constitution, personal jurisdiction is valid if: (i) the party is personally served in state; (ii) the party is domiciled in the forum state; (iii) the party consents to jurisdiction (expressly or implicitly); or (iv) the party's act falls within the state's long arm statute.

1. Due Process Notice Requirements

The defendant must be notified of the lawsuit by a reasonable method and given an opportunity to appear and be heard.

2. Personal Service

Personal service occurs when the defendant is present in the forum state and is personally served with process.

3. Consent to Jurisdiction

a) Actual

Actual consent occurs by making a general appearance so as to defend on the merits of the plaintiff's claim and accept the court's jurisdiction; or answering the complaint.

(1) Special Appearance

The defendant may make a special appearance in court to challenge the jurisdiction by a motion to dismiss or motion to quash service for lack of jurisdiction.

b) Implied Consent

The mere fact the defendant owns property in the state will not give the court personal jurisdiction over the defendant-owner unless the action is directly related to the piece of property.

(1) Domicile

Where the defendant is domiciled in the forum state, the issue usually centers on whether the defendant is in fact domiciled in the state.

4. Long Arm Statute

Long arm statutes (LAS) allow a state to exercise jurisdiction over an out-of-state defendant, provided the prospective defendant has **sufficient minimum contact** with the forum state (infra), in order to satisfy the Due Process Clause of the Constitution. A nonresident defendant whose activities within the state are substantial, continuous, and systematic is subject to "general jurisdiction" in the state, meaning jurisdiction is available on any cause of action. But, if the position is otherwise, that is the activities are not as pervasive in order to satisfy "general jurisdiction," the defendant is subject to "specific jurisdiction" only if:

a) The defendant purposefully availed himself of the benefit of conducting activities in the forum state, thereby obtaining the benefit and protection of the state's laws;
b) The dispute arises out of or has a substantial connection with the defendant's contacts with the state;
c) The exercise of jurisdiction will be fair and reasonable.
d) Note: The court does not simply adopt and apply a mechanistic approach to the jurisdictional question in each case. The court must weigh the facts of each individual case to determine whether a defendant's contact with the forum state is sufficient.

California's Long Arm Statute (§410.10) in short states that a court may exercise jurisdiction on any basis that is not inconsistent with the constitution of California or the USA and which therefore provides California courts with wide jurisdiction over non-residents (subject to any limiting constitutional factors).

5. Minimum Contacts Doctrine

The Fourteenth Amendment's Due Process Clause restricts a state's authority to bind a nonresident defendant to a judgment of its court and requires the nonresident to have "certain minimum contacts" with the forum state.

a) Contacts

The contacts must show that the defendant:

(1) Purposefully availed himself of the forum state's laws; and
(2) Knew, or reasonably should have anticipated, that his activities in the forum state made it foreseeable that he may be "haled into court" there.

b) Fairness

(1) If the claim is related to the defendant's contact with the forum state (specific personal jurisdiction), the court is more likely to find the exercise of jurisdiction to be fair and reasonable; or
(2) If the defendant engages in systematic and continuous activity in the forum state, the court is likely to find this activity to be a sufficient basis for exercising personal jurisdiction over any cause of action (general personal jurisdiction). The court, also, will consider other factors, including:
   (a) Whether the forum is "so gravely difficult and inconvenient" that the defendant is put at a severe disadvantage;
   (b) The forum state's legitimate interest in providing redress for its residents;
   (c) The plaintiff's interest in obtaining convenient and effective relief;
   (d) The interstate judicial system's interest in efficiency; and
   (e) The shared interest of the states in furthering social policies.

B. Quasi In Rem and In Rem Jurisdiction

If personal jurisdiction is not possible or the plaintiff's claim is limited to property interests within the jurisdiction, the court can hear the case under either of these doctrines.

1. Location of the Property (i.e., Situs of the Res)

In rem jurisdiction exists when the court has the power to adjudicate the rights of all persons in the world with respect to a particular item over property located within the physical borders of the state. There is no state court jurisdiction; i.e., no "in rem" power, over property outside the state.

2. Subjecting the Property (Res) to Jurisdiction

Where quasi in rem jurisdiction exists, the court can attach or garnish property in the state belonging to the defendant. The plaintiff's action against the defendant could be litigated but the judgment is limited to the property before the court.

a) Shaffer v. Heitner: In the case of Shaffer v. Heitner, the court determined that there must be a nexus between the defendant and the state, in addition to the mere presence of the property in order to impose jurisdiction.
   (1) A quasi in rem judgment is only enforceable to the extent of the property attached.
   (2) A quasi in rem judgment has no res judicata or collateral estoppel effect.

b) Quasi & in rem jurisdiction requires that the defendant receive notice reasonably calculated to reach the defendant and provide an opportunity to be heard.

3. Effect of Adjudication of Jurisdictional Issue

Parties may waive a jurisdictional issue related to venue.

a) Waiver

(1) Unless there is a timely objection to "venue," any issue relating thereto is deemed to be waived.

(2) Subject matter jurisdiction cannot be waived because it relates to the authority of the court to determine the issue in dispute.

b) If "venue" is correctly identified in the action, then the court will apply the relevant state law in determining the issues in dispute. If "venue" is incorrectly identified and the case is transferred to a court with jurisdiction, it will be the law of the transferee state.

4. Lack of Jurisdiction

a) Procedures for Raising Jurisdictional Defects

A party pursuing a claim must bring proceedings in a court of competent jurisdiction (i.e., one capable of dealing with the action and of entering a valid and enforceable judgment). Rule 12, Federal Rules of Civil Procedure (FRCP) provides that all legal and factual defenses to a claim must be set out in the response to the claim. Generally, unless the time is specified either by Rule 12 or federal statute, the time for serving an answer is within 21 days after being served with the summons and complaint, or if time has been waived, within 60 days after the request for waiver was sent (or 90 days if sent to a defendant outside any judicial district of the United States) and the answer to a counterclaim or cross claim within 21 days after being served with a pleading stating a counterclaim or cross claim.

NOTE : If a motion is served under Rule 12, the time periods referred to are altered as follows (unless the court sets a different time): (i) if the motion is denied or its disposition is postponed until trial, the response pleading must be served within 14 days after receiving notice of the court's action; or (ii) if the court grants a motion for a more definite statement, the response pleading must be served within 14 days after the more definite statement is served.

By Rule 12(b), every defense to a claim for relief in any pleading must be asserted in the responsive pleading if one is required BUT a party may assert the following defenses by motion:

(1) Lack of subject matter jurisdiction (12(b)(1));
(2) Lack of personal jurisdiction (12(b)(2));
(3) Improper venue (12(b)(3));
(4) Insufficient process (12(b)(4));
(5) Insufficient service of process (12(b)(5));
(6) Failure to state a claim for which relief is available (12(b)(6)); and
(7) Failure to join a party under rule 19 (12(b)(7)).

If pursuing a Rule 12 motion to dismiss, all Rule 12 defenses and objections must be included in the motion.

b) Note

The following defenses are not waived by not including them in the answer: (i) failure to state a claim upon which relief can be granted; (ii) failure to join a party under Rule 19; and (iii) lack of subject matter jurisdiction.

c) Special Appearances

The defendant can appear to challenge the jurisdiction by a motion to dismiss or motion to quash service for lack of jurisdiction.

d) General Appearances

When responding to a claim a defendant must:

(1) Set out in short precise terms his defense to each claim pursued against him; and

(2) Admit or deny the allegations asserted against him by the plaintiff and raise jurisdictional defects, if not otherwise pursued by a motion to dismiss.

C. Consequences of Defective Jurisdiction

Jurisdiction and venue are determined by statute, not by the rules of procedure and could result in failure of the proceedings.

D. Collateral Attack on Judgments

Collateral attacks are initiated by commencing a separate action to vacate a judgment for lack of personal jurisdiction. There is no time limit to bring a collateral attack but a party should act diligently on learning of any judgment entered against him. "Laches" is not available as a defense where there has been a complete failure of service of process upon a defendant.

II. FEDERAL COURT SUBJECT MATTER JURISDICTION

A. Federal Courts

Federal courts are courts of limited jurisdiction and a civil action is commenced by filing a complaint with the court (Rule 3, FRCP), and which must comply with the provisions of Rule 4, FRCP. To bring a suit in federal court, the court must have jurisdiction over the subject matter of the dispute. Subject matter jurisdiction can be based either on diversity of citizenship or federal question.

NOTE: Also the provisions of Article III of the United States Constitution which by §1 states the "Judicial Power of the United States shall be vested in one Supreme Court and in such inferior courts as the Congress may from time to time ordain and establish."

B. Federal Questions

The district courts have original jurisdiction over all civil actions arising under the Constitution, laws, or treaties of the United States.

C. Diversity Requirements

1. Diversity of Citizenship

Federal courts can hear a case: (i) between "citizens of different states" (or a citizen and a foreign citizen); and (ii) if the amount in controversy exceeds $75k, excluding costs and interest.

a) Complete Diversity Rule

There is no diversity of citizenship if any plaintiff is a citizen of the same state as any defendant.

(1) Individual Citizenship

Domicile is established by: (1) physical presence in the state; with (2) the intent to make that state her permanent home.

(2) Corporations

Corporations are citizens of: (1) the state where they are incorporated; and (2) the state where they have their principal place of business.

(a) Place of Business:

i. Nerve Center Test: A corporation's place of residence is its principal place of business, which can be defined as the location where its leading officers direct, control, and coordinate its activities. However, simply having an office in a state for the purposes of board meetings is unlikely to satisfy this test.

(3) Partnerships

Courts must look to citizenship of all members, including general and limited.

(4) **Trustee/Executor**

The beneficiary determines diversity.

(5) **Aliens**

Aliens are deemed citizens of another state.

(6) **Replacement**

Replacement of parties can destroy diversity.

(a) **Improper or Collusive Joinder of Parties**

If there is improper or collusive joinder of parties, the court is permitted to dismiss sham parties or join necessary parties with potential effects on diversity.

(7) **Amount in Controversy**

Actions brought under the diversity statute must be in excess of $75,000, exclusive of interest and costs.

(a) **Aggregation**

One plaintiff can aggregate all claims against the defendant to meet the necessary amount.

(b) **Multiple Plaintiffs and Defendants**

When there are multiple plaintiffs and defendants, claims cannot be aggregated. At least one plaintiff's claim must meet the $75,000 requirement.

(c) **Counter Claims**

Claims made against the plaintiff will not be considered in determining whether the amount in controversy has been satisfied.

(d) **Punitive Damages**

If punitive damages are allowed under state law, they can be used to satisfy the dollar requirement.

(e) **Attorney Fees**

Attorney fees recoverable by contract or statute can be used to satisfy the amount in controversy.

(f) **Injunctive Relief**

Injunctive relief is measured by the amount it costs the defendant to comply with the injunction.

(8) **Exceptions**

(a) **Domestic Relations / Probate Proceedings**

Federal courts will not exercise diversity jurisdiction in domestic or probate cases.

(b) **Multiparty, Multiform Trial Jurisdiction Act of 2002**

In an accident where at least 75 people died at a discrete location, minimal diversity is required (one plaintiff diverse from one defendant) and: (i) the defendant must reside in a different state where a substantial part of the accident took place; (ii) any two defendants must reside in different states; and (iii) a substantial part of the accident must have taken place in different states. Anyone with a claim is permitted to intervene if she could not have maintained an action in the district where the case is pending. Nationwide service is allowed.

2. Congressional Power to Limit Jurisdiction

Congress may not add to or take away from the power of the Supreme Court as prescribed by the Constitution.

D. Removal and Remand

If the plaintiff files the case in state court, the defendant may move to have the case removed to federal court, or vice versa. If the court grants the defendant's motion, the plaintiff may move to remand the case back to state court.

1. Removal

An action can be removed from state court to federal court (covering the same geographical area), if the action could have originally been brought in federal court to begin with (Federal Question/Diversity).

a) The defendant must remove within 30 days after service of the first document.
b) All defendants must agree to remove.

2. Remand

The plaintiff may file a motion to remand within 30 days of removal if the plaintiff can show that the federal court does not have original subject matter jurisdiction.

a) A federal court may remand the case back to state court after removal if: (i) there are complex issues of state law that will dominate the case; or (ii) there are ongoing state regulatory hearings.
b) A permissive counterclaim may waive the right to remove. A compulsory counterclaim does not waive the right.

E. Supplemental Jurisdiction

Under the doctrine of supplemental jurisdiction, a court may entertain claims that could not, by themselves, invoke federal question jurisdiction or diversity jurisdiction if the claims arise from the same common nucleus of operative fact as the claim that invoked federal subject matter jurisdiction.

III. CHOICE OF LAW

The California Code of Civil Procedure is the primary source of procedural law for California state courts and deals with matters relating to: jurisdictions, joinder of parties and claims, service of process, pleadings, motions, attachment, trials, appeals and enforcement of judgments. In addition, Rules of Court adopted over time have the force of law and supplement statutory and constitutional provisions.

A. Erie Doctrine

Under the Erie doctrine, a federal court sitting in diversity will apply federal procedural law but must apply the substantive law and conflict of laws rules of the state in which it is sitting.

1. When it is unclear whether a state law rule is substantive or procedural, courts use the outcome determinative test.
2. However, if a federal rule is arguably procedural, it will be applied.
3. Suing in diversity will apply state substantive law and federal procedural law.

B. California Conflict Laws

A federal court sitting in diversity must apply California's conflict of laws rules in determining the applicable substantive law.

1. Tort Claims – Government Interest Approach

a) The court first determines whether the laws of the two or more states are identical. If they are not, the court evaluates whether each state has an interest in the application of its law and if they do, a true conflict arises.

b) If there is a true conflict, the court must evaluate the impact on each state's interest, depending on the law applied for the purpose of determining the issue.

2. Contract Claims – Choice of Law Clauses

a) If the choice of law clause in the contract encompasses all claims, the court must determine whether the clause is enforceable by examining whether the chosen state's law has a substantial relationship to the parties or their transaction or any other reasonable basis exists for the parties' choice of law.

b) If the clause is enforceable, the court then assesses whether the chosen state's law conflicts with a fundamental California policy. If such a conflict exists, the court must decide whether California has a material interest greater than the chosen state in determination of the specific issue.

C. Statute of Limitations

CCP §312 state that "civil actions without exception can only be commenced..." within the statutorily defined period, "... after the cause of action has accrued." It is essential therefore to determine when the cause of action accrued, but the CCP rules do not provide a definition that is generally applicable; but see CCP Part 2 of Civil Actions, which at CCP §335 states "The periods for the commencement of actions other than for the recovery of real property are as follows" and which are then in CCP §333.1 and subsequently including, for example, CCP §340.6 (a) " an action against an attorney for a wrongful act or omission, other than for actual fraud, arising in the performance of professional services shall be commenced within one year after the plaintiff discovers or through the use of reasonable diligence should have discovered, the facts constituting the wrongful act or omission, or four years from the date of the wrongful act or omission, whichever occurs first..." and CCP §340.5 "...in an action for injury or death against a health care provider based upon such person's alleged professional negligence, the time for commencement of action shall be three years after the date of injury or one year after the plaintiff discovers, or through the use of reasonable diligence should have discovered, the injury, whichever occurs first..."

The Supreme Court has held that a state's statute of limitations and any related tolling statutes (i.e., statutes that suspend the running of a statutory limitation period) are substantive.

1. Relation Back Doctrine

An amended complaint by adding a new party after the statute of limitations has expired will relate back to the filing of the original complaint, provided that:

a) Same Transaction or Occurrence

The complaint and amended complaint must involve the same transaction or occurrence.

b) Added Party Must Know or Have Reason to Know

That but for the plaintiff's mistake, it would have been added

CCP §350 provides that "an action is commenced within the meaning of this title (i.e., time for commencing civil actions) when the complaint is filed." Similarly, FRCP Rule 3 (Commencement of Action) provides "...a civil action is commenced by filing a complaint with the court."

D. Federal Law in State Courts

A federal court has subject matter jurisdiction in a civil action arising under federal law or the parties are of diverse citizenship.

1. A choice of law issue may arise because a court with jurisdictional power may not be able to apply its own law.
2. A claim issued in a state court may be removed to federal court if it could have commenced in a federal court and diversity is relevant. The appropriate venue will be the federal court that has effect where the state action commenced.

E. Constitution's Full Faith and Credit Clause

The FFCC applies where a judgment of a state court requires enforcement out of state.

1. This also applies to federal courts. Accordingly, judgments of state and federal courts are recognized between courts, whether state and state, federal and federal, or state and federal.

F. Situs of an Action

1. Local Actions

Venue is proper in the county in which the land is situated, or where the act or omission giving rise to the action occurred.

2. Transitory Actions

For transitory actions, the general rule is that venue is proper in the county in which any defendant resides at the commencement of the action.

a) For contract actions, venue is proper where the obligation is to be performed, or where the contract was executed.
b) For personal injury and wrongful death actions, venue is where the injury or death occurred.

3. Forum Non Conveniens

A court may stay or dismiss a case because there is a court in another jurisdiction considered to be a far more convenient forum to deal with the case. Courts look to similar factors that would justify the transfer. For example, the alternative forum is more suitable and other factors which, when considered together, favor that other forum. Factors to be considered include:

a) Convenience of the parties;
b) Convenience of the witness: availability of the witnesses and evidence;
c) The state's interest in retaining the case: the interest the forum state has in providing a forum for its residents to adjudicate;
d) Whether the laws of the alternative forum will impair a **substantial right** of the plaintiff.

4. Foreign Court's Interest, if any, in Resolving the Dispute

Foreign courts will consider the relative ease or burden which adjudicating the case would impose on them if they decided to review it.

a) Essay Tip: Reach a conclusion by balancing the factors and determining how the court will decide. Note that federal courts are reluctant to grant dismissals as improper venue can be remedied by transferring the case.

G. Venue

1. Federal Venue

Original jurisdiction of the federal court is established where there is subject matter jurisdiction over the dispute and personal jurisdiction over the defendant.

a) Venue is proper in any district where: (i) any defendant resides if all defendants reside in the same state; (ii) a substantial part of the claim arose; or (iii) where a substantial part of the property that is the subject of the action is situated. If no district satisfies (i) or (ii), in diversity actions, a district where any defendant is subject to personal jurisdiction at the time the action is commenced, or for actions not based on diversity, any district in which any defendant may be found (improper venue can be waived).

2. Removal Actions

Venue is proper only in a district that includes the place in which the state action was pending.

3. TRANSFER OF VENUE

Courts can only transfer to a district that is a proper venue and that has personal jurisdiction over the defendant.

a) Transfer may be based on: (i) the convenience of parties and witnesses; and (ii) in the interest of justice (whether laws of the forum will impair a substantial right of the plaintiff).

b) Applicable law: If original venue was proper, the law where transferor sits is applied; for improper venue, the law where transferee sits is applied.

4. STATE VENUE

a) CHANGE OF VENUE

(1) The court has discretion to allow for a change of venue. In making such a determination, the court will consider: (i) the convenience of witnesses (not the parties); and (ii) the interests of justice in obtaining an impartial forum.

(2) The plaintiff or the defendant can move for a change of venue.

(3) Change of venue can cure an improper original venue.

5. TRANSFER OF CASES

If venue is improper, the court may transfer venue to the proper county. On the motion of either party, the court may transfer venue, even if the original venue is proper, when: (i) the court does not have a judge that is qualified to hear the case; (ii) there are reasonable grounds to believe that a fair trial would not take place in the original county; (iii) the interests of justice so require; or (iv) for the convenience of witnesses.

IV. PLEADINGS AND THEIR REQUIREMENTS

A. COMPLAINTS, COUNTERCLAIMS AND CROSS-COMPLAINTS

1. THE COMPLAINT

California is a "code pleading" state, having declined to follow the notice pleading model, but the complaint is required to contain a "...statement of the facts constituting the cause of action in ordinary and concise language" and a "demand for judgment". CCP §425.10(a). California has by case law adopted a more flexible approach and, provided the pleaded allegations give sufficient notice of the factual basis of the claim, not necessarily in a precisely correct format, it will be sufficient.

Pleadings allowed in civil actions are complaints, demurrers, answers, and cross complaints. CCP §422.10

FRCP govern the procedure in all civil actions and proceedings in the United States district courts (except as provided by FRCP Rule 81 – bankruptcy, citizenship, proceedings involving a subpoena, and others) and should be construed and administered to secure the just, speedy, and inexpensive determination of every action and proceeding FRCP 1. By FRCP Rule 2 there is "... one form of action – the civil action ...)", commenced by "...filing a complaint with the court" FRCP 3. The contents of the summons must include: (i) the name of the court and the parties; (ii) be directed to the defendant; (iii) state the name and address of the plaintiff's attorney, or if unrepresented, the name of the plaintiff; (iv) state the time within which the defendant must appear and defend; (v) notify the defendant that a failure to appear and defend will result in a default judgment against the defendant for the relief demanded in the complaint; (vi) be signed by the clerk; and (vii) bear the court's seal.

See FRCP Rule 4 (a), Contents: Amendments (the court may permit amendments to a summons).

a) PROCEDURAL CHALLENGES TO THE COMPLAINT

(1) Motion for Judgment on the Pleadings

An action cannot be dismissed on the pleadings unless, taking everything in the complaint as true, no claim for relief has been stated by the defendant as a matter of law. By CCP §437c(a), any party may move for summary judgment in any action or proceeding if it is contended that the action has no merit or that there is no defense to the action or the proceeding. The motion may be made at any time after 60 days have elapsed since the general appearance in the action or proceedings of each party against whom the motion is directed or at any earlier time after the general appearance that the court, with or without notice, and upon good cause shown, may direct. This rule is extensive and should be referred to for its full terms and effect. Pursuant to Rule 56 FRCP, a party may move for summary judgment, identifying the claim or defense upon which summary judgment is sought. The court shall grant summary judgment if the movant shows that there is no genuine dispute as to any material fact and the movant is entitled to judgment as a matter of law. The court is required to state on the record the reasons for granting or denying the motion. Further, unless a different time is set by local rule or the court orders otherwise, a part may file a motion for summary judgment at any time until 30 days after the close of all discovery.

b) CAUSE OF ACTION ISSUE

To determine the pleading's sufficiency, consider whether it is a notice system or a code system of pleading.

(1) Notice Pleading

The plaintiff must merely allege sufficient facts to put the defendant on notice of what the cause of action is against him.

(2) Code Pleading (State Court)

The complaint must allege all the elements of at least one cause of action or the complaint is subject to dismissal.

(a) Once a cause of action is alleged, the complaint and the judgment entered, the plaintiff must seek all elements of damages or other relief arising from that cause of action. He will be barred from any recovery in subsequent actions.

(b) Inconsistent pleadings: Some code-pleading states do not permit inconsistent allegations in a single count of defense.

(c) Verified complaint: In code-pleading states, a general denial is improper where the complaint is verified. Verified complaints must contain an affidavit stating that the allegations in the complaint are true.

c) PLEADING DAMAGES

(1) General Damages

Those damages that necessarily flow from the defendant's wrongful act, the law will imply them.

(2) Special Damages

Those damages which took place, but which are not a necessary consequence of the defendant's wrongful act. In code and notice pleading jurisdictions, special damages must be alleged in the complaint to be recovered.

B. SERVICE OF PROCESS

CCP §413.10 states that except as otherwise provided by statute, a summons shall be served on a person: (i) within this state, as provided in this chapter; (ii) outside this state, but within the United States, as provided in this chapter, or as proscribed by the law of the place where the person is served; (iii) outside the United States, as provided in this chapter, or as directed by the court in which the action is pending, or if the court before or after service finds that the service is reasonably calculated to give actual notice as proscribed by the law of the place where the person is served, or as directed by the foreign authority in response to a letter interrogatory (subject to the provisions of the convention on the "Service Abroad of Judicial and Extra-Judicial Documents" in civil or commercial matters).

NOTE: Proper service of the complaint/summons on the defendant is a prerequisite to a valid judgment.

1. Service Within California

a) Personal service upon a defendant in California (substituted service may be effected if personal service is not possible with reasonable diligence by leaving a copy of the summons at a person's dwelling house, usual place of abode, usual place of business, in the presence of a competent member of the household (at least 18) and who shall be informed of the contents).

b) Service by mail per CCP §415.30): by mailing copies of the complaint and summons, with two (2) copies of the Notice of Acknowledgment and a prepaid self-addressed return envelope.

c) Constructive service by publication per CCP §415.50: only allowed where the court is satisfied that the party to be served cannot, with reasonable diligence, be served personally or by substituted service.

2. Service on Defendant in Another State

CCP §415.40 permits service on a defendant in another state in any manner provided by the jurisdiction and service of process act for interstate service, plus service by mail (which requires a return receipt). Also, CCP §413.10(b) authorizes service in another state in accordance with the law of the state where the defendant is to be served.

Substituted service is also permitted by California statutes including, for example, service on a designated agent if the defendant is within California.

3. Service Outside the United States

The United States has ratified two multilateral agreements which govern service of proceedings among signatory countries – the Hague Convention and the Inter American Convention.

NOTE: A challenge to the validity of service of process must be made by a valid motion to quash, on or before the last day to plead in response to the complaint. CCP §418.10. This rule does not provide a defendant with the option of pleading lack of proper service as a defense, with the determination of that issue reserved until trial. This is in contrast to FRCP Rule 12(b).

Time Limits on Service of Process

The complaint and summons must be served on the defendant within three (3) years after the action is commenced CCP §583.210(a). Note, failure to serve within the time prescribed resulting in mandatory dismissal of the action §583.250. The time for service requirements do not apply if the defendant enters into a written stipulation or does an act which constitutes a general appearance. By CCP §583.410, if service of a summons is not made within two years after the action is commenced, there is a discretionary power to dismiss for delay in prosecution of the claim.

By FRCP Rule 4(c)1, "A summons must be served with a copy of the complaint. The plaintiff is responsible for having the summons and complaint served within the time allowed by Rule 4(m) and must furnish the necessary copies to the person who makes the service." FRCP Rule 4(e) provides that unless federal law provides otherwise, an individual may be served in a judicial district of the United States by: (i) following state law for serving a summons in an action brought in courts of general jurisdiction in the state where the district court is located or where service is made; or (ii) delivering a copy of the summons and complaint to the individual personally; or (iii) leaving a copy at the individual's dwelling; or (iv) usual place of abode with someone of suitable age and discretion who resides there; or delivering a copy of each to an agent authorized by appointment or by law to receive service of the process.

The rule also addresses service of a minor, an incompetent person, corporation, partnership or an association, service in a foreign country, serving the United States and its agencies, and serving a foreign state, state and/or local government.

If a defendant is not served within 120 days after the complaint is filed, the court on motion, or of its own motion after notice to the plaintiff, must dismiss the action without prejudice against the defendant or order that service be made within a specified time. However, if the plaintiff shows good cause for the failure, the court must extend the time for service for an appropriate period FRCP 4(m).

FRCP Rule 12 addresses defenses and objections, when and how presented, motion for judgment on the pleadings, consolidating motions, waving defenses, and pretrial hearings.

Unless otherwise prescribed by Rule 12 or a federal statute, a defendant must serve an answer within 21 days after being served with the summons and complaint, or within 60 days after the request for a waiver was sent or within 90 days after it was sent to the defendant outside any judicial district of the United States.

After the pleadings are closed but early enough not to delay trial, a party may move for judgment on the pleadings by motion for judgment on the pleadings.

A motion to strike may be made by a party within 21 days after being served with a pleading, or a court on its own motion may strike a pleading alleging: redundant material; or an impertinent or scandalous matter; or where there is an insufficient defense.

C. Answers, General Denials and Affirmative Defenses

1. Answers

An answer is a pleading (like the complaint) that responds to the allegations in the complaint. If a defendant does nothing, he risks entry of default and default judgment. Alternatively, he can attack the complaint and seek a partial or complete dismissal through use of demurrer/other motion(s), or he can respond to the complaint. If the defendant seeks affirmative relief against the complainant, he must proceed by way of separate cross complaint CCP §431.30(c). Note that federal practice combines answers and counterclaims – see FRCP Rules 13 and 14.

CCP §431.20: "Every material allegation of the complaint or cross complaint not controverted by the answer, shall, for purposes of the action, be taken as true," (in other words failing to properly deny an allegation constitutes an admission).

CCP §431.30.(b)(2) provides that an answer must contain a statement of any new matter constituting a defense, with each defense being separately stated and separately numbered. A new matter constituting an affirmative defense must be stated in the answer, and a failure to plead an affirmative defense will be considered a waiver of that defense. A new matter is something relied upon by the defendant, which is put in issue by the defendant.

In short, the answer must admit, deny, or claim lack of knowledge of information sufficient to answer, and where the answer is defective, the court will grant the defendant leave to amend. Entry of default judgment is improper without granting leave to amend first.

2. General Denial

A simple statement denying the whole complaint; i.e., the defendant denies each and every allegation in the plaintiff's complaint.

3. Special Denial

The defendant admits allegations that are true and rejects only those allegations that are specifically untrue.

D. Methods of Challenging Pleadings

1. Demurrer

Demurrers are used in code-pleading states where the complaint fails to state a cause of action or the court lacks subject matter jurisdiction and presents an objection to a complaint, cross complaint or answer when the ground of objection appears on the face of the pleading (see CCP §430.30(a)), and may object to the complaint or cross complaint on one or more of the following grounds:

a) the court has no jurisdiction of the subject of the cause of action alleged in the pleading;
b) the person who filed the pleading does not have the legal capacity to sue;
c) there is another action pending between the same parties on the same cause of action;
d) there is a defect or misjoinder of parties;
e) the pleading does not state facts sufficient to constitute a cause of action;
f) the pleading is uncertain (including uncertain, ambiguous and unintelligible);
g) in an action founded upon a contract, it cannot be ascertained from the pleading whether the contract is written, oral, or implied by conduct;
h) no certificate was filed as required by §411.35 (malpractice action against an architect or engineer); and
i) no certificate was filed as required by §411.36 (association action for negligence against licensed contractor) CCP §430.10.

2. Motion to Dismiss

Under FRCP Rule 12(b)(6), a motion to dismiss can be brought for the following reasons: (i) failure to state a claim upon which relief can be granted; (ii) lack of subject matter jurisdiction; and (iii) improper venue or insufficient service of process.

3. Motion to Strike

Motions to strike challenge irrelevant allegations and the moving party asks to have the irrelevant allegations stricken from the complaint.

4. Motion for Judgment on the Pleadings

If a defendant files an answer that does not respond to the complaint raised in the claim, the defendant will default and a claimant may move for judgment on the pleadings.

5. Motion for Summary Judgment

CCP §437c – any party may move for summary judgment in any action or proceeding if it is contended that the action has no merit or that there is no defense to the action or proceedings. Similarly, FRCP Rule 56 states that a party may move for summary judgment, identifying each claim or defense or the part of each claim or defense on which summary judgment is sought. A motion of summary judgment must be granted if, from the pleadings, affidavits, and discovery materials on file, it appears that no genuine issue of material fact exists and that the moving party is entitled to a judgment as a matter of law.

a) The defending party may move for summary judgment at any time, the plaintiff may not do so until 20 days after the commencement of the action or after an adverse party moves for summary judgment.

6. Pleas in Abatement

At common law, a plea in abatement was a defense in legal proceedings that did not contest the principle of the plaintiff's right to relief but contended the plaintiff had made a procedural error and therefore needed to bring fresh proceedings. This no longer applies in most if not all common law jurisdictions because it has been abolished.

E. Amendment of Pleadings

1. Federal Court

Plaintiff can amend pleadings within 21 days of serving the pleading to be amended or 21 days after the responsive pleading.

a) New Claims – Statute of Limitations

After the statute has run, an amendment to add new claims is only allowed if it relates back to the original complaint—if it arose from the same transaction or occurrence as the original claim.

b) New Parties

An amendment to add a new party only relates back if the defendant had actual knowledge of the suit before the statutory period ran and he knew he was the defendant who should have been sued.

2. State Court

Courts generally do not permit an amendment to add new parties after the statute has run. Such an amendment is seen as a new cause of action.

a) Supplemental Pleadings

Supplemental pleadings set forth events or discoveries occurring after the initial pleadings and face no statute of limitation problems.

b) Note

In California, a party may amend once, as a right, prior to an answer or a demurrer to the complaint being filed. Thereafter, an amendment may only be allowed with the written consent of the other party in the federal court, or by leave of the court in both federal and state court.

F. Statute of Limitations

See New Claims – Statute of Limitations, above.

V. JOINDER

A. Permissive and Compulsory

Permissive Joinder per CCP §378 permits joinder of plaintiffs if they assert any right to relief arising out of the same transaction, occurrence or series of transactions or occurrences and if any question of law or fact common to all these persons will arise in the action; and by CCP §379, all persons may be joined in one action as defendants if there is asserted against them any right to relief arising out of the same transaction, occurrence or series of transactions or occurrences, and if any question of law or fact common to all defendants will arise in the action. FRCP Rule 20, in effect, is the same as the CCP provision.

Further compulsory joinder of parties pursuant to CCP §389 and FRCP Rule 19 (the respective provisions are essentially the same) is required if it will not deprive the court of jurisdiction over the subject matter of the action, and in his absence complete relief cannot be accorded among those already parties, or he claims an interest relating to the subject matter of the action and is so situated that the disposition of the action in his absence may as a practical matter impair or impede his ability to protect that interest or leave any of the persons already parties subject to a substantial risk of incurring double, multiple, or otherwise inconsistent obligations by reason of his claimed interest.

Compulsory or necessary joinder is where parties or claims must be added to the lawsuit in order for the suit to proceed. Permissive joinder is where parties or claims are permitted to be added to the lawsuit; but if they are not added, the court will still allow the lawsuit to proceed.

B. Parties

1. Compulsory Joinder

A party is needed for just adjudication if: (i) complete relief cannot be given to existing parties in his absence; (ii) disposition in his absence may impair his ability to protect his interest in the controversy; or (iii) his absence would expose existing parties to a substantial risk of double or inconsistent adjudications.

Test: Whether the claim against the party involves identical law and facts.

a) Where Joinder Is Impossible

The court must decide whether the action can proceed in the party's absence or it must be dismissed. The court must consider the following: (i) whether the judgment in the party's absence would prejudice him or the existing parties; (ii) whether the prejudice can be reduced by shaping the judgment; (iii) whether a judgment in the other party's absence would be adequate; and (iv) whether the plaintiff will be deprived of an adequate remedy if the action is dismissed.

2. Permissive Joinder

Parties may join as plaintiffs or defendants whenever: (i) there is a question of law or fact that is common to all parties; and (ii) a claim is made by each plaintiff against each defendant that stems out of the same occurrence or transaction.

3. Interpleader

Interpleader permits a person in the position of a stakeholder to require two or more claimants to litigate among themselves to determine, which, if any, has the valid claim where separate actions might result in double liability on a single obligation.

a) Grounds

Interpleader requires: (i) complete diversity between the stakeholder and all adverse claimants, and in excess of $75,000 at issue, or (ii) a federal question claim.

4. Impleader

A defending party may implead a non-party who is or may be liable to him for any part of a judgment that the plaintiff may recover against him.

a) Venue

Venue need not be proper for a third party-defendant.

b) Additional Claims

Such claims may be asserted by the third party-defendant, but they need an independent jurisdiction basis.

c) Defenses

A third party can assert defenses to the plaintiff as well as the defendant. The court may sever claims and try separately for justice.

d) California

Adding a new party must either arise out of the same transaction or occurrence as the original cause of action, or assert a claim/interest in the subject of the plaintiff's action against the third party.

5. Intervention

Upon timely application, any person who has an interest in the matter in litigation, or in the success of either of the parties, or an interest against both, may intervene in the action or proceeding FRCP 24. The California provision reflects FRCP Rule 24. Intervention is available when a petitioner claims an interest in the subject matter of the action, and precluding intervention may hinder his ability to protect a recognized interest CCP §387(b).

6. Permissive Intervention

A third party may intervene if the intervenor has common claims and rights with the main parties. The court has discretion to grant the intervention and will look to see if the intervenor's presence will unduly complicate the case.

C. Claims

A plaintiff can join multiple claims against a defendant. At least one of the claims must arise out of a transaction in which all were involved.

1. Compulsory Joinder

If the defendant's counterclaim arises out of the same transaction or occurrence, failure to raise it bars a subsequent suit. Supplemental jurisdiction is extended to mandatory counterclaims; thus no independent source of federal subject matter jurisdiction is necessary to support a counterclaim arising out of the same transaction as the plaintiff's original claim.

2. Cause of Action v. Primary Rights Theory

Since the federal rules are premised on the "same transaction or occurrence test," if the case is in federal court, discuss whether any claim arising out of the same transaction or occurrence should be barred if the facts give you a state court action as well.

a) Primary Rights Jurisdiction

California and a minority of other jurisdictions look at primary rights (i.e., property damage and personal damages are different primary rights) and thus separate suits are not barred by res judicata from being separately litigated in state court action. Note: Res judicata will arise on failure by a plaintiff or defendant to raise all issues in an original action and which they then seek to raise in subsequent proceedings – they will not be permitted to do so.

3. Permissive Joinder

A defendant may bring counterclaims as long as they are supported by independent subject matter jurisdiction.

4. Cross-Claim

If arising out of the same transaction or occurrence, the defendant can sue a co-defendant, although she is not required to bring a claim. In addition, no independent jurisdictional basis is needed.

D. Class Actions

In California, courts rely upon CCP §382 as the general authority for class action suits, and a party seeking certification as a class action representative must establish the existence of an ascertainable class and a well-defined community of interest involving: (i) common questions of law or fact; (ii) class representatives that have claims or defenses typical of the class; (iii)class representative that adequately represent the interests of the class.

California courts as a generalization follow the procedural provisions of the Consumers Legal Remedies Act and the California Rules of Court govern the management of class actions. Courts also utilize FRCP Rule 23 as appropriate.

1. Federal Rule 23

A representative will be permitted to sue on behalf of a class if the following criteria are met:

a) **NUMEROSITY**

The class is so numerous that joinder of all members is impracticable;

b) **COMMONALITY**

Common questions of law or fact that make the class action suit a superior litigation method;

c) **TYPICALITY**

Persons representing the class have interests typical of the class;

d) **FAIR AND ADEQUATE REPRESENTATION**

The named representative will ensure fair and adequate representation of the interest of absent members of the class; and

e) **ACTION MEETS ANY OF THE REQUIREMENTS OF RULE 23(B)(1) & (2)**

(1) Risk of inconsistent results: Separate actions by class members could create the risk of inconsistent results or would impair the interest of other absent members (persons can opt out); or

(2) Injunctive or declaratory relief is appropriate: A defendant has acted or refused to act on grounds applicable to the class and injunctive or declaratory relief is appropriate (e.g., civil rights actions); or

(3) Class action is superior to alternative methods of adjudication as questions of fact or law common to the class predominate over individual issues.

2. NOTICE REQUIREMENT

In federal court, under Rule 23, notice to all members of the class is required in "common question suits" so that class members can opt out if they so choose.

a) The notice must contain: (i) details of the nature of the claim; (ii) the definition of the class; (iii) the class claims/defenses; and (iv) notice of the binding effect of a class judgment.

b) Notice to other members of the class in other class suits is discretionary with the court.

3. EFFECT OF JUDGMENT

All members of a class are bound by the judgment rendered in a class action, except those individuals in a common question class action who opt out.

a) Members of 23(b)(1), (2) class action cannot opt out. Such cases involve injunctive relief or risk inconsistent results.

4. JURISDICTION

In class actions that are established on diversity, only the citizenship of the named representative is taken into consideration in establishing complete diversity.

a) **AMOUNT IN CONTROVERSY**

One class representative's claim generally must exceed $75,000. Claims can only be aggregated if members are attempting to enforce a single right. Class members with claims not exceeding $75,000 may invoke supplemental jurisdiction as long as complete diversity is not destroyed.

b) **CLASS ACTION FAIRNESS ACT OF 2005**

Under the CAFA, subject matter jurisdiction is established where: (i) there is a minimum of 100 members in the proposed class; (ii) the aggregated amount in controversy is more than five million dollars; and (iii) any class member is different from any defendant.

c) Removal

Any defendant, rather than all defendants, may remove from the state to federal court, even if the defendant is a citizen of the forum.

d) Excluded Actions

No federal jurisdiction exists if primary defendants are states, state officials, or other government entities, or it is a claim regarding federal securities law that relates to internal affairs of a corporation and is based on the law of the state of incorporation.

e) Local Considerations

(1) Mandatory Decline of Jurisdiction

A district court must decline jurisdiction where: (i) two-thirds of the class members are citizens of the state where the action was filed; (ii) principal injuries were sustained in the state where the action was filed; and (iii) a defendant from whom significant relief is sought is a citizen of that state.

(2) Discretionary Decline of Jurisdiction

If more than one-third but less than two-thirds of plaintiffs are citizens of the forum state and the primary defendants are citizens of the forum state, in which circumstances, the court will consider whether the claims involve national interest. The claims will be governed by the law of the state in which the claim is brought, and the state is sufficiently close to the membership of the class and the alleged harm.

VI. DISCOVERY

The purpose of discovery is to narrow the scope of issues for trial and obtain disclosure of documents and evidence to identify and clarify issues to be determined at trial.

A. Discovery in California

CCP §2016.010 (referred to as the Civil Discovery Act), which applies to all civil actions pending in the superior courts (excluding the small claims division), "any party may obtain discovery regarding any matter, not privileged, that is relevant to the subject matter involved in the pending action or to the determination of any motion made in that action" CCP §2017.010.

The scope of discovery extends to any relevant matter that either is admissible in evidence or appears to be reasonably calculated to lead to the discovery of admissible evidence. However, the court shall limit the scope of discovery if it determines that the burden expense or intrusiveness of that discovery clearly outweighs the likelihood that the information sought will lead to the discovery of admissible evidence CCP §2017.020.

CCP 2017.010 provides that any party may obtain discovery regarding any matter "not privileged." Privilege generally refers to information protected from disclosure. NOTE: Rules relating to "privilege" are not set out in the Civil Discovery Act and are provided by the California Constitution and the evidence code.

Absolute Privilege: If protected by absolute privilege, information is protected from disclosure, irrespective of relevance. Absolute privilege applies to, amongst other things: attorney–client privilege, physician–patient privilege, spousal privilege and privilege against self-incrimination.

Qualified Privilege: In some instances, sensitive information may be protected by qualified privilege unless contrary to the interests of justice, for example, relating to trade secrets, newsgatherers' immunity.

FRCP26 Duty to Disclose, General Provisions Governing Discovery: Initial disclosure Unless exempted by Rule 26(a)(1)(B), without awaiting a discovery request, a party is required to disclose: (i) the name and address of each individual likely to have discoverable information that may be used to support a claim or defense; (ii) a copy of all documents, including those electronically stored, that the disclosing party has in his possession, custody or control; (iii) computation of each category of damages, plus supporting, non-privileged documentation; and (iv) any insurance agreement that may be liable to satisfy all or part of a judgment.

Initial disclosure must be made at or within 14 days after the parties' Rule 26(f) conference, unless a different time is set by stipulation or court order – Rule 26(1)(C). A party joined after the Rule 26(f) conference must make initial disclosures within 30 days after being served or joined, unless a different time is set by the court.

A party must also disclose the identity of any witness (expert testimony) it may use at trial to present evidence under Federal Rules of Evidence 702, 703, or 705 – Rule 26 (2)(A). Disclosure must be in accordance with any court order, but in the absence of an order, at least 90 days before the date set for trial, or if solely contradictory or in rebuttal of another party's evidence under Rule 26(a)(2)(B) or (C), within 30 days of the other party's disclosure (Rule 26(2)(D)).

1. Issue

Does the discovery device seek relevant information or information reasonably calculated to lead to the discovery of admissible evidence?

2. Rule

All materials are discoverable unless privileged, and all materials are relevant if they are likely to lead to admissible evidence at trial.

a) Discoverable material does not have to be admissible at trial;

b) "Privilege" and "confidential" are not the same thing; therefore, while privileged documents and communications are not subject to discovery, those that are referred to as "confidential" are discoverable.

3. Required Disclosure

Parties must produce information at three stages without request by the other party.

a) Initial Disclosures

Within 14 days of a Rule 26(f) meeting, identify persons and documents with information relevant to disputed facts alleged with particularity in the pleadings, computation of damages, and insurance for all or part of the judgment.

b) Disclosure of Experts

As directed by the court, a party must identify any expert who may be used at trial and produce a written report containing opinions, dates used, qualifications, and compensation to be paid.

c) Pretrial

No later than 30 days before trial, produce detailed information about trial evidence, including identity of witnesses to testify, live or by deposition, and relevant documents.

B. Types and Mechanics of Discovery Devices

In addition to discovery, the Civil Discovery Act authorizes interrogatories, inspections, medical examinations, expert witness disclosure, depositions and requests for admission. However, in contrast, in FRCP 26(a)(1), there is no requirement for initial disclosure of information that the disclosing party may rely upon to support its claim or defense.

1. Interrogatories

Discovery by written interrogatories, that is questions submitted by one party to any other party, must be answered under oath CCP §2030.010-310.

a) The responding party's obligations and options are set out in CCP §2030.210-310. Responses are required within 30 days. A respondent must answer by providing the information sought or his objection, and each answer shall be as complete and straightforward as possible, as the information available to him permits. It is permissible to say that an answer is not known after reasonable investigation. If it is burdensome to access business records to find the answer, the proponent can be allowed to do it.

b) No more than 25 interrogatories are permitted without court permission.

2. Inspections

CCP §2031.010 provides that a party may obtain discovery by inspecting documents or other relevant material in the possession, custody or control of the other, and this includes documents stored electronically.

3. Medical Examinations

If a party's mental or physical condition is in controversy, discovery by mental or physical examination is permitted by CCP §2032.020. After examination, the person examined may demand in writing a copy of the detailed medical report.

4. Expert Witness Disclosure

CCP 2034.210 provides for the compulsory exchange of the identity of expert witnesses who will testify at trial and the nature of their testimony. If a party unreasonably fails to comply with this requirement, the trial court, after objection, is required to exclude the expert witnesses' evidence CCP §2034.300.

5. Depositions

Testimony taken under oath and upon notice to all other parties. CCP §2025.010-620 provides for oral depositions in California, and unless the parties have agreed otherwise, the depositions must be recorded by a stenographer and transcribed. CCP §2025.620 details the rules applicable for the use of depositions at trial.

Limit: A party cannot take more than 10 depositions or depose the same person more than once, unless by court order or stipulation.

6. Requests for Admissions

Prepared by one party to another party (not a non-party). CCP §2033.010-420 permits the service by one party on another to admit the truth of a factual matter, the genuineness of a document or opinions relating to fact. The other party is required to respond under oath, either with an answer or an objection within 30 days after service. Admissions are binding only in the present action but constitute the conclusive establishment of the fact or matter admitted, and a party can only withdraw or amend such an admission with leave of the Court. If a party denies the truth of something referred to in a notice to admit and which later is proved in court, the requesting party may then seek the costs of proving it.

7. Duty to Supplement

If a party learns that a response to a required disclosure, interrogatory, request for documents, or admission is incomplete or incorrect, it must supplement its response.

C. Limits on Discovery

1. Work Product

Work product consists of documents that reflect the pre-litigation investigation of or by a party or her attorney. In California, "work product" is protected absolutely and which include, "...attorney's impressions, conclusions, opinions or legal research... " with other "work product" only being discoverable if the court determines that non-disclosure will unfairly prejudice the party seeking discovery. Federal rules protect as "work product" any materials "prepared in anticipation of litigation or trial" by a party's attorney.

a) Exception: Good-Cause

Documents or other matters obtained in anticipation of litigation or preparation for trial are discoverable only upon a showing of substantial need and unavailability from other sources. Example: A witness is no longer available.

b) **Exception: Attorney's Handwritten Notes**

A party can never obtain an attorney's handwritten notes, because an attorney's mental impressions are absolutely protected.

D. Use of Discovery at Trial

A party who fails to comply with discovery obligations may be subject to sanctions, unless there is "substantial justification" for the failure.

1. A party who fails to give disclosure will not be permitted to make use of the withheld evidence at trial or hearing, unless the failure was harmless.
2. A jury may be informed of the failure, and the party in default may have to meet reasonable expenses incurred as a consequence of the failure.
3. The court may order the matter to which a failure to disclose relates to be treated as admitted, to prohibit the further pursuit of the claim or defense, and either strike or dismiss pleadings or enter default judgment.

E. Discovery Remedies and Sanctions

1. Subpoena

Used to compel production of a witness at deposition or trial.

2. Subpoena Duces Tecum

An SDT is a court summons ordering the recipient to appear before the court and produce documents and evidence for use at trial or hearing.

3. Sanctions

a) Contempt for violating a court order;
b) Default against non-complying person (provided evidence is within scope of discovery);
c) Costs; and/or
d) Strike pleadings of the non-complying party.

VII. PRE-TRIAL

A. Pre-Trial Conferences

1. FRCP 26(f)

The parties must confer as soon as practicable, and in any event at least 21 days before a scheduling conference is to be held or a scheduling order is due under FRCP 16(b) to consider the nature and basis of their claims and defenses, including the possibility of settlement, initial disclosures, discuss any issues about preserving discoverable information and develop a discovery plan. The parties must submit a proposed discovery plan addressing the timing and form of required disclosures, the subjects on which discovery may be needed, the timing of, and limitations on, discovery, and relevant orders that may be required of the court.

2. Additional Pre-Trial Conferences

Additional conferences may be held to expedite trial and foster settlement. A final pretrial conference may be held to formulate a plan for the trial, including a program for the administration of evidence. An order entered pursuant to a final pretrial conference cannot be modified, except to prevent manifest injustice.

B. Pre-Trial Orders

1. Scheduling Order

The court must hold a scheduling conference and enter a scheduling order limiting the time for joinder, motions, and discovery. The order may also include dates for pretrial conferences, a trial date, and any other appropriate matters. This schedule cannot be modified except by leave of court upon a showing of good cause.

VIII. DISPOSITION WITHOUT TRIAL

A. VOLUNTARY DISMISSAL

A plaintiff may dismiss his action without prejudice as a matter of right only before the defendant files an answer or a summary judgment motion, or by stipulation of all parties. Otherwise, a dismissal without prejudice can be taken only with leave of court.

B. INVOLUNTARY DISMISSAL

A suit can be dismissed against a party for failure to pursue the action; failure to comply with the court orders; or as the result of a ruling on a motion by the opposing party. Dismissal is mandatory if there is:

1. A failure to serve the action within three years of the filing of the complaint. CCP §583.210(a) This can be avoided on a showing of "tolling" or excuse, including defendant not amenable to service, prosecution of the action stayed, service was impossible, or the parties were litigating the validity of service.
2. A failure to bring the case to trial within five years CCP §583.320. The burden is upon the plaintiff to bring the case to trial.
3. A failure to bring a case to a new trial within three years CCP §583.320. Which applies after there has been either a mistrial, hung jury, order for new trial or required following an appeal. The same extensions apply as in (1).

C. DISCRETIONARY DISMISSAL

Is permitted if there is a failure to serve a defendant within two years, there is a failure to bring the case to trial within two years, or there is a failure to bring a case to a new trial within two years CCP §583.420.

D. SUMMARY JUDGMENT

CCP §437c provides that:

1. Any party may move for summary judgment in any action or proceeding if it is contended that the action has no merit or that there is no defense to the action or proceeding.
2. The motion shall be supported by affidavits, declarations, admissions, answers to interrogatories, depositions, and matters of which judicial notice shall or may be taken.
3. The motion for summary judgment shall be granted if all the papers submitted show that there is no triable issue as to any material fact and that the moving party is entitled to a judgment as a matter of law.

For all intents and purposes, the California procedure relating to summary judgment practice conforms with FRPC 56 – Summary Judgment, and pursuant thereto, the court shall grant summary judgment if the movant shows that there is no genuine dispute as to any material fact and the movant is entitled to judgment as a matter of law. The time for filing a motion for summary judgment is any time until 30 days after the close of all discovery, unless the court sets a different timetable FRCP 56(b).

CCP §437c(a) states that summary judgment motions are permissible 60 days after a general appearance of the party against whom the motion is sought. The notice of motion and supporting papers must be served 75 days before the hearing, and opposition papers must be served 14 days before the hearing. CCP §437c(b) details the procedure to be complied with, relating to supporting and opposing papers.

E. DEFAULT JUDGMENT

If a defendant who is properly served with a complaint and summons fails to file an appropriate response in time, the plaintiff may obtain a default judgment CCP §§585;586. After the time for responding to the served complaint has expired, the plaintiff can make written application to the court for entry of a default judgment CCP §585(a) to (c). Note that in some cases, specific statutes impose additional procedural requirements, for example a default judgment in dissolution of marriage proceedings is prohibited. Family Code §2336 Mandatory relief against a default judgment is granted in cases where an attorney files an affidavit of neglect, and in other circumstances there is discretionary relief where it is determined that the mistake was excusable CCP §473.

IX. RIGHT TO A JURY TRIAL

The right to a jury trial is constitutionally guaranteed to the extent that it existed at common law when the federal and state constitutions were adopted.

(California Constitution, Article 1, paragraph 16 preserves the right to a jury trial where there was a right to a jury trial at common law.)

The right exists: (i) when legal and equitable issues are joined; (ii) in a state proceeding; or (iii) federal diversity cases.

A. Joined Issues of Law and Equity

1. Parties have a right to a jury trial when legal and equitable claims or defenses are joined in a single suit.
    a) Issues of fact common to both the legal and equitable claims are triable by the jury. Issues that are solely equitable are tried before a judge.
    b) If there are no common issues, a jury will hear legal claims. A judge will hear equitable claims. The order of the presentation of the claims is determined by first trying the claims, either legal or equitable, which are capable of disposing of the entire action. If the claim is procedurally present in equity, but the underlying claim carries a right to a jury, then the claim must be heard by a jury.
2. **Diversity Cases:** The Seventh Amendment preserves the right to jury trial in federal courts in all suits at common law.
    a) Even if a state court would deny a jury trial, the federal court must allow a jury trial in any diversity suit at common law. The Seventh Amendment prevails over the Erie doctrine. As such, a party may demand a jury trial by serving the other parties with a written demand no later than 14 days after the last pleading directed to the issue is served FRCP 38.
    b) **Waiver:** A timely demand for a jury trial must be made or the right is waived. The party who desires a jury trial must file a written demand with the court and serve it on the parties within 10 days after the filing of the pleading in which the jury triable issue arose. If the party fails to file the written demand, it is waived.
3. **State Court:** The Seventh Amendment right to trial by jury does not apply to the states. California grants the right to civil jury trials for questions of fact where the claim exceeds small claims limits.

X. JURY SELECTION

The Trial Jury Selection and Management Act, CCP §190-237, provides for the selection and formation of trial juries for both civil and criminal cases.

A. Equal Protection Requirements

1. Jury Size

A jury in a civil case must have at least 6 and not more than 12 jurors. A juror may be excused for good cause without causing a mistrial, so long as at least six jurors participate in reaching the verdict.

2. Selection

The selection procedure must meet due process and equal protection requirements of fairness and community representation.

B. Juror Qualifications

All persons are eligible for selection except:

1. Persons who are not citizens of the United States;
2. Persons under 18;
3. Persons who are not domiciled in the state of California;
4. Persons not residents of the jurisdiction where they are summoned to serve;
5. Persons convicted of malfeasance in office;
6. Persons who have insufficient knowledge of the English language;
7. Persons currently serving as jurors in another court of the state;
8. Persons who are the subject of conservatorship.

All persons selected for jury service must be selected at random from panels representing a cross section of the area served by the court and the court clerk must randomly select names of jurors for voir dire from these panels (for example, an approved list of registered voters or DMV licensed drivers).

C. Voir Dire

Voir dire is the process used to determine if any juror is biased or is unsuitable to deal with issues fairly. A trial judge initially examines prospective jurors in a civil trial for the purpose of selecting a fair and impartial jury, and attorneys for the parties have considerable freedom to voir dire prospective jurors.

D. Challenging Jurors

1. Cause

Each party can challenge an unlimited amount of prospective jurors for cause. Challenges for general disqualification arise on two grounds – lack of eligibility and implied bias, see CCP §§ 228 and 229. Challenge also arises for actual bias.

2. Peremptory Challenge

Each party is only granted a set number of peremptory challenges – six per CCP §231(c). Although if there are more than two parties, the number of peremptory challenges is increased to eight. The court may also grant additional challenges if there are more than two sides. Traditionally, peremptory challenges could be made for any reason, without explanation, but a race-neutral-reason is required in exercising peremptory challenges.

XI. ROLES OF JUDGE AND JURY

In trial courts a judge, and sometimes a jury, hears testimony and evidence relating to the issues to be determined in the case for the purpose of determining the outcome by applying the relevant applicable law to the facts found by the jury. The judge is the sole arbiter in relation to matters of law and will provide relevant direction as and when required. The judge's role is impartial, to ensure fairness, to interpret the law and to protect the rights and liberties of citizens guaranteed by the Constitutions of the United Sates and California for the purpose of ensuring legal disputes are resolved fairly and efficiently according to law.

XII. REMOVING A CASE FROM A JURY

A. Nonsuit

A defendant may move for a motion for nonsuit after the plaintiff's opening statement or the completion of the plaintiff's evidence in a jury trial CCP §581c(a). If granted, the judgment of nonsuit constitutes an adjudication on the merits of the case, but if denied the defendant still has the right to present his evidence. Further, after all the evidence, either party may move for an order directing a verdict in its favor.

B. Judgment as a Matter of Law

A motion for a judgment as a matter of law allows judgment to be granted for either party if the evidence is such that reasonable persons could not disagree. A motion for judgment as a matter of law is a prerequisite for the making of a renewed motion for judgment as a matter of law.

C. Renewed Motion for a Judgment as a Matter of Law

A party may file a renewed motion for a judgment as a matter of law no later than 28 days in federal court after entry of judgment.

XIII. POST-TRIAL MOTIONS

A. Setting Aside or Correcting Verdicts

1. Errors Justifying Set Aside

Someone other than a juror can move to have the verdict set aside if:

a) Juror bias or prejudice was not disclosed on voir dire;
b) Jurors received unauthorized evidence; or
c) Jury failed to reach its decision by a rational, group deliberation of the facts.

2. Motion for New Trial

A motion for a new trial must be filed no later than 28 days after judgment has been rendered. If granted, a new trial takes place and proceeds as though the first trial never took place CCP §656. CCP §§657;663 set out the grounds and procedures to be followed and which must be strictly complied with. CCP §657 specifies the grounds for a new trial:

a) Irregularity in proceedings of the court, jury or adverse party, or any order of the court or abuse of discretion, which prevented a party having a fair trial;
b) Misconduct of the jury;
c) Accident or surprise, which ordinary prudence could not have guarded against;
d) Newly discovered evidence which could not have been discovered and produced at trial;
e) Excessive or inadequate damages;
f) Insufficiency of evidence to justify the verdict;
g) Error of law at the trial.

In California, such a motion must be filed no later than 15 days from the date of mailing the notice of entry of judgment, or within 180 days after entry of the judgment, whichever is earliest, and the notice must set out the grounds upon which the motion is made. The court may only grant a new trial on a ground specified within the notice of intention to move for a new trial.

3. Remittitur

If the verdict is excessive, the court may order a new trial or offer the plaintiff remittitur, which allows the plaintiff to choose between a lesser award or a new trial.

4. Additur

If the verdict is more favorable to the defendant than it ought to have been, the defendant must agree either to pay a larger amount than the jury verdict or submit to a new trial (California state courts only).

B. Variation and Modification of Judgment Without a New Trial

1. Motion for Relief from Judgment

This is a motion made in an independent action requesting relief from a prior judgment. The basic grounds for the motion are: mistake; surprise; excusable neglect; newly-discovered evidence; fraud or other misconduct by the other party. The motion must be made within a reasonable time following the judgment.

XIV. EXTRAORDINARY RELIEF FROM JUDGMENT

A. Statutory Relief

Such relief is provided pursuant to statutory authority that has the effect of reversing an otherwise valid judgment.

B. Equitable Relief

1. Injunctive Relief

An injunction is a remedy used to require a person to take, or refrain from taking, a specified action. A court will issue an injunction when necessary to protect a legal right of an individual or group.

a) Classifications

(1) Mandatory

A mandatory injunction requires someone to engage in affirmative conduct.

(2) Prohibitory

A prohibitory injunction prohibits an individual or group from engaging in certain behavior.

(3) Temporary Restraining Order

A TRO may be issued to maintain the status quo pending a ruling by the court on an application for a preliminary injunction. They can be granted ex parte upon a showing of great or irreparable injury.

(4) Preliminary/Provisional Injunction

Such injunctions cannot be granted without an evidentiary hearing where both parties are present. A preliminary injunction does not determine the ultimate rights of the parties, and a factual determination made at the hearing on the preliminary injunction does not bind the court at the trial.

(5) Permanent/Final Injunction

Permanent injunctions are issued following a trial and a final adjudication of the ultimate rights in controversy.

b) Requirements

An injunction can be granted upon a showing of:

(1) An inadequate remedy at law, meaning that compensation would be insufficient;
(2) A serious risk of irreparable harm absent injunctive relief;
(3) A likelihood that the plaintiff will prevail on the merits of the underlying controversy; and
(4) A comparison of the harm to the defendant in issuing an injunction versus the harm to plaintiff in withholding it, which on balance favors the plaintiff.

c) Duration

An injunction may state its date of expiration or may be valid "until further order of the court." A temporary restraining order terminates automatically when the preliminary injunction is granted or denied.

d) Modification

A trial court may modify or dissolve a final injunction on a showing that there has been a material change in the facts on which the injunction was granted or that the ends of justice would be served by the modification or dissolution of the injunction.

XV. APPEAL

A. Appealable Orders

1. Final Judgment Rule

CCP §904.1 identifies judgments and orders that may be appealed. An appeal is submitted to the court of appeal and may be taken from any of the following:

a) From a judgment, except an interlocutory judgment, other than as provided in (h) (i) (k), or a judgment of contempt that is made final and conclusive;
b) From an order made after judgment, made appealable by (a);
c) From an order granting a motion to quash service of summons or granting a motion to stay the action on the ground of inconvenient forum or from a written order of dismissal under Section 581d following an order granting a motion to dismiss the action on the ground of inconvenient forum;
d) From an order granting a new trial or denying a motion for judgment notwithstanding the verdict;
e) From an order discharging or refusing to discharge an attachment or granting a right to attach order;
f) From an order granting or dissolving an injunction or refusing to grant or dissolve an injunction;
g) From an order appointing a receiver;
h) From an interlocutory judgment order or decree hereafter made or entered in an action to redeem real or personal property from a mortgage thereof or a lien thereon determining the right to redeem and directing an accounting;
i) From an interlocutory judgment in an action for partition determining the rights and interests of the respective parties and directing partition to be made;
j) From an order made appealable by the provisions of the Probate Code or the Family Code;
k) From an interlocutory judgment directing payment of monetary sanctions by a party or an attorney for a party if the amount exceeds $5,000;
l) From an order directing payment of monetary sanctions by a party or an attorney for a party if the amount exceeds $5,000;
m) From an order granting or denying a special motion to strike.

Note that sanction orders or judgments of $5,000 or less against a party or an attorney for a party may be reviewed on an appeal by that party after entry of final judgment in the main action, or at the discretion of the court of appeal may be reviewed upon petition for an extraordinary writ.

The California Rules of Court (Rule 8.104(a) to (f)) set out the time limits within which an appeal must be lodged.

Unless Rule 8.108 or Rule 8.702 provides otherwise, a notice of appeal must be filed on or before the earliest of: (i) 60 days after the superior court clerk serves the party filing the notice of appeal with a document entitled "Notice of Entry of Judgment" or a file stamped copy of the judgment showing the date either was served; (ii) 60 days after the party filing the notice of appeal serves or is served by a party with a document entitled "Notice of Entry

of Judgment" or a file stamped copy of the judgment accompanied by proof of service; or (iii) 180 days after entry of judgment.
Note that if a notice of appeal is filed late, the reviewing court must dismiss the appeal.

2. Non-Appealable Orders

Generally, non-final interlocutory orders cannot be appealed. Exception: Under the Interlocutory Appeals Act, review may be taken where: (i) the trial judge certifies that the interlocutory order involves a controlling question of law that may result in the conclusion of the litigation; and (ii) the court of appeals then agrees to allow the appeal.

3. Finality of Judgment

On determination of the evidence and law, judgment is given which is final and binding subject to any right of appeal and which is exercised. The court is not limited to the relief sought in the pleadings and can give such relief as it considers appropriate. In California, the state court is restricted by any applicable jurisdictional issues and cannot issue a declaratory judgment.

4. Limitations of Reviewing Court

If lack of subject matter jurisdiction is not raised until after final judgment and any appeal is dealt with, the judgment may nevertheless be set aside in a subsequent case subject to consideration of:

a) Lack of jurisdiction being clear;
b) The issue of jurisdiction is one of law not fact;
c) The court has a limited not general jurisdiction;
d) The issue of jurisdiction did not arise in the proceedings; or
e) Public policy is against the court acting in excess of jurisdiction.

XVI. FRCP 59 NEW TRIALS; ALTERING OR AMENDING A JUDGMENT

Generally, the court may on motion grant a new trial on all or some of the issues, to any party: (i) after a jury trial for any reason for which a new trial has before been granted in an action at law in federal court; or (ii) after a non-jury trial for any reason for which a rehearing has before been granted in a suit in equity in federal court FRCP 59(a)(1).

By FRCP Rule 59(a)(2), After a non-jury trial the court may, on motion for a new trial, open the judgment if one has been entered, take additional testimony, amend findings of fact and conclusions of law, or make new ones and direct the entry of a new judgment.

A motion for a new trial must be filed no later than 28 days after the entry of judgment FRCP 59(b).

Further, no later than 28 days after the entry of judgment, the court on its own motion may order a new trial for any reason that would justify granting one on a party's motion.

A motion to alter or amend a judgment must be filed no later than 28 days after the entry of judgment FRCP 59(e).

XVII. FRCP RELIEF FROM A JUDGMENT OR ORDER

The court may correct a clerical mistake or a mistake arising from oversight or omission whenever one is found in a judgment order or other part of the record. The court may do so on motion or on its own, with or without notice. But after an appeal has been docketed in the appellate court and while it is pending, such a mistake may be corrected only with the appellate court's leave FRCP 60(a).

FRCP Rule 60(b): The grounds for relief from a final judgment order or proceeding are: (i) mistake, inadvertence, surprise or excusable neglect; (ii) newly discovered evidence that with reasonable diligence could not have been discovered in time to move for a new trial under FRCP Rule 59(b); (iii) fraud (whether previously called intrinsic or extrinsic), misrepresentation or misconduct by an opposing party; (iv) the judgment is void; (v) the judgment has been satisfied, released or discharged; it is based on an earlier judgment that has been reversed or vacated, or applying it prospectively is no longer equitable; or (vi) any other reason that justifies relief.

The court on motion and just terms may relieve a party or its legal representative from a final judgment order or proceeding on any of the above grounds FRCP 60.

A motion under FRCP Rule 60(b) must be made within a reasonable time but no more than a year after the entry of the judgment, order, or the proceeding. The motion does not affect the judgment's finality or suspend its operation FRCP 60 (c)(1) and(2).

XVIII. RES JUDICATA AND RELATED DOCTRINES

A. Claim Preclusion or Res Judicata

Requires that a party seeking relief in a proceeding must pursue all available claims or forms of relief and all available theories at the first proceeding.

1. Res Judicata

This applies only to final judgments or orders by a court of competent jurisdiction on the merits of the case and which is conclusive upon the parties in subsequent litigation involving the same cause of action. The California rule is that a judgment is not final for the purpose of res judicata if it is still open to direct attack by appeal. A judgment must not only be final but also rendered on the merits in order to have res judicata effect. Res judicata must be properly pleaded or proved at trial and, if not, it is deemed to have been waived.

2. Requirements

a) Final Judgment

The prior judgment must be final; all appeals or time for appeal are over.

b) Competent Jurisdiction

The court must have proper subject matter jurisdiction and personal jurisdiction.

c) Judgment On the Merits of the Case

A default judgment is not a judgment on the merits.

d) Parties or Privies

Parties in the present lawsuit, and the previous lawsuit upon which the claim is based, must be identical and identically aligned.

e) Same Cause of Action

The claim itself has to be identical to the one brought in the former lawsuit.

3. Primary Rights Theory

California and a minority of jurisdictions apply the primary rights theory, which allows parties to split their causes of action. Property rights are severable from personal injury rights. Therefore, if their car is in an accident and the plaintiff sues the defendant for property damage in the first suit and then files a separate lawsuit against the defendant later for personal injury, the latter suit is not barred by res judicata. But compare a "breach of contract" which results in injury to person and property, breaches only one primary right and therefore gives rise to only one cause of action.

4. Federal Rules

The federal rules require that all causes of action, including personal injury and property rights arising from the same transaction or occurrence, must be brought at the same time or res judicata will bar subsequent re-litigation. Courts will dismiss the entire lawsuit if res judicata applies.

a) Merger occurs when one of the parties to the suit attempts to assert the same cause of action against the same party in the second suit.

b) Bar prevents the losing party in one suit re-litigating the same cause of action against the winning party in a second suit.

B. Issue Preclusion or Collateral Estoppel

A judgment for the plaintiff or the defendant is conclusive in a subsequent action between them or their privies, as to issues of fact essential to the judgment that were actually litigated and resolved in the first action. This conclusive effect of the first judgment is called collateral estoppel. "The doctrine of collateral estoppel precludes relitigation of an issue previously adjudicated if: (i) the issue necessarily decided in the previous suit is identical to the issue sought to be relitigated; (ii) there was a final judgment on the merits of the previous suit; and (iii) the party against whom the plea is asserted was a party or in privity with a party to the previous suit.

1. Requirements

a) Final judgment

b) Same parties

  (1) Application of CE by a stranger v. former party: In Parkland Hosiery v Shore, the Supreme Court said the use of CE by a stranger against a former party was permissible if:

    (a) The first party had a full and fair opportunity to litigate the issue; and

    (b) Use of CE would not be unfair to the defendant under the circumstances.

  (2) Use of CE can be applied against a party to the first action by someone who was not a party to it, if the party had an opportunity and motive to litigate the issue in the first suit (a break with the traditional mutuality requirement).

  (3) A former party can never use CE against a stranger who had no opportunity to litigate the issue in the previous suit.

c) Identical issues and facts essential to the judgment: The determination of the issue must have been necessary to the prior lawsuit's result. CE applies only to issues that were necessary to the prior judgment.

d) Actually litigated and resolved: Issues and facts must have been actually litigated and resolved in the first lawsuit.

2. Result of a Finding of Collateral Estoppel

Those issues to which collateral estoppel applies are deemed to have been conclusively determined. If those issues are crucial to the plaintiff's prima facie case, or those issues are critical to the defendant's defense, the case may be dismissed on a motion for judgment as a matter of law.

C. Parties Bound by a Judgment

1. Mutuality of Estoppel

Since a judgment cannot be used against a person who was not a party, that person has traditionally been barred from taking advantage of the judgment.

2. Parties and Persons in Privity

A judgment for the plaintiff or the defendant is conclusive in a subsequent action/cause of action between them or their privies.

D. Full Faith and Credit

The U.S. Constitution provides that states must recognize judicial decisions of other states and the full faith and credit provision ensures that judicial decisions of courts of one state are recognized and honored in every other state. The clause prevents "forum shopping."

XIX. Arbitration

Arbitration is a form of alternative dispute resolution in which parties to a dispute agree to participate in.

A. Enforcement of Agreements to Arbitrate

A written contractual provision referring disputes to arbitration is valid and enforceable between the parties to the contract or other relevant agreement.

B. Enforcement of Arbitration Awards

After arbitration, a party can move to have the arbitrator's award confirmed by the court. An opposing party can move to have the arbitrator's award vacated on the grounds of, for example:

1. Fraud; arbitrator failed to act impartially; not adhering to the arbitration agreement;
2. The arbitration award is beyond the scope of the arbitration;
3. The arbitrator showed a clear disregard for the law (federal court only).

If the award is confirmed, it is final and binding and enforceable as a court judgment.

COMMUNITY PROPERTY

Table of Contents

I. RELATIONSHIP OF THE PARTIES

First, the application of California community property law must be appropriate. To make that determination, the relationship of the parties must be established.

A. Valid California Marriage (California Family Code "CFC" 300)

In California, a lawful marriage requires both the legal capacity and performance of formal legal procedures. California does not recognize common law marriages purportedly contracted within or outside California.

B. Non-California Marriage (CFC 308)

California courts generally test the validity of marriages according to the place of celebration.

C. Putative Marriage (CFC 2251)

A putative spouse is one who is not lawfully married. However, if she has a good faith belief that she is lawfully married and that belief is reasonable, she will be given putative spouse status. A putative spouse has the same property rights as a lawful spouse. When the putative spouse learns that she is not lawfully married, she no longer accrues putative spouse property rights.

D. Meretricious/Non-Marital Relationships

California applies general contract principles in such cases. In the absence of a contract, an aggrieved party may seek equitable remedies, such as quantum meruit, for services rendered. Contracts between unmarried cohabitants are not enforceable to the extent that they are explicitly founded on consideration of sexual services.

II. GENERAL PRESUMPTION (CFC 760, 770)

California is a community property state. All property acquired during the course of a marriage is presumed community property. All property acquired before marriage or after permanent separation is presumed to be separate property. In addition, any property acquired by gift, devise, or bequest is presumed to be separate property. In order to determine the character of any asset, courts will trace back to the source of funds used to acquire the asset. A mere change in form of an asset does not change its characterization.

III. ALTERING THE CHARACTER OF PROPERTY

A. Premarital Agreements (CFC 1500)

Such agreements (including ones which waive rights upon death) may circumvent California community property law, provided certain requirements are met.

1. Statute of Frauds (CFC 1611)

In order to satisfy the Statute of Frauds, there must be a writing signed by both parties, although no consideration is necessary.

a) Oral Agreements

An oral premarital agreement may be enforced when: (i) the promise was fully performed; and (ii) the promisee has relied to her detriment on the oral promise.

2. Unenforceable Agreements (CFC 1615)

Premarital agreements that incentivize divorce are invalid. Further, a premarital agreement is invalid if a party did not fully disclose her financial position or if fulfillment of the agreement would yield an unconscionable result.

IV. CHARACTER OF THE PROPERTY

A. When Were the Assets Acquired?

Write out a timeline to assist you in correctly characterizing the subject property; i.e., pre/post marriage, post separation, divorce, etc.

B. Identify the Source of the Funds

1. Separate Property & Exchange Rule, Self-Dealing

Property acquired during marriage that is received by: (i) gift, bequest, devise, or descent; (ii) rents, issues, and profits of separate property acquired before or during marriage; and (iii) property acquired in exchange for separate property, is considered separate property.

a) Property Existing Out of State is within the Purview of Community Property (CFC 2660)

Proof that an asset was acquired during marriage raises a presumption that the asset is community property. By demonstrating that the property was acquired separate property, or is considered separate property (e.g., gift), the presumption can be overcome.

b) Community Payments that Pay Off Purchase Price of Separate Property

In such a case, the community establishes a proportional ownership to the extent that community mortgage payments reduce the principal debt.

2. Community Property (CFC 760)

California is a community property state. All property acquired during the course of a marriage is presumed community property. However, that presumption may be overcome as certain rules apply to specific types of property.

3. Quasi-Community Property (CFC 912)

Such property is acquired by either spouse that would have been community property had the spouse been domiciled in California at the time of acquisition. Quasi-community property retains its separate property nature when the parties become domiciled in California. The quasi-community property label only becomes significant at divorce or death.

4. Quasi-Marital Property (CFC 2251)

Such property is property acquired by putative spouses in the absence of a lawful marriage, provided there was a good faith, objectively reasonable belief that the couple was in fact lawfully wed. Quasi-marital property is acquired like community property until the putative spouse learns her marriage is unlawful.

5. Assets Purchased with Community and Separate Funds (CFC 2640)

When community and separate funds are used to purchase an asset, the community property and separate property acquire a pro rata ownership interest in the asset. The respective share of ownership is calculated by figuring out the percentage that each contributed to the purchase price. The division of ownership also applies to any appreciation. Property purchased with borrowed funds should be characterized by looking to what asset (or labor) the lender relied upon at the time of issuing the loan.

C. Conduct of the Parties

1. Transmutation (CFC 850, 852)

A transmutation is an agreement by the spouses during marriage to alter the character of property. Prior to 1985, transmutations were liberally allowed. After 1985, in order for a transmutation to be valid, it must be in writing signed by the person whose interest is adversely affected. No writing is required for interspousal gifts of a personal nature, which are relatively insignificant in value considering community assets.

2. Improvements

a) Spouse's Community Funds Used to Improve Other Spouse's Separate Property– Gift (CFC 2640(c))

Absent an agreement to reimburse, a gift is presumed when one spouse uses community funds to improve the other spouse's separate estate.

b) Community Funds Used to Improve Own Separate Property

Where a spouse uses community funds to improve her own separate property, the community is entitled to either reimbursement for the cost of the improvement, or by the value of the improvement, whichever is greater.

c) Separate Property to Improve Community Property (CFC 2640(b))

Automatically entitles separate property to reimbursement unless it is waived in writing.

3. Commingling

All funds held in an account or otherwise are presumed to be community property if the source cannot be traced.

a) Tracing

Unless there is an agreement to the contrary, community funds are presumed to have been used to pay for community expenses, and any separate funds used are presumed to be gifted.

(1) Direct tracing

If, at the time of purchase, separate funds were available, the spouse intended for the acquired property to become separate property, and separate property funds were used to acquire the asset, the community property presumption can be overcome.

(2) Exhaustion method

If, at the time of acquisition, community funds in the account had already been exhausted and only separate funds remained, the community property presumption can be overcome.

4. Title of Property (CFC 2581)

Prior to 1984, when a couple took title to an asset in joint and equal form, any separate property used to purchase the property was presumed to be a gift. The separate property was not entitled to a separate ownership interest in the property unless there was an oral or written agreement. In addition, the separate property was not entitled to even reimbursement unless there was an oral or written agreement for reimbursement.

a) When a married couple took title to an asset in joint tenancy after 1984, the asset was presumed to be community property for purposes of divorce unless there was a writing to the contrary. Any separate property used to purchase the asset is reimbursed to the separate property contributor without interest. Beginning in 1987, this rule was extended to all jointly titled assets, except bank accounts.

5. Separation (CFC 910(b))

A separation occurs where there is physical separation and at least one party has no intent to reconcile. If the parties permanently separate, all earnings and appreciation of assets are considered the separate property of each spouse thereafter.

D. Characterize the Property

Determine the nature of the property and then look for property-specific rules below.

V. RULES GOVERNING SPECIFIC PROPERTY

A. Personal Injury Awards (CFC 780, 781, 2603)

Personal injury awards and settlements are community property if the cause of action arose during marriage. If the cause of action arose before marriage or after permanent separation, the award or settlement is separate property. Personal injury awards against the other spouse are always the separate property of the injured spouse. Upon divorce, community property personal injury awards are assigned entirely to the injured spouse so long as they have not been commingled with the other community property funds and so long as the interests of justice do not require otherwise (the other spouse can get up to half where the interests of justice require such).

B. Retirement Benefits (CFC 2610)

Retirement benefits are community property if earned during the course of the marriage. When pensions and other retirement benefits are earned both before and during marriage, courts use the time rule to determine how much of the pension is attributable to community labor and how much is attributable to separate labor. The community's share is calculated by determining the number of years the pension was earned while married and dividing that number by the total number of years the pension was earned.

1. Upon Divorce

A pension may be difficult to divide because of the uncertainty associated with the exact date of retirement. Courts can do several things upon divorce to divide a pension:

a) The court can deviate from equal division and assign the entire pension to the earning spouse and another community asset of equal value to the non-earning spouse;

b) The court can adopt a wait-and-see attitude by dividing the other community assets and reserving jurisdiction over the pension until the age of retirement; or

c) The court can calculate the community's share of the pension and order the pension plan administrator to make payments of one-half of the community's interest directly to the non-earning spouse when the age of retirement is reached.

2. Presumption

Although death does not compromise either spouse's interest, ERISA preempts California law and requires the beneficiary of a private sector pension to be living.

C. Disability Pay and Workers' Compensation Benefits

Disability benefits, including workers' compensation benefits, are characterized as community property or separate property, depending on the wages they are designed to replace. Payments received during marriage are community property because they are designed to replace marital earnings. Likewise, payments received before marriage or after permanent separation are separate property because they are designed to replace separate earnings.

D. Severance Pay

There is no fixed rule with respect to severance pay. Courts will look to the facts and circumstances of each case to determine how to characterize severance pay. To the extent that the severance pay looks like a benefit, which was earned during the course of the marriage, courts are likely to treat it as community property just like other forms of deferred compensation. However, in a few cases, courts have treated severance pay as equivalent to post-separation earnings and have therefore characterized the pay as separate property.

E. Bonuses

Bonuses are treated as community property or separate property, depending on the facts and circumstances of the case. Bonuses, in many cases, will be community property because they are a form of compensation for the spouse's labor during the marriage. In some cases, however, an employee bonus is more analogous to a personal gift from the employer to employee. Likewise, where an incentive bonus is paid to an employee for work after separation, the incentive bonus should be characterized as separate property.

F. Stock Options (CFC 80, 2610)

Stock options are a form of compensation. To the extent stock options are earned during the course of the marriage, the community has the right to share in their value as community property.

G. Education and Training (CFC 2641)

Education and training received during a marriage are not community property assets subject to division. However, the community may be entitled to reimbursement when community funds were used to pay for the education or training of a spouse and that education or training substantially enhanced the earning capacity of the spouse.

1. This right to reimbursement is the exclusive remedy for the community. The right to reimbursement is not absolute. Reimbursement will be reduced or denied in three situations: (i) where the other spouse has also received community-funded education; (ii) where the education or training has reduced the need for spousal support for the educated spouse; or (iii) where the community has already benefited from the education or training. If more than 10 years has passed since the education or training, it is presumed that the community has already benefited. **Note:** Loans obtained to fund education are assigned to the educated spouse upon divorce.

H. Life Insurance

The community has an interest in a whole-life insurance policy to the extent that the community paid the premiums. If a spouse has a community-funded life insurance policy and does not name the other spouse as the beneficiary, the other spouse can claim a one-half interest in the benefits after the death of the covered spouse.

For term-life insurance, courts look at which estate paid the premium for the latest term. If the community paid the premium, the community is entitled to the benefits of the policy. As with whole-life insurance, a spouse may not defeat the other spouse's one-half interest in a life insurance policy by naming some other party as beneficiary of the policy.

I. Growth in Separate Property Business Caused by Community Labor

When community labor is used to enhance the value of a separate property business, the community is entitled to share in the increased value. Courts use one of two formulas for calculating the community's interest in the increased value of a separate property business.

1. Pereira

Used when the increase in value of a separate property business is primarily the result of community labor. Using Pereira, you determine the value of the separate property at the beginning of the marriage and give it a fair rate of return over the course of the marriage. Normally this is the legal interest rate calculated annually. The remainder is community property.

2. Van Camp

Used when the increase in value of a business is primarily the result of the unique nature of the separate property asset. Using Van Camp, you determine what a fair salary would be for the community labor. You multiply that by the years of the marriage. You subtract any salary already received and any amounts paid out of the business for community expenses. The result is the community property share. The rest is separate property.

Pereira is preferred when the management by the spouse was the primary cause of the appreciation of the separate business. Van Camp is applied when the character of the separate business is largely responsible for its success.

J. Growth in Community Property Business Caused by Post-Separation Labor

When labor after separation is used to enhance the value of a community property business, the separate estate is entitled to share in the increased value. Courts use one of two formulas to determine the separate property's share:

1. Reverse-Pereira

Gives the community a fair rate of return for the period after separation; the remainder of the increase belongs to the separate estate.

2. Reverse-Van Camp

Assigns a fair salary to the separate estate and deducts any salary already taken by the spouse after separation and any separate expenses paid out of the business. The remainder belongs to the community.

K. Married Woman's Special Presumption (CFC 803)

The married woman's special presumption applies to property taken in the married woman's name alone prior to 1975. According to the presumption, property taken in the name of a married woman prior to 1975 is presumed to be her separate property. The presumption is based on the fact that prior to 1975, the husband was given sole management and control of the community assets, and thus, any property in the woman's name was presumed to have been a gift to her.

1. Overcoming the Presumption

Husband may rebut the presumption by showing that he did not put title in wife's name (because wife had control over community property at the time title was taken) or that he did not intend to make a gift to wife when he put title in her name.

VI. POTENTIAL RIGHTS

A. Creditors (CFC 910, 911, 913, 914)

Debtor's separate property is liable for debts debtor incurred before or during marriage. The other spouse's separate property is not liable for either debt. A creditor may reach the entire community property of both spouses. However, community property earnings of the non-debtor spouse are not liable for the debtor's premarital obligations held in an account where the debtor spouse has access. Additionally, where one spouse incurs a debt for "necessities of life" during marriage, the other spouse will be held personally liable for the debt.

B. Tort Liability (CFC 903, 1000(b))

A person is not liable for her spouse's torts except in cases where the activity benefited the community. If so, liability is satisfied from community property, then from the separate property of the married person. If there was no community benefit, liability is satisfied from the tortfeasor's separate property and then community property.

C. Spouses' Management/Control

1. Separate Property

Management and control of separate property is vested in the owning spouse. Quasi-community property is considered to be separate property for the purposes of management and control.

2. Community Property

Generally, each spouse has equal management and control of community property. Either spouse acting alone may buy, sell, spend, or encumber all community property.

a) Real Property (CFC 1102)

For real property that is considered community property, both spouses must execute the legal instrument that purports to sell, convey, or lease property for more than one year. If only one spouse's name is on the title, and that spouse misrepresents his marital status, the non-consenting spouse may void the transfer within one year.

b) Personal Property (CFC 1100)

Personal property, including that of minor children, may not be transferred without the written consent of the other spouse. If consent is not obtained, the transfer may be voided at any time (during marriage or post-divorce) and no refund needs to be paid to the transferee. This does not apply to gifts mutually given by both spouses, or gifts from one spouse to another.

c) Special Family Personal Property (CFC 1100(c))

Community personal property used for the family dwelling, furniture, or clothing may not be sold, conveyed, or encumbered without the written consent of the other spouse.

d) Business Exception (CFC 1100(d))

A spouse who is operating a community property business (in whole or in part) has primary management and control of the business and may act alone in executing business transactions. However, the spouse shall give notice of any substantial sale, lease, or exchange of property. Where the managing spouse fails to give notice, and the action infringes on the other spouse's one-half community property interest, the transaction is voidable.

3. Limitations on Power

a) Gifts (CFC 1100(b))

Without the prior written consent of the other spouse, a spouse may not make a gift of community property. In the absence of prior written consent, the non-donor spouse may ratify or revoke the gift in writing. If the donor dies, the non-donor can recover against the donor's estate.

b) Spousal Fiduciary Duties (CFC 1100(e))

In the management of community property assets, each spouse must act in the highest good faith and fair dealing and not act to undermine the other spouse's community property interest.

(1) Managing Spouse

This spouse must give a full accounting to the non-manager when requested and must secure the consent of the non-manager before committing certain acts (such as transferring community property). Before 2003, deliberate dissipation or destruction of property was actionable, but mere incompetence was not. Beginning in 2003, even grossly negligent or reckless conduct breaches a spouse's fiduciary duty.

(2) Breach of Fiduciary Duty (CFC 1100)

If a spouse's interest is substantially impaired by the managing spouse's fiduciary duty, the aggrieved spouse may petition the court for an order for accounting and reformation of title to reflect her interest.

VII. DISTRIBUTION OF PROPERTY

A. Divorce (CFC 2550)

In the absence of a prior writing, at dissolution, each community asset will be divided equally unless a special rule requires deviation from the equal division requirement. Where an asset cannot be divided, in-kind division allows the court to distribute assets between spouses provided division is substantially equal.

1. Specific Rules

a) Misappropriation of Community Property (CFC 2602)

Where one spouse deliberately misappropriates their interest in community property or quasi-community property, the court will adjust any award to the offending spouse in consideration of that spouse's wrongdoing.

b) Negative Assets (CFC 2622(b))

Where a couple's debts exceed their assets, a court may order one spouse to pay more than his or her equal share of the debt after considering each spouse's ability to pay.

c) Student Loans (CFC 2627)

Outstanding student debt is treated as the educated spouse's separate debt and does not factor into the equal division of property and debt.

d) Tort Liability (CFC 1000(b))

Civil judgments for tort liability that arose from conduct that did not benefit the community is the responsibility of the tortfeasor spouse.

e) Separate Debt (CFC 2625)

Financial liabilities a spouse incurs pre-marriage, post-separation, or during marriage, but that were not for the community's benefit, are the responsibility of the spouse who assumed such debt.

f) Personal Injury Recovery (CFC 2603(b))

An award for personal injury is assigned entirely to the injured spouse. However, if such an assignment would result in economic hardship to the other spouse (or the interests of justice require it), the court can award up to one-half of the recovery to the other spouse.

g) Good Will

The value of good will, attributable to repeat patronage, is divisible. Good will is typically measured at market value.

2. Valuation

Assets and liabilities are valued as near to the time of trial as practicable. However, it is important to remember that pre-separation labor is not considered community property and does not add to the community property estate. (See Section IV(C) of the outline for separation rule.)

3. Setting Aside a Decree (CFC 2122)

Where fraud or mistake results in incomplete disclosure to the other spouse of community assets or debt, any award or determination by the court may be set aside and the case reopened.

4. Out-of-State Community Property and Quasi-Community Property (CFC 2660)

The divorce court has the power to distribute all community property and quasi-community assets. Where an asset consists of out-of-state real estate, a court may:

a) Divide all community property and quasi-community property in such a way that it is not necessary to alter the nature of the interests held in out-of-state realty; or

b) Order the parties to execute the legal instruments required to divide the out-of-state property; or

c) Issue a monetary award to one spouse equal to the value of that spouse's interest in the property.

B. Death (CFC 100)

At death, a married person may transfer one-half of all community property/quasi-community property and all separate property by will. The surviving spouse owns the other half of the community property and that may not be devised. The surviving spouse is entitled to one-half of each item of community property. However, the surviving spouse may consent to aggregation of assets where an asset cannot be equally divided.

1. Survivor's Duty to Elect (CPC 13502)

A testator may insert a clause in his will stating that his surviving spouse must either elect to take under the terms of the will or assert her community property ownership rights. **Beware of Omitted Spouse Wills Cross-Over.**

2. Intestate (CPC 6401)

All property that is not transferred by will or testamentary substitute passes by intestacy. An intestate decedent's one-half of community property and quasi-community property passes to the surviving spouse, leaving the surviving spouse with 100% of the community property and quasi-community property. An intestate decedent's separate property passes in whole or in part to the surviving spouse according to the following:

a) Separate property: Spouse 100% - Heirs 0%; Where no issue, parents or issue of parents (siblings, nieces/nephews, etc.)

b) Separate property: Spouse 50% - Heirs 50%; One issue, OR no issue but 1+ parent or issue of parent

c) Separate property: Spouse 33.3% - Heirs 66.6%; Two or more issue, i.e.: 2+ children, 1 child and 1+ grandchild, etc.

3. Out-of-State Community Property and Quasi-Community Property Realty (CPC 101)

Out-of-state realty is normally probated in ancillary administration in the state that the realty is located. When a spouse owning out-of-state realty that would be community property or quasi-community property if it were located in California, exchanges that realty for personalty or California realty, the new property is community property or quasi-community property.

VIII. PREEMPTION

Areas in which federal law preempts California community property law include: (i) federal homestead law; (ii) armed forces life insurance benefits; (iii) U.S. savings bonds (unless there is fraud or breach of trust on the part of spouse managing the community property funds); (iv) Social Security benefits; (v) Employee Retirement Income Security Act (ERISA) benefits (CFC 755); and (vi) supplemental railroad retirement benefits that are subject to state community property distribution.

A. The Uniformed Services Former Spouses' Protection Act (Title 10 USC, Section 1408)

This Act permits a state court to treat federal military retirement benefits as either separate property or community property in accordance with state law. Federal preemption requires that California treat federal military and veterans administration disability benefits received after separation as the worker's separate property. Even when a retired service person elects to take military disability benefits instead of retirement benefits to which she would otherwise be entitled, the USFSPA does not allow the benefits to be treated as community property.

B. Federal Civil Service Retirement Pay

Such compensation is divisible according to California community property law.

C. Copyright Law

Such federal law does not preempt California community property division of copyright proceeds.

CONSTITUTIONAL LAW

Table of Contents

I. JUSTICIABLE CASE OR CONTROVERSY

In order for a case to be justiciable – tried in a court of law – there must be a live case or controversy. A case or controversy is an actual, identifiable dispute between two parties that have adverse legal interests.

A. Ripeness

A court will not hear a case if it is not "ripe." That is, a court will only hear cases where there is an existing substantial controversy warranting judicial intervention. Courts will not hear challenges to statutes before they are enforced, for example. There are exceptions to the ripeness doctrine, such as when a plaintiff is certain to suffer harm.

B. Abstention

Even if there is a case or controversy, courts may abstain from settling a constitutional question where there is an unsettled question of state law. Federal courts may also abstain from enjoining pending state proceedings.

C. Mootness

Much like the doctrine of ripeness, under the doctrine of mootness, a court will not hear a case where the case or controversy has already been resolved or is over. If, however, the controversy is likely to occur repeatedly, courts may choose to hear the case. This exception applies to short events that end before a lawsuit can be brought, such as abortion.

D. Political Question

Courts do not decide political questions – those questions that are reserved for another branch of government.

E. Standing

To bring an action, the plaintiff must have standing, i.e., he or she must have suffered an actual concrete and identifiable injury. There are three elements to standing:

- i. Injury: The plaintiff must show that he has been or will be injured – his constitutional or federal rights violated – by an unlawful government action;
- ii. Causation: The unlawful conduct complained of must have caused the injury.
- iii. Redressability: The court must have the power to grant effective relief as opposed to declaratory relief.

Organizational Standing: In order for an organization to have standing, it must show that (i) the members were injured and would have a right to sue on their own behalf; and (ii) the injury is related to the organization's purpose. Individual members do not, however, have to participate in the lawsuit.

Standing to Assert the Rights of Others: A plaintiff generally has to show that her rights were violated, not a third-person's rights. But courts will allow a plaintiff to assert the constitutional rights of others if:

- i. The third party cannot assert her own rights (e.g., an association may attack a law requiring disclosure of membership lists because members would not be able to attack the law without identifying themselves); or
- ii. There is a special relationship between the claimant and the third party (e.g., a doctor can assert a patient's rights in challenging an abortion restriction).

Taxpayer Standing: Generally, a taxpayer only has standing to challenge a tax bill. Taxpayers do not have standing to challenge government policies, programs, or other expenditures except on First Amendment grounds.

F. Eleventh Amendment Limitations on Federal Courts

Federal courts do not have the authority to hear cases brought by a private party or foreign government against a state government. This includes where the state is named as a defendant or where the state will have to pay retroactive damages. Federal courts can, however, hear lawsuits where local governments are named as defendants, as well as lawsuits brought by the U.S. government or another state.

There are three exceptions:

i. Actions against state officers to enjoin an officer from future conduct that will violate the Constitution or federal law, and actions for damages against an officer in his or her personal capacity;
ii. With state consent, that is expressed and unequivocal; or
iii. When Congress removes immunity.

II. WHAT IS THE CONSTITUTIONAL ISSUE?

A. Separation of Powers

1. Branches of Government

a) Judicial

Established by Article III of the Constitution, the judicial branch has the power to interpret the laws of the United States and declare such laws unconstitutional where appropriate.

b) Executive

Article II of the Constitution establishes the executive branch and confers the following powers: (i) veto power over congressional legislation; (ii) appointment power over federal officials and judges; (iii) making treaties and agreements with foreign governments; (iv) enforcing the laws of the United States; (v) being Commander in Chief of the military; and (vi) granting pardons for violations of federal law.

(1) Foreign Policy

Treaties: Treaties are agreements between the United States and a foreign country that are negotiated by the President and are effective when ratified by the Senate. Treaties prevail over conflicting state law. When in conflict with a statute, the law that was last adopted wins. The United States Constitution prevails over treaties.

Executive Agreement: An executive agreement is an agreement between the United States and a foreign country that is effective when signed by the President and a foreign nation. An executive agreement can be used for any purpose. Such an agreement prevails over state law, but it does not prevail over a federal statute or the United States Constitution.

Commander in Chief: The President has broad powers to use troops in foreign countries without declaring war. Cases brought to challenge the exercise of such powers are dismissed as political questions.

(2) Domestic Affairs

Appointment: The President appoints ambassadors, federal judges, and officers of the United States. Congress may bestow appointment of inferior officers in the President, heads of departments or lower federal courts. Congress may not give itself or its officers' appointment power.

Removal Power: Unless limited by statute, the President may fire any executive branch officer. For Congress to limit removal, there must be an office where independence from the President is desirable and Congress cannot prohibit removal. Removal power is only limited where good cause is found.

Impeachment: The President, Vice President, federal judges, and officers of the United States may be impeached where any of the following are found: treason, bribery, high crimes, or misdemeanors. Impeachment does not remove a person from office. For impeachment to result in removal there must be a majority vote in the House and conviction in the Senate with a 2/3rd vote.

Immunity: The President is immune to civil actions for any acts while in office, but not for conduct engaged in prior to taking office.

Executive Privilege: Executive privilege exists in papers and conversations, unless the papers or conversations are important to a government interest (e.g., evidence in criminal trial).

Pardon: A person can be pardoned by the President for federal crimes only, not state crimes.

c) LEGISLATIVE

Article I of the Constitution establishes the legislative branch and confers the power to pass all federal laws, override Presidential veto, establish lower courts, and conduct Presidential impeachment.

B. SCOPE OF FEDERAL POWERS

1. SOURCE OF POWER

a) COMMERCE CLAUSE

Congress has the exclusive power to enact laws to regulate commerce between states (interstate commerce) and foreign nations. A law regulates commerce – and is therefore a proper exercise of power under the commerce clause – if it:

i. Regulates the channels of interstate commerce;
ii. Regulates the instrumentalities of interstate commerce and persons and things in interstate commerce; or
iii. Regulates activities that have a substantial effect on interstate commerce.

If Congress attempts to regulate non-economic (i.e., non-commercial) intrastate activity, the federal government must prove to the court that the activity in fact affects interstate commerce.

For example, under its broadly construed power to regulate interstate commerce, Congress may prohibit private racial discrimination in activities that have a substantial effect on interstate commerce.

b) Spending

Congress may exercise its power to spend, but only for the "general welfare." Congress can use its spending power to encourage states to comply with specified conditions in exchange for federal funds.

c) Taxing

Congress has the power to lay and collect taxes to raise revenue. If Congress has the separate power to regulate a particular activity that it wishes to tax, it can use the tax as a regulating device. Even if Congress does not have the power to regulate the activity, as long as the tax bears some reasonable relationship to revenue production, it will be upheld. Congress cannot tax exports to foreign countries.

d) Taking of Property

Congress has the power to dispose of and make rules for territories and the other properties in the U.S. While there is no express limitation on Congress' power to dispose of property, federal takings (eminent domain) must be for the purpose of effectuating an enumerated power under some other provision of the Constitution.

e) Citizenship

Congress may establish uniform rules of naturalization. This gives Congress plenary power over aliens.

f) No Federal Police Power

Congress does not have a general police power. It does, however, have certain police powers over the District of Columbia, federal land, military bases, and Indian Reservations.

g) Other Enumerated Powers

Investigatory Power, Property Power, Bankruptcy Power, Postal Power, Power over Citizenship, Admiralty Power, Power to Coin Money & Fix Weights and Measures, Patent/Copyright Power.

2. Necessary and Proper "Power"

Congress has the power to make all laws that are necessary and proper for executing any power granted to it or any other branch, department, or officer of the federal government, anywhere else in the Constitution. The Necessary and Proper Clause, standing alone, is not a source of power; it can only be exercised in conjunction with another federal power granted in the Constitution.

3. Limitations on the Power of the Tenth Amendment

The Tenth Amendment provides that all powers not delegated to the federal government by the Constitution are reserved for the states. Most governmental power is concurrent in that it belongs to both the states and the federal government. When the states and the federal government pass legislation on the same subject matter, the Supremacy Clause provides that the federal law prevails, and the conflicting state law is void.

A valid act of Congress or federal regulation supersedes any state or local action that actually conflicts with the federal rule, whether by commanding conduct inconsistent with that required by the federal rule, or by forbidding conduct that the federal rule is designed to foster. The conflict need not relate to the conduct; it is sufficient if the state or local law simply interferes with achievement of a federal objective.

C. State Interference with Federal System Analysis

1. Supremacy Clause

The Supremacy Clause provides that federal law is the supreme law of the land. Therefore, a federal law may supersede or preempt local laws. If a federal law conflicts with a state law, the state law will be invalid.

a) Preemption

In the absence of an express conflict between state and federal law, the state law may still be invalid where the federal government has intended to "occupy" the entire field, precluding any state or local regulation. To determine whether the federal government has intended to "occupy the field," the court will consider (i) the comprehensiveness of the federal scheme, and (ii) the creation of an agency to administer law.

b) Dormant Commerce Clause

If Congress has not enacted laws regarding the subject, a state or local government may regulate local aspects of interstate commerce. When doing so, however, it must not discriminate against or unduly burden interstate commerce. If it does, the state regulation will violate the Commerce Clause.

Discrimination against out-of-state interests: State or local regulations that discriminate against interstate commerce to protect local economic interests are almost always invalid.

i. *Exception* – Important State Interest: A discriminatory state law may be valid if it furthers an important, non-economic state interest, and there are no reasonable nondiscriminatory alternatives available.
ii. *Exception* – State as "Market Participant": A state may prefer its own citizens when acting as a market participant.

Undue Burden on Interstate Commerce: If a non-discriminatory state law (a law that treats local and out-of-state interests alike) burdens interstate commerce, it will be valid unless the burden outweighs the promotion of a legitimate local interest. The court will consider whether less restrictive alternatives are available.

State Control of Corporations: A different standard may apply to statutes adopted by the state of incorporation regulating the internal governance of a corporation because of the states' long history in regulating the corporations they create and their strong interest in doing so, and even a statute that heavily impacts interstate commerce may be upheld.

2. Privileges & Immunities Clause

Under the Privileges & Immunities Clause, a state cannot unjustly deprive a citizen from another state of any right that is derived from state citizenship solely because the person is not a citizen of that state.

Exception: The Privileges & Immunities Clause does not always prohibit a state from treating in-state and out-of-state citizens differently. A state law discriminating against non-residents may still be valid if the state has a substantial justification for the differing treatment. The state must show that non-residents cause or are part of the problem that the state is attempting to solve and there are no less restrictive means to do so.

D. Individual Rights

1. State Action

As the Constitution generally applies only to government action, a plaintiff must show that a "state action" was involved. This concept applies to government and government officers at all levels – local, state, and federal. Note that state actions can be found in actions of seemingly private individuals who (i) perform exclusive public functions or (ii) have significant state involvement.

Exclusive Public Functions: Activities that are traditionally the exclusive prerogative of the states are considered state actions no matter who performs them.

Significant State Involvement – Facilitating Private Action: State action also exists where a state affirmatively facilitates, encourages, or authorizes acts of discrimination by its citizens. Merely permitting the conduct, granting a license, or providing essential services is insufficient.

A state must be "significantly involved" in the private entity; mere acquiescence by the state in private conduct is not enough. Moreover, states are not constitutionally required to outlaw discrimination. They are only forbidden to facilitate, encourage, or authorize it.

2. Freedom of Speech

The First Amendment prohibits Congress from restricting the press or an individual's right to speak freely, and from interfering with citizens' right to assemble. The Fourteenth Amendment applies these same rules to state governments.

a) Regulation of Content

State regulations of the content of speech are presumptively unconstitutional. The burden is on the state to prove that the regulation is necessary to serve a compelling government interest and that the means are narrowly tailored. However, the Supreme Court has held that certain categories of speech are unprotected despite the First Amendment.

b) Unprotected Speech

These unprotected categories of speech include:

(1) Defamation

Congress may regulate defamatory statements, subject to certain limitations depending on whether the individual is a private or public person.

Public Officials & Figures: The plaintiff must prove that the statement is false and actual malice was present.

Private Persons with a Matter of Public Concern: The plaintiff must prove that the statement is false and the publisher was at least negligent with respect to the falsity of the statement.

Private Persons with a Matter of Private Concern: There is no requirement that the statement be proven false or that malice was present.

Cf: False Statements: The Stolen Valor Act, which prohibited false claims regarding being awarded a military medal, was struck down upon a finding that falsity of a statement by itself is not sufficient to remove First Amendment protections. Further, less restrictive means were available.

(2) Fighting Words

Congress can also regulate fighting words – personally abusive words that are likely to incite immediate physical retaliation in an average person. Words that are merely annoying are not sufficient. The Supreme Court does not tolerate fighting word statutes that are designed to punish only certain viewpoints on race, religion, or gender. However, the Court has upheld a ban on cross burning when done with the intent to intimidate.

(3) Obscenity

Congress may regulate obscene speech. Obscene speech is speech that describes or depicts sexual conduct that, taken as a whole by the average person, is patently offensive and an affront to contemporary community standards, and lacks any serious value. This means that Congress cannot ban literary, artistic, political, or scientific speech even if it would otherwise be considered obscene.

Minors: States are free to adopt specific definitions of obscenity that would apply to the materials sold to minors. Governments cannot, however, prohibit the sale of goods to adults.

Pictures of Minors: In the interest of protecting minors from exploitation, the government may prohibit the sale or distribution of visual depictions of sexual conduct involving minors.

(4) Advocacy of Imminent Lawless Action

Congress can regulate speech if it creates a clear and present danger of imminent lawless action. Under the Brandenburg Test, the government may prohibit speech if:

i. The speech advocates imminent lawless action;
ii. The threatened action poses serious risk of harm;
iii. The speaker specifically intends the unlawful activity to occur; and,
iv. Illegal action is likely to occur.

(5) Commercial Speech (lesser protected speech)

Commercial speech is speech where the audience is potential consumers or the speaker is engaged in commerce. Commercial speech is only protected if it is truthful. The government can regulate commercial speech that proposes illegal activity or if it is fraudulent or misleading. Any other regulation will be upheld if:

i. The regulation serves a significant government interest;
ii. The regulation directly advances that interest; and
iii. The regulation is narrowly tailored to that interest.

c) PROTECTED SPEECH

If the government is regulating the content of speech, the standard of review is strict scrutiny. This means that a law will be upheld only if it is necessary to achieve a compelling government interest. The government must demonstrate that it cannot achieve the goal through a less restrictive alternative.

d) Strict Scrutiny Balancing Test

Government Objective: The objective must be compelling and the means used to achieve that objective must be necessary.

Plaintiff's Interests: What are the plaintiff's interests? What is she trying to achieve or protect?

Less Restrictive Alternative: The government has the burden of showing that it could not achieve the result in a less burdensome way.

e) Content Neutral Regulation of Conduct

The Supreme Court has allowed the government more leeway in regulating conduct-related speech by allowing it to adopt content-neutral time, place, and manner restrictions. The limitations depend on whether the speech involves a public forum or a nonpublic forum.

(1) Time, Place and Manner Restrictions on Speech

The government may regulate the time, place, and manner in which speech and assembly are conducted. The extent of permissible regulations depends on whether the forum is a public, designated public, or non-public forum.

Public Forums and Limited Public Forums: Public forums include public property that has historically been open to speech-related activities such as streets, sidewalks, and public parks. Limited public forums are public properties that the government has opened for speech-related activities on a permanent or limited basis by either practice or policy such as schoolrooms that are open for after-school use by social, civic, or recreation groups.

The government may regulate speech in public and limited public forums as long as the regulations:

i. Are content-neutral;
ii. Are narrowly tailored to serve an identifiable and significant government interest; and
iii. Do not close all channels of communication.

Non-Public Forums: In non-public government-owned forums such as military bases, schools, government workplaces, the government may more broadly regulate speech and assembly as long as the regulations are:

i. Viewpoint-neutral; and
ii. Reasonably related to a legitimate government purpose.

(2) Other Considerations

Prior Restraints: Prior restraints are government regulations that prevent speech before it occurs. Prior restraints are rarely constitutional. In order to put prior restraints on speech, the government must show that there is bound to be a resulting special harm to society. This is a high burden and the government must:

i. Draw narrow, reasonable, and definite standards;
ii. Promptly seek an injunction; and
iii. Promptly seek a final determination of the validity of the restraint.

Unfettered Discretion: A regulation cannot give officials broad discretion over speech issues; there must be defined standards for applying the law. If a statute gives licensing officials unbridled discretion, it is void on its face and speakers need not even apply for a permit. If the licensing statute includes standards, a speaker may not ignore the statute; he must seek a permit and if it is denied, he can challenge the denial on First Amendment grounds. There must be a prompt review process without undue delay.

Overbroad Regulation is Invalid: If a regulation of speech or speech-related conduct punishes a substantial amount of protected speech in relation to a legitimate sweep, the regulation is facially invalid unless a court has limited the construction of the regulation so as to remove the threat to constitutionally protected speech. If the regulation is not substantially overbroad, it can be enforced against persons engaging in activities that are not constitutionally protected.

Void for Vagueness Doctrine: A criminal law or regulation failing to give persons reasonable notice of what is prohibited ("lewd speech," for example) may violate the Due Process Clause. This principle is applied somewhat strictly when First Amendment activity is involved.

Government Speech: The government "is entitled to say what it wishes," Rosenberger (1995). This does not mean that there are no restraints on government speech. Government speech must comport with the Constitution, federal, state and local regulation. For example, the application of the Establishment Clause is the basis for prohibiting religious monuments on government property. *Pleasant Grove City (2009).*

3. Freedom of Association and Belief

The right to join together with other persons for expressive or political activity is protected by the First Amendment. However, the right to associate for expressive purposes is not absolute. Infringements on the right must be justified by compelling state interests, unrelated to the suppression of ideas, that cannot be achieved through less restrictive means.

a) Electoral Process

Laws regulating the electoral process may impact the freedoms of speech, assembly, and association. In determining whether the electoral process is valid, use the following balancing test: If the restriction on First Amendment activities is severe, it will be upheld only if it is narrowly tailored to a compelling state interest; if the restriction is reasonable and nondiscriminatory, it will be upheld under the states' important regulatory interests.

b) Campaign Contributions

Laws limiting the amount of money that a person or group may contribute to a political candidate are valid. But the government may not limit the amount that an individual or group may spend on a political campaign.

4. Freedom of the Press

The press has the right to public information about a matter of public concern. This right can only be restricted by a sanction that is narrowly tailored to further a state interest of the highest order.

The First Amendment guarantees that the public and press have access to criminal trials. This right to attend includes "voir dire," examination of jurors, as well as pretrial proceedings. This right may be outweighed by an overriding interest articulated by the judge.

The government has a compelling interest in protecting children who are victims of sex offenses. Portions of trials wherein children testify may be closed to the public and press if such closure is necessary to protect the child in the individual case.

5. RELIGION

The First Amendment prohibition on the national establishment of a religion and its protections of the free exercise of religion apply to the states through the Fourteenth Amendment.

a) ESTABLISHMENT CLAUSE

The Establishment Clause prohibits Congress from enacting laws respecting an establishment of religion. This clause not only forbids the government from establishing an official religion or endorsing a religion, but also prohibits government actions that unduly favor one religion over another.

If a government regulation or action prefers one religious sect to another, it is invalid unless it is narrowly tailored to promote a compelling interest.
If a government regulation contains no sect preference the court no longer employs the *Lemon Test* or *endorsement test,* but looks to "historical practices and understandings". Under this approach, traditional monuments and practices that have explicit references to religion (for example, "In God we trust") are likely acceptable even though they would not be permitted if created today.

b) FREE EXERCISE CLAUSE

No Punishment of Beliefs: The government cannot punish someone for his or her religious beliefs.

General Conduct Regulation: Regulations that happen to affect religious conduct cannot be challenged under the Free Exercise Clause. A regulation is only invalid if it was designed to interfere with religion. Thus, regulations that apply generally do not have to contain exemptions for religious actions if the regulation happens to burden religious conduct.

i. *Exception*—Unemployment Compensation Cases: If a person quits his or her job for religious reasons, as long as the person is sincere, and is otherwise eligible for unemployment benefits, the state cannot deny benefits.

ii. *Exception*—Right of Amish not to Educate Children: The Amish have received a religious exemption from the requirement that all children must go to school until they are 16. The Supreme Court found the compulsory-attendance law burdened their free exercise of religion.

iii. *Exception*—Prisoners Growth of Facial Hair for Religious Reasons: Once a prisoner shows that a religious practice is grounded in a sincerely held religious belief, the regulation must survive strict scrutiny. In Holt v. Hobbs (2015), the Supreme Court held that an Arkansas prison regulation prohibiting facial hair in the interests of prison safety must survive strict scrutiny, which it did not.

Financial Benefits to Religious Institutions: The government may give financial aid to religious institutions. But courts apply the three-part test articulated above more strictly when the government gives financial aid to schools affiliated with a religion than when the aid is for other religious institutions.

Recipient-Based Aid: The government may give financial assistance to certain groups of individuals as long as those groups are not defined in relation to a religion or by religious criteria. It does not matter if those receiving the aid use it to attend a school affiliated with a religion.

Aid to Colleges and Hospitals: The government may give financial assistance to colleges and hospitals that are associated with a religion as long as the funds are used for non-religious purposes.

Aid to Grade Schools & High Schools: The government may give financial assistance to grade schools and high schools. Courts usually recognize a secular purpose, but it may be harder to meet the other requirements of the test such as government–religion entanglement.

Cases Unconnected to Financial Aid or Education: Laws that favor or place a burden on large segments of society will generally be upheld even if they happen to also favor or burden religious groups. Laws that favor or place a burden on religion or a religious group are unconstitutional.

Religious Activities in Public Schools: Public schools cannot sponsor religious activity but, at the same time, cannot deny a religious organization an accommodation if it makes accommodations for public and private organizations.

Prayers Preceding Legislative Sessions: In *Town of Greece v. Galloway (2014)*, the Supreme Court upheld a local practice that allowed legislative sessions to be preceded by a prayer. The town's practice of opening its town board meetings with a prayer offered by members of the clergy does not violate the Establishment Clause when the practice is consistent with the tradition long followed by Congress and state legislatures, the town does not discriminate against minority faiths in determining who may offer a prayer, and the prayer does not coerce participation of non-adherents.

6. Takings

Under the Takings Clause of the Fifth Amendment, the government may not take private property for public use without just compensation. This applies to the states under the Fourteenth Amendment. A taking is more than the physical taking of property; it extends to regulations that infringe on a property owner's rights. The Takings Clause also applies to more than land-property rights such as contract rights, personal property, and trade secrets.

a) Public Use

The public-use requirement is generally construed broadly. As long as a taking is related to a legitimate public purpose, including public welfare, the government may seize property.

b) Taking vs. Regulation

Determining whether a regulation amounts to a taking is often a fact-intensive inquiry.

(1) Actual Appropriation or Physical Invasion

The seizure or invasion of real property or the seizure of personal property is generally considered a taking.

(2) Use Restrictions

Denial of all Economic Value: If a regulation prevents a property owner from making economic use of his property, the regulation is considered a taking, unless the use is otherwise prohibited under the principles of nuisance or property law.

Temporary: If the regulation only deprives the property owner of economic use of the land temporarily, the court will weigh the relevant facts – the owner's reasonable expectations, length of delay, and the economic effect of delay – to determine whether the principles of fairness and justice require just compensation.

Nolan & Dolan: Municipalities often attempt to condition building or development permits on a landowner's conveying title of part or all of the property to the government, or by granting public access to the property. These conditions are an uncompensated taking, unless: i) the government can show that the condition relates to a legitimate government interest; and, ii) the adverse impact of the proposed development on the area is roughly proportional to the loss caused to the property owner from the forced transfer of occupation rights.

Decreasing Economic Value – Balancing Test: As long as the landowner can still make economically viable use of the property, a regulation is not a taking even if it decreases the value of the property. The court will consider:

i. The social goals sought to be promoted;
ii. The diminution in value to the owner; and
iii. The owner's reasonable expectations regarding the property.

The more drastic the reduction in value or the less it promotes public welfare, the more likely it is to be a taking.

c) Remedy

If the regulation amounts to a taking, the government must:

i. Give the property owner "just compensation," which is generally considered the fair-market value; or
ii. Repeal the regulation and pay the property owner for damages incurred while the regulation was in effect.

"Just compensation" is measured by the loss to the owner, not the gain to the taker. Where the property is worthless in the first place, the government does not have to pay any compensation.

7. Equal Protection

The Equal Protection clause of the Fourteenth Amendment provides that no state shall make or enforce any law that shall deny to any person within its jurisdiction equal protection of the laws. It prohibits governmental regulations that discriminate on the basis of arbitrary classifications, as individuals similarly situated must be treated the same. The Essay Approach is as follows:

a) Determine the Classification

(1) Fundamental Right

i. Privacy Rights: Marriage, contraception, pornography, keeping extended family together, parental decisions, sexual conduct.
ii. Right to Vote
iii. Right to Travel

(2) Suspect Class

Classifications are suspect if they are based on race, alienage, or national origin.

(3) **Quasi-Suspect Class**

Classifications based on legitimacy, gender and orientation are "quasi-suspect."

(4) **Other Classes**

b) **DETERMINE THE STANDARD OF REVIEW**

If a fundamental right or suspect classification is involved, courts will use the strict scrutiny standard to evaluate the regulation. If a quasi-suspect classification is involved, intermediate scrutiny is applied. And if the classification does not affect a fundamental right or involve a suspect or quasi-suspect classification, the rational basis test is applied.

Strict Scrutiny: A law involving a fundamental right or suspect class is constitutional if the government can show it was passed to further a compelling governmental interest and is narrowly tailored to achieve that purpose.

Intermediate Scrutiny: To pass intermediate scrutiny, the government must show that the law furthers an important government interest through regulations that are substantially related to that interest.

Rational Basis: A law has a rational basis if it is rationally related to a legitimate government purpose – not arbitrary or irrational. The party challenging the law generally has the burden of proof.

i. Exception—Facially neutral law: Where a facially neutral law is being applied in a discriminatory manner or there is a discriminatory motive behind the law, the government is said to have the intent to discriminate and strict or intermediate scrutiny will be applied depending on the classification of those targeted.

c) **DETERMINE THE GOVERNMENT'S INTEREST**

d) **DETERMINE WHETHER THE CLASSIFICATION FURTHERS THAT INTEREST**

e) **DETERMINE WHETHER THERE ARE LESS BURDENSOME MEANS AVAILABLE**

8. SUBSTANTIVE DUE PROCESS

Certain fundamental rights are protected under the Constitution. If they are denied to everyone, it is a substantive due process problem. If they are denied to some individuals but not others, it is an equal protection problem. The Essay Approach is as follows:

a) **WHAT FUNDAMENTAL RIGHT IS BEING DEPRIVED OR BURDENED**

(1) **Right of Privacy**

Marriage: The right to marry another individual, regardless of their gender, is a fundamental right, *Obergefell v. Hodges (2015)*. Additionally, the right to end a marriage is also fundamental. Prisoners' rights to marry can be restricted on the basis of legitimate penological interests.

Use of Contraceptives: The right to contraception is a fundamental right and a state cannot prohibit the distribution of non-medical contraceptives to adults.

Abortion: In 2022, the Supreme Court decided Dobbs v. Jackson Women's Health Organization and overturned Roe v. Wade (1973), which held that the federal constitution guarantees the right to abortion.

i. Pre Dobbs—States were allowed to enact regulations before viability only if they did not create an "undue burden" on the right to an abortion. After viability, the states were allowed to regulate and prohibit abortions unless the abortion was necessary to protect the woman's health.
ii. Post Dobbs—Abortion rights are now defined by individual states. Some state courts have held that their state constitution protects abortion as a "privacy" right, others have amended their constitution to explicitly protect abortion rights. Other states have limited abortions to certain circumstances, such as rape, while others have criminalized all abortions.

Obscene Reading Material: The right to privacy also includes the right to read obscene material in one's own home. There is no fundamental right to sell, buy, or transport obscene material.

Keeping Extended Family Together: Related people have a constitutional right to live together as family. The government cannot adopt zoning regulations that infringe on this right.

Rights of Parents: Parents have a fundamental right to direct the upbringing and education of their children.

Intimate Sexual Conduct: Intimate consensual sexual conduct falls under the right to privacy. The Supreme Court has held that states do not have a legitimate interest in interfering with non-commercial conduct.

Collection and Distribution of Personal Data – No Privacy Right: The Fourteenth Amendment's right to privacy does not prohibit states from collecting personal data on their citizens.

(2) Right to Vote

The right to vote is a fundamental right. The government has lawfully placed restrictions on the right to vote on the basis of residence, age, and citizenship, but any other regulation must pass strict scrutiny.

Restrictions on the Right to Vote

i. Residency Requirements: Courts have allowed states to require an individual to live in a state for a reasonable period of time – generally 30 days – before gaining residency for voting purposes. In Presidential elections, Congress can override state waiting periods.

ii. Property Ownership: States cannot condition the right to vote upon the ownership of property.

iii. Poll Taxes: The Twenty-Fourth Amendment prohibits poll taxes.

iv. Primary Elections: Political parties may open their primary elections to anyone, regardless of party affiliation. While states may not prohibit this, they may require voters to register for the primary election.

Dilution of the Right to Vote

i. One Person, One Vote: Applies whenever any level of government decides to select representatives to a government body by a popular election from individual districts.

ii. Gerrymandering: If a state uses race or other suspect classifications as the predominant factor when determining the boundaries of voting districts, it must pass strict scrutiny.

Candidates and Campaigns

i. Candidates: States cannot charge a fee to run for office that would make it impossible for indigents to run. Any regulation on who can run for office must be reasonable, non-discriminatory, and promote an important state interest.

ii. Funding: The government may provide public funds to the two major parties. Minor parties may also receive public funds, but the amount does not have to be equal to that given to public parties.

(3) Right to Travel: Interstate Travel

Individuals have the fundamental right to travel from one state to another. Along with the right to travel to a new state, individuals also have the right to be treated the same as long-time residents. States may, however, place restrictions on travel. Many states impose minimum residency requirements before giving new residents benefits. The constitutionality of these regulations generally depends on the length of time.

Invalid: The Supreme Court has found one-year residency requirements for welfare benefits, voting, and subsidized medical care to be unconstitutional.

Valid: Thirty-day residency requirements, however, have been upheld.

Level of Review: Regulations affecting these rights are reviewed under the strict scrutiny standard.

b) DETERMINE WHETHER STRICT SCRUTINY SHOULD BE APPLIED

c) DETERMINE THE GOVERNMENT'S INTEREST

d) DETERMINE WHETHER THE CLASSIFICATION FURTHERS THAT INTEREST

e) DETERMINE WHETHER THE MEANS AVAILABLE SATISFY THE GOVERNMENT'S BURDEN

9. PROCEDURAL DUE PROCESS

When the federal government or a state government intentionally acts in such a way that denies a citizen of his or her life, liberty, or property, the person must be given notice and an opportunity to be heard. Negligent acts are not subject to the due process clause.

a) Liberty

The Supreme Court has interpreted "liberty" broadly. It is more than freedom from physical restraint, but all conduct that an individual is free to pursue.

b) Property

"Property" under the Due Process Clause includes not only real property and personal belongings, but also intangible property rights such as continued welfare benefits or attendance at a public school. A mere desire for a benefit is insufficient; the individual must have a legal claim or entitlement.

c) What process is due?

"Due process" generally requires: (i) notice; (ii) right to grieve to the governmental actor; and, (iii) the right to appeal. The extent of the procedure necessary is determined by a three-part balancing test that weighs:

i. The importance of the individual's interest that is at stake;
ii. There is risk that the individual will be deprived of the interest through the process used, along with any safeguards; and
iii. The government's interest, such as fiscal and efficiency interests.

d) Waiver

An individual can knowingly and intentionally waive his right to due process.

10. Privileges of National Citizenship

Under the Fourteenth Amendment, states may not deny their citizens the privileges or immunities of national citizenship (e.g., the right to petition congress for redress of grievances, the right to vote for federal officers, and the right to interstate travel). Corporations are not protected by this clause.

11. Full Faith and Credit

If a judgment is entitled to full faith and credit, it must be recognized in sister states. This clause applies only if: (i) the court that rendered the judgment had jurisdiction over the parties and the subject matter; (ii) the judgment was on the merits; and (iii) the judgment is final.

12. Retroactive Legislation

a) Contract Clause – Impairment of Contract

The Contract Clause prohibits states from enacting any law that retroactively impairs contract rights. It does not affect contracts not yet entered into.

Not Applicable to the Federal Government: There is no comparable clause applicable to the federal government. The government may, however, violate the Fifth Amendment's Due Process Clause by impairing a person's right to contract.

Impairment Rules:

i. Private Contracts – Intermediate Scrutiny: State legislation that substantially impairs an existing private contract is invalid unless the legislation: (i) serves an important and legitimate public interest; and (ii) is a reasonable and narrowly tailored means of promoting that interest (e.g., moratorium on mortgage foreclosures).

ii. Public Contracts – Stricter Scrutiny: Legislation that impairs a contract to which the state is a party is tested by the same basic test, but will likely receive stricter scrutiny, especially if the legislation reduces the contractual burden on the state.

b) Ex Post Facto Laws (Criminal Cases Only)

Neither states nor the federal government may pass ex post facto laws. Ex post facto laws are laws that retroactively alter criminal offenses or punishment in a substantially prejudicial manner for the purpose of punishing a person for some past activity. A statute retroactively alters a law in a substantially prejudicial manner if it:

i. Makes criminal an act that was innocent when done;
ii. Prescribes greater punishment for an act than was prescribed for the act when it was done; or
iii. Reduces the evidence required to convict a person of a crime from what was required when the act was committed.

c) Bills of Attainder

Federal and state governments cannot pass bills of attainder -- legislative acts that inflict punishment on individuals without a judicial trial.

d) Due Process Considerations

If a retroactive law does not violate the Contracts, Ex Post Facto, or Bill of Attainder Clauses, it still must pass muster under the Due Process Clause. If the retroactive law does not relate to a fundamental right, it need only be rationally related to a legitimate government interest.

CONTRACTS & UCC ARTICLE 2

Table of Contents

I. APPLICABLE LAW

Determine which law applies to the dispute by identifying the subject matter of the contract.

A. Contract Involving Sale of Goods – UCC

The Uniform Commercial Code ("UCC") – Article 2 applies to transactions in moveable goods. "Goods" means all things (including specially manufactured goods) which are moveable at the time of identification to the contract for sale other than the money in which the price is to be paid, investment securities (Article 8) and things in action.

B. If Both Parties Are Merchants – UCC

Additionally, a number of Article 2 provisions differentiate between merchants and non-merchants. A merchant is defined as one who regularly deals in the kind of goods sold, or who otherwise by his profession designates himself as having special knowledge or skill as to the practices or goods sold (Article 2-104.)

C. Contract Involving Services or Non-Sale of Goods – Common Law

The common law governs contracts for services/non-sale of goods.

D. Predominant Purpose Test

If the contractual transaction involves goods and services, you must then determine the predominant purpose of the contract (i.e., is it the sale of goods or services) and then apply the appropriate law.

II. IS THERE A VALID CONTRACT?

A "contract" is defined as an agreement between two or more persons evidenced by a mutual promise or set of promises supported by consideration. The manifestation of mutual consent usually takes the form of a clear offer by one party, the offeror, and by the other party, the offeree's acceptance.

A. Formation Is Not an Issue

If the fact pattern states there is a valid contract, in your essay answer, provide an introductory paragraph such as: "There appears to be a valid contract. (i) The terms are sufficiently certain and definite: (a) the parties (Dan and Pete); (b) price ($1 per widget); (c) subject matter (100 widgets per month); and (d) time for performance (every Monday). (ii) There was acceptance (i.e., Dan agreed to all the terms of the offer). (iii) Consideration was supplied by the bargained-for-exchange of widgets for money."

B. Where Formation Is An Issue

In order for there to be a valid contract, there must be: (i) mutual assent of the parties (offer and acceptance); (ii) consideration or a substitute to support the contract; and, (iii) no valid defenses to formation.

1. Offer

To be valid, an offer must: (i) be an expression of a promise, undertaking, or commitment to enter into a binding agreement; (ii) contain definite and certain terms; and (iii) be communicated to the offeree.

a) Manifestation of Present Intent

The offeror must intend to contract and not simply negotiate. The test for contractual intent is objective; what a reasonable person would understand from the words or conduct of the offeror in the given circumstances. Statements reasonably understood to be in jest, anger, or the result of duress or intoxication cannot be offers. If, therefore, the person to whom the promise or manifestation is addressed knows, or has reason to know, that the person making the offer does not intend it as an expression of a promise or manifestation of intention, then he will not have made an offer.

b) Definite and Certain Terms

Enough of the essential terms of a contract must be provided in the offer to make it capable of being enforced and make performance relatively certain: (i) identification of the parties; (ii) subject matter; (iii) time for performance; and, (iv) a price, that includes:

(1) Requirement/Output Contract

Offers that designate quantity by requirement or output (UCC 2.306) are certain since these quantity terms can be objectively determined. However, if it is not an output contract, the quantity must be included to create a sales contract.

(2) UCC Sale of Goods

Agreements for the sale of goods controlled by the UCC will not fail due to the omission of an essential term if: (i) the parties make a contract; (ii) there is a reasonably certain basis for remedy in the event of breach; and, (iii) the parties exercise good faith (honesty in fact in the conduct of the transaction). Exception: Quantity term will not be implied by the UCC.

NOTE: Even though a manifestation of intention is intended to be understood as an offer, it cannot be accepted, thereby resulting in the formation of a contract, if the terms of the contract are not reasonably certain.

c) Communication Requirement

The offer must be communicated to the offeree.

2. Termination of the Offer

An offer may be accepted only as long as it has not been terminated. It may be terminated by: (i) an act of either party; or (ii) operation of law.

a) Termination by Acts of Parties

The offeror terminates an offer if he: (i) directly communicated the revocation; or (ii) acts inconsistently with continued willingness to maintain the offer, and the offeree receives correct information of this from a reliable source. Offers made by publication may be terminated only by use of comparable means of publication equal to that given to the offer, and there is no better means of notification reasonably available.

(1) Effective When Received

Revocation is effective when received by the offeree; however, publication of revocation is only effective when published.

(2) Offeror's Power to Revoke

Offers not supported by consideration or detrimental reliance can be revoked at will by the offeror, even if he has promised not to revoke for a certain period of time.

Limitations: The offeror's power to revoke is limited if:

(a) Common Law

There is an option contract supported by valid consideration.

(b) UCC Firm Offer

A written offer signed by a merchant giving assurances that it will be held open will not be revocable for lack of consideration, for the stated period of time or for a reasonable period of time if no period is expressly stated. The period of irrevocability may not exceed three months. (Article 2.205 UCC.)

(c) Reliance

Where the offeree has detrimentally relied on the offer and the offeror could reasonably expect such reliance, revocation is not permitted; or in the case of a unilateral contract, where the offeree has embarked on performance, the contract may not be revoked.

b) Termination by the Offeree

(1) Rejection

An offeree may reject an offer: (i) by express rejection, which terminates his power of acceptance; or (ii) by making a counteroffer (as distinguished from a mere inquiry and which serves as a rejection of the original offer, and the counteroffer creates a new offer by the offeree).

(a) Effective When Received

A rejection is effective when received. Once an offer has been rejected, the original offer is at an end; however, if the offeror restates the offer after it has been rejected, the offeree has the power to accept the new offer.

(b) Rejection of Option

Rejection of an option does not terminate the offer; the offeree is still free to accept the offer within the option period unless the offeror has detrimentally relied on the offeree's rejection.

(2) Lapse of Time

An offer may be terminated by the offeree's failure to accept within the time specified by the offer or within a reasonable period if no deadline was specified. What is a "reasonable period" is a matter of fact depending upon the relevant circumstances applicable to the offer and acceptance.

c) Termination by Operation of Law

The following events will terminate an offer:

(1) Death or insanity of either party;
(2) Destruction of the contract's proposed subject matter; or
(3) Illegality of the contract's subject matter.

3. Acceptance

A valid acceptance of a bilateral contract requires there to be: (i) an offeree with the power of acceptance; (ii) unequivocal terms of acceptance; and (iii) communication of acceptance.

a) Who May Accept

The person to whom the offer is addressed has the power of acceptance, as does a member of the class to whom the offer is addressed, and no other.

b) Acceptance Must Be Unequivocal

(1) Common Law

Acceptance must mirror the offer's terms, neither omitting nor adding terms. Otherwise, it may be a counteroffer.

(2) UCC

Under common law, for an acceptance to be effective, it must conform to the offer, otherwise it will serve as a counteroffer. Under the UCC, however, unless expressly prohibited, an acceptance will be effective even if additional or different terms are contained therein (Article 2.207 UCC).

(3) Additional Terms

Such terms are typically construed as proposed additions to the contract and must be separately accepted to modify the original offer.

Between Merchants: If both parties to the contract qualify as merchants, the new terms do become part of the contract unless:

(a) **Prior Objection**

The original offeror objected in advance to the addition of terms;

(b) **Subsequent Objection**

If the original offeror objects to the new terms within a reasonable time after notice of them is received;

(c) **Material Alteration**

If the new terms would materially alter the original terms (e.g., a disclaimer of warranties; not an arbitration clause) (Article 2.207 UCC).

(4) **Different Terms**

An acceptance form that contains different terms than the offer is considered an acceptance, provided the acceptance does not insist upon the new terms being accepted, and a contract will be formed unless the offeror specifically limits the acceptance to the terms of the offer (if so, it is treated as a counteroffer). There is a split of authority over whether different terms become part of the contract.

(a) **Majority Rule**

Conflicting terms in the offer and acceptance are knocked out of the contract and are replaced by UCC gap-filler provisions. If it concerns a major provision, no contract is formed.

(b) **Minority Rule**

Discrepant terms in the acceptance are ignored.

(5) **Open Terms**

The fact that one or more terms are left open (including price) does not prevent the formation of a contract if the parties intended such, and there is a reasonable basis for giving a remedy. The court can supply reasonable terms for those that are missing.

(6) **Performance**

If the parties have exchanged non-matching forms and begin to perform, a contract has been created. The contract will consist of the terms on which the parties agree, plus supplementary terms supplied by the UCC where the parties are silent (Article 2.207 UCC).

c) **COMMUNICATION OF ACCEPTANCE**

Acceptance is judged by an objective reasonable person standard; the offeree's subjective state of mind is irrelevant. The modern rule and the UCC permit acceptance by any reasonable means unless the offeror unambiguously limits acceptance to particular means.

(1) **Mailbox Rule**

Under the mailbox rule, if the acceptance is by mail or similar means and it is properly addressed and stamped, it is effective at the moment of dispatch. If it is improperly sent, it will be effective on receipt. (Article 2.206 UCC).

(a) **Limitations**

The rule does not apply: (i) if the offer states that acceptance is not effective until received; (ii) if an option contract is involved (effective on receipt); (iii) where the offeree sends a rejection and then sends an acceptance, whichever arrives first is effective; and (iv) where the acceptance is sent first, followed by a rejection – the acceptance is effective unless the rejection is received first and the offeror detrimentally relies on it.

(2) **Acceptance without Communication**

In a bilateral contract, acceptance without communication may occur where: (i) there is an express waiver of communication in the offer; (ii) the offer requires an act as acceptance; or (iii) the offeree silently takes the offered benefits.

(3) **Unilateral Contract**

If the offer requires performance of the bargained-for duties by the offeree, it contemplates a unilateral contract.

(a) **Notice**

Valid notice of performance is required to complete acceptance when: (i) the offeror requires it; or (ii) the offeror has no other way of learning that performance has occurred, and the offeree knows, or should know of this.

4. CONSIDERATION

Courts will enforce a bilateral or unilateral contract only if it is supported by consideration or a substitute for consideration. The parties must exchange something. In the case of a bilateral contract, a mutual exchange of promises constitutes valuable consideration; each party incurs a detriment and a benefit. In the case of a unilateral contract, they exchange a promise for an act.

a) INSUFFICIENT CONSIDERATION

(1) **Gift**

There is no bargain involved when one party gives a gift to another.

(2) **Past Consideration**

A bargained-for exchange cannot occur if one party is induced by a benefit conferred by the other party prior to their present negotiation.

(3) **Moral Consideration**

A bargain does not occur if one party is induced to offer a promise or an act due to a sense of moral obligation.

(4) **Economic Adequacy**

If there is evidence of fraud, undue influence, or duress, there is no valid consideration. If the promise is clearly worthless or a token indicating the transaction is a disguised gift, consideration is invalid.

(5) **Pre-Existing Duty**

A promise or act is not adequate consideration if the party is already obligated to perform it. The necessary detriment can exist if the party tenders some additional performance or if unforeseen and substantial hardship has occurred that will add to the burden of performance.

(6) **Illusory Promise**

A promise is not adequate consideration if the promisor has retained unlimited freedom to determine whether to perform or not. There is no legal detriment.

b) SUBSTITUTE FOR CONSIDERATION

(1) **Promissory Estoppel or Detrimental Reliance**

Promissory estoppel is a sufficient substitute for consideration. The promisor should reasonably expect her promise to induce action or forbearance of a definite and substantial character, and such action of forbearance is in fact induced.

(2) **Specific Circumstances**

An obligation discharged by law (e.g., statute of limitations) can be revived by a gratuitous promise made in writing.

C. Defenses to Formation

Although the requirements for the existence of a contractual relationship appear to be present, in some circumstances, the contract may be voidable due to mistake (a mistake is a belief that is not in accordance with the facts).

1. Absence of Mutual Assent

a) Mutual Mistake

A mistake by both parties at the time the contract is made is a defense to a contention that a valid contract is in place, if: (i) the mistake concerns a basic assumption on which the contract was made; (ii) the mistake has a material adverse effect on the agreed-upon exchange of performance; and (iii) the adversely affected party did not assume the risk of the mistake.

(1) Assumption of Risk

When the parties know their assumption is doubtful, the parties will be deemed to have assumed the risk that their assumption was wrong.

b) Unilateral Mistake

Whether it be of identity, subject matter, or computation, a mistake by one party is generally insufficient to make a contract voidable. However, if the non-mistaken party knew or should have known of the mistake, the contract is voidable by the mistaken party if the effect of the mistake would be to make enforcement of the contract unconscionable or the other party knew of the mistake or she caused it.

(1) Mistake by Intermediary

Where there is a mistake by intermediary, the message will usually be operative as transmitted unless the party receiving the message should have been aware of the mistake.

c) Misrepresentation

If a party induces another to enter into a contract using fraudulent misrepresentation or by using non-fraudulent material misrepresentation (no intent to misrepresent), the contract is voidable by the innocent party if she justifiably relied on the misrepresentation. The misrepresentation can be either an assertion of fact or an omission to disclose a relevant fact. It will be fraudulent if the maker knowingly makes an assertion (or omission) is not in accordance with the facts, and a misrepresentation will be material if it is likely to induce a reasonable person to enter into the contract. A misrepresentation induces a person to contract if it substantially contributes to her decision-making process. If these factors are present, the contract is voidable by the innocent party. Remember to distinguish a misrepresentation from an expression of opinion.

NOTE: If there is fraud in the execution, the contact is void rather than voidable.

d) Illegality of Contract

If the consideration or subject matter of the contract is illegal, the contract is void.

(1) Exceptions

The contract will not be void where: (i) the plaintiff is unaware of illegality while the defendant knows; (ii) the parties are not in pari delicto; and (iii) the illegality is the failure to obtain a license when the license is for revenue raising purposes rather than protecting the public.

D. Defenses to Enforcement

1. Statute of Frauds

Certain agreements within the statute of frauds must be evidenced in writing, signed by or on behalf of the party to be charged, if they are to be enforced. These agreements are promises: (i) in consideration of marriage; (ii) that by their terms cannot be performed within one year; (iii) creating an interest in land; (iv) by executors to pay an estates' debts out of their own pockets; (v) to pay the debts of another (surety); and (vi) for the sale of goods for $500 or more (see Article 2.201 UCC).

a) Memorandum Requirements

The statute is satisfied if the writing contains the following: (i) the identity of the parties; (ii) the contract's subject matter; (iii) the terms and conditions; (iv) a recital of consideration; and (v) the signature of the party to be charged.

NOTE: The memorandum can be contained in more than one document if one of the documents is signed and it is clear from the documents that they relate to the same transaction.

b) Removing the Contract from the Statute of Frauds

(1) Part Performance

Such performance of an oral land sale contract will permit equitable enforcement of the contract.

(2) Detrimental Reliance

An oral contract is enforceable if the promisor represented that a writing would be made, and the other party detrimentally relied on the representation.

(3) Full Performance

Full performance by one party of a multi-year oral contract in less than one year makes the contract enforceable.

(4) Sale of Goods

Oral contracts for the sale of goods will be enforced under the UCC when the merchant sends a written confirmation.

(a) Merchant Confirmatory Memos-Satisfies Statute of Frauds

A written confirmation binds both parties if: (i) between merchants; (ii) a writing in confirmation of the contract and sufficient against the sender is received (signed by the party to be charged); (iii) the party receiving it has reason to know of its contents; and (iv) the recipient does not object to it within ten days of receipt (it will bind the recipient).

(5) Writing

Is not required in the following situations: A contract which does not satisfy the "writing" requirement but is valid in other respects is enforceable.

(a) Specially Manufactured Goods

Where the production of special goods for a buyer has commenced and such goods are not suitable for sale to others in the ordinary course of business.

(b) Delivered Goods

Where goods have been actually received and accepted, the contract is enforceable, but not beyond the quantity accepted or paid for.

(c) Full Payment Received

Where the payment has been received by the seller. However, the oral agreement is not enforceable beyond quantity paid for.

(d) **Admission**

Admission of the contract's existence by the parties removes it from the statute of frauds (but not beyond the quantity of goods admitted).

(e) **Estoppel**

Where a party has caused the other party to detrimentally rely on the oral promise so that to deny enforcement would cause unconscionable injury or loss.

2. UNCONSCIONABILITY

If a contract was unconscionable when made, the court may refuse to enforce it or limit enforcement to avoid unconscionable results. The test for unconscionability is whether, at the time of execution, the contract (or a provision thereof) could result in unfair surprise and was oppressive to a disadvantaged party (see Article 2.302 UCC).

3. LACK OF CAPACITY

Without legal capacity to enter into a contract, the "incapacity" of a party makes the contract voidable.

a) MINORS

A contract made by a minor can be disaffirmed or ratified upon reaching majority by acts manifesting such intent. However, a minor can be bound by a contract for the provision of necessaries or service to the extent of reasonable value.

b) MENTAL INCOMPETENCE

A contract is void if entered into after an adjudication of incompetence, and voidable if entered prior to adjudication. The mentally incompetent contracting party will incur only voidable contractual duties if by reason of mental incapacity, he is unable to understand the nature and consequences of the contract and is unable to act in a reasonable manner and the other party is aware of this. However, if the person regains competence, it can be ratified or disaffirmed.

c) INTOXICATION

Extreme intoxication places a party in the position of the mentally incompetent, rendering him incapable of forming the intent to contract.

NOTE: A contract entered into by an intoxicated person may be later affirmed. Even if the agreement is void, the intoxicated party will be liable for necessaries.

III. MODIFICATION: CHANGING THE TERMS OF AN EXISTING CONTRACT

A. NEW CONSIDERATION

1. COMMON LAW

For modifications to be valid, they need to be supported by additional consideration.

2. UCC

Contract modifications sought in good faith are valid. An agreement modifying a contract within Article 2.209 UCC is binding without consideration. Contract modifications must meet the statute of frauds requirements if the contract, as modified, falls within the statute (Article 2.209 (3) UCC).

B. Oral Modifications

1. Statute of Frauds

a) Modification

Modification of a written contract bringing the subject within the purview of the statute of frauds must be in writing. If goods are over $500, modification must be in writing (Article 2.201(1) UCC). However:

(1) Part-performance takes the contract out of the statute of frauds;
(2) Full performance of an oral agreement by both parties need not be in writing.

b) Writing Prohibiting Oral Modification

A provision that a written contract cannot be modified or rescinded except by a writing is valid and binding. Where a no-oral-modifications provision is provided by a merchant to a consumer, it must be signed by the consumer.

c) Waiver of the Writing Requirement

An invalid oral modification may serve as a waiver of a party's rights to enforce the contract as written if one of the parties relied to her detriment on the modification.

d) Written Confirmations - UCC

Where there is an oral modification that is then followed by a written confirmation, this will satisfy the statute of frauds under UCC 2201.

e) Waiver of Condition

One having the benefit of a condition under a contract may indicate by words or conduct that he will waive that condition and no consideration is required.

(1) Installment Contract

A waiver in an installment contract must be supported by consideration. If not, the waiver can be revoked.

C. By Operation of Law

1. Destruction or Injury to Identified Goods

If goods are destroyed without fault of either party, before the risk of loss passes to the buyer, the contract is avoided. For damaged goods, the buyer may elect to take goods with a reduction in price. If the goods are destroyed or damaged after the risk of loss has passed to the buyer, the buyer will bear the loss.

2. Failure of Agreed-Upon Method of Transportation

If the agreed-upon delivery facilities become unavailable or commercially impractical, any commercially reasonable transportation must be tendered and must be accepted.

IV. WHAT ARE THE TERMS OF THE CONTRACT?

A. Interpretation

1. Where the parties agree upon the meaning of a promise/agreement, the contract will be interpreted in accordance with that meaning. When the contract is made, if one party attaches a different meaning, that meaning will prevail if:
   a) That party did not know of any different meaning and the other party was aware of this; and
   b) That party had no reason to know of any different meaning.

   NOTE: If neither party is bound by the meaning attached by the other, this may result in a failure of mutual assent.
2. A term/condition of the contract may be to the effect that some event or occurrence either must or must not occur (as the case may be) before performance of the contract becomes a

requirement, i.e., a condition precedent to the performance of the contract. The identified event/occurrence may become a contractual condition by agreement of the parties or by imposition of the term by the court.

3. **Interpreting the Terms/Conditions of the Contract:** Generally, an interpretation which gives a lawful reasonable and effective meaning will be applied:
   a) **Specific Express Terms**: Will be given greater weight than terms/conditions implied by a course of dealing or usage in the trade;
   b) **An Integrated Agreement**: an agreement in writing in which one or more of the terms/conditions is expressed, is construed as the final expression of the parties' intentions;
   c) **Different Interpretations**: If the meaning of a term/condition is subject to different interpretations, the preferred meaning adopted is usually that which operates against the person who supplied the words.

B. Parol Evidence Rule

Evidence of prior or contemporaneous agreements are not admissible to contradict or modify a written agreement that was intended as a full and final expression of the parties' bargain. A binding, completely integrated agreement discharges prior agreements (to the extent they are within its scope).

1. Is the Writing Intended as a Final Expression?

Intent is a question of fact determined by:

a) Face of the agreement;
b) All relevant evidence; or
c) Existence of a merger clause.

2. Is the Writing a Complete or Partial Integration?

After establishing that the writing was "final," determine if the integration was complete or partial.

a) If there is complete integration, that is an agreement adopted by the parties as a complete and exclusive agreement, the terms may not be contradicted or supplemented.
b) If there is partial integration (that is an integrated agreement other than a completely integrated agreement), the terms may be supplemented by proving consistent additional terms.

   Test: Would parties similarly situated as these parties were to this contract naturally and normally include the extrinsic matter in the writing?

   (1) Yes – Evidence of extrinsic matter is not admitted.
   Exceptions: The terms of the agreement may be explained or supplemented by: (i) consistent additional terms; (ii) course of dealings; (iii) usage of the trade or business; or (iv) course of performance.
   (2) No – Evidence of extrinsic matter is admitted.

C. Outside the Purview of the Parol Evidence Rule

1. Ambiguities

Where terms of an agreement are uncertain, evidence to clarify the meaning of the terms may be introduced.

2. Conditions Precedent

Evidence that a stated event must take place prior to a contract becoming effective is not precluded by the parol evidence rule.

3. Collateral Agreements

Where the subject matter of an agreement is typically considered independent of the subject matter that is the subject of an agreement precluding parol evidence, such evidence can be admitted to show a collateral agreement exists.

V. WARRANTIES – UCC-SPECIFIC PROVISIONS

A. Warranties

Under the UCC, there are four types of warranties: (i) Article 2.312 UCC - warranty of title and against infringement; (ii) Article 2.314 UCC - implied warranty of merchantability; (iii) Article 2.315 UCC - implied warranty of fitness for a particular purpose; (iv) Article 2.313 UCC - express warranties; and, (v) Article 2.316 UCC - exclusion or modification of warranties.

1. Warranty of Title (Article 2.312 UCC)

In a contract of sale, the seller warrants that he is conveying good title that its transfer is rightful, is free of liens, encumbrances or other security interest of which the buyer has no knowledge.

a) Modification or Exclusion

A warranty of title may only be modified or excluded by: (i) specific language in the contract; or (ii) circumstances that give the buyer reason to know that the seller does not claim title in himself or that the seller is only purporting to sell the rights that he or a third person may have in the goods (Article 2.312(2) UCC).

2. Implied Warranty of Merchantability (Article 2.314 UCC)

In every mercantile contract of sale where it is not expressly disclaimed, the law implies a warranty that the goods shall be of merchantable quality. The UCC imposes the implied warranty of merchantability only upon a seller who is a merchant with respect to goods of that kind. There is an obligation of good faith in every sale transaction so that even a non-merchant seller may be held liable for failure to disclose a known defect. Merchantability is defined as goods that would: (i) pass without objection in the trade; (ii) be of fair average quality; and (iii) be fit for the ordinary purpose for which goods are used.

a) Buyer's Specifications

Where goods are conformed to the buyer's particular specifications, the implied warranty is waived.

b) Disclaimer

To exclude an implied warranty of merchantability, the language must mention merchantability and be conspicuous if in writing.

3. Implied Warranty of Fitness for a Particular Purpose (Article 2.315 UCC) (does not need to be a merchant)

If a seller has reason to know of any particular purpose for which the goods are required by the buyer and is also aware that the buyer is relying on the seller's skill or judgment to select suitable goods, then an implied warranty of fitness for that particular purpose arises.

a) Reason to Know

Apply an objective test.

b) Particular Purpose

Differs from ordinary use and envisages the goods will do something different from their ordinary purpose, i.e., a specific use by the buyer.

c) Buyer's Reliance Essential

The buyer must in fact rely on the seller's superior skill or judgment as part of the transaction for the warranty of fitness for a particular purpose to apply.

d) Disclaimer

To exclude an implied warranty of fitness for a particular purpose, the exclusion must be in writing and must be conspicuous. To exclude all implied warranties, language must be clear. All implied warranties may be excluded by the use of language, which calls the buyer's attention to the exclusion of warranties and makes it clear that there are no implied warranties

e) Buyer Inspection

If the buyer inspects the goods or a sample model before entering the contract or refuses to examine the goods, there is no implied warranty of fitness.

4. Express Warranty (Article 2.313 UCC)

An affirmation of fact or promise made by the seller to the buyer in the course of negotiations that relates to the goods and is part of the basis for the bargain creates an express warranty that the goods will conform to the affirmation or promise.

a) Statement of Fact or Promise

A description of the goods, samples, or models may be sufficient to create an express warranty. *Cf: An opinion that is not objectively measurable, or is otherwise considered "puffery."*

b) Basis of the Bargain

The statement must have been part of the deal and played a part in the buyer's decision to purchase the goods. All statements become part of the basis of the bargain unless a good reason is shown to the contrary.

c) Disclaimer

Words relevant to the creation of an express warranty and words negating or limiting a warranty shall be construed as consistent whenever possible. Where that is not possible, limitations of warranty will be ineffective.

d) Parol Evidence

If admitted, disclaimer will be ineffective. If not admitted, disclaimer will be effective.

5. Exclusion or Modification of Warranties (Article 2.316 UCC)

Wherever possible, words or conduct relevant to the creation of an express warranty or words negating or limiting the warranty shall be construed as consistent with each other where this is possible. Subject to the provisions relating to the parole or extrinsic evidence, negation or limitation is inoperative to the extent that construction is unreasonable.

a) A purported written modification of the implied warranty of merchantability by way of exclusion or limitation must refer to merchantability and the writing must be conspicuous.
b) An exclusion of the warranty of fitness for purpose must be in writing and conspicuous.
c) **NOTE:** Expressions such as "as is" and "with all faults" have the effect of excluding implied warranties; where a buyer fully examines goods before purchase there is no implied warranty with respect to defects the examination ought to have revealed, and implied warranties may be amended by a course of dealing or trade usage.

B. Obligations to Remote Purchasers

Article 2.318 UCC has the purpose of giving certain beneficiaries the same warranty benefit that the original buyer received in the original contract of sale. Any provision, however, negating or limiting the effect of the warranty will have the same effect against the beneficiary as it would against the original buyer.

1. Packaged with a Record

A seller has an obligation to a remote purchaser (not an immediate buyer) that new goods sold or leased that are packaged with a record making an affirmation of fact or remedial promise relating to the goods will conform thereto. Knowledge by a buyer is presumed when the goods are packaged, regardless of whether included documentation is actually read.

2. Communication to the Public

With regard to new goods, if an advertisement to the public provides an affirmation of fact or promise relating to the goods, and the remote purchaser enters into a transaction with **knowledge** of and with the **expectation** that the goods will conform thereto, the seller has an obligation to make the goods conform unless a **reasonable person** would not believe the affirmation/remedial promise. The burden is on remote buyer to establish knowledge.

C. Third Parties

In most states, the seller's warranty extends to any natural person who is in the family or household of the buyer or who is a guest in her home if it is reasonable that such a person may use, consume, or be affected by the goods, and he suffers personal injury because of the breach of warranty.

D. Vouching In

If a reseller is sued (for indemnity, breach of warranty, etc.), the reseller can give the initial seller or other party notice of the suit. If that party does not come and defend, the party will be bound by whatever determination of fact is made that is common to the litigants.

E. Federal Consumer Product Warranties Law

If a consumer product manufacturer issues a full warranty, implied warranties cannot be disclaimed. If a limited warranty is issued, implied warranties cannot be disclaimed or modified, but they can be limited in duration to the length of the limited warranty.

VI. BENEFICIARIES, ASSIGNMENT, DELEGATION, RIGHTS

Following the valid formation of a contract, strangers to the agreement may be found to have rights or obligations traceable to the contract. Third party beneficiary rights arise at the formation of the contract. Assignment of rights and delegation of duties occur due to actions taken after formation.

A. Intended Beneficiary

A person other than the promisee and who will benefit from the performance of the promise, and the performance of the promise will satisfy an obligation of the promisee to pay money to the beneficiary, or the circumstances indicate the promisee intended to give the beneficiary the benefit of the promise.

B. Incidental Beneficiary

Someone who benefits from the performance of the contract but not as an intended beneficiary and in consequence no duty is owed to him.

C. Third-Party Beneficiary

This issue concerns a contract between two parties in which performance is to be rendered to a third person, for whose benefit the contract was made. In order to determine if the third party beneficiary has any rights, the interest must first be characterized:

1. Step 1: Intended vs. Incidental Beneficiary

Intended beneficiaries have contractual rights, whereas incidental beneficiaries do not. To characterize the beneficiary, the court will look to whether the beneficiary: (i) is identified in the contract; (ii) receives performance directly; or (iii) has a relationship with the promisee that demonstrates the promisee's intent to benefit.

2. Step 2: Creditor vs. Donee Beneficiary

Assuming the beneficiary is intended, the intended beneficiary will take one of two forms: (i) a creditor of the promisee; or (ii) a donee who will benefit gratuitously.

3. Step 3: When Does the Beneficiary Acquire Contract Rights?

A contract is enforceable by a third party upon the vesting of contractual rights. Vesting occurs when the third party either: (i) assents to performance; (ii) seeks to enforce performance; or (iii) detrimentally relies on the promise.

4. Step 4: Who Can Sue Whom?

a) Third-Party Beneficiary vs. Promisor

A third-party beneficiary has the same rights of enforcement and/or for breach against the promisor as does the promisee. The third-party beneficiary is subject to the same defenses the promisor has against the promisee.

(1) Restitution

The third-party beneficiary has no right of restitution from the promisor since the benefit conferred was from the promisee.

b) Third Party Beneficiary v. Promisee

Creditors can sue the promisee or the promisor on the basis of any outstanding debt. However, double recovery is not permitted.

c) Promisee v. Promisor

A promisee may seek specific performance where the promisor has failed to perform and remedies at law are insufficient.

D. Assignment of Contract Rights

Assignment is the transfer of a contractual right by the assignor to the assignee (in whole or in part) as a result of which the assignee stands in the place of the original contracting party. An assignment cannot take place if specifically excluded by the contract or is contrary to law, e.g., excluded by statute or the effect of the assignment materially changes the nature of the contract. A valid assignment requires the assignor to intentionally transfer all rights under the contract. Failure to assign all rights results in a delegation. An assignment will be valid even if it is not supported by consideration.

1. Assignment Limitations

An assignment may be invalid where: (i) it is precluded by law; (ii) it is precluded by contract; or (iii) it materially changes the essence of the contract.

2. Non-assignment Provisions

a) Non-assignment clauses eliminate the right, but not the power, to assign contractual rights. Therefore, the obligor must bring suit to set aside an assignment;
b) "Assignment is void" clauses eliminate both the power and right to assign. Any attempt to assign creates no rights in the assignment;
c) A contract is void where an assignment clause provides that the assignment can be avoided in the discretion of the obligor;
d) If the original contract is governed by the UCC, a non-assignment clause can be barred by contractual language.

3. Is the Assignment Revocable?

An assignment for consideration is irrevocable. An assignment without consideration is generally revocable.

a) Revocation

An assignment without consideration is irrevocable where:

(1) Delivery or performance has been rendered;
(2) There is a written agreement; or
(3) There is detrimental reliance on the part of the assignee.

b) Termination

Revocable assignments may be terminated by: (i) death, incapacity or bankruptcy of the assignor; (ii) providing adequate notice of revocation to the assignee or the obligor; or (iii) the conduct of the assignor (receiving performance from the obligor or assigning the right to another party).

4. Who Can Sue Whom?

a) Assignee v. Obligor

As the real party in interest who intends on receiving the benefits of the agreement, the assignee may enforce the contract and be subject to the same defenses as the assignor.

b) Assignee v. Assignor

Where an assignment is supported by consideration the assignee can sue the assignor: (i) if the assignor wrongfully revokes an irrevocable assignment; or (ii) if the obligor successfully asserts a defense against the assignor in an action brought by the assignee against the obligor to enforce the obligation. The assignor will not be liable to the assignee if the obligor is incapable of performing. If the assignor revokes the assignment, the assignee has no remedial rights against the assignor.

5. Successive Assignments

If the first assignment is revocable, a subsequent assignment revokes it. If it is irrevocable, the first assignment will usually prevail over a subsequent assignment.

a) Exceptions

If the second assignee has paid value and did not have notice of the first assignment, the subsequent assignee gets: (i) the first judgment against the obligor; (ii) the first payment of a claim from the obligor; and (iii) delivery of token chose. The subsequent assignee is the party to a novation releasing the assignor and can proceed against the first assignee under an estoppel theory.

E. Delegation of Contract Duties

Delegation occurs when a party to a contract transfers her primary obligation under the contract to a third person. A party may generally delegate any and all duties, subject to certain exceptions.

1. Requirements

The delegor must manifest a present intention to make a delegation. There are no special formalities to be complied with to have a valid delegation. It may be written or oral.

a) Limitations

A party cannot delegate a duty if: (i) it involves the person's personal judgment and skill; (ii) it would change the obligee's expectancy (requirements and output contracts); (iii) the other party reposed a special trust in the delegor; and (iv) the contract forbids it/or the delegation is contrary to public policy.

2. Rights and Liabilities

The obligee must accept performance from the delegate if the duty can be delegated. The delegor is still liable on the contract and the obligee may sue the delegor if the delegate does not perform. If there has been an assumption, the obligee may sue the delegate as an assumption creates a contract between the delegor and the delegee in which the obligee is a third-party beneficiary.

F. UCC Third-Party Rights

1. Entrustment

Article 2.403(3) UCC. Entrusting includes any delivery and any acquiescence in retention of possession, regardless of any condition expressed between the parties to the delivery or acquiescence, and regardless of whether the procurement of the entrusting or the possessor's disposition of the goods have been such as to be larcenous under the criminal law. Entrusting goods to a merchant who deals in goods of that kind gives him power to transfer all rights of the entruster to a buyer in the ordinary course of business (e.g., if you drop a watch off for repair, it can be sold and you have to recover damages from the jeweler).

2. Voidable Title

If a sale is induced by fraud, the title is voidable and the seller can rescind the sale and recover the goods. But the seller cannot recover goods from one who purchases in good faith for value even where:

a) The seller was deceived as to the identity of the buyer;
b) The delivery was in exchange for a check later dishonored;
c) The sale was a cash sale; or
d) The buyer's fraudulent conduct is punishable as larcenous under the criminal law (Article 2.403 UCC).

3. Thief Cannot Pass Good Title

If a thief sells goods that he stole from a true owner, the title is void and the thief cannot pass good title to a buyer. This means that even if the buyer has purchased in good faith for value, the true owner can recover the stolen goods from the buyer.

a) Exceptions

The thief can pass good title if: (i) the goods are money, (ii) the goods are negotiable instruments; (iii) the buyer has made accessions (valuable improvements) to the goods; or (iv) the true owner is estopped from asserting title.

VII. HAVE THE TERMS OF THE CONTRACT BEEN PERFORMED?

A. Promise or Condition

A promise is a commitment to do, or refrain from doing, something. Promises may be conditional or unconditional. A conditional promise is subject to an event, occurrence, or nonoccurrence, which will create, limit, or extinguish the duty to perform. Because it is not always clear whether a contract provision is a promise or a condition, the court will look to the party's intent.

1. Condition Precedent

A condition precedent is a contingency that must occur, or be excused, before a party's own duty to perform matures.

2. Concurrent Condition

A concurrent condition is a contingency that must occur simultaneously with a party's performance.

3. Subsequent Condition

A subsequent condition is a contingency that, by occurring, extinguishes an already matured duty to perform (this can be viewed like discharge).

4. Express Conditions

Express conditions are those conditions that are expressed in the contract in distinction from those implied.

5. Implied In Fact Conditions

Implied in fact conditions are those inferred from evidence of the party's intention and must occur or be present before a party's duty to perform matures.

6. Constructive Conditions

Constructive conditions are those the court imposes after the fact to ensure that the parties receive what they bargained for. Constructive conditions, for example, usually relate to the time of performance of the contract or which party performs first.

B. Have the Conditions been Satisfied or Excused?

A duty of performance becomes absolute when conditions are either performed or excused.

1. Excusing of Conditions By:

a) Failure to Cooperate

A party who wrongfully prevents a condition from occurring cannot claim the benefit of the contract, and the condition is excused.

b) Actual Breach

If one party materially breaches the contract, the other party is excused from performance. A minor breach suspends the duty, but will not excuse it.

c) Right to Demand Assurances

If a party reasonably believes that the other party will not fulfill his duties, he may in writing demand adequate assurance of due performance. He does not have to perform until he receives adequate reassurance. If the other party does not give an assurance within a reasonable time (not over thirty days), the party seeking performance can treat the contract as repudiated.

d) Anticipatory Repudiation

If, through a party's words, actions, or circumstances, it becomes clear that he is unwilling or unable to perform, the other party may:

(1) Ignore the repudiation and urge the other party perform (does not constitute a waiver of any claims if the party does not perform);
(2) Resort to any remedy for a breach; or
(3) Suspend his own performance.
(4) **Retraction of Repudiation**: A repudiating party may withdraw his repudiation at any time unless the other party has cancelled, materially changed his position, or otherwise indicated that he considers the repudiation final (Article 2.611 UCC).

e) Substantial Performance

If a party breaches the contract in a minor way but has almost completely performed his essential duties, he does not forfeit return performance.

f) Divisibility of Contract

When a party performs one part of a divisible contract, she is entitled to the agreed-to equivalent unit from the other party even if she fails to perform the other parts.

(1) **Requirements to Find a Contract Divisible**

(a) The performance of each party is divided into two or more individual matching parts;

(b) The failure to perform one part of the contract does not necessarily put the party in breach of the entire contract.

(2) UCC – Installment Contracts

An installment contract authorizes or requires delivery in separate lots. The buyer may declare a total breach only if defects in an installment substantially impair the value of the entire contract (Article 2.612 UCC).

g) Waiver or Estoppel

(1) Estoppel Waiver

A party may waive a condition by indicating that he will not insist on the other party performing it. He may retract the waiver at any time unless the other party relies on it and detrimentally changes her position.

(2) Election Waiver

If a condition is broken, the party who was to have its benefit may either terminate his liability or continue under the contract. If he chooses the latter, he is deemed to have waived the condition.

(3) No Consideration

A waiver is not enforceable if there is no consideration.

h) Impossibility, Impracticability, or Frustration

Infra.

C. Has the Duty to Perform Been Discharged?

Once it has been established that there is an immediate duty to perform, that duty must be discharged by:

1. Performance or Tender of Performance

A party discharges his duty by complete performance or tender of performance as long as he has the present ability to perform. A failure to carry out a duty under the contract when it is due will be a breach of contract.

2. Condition Subsequent

The duty to perform may be discharged by a condition subsequent.

3. Illegality

The duty to perform may be discharged if the subject matter is illegal.

4. Impossibility/Impracticability/Frustration

a) Impossibility

The duty to perform may be discharged by impossibility of performance, measured by an objective standard where performance is rendered impracticable without the fault of either of the contracting parties. Common examples include: (i) the death or physical incapacity where the presence of a particular person is essential to the performance of the contract; (ii) a law is enacted that renders the subject matter of the contract illegal; and (iii) the subject matter or means of performance are destroyed.

b) Impracticability

If a party who without fault would encounter unanticipated extreme and unreasonable difficulty or expense in performing a promise, a court may discharge the duty to perform. A mere change in the difficulty or expense of performance due to normal risks that the parties could have anticipated (increase in price of raw materials or too many buyers), will not warrant discharge.

c) Frustration of Purpose

A promise to perform a duty may also be discharged if there is a supervening event that the parties could not reasonably know of or reasonably foresee at the time they entered the contract which completely or almost completely destroys the understood purpose of the contract.

5. Mutual Rescission

Both parties may expressly agree to a mutual rescission of the contract and a consequent to discharge of respective duties. A bilateral contract can be rescinded only where the contract has been partially performed. A unilateral contract cannot be rescinded if only one party is left to perform. Parties may mutually rescind a contract orally unless the subject matter is within the statute of frauds or unless the contract requires a writing.

6. Novation

If a new contract substitutes a new party for one of the parties to the original contract, the original party's duty will be discharged. There must be: (i) a previous valid contract; (ii) an agreement among all parties, including the new party; (iii) immediate extinguishment of contractual duties as between the original contracting parties; and (iv) a valid new contract.

7. Release/Covenant Not to Sue

The release must be in writing and supported by consideration or be detrimentally relied upon.

8. Accord and Satisfaction

a) Accord

An agreement in which one party to a contract agrees to accept an identified performance different from that originally promised in satisfaction of the original promise. The performance of the "accord" discharges the original contractual obligation. Pending performance of the accord, the original contractual promise is suspended. Generally, an accord requires consideration, which can be less than the original promised.

(1) Partial Payment of Original Debt

Payment of a smaller amount than is due is valid consideration if the payee does so in good faith and there is a bona fide dispute as to the claim (e.g., marking a check "payment in full").

b) Satisfaction

Satisfaction is the legal consideration that binds the parties.

VIII. MISTAKE, MISREPRESENTATION, DURESS AND UNDUE INFLUENCE

What is the effect if one or both of the contracting parties makes a mistake? Or if the contract is induced by misrepresentation? Or if one party subjects the other to duress or undue influence? Is there a valid contract and is it enforceable?

A. Mistake

A "mistake" arises when one or other of the parties holds a belief that is not in accordance with the facts. If both parties make the same mistake and which has a material effect on the agreed exchange of promises, the contract is voidable at the option of the adversely affected party. When considering "material effect," consideration will be given to effecting relief by, for example, reformation or restitution.

1. Unilateral Mistake

If the mistake is unilateral and has a material effect on the performance of the contract, the contract is voidable by him, if he does not bear the risk of the mistake and to enforce the contract would be unconscionable, or the other party knew of the mistake or it arose because of his fault.

2. Risk of Mistake

A party bears the risk of mistake if pursuant to the contract the risk is his, he was aware of it at the time the contract was made, or only had limited knowledge of the risk and relied upon that limited knowledge, or the court allocates the risk to him because it is reasonable to do so.

B. Misrepresentation

An assertion of an incorrect fact which induces a party to enter into a contractual relationship is a misrepresentation. Silence may amount to a misrepresentation, where, for example, there is a failure to fully disclose details of a material fact or being aware of the other party's misunderstanding of a relevant factual matter, there is a failure to correct that misunderstanding. Misrepresentation will be fraudulent where the maker:

1. Intends to induce a contract by the misrepresentation;
2. He knows his assertion (or silence) is not in accordance with the relevant facts;
3. He does not believe in the truth of the assertion (silence) and will be material if the misrepresentation would be likely to induce a reasonable person to enter into a contract. If an assertion is of "opinion," only the other party will not be entitled to rely upon it unless he believed the maker possessed the necessary skill and judgment regarding the issue in question or there is such trust and confidence in the maker's standing that it is reasonable to rely upon it.

C. Duress

Where a party is compelled by an improper threat to enter into a contractual relationship (duress), the contract is voidable at that party's option. A threat is improper if:

1. It constitutes a crime or a tort (or would if carried into effect);
2. It threatens a criminal prosecution;
3. It threatens civil proceedings; or
4. It breaches good faith.

D. Undue Influence

Undue influence arises where there is unfair persuasion of a party who is subject to the other party's dominance, and if such dominance induces a contract, it will be voidable at the option of the innocent party.

IX. BREACH AND REMEDIES

A. General

Unless indicated otherwise by the contract or the circumstances, the respective contractual obligations are to be performed simultaneously. If each party fully carries out its duty under the contract, the contract is performed and discharged. Failure to do so, however, may constitute a breach of contract by one or other or both of the parties to the contract

1. Breach

If the promisor has an absolute duty to perform and has not yet discharged his duty in accordance with the contractual terms, he may be in breach of contract.

a) Is the Breach Minor or Material?

A minor breach may allow the aggrieved party to recover damages, but she still must perform under the contract. If the breach is material, the aggrieved party does not need to perform and may recover damages.

(1) Test

Whether a breach is minor or material is a factual issue that courts resolve under a reasonable-person test. A party materially breaches a contract when he does not fully perform a promise that goes to the heart of the contract.

(2) **Minor Breach**

If a breach is minor, the aggrieved party is entitled to an award of damages in an amount to compensate for the defective performance. The contract is still in force and enforceable and he must still perform.

(3) **Material Breach**

If the breach is material, the party's duties are discharged, but he must still take affirmative actions. In order to mitigate his damages, he must seek a replacement contract and notify the obligor of the defective performance. If the aggrieved party does mitigate, the amount he is entitled to recover is reduced.

2. DAMAGES

Damages compensate the injured party for the loss suffered arising from the breach of contract. Thus, if a breach occurs but no loss ensues, a plaintiff will only be entitled to a small amount of compensation, i.e., "nominal damages." Generally damages are compensatory, not punitive, and are for the purpose of compensating the injured party for the loss, including consequential loss, caused by the breach.

a) FACTORS TO BE TAKEN INTO ACCOUNT INCLUDE:

(1) Whether compensation will provide an adequate remedy;

(2) The extent to which the injured party will be deprived of the contractual benefit to which she was entitled;

(3) The prospects of the party in breach actually performing her part of the bargain and thereby ending the breach.

b) COMPENSATORY

Compensatory damages award the plaintiff with the monetary amount to give the plaintiff the benefit of the contract had the defendant fully performed. Damages are those that are causal, foreseeable, certain, and unavoidable.

(1) **Causal**

To recover compensatory damages, the plaintiff's harm must have been caused by the defendant's breach.

(2) **Foreseeable**

The damages caused must have been foreseeable at the time the contract was entered into.

(3) **Certain**

Future profits of a new business are difficult to recover because they are uncertain.

(4) **Unavoidable**

The plaintiff cannot recover damages that he could have reasonably avoided.

c) LIQUIDATED DAMAGES

A liquidated damages clause in a contract limits the damages that the plaintiff may recover. They are valid if it would have been too difficult for the parties to determine actual damages when entering into the contract; they must also reasonably forecast the actual harm. Because liquidated damages are a type of actual damages, a court will not enforce them if the clause amounts to a penalty.

d) PUNITIVE DAMAGES

Such damages are intended to punish the conduct of a party and they are not available in contract actions.

e) Interest and Attorney Fees

Courts will only grant prejudgment interest awards as to liquidated sums. A party may recover attorney fees if a statute or contract provides for them.

3. Restitution

An innocent party, who in response to her contractual obligation has conferred benefit upon the party in breach, prior to the breach of contract arising, may be entitled to "restitution," i.e., to receive back the benefit conferred. A party in breach may also be entitled to restitution in circumstances where she is discharged from further contractual obligation by the other party's breach, to the extent that the benefit to be returned will exceed the loss caused by the breach. The law imposes an obligation to pay for unjust gains received pursuant to an unenforceable contract.

a) Where Contract Is Materially Breached

The non-breaching party can recover the value of her performance, even in excess of the contract rate. The breaching party can recover the value of the benefit conferred in excess of the other party's damages.

b) Unenforceable Contract

If a contract is unenforceable, the recovery depends on the nature of the benefit conferred. Specific restitution is available for recovery of tangible property. Where the benefit takes the form of goods or services, the plaintiff is entitled to the value thereof, even in excess of the contract.

4. Specific Performance/Injunction

Specific performance is an order of the court requiring a contracting party to perform what he promised to perform in circumstances where damages will not provide an adequate remedy. The court may order specific performance where: (i) a contract exists; (ii) all of the conditions of the contract have been satisfied; (iii) the legal remedy is inadequate; (iv) the terms are definite and certain; (v) the decree must be feasible to enforce; and, (vi) there must be mutuality of performance.

a) Contract Exists

The parties must have executed a valid contract. An option contract must be supported by consideration.

b) All Conditions are Satisfied

The party seeking specific performance must have performed all of his obligations under the contract, unless an obligation is partial or immaterial.

c) Inadequate Legal Remedy

Even if the parties have executed a valid liquidated damages clause, a court may still order specific performance. (see Torts – Irreparable Harm)

d) Definite and Certain Terms

The contract must be sufficiently definite and certain, so that the court can determine what it is each party must do.

e) Feasible to Enforce

The performance must be feasible to enforce. This issue usually arises only in construction, personal service, and land sale contracts.

f) Mutuality of Performance

The court can only order one party to perform when it can also secure the plaintiff's counter-performance under the contract if the plaintiff has not yet performed.

NOTE: An injunction is also an order of the court restraining a party from doing something which would otherwise be a breach of contract and will be issued where damages would be inadequate to protect the interests of the injured party.

5. DEFENSES

a) LACHES

Laches is an unreasonable delay in pursuing a right. Under the doctrine of laches, a plaintiff who waits an unreasonable amount of time in initiating his equitable claim to the prejudice of the defendant is barred from bringing the claim. The period of delay generally follows the applicable statute of limitations, but can be shorter or longer.

b) UNCLEAN HANDS

The party seeking equitable damages must not have engaged in unfair conduct with respect to the transaction sued upon.

c) HARDSHIP

A court will not order specific performance if it would result in an undue hardship to the breaching party or public that greatly outweighs the harm that the plaintiff would suffer if the court did not grant specific performance. In such situations, the court will award damages in lieu of specific performance.

d) MISTAKE AND MISREPRESENTATION

A court will not order specific performance if one party or both parties were mistaken as to the terms of the contract, or if the contract was induced through misrepresentation.

6. RESCISSION

Where the agreement was induced by fraud, the aggrieved party can rescind the agreement and recover their consideration (voidable title). However, a defrauded seller may not recover the goods from a good faith purchaser.

B. UCC REMEDIES

1. UCC RISK OF LOSS IN THE ABSENCE OF BREACH

a) NON-CARRIER CASES

If the seller is a merchant, risk of loss passes to the buyer only upon buyer taking physical possession of the goods. If the seller is not a merchant, risk of loss passes to the buyer upon tender of delivery. A tender delivery occurs when the seller has the goods ready for the buyer to pick up at the time and place specified in the contract.

b) CARRIER CASES

In a shipment contract, risk of loss passes to the buyer when the goods are duly delivered to the carrier. In a destination contract, the risk of loss passes to the buyer when the goods are tendered to the buyer at the destination.

c) SALE OR RETURN AND SALE ON APPROVAL CONTRACTS

Upon sale or return, the risk of loss is on the seller until acceptance. Upon sale on approval, risk of loss is on the buyer and the buyer must pay for return.

2. UCC RISK OF LOSS UPON BREACH

a) BUYER HAS THE RIGHT OF REJECTION

The seller bears the risk of loss until the buyer receives the goods.

b) BUYER RIGHTFULLY REVOKES ACCEPTANCE

The seller bears the risk of loss, subject to the buyer's insurance.

c) Buyer in Breach

Where the seller is in possession of the goods, the buyer bears the risk of loss, subject to the seller's insurance.

3. Buyer's Remedies

The buyer's remedies depend on whether she rejects the goods prior to acceptance or revokes the acceptance that she has already given.

a) Acceptance

The buyer accepts goods when:

(1) The buyer, after reasonable opportunity to inspect them, indicates to the seller that they conform or that she will keep them in spite of their non-conformance;
(2) The buyer fails to reject the goods within a reasonable time after tender of delivery, or fails to reasonably notify the seller of her rejection; or
(3) The buyer does anything inconsistent with the seller's ownership.

b) Rejection

When the buyer receives goods that do not conform to the contract, the buyer may either keep them and sue for damages or, under some circumstances, reject the goods and either cancel the contract or sue.

(1) Single Delivery

If the goods or the tender fails to conform to the contract, the buyer may: (i) reject all of them; (ii) accept all of them; or (iii) accept some units and reject the rest. The buyer cannot reject the goods just because the seller did not notify the buyer of the shipments, unless the buyer experiences material loss or there is a material delay.

(2) Installment Contracts

The buyer can reject an installment shipment only if the nonconformity substantially impairs the value of that installment and cannot be cured. The seller breaches the whole contract if the nonconformity substantially impairs the value of the entire contract.

c) Revocation of Acceptance

The buyer may revoke her previous acceptance of the goods if the defect substantially impairs their value to her. The buyer must show that when she accepted them, she had a reasonable belief that the buyer would cure the defect; or that it was too difficult to discover the defect or the seller assured the goods conformed to the contract. The buyer must revoke acceptance within a reasonable time after the buyer discovers or should have discovered the defect and before any substantial change occurs in the goods not caused by their own defects.

(1) Seller's Right to Cure

Where a buyer has rejected the goods because of defects, the seller may give the buyer reasonable notice of her intention to cure and make a new tender of conforming goods, which the buyer must then accept.

4. Buyers Damages

a) For Non-Delivery or Upon Rejection or Revocation of Acceptance

The buyer's remedy for undelivered or rejected goods is the difference between the contract price and either the market price or the cost of buying replacement goods, plus incidental and consequential damages, less expenses saved.

b) For Accepted Goods

The buyer may recover the difference between the value of goods delivered and the value they would have had if they had conformed to the contract, plus incidental and consequential damages. The buyer must notify the seller within a reasonable time after he discovers the breach.

c) Specific Performance

5. Seller's Remedies

a) Right to Withhold Goods

If the buyer does not make a payment that is due on or before delivery, the seller may withhold delivery of goods.

b) Seller's Right to Recover Goods

(1) From Buyer on Buyer's Insolvency

When a seller learns that a buyer has received delivery of goods on credit while insolvent, the seller may demand to reclaim the goods within ten (10) days after the buyer receives the goods.

(2) From Bailee

The seller may stop a carrier from delivering goods in its possession when he discovers the buyer is insolvent.

6. Seller's Damages

When the buyer wrongfully refuses to accept conforming goods, the seller can:

a) Accept the goods and recover the difference between the market price and the contract price of the goods;

b) Resell the goods and recover the difference between the market price and the contract price;

c) Accept the goods and recover the difference between the list price and the cost to the seller;

d) Recover incidental damages, including the expense of storing and reselling the goods.

7. Liquidated Damages

Either party may recover liquidated damages as provided by the contract if they are reasonable when measured in light of: (i) the anticipated or actual breach caused; (ii) the difficulties in proof of loss; or (iii) the inconvenience or non feasibility of otherwise obtaining an adequate remedy.

8. Limitations on Damages

Parties may limit or alter the measure of damages otherwise recoverable under the UCC by requiring a seller to repair and replace, or return and refund, for example.

Essay Approach: Is the remedy exclusive? Does it fail its essential purpose? Is it unconscionable?

a) Exclusive Remedy

If the contract provides for its own remedies, a court does not have to resort to only those remedies unless the contract declares such remedies to be exclusive.

b) Failure of its Essential Purpose

If an exclusive or limited remedy would not serve its essential purpose (e.g., it would take too long to repair or replace), the aggrieved party may resort to the usual UCC remedies.

c) Consequential Damages

Parties may limit or exclude consequential damages as an award, unless it would be unconscionable. Courts will presume unconscionability where consumer goods are involved and the goods caused personal injuries.

9. Statute of Limitations

Accrual of statute of limitations is four years; discovery or should-have-discovered statute of limitation is one year; maximum total period of statute of limitations is five years from accrual.

10. When Does Accrual Occur?

a) Breach of Warranty

On delivery of goods, even if the party did not have knowledge of the breach.

b) Repudiation

When a party treats it as a repudiation.

c) Warranty of Title

When the aggrieved party discovers or should have discovered the breach.

d) Remote Purchaser

When the plaintiff remote purchaser receives the goods.

e) "Explicitly Extends to The Future"

When a party discovers or should have discovered the breach. Implied warranties do not extend to future performance; only express warranties do.

f) Remote Purchaser

When the party receives the goods, regardless of when the manufacturer delivered them to dealer.

g) Third-Party Beneficiaries

Third-party beneficiaries are not treated as remote purchasers, rather, they step into the shoes of the dealer.

CRIMINAL LAW

Table of Contents

I. PROPERTY CRIMES

A. LARCENY

Larceny is defined as: (i) a taking (ii) and carrying away (iii) of tangible personal property (iv) of another (v) by trespass (vi) with intent to permanently deprive that person of their property interest.

1. DEFENSES

Mistake of fact and consent of the property owner are valid defenses to larceny.

B. ROBBERY

Robbery is larceny (defined above) that is achieved by force or the threat of force.

C. EMBEZZLEMENT

Embezzlement is defined as: (i) the fraudulent (ii) conversion (iii) of personal property (iv) of another (v) by a person in lawful possession of that property.

D. LARCENY BY FALSE PRETENSES

This crime is defined as: (i) obtaining title (ii) to personal property of another (iii) by making an intentional false statement of fact (iv) with the intent to defraud the other.

E. LARCENY BY TRICK

Larceny by trick is proven with the same elements as larceny by false pretenses; however, the thief obtains possession of property rather than title.

F. LARCENY BY EXTORTION

Larceny by extortion is defined as: (i) obtaining the property (ii) from another (iii) by means of oral or written threats.

G. RECEIPT OF STOLEN PROPERTY

Receipt of stolen property is defined as: (i) receiving possession and control (ii) of stolen personal property (iii) known to have been stolen (iv) by another person (v) with the intent to permanently deprive the owner of his interest in it.

H. FORGERY

Forgery is defined as: (i) the making or altering (ii) of a writing with apparent legal significance (iii) so that it is false.

1. UTTERING OR PASSING A FORGED INSTRUMENT

Such consists of: (i) offering as genuine (ii) an instrument that may be the subject of forgery and is false (iii) with intent to defraud.

I. BURGLARY

Under common law, burglary is defined as: (i) the breaking (ii) and entry (iii) of a dwelling (iv) of another (v) at nighttime (vi) with the intent to commit a felony therein.

1. MODERN APPROACH

Modernly, a dwelling includes any enclosed area, including commercial buildings. Further, the nighttime requirement is relaxed.

J. ARSON

Under common law, arson is defined as: (i) the malicious (ii) burning (iii) of the dwelling (iv) of another.

II. CRIMES OF PROCEDURE

A. PERJURY

Perjury is the intentional making of a false statement of a material fact after taking an oath to be truthful.

B. SUBORNATION OF PERJURY

Such conduct is defined as assisting or inducing another to commit perjury.

C. BRIBERY

Under common law, bribery is the payment or receipt of something of value in exchange for official action. Modern jurisdictions have relaxed the public official requirement and have instituted liability for one who knowingly receives a bribe.

D. OBSTRUCTION OF JUSTICE

Obstruction of justice occurs when an individual intentionally acts to interfere with the administration of justice.

E. COMPOUNDING A CRIME

Under common law, compounding a crime occurs when an individual accepts payment and agrees not to prosecute another for a felony, or to conceal the commission of a felony, or conceal the whereabouts of a felon. Under modern statutes, the definition refers to any crime.

F. MISPRISION OF A FELONY

Under common law, it was a crime not to disclose knowledge of felonious activity. Modernly, this is no longer a crime.

III. CRIMES AGAINST THE PERSON

A. BATTERY

Battery is the unlawful application of force to the person of another resulting in either bodily injury or an offensive touching.

1. AGGRAVATED BATTERY

Battery can be considered aggravated when a deadly weapon is used, bodily injury results, or the victim is of a protected class.

B. ASSAULT

Assault is the intentional creation of reasonable apprehension in the mind of the victim of imminent bodily harm. Words are insufficient to establish an assault, but can rise to the level of criminal threats.

1. AGGRAVATED ASSAULT

Assault with a deadly weapon or the intent to cause great bodily injury or rape is considered aggravated in most jurisdictions.

C. MAYHEM

Under common law, mayhem requires the intentional dismemberment, disfigurement, or disablement of a bodily part.

D. FALSE IMPRISONMENT

False imprisonment consists of the unlawful, unconsented confinement of another. Confinement is not present if reasonable alternative routes of exit or escape are available. If consent is provided, consider its validity, as consent that is the product of duress or incapacity is invalid.

E. Kidnapping

Kidnapping is the unlawful confinement of a person that involves either: (i) some movement of the victim; or (ii) concealment of the victim in a secret place.

1. Aggravated Kidnapping

Kidnapping done for the purpose of ransom, to commit sexual offense, or other enumerated purposes may be considered aggravated.

F. Rape

Under common law, rape is the unlawful carnal knowledge of a woman by a man, not her husband, without her consent.

G. Statutory Rape

Statutory rape is defined as carnal knowledge of a female under the age of consent. Statutory rape is a strict liability crime; therefore, consent or a mistake as to age or consent is irrelevant.

H. Incest

Incest, under common law, consists of a marriage or a sexual act between closely related persons.

I. Seduction

Under common law, seduction consists of inducing an unmarried woman to engage in intercourse by the promise of marriage. The Model Penal Code relaxes the unmarried requirement.

J. Bigamy

Bigamy is a strict liability offense found under common law that provides criminal liability for one who marries another while having a living spouse.

IV. HOMICIDE

Homicide is the unlawful killing of one human being by another. It is criminal when it is done without excuse or legal justification.

Essay Approach:

A. Murder

Murder is the killing of another human being with malice aforethought.

1. Did the defendant have any of the states of mind sufficient to constitute "malice aforethought"? Malice aforethought is defined as one of four states of mind:
   a) Intent to kill (use of a deadly weapon authorizes an inference of intent to kill);
   b) Intent to inflict great bodily injury;
   c) Reckless indifference to an unjustifiably high risk to human life; or
   d) Intent to commit an inherently dangerous felony.

   The four ways to prove malice described above should each be analyzed ("IRAC'd"), in addition to determining whether causation was present, following which you will conclude as to the liability of the defendant for common law murder, modernly known as second degree murder. Then ask:

2. Will the homicide be raised to first degree murder?
   a) **Premeditation and Deliberation:** If the defendant made the decision to kill in a cool and dispassionate manner and actually reflected on the idea of killing, even if only for a brief period, it is first degree murder.

   b) **Felony Murder:** If a murder is committed during the commission of, or in an attempt to commit, an enumerated felony, it is first degree murder. The felonies most commonly listed include: burglary, arson, robbery, rape, kidnapping and mayhem. Some states define first degree murder to include certain victims: police, prison guard on duty, or the elderly. The death, however, must be a foreseeable result of the felony and must have been committed by the accused or co-felon.

3. If the defendant is guilty of murder, can it be reduced to manslaughter?

B. Voluntary Manslaughter

Voluntary manslaughter is a killing that would be murder but for the existence of adequate provocation.

1. Provocation is Sufficient

a) The victim's conduct would arouse sudden and intense passion in the mind of an ordinary person, causing the loss of self-control (threat of deadly force/cheating spouse);
b) The defendant was in fact provoked;
c) There was insufficient time between the provocation and killing for a reasonable person to cool off; and
d) The defendant in fact did not cool off between the provocation and the killing.

2. Imperfect Self-Defense

In jurisdictions that recognize imperfect self-defense, murder may be reduced to manslaughter even where the defendant instigated the altercation, or where the defendant unreasonably, but in good faith, believed that deadly force was necessary given the circumstances.

C. Involuntary Manslaughter

A killing may be considered involuntary manslaughter if it was committed with criminal negligence (defendant was grossly negligent) or during the commission of an unlawful act (a crime not within the purview of the felony murder rule).

D. Second Degree Murder

Second degree murder encompasses all murder that is not first degree and is not made with adequate provocation to qualify for voluntary manslaughter. The prosecution must prove beyond a reasonable doubt that: (i) the defendant intentionally killed a human being (ii) with malice aforethought, and (iii) actual and proximate causation.

1. Year and a Day Common Law Rule

Death of victim must occur within one year and one day from the infliction of the injury/wound.

V. INCHOATE OFFENSES

A. Accomplice Liability

1. Accomplice

An accomplice actively aids and abets the commission of the crime, with the dual intent that the crime be committed by the principal. An accomplice is criminally responsible for the crime committed and will be guilty to the same degree as the principal.

2. Scope of Liability

An accomplice is liable for the crime committed and for other crimes committed that are probable or reasonably foreseeable in furtherance of the criminal objective.

3. Defense

a) Withdrawal

If a co-conspirator (i) voluntarily withdraws; and (ii) communicates his withdrawal to all co-conspirators, then he will cut off liability for any subsequent crimes, but will still be liable for all crimes committed prior to withdrawal. A person has to act to neutralize involvement. The response must be proportional.

B. Accessory After the Fact

An accessory after the fact is one who receives, relieves, comforts, or assists another knowing that the other has committed a felony, in order to help the felon escape arrest, trial, or conviction.

C. Solicitation (Specific Intent "SI" Crime)

Solicitation consists of inciting, counseling, advising, urging, or commanding another party to commit a crime, with the intent that the person solicited commit the crime. It is of no consequence whether the solicited party agrees.

1. Defenses

Impossibility of completion of the solicited crime is not a defense. Withdrawal is not a defense. The Model Penal Code ("MPC") recognizes a defense where the solicitor stops completion of the target crime.

2. Merger

If the person commits (or attempts to commit) the solicited crime, both that person and the solicitor can be found guilty of that crime (or attempt). If the person solicited agrees to commit the crime, but does not attempt to commit the crime, liability for conspiracy may attach. However, under the doctrine of merger, the solicitor cannot be punished for both the solicitation and the completed (or attempted completion of) crime.

D. Conspiracy (SI Crime)

A conspiracy requires: (i) an agreement between two or more people to perform an illicit act or a lawful act in an unlawful manner; (ii) the intent to agree; and (iii) the intent to carry through the agreement to the illicit objective. A majority of states require an overt act in furtherance of the conspiracy, but mere preparation is sufficient. Under common law, two guilty minds were required; thus, a conspirator and an undercover police officer would not suffice. Under the MPC, a unilateral approach is employed where only one "guilty mind" need be present.

1. Liability

Liability for crimes committed by other conspirators attaches if the crimes (i) were committed in furtherance of the objectives of the conspiracy; and (ii) were foreseeable.

2. Defenses:

a) Withdrawal

Withdrawal is not a defense to the conspiracy, but it may be a defense to crimes committed in furtherance of the conspiracy, including the target crime of the conspiracy. To withdraw, a conspirator must notify all members of the conspiracy of her withdrawal and take reasonable steps to reverse any assistance previously provided.

3. No Defense

Factual impossibility is not a defense to conspiracy.

4. No Merger

Conspiracy and the completed crime are separate offenses for which a defendant may be convicted and punished for both.

E. Attempt (SI Crime)

An attempt is an overt act beyond mere preparation, committed with specific intent to commit a crime, which fails to complete the crime.

1. Mental State

The defendant must have specifically intended to perform an act that would result in the completed commission of a crime.

2. Overt Act

The defendant must commit an act beyond mere preparation for the offense. Most states require that the act constitute a substantial step towards the commission of a crime that demonstrates the person's criminal intent.

3. Defenses

a) Legal Impossibility

This means that it is not a crime to do what the defendant intended to do is a defense (e.g., where a person is already dead when he is shot, or where goods were not stolen where receiving stolen goods is alleged).

4. No Defense

a) Factual Impossibility

The fact that it would have been impossible for the defendant to complete the crime is not a defense (e.g., robbing a person who has no money is not a defense).

b) Abandonment

If the defendant had the requisite intent and committed an overt act, she is guilty of attempt despite the fact that she changed her mind and abandoned the plan before committing the intended crime.

VI. DEFENSES

A. Insanity

If a person is legally insane when he commits a criminal act, he is excused. The state must prove beyond a reasonable doubt that the defendant is sane. States may abolish this defense.

1. Four Views

There are four views of what evidence raises an insanity defense. If the defendant raises the defense, he must submit to a psychiatric exam; if not, the court can refuse to allow the defense.

a) M'Naghten Test

Here, a defendant is entitled to acquittal only if he had a mental disease or defect that caused him to either: (i) not know that his act would be wrong; or (ii) not understand the nature and quality of his actions. Loss of control, alone, is no defense.

b) Irresistible Impulse Test

A defendant is not guilty if, due to a mental illness, he was unable to control his actions or conform his conduct to the law.

c) A.L.I. or Model Penal Code Test (Modern View)

A defendant is entitled to a "not guilty" verdict if, as a result of mental disease or defect, he lacked the substantial capacity to either: (i) appreciate the criminality of his actions; or (ii) conform his actions to the requirements of the law.

d) Durham "Product" Test

If the committed act was the product of his mental illness, the defendant is entitled to an acquittal (i.e., the crime would not have been committed but for the disease).

2. Mental Illness

If the defendant is so mentally ill that he is unable to comprehend the proceedings or to assist in his defense, he may not be tried, convicted or sentenced as long as the condition exists. Continuing with prosecution in such circumstances would be a violation of due process.

3. Competency

An accused must have sufficient present ability to consult with her lawyer with a reasonable degree of rational understanding, and a rational and factual understanding of the proceedings against her.

B. Intoxication

Any substance may cause Intoxication. Intoxication can be raised as a defense to negate an element of a crime. Intoxication may take one of two forms: (i) voluntary; and (ii) involuntary. Each form of intoxication carries its own legal significance.

1. Voluntary

Intoxication is the result of the intentional taking of a substance with knowledge of its intoxicating properties, without duress. The person need not have intended to become intoxicated.

a) **Defense to Specific Intent Crime:** A criminal defendant may assert voluntary intoxication as a defense only if the crime requires a purpose, intent, or knowledge (i.e., specific intent), and the intoxication prevented the defendant from formulating the requisite purpose.

b) Voluntary intoxication does not provide a defense to general intent crimes.

2. Involuntary

Involuntary intoxication results from the taking of a substance without knowledge of its intoxicating propensity, under duress, or in accordance with medical advice, without knowledge of its intoxicating properties. Once involuntary intoxication is established, you must apply the insanity tests to determine if the defendant is entitled to acquittal.

C. Infancy

Under common law, a child under the age of 7 is not subject to criminal liability. Children over the age of 7, but younger than 14, were presumed to understand the nature and quality of their conduct. In contrast, children 14 and older were charged as adults. Modernly, each state has set its own adult liability threshold, typically at least 13 years of age.

D. Justification

Such defenses apply where society has deemed punishment to be inappropriate due to the circumstances surrounding the offense.

1. Defense of Self

a) Non-Deadly Force

A person who is without fault may use such force as reasonably appears necessary to protect herself from the imminent application of unlawful force. There is no duty to retreat in such circumstances.

b) Deadly Force

Deadly force maybe used by one who is without fault and who is threatened with the immediate prospect of death or great bodily injury.

(1) Retreat

A majority of jurisdictions do not require retreat before using deadly force. A minority require retreat before using deadly force if the victim can do so safely.

c) Aggressor's Use of Self-Defense

An aggressor may use force if: (i) he communicates his withdrawal; or (ii) the initial victim escalates the level of violence in the confrontation and the initial aggressor does not have the opportunity to withdraw.

2. Defense of Another

A person has the right to defend another to the same degree that the other could have defended herself. This defense is available, provided the defending party has a reasonable belief that the person she is defending possesses the legal justification to use self-defense.

3. Defense of Dwelling

The use of non-deadly force against unlawful entry or attack is permitted. Deadly force is only permitted where there is a reasonable belief that a personal attack or other felonious conduct is forthcoming.

a) Defense of Other Property

(1) Defending Possession

The use of deadly force is unavailable in defense of property. However, non-deadly force may be used following a demand upon the aggressor to cease his conduct.

(2) Reclaiming Property

Force may be used to reclaim property that has been unlawfully taken when the victim is in pursuit of a thief. However, absent a pursuit, force may not be used to recover property.

4. Arrest

Police officers may use reasonable force when necessary to complete an arrest. Deadly force is only permitted where the subject threatens serious bodily injury or death.

a) Private Person

A private party may use non-deadly force to make an arrest if she has reasonable grounds to believe that the person arrested has committed a crime.

5. Necessity

A necessity defense to criminal conduct is available where the person reasonably believed that commission of the crime was necessary to avoid a greater injury than that involved in the crime.

a) Application

An objective test is applied, regardless of subjective intent.

b) Limitation

Causing death of another person is never justified.

c) Exclusion

A necessity defense is not available if the defendant is at fault in creating the situation.

d) In Comparison to Duress

Necessity involves pressure from natural/physical forces; duress involves human threat.

E. Duress

Duress is a defense that the defendant reasonably believed that another person would inflict great bodily injury or cause death to him or a family member. In order for this defense to apply, the threat posed must have been imminent and the conduct engaged in under duress must not have included homicide.

F. Other Defenses

1. Mistake of Fact

Mistake of fact is only a defense if it serves to establish that the defendant lacked the state of mind needed to be convicted of the crime. As a consequence, it is not applicable to strict liability crimes. Where a mistake is offered to negate specific intent, the mistake can be unreasonable, provided it was made in good faith. However, for general intent crimes, the mistake must be reasonable.

2. Mistake of Law

It is not a defense that the defendant believed that her activity would not be a crime. Even where reasonable or upon the advice of counsel, the fact that a defendant believed her conduct was not criminal is not a defense.

a) Exceptions

(i) The punishing law was not published before the defendant engaged in the conduct and thus the defendant lacked notice; (ii) the defendant acted in reasonable reliance upon existing statutory law or a judicial decision; or (iii) the defendant acted in reasonable reliance upon an official position statement made by a government body.

3. Consent

Consent can serve as a defense to crimes where it was freely and voluntarily given by one with the legal capacity to consent. The obtained consent must not have been obtained by fraud or duress.

4. Entrapment

Entrapment may serve as a defense where: (i) the criminal design originated with law enforcement; and (ii) the defendant was not predisposed to commit the crime (prior to contact by the government). It should be noted that merely providing an opportunity for another to commit a crime does not rise to the level of entrapment.

CRIMINAL PROCEDURE

Table of Contents

I. PREREQUISITE TO CONSTITUTIONAL PROTECTIONS

A. Government Conduct Required

The Fourth, Fifth, and Sixth Amendments generally protect only against governmental conduct (i.e., police or other government agents), and not against search by private persons unless deputized as officers of the public police, or otherwise cloaked in governmental authority.

B. Juvenile Courts

All constitutional protections apply except trial by jury, and bail will not be allowed where the child is a "serious risk" to society.

II. ARREST, SEARCH AND SEIZURE: FOURTH AMENDMENT

Generally: The Fourth Amendment establishes the right of the people to be secure in their persons, houses, papers and effects. It protects against unlawful governmental intrusion on a person's reasonable expectation of privacy.

A. Arrests and Other Detention

Government seizures of persons, including arrests, are seizures within the scope of the Fourth Amendment and so must be reasonable.

1. Arrests

An arrest occurs when the police take a person into custody against her will for purposes of criminal prosecution or interrogation. An arrest must be based on probable cause.

a) Probable Cause

Probable cause exists when an officer knows of facts and circumstances that would warrant a person of reasonable caution to believe that an offense has been or is being committed or that the place to be searched contains the fruits or instrumentalities of a crime.

(1) Public Place

No warrant is required before arresting a person in a public place. However, police must have a warrant to effect a non-emergency arrest of a person in his home.

(2) Inventory Search

When incarcerating an individual, police may conduct a full search of the individual and any packages in the possession of the person.

(3) Warrant

When police have probable cause to arrest, they may not enter a suspect's home. An arrest warrant carries with it the authority to enter the suspect's home to make an arrest (but not a third party's home). Probable cause without a warrant is insufficient to allow entry into the suspect's home.

2. Seizures

In determining whether a seizure occurred for purposes of the Fourth Amendment, a court must consider all the circumstances surrounding the encounter to determine whether the police conduct would have communicated to a reasonable person that he was not free to decline. Merely following a suspect does not constitute a seizure for purposes of the Fourth Amendment. A seizure does not occur until a suspect actually yields to a police officer's show of authority or physical force.

a) Investigatory Detentions (Stop and Frisk)

Police may briefly detain an individual for investigation if they have a reasonable suspicion that criminal activity is afoot. Police may frisk the individual and retrieve any items that feel like weapons if the police have reasonable suspicion that the individual is armed. Police may also retrieve and seize any items that they can immediately identify as contraband.

(1) **Reasonable Suspicion**

Facts or circumstances that would lead a reasonable person to suspect that a crime has been, is being, or will be committed.

(2) **Duration and Scope**

The detention must be no longer than necessary to conduct a limited investigation to verify the suspicion. The police may ask the detained person to identify himself and generally may arrest for failure to comply with such a request. The detention will also turn into an arrest if, during the detention, other probable cause for arrest arises. Brief property seizures are similarly valid if based on reasonable suspicion.

(3) **Anonymous Tip**

Reasonable suspicion can be found on the basis of an anonymous tip where sufficiently corroborated, but not where it merely describes an individual and makes an assertion of criminal conduct.

(4) **Search Warrants**

Occupants of and in the immediate vicinity of a location searched pursuant to a warrant may be detained to facilitate completion of the search, prevent flight and for officer safety.

b) AUTOMOBILE STOPS

Generally, the police may not stop a car unless they have reasonable suspicion to believe that a law has been violated. However, if special law enforcement needs are involved, the Supreme Court allows police to set up roadblocks to stop cars without individualized suspicion that the driver violated some law. To be valid, the roadblock must: (i) stop cars on the basis of some neutral, articulable standard; and (ii) be designed to serve purposes closely related to a particular problem related to automobiles and their mobility (DUI checkpoints for drunk drivers are allowed; however, they are not allowed to search for illegal drugs).

(1) **Police May Order Occupants Out**

After lawfully stopping a vehicle, in the interest of officer safety, an officer may order the occupants out of the vehicle. Moreover, if the officer reasonably believes the detainees to be armed, he may frisk the occupants and search the passenger compartment for weapons, even after he has ordered the occupants out.

(2) **Pre-textual Stops**

If the police reasonably believe a driver violated a traffic law, they may stop the car, even if their ulterior motive is to investigate whether some other law, for which the police lack reasonable suspicion, has been violated.

c) OTHER DETENTIONS

(1) **To Obtain a Warrant**

If the police have probable cause to believe that a suspect has hidden drugs in his home they may, for a reasonable time, prevent him from going into the home unaccompanied so that they can prevent him from destroying evidence while they obtain a warrant.

(2) **Occupants of the Premises**

A valid warrant to search for contraband allows the police to detain occupants of the premises during a proper search.

(3) **Station House Detentions**

The police must have full probable cause for arrest to bring a suspect to the station for questioning or fingerprinting.

(4) **Grand Jury**

Seizure of a person by subpoena for a grand jury appearance is not within the Fourth Amendment's protection.

(5) **Deadly Force**

A police officer may not use deadly force to apprehend a suspect unless the officer had probable cause to believe that the suspect poses a significant threat of death or serious physical injury. On the other hand, a mere attempt to arrest that results in the death of a suspect is not necessarily a seizure governed by the Fourth Amendment.

B. SEARCH AND SEIZURE

Essay Approach:

1. DOES THE DEFENDANT HAVE A FOURTH AMENDMENT RIGHT?

a) REASONABLE EXPECTATION OF PRIVACY

To have a Fourth Amendment right, a person must have his own reasonable expectation of privacy with respect to the place searched or the item seized. The determination is made on the totality of the circumstances and must be an expectation that society is prepared to recognize, but a person has a legitimate expectation of privacy any time:

(1) He owned or had a right to possession of the place or property searched (including the contents and location of a cell phone and property tracked by GPS);
(2) The place searched was in fact his home, whether or not he owned or had a right to possession of it; or
(3) He was an overnight guest of the owner of the place searched.

b) EXCEPTION: THINGS HELD OUT TO BE PUBLIC

One does not have a reasonable expectation of privacy in objects held out to the public.

c) SPECIFIC EXAMPLES

(1) **Sense Enhancing Technology**

Technology that is not in general public use to obtain information from inside a suspect's home that could not otherwise be obtained without physical intrusion violates the suspect's reasonable expectation of privacy.

(2) **Location Tracking**

Attaching a GPS tracker to a car, or obtaining cell phone location data, is a search within the meaning of the Fourth Amendment.

(3) **Police Dog**

Bringing a trained police dog within the curtilage of a home for the purpose of obtaining evidence to secure a search warrant is a search in violation of the Fourth Amendment.

(4) **Cell Phones**

The Supreme Court has held that individuals have a reasonable expectation of privacy in their cell phones and, as a result, warrantless searches are impermissible absent exigent circumstances.

2. Did the Government Have a Valid Warrant?

To be valid, a warrant must be issued by a neutral and detached magistrate upon submission of a sworn statement by law enforcement that provides probable cause to believe that evidence of criminal conduct subject to seizure is located at the premises listed, or on the person named.

a) Probable Cause

As defined above.

(1) Informants

Where an affidavit submitted by law enforcement in support of a warrant contains information that has been obtained by a confidential informant, the information must be considered within the totality of the circumstances.

b) Particularity

To pass constitutional muster, a warrant must articulate with reasonable precision the place or person to be searched and the items to be seized.

c) Neutral and Detached Magistrate

A neutral and detached magistrate is one who possesses no financial or personal incentives.

d) Proper Execution

The search must be limited in scope to the places and items contained in the warrant. The police must knock and announce prior to entry unless doing so would risk harm to the officers or destruction of evidence. The police must have reasonable suspicion that a person is armed and dangerous to conduct a frisk even when the person is at a location where a search warrant is being executed. However, the police may detain those present within a house that is being searched pursuant to a warrant.

Invalidating the Warrant: A search warrant issued on the basis of an affidavit will be held invalid if the defendant establishes all of the following: (i) a false statement was included in the affidavit by the affiant; (ii) the affiant intentionally or recklessly included the false statement; and (iii) the false statement was material to the finding of probable cause.

However, evidence obtained by the police in reliance on a facially valid warrant may be used by the prosecution, despite an ultimate finding that the warrant was not supported by probable cause.

3. If There Is No Valid Warrant, Is There an Exception to the Warrant Requirement?

A warrantless search violates the Fourth Amendment unless the search falls within the purview of one of the warrantless search exceptions:

a) Search Incident to Lawful Arrest

Incident to lawful arrest, the police may search the person and the areas into which he might reach to obtain weapons or destroy evidence related to the grounds for arrest. The police may also make a protective sweep of the area if they believe accomplices may be present or persons that pose a threat to those on the scene. The search must be contemporaneous in time and place with the lawful arrest.

(1) Contemporaneous to Lawful Arrest Required

If an arrest is unlawful, any search incident to that arrest is also considered unlawful.

(2) **Search Incident to Incarceration**

Following arrest and transportation to a custodial facility, the police may make an inventory search of the arrestee's belongings, including any vehicle in the arrestee's possession at the time of the arrest.

(3) **Curtilage**

If a suspect is arrested on his front steps, police may not search the home incident to the arrest.

b) **AUTOMOBILE EXCEPTION**

If law enforcement has probable cause to believe that a vehicle contains instrumentalities or evidence of a crime, they may search the vehicle and any container that might reasonably contain the item(s). If a warrantless search of a vehicle is valid, the vehicle may be towed and later searched. If the car itself is considered evidence, it may be seized with probable cause. This exception may not be used to enter private property and perform a search of a vehicle parked next to the owner's home.

(1) **Passenger's Belongings**

The search may extend to packages belonging to passengers.

(2) **Locked Containers Placed in Vehicle**

The police may search locked containers that are placed in the vehicle if they have probable cause.

(3) **Motor Home**

A motor home is a vehicle for purposes of the automobile exception so long as it retains its mobility.

c) **PLAIN VIEW**

When a law enforcement officer is lawfully situated and observes in plain view what is believed to be contraband or evidence of a crime, the officer may seize the evidence without a warrant, provided the officer has probable cause to believe that the seized evidence is contraband or a fruit or instrumentality of a crime.

d) **CONSENT**

Knowing and voluntary consent to search by a person with the apparent right to use or occupy the area searched is an exception to the warrant requirement. However, if a tenant is physically present at the place to be searched and objects to a search, consent to search that is provided by a co-tenant is invalidated.

(1) **Scope of the Search**

If the consenting party does not expressly limit the scope of the search, the scope will extend to all areas that a reasonable person would believe are included in the search area. It is important to note that knowledge of the right to refuse to provide consent is not relevant.

e) **STOP AND FRISK**

The police may briefly detain an individual for investigation if they have reasonable suspicion that criminal activity is afoot. The police may frisk the individual and retrieve any items that feel like weapons if they have reasonable suspicion that the individual is armed. The police may also retrieve and seize any items that they can immediately identify as contraband.

f) **INVENTORY SEARCH**

When police operate pursuant to a standard operating procedure, they can inventory the contents of a vehicle that has been lawfully impounded. The police may conduct the inventory search in the field or at the station. If there are no standards to guide police actions, the search will not be upheld.

g) Hot Pursuit, Evanescent Evidence, and Other Evidence

(i) Police in hot pursuit of a felon may make a warrantless search and seizure and seize items that impose an immediate threat to public safety; (ii) the police may enter private residences in order to capture the fleeing felon; (iii) the police may seize without a warrant evidence likely to disappear or be destroyed before a warrant can be obtained; or (iv) contaminated food or drugs, children in trouble, and burning fires and other threats to public safety may justify warrantless search and seizures.

(1) Blood Draws

Nonconsensual warrantless blood draws generally violate an individual's Fourth Amendment rights. However, in drunk driving incidents when a driver is unconscious and cannot be given a breath test, the exigent-circumstances doctrine generally permits a blood test without a warrant. [Mitchell vs. Wisconsin 2019]

4. Other Inspections and Searches

a) Administrative Inspections and Searches

Administrative warrants are permitted upon a showing of a general and neutral enforcement plan. Such warrants may be used to gain entry in private residences and commercial buildings.

(1) Exceptions

The following warrantless searches have been upheld:

- (a) The search of airline passengers prior to boarding;
- (b) Inventory searches of those lawfully arrested;
- (c) The seizure of contaminated food;
- (d) Probation searches;
- (e) The search of government employee's desks and files for a work-related purpose;
- (f) Drug testing of employment applicants;
- (g) Drug testing of students engaging in extracurricular activities; or
- (h) Drug testing of employees who operate vehicles during the scope of their employment.

b) Foreign Countries and Border Searches

(1) Foreign Countries

The Fourth Amendment does not apply to searches and seizures of non-citizens conducted by United States officials while outside of the United States.

(2) Searches at the Border

No warrant is necessary for border searches. Neither citizens nor non-citizens have any Fourth Amendment rights at the border. Officials may stop a vehicle inside of the United States border for questioning upon reasonable suspicion that the vehicle contains illegal aliens. Search and seizures by border officials at fixed checkpoints inside of the United States are permissible without reasonable suspicion.

(3) Opening International Mail

The scope of border searches includes the opening of international mail upon reasonable cause that contraband is contained therein.

(4) **Detentions**

Officials with reasonable suspicion that a person crossing the border is smuggling contraband in or on his person may detain the traveler for further investigation.

c) Wiretapping

Wiretapping and electronic surveillance are considered a search under the Fourth Amendment and thus require a warrant. To be issued, a warrant for electronic surveillance requires an affidavit demonstrating: (i) probable cause of criminal activity; (ii) the name of the persons to be recorded and the nature of their conversations; and (iii) the limited duration of the electronic surveillance. Upon completion of service of the warrant, law enforcement must provide to the court details of what conversations have been recorded.

(1) **Exceptions**

In the case of an individual wearing "a wire," the speaker assumes the risk that the hearer is wearing a surveillance device.

d) Shocks the Conscience

Under the Due Process Clause, any evidence that is acquired in a way that shocks the conscience or infringes on society's sense of justice is excludable. Most commonly, courts will balance society's interest in obtaining the information or evidence against the individual's rights.

III. CONFESSIONS

A. Due Process

The Due Process Clause is violated by the use of a suspect's confession obtained when his free will was/is overborne by official pressure, fatigue, and falsely-aroused sympathy. In order for the statement to be excluded as involuntary, some coercive police conduct must be present. The mere fact that a suspect has heard voices, which command him to confess, is not sufficient to dictate that a statement is involuntary.

B. Sixth Amendment – Right to Counsel

The Sixth Amendment guarantees the right to assistance of counsel in all criminal proceedings. Unlike the Fifth Amendment right to counsel during interrogation, the Sixth Amendment right attaches to all critical stages of criminal prosecution, beginning with the filing of formal criminal charges. Once this right has attached, law enforcement cannot question the defendant about the crime for which he has been charged.

1. Offense-Specific

The Sixth Amendment right to counsel is offense-specific. As a result, when a defendant is charged with a crime and counsel has been appointed, the defendant may be questioned about any uncharged offenses that do not relate to the current prosecution without counsel being present. Note: Although the Sixth Amendment protections may not apply, the Fifth Amendment's protections against custodial interrogation will likely apply.

2. Informants

The use of informants, who are paid and acting under instructions of the government, violates the defendant's Sixth Amendment rights when the suspect is in custody after the indictment. However, a defendant's Sixth Amendment rights are not violated when the statements are voluntarily made and the informant took no action to elicit the statements.

C. Fifth Amendment – Privilege Against Compelled Self-Incrimination

1. Miranda Warnings

Anyone in the custody of the government and subject to interrogation, must be given Miranda warnings prior to interrogation by the police. For an admission or confession to be admissible under the Fifth Amendment right against self-incrimination, prior to interrogation a person must be informed that:

a) He has the right to remain silent;
b) Anything he says can be used against him in the court;
c) He has the right to the presence of an attorney; and
d) If he cannot afford an attorney, one will be appointed for him if he so desires.

2. Custody

A person is in custody when he has been deprived of freedom of action in a significant way. Custody is present when a reasonable person would feel that he was not free to leave. **Note:**

a) A suspect who goes to a police station voluntarily upon police request is not in custody for the purposes of Miranda;
b) A traffic stop does not constitute custody until arrest;
c) Incarcerated individuals subject to interrogation about crimes unrelated to their current incarceration do not have to be provided Miranda rights prior to questioning as "imprisonment alone is not enough to create a custodial situation." The Supreme Court held that a simple advisement that the individual may terminate questioning at any time is sufficient.

3. Interrogation

An interrogation consists of any direct questioning by the police of any words or actions which they should have known were reasonably likely to elicit an incriminating response.

a) Undercover Agents

Undercover agents do not have to give Miranda warnings unless the suspect knows that he is being interrogated and not having a conversation.

b) Psychological Manipulation

Psychological coercion of a suspect by police will be considered an interrogation for the purposes of Miranda.

4. Waiver

A suspect can waive his Miranda rights so long as the waiver is knowingly and voluntarily made. The suspect's silence is not an adequate waiver of Miranda.

5. Invocation of Right to Counsel

Once a suspect invokes his right to counsel, all interrogation must cease and the suspect may not be re-questioned. When a suspect requests counsel, all-questioning must cease and officials may not reinitiate questioning without counsel being present, even if the suspect has already consulted with his attorney.

6. Invocation of Right to Remain Silent

When a suspect invokes his right to remain silent, police may resume questioning after the passage of a significant period of time and the giving of fresh Miranda warnings, so long as the second interrogation is restricted to a crime that had not been the subject of the earlier interrogation.

7. Scope

The protection applies only to testimonial evidence, not real or physical. A person served with a subpoena requiring production of documents tending to incriminate him generally has no basis in the privilege to refuse to comply, because the act of producing the documents does not involve testimonial self-incrimination. It is a violation of Miranda for a prosecutor to comment on the defendant's silence. However, if the prosecution does comment on the defendant's silence, the harmless error test applies.

IV. PRETRIAL IDENTIFICATION

A. Sixth Amendment – Right to Counsel

A defendant has a right to the presence of an attorney at any post-charge lineup. This right does not extend to photo identifications or the collection of physical evidence, including handwriting exemplars, fingerprints, or DNA.

B. Due Process

A defendant can attack an identification as denying due process if the identification is unnecessarily suggestive and there is a substantial likelihood of misidentification. The Due Process Clause does not require a pretrial judicial inquiry into the reliability of an eyewitness identification when the identification was not procured under unnecessarily suggestive circumstances arranged by law enforcement [Perry v. New Hampshire (2012)].

V. REMEDY FOR CONSTITUTIONAL VIOLATIONS

A. The Exclusionary Rule

The Exclusionary Rule prohibits the introduction of evidence that was obtained in violation of a defendant's Fourth, Fifth, and Sixth Amendment rights. Under this rule, illegally obtained evidence is inadmissible at trial and all "fruits of the poisonous tree" (evidence obtained from the use of the illegally obtained evidence) are also excluded. **Exceptions:**

1. Independent Source

Evidence obtained from an independent source of the original illegality is not excluded under the Exclusionary Rule.

2. Attenuation

The Exclusionary Rule does not mandate the exclusion of derivative evidence that is sufficiently attenuated from the initial illegality so as to purge the taint of the illegality.

3. Inevitable Discovery

The Exclusionary Rule does not bar the admission of evidence where the prosecution can show that the police would have ultimately discovered the evidence, regardless of any constitutional violation.

4. Good-Faith

The police relied in good faith on a warrant that was issued by a neutral magistrate that was later found to be defective.

B. Impeachment

The Exclusionary Rule does not apply to statements and tangible evidence used to impeach the defendant's testimony at trial [Harris v. New York, U.S. v. Havens]. The defendant's testimony can be on either direct or cross-examination. The Exclusionary Rule is not a shield for perjury.

VI. PROCEDURAL REQUIREMENTS

A. Pretrial

1. Preliminary Hearing

A defendant can only continue to be detained upon a finding of probable cause that the defendant has committed the crime charged. If probable cause has already been determined through an indictment, no preliminary hearing to establish probable cause need be conducted.

2. Detention – Bail

Bail can be set no higher than is necessary to assure the defendant's appearance at trial. Bail is typically set according to a bail schedule. For the purposes of setting bail, the court must assume that the charges are true. Refusal to grant or the setting of excessive bail is subject to immediate appeal. However, the Supreme Court has upheld portions of the Federal Bail Reform Act that allow defendants to be held without bail where they pose a danger to the public or it is likely that they would fail to appear at trial.

3. Grand Juries

The Fifth Amendment right to indictment by grand jury has not been incorporated into the Fourteenth Amendment. However, the constitutions of some individual states require a grand jury indictment.

a) Proceedings

(1) Secrecy

Grand jury proceedings are conducted in secret. The defendant has no right to notice of the proceeding, to be present, to confront witnesses, or to introduce evidence on his behalf.

(2) Witnesses

A witness does not have the right to: (i) Miranda warnings; (ii) notice that he is a potential defendant; or (iii) the right to have an attorney present.

(3) No Right to Exclude Evidence

A grand jury can consider evidence in support of an indictment that would be inadmissible at trial.

(4) No Right to Challenge Subpoena

A defendant has no right to challenge a subpoena on the grounds that the grand jury lacked probable cause to call a witness.

(5) Exclusion of Minorities

A conviction will be reversed (regardless of harmless or harmful error), if said conviction was the result of an indictment handed down by a grand jury where minority members were excluded.

4. Speedy Trial

A determination of whether a defendant's Sixth Amendment right to a speedy trial has been violated is made by an evaluation of the totality of the circumstances. Factors to consider are: (i) the length of the delay; (ii) reason for the delay; (iii) whether defendant asserted his right; and (iv) prejudice to the defendant. The right does not attach until the defendant has been arrested or charged.

5. Brady

The government has a duty to disclose material, exculpatory evidence to the defendant. Failure to disclose such evidence, whether willful or inadvertent, violates the Due Process Clause and is grounds for reversing a conviction if the defendant can prove that: (i) the evidence is favorable to him because it either impeaches or is exculpatory; and (ii) prejudice has resulted and there is a reasonable probability that the result of the case would have been different if the undisclosed evidence had been presented at trial.

6. Affirmative Defenses

If the defendant is going to use an alibi or the insanity defense, he must notify the prosecution and provide a list of his witnesses who establish the alibi. The prosecution must provide the defense a list of rebuttal witnesses. The prosecutor may not comment on the defendant's inability to produce an alibi witness or alibi itself.

7. Competency to Stand Trial

Incompetency to stand trial is not a defense to the charge, but rather is a bar to trial. It is based on the defendant's mental condition at the time of trial. Incompetency to stand trial is established by: (i) the defendant's lack of a rational and factual understanding of the charges and proceedings; or (ii) the defendant's lack of sufficient present ability to consult his lawyer with a reasonable degree of understanding. The burden is on the defendant to establish by clear and convincing evidence. If the defendant later regains his competency, he can then be tried and convicted.

B. Trial

1. Public Trial

The Sixth and Fourteenth Amendments guarantee the right to public trial.

a) Due Process Rights

Due Process is violated if: (i) the trial is conducted in a manner making it unlikely that the jury gave the evidence reasonable consideration; (ii) the state compels the defendant to stand trial in prison clothing; and (iii) the jury is exposed to influence favorable to the prosecution.

2. Trial by Jury

There is no constitutional right to a jury trial for petty offenses, but only for offenses where imprisonment for more than six months is authorized. There is no right to a jury trial in juvenile proceedings.

a) Contempt

For civil contempt, an individual has no right to a jury trial. For criminal contempt, cumulative penalties totaling more than six months cannot be imposed without affording the defendant a right to a jury trial. However, penalties incurred during trial may aggregate to more than six months without a jury trial.

(1) Probation

A judge may place the contemnor on probation for up to five years without a jury trial as long as revocation of probation would not result in more than six months imprisonment.

b) Jurors

A jury must be comprised of at least six jurors. A unanimous verdict is now required in all states and federal courts for a defendant to be convicted.

(1) Batson

A defendant has a right to have a jury selected from a representative cross-section of the community. The Equal Protection ("EP") Clause forbids the use of peremptory challenges to exclude jurors solely on the basis of race. An EP-based attack on peremptory challenges involves that: (i) the defendant must show facts or circumstances that raise an inference that the exclusion was based on race or gender; (ii) upon such a showing, the prosecutor must come forward with a race neutral explanation for the strike; and (iii) the judge then determines whether the prosecutor's explanation was the genuine reason for striking the juror, or merely a pretext for purposeful discrimination.

(2) Capital Punishment

A state may not automatically exclude for cause all those who express doubt or scruple about the death penalty. It must be determined whether the juror's views would prevent or substantially impair performance of his duties in accordance with his instructions and oath. A death sentence imposed by a jury from which a juror was improperly excluded is subject to automatic reversal.

c) SENTENCE ENHANCEMENT

In certain circumstances, if additional facts are proven, substantive law may allow for a sentence to be increased. The additional facts must be presented to the jury, proven and found to be true beyond a reasonable doubt. Only a jury has the power to make this determination; a judge may not. If a judge makes the determination as to the truth of the additional facts, the defendant's right to a jury trial is violated.

3. RIGHT TO COUNSEL

A defendant has a right to counsel and any conviction obtained in violation of that right is reversible.

a) APPLICABLE STAGES

A defendant has the right to have private counsel or have counsel appointed during the following stages: (i) custodial police interrogation; (ii) post-indictment interrogation; (iii) preliminary hearing; (iv) arraignment; (v) post-charge line-ups; (vi) guilty pleas and sentencing; (vii) felony trials; (viii) misdemeanor trials when imprisonment is actually imposed or when a suspended sentence is imposed; (ix) overnight recesses during trial; and (x) appeals as a matter of right.

b) NON-APPLICABLE STAGES

A defendant does not have the right to have private counsel or have counsel appointed during the following stages: (i) blood sampling; (ii) taking of handwriting/voice exemplars; (iii) pre-charge or investigative line-ups; (iv) photo line-ups; (v) discretionary appeals; (vi) parole and probation revocation proceedings (unless involves the imposition of a new sentence); and (vii) post-conviction proceedings.

c) WAIVER

A defendant has the right to waive the assistance of counsel and defend himself at trial if the judge finds that the defendant's waiver is knowing and intelligent. This determination does not consider the legal abilities of the defendant.

d) EFFECTIVE ASSISTANCE

The Sixth Amendment right to counsel includes the right to effective counsel. This right extends to the first appeal. An ineffective assistance claim must demonstrate: (i) a deficient performance by the defendant's attorney; and (ii) that but for the deficiency, the result of the proceedings would have been different.

Note:

(1) Failure of an attorney to communicate a plea offer is ineffective assistance of counsel where prejudice is shown. Example: Where an attorney fails to communicate the offer of a reduced sentence and the defendant receives significantly more time upon conviction at trial.

(2) Circumstances not constituting ineffective assistance include: (i) trial tactics; (ii) failure to argue frivolous issues; (iii) rejection of defendant's request for a continuance; and (iv) failure to raise a constitutional defense that is later invalidated.

4. RIGHT TO CONFRONT WITNESSES

The defendant's Six Amendment right to confront adverse witnesses in a criminal prosecution is not absolute where: (i) the defendant is disruptive and the judge removes him from the courtroom; (ii) the defendant leaves the courtroom on his own volition; or (iii) a greater public purpose will be served by not allowing the defendant to confront the adverse witness face to face (e.g., protecting a child witness from upset and distress).

a) CO-DEFENDANT'S CONFESSION

In certain circumstances, a criminal defendant's Sixth Amendment right of confrontation may prohibit the use of confessions made by co-defendants.

(1) Co-Defendant's Confession May Not be Admitted

A co-defendant's confession may not be admitted, even if it interlocks with the defendant's own confession which is admitted when: (i) two defendants are tried together; and (ii) one defendant gives a confession that incriminates the other defendant.

(2) Co-Defendant's Confession May be Admitted

A co-defendant's confession may be admitted: (i) when the confessing defendant decides to testify and be subject to cross-examination; (ii) where the confessing defendant declines to testify, in which case all portions referring to the co-defendant's statement are eliminated; or (iii) when the confession of the defendant that is not testifying is used in order to impeach the testifying defendant's assertion that his confession was obtained through force.

b) HEARSAY

A prior testimonial statement of an unavailable witness will be admitted only if the defendant had the opportunity to cross-examine the declarant at the time the statement was made.

C. GUILTY PLEAS AND PLEA BARGAINING

1. TAKING THE PLEA

A guilty plea must be made voluntarily and knowingly and is a waiver of the Sixth Amendment right to a jury trial. When entering a plea of guilty or no contest, the defendant must be advised of the following by the judge: (i) he has the unequivocal right to not enter a plea of guilty or no contest; (ii) by entering such a plea, he is waiving his constitutional right to a trial by jury; (iii) the charge and the nature of the charge to which he is entering a plea; and (iv) the mandatory minimum penalty and the maximum penalty of the charge.

2. SETTING ASIDE A PLEA

A plea may be set aside when: (i) the court did not have jurisdiction over the defendant; (ii) the defendant did not have effective assistance of counsel; (iii) the plea bargain could not come to fruition; or (iv) the plea was found to be involuntary. A plea may not be set aside and is immune from collateral attack when it is intelligently and voluntarily made by the defendant.

3. PLEA BARGAINING

If a plea bargain is agreed upon and entered into by the prosecution and the defendant, neither party may back out. The plea bargain will be enforced against them. However, a plea bargain cannot be enforced against the judge because the judge does not have to accept the plea.

VII. CONSTITUTIONAL RIGHTS IN SENTENCING & PUNISHMENT

A. PROCEDURAL RIGHTS IN SENTENCING

1. RIGHT TO COUNSEL

The defendant has the right to counsel at sentencing. Normally, sentences are based on reports where the witnesses have not been examined and evidence is considered to be hearsay. On the other hand, statutorily based sentence enhancements require that the jury make a determination on the truth of the evidence presented.

2. Resentencing After Appeal

A defendant cannot be penalized for exercising his right to an appeal. If, after a successful appeal, the defendant is reconvicted and given a harsher punishment, the sentencing judge must state on the record all the reasons for the greater sentence.

B. Substantive Rights in Punishment

The Eighth Amendment prohibits cruel and unusual punishment. A penalty that is grossly disproportionate to the seriousness of the offense committed is considered by the Supreme Court to be cruel and unusual.

1. Death Penalty

a) For Murder

There are certain requirements that must be met under a statutory scheme that imposes the death penalty. The statutory scheme must: (i) give the judge or jury guidance in making the decision; (ii) provide all the information regarding the defendant; and (iii) give reasonable discretion to the judge or jury. If the death penalty is imposed based on the defendant's prior convictions, it must be reversed if the aggravating prior conviction is later vacated.

b) Rape or Felony Murder

The Supreme Court has ruled under the Eight Amendment that imposition of the death penalty for rape or felony murder are prohibited due to the punishment being disproportionate to the offense. In the case of felony murder, a participant may be sentenced to death where it can be shown that he acted with reckless indifference to human life.

c) Sanity

The Supreme Court has ruled that it constitutes cruel and unusual punishment to execute a prisoner who is insane at the time of execution, regardless of whether he was sane when the crime was committed.

d) Mental Retardation

The Supreme Court has ruled that it constitutes cruel and unusual punishment to sentence a person who is mentally retarded to death.

e) Minors

The death penalty may not be imposed on murderers who were under 18 years of age at the time they committed the murder.

2. Status

A statute that makes it a crime to have a given status violates the Eighth Amendment because it punishes mere propensity to engage in dangerous behavior. However, it is permissible to enhance punishment for a new crime based on prior criminal activity.

3. Considering Defendant's Perjury

The trial judge may take into account a belief that the defendant committed perjury while testifying at trial on his own behalf.

4. Imprisonment of Indigents for Nonpayment

Where the aggregate imprisonment exceeds the maximum period fixed by statute and results directly from involuntary nonpayment of a fine or court costs, there is an impermissible discrimination and violation of the Equal Protection Clause.

5. Juvenile Life Sentences

Miller v. Alabama (2012) – A mandatory life sentence without the possibility of parole is unconstitutional when applied to juvenile offenders.

6. Excessive Fines Clause of the Eighth Amendment

Fines are not excessive unless grossly disproportionate to the gravity of the offense.

a) Forfeiture

The owner of property is not constitutionally entitled to notice and a hearing before the property is seized for purposes of a forfeiture proceeding. However, a hearing is required before final forfeiture of the property.

VIII. APPEALS

A. No Right to Appeal

There is no federal constitutional right to an appeal.

B. Equal Protection and Right to Counsel on Appeal

The Equal Protection Clause provides that convicted persons should have access to appellate review regardless of their ability to pay. As a result, indigent defendants have the right to appointed counsel upon their first appeal.

C. Retroactivity

Procedural rules that become applicable after an appeal has been filed must be applied to all outstanding direct appeals in addition to any new appeals filed.

IX. COLLATERAL ATTACK UPON CONVICTION

A. Availability of Collateral Attack

Once a defendant has exhausted his appeals, he may still bring a collateral attack to challenge a conviction. The most common vehicle for such an attack is a habeas proceeding.

B. Habeas Corpus

Such a proceeding is brought to establish unlawful detention while in custody. There is no right to appointed counsel in a habeas proceeding.

X. DOUBLE JEOPARDY

Under the Fifth Amendment, an individual may not be retried for the same offense once jeopardy has attached. The Double Jeopardy provision attaches in a jury trial once the jury is sworn in or in a bench trial once the first witness is called to testify and duly sworn.

Exceptions Permitting Retrial: (i) where the jury fails to reach a verdict in the first trial due to a mistrial or a hung jury; (ii) the defendant's appeal for a new trial was granted; or (iii) the defendant failed to honor a plea agreement.

A. Same Offense

1. General Rule

Two crimes are considered to be the same offense unless each crime requires proof of an additional element that the other does not.

a) Lesser Included Offenses

The attachment of jeopardy for a greater offense bars retrial for lesser-included offenses, except that retrial for murder may be permitted where the victim dies after attachment of jeopardy for battery. The state may continue to prosecute for a charged offense despite a plea to a lesser included.

(1) **Exception – Subsequent Conduct**

Double jeopardy does not apply where the defendant, following conviction of a lesser offense, engages in conduct that constitutes a more serious offense involving the same circumstances of the lesser offense.

2. **CIVIL ACTIONS**

The clause only applies to repetitive criminal prosecutions. Thus, a state may bring, or have brought, a subsequent civil action.

B. SEPARATE SOVEREIGNS

The federal and state governments are considered separate sovereigns and each sovereign has the right to prosecute an individual for the same course of conduct. It is important to note that a prosecution by a local authority (such as a county District Attorney's Office) will preclude criminal prosecution by any other state agency (such as the Attorney General's Office).

1. **IMMUNITY**

Testimony obtained by a promise of immunity is coerced and therefore involuntary. Thus, immunized testimony may not be used for impeachment of a defendant's testimony at trial; however, it can be used in a perjury trial. Further, federal prosecutors may not use evidence obtained as a result of a state grant of immunity, and vice versa.

C. PROSECUTION APPEALS

A prosecuting agency has the right to appeal a dismissal of a case, or the denial or grant of a motion, provided that the appeal does not concern the defendant's acquittal of criminal charges, on the merits of such charges, following the attachment of jeopardy.

EVIDENCE

Table of Contents

Statutory References:

"FRE" = Federal Rules of Evidence

"CEC" = California Evidence Code

I. RELEVANCE

A. Logical Relevance

Evidence is relevant if it has a tendency to make a fact that is of consequence to the determination of the case more or less probable [FRE 401; CEC 350]. California requires the fact to be in dispute [CEC 210].

Consider:

1. What proposition is the evidence being used to prove?
2. Is this a material issue in the case?
3. Is the evidence probative?

B. Proposition 8

California's Truth-in-Evidence Amendment requires the admission of all relevant evidence, even that which is obtained in violation of an individual's constitutional rights. However, as the supremacy clause requires courts to enforce an individual's rights under the U.S. Constitution, Proposition 8 has little effect and does not apply to: (i) the exclusionary rule; (ii) hearsay (right to confront); (iii) limitations on character evidence concerning a victim in a rape case; (iv) the preclusion of offering bad character evidence of a defendant before he opens the door; (v) the secondary evidence rule; and (vi) legal relevance.

II. FORM OF EVIDENCE

A. Documents

1. Authentication

As a general rule, a writing or any secondary evidence of its content will not be received in evidence unless the writing is authenticated by proof that shows that the writing is what the proponent claims it is. The proof must be sufficient to support a jury finding that the document is genuine [FRE 901; CEC 1400].

a) Authentication by Pleadings or Stipulation

The genuineness of a document may be admitted by pleadings or by stipulation.

b) Evidence of Authenticity

(1) Admissions

A writing may be authenticated by evidence that the party against whom it is offered has either admitted its authenticity or acted upon it as authentic [CEC 1414].

(2) Eyewitness Testimony

A writing can be authenticated by testimony of one who sees it executed or hears it acknowledged. The subscribing witness need not give the testimony [FRE 901(b)(1); CEC 1413].

(3) Handwriting Verifications

A writing may be authenticated by evidence of the genuineness of the handwriting of the maker. This evidence may be the opinion of a non-expert with personal knowledge of the alleged writer's handwriting, or the opinion of an expert who has compared the writing samples of the maker's handwriting. Genuineness may also be determined by the trier of fact through comparison samples [FRE 901(b)(1)-(3); CEC 1415-17].

(4) **Ancient Documents**

A document may be authenticated by evidence that it is: (i) at least 20 years old; (ii) in such condition as to be free from suspicion as to authenticity; and (iii) found in a place where such a writing would likely be kept [FRE 901(b)(8)]. In California, the writing must be more than 30 years old [CEC 1419].

(5) **Reply Letter Doctrine**

A writing may be authenticated by evidence that it was written in response to a communication sent to the claimed author [CEC 1420].

(6) **Photographs**

Photographs are admissible only if identified by a witness as a portrayal of certain facts relevant to the issue and verified by the witness as a correct representation of those facts [FRE 901(b)(1)].

(7) **X-Ray Pictures, MRIs, ECG etc.**

It must be shown that the process used was accurate, the machine was in working order, and the operator was qualified to operate it. Finally, the chain of custody must be established to assure that the X-ray has not been tampered with [FRE 901(b)(9)].

c) **Self-Authenticating Documents**

Certain writings are said to "prove themselves." Extrinsic evidence of authenticity is not required for the following: (i) certified copies of public records; (ii) official publications; (iii) newspapers and periodicals; (iv) trade inscriptions; (v) acknowledged documents; (vi) commercial paper and related documents; and (vii) certified business records [FRE 902; CEC 1450-54].

2. **Best Evidence Rule**

To prove the terms of a writing (including a recording, photograph, or x-ray), the original writing, or a duplicate, must be produced if the terms of the writing are material or the knowledge of a witness concerning a fact results from having read the document [FRE 1002-03].

a) **Admissibility of Secondary Evidence of Contents**

If the proponent cannot produce the original writing in court, he may offer secondary evidence of its contents if a satisfactory explanation is given for the non-production of the original [FRE 1004].

(1) **Satisfactory Foundation**

Valid excuses for justifying the admissibility of the secondary evidence include:

(a) Loss or destruction of the original;

(b) If the original is in possession of a third party outside the jurisdiction and is unobtainable;

(c) If the original is in the possession of an adversary, who, after due notice, fails to produce the original.

(2) **California**

California has replaced the Best Evidence Rule with the Secondary Evidence Rule, where secondary evidence is admissible as the original, unless: (i) there is a genuine dispute as to the material terms of the writing; or (ii) admission would be unfair [CEC 1520-23].

3. Parol Evidence Rule

If an agreement is reduced to writing, that writing is the agreement and hence constitutes the only evidence of it. Prior or contemporaneous negotiations or agreements are merged into the written agreement, and they are inadmissible to vary the terms of the agreement.

a) Exceptions

The parol evidence rule does not apply in the following circumstances:

(1) Incomplete or Ambiguous Contract

Parol evidence is admissible to complete an incomplete contract or explain ambiguous terms.

(2) Reformation of Contract

The rule does not apply where a party alleges facts entitling him to reformation (mistake).

(3) Challenge to Validity of Contract

Parol evidence is admissible to show that the contract is void or voidable, or was made subject to a valid condition precedent that has not been satisfied.

b) Subsequent Modifications

The rule applies only to negotiations prior to, or at the time of, the execution of the contract. Parol evidence is admissible to show subsequent modification or discharge of the written contract.

B. Testimony

1. Competency of the Witness

The rules do not specify any mental or moral qualifications for witness testimony, other than: (i) the witness must have personal knowledge of the matter about which he is to testify; and (ii) the witness must declare he will testify truthfully [FRE 601-03; CEC 700-01].

a) Infants

The competency of an infant depends on the capacity and intelligence of the particular child as determined by the trial judge.

b) Insanity

An insane person may testify, provided he understands the obligation to speak truthfully and has the capacity to testify accurately.

c) Judge and Jurors

The presiding judge and jurors are incompetent to testify before the jury in which they are sitting.

d) Dead Man Acts

Most states have dead man acts, which provide that a party or person of interest in the event is incompetent to testify to a personal transaction or a communication with the deceased, when such testimony is offered against the representative or successors in interest of the deceased.

2. Form of Examination of Witness

a) Leading Questions

These are questions that suggest the answer desired and are generally improper on direct examination. However, they are permitted: (i) on cross-examination; (ii) to elicit a preliminary matter; (iii) when a witness needs aid because of loss of memory, immaturity, or physical or mental weakness; or (iv) when the witness is hostile.

b) Assumes Facts Not in Evidence

The question contains facts relevant to the case that have not been previously introduced into evidence.

c) Compound

The single question asked seeks to elicit two separate answers.

d) Non-Responsive Answers

Here, the witness fails to answer the question.

e) Argumentative

A question that includes inferences or conclusions.

f) Asked and Answered

A question that has previously been asked.

III. CATEGORY OF EVIDENCE

A. Judicial Notice

Judicial notice is recognition of a fact as true without formal presentation of evidence. Courts take notice of indisputable facts that are either matters of common knowledge in the community or capable of verification by resorting to easily accessible sources of unquestionable accuracy/scientific facts [FRE 201; CEC 450-51].

B. Hearsay

1. Essay Approach

a) Is there an assertion or communication?
b) Was the statement made out of court?
c) Who is the declarant?
d) Is it offered for the truth of the matter stated? The evidence might be offered to prove a relevant state of mind, for impeachment, rehabilitation, or if it constitutes words that have legal significance.
e) Does an exception to the hearsay rule apply?
f) If the hearsay is a document, is there a multiple hearsay issue?
g) Is the Sixth Amendment implicated? A criminal defendant's right of confrontation requires exclusion of hearsay despite the application of a hearsay exception. Testimonial statements include pretrial statements that declarants would reasonably expect to be used in a criminal prosecution.

2. Definition

Hearsay is an out-of-court statement offered for the truth of the matter asserted [FRE 801(c); CEC 1200]. Hearsay is typically excluded because it lacks reliability and hinders cross-examination. For the purposes of the hearsay rule, a statement is an oral or written assertion, or nonverbal conduct intended as an assertion [FRE 801(a)].

3. Out-of-Court Statements Not Offered for the Truth

a) Verbal Acts of Legally Operative Facts

These involve out-of-court statements that have a legal significance. Evidence of such statements is not hearsay because the issue is simply whether the statement was made. Examples: Defamation, threats, offer, acceptance, assignment, or donation.

b) Statements Offered to Show the Effect Upon Listener

A statement that is hearsay to prove the truth of the statement may still be admitted to show the statement's effect on the hearer or reader.

- Notice; knowledge; providing motive.

c) **Statements Offered as Circumstantial Evidence of Declarant's State of Mind**

A statement that serves as circumstantial evidence of the declarant's state of mind is not hearsay, as it is not offered for the truth, but to show knowledge or lack of capacity.

d) **Nonhuman Declarations**

There is no such thing as animal or machine hearsay. There must be an out-of-court-statement by a person. Time of day, radar readings, etc. are not hearsay.

4. **Not Considered Hearsay Under Federal Rules of Evidence (FRE) [California Hearsay Exceptions]**

a) **Admission by Party Opponent**

Any statement by a party offered against that party at trial is non-hearsay under the Federal Rules of Evidence. In state proceedings, the statement fits within the exception to the hearsay rule for admissions of a party [FRE 801(d); CEC 1204, 1220-28].

(1) **Adoptive Admission**

A party may expressly or impliedly adopt someone else's statement as his own.

(2) **Silence**

If a party fails to respond to accusatory statements where a reasonable person would have spoken up, his silence may be considered an implied admission if it can be shown the defendant must have heard and understood the statement.

(3) **Vicarious Admission**

A statement made by the party's agent or employee on a matter within the scope of that relationship while it existed. (No California provision)

(4) **Principal-Agent/Partnership**

A statement made by an agent during the scope of her agency, made during the existence of an employment relationship, is admissible.

(5) **Co-Conspirators**

An out-of-court statement made by a co-conspirator in furtherance of a conspiracy is admissible against other co-conspirators as a vicarious admission, provided the statement was made at a time when the declarant was participating in the conspiracy, and it is only admissible when the defendant has an opportunity to cross-examine the declarant.

(6) **Wrongful Death (California Only)**

A statement of the deceased can be used against the family as though he were a party [CEC 1227].

b) **Prior Statements of a Witness**

Under the Federal Rules [FRE 801(d)] and California Evidence Code [CEC 1235-38], a prior statement by a witness is not hearsay if:

(1) **Prior Inconsistent Statement**

The prior statement is inconsistent with the declarant's in-court testimony and was given under oath at a prior proceeding. In California, "under oath" is not required [CEC 1235].

(2) **Prior Consistent Statements**

The prior statement is consistent with the declarant's in-court testimony and is offered to rebut a charge that the witness is lying or exaggerating because of some motive and the statement was made before any motive to lie or exaggerate arose.

(3) **Prior Statements of Identification**

The prior statement is one of identification of a person made after perceiving him. The witness must be on the stand.

5. Hearsay Exceptions

a) Documentary

(1) **Past Recollection Recorded**

Where a witness states that she has insufficient recollection of an event to enable her to testify fully and accurately, even after she has consulted a writing given to her on the stand (recollection refreshed), the writing itself may be read into evidence if a proper foundation is laid. The foundation must include proof that: (i) the witness at one time had personal knowledge of the facts in the writing; (ii) the writing was made by the witness, at her direction, or was adopted by the witness; (iii) the writing was timely made when the matter was fresh in the witness's mind; (iv) the writing is accurate; and (v) the witness has insufficient recollection to testify fully and accurately [FRE 803; CEC 1237].

- Present Recollection Refreshed *(Not a Hearsay Issue)*: Any writing may be used to refresh a witness's memory. However, they cannot read directly from it [FRE 612].

(2) **Business Records**

Business records are entries made in the regular course of business by a person who has a business duty to accurately record the information and who either has personal knowledge, or receives the information from one person with personal knowledge, and a business duty to accurately report. The entry has to have been made at or near the time of the transaction or event [FRE 803(6)]. California does not permit opinions or diagnoses to be admitted through business records, only acts and observations [CEC 1271]. The rule also includes the absence of a business record [CEC 1272].

(3) **Official Records**

Records and reports of a public agency or office are admissible if the record was made at or near the time of the occurrence by one with a duty to accurately record the information [FRE 803(8); CEC 1280]. California case law prohibits the admission of opinions contained within such records without personal knowledge.

- Police Reports: Such reports cannot be used against a criminal defendant but can be used by a criminal defendant. However, they can be used in civil cases.

(4) **Ancient Documents**

Statements made in documents, which are authenticated as being more than 20 years old, are admissible under the ancient documents exception to the hearsay rule [FRE 803(16)]. In California, the document must be more than 30 years old [CEC 1419].

(5) **Learned Treatises**

A learned treatise is admissible if the treatise is established as reliable and if it was utilized in examining or cross-examining an expert witness or if the expert relied on the treatise during testimony [FRE 803(18); CEC 1341].

b) Declarant's Availability Is Irrelevant

(1) **Excited Utterance**

Such is a statement made in response to a startling or exciting event, which relates to the event and is made contemporaneously with the event [FRE 803(2)]. An excited utterance is an exception to the hearsay rule. The rationale is that such statements have their own indicia of trustworthiness. In California, they are known as spontaneous statements [CEC 1240].

(2) **Present Sense Impression**

Such is a statement made while describing an event as it takes place or shortly thereafter [FRE 803(1)]. Like an excited utterance, a present sense impression is an exception to the hearsay rule because it is believed that such statements have their own indicia of trustworthiness. There is no California parallel.

- Contemporaneous Statement – California Only: Such a statement describes the conduct of the declarant while he is engaged in the conduct and is offered to explain or qualify the conduct [CEC 1241].

(3) **Present State of Mental, Emotional, or Physical Condition**

A declarant's statement regarding his present state is an exception to the hearsay rule [FRE 803(3)]. Thus, a declarant's statement that he is angry, bored or frightened, or has some other state of mind, is not excluded under the hearsay rule. Additionally, a declarant's statement of intent is also included with the state of mind exception [CEC 1250-51].

(4) **Statement of Physical Condition for Medical Diagnoses:**

(a) **Past or Present Physical Condition**

Statements of past or present physical condition are admissible if made to medical personnel to assist in diagnosing or treating the condition. Such statements are allowed to include the cause or source of the condition insofar as it is relevant to the diagnosis [FRE 803(4)]. California requires that the declarant be unavailable but also admits statements of the declarant's prior emotional, mental, or physical state, including statements of future intent [CEC 1253].

(b) **Statements in Contemplation of Litigation**

Courts will prevent statements of physical symptoms where the patient-declarant has consulted a physician for the purpose of preparing for litigation.

(c) **California**

There is no broad exception for statements of medical diagnoses. The physical state must be at issue and the witness is unavailable or victim is under 12 and action is for child abuse or neglect [CEC 1253].

c) **DECLARANT MUST BE UNAVAILABLE**

(1) **Statements Against Interest**

A declarant's statement against his penal or pecuniary interest is an exception to the hearsay rule when the declarant is unavailable. The statement has to be against the declarant's interest when it is made and it has to be based on personal knowledge of the declarant. Where the statement is against a penal interest, corroboration must be present [FRE 804(b)(3); CEC 1230].

(2) **Dying Declaration**

A dying declaration is a statement made under fear of impending death, which relates to the cause or circumstances of that death. Such a statement is admissible in a civil case or in a homicide prosecution so long as the declarant is unavailable. The declarant need not have died [FRE 804(b)(2)].

(a) **California**

The declarant must really be dead and the statement must concern cause of death [CEC 1242].

(3) Former Testimony

Former testimony is admissible when the testimony was under oath and the person who testified is now unavailable. The declarant has to have been subject to cross-examination by a party who had an opportunity and similar motive to cross-examine the declarant [FRE 804(b)(1); CEC 1290].

(4) Statements of Personal Family History

Statements of an unavailable declarant's personal family history, or another related person, are admissible [FRE 804(b)(4); CEC 1310-11].

(5) Statements Offered Against a Party That Caused the Declarant's Unavailability

Such statements are admissible, provided the party engaged in wrongdoing or allowed wrongdoing, resulting in the declarant's unavailability [FRE 804(b)(6)]. California requires a prosecution for a "serious felony" [CEC 1350].

d) Catch-All Exception

A statement not specifically covered by any of the foregoing exceptions – but having equivalent guarantees of trustworthiness – may be admissible if the court determines:

(1) It is offered as evidence of a material fact;
(2) It is more probative than other evidence which can be procured through reasonable efforts; and
(3) The interests of justice will be served by its admission [FRE 807].

6. Sixth Amendment Right to Confrontation

Because the use of hearsay evidence in a criminal case may violate the Confrontation Clause, prior testimonial evidence is inadmissible against a criminal defendant unless the hearsay declarant is unavailable and the defendant had the opportunity to cross-examine the hearsay declarant at the time the statement was made. In addition, hearsay rules and other exclusionary rules cannot be applied where such application would deprive the accused of her right to a fair trial or deny her right to compulsory process. This exclusion is not available if the defendant caused the unavailability.

C. Character

1. Substantive Purposes

a) Criminal Case

Evidence of a person's character, or a trait of his character, is not admissible for the purpose of proving that he acted in conformity therewith on a particular occasion [FRE 404; CEC 1101-02].

(1) Exception – Mercy Rule

This rule allows a defendant to offer evidence of his good character to establish his innocence in the form of:

(a) Opinion testimony;
(b) Reputation testimony;
(c) No specific instances are permitted.

Once the defendant opens the door, the prosecution can put on evidence of the defendant's bad character by [FRE 404(a)(2)]:

(a) Opinion testimony;
(b) Reputation testimony; or
(c) Cross-examination of the defendant's witnesses about their knowledge of the defendant's specific instances of misconduct. [FRE 405]. This is not allowed to be proved up with extrinsic evidence except in California where Prop 8 allows extrinsic evidence.

(2) **Exception – Specific Acts**

Evidence of other crimes or misconduct is admissible if these acts are relevant to some issue other than the defendant's character or disposition (MIMIC) [FRE 404(b)(2); CEC 1101(b)].

(a) **Admissibility**

To be admissible, there must be sufficient evidence to support a jury finding that the defendant committed the prior act, and its probative value must not be substantially outweighed by its prejudice.

- Motive; identity; mistake; intent; common plan/scheme; knowledge; notice.

(3) **Exception – Sexual Assault/Child Molestation Cases**

In sexual assault and child molestation cases, specific instances of the defendant's prior acts of sexual assault or molestation are admissible [FRE 413, 414]. California expands this exception to also include prior possession of child pornography, exploitation of children, and prior domestic violence [CEC 1108-09].

(4) **Exception – Character of Victim**

Except in rape cases, the defendant may introduce reputation or opinion evidence of a bad character trait of the alleged crime victim when it is relevant to show the defendant's innocence [FRE 404(a)(2)(B)]. In addition, California allows the introduction of specific instances of the victim's conduct [CEC 1103]. Once the defendant has introduced evidence of a bad character trait of the victim, the prosecution may counter with reputation or opinion evidence of: (i) victim's good character, or (ii) defendant's bad character for the same trait. California allows the prosecution to rebut with specific instances.

(a) **Sexual Assault Exceptions**

In any civil or criminal proceeding involving alleged sexual misconduct, evidence offered to prove the sexual behavior or sexual disposition of the victim is generally inadmissible [FRE 412; CEC 1106].

Exceptions:

- Prior consensual conduct with the defendant; or
- Conduct with others offered to show an alternative source of physical evidence.

b) **CIVIL CASES**

Unless character is directly in issue, evidence of character being offered by either party to prove the conduct of a person in the litigated event is generally not admissible in a civil case. Where it is admissible, reputation and opinion testimony may be offered, with inquiry into specific instances of conduct on cross-examination allowed [FRE 404]. Where character is essential to the cause of action or defense, specific instances of conduct are allowed [FRE 405]. California permits all three forms of character evidence when admissible [CEC 1100 et seq.].

(1) **Character in Issue**

(a) Child custody – the character of parents in issue;
(b) Defamation;
(c) Negligent entrustment;
Example: Loan of a gun to a person with a history of violence.

(2) **Sexual Assault Cases**

If not placed in issue, the same rule as for criminal proceedings applies. If placed in issue, evidence of the alleged victim's sexual behavior is admissible if it is not excluded by any other rule and its probative value substantially outweighs the danger of harm to the victim and of unfair prejudice to any party [FRE 412(b)(2); CEC 1106].

D. HABIT/CUSTOM

While character is a generalized description of one's disposition, habit describes one's regular response to a repeated specific situation. Evidence of the habit of a person or of the routine practice of an organization, whether corroborated or not and regardless of the presence of eyewitnesses, is relevant to prove that the conduct of the person or organization on a particular occasion was in conformity with the habit or routine practice [FRE 406; CEC 1105].

Similar happenings: Evidence of chronic litigation is not admissible. Similar false claims can be introduced under a common plan or scheme theory. Prior contracts between the same parties can be used to establish the terms of another agreement. Prior accidents can be used to show knowledge, ownership, or the existence of a condition, etc.

E. OPINION

1. LAY

A lay witness is allowed to testify in the form of an opinion when: (i) the opinion would be helpful to the trier of fact; (ii) the opinion is based on the perception of the witness; and (iii) the subject is a proper subject for lay opinion (weather, speed, intoxication, sanity, handwriting, distance) [FRE 701; CEC 800].

2. EXPERT OPINION

An expert is allowed to testify in the form of an opinion when: (i) the opinion would be helpful to the trier of fact; (ii) the opinion is based upon a matter on which an expert might reasonably rely; and (iii) the expert is properly qualified based on education, training or experience [FRE 702]. In addition, if the expert is testifying regarding some novel theory, the expert's opinion has to be based on methods or processes of scientific thought. In federal courts, the theory need not have been generally accepted within the scientific community [FRE 703].

a) CALIFORNIA GENERAL TEST

In California, the proponent of the scientific evidence must prove that the underlying scientific theory, and the instruments that it uses, have been generally accepted as valid and reliable in the relevant scientific field [CEC 801]. Hypothetical questions can be asked and the opinion may be based on inadmissible evidence. The ultimate issue can be embraced, but cannot draw a legal conclusion.

F. IMPEACHMENT

1. CONVICTIONS

A witness can be impeached with evidence that the witness has been convicted of a felony or of any crime involving perjury or false statements [FRE 609(a)]. These convictions cannot be too remote. Generally, if more than 10 years have passed from the date of the conviction, the conviction is not admissible for impeachment purposes [FRE 609(b)]. In California, any witness may be impeached with any prior felony conviction or the facts of any misdemeanor where the adjudicated elements necessarily involve moral turpitude.

2. BAD REPUTATION FOR TRUTH OR VERACITY

A witness can be impeached by the introduction of other witnesses who can testify to the reputation of the witness for untruthfulness. Similarly, another witness who is familiar with the witness can express an opinion about whether the witness is generally truthful [FRE 608(a)]. Specific instances can be inquired into on cross-examination, but extrinsic evidence is not permissible [FRE 608(b)]. In civil cases, California precludes such cross-examination unless a conviction resulted [CEC 780]. Prop 8 allows cross-examination as to specific instances in criminal cases.

3. Bias and Prejudice

Evidence that a witness is biased or prejudiced against one of the parties is admissible for impeachment purposes. Extrinsic evidence is admissible to show that a witness suffers from bias or prejudice [FRE 608; CEC 780].

4. Prior Bad Acts Involving Dishonesty

Under the FRE, a witness can be cross-examined regarding prior bad acts involving dishonesty so long as the questioning is conducted in good faith. Extrinsic evidence is not admissible to prove the prior bad act. If the witness denies the bad act in response to the question, no further evidence is admissible [FRE 608]. However, in California, such questioning is precluded in civil cases [CEC 780]. California permits cross-examination in criminal cases and the use of extrinsic evidence under Prop 8. However, such evidence is still subject to legal relevance limitations.

5. Prior Inconsistent Statements

Prior inconsistent statements are admissible for impeachment purposes. Under the FRE, if the statements were made under oath, they are admissible not only for impeachment purposes but as substantive proof. If the statements were not made under oath, they are admissible only for impeachment in federal court. Extrinsic evidence is only admissible where the witness is given an opportunity to explain or deny the statement [FRE 613].

California: Such statements can be used for the truth regardless of whether they were made under oath [CEC 1235].

6. Evidence of Poor Memory/Poor Sight

Such evidence is admissible to impeach a witness.

IV. PRIVILEGE & WAIVER

FRE: Privileges are governed by common law [FRE 501].

A. Attorney-Client

Communications between an attorney and a client, made during professional consultation, are privileged from disclosure. The client must be seeking the professional services of the attorney at the time of the communication. Disclosures made before the attorney accepts or declines the case are covered by the privilege and apply indefinitely [CEC 950-62].

1. Corporate Clients

Corporations are clients and statements made by corporate officials or employees to an attorney are protected if the employees were authorized to make such statements.

2. Holder of the Privilege

The client holds the privilege and she alone may waive it. The attorney's authority to claim the privilege on behalf of the client is presumed in the absence of contrary evidence.

3. Exceptions

There is no privilege:

a) If the attorney's services were sought to aid in the planning or commission of something the client should have known was a crime or fraud;
b) Regarding a communication by a deceased client that is relevant to a current dispute; and
c) For a communication relevant to an issue of breach of duty in a dispute between the attorney and client.

B. Doctor-Patient

The privilege belongs to the patient, and he may decide to claim or waive it. Confidential communications between a patient and his physician are privileged, provided that: (i) a professional relationship exists; (ii) the information was acquired while attending the patient in the course of treatment; and (iii) the information was necessary for treatment [CEC 990-95]. This is not recognized in federal court.

1. Exceptions

The privilege does not apply or is waived if:

a) The patient has put his physical condition in issue;
b) The physician's assistance was sought to aid wrongdoing;
c) The communication is relevant to an issue of breach of duty in a dispute between the physician and patient;
d) The patient agreed by contract; or
e) It is a federal case applying the law of privilege.

2. Criminal Proceedings

In some states, the privilege applies in both criminal and civil proceedings. In a number of others, it generally cannot be invoked in criminal cases. In other states, the privilege is denied in felony cases, and in a few states, it is denied only in homicide cases.

C. Psychiatrist/Psychotherapist/Social Worker-Client Privilege

The Supreme Court recognizes a federal privilege for communications between a therapist and his client. Thus, the federal courts and virtually all of the states recognize a privilege for this type of confidential communication [CEC 1010-38].

D. Clergy-Penitent

A privilege exists for statements made to a member of the clergy, the elements of which are the same as the attorney-client privilege [CEC 1038].

E. Husband-Wife Privilege

1. Spousal Immunity

A married person whose spouse is a defendant in a criminal case may not be called as a witness by the prosecution without the witness' consent. Moreover, a married person may not be compelled to testify against his spouse in any criminal proceeding, regardless of whether the spouse is the defendant. There must be a valid marriage for the privilege to apply, and the privilege lasts only during marriage.

a) Holder of the Privilege

In federal court and California, the privilege belongs to the witness-spouse. Thus, the witness-spouse cannot be compelled to testify, but may choose to do so. In most states, the privilege belongs to the party-spouse [CEC 970-71].

2. Privilege for Confidential Marital Communications

In any civil or criminal case, confidential communications between a husband and wife during a valid marriage are privileged. For the privilege to apply, the marital relationship must exist when the communication is made. Divorce will not terminate the privilege, but communications made after divorce are not privileged. In addition, the communication must be made in reliance on the intimacy of the marital relationship (confidential) [CEC 980]. Here, either spouse can invoke the privilege.

3. When Neither Marital Privilege Applies

Neither privilege applies in actions between the spouses or in cases involving crimes against the testifying spouse or either spouse's children.

F. Self-Incrimination

Under the Fifth Amendment, a witness cannot be compelled to testify against himself. Any witness compelled to appear in a civil or criminal proceeding may refuse to give an answer that ties the witness to the commission of a crime [CEC 930].

G. Work Product

Privilege protects material prepared by an attorney in preparation of litigation, regardless of its content [CEC 915].

1. Absolute Privilege

Documents containing the attorney's impressions, conclusions, opinions, research, theories of the case, significant facts, and persons talked to by the attorney are never discoverable.

2. Qualified Privilege

Documents not protected by the absolute privilege will be discoverable unless the opposing party can show substantial hardship and that unfair prejudice would result from the inability to pursue a claim or defense.

3. Not Privileged

The locations of witnesses, evidence, statements, and those who you plan to call at trial are not privileged.

4. Expert Reports

If the report was made based upon privileged communications, it will be protected. If the report was not made based upon privileged communications, the privilege will not apply.

- Testifying expert: Where an expert will testify at trial, the privilege is deemed waived.

H. Waiver

Any privilege is waived by: (i) failure to claim the privilege; (ii) voluntary disclosure of the privileged matter by the privilege holder; or (iii) a contractual provision waiving in advance the right to claim the privilege.

1. Eavesdropper

A privilege based on confidential communications is not abrogated because it was overheard by someone whose presence is unknown to the parties. Under the modern view, in the absence of negligence by the one claiming the privilege, even the eavesdropper would be prohibited from testifying.

V. POLICY EXCLUSIONS

A. Subsequent Remedial Measures

Such are inadmissible to prove liability or fault. They are admissible to show ownership or control if it is in dispute or to show the feasibility of repair [FRE 407; CEC 1151].

B. Proof of Insurance

Such is inadmissible to show liability or fault or to show the ability to pay. Proof of insurance is admissible to show ownership or control if in dispute [FRE 411; CEC 1155].

C. Offers to Settle/Withdrawn Guilty Pleas

Disputed claims are inadmissible for policy reasons. The law wants to encourage parties to settle disputes without litigation. Any statement made in conjunction with the offer to settle is also inadmissible [FRE 408; CEC 1152-53].

D. OFFERS TO PAY MEDICAL EXPENSES

Such offers are inadmissible for policy reasons. The law wants to encourage parties to act as good Samaritans and to offer aid to those who are injured. [FRE 409]. In California, all statements surrounding negotiations are inadmissible, including admission of fault [CEC 1152].

E. DOCTRINE OF COMPLETENESS

When part of a writing or recorded statement is introduced, an adverse party may require the immediate admission of any other part of the writing, which, in fairness, ought to be considered.

F. DOCTRINE OF LIMITED ADMISSIBILITY

When evidence which is admissible only as to one party or for one purpose is admitted, the court should restrict the evidence to its proper scope and instruct the jury accordingly.

VI. LEGAL RELEVANCE

Although relevant, evidence may be excluded if its probative value is substantially outweighed by the danger of unfair prejudice, confusion of the issues, or misleading the jury, or by considerations of undue delay, waste of time, or needless presentation of cumulative evidence [FRE 403; CEC 352].

PROFESSIONAL RESPONSIBILITY

Table of Contents

New California Rules of Professional Conduct became effective on November 1, 2018. The numbering in this outline follows the new California rule numbering system, except where noted that the rule is an American Bar Association (ABA) Model Rule.

Function of the Rules of Professional Conduct

(a) A willful violation of the rules of Professional Conduct is a basis for discipline. However, a violation of these rules alone does not establish a civil cause of action or a basis for civil liability.

Terminology

(a) "Informed consent" means a person's agreement to a proposed course of conduct after the lawyer has communicated and explained (i) the relevant circumstances and (ii) the material risks, including any actual and reasonably foreseeable adverse consequences of the proposed course of conduct.

(b) "Informed written consent" means that the disclosures and the consent required must be in writing.

(c) "Reasonable" or "reasonably" when used in relation to conduct by a lawyer means the conduct of a reasonably prudent and competent lawyer.

(d) "Reasonable belief" or "reasonably believes" when used in reference to a lawyer means that the lawyer believes the matter in question and that the circumstances are such that the belief is reasonable.

(e) "Reasonably should know" when used in reference to a lawyer means that a lawyer of reasonable prudence and competence would ascertain the matter in question.

1 LAWYER-CLIENT RELATIONSHIP

1.1 COMPETENCE

(a) A lawyer shall not intentionally, recklessly, with gross negligence, or repeatedly fail to perform legal services with competence.

(b) "Competence" requires the lawyer to have the requisite (i) learning and skill, and (ii) mental, emotional, and physical ability reasonably necessary for the performance of such service.

(c) A lawyer who is not sufficiently competent may still accept representation of a client where: (i) the lawyer associates or consults with a lawyer reasonably believed to be competent; (ii) the lawyer acquires sufficient competence through learning before performing; (iii) the lawyer refers the client to a competent lawyer.

(d) In emergency situations where a lawyer cannot consult with another competent lawyer, the lawyer may provide assistance in an area in which the lawyer is not competent provided the representation is reasonably limited based on the emergency.

1.2 SCOPE OF REPRESENTATION AND ALLOCATION OF AUTHORITY

(a) A lawyer shall abide by a client's decisions concerning the objectives of representation and shall reasonably consult with the client as to the means by which they are to be pursued, provided that such decisions do not constitute a violation of law, as discussed below. A lawyer may take such action on behalf of the client as is impliedly authorized to carry out the representation. If a client wishes to settle a civil case, or plead guilty in a criminal case, or testify in a criminal case, a lawyer must defer to the client's wishes after fully advising the client.

(b) **Limited Scope:** A lawyer may limit the scope of the representation if it is reasonable under the circumstances and the client provides informed consent.

1.2.1 Advising or Assisting the Violation of Law

(a) A lawyer shall not counsel a client to engage or assist a client in conduct that the lawyer knows is criminal, fraudulent, or a violation of any law, rule, or ruling of a tribunal. However, a lawyer can discuss the legal consequences of any proposed conduct, and help the client make a good faith effort to determine the validity, scope, meaning, or application of a law, rule, or ruling of a tribunal.

1.3 Diligence

(a) A lawyer shall not intentionally, repeatedly, recklessly or with gross negligence fail to act with reasonable diligence in representing a client.

1.4 Communication with Clients

(a) Where not otherwise prohibited by law, a lawyer shall:

(1) Explain issues to a client so that informed decisions can be made;

(2) Promptly inform of any circumstance where the client's informed consent is required;

(3) Reasonably consult with the client about the means used to accomplish the client's objectives;

(4) Keep the client reasonably informed of significant developments relating to the representation, including providing copies of documents when necessary;

(5) Advise the client whenever representation is limited in some way.

(b) A lawyer may delay communicating information to a client if there is a reasonable basis to believe that the client may cause harm to the client or third-party.

1.4.1 Communication of Settlement Offers

(a) A lawyer shall promptly communicate all terms of a proposed settlement, regardless of whether the matter is civil or criminal in nature.

1.4.2 Disclosure of Professional Liability Insurance

(a) A lawyer must disclose in writing that the lawyer does not have liability insurance at the time of hiring. If the lawyer later learns that the lawyer no longer has insurance or discovers that it was not disclosed at the time of hiring, it must be disclosed within thirty days of learning of the deficiency.

(b) **Exceptions**:

(1) a lawyer previously provided written notification to the client that the lawyer does not have insurance;

(2) a lawyer knows or reasonably should know that the lawyer's legal representation of the client in the matter will not exceed four hours. If the representation exceeds four hours, disclosure is required;

(3) a government lawyer or in-house counsel need not comply provided the advice is being given to the government agency or company;

(4) a lawyer who is providing emergency legal services to protect the client's rights.

1.5 Fees for Legal Services

(a) A lawyer shall not make an agreement for, charge, or collect an unconscionable or illegal fee.

(b) Whether a fee is unconscionable is determined by the facts and circumstances existing at the time of the agreement. It is important to consider: whether the lawyer overreached or engaged in fraud; whether the lawyer failed to disclose material facts; the sophistication of the client; the value of the services rendered relative to the labor; the skill, experience, and reputation needed to execute the representation; the nature, scope, and length of the representation.

(c) **Contingent Fees:** Such fees are not permissible in criminal cases or in a family law case where fees are contingent upon dissolution or nullification of a marriage, or upon the amount of spousal or child support, or the amount or value of property obtained in settlement.

(d) **Earned on Receipt:** Fees considered to be "earned on receipt" or "non-refundable" are permissible where a client agrees in writing after disclosure that the client will not be entitled to a refund of all or part of the fee charged.

(e) **Flat Fee:** Such fees are permissible. A flat fee is a fixed amount that constitutes complete payment for the stated representation regardless of the amount of work ultimately involved.

1.5.1 Fee Divisions Among Lawyers

(a) Lawyers who are members of the same firm may divide fees earned. However, lawyers who are not members of the same law firm shall not divide a fee for legal services unless:

(1) the total fee charged for legal services is not increased because of the fee splitting;

(2) the fee splitting agreement is in writing;

(3) the client provides written consent after disclosure of terms of the division, including the identity of the lawyers or firms involved.

(b) The ABA requires the fee division to be proportional to the services performed by each lawyer, or each lawyer assumes joint responsibility for the case.

1.6 Confidential Information of a Client

(a) **California:** A lawyer shall not reveal confidential information unless the client gives informed consent, or the lawyer reasonably believes the disclosure is necessary to prevent a criminal act likely to result in death or substantial bodily harm. Prior to revealing confidential information to thwart a criminal act, the lawyer must attempt to persuade the client not to commit the act, or to prevent the potential harm. The lawyer must not disclose more information than necessary and must reasonably inform the client of the disclosure.

(b) **ABA Model Rule:** The ABA rule expands upon California's exception to also include: preventing the client from committing a crime or fraud that is reasonably certain to result in substantial injury to the financial interests or property of another and in furtherance of which the client has used or is using the lawyer's services; and to prevent, mitigate or rectify substantial injury to the financial interests or property of another that is reasonably certain to result or has resulted from the client's commission of a crime or fraud in furtherance of which the client has used the lawyer's services.

(c) **Self-Defense:** The ABA rules provide that an attorney may reveal confidential information to defend him or herself against a civil or criminal action involving the client. The

California rules do not explicitly provide such an exception. However, California Evidence Code § 958 provides that "there is no privilege ... relevant to an issue of breach, by the lawyer or by the client, of a duty arising out of the lawyer-client relationship."

1.7 CONFLICT OF INTEREST: CURRENT CLIENTS

(a) A lawyer shall not, without informed written consent from each client represent a client if the representation is directly adverse to another client in any matter.

(b) A lawyer shall not, without informed written consent from each affected client, represent a client if there is a significant risk the lawyer's representation will be materially limited by the lawyer's responsibilities to another or former client.

(c) A lawyer shall not represent a client without written disclosure of the relationship to the client, where the lawyer or firm has a relationship with a party in the same matter.

(d) Representation is permitted under this rule only if the lawyer complies with paragraphs (a), (b), and (c), and:

(1) the lawyer reasonably believes that they can provide competent and diligent representation to each affected client;

(2) the representation is not prohibited by law; and

(3) the representation does not involve the assertion of a claim by one client against another client represented by the lawyer in any proceeding before a tribunal.

1.8 CONFLICTS OF INTEREST (CALIFORNIA & ABA RULE COMPARISON)

(a) **ABA Model Rule 1.8** lists specific conflicts of interest. California articulates such conflicts as Rules 1.8.1 *et seq.* As a reminder, the rule numbering herein tracks California's number system.

(b) **Media Rights:** Under the ABA rules, prior to the conclusion of representation of a client, a lawyer shall not make or negotiate an agreement giving the lawyer literary or media rights to a portrayal or account based in substantial part on information relating to the representation. There is no California corollary.

(c) **Interest In The Case Subject Matter:** A lawyer shall not acquire a proprietary interest in the cause of action or subject matter of litigation the lawyer is conducting for a client, except that the lawyer may: (i) acquire a lien authorized by law to secure the lawyer's fee or expenses; and (ii) contract with a client for a reasonable contingent fee in a civil case. There is no California corollary, however see CA Rule 1.8.9.

1.8.1 BUSINESS TRANSACTIONS WITH A CLIENT AND PECUNIARY INTERESTS ADVERSE TO A CLIENT

A lawyer shall not enter into a business transaction with a client, or knowingly acquire any pecuniary interest adverse to a client, unless (i) the terms are fair, reasonable, and fully disclosed in writing; (ii) the client has been advised or has independent counsel; and (iii) informed written consent is provided.

1.8.2 USE OF CURRENT CLIENT'S INFORMATION

A lawyer shall not use a client's confidential information to the disadvantage of the client unless the client gives informed consent, except as permitted by these rules or the State Bar Act.

1.8.3 GIFTS FROM CLIENTS

(a) A lawyer shall not:

(1) solicit a client for a substantial gift unless the lawyer or recipient is related to the client, or

(2) prepare an instrument for the client giving the lawyer or person related any substantial gift unless they are related to the client or the client has been advised by independent counsel.

1.8.4 [RULE RESERVED FOR FUTURE USE BY THE CALIFORNIA BAR]

1.8.5 PAYMENT OF PERSONAL OR BUSINESS EXPENSES INCURRED BY OR FOR A CLIENT

(a) A lawyer shall not pay or agree to pay the expenses of a prospective or existing client.

(b) Notwithstanding paragraph (a), a lawyer may:

(1) pay such expenses to third persons, from funds collected for the client based on representation and with consent;

(2) after the lawyer is retained, agree to lend money to the client based on the client's written promise to repay the loan, provided no material conflict is present;

(3) advance the costs of representing the client where the repayment is contingent on the outcome of the matter; and

(4) pay the costs of representing the interests of an indigent person in a matter in which the lawyer represents the client.

(c) "Costs" includes any reasonable expenses of litigation.

1.8.6 COMPENSATION FROM ONE OTHER THAN CLIENT

A lawyer shall not accept compensation for representing a client from someone other than the client unless:

(a) there is no interference with the lawyer's independent professional judgment or with the lawyer-client relationship;

(b) confidential information is protected; and

(c) the lawyer obtains the client's informed written consent, unless:

(1) nondisclosure or the compensation is otherwise authorized by law or a court order; or

(2) the lawyer is rendering legal services on behalf of any public agency or nonprofit organization that provides legal services to the public.

1.8.7 AGGREGATE SETTLEMENTS

(a) A lawyer who represents two or more clients shall not enter into an aggregate settlement of the claims in a civil or criminal matter unless each client gives informed written consent.

(b) This rule does not apply to class action settlements subject to court approval.

1.8.8 LIMITING LIABILITY TO CLIENT

A lawyer shall not:

(a) Contract with a client limiting their liability for malpractice; or

(b) Settle a malpractice claim for their liability to a client unless the client is:

(1) represented by independent counsel; or

(2) advised in writing by the lawyer to seek the advice of independent counsel and given a reasonable opportunity to seek that advice.

1.8.9 PURCHASING PROPERTY AT A FORECLOSURE OR A SALE SUBJECT TO JUDICIAL REVIEW (NO ABA MODEL RULE COUNTERPART)

(a) A lawyer shall not purchase property in an action when they or their affiliates represent a party or as executor, trustee, administrator, or conservator from that action.

(b) A lawyer shall not represent the seller at a probate, foreclosure, receiver, trustee, or judicial sale in an action where the purchaser is a relative of the lawyer or their affiliates.

1.8.10 SEXUAL RELATIONS WITH CURRENT CLIENT

(a) A lawyer shall not have sexual relations with a client who is not their spouse unless the relationship existed before the representation.

(b) "Sexual relations" means intercourse or intimate touching.

1.8.11 IMPUTATION OF PROHIBITIONS UNDER RULES 1.8.1 TO 1.8.9

While lawyers are associated in a law firm, a prohibition in rules 1.8.1 through 1.8.9 that applies to any one of them shall apply to all of them.

1.9 DUTIES TO FORMER CLIENTS

(a) A lawyer who has formerly represented a client shall not represent another person in the same or substantially related matter where interests are adverse without informed written consent from the former client.

(b) A lawyer shall not knowingly represent a person in the same or a substantially related matter if their prior firm previously represented a client who has adverse interests, and whom the lawyer has material confidential information about, without informed written consent from the former client.

(c) A lawyer or prior firm formerly represented a client shall not thereafter use or reveal confidential information gained from that former representation unless allowed to by law or the information has become generally known.

1.10 IMPUTATION OF CONFLICTS OF INTEREST: GENERAL RULE

(a) While lawyers are associated in a firm, they cannot knowingly represent a client when any of them would be prohibited from doing so by rules 1.7 or 1.9, unless:

(1) it is based on a personal interest of a lawyer and there is not a significant risk of limiting the representation of the client by other lawyers in the firm; or

(2) the prohibition is based upon rule 1.9(a) or (b) and arises out of the prohibited lawyer's association with a prior firm, and the prohibited lawyer did not substantially participate in the matter, is timely screened, and written notice is given to any affected former client.

(b) When a lawyer is not with a firm anymore, that firm can later represent a person with adverse interests to a former client of that lawyer, unless the matter is the same or related to a prior matter and the firm has material or confidential information of the former client.

(c) A prohibition under this rule may be waived by each affected client under the conditions stated in rule 1.7.

(d) The imputation of a conflict of interest to lawyers associated in a firm with former or current government lawyers is governed by rule 1.11.

1.11 Special Conflicts of Interest for Former/Current Government Officials & Employees

(a) Except as law may otherwise expressly permit, a lawyer who has formerly served as a public official or employee of the government:

(1) cannot use or reveal confidential information; and

(2) shall not represent a client connected to any matter the lawyer participated in as a government employee, without informed written consent from the government. This paragraph shall not apply to matters governed by rule 1.12(a).

(b) A lawyer's prohibition under (a) also prohibits their firm unless that lawyer is timely screened and written notice from the government.

(c) A lawyer who was a public official or employee and received confidential government information about a person may not represent a client whose interests are adverse in a matter to that person. That lawyer's firm may continue representation in the matter if there is timely screening and no fee sharing.

(d) Except as law may otherwise expressly permit, a lawyer currently serving as a public official or employee:

(1) is subject to rules 1.7 and 1.9; and

(2) shall not:

(i) participate in a matter where the lawyer personally participated while in nongovernment employment without informed written consent from the government; or

(ii) negotiate for private employment with any person involved in a matter the lawyer is participating in except if a law clerk to a judge as permitted by rule 1.12(b) and subject to the conditions stated in rule 1.12(b).

1.12 Former Judge, Arbitrator, Mediator, or Other Third-Party neutral

(a) A lawyer shall not represent anyone connected to a matter where they participated as a judge, arbitrator, or other third-party neutral without informed written consent from all parties.

(b) A lawyer shall not seek employment from any person involved in a matter where they participated as a judge, arbitrator, or other third party neutral, except if that lawyer was a staff attorney or law clerk.

(c) If a lawyer is prohibited from representation by paragraph (a), their firm may continue representation if the lawyer was not a settlement judge, that lawyer is timely screened, and written notice is given.

(d) An arbitrator selected as a partisan of a party in a multimember arbitration panel is not prohibited from subsequently representing that party.

1.13 Organization as Client

(a) A lawyer employed or retained by an organization shall recognize that the client is the organization itself.

(b) If a lawyer representing an organization knows that a constituent intends to or has acted in a way that violates the law with respect to the organization which will likely result in substantial injury to the organization, the lawyer shall act as reasonably necessary in the best interest of the organization including referring the matter to a higher authority in the organization.

(c) In taking any action pursuant to paragraph (b), the lawyer shall not reveal any confidential information.

(d) If, despite the lawyer's actions, the highest authority continues in unlawful action, the lawyer shall maintain the best interest of the organization and may withdraw or resign if necessary.

(e) A lawyer may represent constituents of the organization with consent, however, must disclose the lawyer's client as the organization initially.

1.14 Client with Diminished Capacity (ABA Model Rule Only)

(a) An attorney must maintain a normal attorney-client relationship to the extent possible. If the attorney believes the client is at risk of substantial physical or financial harm, he may take reasonable protective action. The attorney may seek the appointment of a guardian if necessary. There is no California corollary.

1.15 Safekeeping Funds and Property of Clients and Other Persons

(a) All funds received or held by a lawyer shall be deposited in a "Trust Account" in the State of California, or with written consent of the client in another jurisdiction.

(b) Notwithstanding paragraph (a), a flat fee paid in advance for legal services may be deposited in the operating account if disclosed in writing to the client that they may require a Trust Account and that the client gets a refund if services are terminated. If the fee is over $1000, the disclosure must be signed by the client.

(c) Funds belonging to the lawyer cannot be commingled with the Trust Account unless funds are needed to pay bank charges. However, if there are funds belonging to both client and lawyer, the lawyer's funds must be withdrawn whenever the lawyer's interest in the money becomes fixed.

(d) A lawyer shall:

(1) promptly tell a client when they receive funds for the client;

(2) place in safekeeping any securities received for the client;

(3) maintain records of client interests received by the lawyer;

(4) promptly account in writing to the client;

(5) preserve these records for no less than five years after final distribution;

(6) comply with any order for an audit of such records issued pursuant to the Rules of Procedure of the State Bar; and

(7) promptly distribute, as requested, any undisputed interests in the lawyer's possession that the client is entitled to receive.

1.16 Declining or Terminating Representation

(a) A lawyer shall not represent a client, or shall withdraw from representation, if (i) they know the action is without probable cause and is malicious; (ii) they know it will violate the rules of conduct; (iii) their mental or physical condition affects the representation; or (iv) the client discharges the lawyer.

(b) A lawyer may withdraw from representing a client if (i) the client insists on unwarranted or bad faith litigation; (ii) the representation pursues crime or fraud; (iii) the client's behavior causes unreasonable or ineffective representation; (iv) there is a material breach of the client agreement; (v) the client agrees to termination; (vi) it serves the best interest of the client; (vii) the lawyer's mental or physical condition requires it; (viii) a violation of State Bar rules will occur; or (ix) the tribunal will find good cause to withdraw.

(c) If permission for termination of representation is required by a tribunal, the lawyer cannot terminate without tribunal permission.

(d) A lawyer shall not terminate representation until they have taken reasonable steps to avoid prejudice to the client.

(e) Upon the termination of representation, the lawyer shall promptly release all client materials and property to the client and shall refund any fees not earned other than a retainer fee.

1.17 Sale of a Law Practice

All, or substantially all, of the law practice of a lawyer, living or deceased, including goodwill, may be sold to another lawyer or law firm subject to all the following conditions:

(a) Fees charged to clients do not increase by the sale only;

(b) If the sale includes transfer of unfinished work or confidential client information, then written notice must be given to each client included in the sale, and the purchaser shall obtain written consent of the client. If after 90 days there is no response, consent by the client is presumed;

(c) If substitution is required by the rules of a tribunal in which a matter is pending, all steps necessary to substitute a lawyer shall be taken;

(d) The purchaser shall comply with all conflict rules of current/former clients;

(e) Confidential information shall not be disclosed to a nonlawyer in connection with a sale under this rule;

(f) This rule does not apply to the admission to or retirement from a law firm.

1.18 Duties to Prospective Clients

(a) A prospective client is a person who consults a lawyer for securing legal service or advice from the lawyer.

(b) Even when no relationship ensues, a lawyer who communicated with the prospective client shall not use or reveal confidential information. A lawyer or firm shall not represent a client who is adverse to that prospective client unless there is informed written consent from both parties, or the lawyer is timely screened and written notice given to the prospective client.

2 COUNSELOR

2.1 Advisor

In representing a client, a lawyer shall exercise independent professional judgment and render candid advice.

2.2 [Rule Reserved for Future Use By The California Bar]

2.3 Evaluation for Use by Third Persons (ABA Model Rule Only)

Under the ABA rules only, a lawyer may provide an evaluation affecting a client if the lawyer believes that the evaluation is in keeping with the attorney-client relationship. An evaluation that is likely to materially and adversely affect the client's interest shall not be provided without the client's informed consent. There is no California corollary to this rule.

2.4 Lawyer as Third-Party Neutral

A lawyer is a third-party neutral when they assist two or more persons who are not clients to resolve a dispute. They shall inform unrepresented parties that they are not representing them.

2.4.1 Lawyer as Temporary Judge, Referee or Court-Appointed Arbitrator (No ABA Model Rule Counterpart)

A lawyer who is serving as a temporary judge or arbitrator shall comply with the California Code of Judicial Ethics.

3 ADVOCATE

3.1 Meritorious Claims and Contentions

(a) A lawyer shall not:

(1) bring or continue an action or a position without probable cause, that is malicious, or that is not warranted by law or is in bad faith.

(b) A lawyer for the defendant in a criminal proceeding may defend the charge by requiring every element be established.

3.2 Delay of Litigation

In representing a client, a lawyer shall not use means that have no substantial purpose other than to delay or prolong the proceeding or to cause needless expense.

3.3 Candor Toward the Tribunal

(a) A lawyer shall not:

(1) knowingly make or fail to correct a false statement to a tribunal;

(2) fail to disclose adverse legal authority;

(3) knowingly offer false evidence. If the lawyer knows a witness has given false evidence, they must take reasonable measures to remedy the admission of such evidence, unless the information is privileged and cannot be disclosed;

(4) offer evidence in a criminal matter that is believed to be false, other than the testimony of the defendant.

(b) A lawyer who represents a client who knows a person is going to engage in crime or fraud related to the proceeding shall take reasonable remedies.

(c) The duties stated in paragraphs (a) and (b) continue to the conclusion of the proceeding.

(d) In an ex parte proceeding, the lawyer shall inform the tribunal of all material facts whether adverse or not to the client.

3.4 Fairness to Opposing Party and Counsel

(a) A lawyer shall not:

(1) unlawfully obstruct access to, alter, suppress, or destroy evidence;

(2) falsify evidence, counsel or assist a witness to testify falsely;

(3) pay a witness contingent on the content of their testimony or the outcome of the case, unless they are for expenses incurred by the witness for attending, loss of time, or professional expert services;

(4) advise or direct a witness to leave the jurisdiction to become unavailable;

(5) knowingly disobey an order of the court unless not valid; or

(6) in trial, assert personal knowledge of facts unless testifying, or state a personal opinion as to guilt or innocence.

3.5 Contact with Judges, Officials, Employees, and Jurors

(a) A lawyer shall not give anything of value to a judge or official unless permitted by statute. This rule does not apply to campaign contributions.

(b) Unless permitted to do so by law, a lawyer shall not communicate with a judicial officer about a contested matter, except: (i) in open court; (ii) with consent from other counsel; (iii) in the presence of all other counsel; (iv) in writing given to all parties; or (v) in ex parte matters.

(c) As used in this rule, "judge" includes all judges, arbitrators, or personnel.

(d) A lawyer connected with a case shall not knowingly communicate with or investigate any juror during the proceeding, nor after the proceeding if the juror does not consent or is coerced.

(e) These restrictions also apply to family members of the jury.

(f) For purposes of this rule, "juror" means any impaneled, discharged, or excused juror.

3.6 Trial Publicity

(a) A lawyer involved in litigation shall not make an extrajudicial statement that will be public and will likely prejudice the proceeding.

(b) Notwithstanding paragraph (a) and subject to any court order, a lawyer may state the claim/offense involved, identity, public records, scheduling, or reasonable warnings to the public if necessary.

(c) In a criminal case, this can also include arrest and officer information.

(d) Notwithstanding paragraph (a), a lawyer may make a statement reasonably necessary to protect a client from undue prejudice of recent publicity.

(e) No lawyer associated in a law firm or government agency with a lawyer subject to paragraph (a) shall make a statement prohibited by paragraph (a).

3.7 Lawyer as Witness

(a) A lawyer shall not act as an advocate in a trial in which the lawyer is likely to be a witness unless:

(1) the lawyer's testimony relates to an uncontested issue or matter;

(2) the lawyer's testimony relates to the nature and value of legal services rendered in the case; or

(3) the lawyer has obtained informed written consent.

(b) A lawyer may act as advocate in a trial in which another lawyer in the lawyer's firm is likely to be called as a witness unless precluded from doing so by law.

3.8 Special Responsibilities of a Prosecutor

The prosecutor in a criminal case shall:

(a) not prosecute without probable cause;

(b) make reasonable efforts to assure the rights of the accused to counsel;

(c) timely disclose all evidence negating guilt including any new evidence;

(d) prevent extrajudicial statements;

(e) make efforts to remedy any wrong convictions.

3.9 Advocate in Non-adjudicative Proceedings

A lawyer shall disclose an appearance before a legislative body when appearing as a representative in connection with a pending non-adjudicative matter.

3.10 Threatening Criminal, Administrative, or Disciplinary Charges (No ABA Model Rule Counterpart)

(a) A lawyer shall not threaten charges to gain an advantage in a dispute.

4 TRANSACTIONS WITH PERSONS OTHER THAN CLIENT

4.1 Truthfulness in Statements to Others

In the course of representing a client, a lawyer shall not knowingly:

(a) make a false statement of material fact or law or fail to disclose such fact to avoid crime or fraud unless it would violate confidentiality.

4.2 Communication with a Represented Person

(a) In representing a client, a lawyer shall not communicate about the representation with a person they know to be represented by another lawyer, without consent from the other lawyer.

(b) In the case of a represented organization, a lawyer cannot communicate with current officers or directors, or employees, if they are the subject of the matter.

(c) This rule shall not prohibit:

(1) communications with a public official, board, committee, or body; or

(2) communications otherwise authorized by law or a court order.

4.3 Communicating with an Unrepresented Person

(a) In communicating on behalf of a client with a person who is not represented by counsel, a lawyer shall not state or imply that the lawyer is disinterested and should remedy any confusion.

(b) A lawyer cannot seek to obtain privileged information they are not entitled to.

4.4 Duties Concerning Inadvertently Transmitted Writing

Where it is reasonably apparent to a lawyer who receives a writing relating to a lawyer's representation of a client that the writing was inadvertently sent and is work product, the lawyer shall refrain from reading it and promptly notify the sender.

5 LAW FIRMS AND ASSOCIATIONS

5.1 Responsibilities of Managerial and Supervisory Lawyers

(a) A lawyer with managerial authority in a firm shall make reasonable efforts to ensure that all lawyers comply with State Bar rules.

(b) A lawyer shall be responsible for another lawyer's violation of these rules and the State Bar Act if:

(1) the lawyer orders or, with knowledge of the relevant facts and of the specific conduct, ratifies the conduct involved; or

(2) the lawyer with authority in the firm knows of the conduct and fails to take remedial action.

5.2 Responsibilities of a Subordinate Lawyer

(a) A lawyer shall comply with these rules regardless if acting at the direction of another lawyer, however, a lawyer does not violate these rules if acting in accordance with a supervisor's reasonable acts.

5.3 Responsibilities Regarding Nonlawyer Assistants

With respect to a nonlawyer employed or retained by or associated with a lawyer:

(a) A lawyer with managerial authority in a firm shall make reasonable efforts to assure the nonlawyer's conduct is compatible with the professional obligations of the lawyer; and

(b) A lawyer shall be responsible for another person's violation of these rules and the State Bar Act if:

(1) the lawyer orders or, with knowledge of the relevant facts and of the specific conduct, ratifies the conduct involved; or

(2) the lawyer with authority in the firm knows of the conduct and fails to take remedial action.

5.3.1 Employment of Disbarred, Suspended, Resigned, or Involuntarily Inactive Lawyer (No ABA Model Rule Counterpart)

(a) A lawyer shall not in a legal capacity employ, associate in practice with, or assist a person the lawyer knows or reasonably should know is an ineligible person to practice law per the State Bar.

(b) A lawyer may employ, associate in practice with, or assist an ineligible person to perform research, drafting or clerical activities, including but not limited to:

(1) Legal preparation, research, drafting, billing, or clerical work.

(c) Prior to or at the time of employing, associating in practice with, or assisting an ineligible person, the lawyer shall provide written notice to the State Bar and to affected clients.

5.4 Financial and Similar Arrangements with Nonlawyers

(a) A lawyer shall not share legal fees with a nonlawyer except to: (i) pay to a deceased lawyer's estate; (ii) pay to employees for retirement / compensation; (iii) as part of a lawful lawyer referral service; or (iv) in sharing a court-awarded legal fee with a nonprofit organization.

(b) A lawyer shall not form a partnership for the practice of law with a nonlawyer.

(c) A lawyer shall not allow a person paying for the legal services of another to interfere with independent professional judgment.

5.5 Unauthorized Practice of Law; Multijurisdictional Practice of Law

(a) A lawyer admitted to practice law in California shall not practice or assist in another jurisdiction if that would violate the rules of the jurisdiction.

(b) A lawyer who is not admitted to practice law in California shall not maintain a legal practice presence, nor represent that they can practice in, California.

5.6 Restrictions on a Lawyer's Right to Practice

(a) Unless authorized by law, a lawyer shall not participate in offering or making an agreement to restrict the right of another lawyer to practice after the termination of a relationship, unless upon retirement.

6 PUBLIC SERVICE

6.1 Pro Bono Service (ABA Model Rule Only)

(a) A lawyer should aspire to render at least (50) hours of pro bono legal services per year and provide additional assistance in the form of reduced fee or no fee services to individuals in need, and charitable or religious organizations.

6.2 Accepting Appointments (ABA Model Rule Only)

(a) A lawyer shall not avoid being appointed on a case, unless there is good cause to do so. Such as, representation would violate a rule of conduct, an unreasonable financial burden would be imposed on the attorney, or the attorney finds the client repugnant such that it would impair the attorney-client relationship.

6.3 Membership in Legal Services Organization

(a) A lawyer may serve as a director, officer or member of a legal services organization, apart from their law firm even if that organization has adverse interests to a client. However, they cannot knowingly participate in a decision if doing so would violate confidentiality or have a material adverse effect on the client.

6.4 Law Reform Activities Affecting Client Interests (ABA Model Rule Only)

(a) A lawyer may serve as a director, officer or member of an organization involved in reform of the law or its administration notwithstanding that the reform may affect the interests of a client of the lawyer. When the lawyer knows that the interests of a client may be materially benefitted by a decision in which the lawyer participates, the lawyer shall disclose that fact but need not identify the client.

6.5 Limited Legal Services Programs

(a) A lawyer who works as part of a program sponsored by a court, government agency, bar association, law school, or nonprofit organization, and provides short-term limited legal services is subject to conflict rules only if they know of it. Any disqualification under this section is not imputed to the firm.

7 INFORMATION ABOUT LEGAL SERVICES

7.1 Communications Concerning a Lawyer's Services

(a) A lawyer shall not make a false or misleading communication about the lawyer or the lawyer's services that includes any material misrepresentation.

7.2 Advertising

(a) A lawyer may advertise through any written, recorded, or electronic communication.

(b) A lawyer shall not compensate a person for the purpose of recommending or securing the services of the lawyer, except a lawyer may: (i) pay for lawful advertisements; (ii) pay for a lawful lawyer referral service; or (iii) offer a gift for a past recommendation if there is no future agreement.

- (1) A lawyer may refer clients to another lawyer or professional pursuant to a lawful arrangement to refer clients to the lawyer if it is not an exclusive arrangement and the client is informed.

(c) Any communication made pursuant to this rule shall include the name and address of at least one lawyer or law firm responsible for its content.

7.3 Solicitation of Clients

(a) A lawyer shall not by in-person, live telephone or real-time electronic means, contact, solicit services for pecuniary gain unless that person is another lawyer, a relative, or has a prior relationship with the lawyer.

(b) A lawyer shall not solicit employment from a person who is known to not desire solicitation, or in a manner that is coercive or harassing in nature.

(c) Any solicitation to a person known to be in need of legal services shall include the word "Advertisement" or similar on the outside envelope, and at the beginning/end of a recording, unless it is apparent that it is an advertisement.

(d) A lawyer may participate in a prepaid legal service plan that uses live contact to solicit clients if it is not operated by the lawyer and it is sent to persons not known to need services.

7.4 Communication of Fields of Practice and Specialization

(a) A lawyer shall not state that the lawyer is a certified specialist in a particular field of law, unless they are currently certified by that Board or the State Bar and the name of that organization is on the communication.

7.5 Firm Names and Trade Names

(a) A lawyer shall not use a firm or trade name that is fraudulent or misleading including implying a government relationship.

7.6 Political Contributions to Obtain Legal Engagements or Appointments by Judges (ABA Model Rule Only)

(a) A lawyer or law firm shall not accept a government legal engagement or an appointment by a judge if the lawyer or law firm makes a political contribution or solicits political contributions for the purpose of obtaining or being considered for that type of legal engagement or appointment.

8 MAINTAINING THE INTEGRITY OF THE PROFESSION

8.1 False Statement Regarding Application for Admission to Practice Law (No ABA Model Rule Counterpart)

(a) An applicant for admission to practice law shall not make a false statement on that application.

(b) A lawyer shall not make a false statement on another person's application to practice law.

8.1.1 Compliance with Conditions of Discipline and Agreements in Lieu of Discipline

A lawyer shall comply with the terms of any discipline imposed.

8.2 Judicial Officials

(a) A lawyer shall not knowingly make a false statement about a judicial officer or candidate.

(b) A lawyer who is a candidate or seeks appointment to judicial office shall comply with the Canons of Judicial Ethics.

8.3 Reporting Professional Misconduct (ABA Model Rule Only)

(a) A lawyer who knows that another lawyer or Judge has violated the relevant rules of conduct, or a substantial question as to the person's honesty, trustworthiness, or fitness for practice, shall inform the relevant professional governing body.

8.4 MISCONDUCT

It is professional misconduct for a lawyer to:

(a) violate the Rules of Professional Conduct or the State Bar Act;

(b) commit a criminal act or engage in conduct regarding honesty or fitness as a lawyer;

(c) knowingly assist or induce a judicial officer to violate the law.

8.4.1 PROHIBITED DISCRIMINATION, HARASSMENT, AND RETALIATION

(a) A lawyer shall not unlawfully harass, discriminate, or retaliate on the basis of any protected characteristic in representation or termination of a client, employee, or volunteer.

(b) A lawyer who is the subject of a State Bar investigation shall notify the proceeding of any criminal, civil, or administrative action based on the same conduct.

(c) This rule shall not preclude a lawyer from:

(1) representing a client alleged to have engaged in unlawful discrimination, harassment, or retaliation;

(2) providing advice and engaging in advocacy as otherwise required or permitted by these rules and the State Bar Act.

8.5 DISCIPLINARY AUTHORITY; CHOICE OF LAW

(a) **Disciplinary Authority**

(1) A lawyer admitted to practice in California is subject to the discipline of California regardless of where the conduct occurs.

(2) A lawyer not admitted in California is subject to the discipline of California if they provide services in California.

(b) **Choice of Law**

In any exercise of the disciplinary authority of California, the rules of professional conduct to be applied are based on the rules of the jurisdiction where the tribunal sits or the rules of the jurisdiction where the conduct occurred.

REAL PROPERTY

Table of Contents

I. LANDLORD AND TENANT

A. NATURE OF LEASEHOLD

A leasehold is an estate in land under which the tenant has a present long-term possessory interest in the leased premises. The landlord has a reversion.

1. TENANCY FOR YEARS

A fixed-term lease does not have to be for years; however, it may also be defined by weeks or months (e.g., A rents to B for 2 years).

a) CREATION

Usually created by written leases. If the lease is for more than one year, it must be in writing under the Statue of Frauds.

b) TERMINATION

Ends automatically on its termination date. In most leases, the landlord reserves the right of entry, which allows him to terminate the lease if the tenant breaches any of the covenants.

c) SURRENDER

Tenant may surrender the tenancy in writing.

2. PERIODIC TENANCY

A periodic tenancy continues for successive periods (month to month) until one party terminates it by giving proper notice.

a) CREATION

(i) Express agreement – the landlord to the tenant from month to month; (ii) Implied agreement – the landlord to the tenant at a rent of $100 payable monthly; (iii) Operation of Law – the tenant remains in possession after the lease expires, or lease is invalid and the tenant remains anyway.

b) TERMINATION

The tenancy continues until one party gives proper notice, generally one full period in advance. For a year-to-year lease, the party must give six months' notice.

3. TENANCIES AT WILL

Either the landlord or the tenant may terminate the tenancy at his or her will.

a) CREATION

A tenancy at will often arises when there is a defect in the original lease, but it can also be created by an express agreement. The courts will also treat periodic rent payments as a periodic tenancy.

b) TERMINATION

The landlord and tenant must have the same rights to termination. Either party may terminate without notice.

4. TENANCIES AT SUFFERANCE

a) CREATION

A tenancy at sufferance arises when a tenant continues to occupy the premises after the expiration of a lawful tenancy without the landlord's consent.

b) TERMINATION

A tenancy at sufferance lasts only until the landlord takes steps to evict the tenant, which the landlord may do at any time without notice.

5. Hold-Over Doctrine

If a tenant does not vacate the premises after his right to possession has ended, the landlord may: (i) evict him; or (ii) bind him to a new periodic tenancy. Generally, the terms and conditions that governed the expired tenancy will govern the new tenancy unless the landlord notifies the tenant otherwise and the tenant remains in possession.

a) Exceptions

The hold-over doctrine does not apply where: (i) the tenant remains in possession for only a few hours or only leaves a few pieces of property; (ii) the delay is not the tenant's fault (severe illness); or (iii) the lease is seasonal. In these situations, the landlord can only evict the tenant, not bind the tenant to a new tenancy.

B. Tenant Duties and Landlord Remedies

1. Tenant's Duty to Repair (Doctrine of Waste)

The tenant cannot damage (commit waste on) the leased premises. There are three types of waste:

a) Voluntary (Affirmative) Waste

The tenant intentionally or negligently damages the premises or exploits minerals on the property.

b) Permissive Waste

The tenant fails to take reasonable steps to protect the premises from damage. The tenant is liable for all ordinary repairs, but not ordinary wear and tear. If the landlord has a duty to make repairs, the tenant must promptly report problems.

c) Ameliorative Waste

The tenant alters the leased property, increasing its value. Generally, the tenant is liable for restoration. Today, most courts allow a tenant to make improvements if he is a long-term tenant and the change reflects changes in the neighborhood.

d) Tenant's Liability for Covenants to Repair

The tenant has a duty to repair ordinary wear and tear unless expressly excluded, but has no duty to repair structural failures or damage from fire or other casualty unless expressly included. Where the premises are destroyed, neither party has a duty to repair, but the tenant has a duty to continue to pay rent.

2. Duty to Not Use Premises for Illegal Purpose

The landlord may terminate the lease if the tenant regularly, as opposed to occasionally, uses the premises for an illegal purpose.

3. Duty to Pay Rent

If the lease ends before the end of a rental period, the tenant must pay a proportional amount of rent. After the tenant surrenders the property, his duty to pay rent ends.

4. Landlord Remedies

a) Tenant on Premises but Fails to Pay Rent – Evict or Sue for Rent

Under common law, a tenant's failure to pay rent served as a basis for a cause of action for money damages; the landlord could not terminate the lease. Most modern leases give the landlord the right to terminate under the unlawful-detainer statute and the tenant cannot raise counterclaims.

b) Tenant Abandons – Do Nothing or Repossess

If the tenant unjustifiably abandons the property, the landlord is entitled to damages, but must mitigate damages by seeking to re-let the premises. The landlord can recover the difference between the promised rent and the fair rental value of the property (if re-let, difference between promised rent and amount received from re-letting).

C. Landlord Duties and Tenant Remedies

Unless required by lease, statute, or implied warranty of habitability, the general rule is that a landlord does not have to repair or maintain the premises.

1. Duty to Deliver Possession of Premises

Most states require the landlord to give the tenant actual possession of the premises at the beginning of the leasehold term. The landlord breaches the lease if he does not evict a holdover tenant by the beginning of the new lease term.

2. Quiet Enjoyment

Every lease has an implied covenant that neither the landlord nor a paramount titleholder (bank foreclosing on a mortgage) will interfere with the tenant's quiet enjoyment and possession of the premises. This covenant may be breached—and the tenant evicted—in the following ways:

a) Actual Eviction

The landlord or a paramount titleholder excludes the tenant from the entire leased premises. The tenant has no obligation to pay rent.

b) Partial Eviction

The tenant is physically excluded from part of the leased premises. The tenant does not have to pay rent on the entire premises. If a third-party excludes the tenant from part of the leased premises, the tenant pays an apportion based on the reasonable rental value of the portion she continues to possess.

c) Constructive Eviction

If the landlord – not a third party – does something or fails to provide a service he has a duty to provide, that renders the property uninhabitable the tenant may vacate the premises, terminate the lease and seek damages.

3. Implied Warranty of Habitability

Most jurisdictions imply a non-waivable covenant of habitability into residential leases, in which the premises must meet local housing codes. If the premises are uninhabitable, the tenant may: (i) terminate the lease; (ii) make repairs and offset the cost against future rent; (iii) abate the rent to an amount equal to the fair rental value in view of the defects; and (iv) remain in possession, pay full rent, and sue for damages. This does not apply to commercial tenants.

4. Retaliatory Eviction

A landlord may not terminate a lease or otherwise penalize a tenant for exercising a legal right, including reporting housing or building code violations. Many statutes presume a retaliatory motive if the landlord acts within a certain number of days – generally 90-180 days – after the tenant exercises her rights. To overcome the presumption, the landlord must show a valid, non-retaliatory reason for his actions.

D. Assignments and Subleases

A tenant may freely transfer her leasehold interest, in whole or in part, unless the lease states otherwise. An assignment is a complete transfer of the entire remaining term. If the tenant retains any part of the remaining term (other than a right to renter upon breach), the transfer is a sublease. **Note:** For the bar exam, a transfer is a sublease only when the original tenant reserves time for herself (e.g., the last month of the lease).

1. Consequences of Assignment

When a tenant transfers his entire interest, the assignee stands in the shoes of the original tenant, and the landlord and assignee are in privity of estate and both are bound on all covenants that "run with the land." There is no longer privity between the landlord and the original tenant.

a) Covenants That Run with the Land

Covenants that run with the land are those that are tied to the land, not the owner, and are transferred as the land is transferred. The covenants either benefit the landlord and burden the tenant, or vice versa, with respect to their interests in the property.

b) Rent Covenants

A covenant to pay rent runs with the land so the assignee must pay rent to the landlord. After assignment, the original tenant and the landlord are no longer in privity of estate, but they are in privity of contract and the original tenant remains liable on the original contract obligation to pay rent. If the assignee reassigns his leasehold interest, his privity of estate with the landlord ends and he has no liability for the subsequent assignee's failure to pay rent because there was no contract between the assignee and the landlord.

2. Consequences of Sublease – Sublessee Not in Privity with Landlord

A sublessee is the tenant of the original lessee and usually pays rent to the original lessee, who then pays the landlord. Because a sublessee is not in privity with the landlord, he is not personally liable to the landlord for rent or for the performance of any of the covenants in the original lease.

a) Landlord's Remedies

If the landlord does not receive rent or there is a breach of any other covenant that serves as a basis for termination, the landlord may terminate the lease and the sublease automatically ends. A number of jurisdictions allow a landlord who does not receive rent to assert a lien on personal property found on the premises; this applies to a sublessee's property, as well as that of the original tenant.

b) Rights of Sublessee

A sublessee cannot enforce any of the landlord's obligations in the main lease, except for the implied warranty of habitability in a residential sublease.

3. Covenants Against Assignment of Sublease

Courts will strictly construe lease restrictions on assignment and sublease against the landlord. Thus, a prohibition against assignment does not preclude a sublease (and vice versa).

a) Waiver

A landlord can waive a valid covenant against lease assignment expressly, or implicitly by accepting rent with knowledge of the assignment and without making an objection.

b) Transfer in Violation of Lease

An assignment or sublease that violates a lease provision is not void, but the landlord may generally terminate the lease or sue for damages.

4. Assignments by Landlords

A landlord may assign rents and his reversion without the tenant's consent. This is generally done by deed when he sells the building to a new owner.

a) Rights of Assignee Against Tenants – Attornment

Once the assignment is made and the tenants are given reasonable notice, they must pay rent to the new owner. The beneficial covenants that run with the land are transferred to the new owner.

b) Liabilities of Assignee to Tenants

Likewise, the burdens and liabilities of the landlord's covenants that run with the land are transferred to the assignee. The original landlord will also remain liable on all of the covenants he made in the original lease.

E. Condemnation of Leaseholds

If the entire leasehold is taken by eminent domain, the tenant is entitled to compensation and no longer has to pay rent as there is no longer a leasehold estate when the leasehold and reversion have merged in the condemnor. If, however, the taking is only temporary or partial, the tenant must pay rent, but is still entitled to compensation (a share of the condemnation award).

F. Tort Liability of Landlord and Tenant

1. Landlord's Liability

Under common law, the landlord does not have a duty to make the premises safe. Today, there are several exceptions:

a) Concealed Dangerous Condition (Latent Defect)

If, at the time the lease is entered into, the landlord knows or should have known of a dangerous condition that the tenant could not discover by reasonable inspection, the landlord must disclose it when the parties enter into the lease. A landlord who fails to disclose a dangerous condition will be liable for any injuries resulting from the condition. If the tenant accepts the premises after disclosure, she assumes the risk for herself and others, relieving the landlord of any liability.

b) Public Use

The landlord is liable for injuries to the public if he:
(i) knows (or should know) of a dangerous condition; (ii) has reason to believe the tenant may admit the public before the landlord repairs the condition; and (iii) fails to repair the condition.

c) Repairs

Although the landlord is not liable for injuries from dangerous conditions arising after the tenant takes possession, if the landlord undertakes such repairs, he owes a duty of reasonable care. The landlord also has a duty of reasonable care in maintaining common areas (e.g., halls, elevators). If the landlord covenants to repair or has a statutory duty to repair, he is liable for injuries resulting from failure to repair or negligent repair.

d) Furnished Short-Term Residence

A landlord who rents a fully furnished premises for a short period is liable for injuries resulting from any defect, whether or not he knew of the defect or disclosed it.

e) Modern Trend – General Duty of Reasonable Care

Courts have found that a landlord owes a general duty of reasonable care to residential tenants, under which he is liable for injuries resulting from ordinary negligence if he had notice of a defect and an opportunity to repair it, but failed to do so.

2. Tenant's Liability

For the duty of care by the tenant, as an occupier of land, see Torts.

II. COOPERATIVES, CONDOMINIUMS, AND ZONING

A. COOPERATIVE

In a cooperative, a corporation holds title to the land and buildings and leases individual apartments to shareholders. Because they are economically interdependent and the individual owners are regarded as tenants, a direct restraint on the alienation of an individual interest is valid.

B. CONDOMINIUMS

In a condominium, each owner owns the interior of his individual unit, plus an undivided interest in the exterior and common areas. Since condominium unit ownership is treated as fee ownership, the ordinary rules against restraints on alienation apply.

C. ZONING

The state may enact statutes to reasonably control the use of land for the protection of the health, safety, morals, and welfare of its citizens. The zoning power is based on the state's police power and is limited by the Due Process and Equal Protection Clauses of the Fourteenth Amendment, and the "no taking without just compensation" clause of the Fifth Amendment. Cities and counties can exercise zoning power only if so authorized by a state enabling act. Remember these terms:

1. NONCONFORMING USE

A use that exists when the state passes a zoning act that does not conform to the statute cannot be eliminated at once.

2. SPECIAL USE PERMIT

A special use permit is one that must be obtained even though the zoning is proper for the intended use. It is often required for hospitals, funeral homes, drive-through businesses, etc.

3. VARIANCE

A variance is a departure from the literal restrictions of a zoning ordinance, granted by administrative action.

4. ZONING ORDINANCES

Zoning ordinances are generally invalid if: they have no reasonable relation to public welfare; are too restrictive; are discriminatory as to a particular parcel; are beyond the grant of authority; violate due process; or are racially discriminatory.

D. UNCONSTITUTIONAL TAKINGS AND EXACTIONS

See Constitutional Law.

III. FIXTURES

A fixture is a chattel that has been so affixed to land that it is no longer personal property, but a part of the realty. A fixture passes with the land.

A. CHATTELS INCORPORATED INTO STRUCTURE

Fixtures include items that are incorporated into the realty so that they lose their identity (e.g., bricks, concrete), and items that, if removed, would cause damage (e.g., plumbing, heating ducts).

B. COMMON OWNERSHIP CASES

A common ownership case is one in which the person who brings the chattel to the land owns both the chattel and the land (X installs a furnace in his home). These become "fixtures" if the owner intended to make the item part of the realty. Intention is inferred from: (i) the nature of the article; (ii) the manner of attachment; (iii) the amount of damage that would be caused by its removal; and (iv) the adaptation of the item to the use of the realty.

1. Constructive Annexation

An article of personal property that is so uniquely adapted to the real estate that it makes no sense to separate it (keys to doors, custom curtain rods) may be a fixture even if it is not physically attached to the property.

C. Divided Ownership Cases

In divided ownership cases, the chattel is owned and brought to the realty by someone other than the landowner, such as a tenant or licensee.

1. Landlord-Tenant

Whether an annexed chattel is a fixture depends on whether there is a relevant agreement between the landlord and tenant. Absent an agreement, a tenant may remove his annexed chattels if removal would not damage the premises or destroy the chattel. If the tenant does not remove it by the end of the lease term (or within a reasonable time), the tenant must pay for any damage.

2. Life Tenant and Remainderman

The same rules apply for life tenants, except that the life tenant must remove annexations before the end of his tenancy.

3. Licensee or Trespasser and Landlord

Licensees are treated as tenants; however, trespassers normally lose their annexations. Thus, absent a statute, an adverse possessor or good-faith trespasser cannot remove fixtures.

D. Third-Party Cases

1. Third Party Lien on Land to which Chattel is Affixed

Generally, the mortgagee has no greater rights than the mortgagor. Thus, chattels annexed by the mortgagor's tenant are generally not within the lien of the mortgagee, except where the mortgage is made after the lease and the mortgagee is without notice of the tenant's rights.

2. Third-Party Lien on Chattel Affixed to Land

If a landowner affixes a chattel, of which the seller retains a security interest, to mortgaged land and defaults on both the chattel and mortgage payments, the general rule is that the first to record his interest wins possession of the chattel. The UCC, however, provides that the seller wins if she records a "fixture filing" within 20 days after the chattel is affixed to the land. The seller must compensate the mortgagee for damage or repair caused by removal.

IV. RIGHTS IN THE LAND OF ANOTHER

A. Easements

An easement is a non-possessory interest in land that creates a right to use land possessed by someone else.

1. Creation

An easement can be created by express grant or reservation, implication, or by prescription.

a) Express Grant

Any easement expressly granted must be in writing to satisfy the Statute of Frauds.

b) Express Reservation

A grantor creates an easement by reservation when she conveys title to land but reserves the right to continue to use a tract for a special purpose. As an interest in land, the Statue of Frauds must also be satisfied. Under the majority view, an easement can be reserved only for the grantor. An attempt to reserve an easement for anyone else is void.

c) Implication

An easement by implication is created by operation of law as a result of surrounding circumstances that indicate they must have intended for an easement. This is an exception to the Statute of Frauds, as it is not in writing.

(1) Implied from Existing Use

An easement may be implied from existing use if: (i) the single tract was owned by the same person; (ii) that person continuously and actively used it at the time of the conveyance; (iii) that person used it for a purpose that is reasonably necessary for the enjoyment of the property; and, (iv) the court determines that the parties intended the use to continue after the transfer of the property.

(2) Implication Without Existing Use

(a) Subdivision Plat

Buyers of the lots that refer to a recorded plat or map, with streets leading to the lot, have implied easements to use the streets to access their lots.

(b) Profit a Prendre

The holder of a profit (a prendre) has an implied easement to pass over the surface of the land to use it as reasonably necessary to exercise his right to take something off the land or extract it.

(3) Necessity

An easement by necessity arises when a landowner divides his property in a way that deprives one of the subdivisions access to something that is necessary for the use and enjoyment of the property.

d) Prescription

A person can acquire an easement by prescription in the same way a person can acquire property by adverse possession. The use must be: (i) open and notorious; (ii) adverse (without the owner's permission); (iii) continuous and uninterrupted; (iv) for the statutory period of time. Generally, one cannot acquire a prescriptive easement over public land.

2. Characteristics

a) Affirmative or Negative

(1) Affirmative

The holder is entitled to make affirmative use of the servient tenement.

(2) Negative

The holder can forbid the possessor of the servient tenement to refrain from engaging in an activity on the servient estate. Negative easements are generally limited to: (i) light; (ii) air; (iii) lateral and subjacent support; and, (iv) flow of an artificial stream. **Note:** Restrictions relating to anything else are considered restrictive covenants.

b) Appurtenant or In Gross

(1) Appurtenant

An easement is appurtenant when it benefits the holder in his physical use or enjoyment of another tract of land. The owner of the easement holds it in his capacity as the owner of another tract of property. Thus, there are two tracts: (i) the dominant tenement; and, (ii) the servient tenement. An easement appurtenant passes with the transfer of the benefited land, regardless of whether it is referenced in the conveyance. The burden of the easement also transfers with the servient estate unless the new owner is a bona fide purchaser with no actual or constructive notice of the easement.

(2) In Gross

The holder of an easement in gross has a right to use the servient tenement independent of his possession of another tract of land (i.e., the easement benefits the holder rather than another parcel). An easement in gross is for the holder's pleasure (e.g., swim on Blackacre) and is not transferable, unless it is an economic or commercial interest (e.g., the right to erect billboards).

c) Scope

Unless the grant provides otherwise, courts assume the easement was intended to meet both present and future needs of the dominant tenement (e.g., widening to accommodate new wider cars). If, however, the dominant parcel is subdivided, the lot owners will not succeed to the easement if to do so would unreasonably overburden the servient estate.

d) Termination

(1) Stated Conditions

The original grant may specify when or under what conditions the easement will end.

(2) Unity of Ownership (Merger)

The easement is destroyed when the same person acquires ownership of both the easement and the servient estate, thus merging the two. The easement will not be automatically revived if there is a later division. The easement is not destroyed, however, if the interest in the servient tenement is not of equal or greater duration than the duration of the easement privilege.

(3) Release

The owner of the easement can terminate the easement, even an easement in gross, by executing a deed of release.

(4) Abandonment

An easement owner who abandons an easement through physical action (building a structure that renders the easement unusable) extinguishes the easement. Merely stopping use of the easement or expressing a wish to abandon it does not extinguish the easement.

(5) Estoppel

While oral expressions of intent to abandon do not terminate an easement unless they are put in writing (a release) or accompanied by an action (abandonment), if the owner of the servient estate changes his position in reasonable reliance on the oral representations, the easement ends through estoppel.

(6) Prescription

An easement by prescription ends when the owner of the servient tenement excludes the easement holder for a prescribed statutory period, typically 20 years.

(7) Necessity

Easements created by necessity end once the necessity ends.

(8) Condemnation and Destruction

All easements end if the servient estate is condemned. Courts are split as to whether easement holders are entitled to compensation. If the easement is destroyed involuntarily, the easement ends; if it is destroyed voluntarily, the easement is not destroyed.

e) Failed Attempt

A failed attempt to create an easement results in a license.

B. Licenses

A holder of a license has the privilege to go upon the land of another. It is merely a privilege, not an interest in the land, revocable at the will of the licensor. A license is personal to the licensee and thus inalienable. Any attempt to transfer a license results in revocation.

1. Irrevocable Licenses

A license cannot be revoked in the following situations:

a) Estoppel

If a licensee relies on the license and invests substantial amounts of money or labor, the licensor is estopped to revoke the license. The license becomes an easement by estoppel, which lasts until the holder receives a sufficient benefit to reimburse him for his expenditures.

b) License Coupled with an Interest

A license, coupled with an interest, is irrevocable as long as the interest lasts.

C. Profits

A profit entitles the holder to take identified resources (soil, timber, materials, fish, etc.) from the servient estate. Implied in every profit is an easement entitling the benefit holder to enter the servient estate to remove the resources. The rules governing creation, alienation, and termination of easements also apply to profits. A profit may also be extinguished by trough surcharge – misuse that overly burdens the servient estate.

D. Covenants Running with the Land at Law (Real Covenants)

A real covenant running with the land is a written promise to do something on the land (maintain a fence) or a promise not to do something on the land (not build a multi-family dwelling). Because they run with the land, subsequent owners may enforce or be burdened by the covenant, provided certain requirements are met.

1. Requirements for Burden to Run

If the following elements are present, any successor in interest to the burdened estate will be bound by the covenant as if she expressly agreed to it:

a) Intent

The parties to the covenant intended that successors be bound by its terms. Courts may infer intent from the circumstances surrounding the creation of the covenant, or, more often, the language of the conveyance itself.

b) Notice

Under modern recording acts, a subsequent purchaser for value must have had actual, inquiry, or record notice of the covenant at the time of purchase.

c) Horizontal Privity

When entering into the covenant, the parties must have shared some interest in the land independent of the covenant (grantor-grantee / landlord-tenant / mortgagee-mortgagor).

d) Vertical Privity

The successor in interest to the covenanting party must hold the entire durational interest that the covenantor held at the time he made the covenant.

e) Touch and Concern

Negative covenants touch and concern the land if they restrict the servient estate holder's use of the parcel. Affirmative covenants touch and concern the land if they require the servient estate holder to do something that increases his obligation in connection with his enjoyment of the land.

2. Requirements for Benefit to Run

The promisor's successor in interest may enforce the covenant if the following elements are present:

a) Intent

The covenanting parties intended that the successors in interest to the covenantee would be able to enforce the covenant.

b) Vertical Privity

The benefits run to the assignees of the original estate or any lesser estate (i.e., any succeeding possessory estate may enforce the benefit).

c) Horizontal Privity

While the parties do not have to be in horizontal privity, if they are not, the promisee's successors can only enforce the covenant against the promisor, not the promisor's successors.

d) Touch and Concern

The benefit of a covenant touches and concerns the land if the promised performance benefits the covenantee and her successors in their use and enjoyment of the land.

3. Specific Situations Involving Real Covenants

Generally, promises to pay money to be used in connection with the land (homeowner association fees) and covenants not to compete run with the land. Courts will not enforce racially restrictive covenants.

4. Remedy – Damages Only

A non-breaching party to a real covenant may receive money damages, which can be collected from the defendant's general assets. If the party asks for an injunction to enforce a promise, it will be enforced as an equitable servitude, rather than a real covenant.

5. Termination

As with all other non-possessory interests, a party may terminate a covenant by a written release; or it may end where there is a merger of the benefited and burdened estates; or the burdened property is condemned.

E. Equitable Servitudes

An equitable servitude is a covenant that can be enforced against assignees who have notice of the covenant, regardless of whether it runs with the land at law. The usual remedy for enforcement is an injunction – this is the crucial difference between real covenants and equitable servitudes. If money damages are sought, a real covenant analysis is appropriate. A single promise creates both a real covenant and an equitable servitude.

1. Creation

Generally, equitable servitudes are created by covenants contained in a writing that complies with the Statute of Frauds. A negative equitable servitude may be implied from a common scheme or plan for the development of a residential subdivision.

a) Common Scheme

Reciprocal negative servitudes will be implied only where the developer planned that all parcels would be subject to the same restriction when sales began. Evidence includes: (i) a recorded plat; (ii) a general pattern of restrictions; or (iii) oral representations to early buyers.

(1) If the scheme arises after some lots are sold, no previous buyers can be bound unless they agree under an express covenant.

b) Notice

To be bound by an implied covenant not in her deed, a grantee must have had notice of the covenants in the deeds of others in the subdivision. Notice may be actual (direct knowledge of the covenants), inquired (neighborhood appears to conform to common restrictions), or recorded (prior deed with covenant in grantee's chain of title).

2. Requirements For the Burden to Run

a) Intent

The covenanting parties intended that the servitude be enforceable by and against assignees;

b) Notice

The successor of the promisor has actual, inquiry, or record notice of the servitude; and

c) Touch and Concern

The covenant touches and concerns the land (i.e., it restricts the holder of the servient estate in his use of that parcel).

3. Requirements For the Benefit to Run

The benefit of an equitable servitude runs with the land and is enforceable by the promisee's successors as long as: (i) the original parties so intended; and, (ii) the servitude touches and concerns the benefited property. No privity of estate is required.

4. Equitable Defenses to Enforcement

A court will not enforce an equitable servitude if:

a) Unclean Hands

The person seeking enforcement violates a similar restriction on his own land;

b) Consent

A benefited party acquiesced in a violation;

c) Estoppel

A benefited party acted in a way that a reasonable person would believe he was abandoning the covenant;

d) Laches

The benefited party failed to bring a lawsuit against the violator within a reasonable time; or

e) Inequitable

The neighborhood has changed so significantly that enforcing the covenant would be inequitable.

5. Termination

Like other non-possessory interests, an equitable servitude ends when: (i) the benefit holder executes a written release; (ii) the benefited and burdened estates are merged; or (iii) the burdened property is condemned.

F. Party Walls and Common Driveways

A wall erected partly on the property of each of two adjoining landowners generally belongs to each owner to the extent it rests upon her land. Courts will also imply mutual cross-easements of support, meaning that each owner can use a wall or driveway, and neither party can unilaterally destroy it.

1. Creation

A written agreement is required, as the Statute of Frauds applies to the creation of a party wall or common driveway agreement. If there is no writing, an irrevocable license can arise if a party detrimentally relies on an oral agreement. Implication or prescription can also create party walls and common driveways.

2. Running of Covenants

An agreement by party wall or common driveway owners who agree that they will both be mutually responsible for maintaining the wall or driveway runs to the successive owners of each parcel.

G. Adverse Possession

A person may acquire title to real property through adverse possession if an owner does not, within a statutory period, take action to eject a possessor whose claim is adverse to the owner. At the end of the statutory period, title vests in the possessor. In order to take title by adverse possession, the possession must be:
(i) hostile; (ii) open and notorious; (iii) actual and exclusive; and (iv) continuous.

1. Hostile

Possession is hostile if the possessor enters without the owner's permission. If the possessor was previously allowed on the land (lease), possession does not become hostile until the possessor makes it clear to the true owner the fact that she is claiming hostilely.

a) Co-Tenants

A co-tenant generally does not possess adversely to other co-tenants unless he declares his intention to claim exclusive dominion.

b) Grantor Stays in Possession

A grantor who remains in possession of land after she conveys it is presumed to be there with permission. (Likewise, a tenant who holds over is presumed to have permission of the landlord.)

2. Open and Notorious

Possession is open and notorious when it is the kind of use the owner would make of the land. The adverse possessor's occupation must be sufficiently apparent to put the true owner on notice that a trespass is occurring.

3. Actual and Exclusive

An adverse possessor will gain title only to land she actually occupies. If an adverse possessor occupies a reasonable portion of the parcel, then she will be deemed to have constructively possessed the entire parcel. Exclusive means that the possessor is not sharing with the true owner or the public. Two or more people may obtain title by adverse possession; they take title as tenants in common.

4. Continuous Possession

Possession must be continuous, not intermittent, throughout the statutory period, unless the intermittent possession is of a type that the usual owner would make (e.g., a summer home).

a) Tacking

An adverse possessor can tack her own possession onto the periods of adverse possession of her predecessors, but privity is required.

H. Disability

The statutory period does not begin to run if the true owner was under some disability (minority, prison, insanity) to sue when the cause of action first accrued.

I. Future Interests

The statutory period does not begin to run against a holder of a future interest until the interest becomes possessory.

J. Restrictive Covenants

If an adverse possessor violates a restrictive covenant in the owner's deed for the limitations period, she takes title free of that restriction. If the possession is consistent with the covenant, her title remains subject to the restriction. **Note:** Government land and land registered under the Torens system is not subject to adverse possession.

V. ESTATES IN LAND

A. Present Possessory Interests

1. Fee Simple Absolute

A fee simple represents absolute ownership and is the largest estate in land that is recognized by law. The owner has the exclusive right to use it, sell it, divide it, devise it – whatever she chooses to do with it. A fee simple has the potential to last for an infinite duration. Under common law, a grantor created a fee simple by using the language "to A and his heirs…"; today, it is created by simply using "to A."

2. Defeasible Fee

A defeasible fee is an estate in land that can be terminated upon the occurrence of an event stated in the granting document.

3. Fee Simple Determinable ("FSD") - Possibility of Reverter

A fee simple determinable automatically terminates upon the happening of the stated event. The estate will then be automatically transferred to the grantor. The grantor creates an FSD with language such as: "as long as" and "until." "For the purpose of" or "to be used for" are simply expressions of motive and do not create an FSD. It can be conveyed, but is still taken subject to the estate being terminated by the specific event.

a) Possibility of Reverter

When a grantor conveys an FSD, he automatically retains a future estate of a possibility of reverter. The grantor may transfer or devise a possibility of reverter.

4. Fee Simple Subject to Condition Subsequent (Right of Entry)

This estate is similar to a fee simple but it has a condition attached. The grantor reserves the right to terminate the estate upon the happening of a certain stated event. The estate is created by use of conditional words such as: "upon condition that"; "provided that"; "but if"; and, "if it happens that."

a) Right of Entry

The grantor has a right of entry if the triggering event occurs. When the event occurs, the grantor must take steps to establish possession of land; it does not automatically revert to the grantor. Some courts have held that a holder of a right of entry cannot transfer it while he is alive, but most states agree that the right is descendible.

5. Fee Simple Subject to Executory Interest

This estate automatically terminates upon the happening of a stated event and then passes to a third party, not the grantor. The third party then has an executory interest.

6. Fee Tail

A fee tail in an estate is a restriction on the sale or inheritance of the property in which it can only be sold, devised, or inherited by lineal heirs. A grantor creates a fee tail with the language "to A and the heirs of his body." Most jurisdictions have abolished the fee tail, and any attempt to create one results in a fee simple.

7. Life Estate

A life estate gives the holder the use of the estate for the duration of a life. It is usually for the life of a tenant, but it could be for the life of a third party. A grantor creates a life with language such as: "To A for life, then to B."

a) Duration

(1) Life of Grantee

A life estate is usually measured by the life of the grantee.

(2) Life Estate Pur Autre Vie

A life estate pur autre vie is measured by the life of a third party. Such an estate may result when the life tenant conveys his life estate to another (e.g., B holds a life estate, conveys it to C, so C has a valid life estate for as long as B lives), or the grantor may create one through language such as "To A for the life of B, then to C."

(3) Condition Subsequent/Executory Interest

A life estate can be characterized as subject to a condition subsequent or executory interest.

b) Rights and Duties of Life Tenant – Doctrine of Waste

A life tenant has the right to live on the property until death and enjoy any ordinary use and profits of the land, as long as it does not injure the interests of a remainderman or reversioner. A future interest holder may sue for damages or enjoin such acts.

(1) Affirmative (Voluntary) Waste

A life tenant can consume or exploit natural resources on the land where it is: (i) necessary to repair or maintain the land; (ii) the land is suitable only for such use; or (iii) it is expressly or impliedly permitted by the grantor. Some jurisdictions follow the open mines doctrine, which allows mining on the land, limited to mines already open. Many jurisdictions allow any activity if the land has already been used for that purpose.

(2) Permissive Waste

Permissive waste occurs when a life tenant fails to protect or preserve the land. A life tenant must: (i) maintain the land and structures; (ii) pay interest on mortgages (not principal); (iii) pay ordinary taxes on the land; and (iv) pay special assessments for public improvements of short duration (long duration are apportioned between the life tenant and future interest holder). A life tenant does not have to insure the premises for the benefit of the remaindermen and is not responsible for damages caused by a third-party tortfeasor.

(3) Ameliorative Waste

Even if an improvement increases the property's value, if it changes the property's character, it is waste. Under common law, the remaindermen could recover the cost of restoring the land to its original condition. Life tenant may now, however, alter or even demolish existing buildings if: (i) it does not diminish the market value of the future interests; and (ii) either (a) the remaindermen do not object, or (b) the neighborhood has substantially and permanently changed so that the property is no longer useful (a change from residential to commercial).

(a) Cf – Leasehold Tenant

Remains liable for ameliorative waste if market value was increased.

(b) Cf – Worthless Property

If the land is worthless, the life tenant may seek a partition sale and put the proceeds in trust with the income paid to the life tenant.

c) Renunciation of Life Estate

If a life tenant renounces his interest in a life estate, the future interest immediately goes to the remaindermen.

B. Future Interests

A future interest gives the holder the right or possibility of future possession of an estate. A future interest is a present legally protected right in property.

1. Reversionary Interests

a) Possibilities of Reverter and Rights of Entry: *supra.*

b) Reversion: If a grantor conveys less than she owns, the remaining is a reversion. It arises simply by operation of law; it does not have to be expressly reserved in the granting documents. A reversion is alienable, devisable, and inheritable. Its holder can sue for waste and for tortious damage to the reversionary interest ("to B for life"; A has a reversion).

c) Reversions are not subject to the Rule Against Perpetuities ("RAP"), as they are vested future interests.

2. Remainder

A remainder is a future interest that becomes possessory on the natural expiration of the preceding estate created by the same instrument – not before and not after a gap in time. A remainder must be expressly created in the instrument creating the preceding possessory estate.

Example: A conveys to B for life then to C; C has a remainder.

Example: A conveys to B for life then to C one day after B's death; C does not have a remainder. A remainder cannot cut short a preceding estate; it can never follow a fee simple estate.

a) Indefeasibly Vested Remainder

An indefeasibly vested remainder must be given to an existing and ascertained person, and cannot be subject to a condition precedent, nor can the remainder be taken away. The remainderman has a right to immediate possession upon termination of the preceding estate.

b) Vested Remainder Subject to Open

This is created in a class of persons (children), of which at least one member is known, but others may be added to the class. While the interest is certain to become possessory, it is subject to diminution if it will be shared among additional members. Example: A conveys to B for life then to children of C. B and C are living and C has one child, D. D has a vested remainder subject to open.

c) Vested Remainder Subject to Total Divestment

A vested remainder subject to total divestment is a vested remainder subject to a condition subsequent and can thus be taken away.

Example: A to B for life, then to C, but if C dies unmarried, then to D. C has a vested remainder subject to complete divestment by D's executory interest.

d) Contingent Remainder

When the identity of the person to take possession is uncertain, or the fact the person will actually take possession is uncertain, it is a contingent remainder.

(1) Subject to Condition Precedent

A condition precedent is an event or state of affairs that must be present or satisfied before the remainderman has a right to possession.

Example: A to B for life and then to C if C marries D. C's remainder is contingent upon marriage to D.

Example: A to B for life, then to C if C marries D, otherwise to E. C and E have alternative contingent remainders. Cf: To B for life then to C, but if C marries D, then to E. C has a vested remainder subject to divestment by E's executory interest.

(2) **Unborn or Unascertained Persons**

When a remainder is given to an unborn or unascertained person, it is contingent because no one is ready to take possession if the preceding estate ends until the remainderman is ascertained.

Example: To B for life then to children of C. If C has no children, the remainder is contingent

(3) **Destructibility of Contingent Remainders**

Under common law, if a contingent remainder does not vest by the time the preceding estate is terminated, it is destroyed.

Example: To B for life, then to C if she reaches age 21. If B dies before C reaches age 21, C's remainder is destroyed.

(a) **Modern Jurisdictions**

Modern jurisdictions have abolished the destruction rule. In those states, C's interest would be converted to an executory interest upon B's death because it will divest A's reversionary estate when C turns 21.

(b) **Doctrine of Merger**

Under common law, a contingent remainder is destroyed when one person acquires all of the present and future interests in land, except a contingent remainder.

Example: X to Y for life, then to Z's children. If Z has no children, X's life estate pur autre vie and reversion merge, the contingent remainder in Z's children is destroyed.

(4) **Rule in Shelley's Case (Rule Against Remainders in Grantee's Heirs)**

If an instrument creates a life estate in A and gives the remainder to A's heirs, common law did not recognize the remainder and A took the life estate and the remainder.

(5) **Doctrine of Worthier Title**

Under the doctrine of worthier title, any remainder in the grantor's heirs becomes a reversion in the grantor.

Example: To B for life, then to A's heirs. B has a life estate and A has a reversion. Applies only to lifetime transfers, not wills.

e) **EXECUTORY INTERESTS**

Executory interests are future interests in a third party that will be triggered on the happening of a specified event. They can cut short the estate before its natural termination. Executory interests can be "shifting" – previous interest was held by the grantor – or "springing" – the previous interest was held by someone other than the grantor. Executory interests are not considered vested and thus subject to RAP. However, they cannot be destroyed; if a future interest does not follow the natural termination of the preceding estate, it must be an executory interest. Thus, only an executory interest can follow a fee simple. Where ambiguous, courts favor vesting of estates.

(1) **Springing**

A to B and his heirs when B marries C. B has a springing executory interest because it divests the grantor's estate.

(2) Shifting

A to B for life, then to C, but if C predeceases B, then to D and his heirs. D has a shifting executory interest because it divests a transferee's preceding estate.

f) Transferability of Remainders and Executory Interests

Vested remainders are fully transferable, descendible, and devisable. Under common law, contingent remainders and executory interests could not be transferred inter vivos, but most courts today hold that they can be transferred just as any other estate. Contingent remainders and executory interests are descendible and devisable, as long as survival is not a condition precedent.

g) Class Gifts

A "class" is a group of persons having a common characteristic (children, nephews). The total number of persons in the class will determine each member's share. Where a remainder is a class gift, it may be vested subject to open (at least one group member exists) or contingent (where all group members are unascertained).

(1) When the Class Closes

Unless the governing documents provide otherwise, under the rule of convenience, the class closes when any member of the class is entitled to her share of the class gift. Persons in gestation at the time the class closes are included.
Example: Will to children 21 and over at death. Class closes at death.

(2) Survivorship

Generally, descendants of a deceased class member do not share in the gift. If, however, the gift references descendants or heirs, they are automatically included if the class member dies (e.g., to B for life, then to his surviving children).

C. Rule Against Perpetuities

The rule against perpetuities limits an owner's power to control future dispositions of the property by stating that any present or future interest in property is invalid if it does not vest within 21 years after the death of some life in being at the creation of the interest.

1. When the Period Begins to Run

In a will, the period begins to run at the time of death. In a deed, the period begins to run upon delivery. In an irrevocable trust, the period begins to run at the time of creation.

2. Must Vest

An interest vests for purposes of the rule when: (i) it becomes possessory; or (ii) there is an indefeasibly vested remainder or a vested remainder subject to total divestment. If there is any possibility that it could vest beyond the period, it is void.

3. Lives in Being

Unless other measuring lives are specified, any life of an identifiable person alive at the time the interest is created can be used.

4. Exemptions from the Rule

The rule applies: to contingent remainders; executory interests; vested remainders subject to open (class gifts); options to purchase (not attached to a leasehold); rights of first refusal; and, powers of appointment. It does not apply to a grantor's interests (e.g., reversion; possibility of reverter; rights of entry).

5. Applications of the Rule

a) Age Contingency Beyond 21 in Open Class

A gift to an open class conditioned on members surviving beyond age 21 violates the RAP.
Example: To X for life, then to his children who attain 25 years of age.

b) Unborn Widow or Widower

A gift to an unborn widow or widower violates RAP because a person's widow is not determined until his death and the widow may not be in existence at the time of the gift.

c) Administrative Contingency

"To my issue surviving at the time my estate is distributed" is invalid because the estate might not be distributed within 21 years.

d) Options and Rights of First Refusal

An option to purchase or right of first refusal that may be exercised after life plus 21 years has passed is void. Exception: RAP does not apply to options to purchase held by the current lessee.

e) Class Gifts

(1) Bad-as-to-One, Bad-as-to-All

If the interest of any class member may vest after the perpetuities period, the whole class gift fails. For a class to be used as valid measuring lives, the class must be closed; to vest, all conditions precedent must be satisfied for every member within the perpetuities period.

(2) Gift to Subclass Exception

Each gift to a subclass is treated as a separate gift under RAP.

Example: Income to A for life, then to A's children for their lives, then to A's children's issue. The gifts to each of A's children living at the time of the disposition are valid, but the gift to their not-yet-born children is void.

(3) Per Capita Gift Exception

A fixed-amount gift to each member of a class is not treated as a class gift under RAP. Each is judged as a separate gift.

D. The Rule Against Alienation

Generally, any restriction on the sale or transferability of property forever or an extremely long period of time is void. There are three types of restraints on alienation: (i) disability restraints, where the grant states that a transfer by the grantee is ineffective; (ii) forfeiture restraints, under which a grantee forfeits his interest if he attempts to transfer it; and (iii) promissory restraints, under which an attempted transfer is a breach of the covenant.

1. Disabling Restraints on Legal Interests are Void

A disability restraint on any type of legal interest (fee simple, life estate) is void.

2. Absolute Restraints on Fee Simple are Void

All absolute restraints on the alienation of fee simple estates are void and the grantee may transfer the property as he or she chooses. Other restraints that are limited to a certain period and for a reasonable purpose are enforceable.

3. Valid Restraints on Alienation

(i) Forfeiture and promissory restraints on life estates; (ii) forfeiture restraints on transferability on future interests; (iii) reasonable restrictions on commercial transactions; (iv) rights of first refusal; (v) restrictions on assignment and sublets of leaseholds (e.g., requiring landlord's consent).

E. Concurrent Estates

More than one person may hold an estate in land at the same time. All persons have the right to the enjoyment and possession of the land.

1. Joint Tenancy

In a joint tenancy, each individual shares equal ownership of the property and has the equal, undivided right to keep or dispose of the property. A joint tenant has the right to survivorship – when one joint tenant dies, the property passes to the other joint tenants, not the heirs or descendants.

a) Creation

The interests of joint tenants must be equal in every way; no tenant may have a larger share, the interests must be vested for the same time, by the same instrument, with the same right to possession until one of them dies.

b) Severance of the Right of Survivorship

(1) Inter Vivos Conveyance

A joint tenancy is destroyed if a joint tenant conveys his or her interest; the transferee holds a tenancy in common. Where there are more than two joint tenants, conveyance by one destroys the joint tenancy only to the extent of the conveyor's interest. A joint tenancy may not be converted into a tenancy in common – severed – unless the joint tenant transfers her entire interest.

(a) Judgment Liens

These liens do not sever the joint tenancy until sold at foreclosure.

(b) Mortgages

A mortgage is a lien on title and will not sever a joint tenancy. The joint tenancy turns into a tenancy in common only if the mortgage is foreclosed upon and the property is sold.

(c) Leases

There is a split among states as to whether a lease will sever a joint tenancy.

(2) Testamentary Disposition

A testamentary disposition has no effect because the testator's interest vanishes at her death and the interest passes to the other joint tenants.

(3) Murder

Some state statutes provide for a constructive trust on one joint tenant's interest where she murders the other.

2. Tenancy by the Entirety

A tenancy by the entirety is a marital estate with a right of survivorship. Under common law, it arises presumptively in any conveyance to a husband and wife. It is severed upon death, divorce, or mutual agreement, or execution by a joint creditor. One spouse cannot convey a tenancy by the entirety; any deed doing so is void.

3. Tenancy in Common

A tenancy in common is a concurrent estate where the tenants are each entitled to possession and enjoyment of the whole, but there is no right of survivorship and tenants can hold different interests in the property. If a grant is made to multiple individuals, they are presumed to take as tenants in common, not as joint tenants.

4. Rights and Duties of Co-Tenants

a) Possession

Each co-tenant has the right to possess all portions of the property but no co-tenant has a right to exclusively possess any portion. A co-tenant that does not have possession cannot bring a possessory action unless she is wrongfully ousted by another co-tenant claiming an exclusive right to possession.

b) Rents and Profits

A co-tenant can keep profits from her own use of the property absent an agreement to the contrary. However, she must share any net rents from third parties and net profits from exploitations of the land, such as mining, with the other co-tenants.

c) Effect of One Concurrent Owner's Encumbering the Property

A joint-tenant or tenant in common may encumber her own interest (by mortgage/judgment lien), but not the interests of other co-tenants. In the case of a joint-tenancy, the lender bears the risk that obligated co-tenant will die before foreclosure, extinguishing the lender's interest.

d) Remedy of Partition

Any co-tenant has a right to demand that the property be partitioned and split among the tenants, either in kind by a physical division of the land or by sale with a division of proceeds. Restraints on alienation are valid provided they are limited to a reasonable time.

5. Expenses for Preservation of Property – Contribution

a) Repairs

A co-tenant who pays more than her pro rata share of necessary repairs, and has provided notice to the other co-tenants, is entitled to contribution.

b) Improvements

No co-tenant has a duty to improve the property and there is no right of contribution for improvements.

c) Taxes and Mortgages

A co-tenant is entitled to contribution for taxes or mortgage payments paid on the entire property. If the co-tenant is in sole possession, however, reimbursement is limited to expenditures that exceed the rental value of her use.

6. Duty of Fair Dealing

Co-tenants enjoy a confidential relationship among themselves. Acts by one co-tenant are presumed to be on behalf of other co-tenants.

VI. CONVEYANCING

A. Land Sale Contracts

1. Statute of Frauds

A contract for the sale of land must be in writing and contain the signature of the party to be charged and the essential terms (parties, description of land, price). If the parties partly perform the contract (possession, substantial improvements, payment of purchase price), the Statute of Frauds may no longer apply.

2. Doctrine of Equitable Conversion

Once both parties sign a contract, the buyer is considered the owner of the property. The seller's interest (right to the proceeds of sale) is considered personal property. Legal title to the property, which remains with the seller, is considered to be held in trust for the buyer. But because the right to possession follows the legal title, the seller possesses the property until closing.

a) Risk of Loss

If the property is destroyed (without fault of either party) before closing, the majority rule places the risk on the buyer. Some jurisdictions have adopted the Uniform Vendor and Purchaser Risk Act, which places the risk on the seller. Even though the buyer assumes the risk of loss, the seller must credit any insurance proceeds against the purchase price the buyer is required to pay if the property is damaged or destroyed.

b) Passage of Title on Death

If one party dies before the contract is completed, the seller's interest passes as personal property and the buyer's interest passes as real property. Thus, the seller's heirs or devisees must give their legal title to the buyer at closing. Or the buyer's heirs can demand conveyance of the land at closing. **Note:** If property is specifically devised by will, ademption rules may change the result of the equitable conversion doctrine.

3. Marketable Title

Every contract contains an implied warranty that the seller will provide marketable title (title reasonably free from doubt) at closing. It does not have to be perfect, but it must be free of valid claims from outside parties that would present an unreasonable risk of litigation.

a) Defects in Record Chain of Title

Title may be unmarketable if there is a defect in the chain of title such as a variation in the description in deeds, a defectively executed deed, or evidence that a prior grantor did not have the capacity to convey.

(1) Adverse Possession

On the MBE, title acquired by adverse possession is unmarketable. Recent cases hold that it is marketable.

(2) Future Interests Held by Unborn or Unascertained Parties

While most states consider all types of future interests transferable, an unborn or unascertained future interest holder cannot convey marketable title. Courts refuse to appoint a guardian ad litem to do so.

b) Encumbrances

Encumbrances such as mortgages, liens, restrictive covenants, easements, and significant encroachments generally render title unmarketable. A visible or known beneficial easement, however, will not impair the marketability of title. And if a seller will satisfy a mortgage or lien at closing, the title is marketable.

c) Zoning Restrictions

Zoning restrictions do not affect marketability; existing violations of a zoning ordinance do.

d) Time of Marketability

If the seller has agreed to furnish marketable title on the date of closing, the buyer cannot rescind before then on grounds that the seller's title is not marketable. Note that if the buyer is paying in installments, the seller does not have to provide marketable title until the buyer makes his last payment.

Exam Tip: Avoid answer choices referring to the implied warranty of marketability of title if the closing has already occurred. Once the closing occurs, the seller is no longer liable on this contractual warranty. The seller is then liable only for promises made in the deed.

e) Remedy If Title Not Marketable

If title is unmarketable, the buyer must notify the seller and give him a reasonable amount of time to cure the defect. If the seller fails to do so, the buyer may rescind the contract, seek damages, specific performance with abatement, or file a lawsuit to quiet title. If closing has already taken place, the contract and deed merge so that the seller is no longer liable on the implied contractual warranty.

Exam Tip: Do not be fooled into choosing the answer that lets the seller off the hook for title defects because the contract calls for a quitclaim deed. A quitclaim deed does not affect the warranty to provide marketable title.

4. Time of Performance

A closing date is not binding, as courts will presume that time is not "of the essence." Thus, a party late performing her end of the contract can still enforce the contract if she tenders within a reasonable time (e.g., two months) after the closing date.

a) When Presumption Overcome

Time is of the essence, however, if:
(i) the contract so states; (ii) an intent is indicated by the circumstances; or (iii) one party tells the other that time is of the essence.

b) Liability

If time is of the essence, a party who does not tender performance on the closing date breaches the contract and may not enforce it. Regardless of whether time is of the essence or not, a party who tenders late is liable for incidental losses.

5. Tender of Performance

The buyer's obligation to pay and the seller's obligation to convey are concurrent conditions. Thus, neither party is in breach until the other tenders performance, even if after the closing date. If neither party tenders performance on the closing date, it is extended until one of them does so.

a) When Party's Tender Is Excused

A party does not have to perform if the other party repudiates the contract or it is impossible for the other party to perform (e.g., unmarketable title that cannot be cured).

6. Remedies for Breach of Sales Contract

The non-breaching party is entitled to damages (difference between contract price and market value on date of breach, plus incidental costs) or specific performance. If the buyer wishes to proceed despite unmarketable title, she can request specific performance with an abatement of the purchase price.

a) Liquidated Damages

A contract for the sale of land usually requires the buyer to deposit earnest money with the seller. If the buyer does not perform, the seller may keep this money as liquidated damages. As long as the amount is reasonable in light of the seller's anticipated and actual damages, courts will uphold the seller's retention of the earnest money.

7. Seller's Liabilities for Defective Property

a) Warranty of Fitness or Quality--New Construction Only

Contracts for the sale of real property carry no implied warranty of quality or fitness for purpose. Most courts will recognize a warranty of fitness/quality if a house is new.

b) Sale of Existing Land and Buildings--Liability for Defects

The seller of an existing building (not new construction) may be liable to a purchaser for defects such as a leaky roof, flooding basement, termites, on any of several different theories:

(1) Misrepresentation (Fraud)

The seller is liable for defects about which he knowingly or negligently made a false statement of fact to the buyer. The buyer must have relied on the statement, which must have materially affected the value of the property.

(2) **Active Concealment**

The seller is liable for defects if he takes steps to conceal the defects.

(3) **Failure to Disclose**

Most states will hold a seller liable for not disclosing defects if: (i) he knows or has reason to know of the defect; (ii) the defect is not apparent to the buyer upon ordinary inspection; and (iii) the defect is of a serious nature so that the buyer would likely reconsider if known. If the property is a personal residence, the defect is dangerous, or the seller created the defect or made a failed attempt to repair it, a court is more likely to hold the seller liable.

(4) **Negligence**

A person may sue a builder for negligence in performing a building contract. Some courts permit the ultimate vendee to sue the builder despite lack of privity.

c) **DISCLAIMERS OF LIABILITY**

A general disclaimer in the sales contract ("property sold as is" or "with all defects") will not relieve a seller from liability for fraud, concealment, or failure to disclose. The disclaimer must identify specific types of defects (seller is not liable for any defects in the roof).

8. **REAL ESTATE BROKERS**

While a real estate broker is an agent of the seller, she should disclose material information if she has actual knowledge.

B. DEEDS – FORM AND CONTENT

Deeds transfer title to an interest in real property.

1. FORMALITIES

A deed must be in writing, signed by the grantor, and identify the parties and land.

a) If a deed is delivered with the name of the grantee left blank, the court presumes the person taking delivery has authority to fill in the name of the grantee. If the person fills in a name, the deed is valid. If the land description is left blank, the deed is void unless the grantee was explicitly given authority to fill in the description.

2. DEFECTIVE DEEDS

A void deed will be set aside even if the property has passed to a bona fide purchaser. A voidable deed will be set aside only if the property has not passed to a bona fide purchaser.

a) **VOID DEEDS**

A deed is void if it was forged, never delivered, or obtained by fraud in the factum (i.e., the grantor was deceived and did not realize that she was executing a deed).

b) **VOIDABLE DEEDS**

A deed is voidable if it was executed by minors or incapacitated persons, or if it was obtained through fraud in the inducement, duress, undue influence, mistake, or breach of fiduciary duty.

Example: If a joint owner tries to convey property by forging the signature of the other owner, the conveyance is valid as to the interest of the owner whose signature is genuine but void as to the other owner. The conveyance works a severance and the buyer is a tenant in common with the joint tenant whose signature was forged.

3. FRAUDULENT CONVEYANCES

Even if a deed complies with the required formalities, the grantor's creditors may set it aside if it was made: (i) with an actual intent to hinder, delay, or defraud a creditor; or (ii) without receiving a reasonably equivalent value in exchange for the transfer and the debtor was insolvent or became insolvent as a result of the transfer.

4. Description of Land Conveyed

A description of the land only has to provide a good lead to the identity of the property (e.g., "all my land in Newport"). If a court finds the description is too indefinite, the grantor keeps title but the court may order that the deed be reformed. Parol evidence is generally admissible to resolve patent or latent ambiguities if the description gives a good lead. It may not be admissible where the description is simply inadequate.

a) Rules of Construction

If descriptions are inconsistent or conflicting, courts will look to the following, in this order of importance: (i) natural monuments [oak tree]; (ii) artificial monuments [stakes, buildings]; (iii) courses [angles]; (iv) distances [feet, yards]; (v) name [Blackacre]; and, (vi) quantity [200 acres].

5. Boundary Cases

If there is a right-of-way or water boundary, the title to land presumptively passes in the center. This presumption can be rebutted by language in the deed. If there is a variable boundary (i.e., water boundary), a slow and imperceptible change will change the legal boundary; an accretion (slow deposit of soil on land abutting water) belongs to the abutting owner. Avulsion (sudden change of water-course) will not change ownership rights. Fixed boundaries are also not changed by the encroachment of water.

6. Reformation of Deeds

A court will reform a deed if it does not represent the parties' agreement due to: (i) mutual mistake; (ii) a scrivener's error; or (iii) a unilateral mistake caused by misrepresentation or other inequitable conduct.

C. Delivery and Acceptance

A deed is ineffective until it is delivered and accepted. A deed to a dead person is void even if the grantor did not know the grantee had died. The grantor retains title, it does not pass to the intended grantee's heirs.

1. Delivery

Delivering a deed refers to some action intended to make a deed presently effective. Delivery may be satisfied by manual delivery, notarized acknowledgment by the grantor, recording, or anything else showing the grantor's intent to deliver. Parol evidence may show an intent to deliver, but not show that delivery was conditional.

a) Title Passes Upon Delivery

Delivery cannot be canceled or taken back. **Note:** If the grantee in an exam fact pattern returns a deed to the grantor, the return has no effect; it is not a cancellation or a re-conveyance. To return title to the grantor, the grantee must draw up a new deed and deliver it to the grantor.

2. Retention of Interest by Grantor or Conditional Delivery

If the grantor retains control or interest (right to revoke), the grantor shows a lack of intent to pass title. Failure to record a delivered deed does not affect the passage of title even if the parties believe that the deed is ineffective until recording.

a) Express Condition of Grantor's Death

A properly executed and delivered deed that provides that title will not pass until the grantor's death is valid, giving the grantee a future interest.

b) Conditions Not Contained in Deed

If a deed is complete on its face when delivered, any oral condition made upon delivery is disregarded and the delivery is absolute.

c) Where Grantor Gives Deed to Third Party

A grantor may make a delivery conditional when giving deed to a third party.

d) Transfer to Third Party with No Conditions

A grantor who gives a deed to a third party with instructions to give it to the grantee makes a valid delivery. If the grantor does not provide instructions and the third party is the grantor's agent, there is no delivery.

e) Transfer to Third Party with Conditions (Commercial Transaction)

When a grantor gives a deed to a third party with instructions to give it to the grantee when a certain condition occurs (if grantee pays purchase price before a certain date), he has made a valid conditional delivery. Parol evidence is admissible to show that delivery is conditional. (Remember that parol evidence is not allowed where the grantor gives the deed ***directly*** to the grantee.)

(1) Grantor's Right to Recover Deed

A grantor can revoke a deed only if: (i) the condition has not yet occurred; and, (ii) there is no enforceable written contract to deliver the deed.

(2) Breach of Escrow Conditions

If a grantee wrongfully acquires the deed from the escrow holder before the condition occurs, title does not pass to the grantee and the grantee cannot give marketable title to a subsequent purchaser.

(3) Relation Back Doctrine

Title generally passes when the condition occurs. It may relate back to the time the grantor gave the deed to the third party when justice requires (grantor dies or becomes incompetent) and there is an enforceable contract to convey. Rights of intervening bona fide purchasers are thus protected.

f) Transfer to Third Party with Conditions (Donative Transaction)

When a grantor gives a deed to a third party to give to a donee upon the occurrence of a specified condition, the main issue is whether the grantor can revoke the deed before the condition occurs. The deed is not revocable unless the condition is the grantor's death, which gives the donee a springing executory interest and is revocable unless there is an enforceable contract to convey.

3. Acceptance

Once the grantee accepts the deed, delivery is complete. Most states will presume acceptance. Acceptance relates back to the date the deed was delivered into escrow unless doing so would defeat the rights of intervening third parties.

a) Dedication

Land may be transferred to a public body (city, county) by dedication. A dedication may be express or implied and done through written or oral statement, submission of a map or plat showing the dedication, or opening the land for public use. A dedication must be accepted for such use by a formal resolution, approval of map or plat, or actual assumption of maintenance or improvements.

D. Covenants For Title And Estoppel By Deed

There are three types of deeds that a property can use to convey an interest other than a leasehold: a general warranty deed, a special warranty deed, and a quitclaim deed. These differ in the scope of title assurance (i.e., covenants for title). Be careful not to confuse covenants for title with real covenants (written promises to do or not do something on the land).

1. Covenants in General Warranty Deed

a) Covenant of Seisin

The grantor covenants that she has both title and possession of the estate she purports to convey.

b) Covenant of Right to Convey

The grantor covenants that she has the authority to make the grant, which is satisfied by title alone.

c) Covenant Against Encumbrances

The grantor covenants there are no physical (encroachments) or title (mortgages) encumbrances.

d) Covenant of Quiet Enjoyment

The grantor covenants that no third party will disturb the grantee's possession by a lawful claim of title.

e) Covenant of Warranty

The grantor covenants to defend against a third party's reasonable claims of title and compensate the grantee for any loss sustained by a claim of superior title.

f) Covenant for Further Assurances

The grantor covenants to perform acts reasonably necessary to perfect the title.

(1) Breach of the Covenants

The covenants of seisin, right to convey, or encumbrances are breached, if at all, when the property is conveyed. Quiet enjoyment, warranty, and further assurances are future covenants that are breached when the grantee's possession is disturbed.

(2) Damages and Remote Grantees

If the last grantee in a line of successive conveyances by general warranty deed is evicted by lawful claim of title, he may sue anyone up the line. Some states allow him to recover to the extent of consideration received by a defendant-covenantor. Other states limit recovery to the lesser of what he paid or what the defendant-covenantor received.

2. Statutory Special Warranty Deed

In many states, use of the word "grant" in a deed implies two limited assurances against acts of the grantor (not her predecessors): (i) that the grantor has not conveyed the same estate or any interest therein to anyone other than the grantee; and (ii) that the estate is free from encumbrances.

3. Quitclaim Deeds

When a grantor transfers property by a quitclaim deed, he releases whatever interest he has and quits any right to claim the property. There are no express or implied covenants of title.

4. Estoppel by Deed

If the grantor purports to convey an estate in property that she does not own at the time, her subsequent acquisition of the estate will inure to the benefit of the grantee. This doctrine applies where the conveyance was by warranty deed or where the deed purported to convey a particular estate. It does not usually apply to quitclaim deeds.

a) Rights of Subsequent Purchasers

Most courts hold that title inures to the benefit of the grantee only as against the grantor. If the grantor transfers her after-acquired title to a bona fide purchaser ("BFP") for value, the BFP will prevail over the original grantee.

b) Remedies of Grantee

The original grantee can either accept title or sue for damages for breach of covenant.

E. Recording Acts

Recording acts generally protect all bona fide purchasers from secret interests and provide a mechanism for "earlier" grantees to give notice through a record and determine priority between parties claiming an interest in the same property.

Notice Statutes: Under a notice statute, a subsequent BFP (one who pays value and has no notice – actual/constructive/inquiry – of a prior instrument) prevails over a prior grantee who failed to record his interest. The subsequent purchaser must have had no actual or constructive notice at the time of the conveyance, but he does not have to record his interest for it to be protected.

Race-Notice Statutes: Under a race-notice statute, a subsequent BFP is protected only if she records before the earlier grantee and lacks notice of prior unrecorded claims.

Race Statutes: Under a pure race statute, whoever records first wins, regardless of whether either party had notice.

1. Without Notice

The purchaser had no actual, constructive (record), or inquiry notice of a prior conveyance when she paid consideration and received the interest.

2. Actual Notice

A grantee may obtain notice from any source (newspaper, word-of-mouth).

3. Record Notice--Chain of Title

Recordation gives prospective subsequent grantees constructive notice of the existence and content of recorded instruments. A subsequent purchaser is charged with notice of only those conveyances that are recorded and appear in the chain of title.

a) Wild Deeds

A "wild deed" is a recorded deed that is not connected to the chain of title. A subsequent purchaser cannot have constructive notice of a wild deed because he cannot feasibly find it.

Example: A conveys Blackacre to B. B does not record. B conveys it to C, and C records. A conveys Blackacre to D. D does not have notice of C's claim.

b) Deed in Chain Referring to Instrument Outside Chain

A reference to another instrument, regardless if it is recorded or in the chain of title, in a recorded document that is in the chain of title may impart constructive notice to the BFP.

c) Restrictive Covenants--Deeds from Common Grantor

Courts are split on whether deeds are in the chain of title of a subject lot if they are for adjacent lots or lots in the same subdivision, executed by the same grantor, and contain restrictions and easements involving the subject lot.

4. Inquiry Notice

In certain circumstances, a purchaser must make reasonable inquiries and will be charged with whatever an inquiry would have revealed. References in recorded instruments to unrecorded transactions, unrecorded instruments in the chain of title, and possession unexplained by the record, all put a purchaser on inquiry notice. The mere fact that a quitclaim deed was used does not charge the purchaser with inquiry notice.

5. Valuable Consideration

To be protected by a recording statute, the subsequent grantee must show that he is a purchaser, not a donee. Consideration must be of some pecuniary value (love and affection is not valuable consideration). Property received as security for an antecedent debt is not sufficient. A purchaser is protected by a recording statute only after he pays consideration. Thus, even if the deed was delivered and recorded before the consideration was paid, a purchaser will not prevail over deeds recorded before he paid the consideration.

6. Those Protected by Recording Acts

Only BFPs are protected from the claims of a prior transferee under "notice" and "race-notice" statutes. To be a BFP, a person must be a purchaser, without notice and pay valuable consideration.

a) Purchasers

All statutes protect purchasers (of the fee or lesser estate). Mortgagees for value are purchasers. Donees, heirs, and devisees are not protected because they do not give value.

b) Judgment Creditors

Most states permit a plaintiff who obtains a money judgment to place a judgment lien on the defendant's real property. The majority, however, hold that such a judgment creditor is not protected by the recording statute against a prior unrecorded conveyance by the defendant.

c) Purchaser from Heir

A purchaser from an heir or devisee of the record owner is protected against prior unrecorded conveyances of the record owner (now deceased).

d) Transferees from Bona Fide Purchaser--Shelter Rule

A person who takes from a BFP will prevail against any interest the transferor-BFP would have prevailed against. This is true even if the transferee had actual notice of a prior unrecorded conveyance.

e) Recorder's Mistakes

An instrument is recorded when the purchaser files it with the recorder's office, regardless of whether it is thereafter properly indexed. A subsequent purchaser is charged with notice of a mis-indexed instrument, but has a cause of action against the recorder's office.

f) Effect of Recording Unacknowledged Instrument

An unacknowledged instrument is not entitled to recordation, and it does not give a subsequent purchaser constructive notice.

F. Crops (Emblements)

Generally, the conveyance of land includes the conveyance of all crops growing on it. Exceptions: (i) crops that have already been harvested or severed from the land; and, (ii) crops planted by a tenant during the term of the tenancy as long as the tenancy was for an uncertain duration and was terminated without fault on the part of the tenant.

VII. RIGHTS INCIDENTAL TO OWNERSHIP OF LAND (NATURAL RIGHTS)

A. Generally

An owner of real property has the exclusive right to use and possess the property's surface, airspace, and soil.

B. Rights to Lateral and Subjacent Support of Land

1. Lateral Support

Ownership of land comes with the right to lateral support in the land's natural state by adjoining land.

a) SUPPORT OF LAND IN NATURAL STATE

An adjacent landowner is strictly liable if he excavates his land so as to cause adjacent land to subside (slip or cave-in).

b) SUPPORT OF LAND WITH BUILDINGS

An adjacent landowner is strictly liable for damage to buildings caused by his excavation if the land would have collapsed in its natural state. Otherwise, he is liable for such damage only if he was negligent.

2. SUBJACENT SUPPORT

An underground occupant of land, such as a mining company, must support the surface and buildings that existed when the subjacent estate was created. The owner is only liable for damage for subsequently erected buildings upon a showing of negligence.

C. WATER RIGHTS

Courts apply different rules to watercourses, ground water, and surface waters:

1. WATERCOURSES (STREAMS, RIVERS, AND LAKES)

The two doctrines courts use when determining allocation of water in watercourses are the riparian doctrine and the prior appropriation doctrine:

a) RIPARIAN DOCTRINE

Those who own the land bordering the watercourse, own the water. Riparian rights attach to all contiguous tracts held by the same owner as long as the land abuts the water. Riparian owners can use the water only in connection with the riparian parcel.

(1) Natural Flow Theory

A riparian owner can be enjoined from using the water in a way that substantially or materially decreases the water's quantity, quality, or velocity.

(2) Reasonable Use Theory

All riparians have a right of "reasonable use" of the water, and one owner cannot be enjoined from use unless that use substantially interferes with the use of other riparian owners. In determining "reasonable" use, courts balance the utility of the owner's use against the gravity of the harm. Six factors are helpful in making this determination: (i) alteration of flow; (ii) purpose of use; (iii) pollution; (iv) extent of use; (v) destination of water taken; and (vi) miscellaneous conduct that may give rise to litigation.

(3) Natural Flow Theory vs. Artificial Use

Under either theory, natural uses (consumption, gardening) prevail over artificial uses (irrigation, manufacturing).

b) PRIOR APPROPRIATION DOCTRINE

Individuals acquire rights by actual use. Appropriation rights are determined by priority of beneficial use. The first person to use or divert water for beneficial use can acquire rights to the water. He can lose it by abandoning it.

2. GROUND WATER (PERCOLATING WATER)

Courts use four doctrines when determining rights in diffuse underground water recovered through wells:

a) **Absolute Ownership Doctrine**

This doctrine is followed by about 12 eastern states. The owner of overlying land owns the water and can take all the water she wishes, for any purpose, including export.

b) **Reasonable Use Doctrine**

About 25 states follow this doctrine. The overlying landowner owns the water but may only take it for export if doing so does not harm other owners who have rights in the same aquifer.

c) **Appropriative Rights Doctrine**

This doctrine is followed in some western states. The rights to the ground water are determined by priority of use (not ownership of overlying land).

3. **Surface Waters**

A landowner can use surface water (water without a channel that passes over land such as rainfall, seepage) within her boundaries for any purpose she desires. Questions on surface water usually concern liability for changing natural flow by dikes, drains, etc. Whether the landowner is liable depends on the theory the state follows:

a) **Natural Flow (Civil Law) Theory**

Under this theory, followed by half of the states, owners cannot alter natural drainage patterns. Most states have "softened" the rule to allow for "reasonable changes."

b) **Common Enemy Theory**

Under this theory, followed by most of the other states, an owner can take protective measures to get rid of the water (e.g., dikes). But many courts have modified the rule to prohibit unnecessary damage to others' lands.

c) **Reasonable Use Theory**

There is a growing trend among courts to apply this theory, in which the court balances the utility of the use against the gravity of the harm.

d) **Redirecting Surface Water**

The above theories apply to redirecting surface water. A landowner can capture (by a dam or in barrels) as much surface water as he wishes and divert it for any purpose on or off the land. Owners below have no cause of action unless the landowner maliciously diverted the water.

D. **Right in Airspace**

A landowner does not have an exclusive right to airspace above a parcel, but she is entitled to freedom from excessive noise.

E. **Right to Exclude – Remedies of Possessor**

The possessor of real property has the right to exclude others. His remedies for invasions include actions for:

1. Trespass (land invaded by tangible physical object);
2. Private nuisance (land invaded by intangibles such as odors or noise);
3. Continuing trespass (land repeatedly invaded by trespasser); and
4. Ejectment or unlawful detainer to remove a trespasser or tenant. This action can be joined with a demand for money damages.

VIII. SECURITY INTERESTS IN LAND

A. TYPES OF INTEREST

1. MORTGAGE

The borrower is the mortgagor. The lender is the mortgagee. On default, the lender can realize on the mortgaged real estate only by having a judicial foreclosure sale.

2. DEED OF TRUST

The individual who transfers legal title in real property is the trustor. He transfers a deed of trust to a third-party trustee, who is usually closely connected to the lender (the beneficiary). On default, the lender will instruct the trustee to foreclose the deed of trust by sale.

3. INSTALLMENT LAND CONTRACT

An installment purchaser obtains legal title only when he pays the contract price in full. These contracts usually have forfeiture clauses that allow the vendor to cancel the contract upon default, retake possession, and keep all money paid.

4. ABSOLUTE DEED

This deed conveys an unrestricted title to a property. If it is conveyed for security purposes, courts may treat it as an "equitable" mortgage, which is treated as any other mortgage (creditor must foreclose by judicial action).

5. SALE-LEASEBACK

A landowner may sell a property and then lease it back from the purchaser for a period of time with the proceeds. Like an absolute deed, a court may treat it as a disguised mortgage.

B. TRANSFERS BY MORTGAGEE AND MORTGAGOR

1. TRANSFER BY MORTGAGEE

a) TRANSFER OF MORTGAGE WITHOUT NOTE

Some states hold that a note is automatically transferred with the mortgage, unless the mortgagee-transfers or expressly reserves the rights to the note. In these states, the transferee can file an equitable action to compel a transfer of the note. In other states, a mortgage without a note is void because the note is the principal evidence of the debt.

b) TRANSFER OF NOTE WITHOUT MORTGAGE

If a note is transferred without a mortgage, the mortgage will automatically follow with a separate assignment unless the mortgagee-transferee expressly reserves the rights to the mortgage.

c) METHODS OF TRANSFERRING THE NOTE

The mortgagor-transferor may transfer the note by endorsing it and delivering it to the transferee, or a separate document of assignment.

2. TRANSFER BY MORTGAGOR-GRANTEE TAKES SUBJECT TO MORTGAGE

A grantee of mortgaged property takes the property subject to the mortgage.

a) ASSUMPTION

A grantee who signs an assumption agreement becomes primarily liable to the lender; the original mortgagor is secondarily liable as a surety. If no assumption agreement is signed, the grantee is not personally liable on the loan, and the original mortgagor remains primarily and personally liable. However, if the grantee does not pay, the loan may be foreclosed, wiping out the grantee's investment. Once a grantee has assumed a mortgage, any modification of the obligation by the grantee and mortgagee discharges the original mortgagor of all liability.

b) Due-on-Sale Clauses

Due-on-sale clauses stipulate that the lender may demand full payment of the loan if the mortgagor transfers any interest in the property without the lender's consent.

3. Possession Before Foreclosure

The mortgagee can foreclose on the mortgage when the mortgagor defaults on the loan. A mortgagee may be able to take possession of the property or begin receiving the rents from the property before foreclosing.

a) Theories of Title

Whether the mortgagee can take possession before foreclosing depends on the state. Most states follow either the title or the lien theory:

(1) The Lien Theory

The mortgagee is the holder of a security interest and the mortgagor is the owner of the land until foreclosure. Thus, the mortgagee may not take possession before foreclosure.

(2) The Title Theory

The mortgagee has legal title until the mortgage has been satisfied or foreclosed, and the mortgagee is entitled to possession upon demand at any time.

(3) The Intermediate Theory

The mortgagor has legal title until default. Upon default, the mortgagee has legal title and may demand possession when the mortgagor defaults.

b) Mortgagor Consent and Abandonment

The mortgagee may take possession if the mortgagor consents or abandons the property.

c) Risks of Mortgagee in Possession

Most mortgagees do not take possession because there are liability risks involving the duty to account for rents, the duty to manage the property in a prudent manner, and potential tort liability for those injured on the property.

d) Receiverships

Most mortgagees attempt to intercept rents before foreclosure by asking the court to appoint a receiver to manage the property, which courts will generally do upon a showing: (i) that waste is occurring; (ii) that the value of the property is inadequate to secure the debt; and (iii) that the mortgagor is insolvent.

4. Foreclosure

Almost all states require foreclosure by sale, where the mortgagee sells the property to satisfy the debt in whole or part. This is usually done by auction and the lender is permitted to bid on the property.

a) Redemption in Equity

The mortgagor may redeem the property by paying the amount due any time before the foreclosure sale. This right cannot be waived.

b) **Statutory Redemption**

About half of the states allow the mortgagor to redeem the property for some fixed period (e.g., six months) after a foreclosure sale.

5. **Priorities**

Priority is usually determined by reference to the time it was placed on the property. While foreclosure does not destroy any interests senior to the interest being foreclosed, it generally destroys all junior interests. But a failure to include a junior interest holder in a foreclosure action preserves that party's interest.

a) **Modification of Priority**

Priority among mortgages generally follows the chronological order in which they were placed on the property. This priority may be changed by: (i) the operation of a recording statute if a prior mortgagee fails to record; (ii) a subordination agreement between a senior and junior mortgagee; (iii) a purchase money mortgage; (iv) the modification of a senior mortgage (junior mortgage has priority over the modification); or (v) the granting of optional future advances by a mortgagee with notice of a junior lien (junior lien has priority over advances).

b) **Purchase Money Mortgages**

A purchase money mortgage ("PMM") is a mortgage given by the seller in exchange for funds used to purchase the property. PMMs have priority over non-PMMs executed around the same time even if the non-PMM was recorded first. A seller's PMM has priority over a third-party's PMM. If there are two third-party PMMs, priority is determined by whichever came first. Usually two PMMs have notice of the other's existence; thus, the recording acts are of no use in determining priority.

6. **Proceeds of Sale**

Proceeds of a sale are first applied to the expenses of the sale, attorney fees, and court costs; then applied to the principal and accrued interest on the foreclosed loan; next to any other junior interests in the order of their priority; and finally to the mortgagor.

7. **Deficiency Judgments**

If the sale proceeds do not satisfy the mortgage debt, the mortgagee retains a personal cause of action against the mortgagor for the deficiency.

C. **Installment Land Contracts**

Most installment contracts provide that the vendor's remedy for default is forfeiture rather than foreclosure. To avoid such a harsh result, courts will use the following theories:

1. **Equity of Redemption**

Several courts give the purchaser a grace period in which to pay the accelerated full balance of the contract and keep the land.

2. **Restitution**

A number of courts grant a forfeiture but require the vendor to refund to the purchaser any amount by which his payments exceed the vendor's damages.

3. **Treat as a Mortgage**

A few courts treat installment contracts as mortgages and require a judicial foreclosure sale.

4. **Waiver**

Courts have also held that a vendor's pattern of accepting late payments constitutes a waiver of the right of strict performance. To reinstate strict performance, the vendor must send the purchaser a notice of his intention to do so and allow a reasonable time for the purchaser to make up any late payments.

5. Election of Remedies

The vendor can choose only one remedy (damages or specific performance).

TORTS

Table of Contents

I. INTENTIONAL TORTS

Generally, a person acts with intent to cause an outcome. General requirements for torts relating to intentional harm to persons are: (i) an intention to cause harm and which harm is the likely outcome of that action; and (ii) recklessness – being aware of the risk of harm caused by the intended action.

A. To the Person

1. Battery

Battery is the intended harmful offensive contact with another person. To recover for battery, a plaintiff is required to show: (i) harmful or offensive contact to the plaintiff's person; (ii) intent; and (iii) causation.

a) Harmful or Offensive Contact

A contact is judged by a reasonable person standard and is always considered offensive if it has not been consented to. The usual interaction of everyday life does not constitute harmful or offensive contact. The contact can be direct (strike) or indirect (trap).

(1) Volitional Act

A volitional act is required by the defendant for all intentional torts.

b) Person

Includes the plaintiff's physical being and clothing and anything else that may be connected to them on that particular occasion.

c) Intent

May be either: (i) specific – where the goal is to bring about a specific consequence; or (ii) general – where the actor knows with substantial certainty that some harm will result from his tortious conduct.

(1) Transferred Intent

The transferred intent doctrine applies when the defendant intends to commit a tort against one person but instead: (i) commits a different tort against that person; (ii) commits the same tort as intended but against a different person; or (iii) commits a different tort against a different person. In such cases, the intent to commit a certain tort against one person is transferred to the tort actually committed or to the person actually injured

Applies to Battery, Assault, False Imprisonment, and Trespass to Land or Chattel.

d) Causation

The result must have been legally caused by the defendant's act or something set in motion by him. Causation is satisfied if the defendant's conduct was a substantial factor in bringing about the injury.

2. Assault

Whereas battery involves physical contact, assault is the creation of an apprehension of unlawful harmful contact. This is an act by an individual (the defendant) by which he intends to create fear in an individual (the plaintiff) that the plaintiff is about to be harmed. The fear of potential harm is subject to a test of reasonableness, taking into account factors such as the physical state of the plaintiff. What may cause fear in someone who is both elderly and infirm may not be deemed to reasonably cause fear in someone who is young, fit and able-bodied. The elements of assault are: (i) an act by the defendant creating a reasonable apprehension of unlawful physical contact in the plaintiff; (ii) immediate harmful or offensive contact to the plaintiff's person; (iii) intent; and (iv) causation.

a) Reasonable Apprehension

If the defendant has the apparent ability to commit a battery, this will be enough to cause a reasonable apprehension. Words alone are not sufficient as they can negate apprehension.

b) Immediate Harmful or Offensive Contact

The plaintiff must be apprehensive that she is about to become the victim of an immediate battery. If the other person is not aware of the attempt to inflict unlawful harm, before it is terminated, a tort will not be committed.

c) Intent & Causation

As defined above.

3. False Imprisonment

False imprisonment is either a deliberate act or omission by one person (the defendant) intending to confine another (the plaintiff) to a defined area or place; his act directly or indirectly results in such confinement; and, the other is aware and is harmed by it. Again, it must be evidenced that the defendant showed intent to this effect. The elements of this tort are: (i) an act or omission by the defendant that confines or restrains the plaintiff to a bounded area; (ii) intent; and (iii) causation.

a) Confinement

Confinement may be demonstrated by physical barriers and the physical force of one person against another, for example, one individual bars the way of another. A threat of force that causes the plaintiff to fear violence upon leaving a designated area even though there is no actual, physical restraint (e.g., a locked door) is also sufficient to demonstrate confinement. The confinement or threat must be current and present; a future event or threat of a future event is not sufficient to demonstrate confinement. Sufficient acts of restraint include: (i) physical barriers; (ii) physical force; (iii) threats of force; (iv) failure to release; and (v) invalid use of legal authority. The plaintiff must know of the confinement.

b) Bounded Area

This is an area that is inescapable by the plaintiff, whether it is because of a physical or other type of restriction. There must be no reasonable means of escape known to the plaintiff – if there is and the plaintiff is aware of it, there will be no unlawful confinement. Further, it is not an unlawful confinement to prevent a person taking a particular route when there is a suitable alternative route available to him.

4. Intentional Infliction of Emotional Distress

This is conduct by the defendant toward another that is extreme and outrageous and with which the defendant is intent on causing emotional distress and/or is reckless in the outcome of his actions in this regard. Further, if the emotional harm causes bodily harm, liability will attach for that harm. Also, the plaintiff must be able to show damage. The elements of this tort are: (i) an act by the defendant amounting to extreme and outrageous conduct; (ii) intent or recklessness; (iii) causation; and (iv) damages.

a) Extreme and Outrageous Conduct

In general, this is conduct that transcends all bounds of human decency. This also applies to conduct that is not normally considered extreme or outrageous but becomes so either because of the identity or characteristics of the defendant, the physical and mental characterization of the plaintiff, or because it is continuous in nature.

b) Intent or Recklessness

If the defendant gives no consideration to the effect of his actions, then he will demonstrate the requisite level of intent.

c) Causation

Causation is demonstrated when the plaintiff suffers severe emotional distress because the defendant with intent causes physical harm to a third party. The third party must be a close relative of the plaintiff and the defendant must be aware of this relationship at the time. The plaintiff must also be present during the assault/battery. The plaintiff also must be a witness to it.

d) Damages

There must be actual evidence of damages in order to sustain a claim for severe emotional distress, as token or minimal damages will not support this claim.

B. To Property

Intentional harm to land or chattels

1. Trespass to Land

Consists of: (i) actual physical entry by the defendant onto the plaintiff's real property which is in the possession of the plaintiff, or causes a third party or thing to do so; (ii) the defendant remains on the land; or (iii) the defendant fails to remove from the land something which he is under a duty to remove; and (iv) causation.

a) Physical Entry

Physical invasion is entry by a person or object. If the entry takes place by something intangible and remains upon the land (e.g., noise), the plaintiff may find that they have instead a case for nuisance.

b) Real Property

Real property is defined as the structure of an object, its surface, the air space around it, and the underground depths to what is defined as a reasonable level (e.g., mineral rights).

c) Intent

To evidence intent, it is not necessary for the defendant to show that he did not know the land or property belonged to someone else; he merely needs to intend to enter it.

d) Causation

As defined above.

e) Potential Plaintiffs

This includes the owner of the land and anyone in possession of the land who may be distinct from the owner (e.g., a tenant).

A person who intentionally enters upon land in the possession of another is liable for trespass even though his trespass causes no harm to the land. Furthermore, a person who enters upon the land in the possession of another in the mistaken belief that he is entitled to do so, whether in law or fact, is liable for trespass provided the mistake has not been caused by the conduct of the possessor.

2. Trespass to Chattels

Trespass to chattels is defined as: (i) an act by the defendant that interferes with the plaintiff's right of possession in a chattel by either taking possession of the chattel or otherwise interfering with it while in the possession of another; (ii) intent; (iii) causation; and, (iv) damages.

a) Interference

Interference may be shown by the following:
(i) Intermeddling: directly damaging the chattel by intentional physical contact; or (ii) Dispossession: depriving the plaintiff of his lawful right of possession of the chattel.

b) Intent & Causation

Intention is present when something is done for the purpose of interfering with the chattel by using it or otherwise intermeddling with it in contravention of the possessor's rights. It is irrelevant if the wrongdoer acts under a mistake of fact or law.

c) Damages

Actual damages, not necessarily to the chattel, but at least to a possessory right, are required. Liability attaches if:

(1) the lawful owner of the chattel is dispossessed;
(2) the chattel is damaged;
(3) the lawful owner is deprived of use of the chattel.

3. Conversion

Conversion is the assumption of ownership / control over a chattel to the detriment of a lawful owner, and which may require the wrongdoer to pay the owner the full value of the chattel. Conversion consists of: (i) an act by the defendant that interferes with the plaintiff's right of possession in a chattel to the extent that it warrants requiring the defendant to pay the chattel's full value; (ii) intent; and (iii) causation.

a) Acts of Conversion

Acts include theft, an incorrect transfer of title, (including, for example, a purported sale of a chattel the seller does not own and therefore has no power to sell), retaining an item (e.g., after a loan), or damaging or changing an item in some material way or misusing it.

b) Seriousness of Interference

The longer the plaintiff is deprived of the item and the more it is used by the defendant, the more likely it is that the tort of conversion will be demonstrated. Only items that have a physical form or have been converted into a physical form can be the subject of interference. **Note:** In certain cases, it may be relevant to consider the less serious tort of trespass to chattels where the measure of damages will reflect the diminished value of the chattel as opposed to the full value of the chattel, in conversion.

c) Intent & Causation

As defined above.

d) Potential Plaintiff

This is any plaintiff who is in physical possession of the chattel or a plaintiff who has the right of immediate possession of the chattel.

e) Remedies

The remedies include reimbursement for fair market value at the time of the conversion or the item may be returned to the plaintiff under a right called replevin. The right of replevin entitles the plaintiff to compensation for any financial losses resulting from the absence of that item.

C. Defenses

1. Consent

If the plaintiff gives permission to the defendant to behave in a particular way, which can be manifested by action or inaction, then this acts as an acceptance of the defendant's behavior and **MAY** therefore be relied upon by the defendant as a defense. The consent must be valid and the defendant must stay within the boundaries of the consent.

a) Express Consent

If the plaintiff gives express agreement to the defendant's conduct, then the defendant will not be liable at law unless the plaintiff is mistaken in giving his consent and the defendant knows of the mistake. Additionally, if the defendant uses duress or deceives the plaintiff by some fraudulent act into giving consent, it is not valid.

b) Implied Consent

Consent is implied legally when the life of a person is at stake or there is a lesser but nevertheless important interest in the person or property.

c) Apparent Consent

is subject to the reasonable person test: that which an ordinary person would assume from the circumstances of the particular situation and the plaintiff's behavior. Such that even though actual consent is absent, the words or conduct of the plaintiff may be sufficient to manifest consent entitling the defendant to rely upon it.

d) Capacity

An individual who lacks mental capacity, whether by age or infirmity, is not capable of giving consent.

e) Scope

The defendant must remain within the boundaries of the consent; straying outside these may result in liability:

(1) A conditional consent to enter land only permits entry upon the land pursuant to that condition or such other restriction that might have been put in place, e.g., a time restriction;

(2) Similarly, a consent which restricts entry upon land to a particular area does not permit entry upon any other part of the land.

2. Self-Defense, Defense of Others, and Defense of Property

a) Self-Defense

Reasonable action may be taken to protect against attack or injury but the act of defense must be commensurate with the level of threat. It is possible to be mistaken about the immediate danger but a test of reasonableness is applied to this. Where the person reasonably believes that the other's conduct threatens him with death or serious bodily harm, then the right to use force does extend to including the possibility of causing death or serious bodily harm.

b) Defense of Others

One person may defend another using force if he has a reasonable belief that the individual he is defending would have taken the same action himself. In such circumstances, it is necessary for the intervening person to reasonably believe that the circumstances would give the third person the right of self defense and that his intervention is necessary for the protection of the third person.

c) Defense of Property

Reasonable force, not intended to cause death or serious bodily harm, is permitted to defend real and personal property and to prevent the commission of a tort. If possible, a request to cease the action must be made to the defendant, subject to a test of danger to the plaintiff or general futility. The defense is only available prior to and during the commission of any tortious act by the defendant or in the very immediate aftermath.

(1) Reasonable Force

One may not use force causing death or serious bodily injury unless the invasion also entails a serious threat of bodily harm.

(2) **Mistake**

The act of intrusion is subject to a test of reasonable mistake unless the defendant has a right of privilege that will override the protection of the property. The test of mistake is not allowed if the defendant is reasonably led to believe that there is no right of privilege.

(3) **Public Safety**

Entry upon the land of another may be permissible if it is reasonably believed it is necessary to do so for the purpose of averting an imminent threat to public safety, e.g., threat of flood. It may also be permissible to enter the land of another where to do so is necessary for self protection or for protecting the landowner, provided the entry is done reasonably both in time and manner.

(4) **Consent**

If a landowner consents to a person entering upon his land for a particular purpose, once that purpose is completed, the consent expires and the right to remain upon the land or to reenter the land no longer applies.

d) **RE-ENTRY ONTO LAND**

There are modern processes to allow re-entry onto property and therefore, the old common law remedies such as force no longer apply. The correct legal procedures have to be followed.

e) **RECAPTURE OF CHATTELS**

If a chattel passes to another lawfully, then it may only be recovered using methods that are non-violent. If the possession of the chattel has passed illegally, then force may be used to recover it but this force must be reasonable.

(1) **Demand**

In the first instance, a request must be made to return the item before any further action may be taken.

(2) **Innocent Party**

If the chattel has passed to an innocent third party, then force cannot be used to recover the item from that individual.

(3) **Entry**

If the chattel is physically located on land belonging to the defendant (i.e., the person who has illegally taken the item), then the owner of the chattel may enter the land without this constituting trespass in order to take the item back. The reclaim of the item must be conducted in a reasonable manner and this must be preceded by a request to return the chattel in the first instance.

(4) **Owner's Fault**

If a chattel is on someone else's property because of the negligence of the owner, then the owner of the item has no right at law to enter that land in order to recover it. The appropriate legal processes must be followed.

(5) **Mistake**

Reasonable mistake is not normally applied to the right of recovery of chattels and the land on which they may be located.

(6) **Shopkeepers**

A shop owner or its representative (e.g., the manager) may detain an individual if they suspect that he has been shoplifting. For this privilege to apply, there must be: (i) a reasonable belief as to the fact of theft; (ii) reasonable detention and only non-deadly force; and, (iii) a reasonable period of time for the detention for the purpose of investigating.

3. Privilege of Arrest

a) Invasion of Land

The privilege of arrest carries with it the ability to enter the land of another in order to affect the arrest.

b) Subsequent Misconduct

Although the arrest may attract privilege, the arrestor must act in a reasonable manner and so could be liable for any subsequent misconduct.

c) Misdemeanor

Privilege applies only in the event of a breach of the peace and the act must have taken place in front of the defendant.

d) Felony

There is a difference in the standard applied to a felony depending on whether the arrestor is a citizen or a police officer. The citizen must be able to satisfy a reasonable test that the person he arrested has committed the felony. The police officer must be able to demonstrate that he reasonably believes that a felony has taken place and that the person he has arrested has committed it. An officer/citizen can use a degree of force reasonably necessary to make the arrest. Deadly force is only available when the suspect poses a serious threat of harm.

4. Necessity

Necessity is only a defense to property torts. There are two types of necessity: public and private. Public necessity is for the public good. Private necessity is to protect the person or property of an individual. Interference is permitted when it is deemed reasonably necessary to avoid injury from a natural or other force and the act of invasion is less serious or intrusive than the possible damage that may occur if it were not undertaken.

5. Discipline

A parent, teacher or other person in loco parentis may discipline a child but the level of force must be reasonable.

II. NUISANCE

A "nuisance" may be either a private nuisance or a public nuisance. Examples of nuisance include: Noise; Smoke; Noxious fumes.

A. Private Nuisance

This is a substantial and unreasonable interference with a private individual's use of or enjoyment of property that is in the possession of that individual or which he has a right to possess but which does not constitute trespass to that property. Possession/interest, is construed in a broad sense in this context.

1. Substantial Interference

Substantial interference is interference that may be deemed to be offensive, inconvenient or annoying, subject to the reasonable man test. If the plaintiff shows an unusual predisposition or sensitivity to the interference, then this is not classified as substantial interference, or if his use of his own property is specialized in some way.

2. Unreasonable Interference

The test of reasonableness means that the level of nuisance must outweigh the utility of the defendant's conduct.

3. Compare to Trespass to Land

Trespass is a physical interference with the landowner's possession. In nuisance, the interference is not physical but instead disturbs in some way the landowner's use and/or enjoyment of the land so that the pleasure/enjoyment that the landowner would normally expect to enjoy from the occupation of the land is impaired or destroyed.

B. Public Nuisance

Public nuisance is an unreasonable interference with a right common to the general public that affects the community at large. Recovery of damages by a private individual is not available for public nuisance unless the private individual suffers a unique damage that does not affect the rest of the community. It is not sufficient for him to have suffered the same harm or injury as everyone else but to a greater extent. Additionally, a public official may have authority on behalf of the state or other public body to take action to abate the public nuisance.

C. Remedies

1. Damages

Compensatory and punitive damages may be awarded where appropriate. If the complaint is of a public nuisance, in order for an individual to succeed in a claim for damages, a plaintiff must show that he has suffered damage over and above that suffered by the general public. Further, damages will be ordered after the event, whereas an injunction may be granted where harm is threatened or before any harm or injury is sustained.

2. Injunctive Relief

Injunctive relief is available where damages are not or are otherwise inadequate. The Court will consider the relative hardships but no deference to the defendant will be provided where there is intentional wrongdoing. Consider whether the effect of the nuisance is so harmful and unreasonable that it must be stopped. If it is, an injunction will be granted.

3. Abatement by Self-Help

Abatement by self-help is available after notice has been given to the defendant and he has refused to act. Any force used must be reasonable and commensurate with the original act. In public nuisance, the only claimants, whether public or private, are those who have suffered some unique damage.

D. Defenses

1. Legislative Authority

Legislative authority may be a partial defense in nuisance – the nuisance complained of is authorized by appropriate legislation.

2. Conduct of Others

No one person is liable for all damage caused by concurrent acts and those of others.

3. Contributory Negligence

Contributory negligence is not usually a defense to nuisance unless the plaintiff's case relies on a theory of negligence.

4. Coming to the Nuisance

The general rule is that coming to a nuisance will not defeat a plaintiff's claim. It is possible to come to a nuisance and still pursue an action for nuisance. The exception to this may be if the plaintiff is seeking to make a claim of harassment.

III. ECONOMIC HARM AND DIGNITARY INTERESTS

A. DEFAMATION

Defamation is the communication of any intentional false communication that has the effect of harming another's reputation, thereby reducing the respect in which they are held and comprises: (i) Libel: defined as defamation by written / printed words, pictures or other permanent form; and (ii) Slander: defined as defamation by spoken words or some other transient (as opposed to permanent) form.

The law of defamation is actionable under common law, subject to constitutional limitations, upon a showing of: (i) defamatory language of or concerning the plaintiff, i.e., language that is false (written or spoken, as the case may be, and unprivileged); (ii) publication thereof by the defendant to a third person; and
(iii) damage to the plaintiff's reputation. If the defamation is a matter of public concern, the Constitution requires the plaintiff to prove two additional elements: (v) falsity of the defamatory language; and (vi) fault on the part of the defendant.

1. DEFAMATORY LANGUAGE OF OR CONCERNING PLAINTIFF

Defamatory language is language that damages the reputation of the plaintiff. Verbal insults are not sufficient to evidence reputational damage. The plaintiff must demonstrate at law that a third party would reasonably associate the alleged defamatory statement with the plaintiff. It is possible that additional evidence can be offered to link the statement to the plaintiff. If the statement is made about a small group, each member may establish that the statement refers to them. If the statement is made about a large group, no member can prove the statement refers to them.

2. PUBLICATION

Publication means communication of the defamation to someone other than the plaintiff, made intentionally or negligently. Liability attaches to the author, speaker, primary publishers, and one selling papers or playing tapes only if he knows or should know of the defamatory content.

3. DAMAGE TO PLAINTIFF'S REPUTATION

The type of damage that may be claimed is specific to the type of defamation being claimed. Specifically, libel, which involves the publication of the defamatory statement, carries with it a presumption of general damage, and special damages need not be proven. However, in the case of slander, which is a spoken defamation, the plaintiff must prove special damages, unless the statement falls within defamation-slander per se, such that it defames the plaintiff on its face and extrinsic evidence is not required to explain the statement's defamatory nature: (i) the slander adversely reflects on one's conduct in a business, trade profession or occupation; (ii) an individual has a loathsome disease; (iii) an individual is or was guilty of a crime involving moral turpitude; or (iv) a woman is unchaste.

4. FIRST AMENDMENT PROTECTIONS FOR "PUBLIC CONCERN"

Falsity: The plaintiff must prove that the statement is false.
Fault on Defendant's Part: The fault the plaintiff must prove depends on the plaintiff's status.

a) PUBLIC OFFICIALS / FIGURE

Under New York Times v. Sullivan, it was established that public officials are persons who have substantial responsibility or control over the conduct of government affairs, e.g., police officer, or Assistant District Attorney. Malice, which is knowledge that the statement was false, or the maker was reckless as to whether it was false (for example, altering a quotation constitutes malice where the meaning of the quotation is changed) must be proved in defamation proceedings brought by public officials and public figures. A "public figure" is someone who has achieved fame or notoriety.

b) Private Citizens

Where the plaintiff is a private individual, he must show that the defendant was negligent with respect to the falseness of the alleged defamation only if it is a matter of public concern. Where the defendant is shown to be negligent, only damages for actual injury are recoverable. However, if the plaintiff can demonstrate malice on the part of the defendant, damages may be presumed and the plaintiff may then recover punitive damages.

5. Defenses

a) Consent of the Plaintiff

The consent of the plaintiff provides a complete defense to a claim of defamation.

b) Truth

Truth may also be offered as a complete defense by the defendant in cases where it is not necessary for the plaintiff to demonstrate falseness (i.e., in a private matter).

c) Privilege

A defendant who has made a defamatory statement may be able to rely upon "privilege" as a ground of defense, in which context the defendant is not arguing that the statement is true or that it did not harm the plaintiff's reputation, but that in the circumstances in which it was made, he cannot be held liable because it is protected by either absolute privilege or qualified privilege.

d) Absolute Privilege

Absolute privilege protects a statement even if it was made with actual malice, i.e., knowing it to be false or recklessly without caring whether it be true or false. The defendant may have an absolute privilege in the following instances: (i) comments made during the course of judicial proceedings; (ii) legislative sessions; (iii) comments made by federal officials; and (iv) comments made between spouses.

e) Qualified Privilege

Qualified privilege differs from absolute privilege in that it does not protect statements made with actual malice but will protect statements made by a defendant who reasonably believed it was true when he made it. The defendant may have a qualified privilege in the following instances: (i) reports of official proceedings; and (ii) statements in the interest of the public. If the statement is deemed to be in the public interest, the defendant may claim qualified privilege in certain circumstances – namely defense of his own actions, defense of his property or reputation, statements which can be shown to be in the interest of the recipient and a general, common public interest. The privilege is lost when made not within the scope of the privilege or made with malice. The defendant bears the burden to show that:

(1) he had a good faith reason to believe a statement was true;
(2) he had a personal or professional interest in knowing the information in the statement; and
(3) he shared it only with others who had the same interest in knowing the information in the statement.

B. Invasion of Right to Privacy

1. Appropriation of Picture or Name

Such occurs when the defendant uses the name or image of the plaintiff for personal or commercial gain. The plaintiff must show that the defendant has used his name or image without his permission and to the defendant's personal or commercial advantage. Nominal damages available.

2. Intrusion upon Affairs or Seclusion

Comprises intrusion upon the privacy or the private affairs of another by physical, electronic or other means, e.g., computer hacking. The act of prying or intruding must be objectionable to a reasonable person and be in an area where privacy would be expected. The intrusion must be into something private. Public photographs are not actionable.

3. Publication of Facts Placing Plaintiff in False Light

False light exists where views or actions are attributed to the plaintiff, which he either does not hold or did not take and which put him in a false light with the public. To recover, the plaintiff must show the publication of information placing the plaintiff in a false light that is offensive to a reasonable person under the circumstances. If the matter is in the public interest, malice by the defendant must be proven. Generally, a plaintiff will need to establish:

a) a publication by the defendant (remember to consider libel also);
b) made with actual malice (see *New York Times v. Sullivan*);
c) he is placed in a false light; and
d) is offensive/embarrassing to a reasonable person.

Note: that in distinction to defamation, the plaintiff does not have to show actual harm or damage.

4. Public Disclosure of Private Facts

Public disclosure of private facts involves publication of the plaintiff's private facts which are not of public concern, and which is highly offensive to a reasonable person. Liability may attach even if the statement is true. Malice and fault must be proven if the matter is of public concern.

a) Causation

There must be a direct and clear link between the defendant's conduct and the invasion of the plaintiff's privacy.

b) Damages

The plaintiff does not need to demonstrate special damages; it is sufficient to evidence mental anguish and emotional distress.

c) Defenses

Consent, truth and good faith are not valid defenses.

d) Personal

These rights are personal and do not apply to family members or corporations.

C. Misrepresentation

A person who sells or distributes products, who in the course of doing so makes a fraudulent, negligent or innocent misrepresentation of a material fact about the product, is liable to persons or property for harm caused by the misrepresentation.

1. Intentional (Fraud/Deceit)

Intentional misrepresentation is defined as: (i) misrepresentation; (ii) scienter; (iii) intent; (iv) causation; (v) justifiable reliance; and (vi) damages.

a) Misrepresentation

Affirmative misrepresentation of a material fact. Silence is not enough.

b) Scienter

Scienter is defined as making a statement knowing it to be false or knowing that it lacks any basis in fact.

c) Intent

The defendant must intend that the plaintiff rely on the misrepresentation either in the committal of an act or by refraining to act.

d) Justifiable Reliance

There must be a justifiable reliance by the plaintiff based on a statement of fact, not opinion.

e) Damages

The plaintiff must suffer pecuniary loss.

2. Negligent Misrepresentation

Negligent misrepresentation is shown where there is a: (i) misrepresentation by the defendant in a business or professional capacity; (ii) breach of duty toward a particular plaintiff; (iii) causation; (iv) justifiable reliance; and (v) damages. This is typically found in commercial settings. Liability will attach only where reliance by a particular plaintiff could be contemplated.

D. Misuse of Legal Proceedings

1. Malicious Prosecution

Malicious prosecution (i.e., the pursuit of a lawsuit against another and which is without merit) is defined as: (i) the institution of criminal/civil proceedings against the plaintiff; (ii) termination in the plaintiff's favor; (iii) absence of probable cause for prior proceeding (insufficient facts for a reasonable person to believe the guilt or liability); (iv) improper purpose or malice; and (v) damages (pecuniary loss is not required).

2. Abuse of Process

A person who uses legal process (civil or criminal) against another person with the intention of achieving a purpose for which it was not intended is liable to that other person for harm caused by the abuse of process. Abuse of process is shown where there is: (i) the use of a legal process or procedure for an improper purpose; or (ii) a definite act or threat against the plaintiff for an improper purpose.

E. Interference with Business

A person who, with intent and acting improperly, interferes with the contractual relationship between the plaintiff and a third party by either preventing performance or causing performance to be more expensive, is liable for the financial loss suffered. Interference with business requires: (i) an existence of a valid contractual relationship between the plaintiff and a third party or a valid business expectancy of the plaintiff; (ii) the defendant's knowledge of the contractual relationship or expectancy; (iii) intentional interference by the defendant inducing a breach or termination or disruption of the contractual relationship or expectancy; and (iv) resulting damage.

1. Privilege

The defendant's conduct may be privileged where it is a proper attempt to obtain business for itself or protect its interest, especially if it concerns prospective business and not existing contracts.

IV. Strict Liability

In certain circumstances, liability will attach to a defendant, notwithstanding an absence of fault and/or intent and which is generally referred to as "strict liability," examples of which include possession of certain animals, and abnormally dangerous activities.

Prima Facie Case: There is a prima facie case for strict liability when: (i) there is an existence of an absolute duty on the part of the defendant to make safe; (ii) there is a breach of that duty; (iii) the breach of duty was the actual and proximate cause of the plaintiff's injury; and (iv) there is damage to the plaintiff's person or property.

A. Liability for Animals

1. Trespassing Animals

An owner or possessor of livestock or other animals (excluding cats and dogs) is strictly liable at law for damage incurred/physical harm caused by the trespassing or wandering of his animals onto the land of another, provided it is reasonably foreseeable.

2. Personal Injuries

a) Strict Liability for Wild Animals

An owner or possessor of a wild animal (i.e., animals that have not been domesticated and but for restraint are likely to cause personal injury) is strictly liable for personal injury caused to licensees and invitees by wild animals, as long as the injured person did nothing to bring about the injury.

b) No Strict Liability for Domestic Animals

An owner is not strictly liable for injury caused by a domestic animal unless that animal has particular issues with its behavior that are not usually common to the breed or species and the owner is aware of this or has reason to know of the propensity.

c) Strict Liability Not Available to Trespassers

Strict liability does not usually apply in the event of trespass and when the owner has not been negligent. However, a landowner may be liable for injury caused by guard dogs on the basis of an intentional tort.

B. Abnormally Dangerous Activities

A person who carries on an abnormally dangerous activity, one that creates a foreseeable and significant risk of physical harm even when reasonable care is exercised, is subject to strict liability for any physical harm arising from that activity. There are three requirements for the application of strict liability to abnormally dangerous activities: (i) the activity must involve risk of serious harm to person or property; (ii) the activity must be one that cannot be performed without risk of serious harm no matter how much care is taken; and (iii) the activity is not commonly engaged in in the particular community (blasting explosives, etc.). No amount of due care on the part of the defendant will relieve him of liability in a strict liability situation.

C. Extent of Liability

The duty of care is to remove or control by making safe the usual dangerous behavior of the animal/activity. The potential plaintiff must be foreseeable.

D. Defenses

Contributory negligence is not a defense if the plaintiff failed to realize the danger or guard against it. The defendant may rely upon contributory negligence, if he can show that: (i) the plaintiff was aware of the danger; (ii) his conduct was unreasonable; and (iii) this conduct was the cause of the failure of the activity to conclude safely. States that apply comparative negligence rules tend to apply these to strict liability cases only.

V. NEGLIGENCE

A person is negligent, if, when carrying out a duty, he fails to exercise proper care commensurate with the duty being performed, and as a result, damage or injury results. Accordingly, persons are required to conduct themselves in accordance with those standards of care applicable to the situation. For example, a surgeon when carrying out surgery is required to exercise that duty of care that equates with the skill and judgment he must display when undertaking the surgery.

Negligence is established where there is: (i) a duty of care on the part of the defendant to conform to a specific standard of conduct for protection of the plaintiff against an unreasonable risk of injury; (ii) the defendant's conduct falls below the duty of care owed to the plaintiff, i.e., there is a breach of the duty of care; (iii) the breach is the actual and proximate cause of the plaintiff's injury; and (iv) damage/injury results from the defendant's breach of the applicable duty of care.

A. Duty of Care

A duty of care is owed to all foreseeable plaintiffs. The extent of the duty is determined by the applicable standard of care.

1. Foreseeable Plaintiff

A duty of care is owed only to foreseeable plaintiffs. However, an issue arises where the defendant breaches a duty to one plaintiff and a second plaintiff is harmed.

a) Zone of Danger

Under the Cardozo view (majority), a second plaintiff can recover if she was located within the zone of danger created by the negligent conduct.

b) Everyone is Foreseeable

Under the Andrews view (minority), a second plaintiff can establish a duty of care which extends from a breach of duty to a first plaintiff, even though that second plaintiff is more remote.

2. Specific Situations

a) Rescuers

Where a defendant negligently puts himself or a third party in danger, a rescuer is deemed to be a reasonably foreseeable plaintiff.

b) Prenatal

A duty of care is owed at law to a fetus, providing the fetus is viable. Parents may recover for a wrongful birth or pregnancy, and recovery would include additional medical costs and damages for pain in pregnancy and childbirth, but childcare costs thereafter are not covered. A child has no right of recovery for wrongful birth.

c) Intended Beneficiaries

Any person for whose economic or financial benefit a legal or business transaction is made may be classified as a foreseeable plaintiff.

3. Standards of Care

a) Basic – Reasonable Person

The reasonable person test is an objective standard against which behavior is measured. The standard is gauged in general terms by what the reasonable person in the street would do in those particular circumstances.

b) Particular Standards

(1) Professionals

A professional is deemed to possess the level of skill and knowledge of an appropriate member of that profession, bearing in mind age and experience and in consequence a higher duty of care is required when carrying out professional duties, e.g., medicine / law. A doctor has a duty to disclose the risks of treatment to enable a patient to make an informed consent.

(2) Children

A child is judged against a level of other children of similar age, intelligence, background and experience, and if the child's conduct does not conform with that "level," liability for negligence will attach. However, if a child is engaged in adult activities, then the appropriate duty of care may be that of an adult in those circumstances, i.e., the child's conduct will be judged against the duty of care to which the adult is subject. Note that a child below the age of five cannot be liable for negligence because such a child is deemed incapable of committing a negligent act.

(3) **Common Carriers and Innkeepers**

These individuals have a higher duty of care to aid or assist patrons and prevent injury from third persons. A common carrier/an innkeeper is under a duty of care to its passengers/guests to take such action (or as the case may be, to cease action) as is reasonable to protect them from unreasonable risk of physical injury.

(4) **Automobile Driver to Guest**

A guest is owed a duty of ordinary care.

(5) **Bailment/Bailment Duties**

Bailment is the placing of property belonging to the bailor in the custody and control of another (the bailee) who has responsibility for its safekeeping and eventual return to the bailor. A bailment may be gratuitous or for hire, although the bailee is still subject to a duty of care, albeit of a lower standard.

(a) For a gratuitous bailment, the bailor must inform the bailee of known defects in the chattel.

(b) For a bailment for hire, the bailor must also inform the bailee of chattel defects of which he is or should be aware.

Bailee Duties: The duty of care for a bailee is dependent on who is to benefit from the bailment. If it is just the bailor, the standard of care is low; if it is for the exclusive benefit of the bailee, then the bailee owes a duty of extraordinary care. The level is pitched somewhere between these two points if the benefit is deemed to be for the mutual benefit of the bailor and the bailee, in which case the bailee will owe a duty of ordinary care.

(6) **Emergency Situations**

The defendant must act as a reasonable person would under the same emergency conditions. This does not apply if the emergency is of the defendant's own making.

c) **OWNERS AND/OR OCCUPIERS OF LAND**

(1) **Duty of Possessor to Those Off Premises**

There is no duty to protect one off the premises from natural conditions on the premises; however, there is a duty for unreasonably dangerous artificial conditions or structures abutting adjacent land. In urban areas, the owner/occupier is liable for damage caused off the premises by trespass on the premises.

(2) **Duty of Possessor to Those On Premises**

(a) **Trespassers**

There is no duty of care owed to an unknown trespasser. If a trespasser is discovered, the landowner has a duty of care to either warn the trespasser of unsafe conditions or make them safe if they involve the risk of serious injury or death to the trespasser. When conducting operations on the land, the landowner must exercise care. Those holding easements or licenses also owe a duty of care to a known trespasser in addition to those owed by the landowner.

(b) **Infant Trespassers – Attractive Nuisance Doctrine**

Landowners owe an ordinary duty of care to avoid reasonably foreseeable risks of harm to children caused by artificial conditions on his property. For this standard to apply, the plaintiff must show: (i) there is a dangerous condition existing on the land that the owner knew, or should have known of; (ii) the owner knew, or should know, that children frequent the area; (iii) the condition is likely to cause injury; and (iv) the expense of remedying the situation is small compared with the magnitude of the risk.

(3) **Duty Owed to Licensees**

A licensee is one who enters land not open to the public with permission. The landowner or their agent has a duty to warn of dangerous conditions which may not be deemed to be evident to the licensee and conduct their operations with reasonable care towards the licensee, although this duty does not extend to include a duty to inspect or repair.

(4) **Duty Owed to Invitees**

People entering land by the invitation of the landowner are termed invitees at law. This may be in a private capacity for business with the landowner or as a member of the public because the land is open to the public. The landowner owes a duty of care to invitees, whether public or private, including a duty to inspect and discover non-apparent unsafe conditions and make them safe. If an invitee exceeds the scope of their invitation, then this status is lost.

(5) **Duty Owed to Users of Recreational Land**

A landowner who allows members of the public to access his land for recreational purposes without charge is not liable for any injuries suffered by those people unless he has deliberately and with malicious intent failed to mitigate or warn against a dangerous condition or activity.

(6) **Modern Trend**

Certain states (albeit a minority) do not accept a distinction between licensees and invitees and simply apply the reasonable person test to dangerous issues present on the land.

d) Duties of Lessor and Lessee of Realty

A lessee has a general duty to maintain the leased premises. The lessor must warn of current defects of which he is aware and which he knows may not be evident from an inspection by the lessee. If the lessor is bound by a covenant to repair the premises, he will be liable if there are dangerous conditions, subject to a test of reasonableness. If the lessor volunteers to repair, he will also be subject to a duty of care and must not be negligent, if he is, he may then be held liable. **Note:** If a guest is injured, consider the landlord's liability as lessor and lessee's liability as occupier.

e) Duties of Vendor of Realty

The vendor must reveal any dangerous conditions that are not apparent to the vendee upon reasonable inspection and which the vendor knows will not be apparent upon such inspection.

f) Negligence Per Se

Instead of relying upon the common law negligence criterion of a reasonable person for the purpose of establishing the applicable duty/standard of care, in some instances a statutory or regulatory provision will determine the extent of a duty and whether there has been a breach of that duty. A statute's specific duty may replace the more general common law duty of care if: (i) the statute provides for a criminal penalty; (ii) the statute clearly defines the standard of conduct; (iii) the plaintiff is within the protected class; and, (iv) the statute was designed to prevent the type of harm suffered by the plaintiff.

(1) Excuse for Violation

Where compliance is beyond the defendant's control or where compliance would cause more harm or damage than the original violation, a defendant's conduct may be excused.

(2) Effect of Violation

A majority of jurisdictions hold that a statutory violation is negligence per se. It establishes a conclusive presumption of duty and breach. However, in contrast, compliance with a statute will not establish that due care was exercised.

g) Negligent or Reckless Infliction of Emotional Distress (NIED)

The duty to avoid causing emotional distress to another is breached when the defendant creates a foreseeable risk of injury to the plaintiff, either by: (i) causing a threat of physical impact that leads to emotional distress; or (ii) directly causing severe emotional distress that by itself is likely to result in physical symptoms.

(1) Injury Requirement

The plaintiff can recover damages only if the defendant's conduct caused some physical injury. However, physical injury is not required in the case of: (i) an erroneous report of a relative's death; or (ii) the mishandling of a relative's corpse.

(2) Third-Party Recovery

A 3rd party may recover for NIED if: (i) the plaintiff and the person injured by the defendant are closely related; (ii) the plaintiff was present at the scene; and (iii) the plaintiff observed or perceived the injury.

h) Contractual Obligations

Previously, in order for a plaintiff to sue under a tort theory for contractual obligations, privity was required. However, that requirement has since been broken down. Nonfeasance (not performing at all) requires privity and a contract action. Misfeasance does not.

i) Affirmative Duties to Act

The general proposition is that a person must exercise a duty of reasonable care when his conduct creates a risk of harm, but that no duty of care arises when his conduct has not created a risk of harm.

(1) Assumption of a Duty of Care

Once a person, who has no duty to do so, acts by coming to the aid of another who is at risk of harm, then that person has a duty to exercise reasonable care while carrying out the rescue. Further on ceasing to act, there is a duty not to place that other person in a worse position than they were in before the intervention.

(2) Peril Due to Defendant's Negligence

If a person's conduct (which itself may not be negligent) places another at risk of injury, there is a duty to exercise reasonable care to either prevent or restrict the level of harm inflicted.

(3) Special Relationship Between Parties

A person who is in a special relationship with another owes a duty of reasonable care to that person with respect to risks that fall within that special relationship, examples of which include:

(a) Parent/Dependent children;
(b) School/Student;

(c) Hotel/Guest;
(d) Common carrier/Passengers;
(e) Employer/Employee (while at work);
(f) Landlord/Tenant;
(g) Occupier of land open to the public/the public lawfully upon the land.

(4) **Duty to Control Third Persons**

There is no implied duty to prevent one person from injuring another. If one person is in a position to control another's actions, either because of their ability or authority over that person, liability could arise if action is not taken to prevent harm.

(5) **Duty Based on an Undertaking**

A person who carries out an undertaking (gratuitous or pursuant to a contract), owes a duty of reasonable care in carrying out the undertaking, where the undertaking creates additional risk that was not previously present. The duty also extends to third parties.

B. BREACH OF DUTY

Generally, liability in tort is dependent upon the establishment of a breach of duty of care owed by the tortfeasor (wrongdoer/defendant) to the plaintiff. Breach of duty occurs where a defendant fails to discharge their duty of care towards a plaintiff, which will vary based upon the particular applicable circumstances and the status of the defendant.

1. CUSTOM OR USAGE

A defendant who complies with the custom/usage of a community may have discharged any relevant duty of care owed to the plaintiff. However, existing practices may be relevant to a cause of action because simply conforming to an industry practice does not mean there has been no breach – the entire industry could be negligent, for example.

2. VIOLATION OF A STATUTE

Statutes may prescribe that certain precautions/protections/restrictions etc., be put in place to protect against accident and resultant injury to a person, which the statute is designed to protect and which a defendant's wrongdoing may cause. Such circumstances are considered to be "negligence per se". However, simply because a defendant has complied with a statutory requirement does not preclude a finding of negligence. If, for example, a defendant should have taken further additional precautions to those required by the statute, the defendant can be found to be in breach.

3. RES IPSA LOQUITUR

The essence of an event occurring may itself demonstrate a breach of duty by its very nature, as it could not have occurred without inherent negligence on the part of one party, i.e., the defendant. Res Ipsa Loquitur requires the plaintiff to show: (i) the accident causing the injury is a type that would not normally occur unless someone was negligent; (ii) the negligence is attributable to the defendant, commonly established by showing that the instrumentality causing the injury was in the exclusive control of the defendant; and (iii) the plaintiff was not at fault.

4. FAILURE TO WARN

If by his conduct a person creates a situation that could result in physical or emotional harm, then he may fail to exercise reasonable care, if being aware of the risk he fails to warn those who may encounter the risk and a warning would be effective in reducing or eliminating the risk. Furthermore, even if a defendant does warn of the potential risk, he may still be liable for failure to take additional precautions to protect against the risk.

C. Causation

The plaintiff must be able to demonstrate that the negligent behavior/conduct of the defendant was the direct cause of his injury. For liability to attach, the plaintiff must show both actual and proximate cause.

1. Actual (Factual) Cause

To determine whether the defendant's conduct was the actual cause of the plaintiff's injury, three tests exist:

a) "But For" Test

In some factual situations, it is possible to say that the accident/conduct resulting in the injury would not have occurred "but for" a failure of the defendant to adequately and properly adhere to the applicable duty of care, i.e., the injury would not have occurred but for this act or omission.

b) Substantial Factor Test

Where several factual causes combine to establish an injury upon the plaintiff, and any one factual cause by itself would have been sufficient to cause the injury, each act is regarded as a factual cause of the injury.

c) Alternative Causes Approach

A distinction is made when there is more than one cause of the injury/damage, but it is not known which factual cause caused the injury/damage. Each act attaches to a defendant, and if there is more than one defendant, each defendant must demonstrate that he has not been negligent.

2. Proximate Cause

The defendant's conduct must be the proximate cause of the plaintiff's injury/damage.

a) General Rule

Generally, a defendant is liable for those losses/injuries that result from the defendant's tortious conduct/behavior. The defendant's behavior is subject to a test of foreseeability (i.e., what are the usual possible harmful outcomes if a defendant engages in the type of conduct/behavior?).

b) Direct Cause Cases

The defendant is liable for all reasonably foreseeable harmful results of his conduct/behavior, even if the events occurred in a sequence characterized by an unusual manner or timing. The test of foreseeability is paramount and the defendant is not liable for any harm/damage if the harm/damage is an unforeseeable consequence of his conduct/behavior.

c) Indirect Cause Cases

If a defendant is negligent and a secondary indirect act combines with the defendant's act to cause a plaintiff injury, the defendant is liable to the extent those injuries (or loss) are the result of the defendant's tortious conduct.

(1) Almost Always Foreseeable:

(a) Rescuers

In cases where a defendant's conduct is the cause of injury to another (and for which the defendant is liable) the defendant will also be liable for additional harm arising from the efforts of a third person, e.g., a medical practitioner who provides aid, provided that the additional harm arises from such normal efforts to render aid. Further, the defendant may also be liable to the person who comes to the aid of that other, even though the "rescuer" might have been unforeseeable. However, a defendant will not be liable for any additional harm that arises and which is the result of an unusual or extraordinary consequence of providing the aid.

(b) **Foreseeability**

Is consistently found by courts in certain circumstances, which include: (i) negligence of rescuers; (ii) the conduct of rescuers; (iii) efforts to protect and defend another; and (iv) subsequent illness caused by a weakened condition.

(2) **Unforeseeable Results Caused by Foreseeable Intervening Forces**

In cases (which are rare) where a totally unforeseeable result is caused by a foreseeable intervening force, most courts hold the defendant not liable.

(3) **Unforeseeable Results Caused by Foreseeable Intervening Forces**

For liability to attach following the intervention of an extraneous factual cause, the intervening factual cause (i.e., the "intervening force") must be foreseeable. A subsequent, unforeseen factual cause may break the causal connection between the defendant and the plaintiff following the defendant's initial tortious act. This will remove liability from the defendant for any additional harm suffered by the plaintiff post intervention.

D. DAMAGE & DAMAGES

When pursuing a negligence claim, a plaintiff must establish that loss, damage, or injury has arisen as a result of the tortious conduct / behavior of the defendant. Damage to the plaintiff is never presumed and cannot be nominal. Punitive damages are rarely awarded. In cases where liability is established, the plaintiff will be compensated with "damages," the primary purpose of which is to try and place the plaintiff in the same position he would have been but for the commission of the tort.

1. CATEGORIES

Damages can be categorized as:

a) COMPENSATORY

i.e., to compensate the plaintiff for the loss/injury suffered by him. Compensatory damages may be further subdivided into:

(1) **General Damages**

Compensatory in nature for the loss/injury suffered, without proof of pecuniary loss, e.g., bodily injury, emotional distress;

(2) **Special Damages**

To compensate for losses other than those for which general damages are awarded and for which proof of pecuniary loss is required, e.g., loss of income, or the loss of earning capacity.

b) PUNITIVE

Punitive damages, sometimes referred to as "exemplary damages," the purpose of which is to punish the defendant and to deter others from committing the same type of conduct in the future. Generally, the conduct required is categorized as "outrageous" because of evil motive or without any concern for the rights of others. In negligence, punitive damages are allowed only where the defendant's conduct is deemed to be wanton and willful, reckless or malicious.

2. COMMON EXAMPLES & CONSIDERATIONS

a) PERSONAL INJURY

In personal injury cases, the plaintiff may recover for all damages: past; present; and, prospective. Additionally, special and general awards are available.

b) Property Damage

For property damage, the amount of recovery is deemed to be the reasonable cost of repair or, if beyond repair, the market value at the time of the event.

c) Non-Recoverable Items

Interest is not recoverable in a personal injury action, nor are attorneys' fees.

d) Duty to Mitigate

There is always a duty upon the plaintiff to mitigate damage and therefore, a plaintiff is not entitled to recover damages for any loss or damage that could have been avoided by his own reasonable effort or expense, after the tortious act.

e) Collateral Source Rule

The defendant may not claim a reduced level of damage because the plaintiff is receiving benefits from other sources (e.g., health insurance).

E. Defenses

Liability for a tortious act will attach to a defendant, subject to any defenses he may have available to him, including:

1. Contractual Limitation

Subject to satisfying any contractual law requirement, a contractual provision absolving a defendant from liability will have the effect of preventing a plaintiff from succeeding on his claim.

2. Assumption of Risk

If a plaintiff is aware of potential risk but nevertheless agrees to continue with the act and / or to permit the defendant to continue in light of this knowledge, in the event of the plaintiff suffering loss or damage, recovery may be denied to the plaintiff. The plaintiff must have: (i) known of the risk; and (ii) voluntarily proceeded in the face of the risk.

a) Implied

Knowledge may be implied subject to the reasonable man test. The plaintiff does not assume the risk where there is no available alternative, or where there is fraud, force, or an emergency situation. Certain parties, such as carriers and public utility companies, may limit their liability by issuing a disclaimer. Some individuals are protected by statute and implied risk may not be attributed to them.

b) Intentional Torts

If the plaintiff assumes a risk, this may not be relied upon by the defendant as a defense to intentional torts (but it may be a defense to wanton and willful misconduct by the plaintiff).

3. Contributory Negligence or Fault

A defendant may be able to mitigate his exposure to compensation by claiming that the plaintiff is in some part responsible for the damage or harm that has arisen and which he has suffered. The standard of care applicable to the plaintiff is the same as the standard of care employed to assess the defendant's conduct.

a) Effect

At common law, contributory negligence acted as a total bar to a plaintiff's recovery of damages, even where the plaintiff was 1% at fault and the defendant was 99% at fault. Today, only four jurisdictions recognize this "pure contributory negligence rule." Most jurisdictions favor a comparative negligence system.

b) Intentional Torts & Wanton/Reckless Conduct

Contributory negligence is not applicable to intentional torts and wanton and reckless conduct.

c) Last Clear Chance

The last clear chance rule allows recovery by the plaintiff despite contributory negligence. Under the last clear chance rule, the negligence falls upon the last individual who has an opportunity to take avoiding action to prevent harm and who fails to do so. This rule permits the plaintiff to recover despite his contributory negligence. Under this rule, the person with the last clear chance to avoid an accident, but who fails to do so, is liable in negligence.

d) Imputed

Contributory negligence will be imputed to the plaintiff from a third party where there is a master-servant, partner, or joint venture relationship. Contributory negligence is not imputed between husband and wife, parent and child, or automobile owner and driver.

4. Comparative Negligence

In comparative negligence cases, the plaintiff's contributory negligence is not a complete bar to recovery of damages, but the contributory negligence will act as a reducing factor on the level of damages recoverable. A majority of states allow the plaintiff to recover only if his negligence was less serious or no more serious than that of the defendant (i.e., the plaintiff was 50% at fault, or less). Pure comparative negligence states allow recovery no matter how great the plaintiff's negligence (e.g., a plaintiff can recover where he was 99% at fault).

a) Last Clear Chance Doctrine

Defined above, and is not used in jurisdictions that consider the application of comparative negligence.

VI. PRODUCTS LIABILITY

Generally, a party who carries on business selling or otherwise distributing products and who sells or distributes a defective product, is liable for injury to persons or damage to property caused by the defect. A "defective product" is one which at the point of sale or distribution: (i) contains a manufacturing defect; (ii) is defective in design; or (iii) is not sold/distributed with adequate safety warnings/instructions. A "product" is an item of tangible personal property sold or distributed on a commercial basis for use or consumption. As a result, "services" do not fall within the definition of product (a cause of action for negligence may be appropriate). However, the definition of product may extend to include such things as electricity, when its sale or distribution is akin to the sale of tangible personal property.

A. Theories of Liability

There are five theories of liability that the plaintiff may use in a products liability case: (i) strict liability; (ii) negligence; (iii) intent; (iv) breach of implied warranties; and/or (v) representation theories – i.e., express warranty and misrepresentation.

B. Strict Liability

If a product contains a defect, in the event of loss or damage arising, liability will attach. A defendant is strictly liable when: (i) a defendant is a commercial supplier; (ii) a product reaches a consumer without substantial alteration; (iii) the product is defective; (iv) the product is unreasonably dangerous to the consumer; (v) there is actual and proximate cause; and (vi) damages are proven (i.e., loss/injury results).

1. Defendant is a Commercial Supplier

For example, a manufacturer, wholesaler or retailer.

2. Without Substantial alteration

The defect must have existed when the product left the defendant's control. This will be inferred if the product moved through normal channels of distribution. Privity is not required.

3. Types of Defects

a) Manufacturing Defect

A manufacturing defect is found when a product differs from the manufacturer's specification and is made dangerous or more dangerous as a result. The defendant will be liable if the plaintiff can show that the product failed to perform as safely as an ordinary consumer would expect (the defendant must anticipate misuse – also applies to food).

b) Design Defects

If all the products are identical and all demonstrate dangerous capabilities, they may be deemed to have a design defect. The plaintiff must show that the defendant could have made the product safer without serious impact on the product's price/utility.

c) Inadequate Warnings

A product may also be deemed to be defective in some way if the manufacturer fails to accompany the product with adequate safety instructions/warnings as to the risks incurred when using the product. For liability to attach, the danger must not be apparent to users. A product's noncompliance with government safety standards establishes that it is defective, while compliance with safety standards is evidence (not conclusive) that the product is not defective. The defendant will not be held liable for dangers not foreseeable at the time of market and will not be held liable for some dangerous products (knives) if the danger is apparent and there is no safer way to make the product.

4. Causation

The plaintiff must demonstrate that the defect was present when the product left the manufacturer's control. Proximate cause is the same as in cases of negligence.

5. Damage

Damages are only recoverable if physical injury or damage to property is evidenced. Economic loss is not recoverable.

6. Defenses (*see Negligence – Defenses for rule statements*)

a) Contributory/Comparative Negligence

In states where contributory/comparative negligence is available as a defense, it will not be available as a defense where: (i) the plaintiff failed to discover the defect and guard against it; or (ii) the plaintiff's act was reasonably foreseeable.

b) Assumption of Risk

Assumption of risk does act as a defense and is a particularly relevant discussion where there is the failure to warn of a non-obvious, dangerous propensity of the product. However, disclaimers may not be relied upon as a defense if personal injury occurs or there is damage to property in cases of negligence or strict liability.

C. Liability Based on Negligence

Liability based on negligence is found where there is: (i) a duty of care; (ii) breach of that duty; (iii) actual and proximate causation; and (iv) damage.

1. Duty of Care

A duty of reasonable care is owed to any foreseeable plaintiff. Privity with the defendant is no longer required, so any foreseeable plaintiff can sue: users, consumers, bystanders. Commercial suppliers (e.g., manufacturers, wholesalers, and retailers) can be held liable.

2. Breach of Duty

A breach of duty is shown by the negligent conduct of the defendant in the supplying of a defective product (as defined above).

a) Negligence

Negligence is established just as it would be in standard negligence cases. Where applicable, a plaintiff may invoke Res Ipsa Loquitor.

b) Retailers and Wholesalers

In contrast to a manufacturer, a retailer and/or wholesaler, although potentially liable for their own negligence, will be able to avoid liability for the defective product by satisfying their duty of care by a cursory inspection.

3. Causation

See negligence discussion for rule statements - An intermediary's negligent failure to discover a defect does not supersede the original manufacturer's negligence unless the intermediary's conduct exceeds ordinary foreseeable negligence.

4. Damage

See negligence discussion for rule statements - Physical injury or property damage must be shown. Recovery will be denied if there is solely economic loss.

5. Defense

See negligence discussion for rule statements.

D. Intent

The defendant will be liable to anyone injured by an unsafe product if the defendant intended the consequences or knew that they were substantially certain to occur. If intent is present, the tort of battery is applicable and may be the primary tort relied upon by the plaintiff. If the plaintiff suffers any injury, he can sue. Compensatory and punitive damages are available. The defenses applicable to intentional torts apply.

E. Implied Warranties

In a contract for the sale of goods, two warranties are implied, which a purchaser can rely upon.

1. Merchantability

That is the products supplied are of merchantable quality and fit for the purpose for which they are intended. The defendant is liable for a breach of this warranty where: (i) he is a commercial supplier who deals in goods of the kind; (ii) the product is unsafe (breach); (iii) there is actual and proximate causation; and (iv) damage results.

2. Fitness for a Particular Purpose

Fitness for a particular purpose arises when it is brought to the vendor's attention that the purchaser requires the goods for a particular purpose, and the purchaser is relying upon the vendor's knowledge and skill when recommending that purchase. Liability attaches where: (i) the product is not fit for the particular purpose required; (ii) there is actual and proximate causation; and (iii) damage arises.

3. Standing

Standing in most cases may be extended beyond the parties privy to the contract, to include, for example, third party beneficiaries (e.g., buyer, family, household, and guests) and who may sue for damage suffered by reason of the defective product.

4. Damages

Damages are recoverable for personal injury, property damage, and pure economic loss.

5. Disclaimers

Disclaimers may be relied upon for cases involving economic loss but are generally rejected in personal injury cases.

F. Representation Theories

1. Express Warranty

An express warranty is any statement, or promise, or representation, concerning the product sold or distributed and which is relied upon by the purchaser to form part of the contract conditions.

a) Standing

Redress is available to any consumer, user, or bystander. If the redress is sought by the purchaser, the warranty must be present in the contract made between the purchaser and the vendor. If the plaintiff is not a party to the contract, then it is not necessary to show any reliance on the representation, as long as reliance on that fact/facts can be demonstrated by a third party.

b) Breach

It is not necessary to evidence fault to establish a breach. The plaintiff is merely required to demonstrate that the product supplied has not fulfilled the warranty made.

c) Causation, Damage, and Defenses

See implied warranties, above.

d) Disclaimers

A disclaimer may only be relied upon when it is consistent with the warranty.

2. Misrepresentation of Fact

A vendor engaged in the business of selling or distributing products is liable for misrepresentation of a material fact concerning a product and which results in injury to a person or damage to property caused by the misrepresentation:
(i) the statement concerns a material fact relating to the quality of the goods and their potential uses, ignoring at this juncture any merchandising hype; and (ii) the vendor intended the representation to be relied upon by the purchaser in a specific transaction.

a) Liability

Liability is usually based on strict liability, but can also be relevant to misrepresentation, both intentionally and negligently.

b) Justifiable Reliance

It is necessary to show reliance on the misrepresentation and that the misrepresentation is a substantial determinant in the purchaser's decision to acquire the product.

c) Causation and Damage

Reliance is sufficient to show actual cause. Proximate cause and damage remain the same as for strict liability.

d) Defenses

If the plaintiff is entitled at law to rely on the (mis)representation, then assumption of risk is not a defense available to a defendant.

VII. GENERAL CONSIDERATIONS

A. VICARIOUS LIABILITY

Vicarious liability applies where one person commits a tort against another in circumstances where a third person is held liable. The third person, "the principal," will be directly liable for the tortious act of his agent, when the agent acts with actual authority of his principal or the agent's conduct is ratified by the principal. A common example is of an employee, who, while acting within the scope of his employment, commits a tortious act. In such circumstances, the employer will be vicariously liable to the third party under the doctrine of Respondeat Superior, discussed below.

1. DOCTRINE OF RESPONDEAT SUPERIOR

This doctrine is limited to the employer/employee relationship and arises where an employee in the course of his employment, by his negligence (or other tortious act), causes loss of, or injury to, property or a person. If an employee acts outside the scope of his employment and while doing so commits a tortious act, generally, the principal (employer) will not be vicariously liable. However, the employee will have a direct liability for his own tortious act.

a) MINOR DETOUR

What constitutes an act within the scope of employment will differ from case to case and will be fact dependent. The scope of employment may be defined by, for example, a time factor or a physical geographic factor. If an employee commits a tortious act while acting outside such restrictions, or deviates from his normal routine (to carry out some personal business), then the tortious act may not be within the scope of employment, and vicarious liability will not apply.

b) INTENTIONAL TORTS

If the tort is a deliberate and intended act, then it may not fall within the scope of employment. There are exceptions to this, for example, for those who use force in the course of their employment.

c) EMPLOYERS

An employer will be held liable for damage or injury to employees arising out of the employer's negligence.

2. INDEPENDENT CONTRACTORS

The general rule is that a party (i.e., the principal) is not vicariously liable for the tortious conduct of an independent contractor, who will be directly liable for such conduct, subject to exceptions, including:

a) The activity for which the independent contractor is engaged is highly dangerous and it is the highly dangerous activity which is the factual cause of the liability;

b) The activity for which the independent contractor is engaged is likely to involve trespass or the commission of a public/private nuisance and which is the factual cause of the liability;

c) An owner/occupier of land is liable for activity on the land carried out by the independent contractor. A duty of care is owed by the landowner/occupier (for example, to those entering onto the land) and the owner/occupier will be vicariously liable for loss or damage arising from the tortious conduct of the independent contractor;

d) Although a principal will not be liable for the manner in which work is carried out by an independent contractor, vicarious liability will attach if the principal retains control over any part of the work, in which case the principal has a duty to exercise reasonable care; and

e) A principal may be directly liable in negligence arising out of the inadequate selection or supervision of an independent contractor.

3. Partnerships and Joint Ventures

Each partner is jointly and severally liable for the tortious conduct of the other partners for acts conducted within the scope and pursuance of their business. Further, the partners will be vicariously liable for the tortious conduct of an employee while acting in the course of his employment. In circumstances where two or more partners are jointly liable for the same harm, partners are entitled to recover a "contribution" from each of his fellow partners equivalent to the fellow partner's comparative share.

4. Automobile Owner for Driver

The liability of an automobile owner for the actions of the driver depends somewhat on the location and within which state. In principle, the car owner is not vicariously liable for the tortious conduct of another driver of his vehicle. However, in some states the rule of vicarious liability will apply and, in others, the principle is only extended to those immediate members of the family and household driving with the car owner's permission, actual or implied.

a) Permissive Use

Some states have gone further and extended the principle to include any damage caused by an individual driving with the consent of the owner.

b) Negligent Entrustment

Some states impose a duty of care on a car owner present in the vehicle when the negligent act occurred on the basis that this individual could have prevented it.

5. Parent/Child

Generally, a person's childhood is a relevant fact to take into consideration when considering a child's tortious conduct. Children under five years of age are considered to be incapable of negligence, although a parent may be liable for negligent supervision. For older children, a child's negligent conduct needs to be measured against that of a reasonably careful person of the same age, intelligence and experience of the child in question. At common law, a parent was not vicariously liable for the tortious acts of a minor. However, most states impose liability on a parent for the intentional torts of their children up to a set financial limit. Children may act as agents for their parents, which may attract vicarious liability if the child commits a tort while an agent for the parent. Similarly, a cause of action against the parent may exist for negligent supervision.

6. Tavern Keepers

Under common law, Publicans do not have a duty of care to those who sustain injury as a result of alcoholic intoxication, and this extends to a third party who may be injured by an intoxicated individual. Under modern law, several jurisdictions impose liability on tavern keepers based on ordinary negligence principals (e.g., the foreseeable risk of serving alcohol to a minor or an obviously intoxicated adult) for which the tavern keeper has direct liability, rather than vicarious liability.

B. Multiple Defendants

1. Joint and Several Liability

Two or more persons will be jointly and severally liable for their tortious conduct resulting in injury to another, and the injured person may recover any damages in full from any one of the jointly and severally liable defendants.

2. Satisfaction and Release

a) Satisfaction

Full payment of damages discharges the responsibility of all jointly and severally liable parties. If full payment is not received, the plaintiff may proceed against all or any of the jointly and severally liable parties to effect full recovery.

b) Release

Under common law, a release of one joint tortfeasor was a release of all joint tortfeasors. A majority of jurisdictions now provide that a release of one tortfeasor does not discharge the other tortfeasors unless expressly provided in the release.

3. Contribution and Indemnity

Contribution and indemnity provide a mechanism by which joint tortfeasors who have been found jointly and severally liable may apportion between them the damages payable to a plaintiff.

a) Contribution

Contribution allows a jointly and severally liable defendant who pays more than his share of damages to recover a contribution from other jointly and severally liable parties for the excess. Provided, however, that the other party(ies) does/do not have a valid settlement and release from the plaintiff. Contribution is only available from another defendant where he is liable to the plaintiff, and does not apply to intentional torts that are not committed in concert.

(1) Amount of Contribution

This is a fault-based process, which determines the amount of contribution of multiple defendants. A person entitled to a contribution may recover no more than the amount paid to the plaintiff in excess of the person's comparative share of responsibility. This is applicable in most states but not all, and some states (a minority) apportion blame equally amongst all defendants regardless of the level of fault.

b) Indemnity

Generally, the purpose of an indemnity is to place a person in the same position they would have been but for the occurrence which brings the indemnity into operation. In situations where two or more persons are liable for the same tortious act resulting in loss, and one of them discharges the liability of another, then he is entitled to an indemnity (i.e., to be reimbursed for the amount paid to the plaintiff). If the indemnity is based on a contractual obligation, indemnity must be paid even where the party providing the indemnity would not be liable to the plaintiff.

4. Survival and Wrongful Death

a) Survival of Tort Actions

In certain circumstances, the right to continue to pursue a tortious claim survives the death of one or more of the parties. This applies to property and personal injury actions, but not to those relating to an intangible interest (e.g., defamation or invasion of privacy).

b) Wrongful Death

A wrongful death action arises when a person is killed because of the tortious conduct of another. **Note:** while a wrongful death may be criminal, it does not preclude civil proceedings. Damages for wrongful death may include economic and non-economic loss. Economic damages include: loss of support and income, medical and funeral expenses, loss of services. Non-economic damages relate to pain and suffering.

In wrongful death actions, the spouse and next of kin of the plaintiff have a right of recovery of pecuniary injury. Any financial award to the plaintiff's estate is protected against claims by potential creditors. The level of recovery and damages awarded may be no greater than that which the defendant could have claimed while living.

5. Tortious Interferences with Family Relationships

a) Husband – Wife

Either spouse has the right to claim for indirect interference by the defendant to the other spouse, whether it be intentional or negligent.

b) Parent – Child

A parent may claim on behalf of a child, but a child has no corresponding right to claim for damages inflicted upon the parent as the result of a tortious act.

c) Nature of Action

A defense that prohibits recovery by an injured party will also prevent recovery for claims of interference with the family relationship.

6. Tort Immunities

a) Intra-Family Tort Immunities

Under common law, one member of a family unit could not sue another in tort for personal injury. Most states have abolished such immunity, but those that retain it do not apply it to: (i) intentional tortious conduct; and (ii) automobile accident cases, to the extent of insurance coverage.

b) Government Tort Immunity

(1) Federal Government

The U.S. government has waived immunity for tortious acts other than in certain circumstances, including: assault; battery; false imprisonment; false arrest; malicious prosecution; abuse of process; slander; libel; misrepresentation; deceit; and, interference with contractual rights.

(2) State and Local Governments

For the most part, state and local governments have waived their immunity to the same degree as the U.S. government.

(3) Immunity of Public Officials

Public officials carrying out their designated duties are immune from prosecution for discretionary acts, provided they are done without malice or improper purpose. However, this immunity does not apply to ministerial acts that do attract liability, even in the absence of malice or improper purpose.

TRUSTS

Table of Contents

I. CREATION OF A VALID TRUST

A trust is a fiduciary relationship concerning property where one person, the trustee, holds legal title to the trust property (or the res), subject to the enforceable equitable rights of the beneficiary who holds equitable title. A trust is essentially a device whereby one or more persons manage property for the benefit of another.

In order for a valid trust to be created, the settlor must: (i) manifest an intention to create a trust; (ii) for a valid trust purpose; (iii) with ascertainable property, the res; (iv) that is delivered; (v) to the trustee; (vi) for the benefit of beneficiaries.

A. METHOD OF CREATION

1. TESTAMENTARY TRUST

This trust is created in a will.

2. POUR-OVER TRUST

Statutorily allowed in California, where property disposed of by will is placed into a preexisting trust. This is simply a way to plan for incapacity. *Cross-Over Issues: See Wills & Intestate Succession: Incorporation by Reference & Acts of Independent Significance.*

3. INTER VIVOS (OR "LIVING") TRUST

An inter vivos trust starts when created by the settlor. This type of trust can be created by transfer of property to another as trustee or by an individual claiming to be the trustee. Intent must be shown by conduct or words (e.g., delivery of the trust property or declaring oneself a trustee of the trust). Delivery of trust property requires placing the trust property out of the settlor's control (unless the settlor also serves as trustee) and in trust with a trustee.

Oral Trusts: The majority of states do not require a written instrument for a trust of personal property; oral trusts are sufficient. However, written instruments are required for land trusts. Failure to provide a written instrument may result in the imposition of a constructive trust.

B. INTENT

In order for a valid trust to exist, the settlor of the trust must have the requisite intent to create a trust. Such intent is established by oral or written statements of the settlor. An oral trust is valid, except where the purported terms of the trust bring it within the purview of the statute of frauds or the statute of wills.

Immediate Effect: The settlor must intend that the trust be immediately created rather than at a future time. However, it is permissible for trust property to include a future interest.

C. VALID TRUST PURPOSE

A trust will not be valid if it is illegal or contrary to public policy. If a condition violates public policy or is illegal, argue severance of the offending provision.

D. TRUST PROPERTY (RES)

Where there is no trust property, the trust fails, as the trustee has no property to manage. Therefore, the settlor must have a present existing property interest that is certain and identifiable. If the property interest comes into existence in the future, the settlor must renew his intention to create a trust.

Presently Existing Property Interest: An intention to create a present trust must have been externally manifested by the settlor at the time he owned the property and prior to its conveyance to another.

E. DELIVERY

Although a trust will not fail for want of delivery, delivery of the trust property helps establish the intention of the settlor to create a trust. Where trust property is real property, delivery may be made by conveying title or delivery of a deed. Where trust property is personal, delivery may be made by the following: (i) physical delivery; (ii) symbolic delivery where something symbolic of the property is given, as manual delivery is impractical (executing deed); or (iii) constructive delivery, giving the trustee the means to obtain the property or an item that represents the property.

F. TRUSTEE

A trustee is the person who manages and holds legal title to the trust property. A trust will not fail for want of a trustee, as a court can appoint one. However, where trustee is the only beneficiary, merger takes place and terminates the trust.

G. BENEFICIARIES

For a private trust, there must be ascertainable beneficiaries. Without them, there would be no one to enforce the trust and the trustee could appropriate the property for himself (contrary to the settlor's intent).

1. UNASCERTAINED BENEFICIARIES

Beneficiaries need not be identified at the time the trust is created, but they must be susceptible to identification at the time the trust comes into effect (e.g., children). As such, a private trust may exist for the benefit of members of the class, provided that it is sufficiently definite. If it is too broad, it may be unenforceable.

2. POWER OF APPOINTMENT

Modernly, a power of appointment may be granted to the trustee to carry out the settlor's intent where there are not ascertainable beneficiaries. Under a Power of Attorney, there is no obligation on the trustee to pick anyone. The trustee may choose whomever he pleases. Therefore, there are no fiduciary obligations beneficiaries can enforce.

Exception: Charitable Trusts, *infra*.

II. TYPES OF TRUSTS

A. CHARACTERIZATION

1. MANDATORY TRUST (A.K.A. SIMPLE TRUST)

A mandatory trust is one where the trustee lacks discretion and must distribute its principal or income in accordance with the schedule set by the trust.

Example: Trustee shall distribute $1,000.00 per year to B. If the trustee does not, B can sue the trustee.

2. DISCRETIONARY TRUST

In a discretionary trust, the trustee is given discretion to determine which of the beneficiaries may receive the capital/income of the trust and how much each will be allotted to meet the intent of the settlor.

Duty to Inquire: A trustee of a support trust has a duty to inquire as to the financial situation of the beneficiaries, regardless of absolute discretion. A trustee with absolute discretion still must act with prudence and within reason. Inclusion of an exculpatory clause in an instrument in which the drafter is the trustee is not, per se, invalid, but may be viewed with some suspicion by the courts. There must be some evidence of undue influence or overreaching.

3. Revocable Trust

In a revocable trust, the settlor retains the right to amend or revoke during the settlor's lifetime.

B. Spendthrift Trust

A spendthrift trust is an irrevocable trust. It is created for the benefit of a recipient (often because he is unable to manage money prudently), and gives an independent trustee full authority to make decisions as to how the trust funds may be spent for the benefit of the beneficiary. Creditors of the beneficiary generally cannot access the funds in the trust, as payments are immune from voluntary and involuntary alienation. Therefore, a beneficiary's creditors cannot reach his interest until income has been paid to him.

Exceptions:

i. Creditors of the beneficiaries have a right to the distributions of the trust – but not the corpus – in the following circumstances:
   1. Suppliers of necessities (food, medical care);
   2. Alimony & child support obligations;
   3. Tort claims – Majority cannot go after trust res, while minority can;
   4. Claims by government entities (e.g., taxes).

ii. A trust that provides for voluntary, not involuntary, alienation is invalid for public policy reasons.

C. Support Trust

A support trust requires the trustee to pay or apply only so much of the income or principal as is necessary for the support of the beneficiary. Even without a spendthrift clause, the interest is not assignable, as that would defeat the purpose of the trust.

D. Honorary Trust

An honorary trust is a device by which a person establishes a trust for which there is neither a charitable purpose nor a private beneficiary to enforce the trust. Since there is no named beneficiary, the implementation of the trust depends on the honor of the trustee. If the person does not execute the trust duties, he holds the property for the settlor or settlor's heirs on the theory of a resulting trust.

E. Secret Trust

A secret trust is a trust in which property is left to a person under a will, which makes an absolute gift, on its face, to a named beneficiary. However, in reality, the gift is made in reliance upon the beneficiary's promise to hold the gift in trust for another. To prevent unjust enrichment, the court will allow the intended trust beneficiary to present extrinsic evidence of the agreement, and if proved by clear and convincing evidence, a constructive trust will be placed on the gift.

F. Semi-Secret Trust

In the case of a semi-secret trust, the will makes a gift to a person in trust, but does not designate a beneficiary. As no beneficiary is named, the trust is unenforceable and the assets go into a resulting trust.

G. Pour-Over Trust

A pour-over clause in a will gives probate property to a trustee of the testator's separate trust to be distributed by the terms of the trust. The pour-over clause must be validated either under incorporation by reference to the previously existing trust into which the property will be poured, or under the doctrine of acts of independent significance by referring to some act that has significance apart from disposing of probate assets, namely the revocable inter vivos trust.

1. Incorporation by Reference

(Cannot incorporate post-will amendments) A will can incorporate by reference a trust instrument in existence at the time the will is executed, but it cannot incorporate trust amendments made thereafter. The writing must be in existence when the will is made, specifically identified with the intent to incorporate. If changes are made to a trust after the will is created, changes will not take effect.

2. Acts of Independent Significance

(Solves the problem of post-will amendments, but creates a problem if you do not want to fund it yet) The pour-over clause may be validated under an act of independent significance by referring to some act that has significance apart from disposing of probate assets -- in this context, by reference to an inter vivos trust that disposes of assets transferred to the trust during life. The settlor must fund the trust (with res) while he or she is alive.

3. UTATA

The UTATA allows for incorporation of a trust even if it is amended after the will is executed, provided that the amendments are communicated to the trustee while the settlor is alive. It is deemed an inter vivos trust, not as a testamentary trust, and does not need to be funded. The Supremacy Clause provides that federal law is the supreme law of the land. Therefore, a federal law may supersede or preempt local laws. If a federal law conflicts with a state law, the state law will be invalid.

H. Charitable Trust

There are four differences between the rules governing charitable trusts and private trusts. The charitable trust: (i) may be perpetual; (ii) it must benefit a charitable purpose; (iii) the trust must have indefinite beneficiaries; and (iv) the Cy Pres doctrine applies.

1. Purpose

Charitable trusts serve to benefit the public through the advancement of particular social goals, including: health, education, cultural awareness, poverty, and religion. Although the class of beneficiaries may be limited, they cannot be so limited as to be considered excessively restricted.

2. Indefinite Beneficiaries

The courts consider the community at large the beneficiary of a charitable trust, and a particular individual eligible for its benefits has no standing to enforce its terms. The duty of enforcement is placed upon the Attorney General of the state in which the trust is located.

3. DURATION

Charitable trusts are not subject to the Rule Against Perpetuities and may continue as long as their purpose exists.

Cy Pres: Where a settlor creates a trust with charitable intent, yet for some reason the execution of the trust becomes impossible or impracticable, under the Cy Pres doctrine, the court may reform the trust to achieve the charitable intent.

I. TOTTEN TRUST

A totten trust is a bank account for the benefit of a third party.

J. RESULTING TRUST

When a trust fails for want of a beneficiary or other reason, by operation of law, the trustee will hold a resulting trust in favor of the settlor's heirs.

K. CONSTRUCTIVE TRUST

A constructive trust is not really a trust but rather a flexible equitable remedy to prevent unjust enrichment. The constructive trustee's only duty is to convey the property to the person who would have owned it but for the wrongful conduct, or failure of the trust or will.

III. MODIFICATION AND TERMINATION OF TRUSTS

A. GENERAL RULE

If the settlor and all beneficiaries consent, the trust may be modified or terminated.

B. THE CLAFLIN DOCTRINE

Under the Claflin Doctrine, the trust cannot be modified or terminated, even if all beneficiaries agree, if to do so would be contrary to a material purpose of the settlor. Material purposes include spendthrift, support, and discretionary trusts.

C. CHANGED CIRCUMSTANCES

In California, a court may also, upon a change of circumstances unanticipated by the settlor, authorize a modification to the terms of the trust in order to realize the trust purpose. However, changes to a trust may not serve to deprive a beneficiary of an interest in the trust. In cases in which the primary purpose of the trust was to support the income beneficiary, recent statutes have given the court power to invade the corpus. In addition, a court can accelerate vested rights.

D. EQUITABLE DEVIATION

Equitable deviation allows the court to authorize the trustee to change the terms of the instrument to reflect not what the settlor meant to say, but what the court *believes* the settlor would have said had she anticipated the changed circumstances.

E. REFORMATION

Reformation is an equitable remedy that conforms the instrument to reflect what the settlor actually intended at the time of its execution.

F. PREMATURE TERMINATION

A court may prematurely terminate the trust in situations in which the trust's purpose has become impossible or illegal, or has been completed.

G. Charitable Trusts and Cy Pres

supra.

IV. RIGHTS OF CREDITORS

A. General

1. Voluntary Alienation

Unless a beneficiary is restricted by the trust itself or a provision of law, a beneficiary may assign his interest in the trust. Once the interest is assigned, the original limitations and conditions imposed by the trust document remain.

2. Involuntary Alienation

Unless a beneficiary is restricted by the trust itself (e.g., a spendthrift trust) or a provision of law, an insolvent trust beneficiary's creditors may levy on his beneficial interest, which is subject to judicial sale. The beneficiary cannot force payment, nor can the creditors. However, if the trustee has notice of the debt and the judgment against the beneficiary and the trustee decides to pay, a court may order the trustee to pay the beneficiary's income directly to a creditor until any debt is satisfied.

B. Application to Specific Trusts

1. Spendthrift Trusts

supra.

2. Discretionary Trusts

In a discretionary trust the beneficiaries do not have a fixed interest in the trust funds, and the trustee is given discretion to determine whether (and when) to apply or withhold income or capital to the beneficiary. Creditors take only if the trustee exercises his discretion to pay, unless the beneficiary's interest is also protected by a spendthrift provision.

3. Support Trusts

A support trust directs the trustee to pay to the beneficiary as much of the income or principal as is necessary for the beneficiary's support (e.g., education, housing, food, etc.). The interest of the beneficiary cannot be assigned or reached by creditors. In some cases, the trust may require the beneficiary to prove why payment is necessary for her support, and the trustee must also carefully examine why such a request should be granted.

V. TRUST ADMINISTRATION AND DUTIES

A. Powers of the Trustee

A trustee's powers are expressly conferred by the trust instrument, by state law, and by court decree. Additionally, further powers may be implied as necessarily required to fulfill the trust's purpose.

B. Fiduciary Duty

A trustee owes a fiduciary duty to administer the trust solely in the interest of the beneficiaries. A breach can mean personal liability for the trustee.

1. Self-Dealing

Unless there is court approval or an express waiver in the trust instrument, self-dealing is not tolerated in the relationship between a fiduciary and those whose interests he or she is protecting. A trustee owes a duty of undivided loyalty to the trust and its beneficiaries. In self-dealing scenarios, the court applies the "no further inquiry" rule, which asserts that a trustee will be liable, no matter how fair and reasonable the transaction may have been to the beneficiaries, and the fairness or unfairness of a transaction is not even considered.

a) Trustee Options

Obtain settler authorization, court approval, or authorization from the beneficiaries. For this to work, there must be full disclosure to all beneficiaries, and the transaction must be objectively reasonable.

b) Beneficiary's Rights

If a prohibited transaction takes place, the beneficiary may: (i) set aside the transaction, trace, and recover the property until they encounter a bona fide purchaser who had no knowledge of the breach of the trust; (ii) recover any profit made by the trustee; or (iii) affirm the transaction.

2. Conflict of Interest

A trustee breaches the duty of loyalty by not acting in the best interest of the beneficiaries. Remedies include ratification by the beneficiaries or surcharge of the trustee and a suit for any loss.

3. Prudent Investor Rule

The trustee has a duty to invest and manage trust assets as a prudent investor would, in light of the trust purpose, terms, distribution requirements, and other circumstances of the trust.

4. Duties Relating to Care of Trust Property

a) Duty to Preserve Trust Property and Make it Productive

The trustee has a primary responsibility to preserve the trust res and make the trust property productive. The trustee is expected to take charge of leasing land, collecting claims, and investing money, among other duties. A trustee may be held liable for the amount of income that would normally have been received from proper investment.

b) Duty to Separate and Earmark Trust Property – Commingling

A trustee has a duty to keep trust assets separate from other assets. Trust property must be titled in the trustee in accordance with a specific trust. Where the trustee commingles trust assets with his or her own and there is a loss, it is presumed that the lost property belonged to the trustee, and the remaining property belongs to the trust. Where a portion of the blended assets increases in value and another portion decreases in value, it is presumed that the former applied to the trust's assets and the latter to the trustee's assets.

c) Duty Not to Delegate

A trustee may not delegate trustee functions that could otherwise be executed by the trustee, especially those that require his or her discretion and judgment. Further, he may never delegate the entire administration of a trust.

Investment and Management Decisions: Investment decisions may be delegated by the trustee to appropriate individuals in order for the trust property to be correctly invested.

Remedy: If a trustee improperly delegates, limits, or surrenders his or her control over the management of the trust property, the trustee becomes a guarantor of the trust asset and is responsible for actual losses, regardless of the manner in which the loss occurred.

Co-Trustee Liability: A trustee will be liable for acts of a co-trustee if he: (i) approved, acquiesced to, or participated in the breach or negligently disregarded his or her own duties; (ii) concealed the breach or failed to take steps to compel redress; or (iii) imprudently delegated authority to the co-trustee.

d) Duty to Diversify Investments

A trustee must diversify the investments of the trust unless he or she reasonably determines that its purposes are better served without diversification.

e) Duty to Account

The trustee has the role of keeper of records and provider of transactional details, which ensures that the trustee is meeting his or her obligation of loyalty.

f) Duty to Defend Trust from Attack

A trustee has a duty to investigate and form an opinion on the merits of a legal attack against the trust, unless examination reveals the challenge is well founded and a defense would be meritless.

g) Duty of Impartiality Between Beneficiaries

Income Beneficiaries want to maximize profits, even at the expense of burning up the principal.

Remainder Beneficiaries want to protect principal because they want money to be left for them.

h) Duty of Impartiality

The duty of impartiality requires that the trustee protect the interests of both types of beneficiaries and treat them fairly and equitably. He must produce reasonable income for the income beneficiaries while preserving the corpus for the principal beneficiaries.

i) Equitable Adjustment Power

The equitable adjustment power empowers the trustee to invest in whatever maximizes overall return. If there will be too much or too little for one class of beneficiaries, then it allows the trustee to reallocate the investments to comply with his duty of impartiality to both types of beneficiaries.

WILLS AND INTESTATE SUCCESSION

Table of Contents

I. IS THERE A VALID WILL?

A. Formal Attested Will (California Probate Code "CPC" § 6110)

To be valid, a formal will must: (i) be in writing; (ii) be signed by the testator (or a conservator, or by another person in his presence at his discretion); (iii) be signed (or the signature needs to be acknowledged by testator) in the joint presence of at least two witnesses; and (iv) ensure that the witnesses understand that the instrument being witnessed is the testator's will.

1. Subscription

A signature may consist of an informal name or the testator's initials. Under California law, an attested will need not be signed at the end of the document.

2. Witnesses

Witnesses must be legally competent and understand that they are witnessing the execution of a will. The will must be signed by at least two witnesses, before the testator dies. However, witnesses need not sign in the presence of the testator or of each other. In California, the witnesses need not sign at the end of the will. Further, no signing order is required.

B. Holographic Wills (CPC § 6111)

California allows holographic wills if the signature and material provisions of the will are in the testator's own handwriting. Provisions of an inconsistent will may govern unless evidence establishes that the holographic will was executed later in time.

C. Falling Short of Compliance (CPC § 6110(c)(2))

1. Dispensing Doctrine

If established by clear and convincing evidence ("CCE") that the decedent intended the document to constitute his will at the time of signing, the court will ignore the lack of formality and probate the will. This doctrine only applies to lack of formalities relating to the witness requirements.

D. California Statutory Will (CPC § 6240)

To be a valid statutory will, the testator must fill in the blanks and sign the will in the presence of two witnesses, consistent with a formal will.

E. Testamentary Capacity (CPC §§ 6100, 6100.5)

1. Mental Capacity

A testator must be at least 18 years old and be able to communicate his wishes and understand the nature of the disposition he is making and its effects. To prove that a testator lacked capacity at the time he executed his will, the challenger must produce evidence of a deficit in at least one of the following: (i) alertness and attention; (ii) the ability to process information; (iii) thought processes (delusions); or (iv) the ability to modulate mood. Such a deficit may be considered only if it significantly impairs the person's ability to understand and appreciate the consequences of his actions with respect to the will.

2. Insane Delusion

An "insane delusion" can invalidate an entire will or portion thereof when it caused the disposition. An insane delusion is a belief to which the testator adheres when a rational person in the same situation would not have drawn the same conclusion as was reached by the testator.

3. Mistake

Where there has been a mistake in the execution or composition of a will, it will fail for lack of testamentary intent. When a single provision of a will is invalid due to a mistake, the will's remainder will be probated unless it would undermine the testator's intent.

4. UNDUE INFLUENCE

Undue influence is a mental or physical coercion that deprives the testator of his free will, causing him to substitute another person's desire for that of his own. Undue influence requires that: (i) the testator be susceptible to influence; (ii) the other person be given the opportunity to influence; (iii) the other person be disposed to influence; and (iv) the provisions of the will be unnatural. The will may fail in whole or in part because of undue influence.

a) PRESUMPTION (CPC § 21380)

Presumption of undue influence arises if: (i) the beneficiary was in a confidential relationship with the testator; (ii) the beneficiary witnessed the execution of the will; and (iii) the disposition appears unnatural.

b) CONFIDENTIAL RELATIONSHIPS

Confidential relationships include attorney-client and doctor-patient.

5. FRAUD

Any gift resulting from fraud is invalid.

a) FRAUD IN THE EXECUTION

Fraud is present where there is a misrepresentation as to the nature or contents of an instrument.

b) FRAUD IN THE INDUCEMENT

Fraud is present where there is a misrepresentation of facts that influences the testator's motivation.

c) REMEDY

The denial of probate of tainted portions of the will and constructive trust are remedies for these types of fraud.

F. CHOICE OF LAW (CPC § 6113)

The law of the testator's domicile controls the disposition of personal property. The law of situs controls the disposition of real property. The California Probate Code validates wills not made in California if: (i) they are executed in accordance with California law; or (ii) executed in accordance with the law of the state where the will was executed; or (iii) in accordance with the law of where the testator died.

II. HAS THE WILL BEEN REVOKED?

A. METHODS OF REVOCATION (CPC § 6120)

1. WRITTEN INSTRUMENT

a) EXPRESS REVOCATION

A will may be expressly revoked by a later will (formal, holographic, or statutory) or codicil executed with the formalities required for a valid will.

b) IMPLIED REVOCATION

Revocation by implication occurs where the contents of a subsequently executed testamentary instrument contradict the terms of a prior instrument. The terms of the prior will are invalidated where a contradiction exists.

2. PHYSICAL ACT

To be a valid revocation, the will must be torn, burned, canceled, obliterated, or destroyed with concurrent intent to revoke the will. Revocation by physical act may be done by another, provided it is at the testator's direction.

3. Interlineation

California allows partial and complete revocation by physical act. Interlineation of a holographic will revokes a prior disposition and replaces it with a new valid disposition. The prior signature of a holographic will is adopted at the time of the interlineation. Interlineation of a formal will must be accompanied by the testator's signature and it must be witnessed.

4. Effect of Revocation

a) Revocation of a will revokes all codicils;

b) Revocation of a codicil does not revoke a will;

c) Destruction of a duplicate will revokes all copies.

B. Dependent Relative Revocation ("DRR")

Such applies when the testator revokes his will or provision of a will upon the mistaken belief that another disposition of the property is valid and, but for this mistake, he would not have revoked the will. Where the other disposition fails, the revocation is set aside and the original will remains in force.

C. Revival (CPC § 6123)

If will-2 is revoked by physical act, extrinsic evidence may be introduced to show the testator's intent to revive will-1. If will-2 was revoked by a subsequent will (will-3), will-1 is not revived unless the terms of will-3 indicate that the testator intended will-1 to be probated; no extrinsic evidence may be used to establish the intent to revive will-1.

D. Missing Will (CPC § 6124)

Where the will of a competent testator cannot be found at her death, it is presumed that the will was destroyed with the concurrent intent to revoke.

1. Rebuttable

If there is evidence that rebuts the presumption of revocation (i.e., that the decedent lost the will), the copy of the will can be used to prove the contents of the lost original will, and the original would be probated.

E. Revocation by Operation of Law (CPC § 6122)

1. Divorce

If after executing a will, the testator's marriage or domestic partnership is dissolved or annulled, any appointment, or disposition of property to the former spouse or domestic partner will be revoked. However, a testator may expressly waive this in the will and allow property to pass to the former spouse or domestic partner. Remarriage revives a disposition, but separation does not count.

III. COMPONENTS OF A WILL

A. Integration

All papers actually present at execution are integrated into the will if the testator so intended. The intent of the testator will be demonstrated by the circumstances of the execution.

B. Republication by Codicil (CPC § 6132)

1. Codicil

A codicil is a testamentary instrument that modifies an earlier will and must be executed with the same formalities as a will.

2. Republication by Codicil

A codicil republishes a will. As a result, when a codicil is executed, the will to which the codicil attaches is deemed republished upon execution of the codicil.

NOTE: Where a codicil is present, consider the issues of omitted children and spouses, as republication of a will by codicil may preclude their claim. Also, a validly executed codicil may cure a will that is defective.

C. Incorporation by Reference (CPC § 6130)

A separate document may be incorporated into the will by reference if: (i) the document is in existence upon execution of the will; (ii) the will specifically names the document; and (iii) the document can be proven to be the one referenced in the will. California permits a document that is incorporated by reference to be modified by the testator after the execution of the will.

NOTE: The doctrines of incorporation by reference and republication often apply to the same facts with different results. A writing not in existence at the time of the will can be later incorporated indirectly through republication.

D. Act of Independent Significance (CPC §6131)

Omissions in a will can be completed by referring to acts or documents executed during the testator's life, provided it has significance that is independent from its testamentary disposition. For instance, a gift to "each book club member" has significance that is independent of the will. "Book members" may change during the testator's life, which in turn changes the beneficiaries in the will. However, the "book members" come and go for reasons independent of changing the will; therefore, there is no need to follow formalities even though the beneficiaries are changing.

IV. INTERPRETATION OF THE WILL

A. Admission of Extrinsic Evidence (CPC § 6111.5)

1. Ambiguity

California permits the admission of extrinsic evidence to explain any ambiguity. As a result, extrinsic evidence of the testator's intent and/or the identity of particular gifts may be introduced, provided such evidence relates to a reasonable interpretation.

V. RIGHTS OF OMITTED SPOUSES AND CHILDREN

A. Omitted Spouse (CPC § 21610)

Where a testator fails to provide in a will for the surviving spouse, and the marriage took place following the execution of the will, California law presumes that the testator forgot to amend the will. As a result, the omitted spouse receives: (i) the one-half of the community property that belongs to the decedent; (ii) the one-half of the quasi-community property that belongs to the decedent; (iii) the separate property of the decedent equal to one-half or one-third, depending on the number of children that survive the testator; or, where the testator leaves no issue, the spouse will receive all separate property.

1. Exceptions (CPC § 21611)

(i) the failure to provide for the omitted spouse was intentional and it appears in testamentary instruments; (ii) the decedent provided for the spouse by transfer outside of the will, and the intention that the transfer be in lieu of a provision in the will is shown by statements of the decedent or from the amount of the transfer or by other evidence; and (iii) spousal Waiver.

2. Spousal Waiver

A spouse can waive her right to the other spouse's estate: (i) by executing a signed writing; (ii) after the benefiting spouse fully discloses their financial status; and (iii) given the waiving spouse must have had independent counsel.

NOTE: If #2 is not met, the court may enforce a waiver if it finds that it was a fair and reasonable disposition under the given circumstances or that the spouse had sufficient bargaining power.

B. Omitted Children (CPC § 21620)

If the testator fails to provide in a testamentary instrument for a child born or adopted after executing the will, the omitted child shall receive a share of the decedent's estate equal in value to that which the child would have received intestate.

1. Exceptions (CPC § 21621)

(i) the failure to provide was intentional and it appears on the face of the will; (ii) the testator directed the disposition of substantially all the estate to the parent of the child; or (iii) the testator provided for the child by transfer outside of the will and the intention that the transfer be in lieu of a provision in the will is shown by statements of the testator or other evidence.

2. Decedent's Erroneous Belief (CPC § 21622)

If, at time of execution, the testator decedent believed the child to be dead or was unaware of the birth of the child, the child shall receive her intestate share. **Consider the republication doctrine. In that case, where the child is known and alive at the time of the republication, she would not be considered omitted.**

VI. BARS TO SUCCESSION

A. Interested Witnesses (CPC § 6112)

If the will is signed by an interested party, that fact alone does not invalidate the will or any provision. Unless there are at least two other subscribing disinterested witnesses, there is a presumption that the witnesses procured the devise by duress, menace, fraud, or undue influence.

1. Rebuttable Presumption

The failure to rebut the presumption results in the witness losing his share above, which he would have received through an intestate disposition.

B. Prohibited Transferees (CPC § 21350)

California presumes invalid any will provision making a donative transfer to: (i) a person who drafted the will; (ii) a person related to, living with, or employed by the drafter; (iii) a partner or shareholder of a law partnership in which the drafter has an ownership interest, as well as an employee of that partnership; (iv) any person who has a fiduciary relationship with the testator who transcribes the will or causes it to be transcribed; (v) any person who is related to, lives with, or is employed by a person referred to in (iv); or (vi) a care custodian of a dependent child.

1. Exceptions (CPC 21351)

A will provision in favor of the drafter is valid if the testator is related to, lives with, or is the domestic partner of the drafter, or if the will is reviewed by an independent lawyer.

2. Rebuttable Presumption

The transferee may establish by clear and convincing evidence that the transfer was not the product of fraud, menace, duress, or undue influence. Failure to rebut loses share above intestate succession.

C. Slayer Statute (CPC 250)

One who feloniously and intentionally kills the decedent is not entitled to: (i) any property, interest, or benefit under a will or trust of the decedent, including any power of appointment as executor, trustee, guardian; (ii) decedent's property by intestate succession, including the community property the killer could receive; or (iii) any of the decedent's quasi-community property the killer would acquire.

Determination of whether the killing was felonious and intentional:

1. A final judgment of conviction of felonious and intentional killing;

2. Absent a conviction, the court may determine by a *preponderance of evidence* whether the killing was felonious and intentional for purposes of this statute. The burden rests with the challenger.

D. Elder Abuse (CPC § 259)

An individual is deemed to have predeceased a decedent where all of the following apply:

1. It is proven by clear and convincing evidence that the person is liable for physical abuse, neglect, or fiduciary abuse of the decedent, who was an elder or dependent adult;
2. The person is found to have acted in bad faith;
3. The person has been found to have been reckless, oppressive, fraudulent, or malicious in the commission of any of these acts upon the decedent; and
4. Decedent was substantially unable to manage her finances or resist fraud or undue influence.

E. No-Contest Clause (CPC §§ 21310, 21311)

A no-contest clause is enforceable against a beneficiary who brings a contest within the terms of the no-contest clause.

1. Actions Not Constituting a Contest

The following actions do not constitute a contest unless they are *expressly identified* in the will:

a) The filing of a creditor's claim;
b) An action to determine the character, title, or ownership of property;
c) A challenge to the validity of a document other than the document containing the clause.

2. Not a Contest as a Matter of Public Policy

Certain actions are not considered contests as a matter of public policy and cannot be drafted around, including:

a) An action for the interpretation of the instrument containing the no-contest clause or a document expressly identified in the clause; or
b) An action for reformation of the testamentary instrument in order to carry out the testator's intent.

3. Unenforceable No-Contest Clauses

Certain clauses are not enforceable as per the following circumstances:

a) Reasonable cause

The beneficiary brings a contest on the following grounds: a) alleging forgery of the document; b) to establish prior revocation of the document; and c) to establish whether someone is a prohibited transferee.

b) Reasonable cause – defined

A person is in possession of facts that would cause a reasonable person to believe that the allegations filed with the court may be proven, or are likely to be proven, after a reasonable opportunity for investigation or discovery.

c) Probable cause

The beneficiary contests a provision that benefits: a) a person who drafted/transcribed the instrument; b) a person who gave directions to the drafter; or c) a person who acted as a witness.

F. Non-Probate Issues

1. Joint Tenancies

A joint tenant who feloniously and intentionally kills another joint tenant thereby affects a severance of the interest so that the share of the decedent passes as the decedent's property and the killer has no rights by survivorship.

2. Life Insurance

A named beneficiary of a life insurance policy, who feloniously and intentionally kills the insured person, is not entitled to any benefit under the policy, and it becomes payable as if the killer had predeceased the decedent.

VII. DEVISES UNDER THE WILL

A. Lapse

At common law, when a beneficiary dies after the testator executes his will but before the testator dies, the gift to the beneficiary fails.

1. Anti-Lapse (CPC §§ 21110, 21111)

California provides an anti-lapse statute to provide a replacement beneficiary in the event a beneficiary predeceases the testator. The anti-lapse statute applies only if the testator was kindred of the predeceased beneficiary, or kindred of a surviving, deceased, or former spouse of the testator. Where anti-lapse is applicable, issue of a deceased devisee take in his place. Anti-lapse will not operate where the will expressly precludes it or otherwise provides an alternate disposition schedule.

Approach

Step 1: Will the beneficiary be deemed to have predeceased the testator? (Commonly satisfied by death; the failure to meet survival requirement; or the application of a slayer statute)

Step 2: Does anti-lapse apply? – (Protected transferee)

a) Is the beneficiary kin of the testator, kin of a former, predeceased, or surviving spouse; and

b) Has the beneficiary left issue?

If a and b do not apply, go to Step 3.

If a and b apply:

i. Does the will express contrary intention?

ii. Is anti-lapse precluded by statute?

iii. Is the beneficiary a member of a class but died before the testator executed the will and the testator knew about it?

If any apply, anti-lapse does not apply. Go to Step 3.
If they do not apply, anti-lapse applies and the kin will receive the gift by right of representation.

Step 3: Anti-lapse does not apply. Is an alternative disposition specified? If yes, follow the alternate disposition; if no, go to Step 4.

Step 4: Is the gift an individual or class gift?
Class gift: In this circumstance, the gift goes to other members of the class.
Individual gift: The residuary beneficiary takes the gift. If there is no residuary beneficiary, property is distributed per intestate scheme.

B. Ademption (CPC § 21134)

If a gift is made in a will and it was sold before death, it is presumed that the testator did not want the person to take it. Only specific gifts adeem.

1. Types of Gifts

Specific gifts (e.g., car); Demonstrative gifts (e.g., Proceeds from the sale of the car); and General gifts (e.g., cash).

2. Mitigation Doctrines

a) Satisfaction

Property given to a person by the testator during his lifetime is treated as a satisfaction of an at-death transfer if one of the following is satisfied: (i) the will provides for the deduction of a lifetime gift from an at-death transfer; (ii) the testator declares in a contemporaneous writing that the gift is in satisfaction of an at-death transfer; (iii) the transferee acknowledges in writing that the gift is in satisfaction; and (iv) property given is the same as the specific gift to that person.

b) Specific Gifts and Money Owed to the Testator

A transferee may receive: (i) the balance of the purchase price owing from the sale of property; (ii) eminent domain award; (iii) insurance for injury to property; (iv) property acquired as a result of foreclosure, or obtained in lieu of foreclosure, of the security interest for a specifically given obligation.

c) Gifts Sold by Conservator

The recipient gets the sale price of the property, any eminent domain award, and proceeds of insurance on the gifted property.

d) Exoneration of Liens

Gifted property is transferred subject to any deed of trust, lien, without right of exoneration, regardless of a directive to pay debts.

e) Securities

If the will provides for transfer of securities owned by the testator, the gift includes stock acquired as a result of a merger, consolidation, purchase, or split.

C. Abatement (CPC § 21402)

Upon the death of the testator, when the estate is not sufficient to pay all debts, gifts to beneficiaries will be abated. An order of abatement may be specified in the will. Absent instructions by the testator, gifts abate in the following order: (i) intestate property; (ii) residuary gifts; (iii) general gifts to non-relatives; (iv) general gifts to relatives; (v) specific gifts to non-relatives; (vi) specific gifts to relatives. Gifts are abated pro-rata within a class. Anti-lapse is considered under the instrument.

D. Advancements (CPC § 6409)

A gift is an advancement against that heir's share of the intestate estate only if one of the following conditions is satisfied:

1. The decedent declares in a *contemporaneous* writing that the gift is an advancement against the heir's share of the estate; or
2. The heir acknowledges in writing that the gift is to be deducted or is an advancement from her share.
3. **Hotchpot**: If an advancement is greater than the share to be received at death, the beneficiary does not have to give money back, but devises will be adjusted to ensure equitable distribution.

VIII. TOTAL OR PARTIAL FAILURE OF THE WILL: INTESTATE SUCCESSION

A. Who are the Decedent's Heirs?

1. Adoption (CPC § 6451)

Adoption severs familial relationship with the natural family and establishes familial relationship with the adoptive family.

a) Exceptions

Adoptive child still inherits **from** natural parents where:

(1) The natural parent lived with the adopted child as parent (or would have but for dying too soon); **AND**

(2) a) Adoption follows the death of one of the natural parents; **OR** b) The adoption is conducted by a step-parent.

b) **TRUE WHOLE-BLOODED SIBLINGS**

True whole-blooded siblings of the adopted child inherit from him whenever he would have inherited from the natural parent (Steps 1+2).

c) **OTHER THAN WHOLE-BLOODED SIBLINGS**

The natural family inherits from the adopted child only where 1 + 2b above are met (i.e., only the parent who is still part of the adoptive child's nuclear family is deemed his relative).

2. EQUITABLE ADOPTION (CPC § 6455)

Under common law, if a natural parent gives up custody to a third party with the understanding that the third party adopt and treat the child as their natural heir when the third party dies, the courts will equitably enforce a child's right to claim as though she had been formally adopted.

3. FOSTER OR STEP-PARENT (CPC § 6454)

Intestate succession by a person or the person's issue from or through a foster parent or step-parent is permitted where:

a) The relationship began during the person's minority and continued throughout the joint lifetimes of the person and the person's foster parent or step-parent; **AND**

b) It is established by clear and convincing evidence that the foster/step-parent would have adopted the person but for a legal barrier (e.g., the natural parent would not consent).

4. WHO IS A NATURAL PARENT? (CPC § 6453)

A natural parent/child relationship is established where that relationship is presumed and not rebutted pursuant to the Uniform Parentage Act.

5. CHILDREN BORN OUT OF WEDLOCK (CPC § 6452)

If a child is born out of wedlock, neither a natural parent nor a relative of that parent inherits from or through the child unless **both** of the following requirements are satisfied:

a) The parent or a relative of the parent acknowledged the child; **AND**

b) The parent or a relative of the parent contributed to the support or the care of the child.

6. HALF-BLOODS (CPC § 6406)

Relatives of the half-blood inherit the same share they would inherit if they were of the whole blood.

a) **EXCEPTION**

They do not inherit through an adopted sibling.

7. UNBORN RELATIVES OF THE DECEDENT (CPC § 6407)

Relatives conceived before the decedent's death but born after it inherit as if they had been born in the lifetime of decedent.

a) **EXCEPTION**

Rebuttable presumption that a child born 300 days after the decedent's death was not conceived prior to his death.

B. DID THE HEIRS/BENEFICIARIES SURVIVE THE DECEDENT?

1. GENERAL INTESTATE (CPC § 6403)

If devolution of property depends upon priority of death and it cannot be established by clear and convincing evidence ("CCE") that one person survived the other by 120 hours, property of each person shall be distributed as if that person had survived the other.

2. SPECIFIC CALIFORNIA PROBATE CODE PROVISIONS

Technically not intestate succession

a) JOINT TENANTS (CPC § 223)

Without clear and convincing evidence that one survived the other, property shall be administered one-half as if one joint tenant had survived and one-half as if the other joint tenant had survived.

b) LIFE OR ACCIDENT INSURANCE (CPC § 224)

Without clear and convincing evidence that the beneficiary survived the insured, the proceeds shall be administered as if the insured had survived the beneficiary.

c) EXCEPTIONS TO APPLICABILITY

A provision is made dealing explicitly with simultaneous deaths OR survival for a stated period needed.

C. IS SUCCESSION BARRED?

See prohibited transferees above.

D. SHARE OF SURVIVING SPOUSE (CPC § 6401)

In California, the surviving spouse always gets the deceased spouse's community property and quasi-community property. As the surviving spouse already owned the other one-half of the community property and quasi-community property, the decedent's spouse owns 100% of the community property and quasi-community property. However, the surviving spouse's share of the deceased spouse's separate property depends on which other heir(s) survive:

1. Separate Property Division: **Spouse 100% - Heirs 0%**
   Occurs where no issue, parents or issue of parents (siblings, nieces/nephews, etc.) remain.
2. Separate Property Division: **Spouse 50% - Heirs 50%**
   Occurs where one issue, OR
   No issue but 1+ parent or issue of parent remains.
3. Separate Property Division: **Spouse 33.3% - Heirs 66.6%**
   Occurs where two or more issue, i.e., 2+ children, 1 child & 1+ grandchild, etc., remain.

E. SHARE NOT PASSING TO SURVIVING SPOUSE (CPC § 6402)

1. Each category takes to the exclusion of all others:
   a) Issue (children, grandchildren, great-grandchildren, etc.);
   b) Parents;
   c) Issue of Parents (nieces and nephews, or issue of nieces and nephews);
   d) Grandparents;
   e) Issue of Grandparents (cousins);
   f) Issue of a Predeceased Spouse;
   g) Next of Kin (blood relatives, no matter how remote);
   h) Parents of Predeceased Spouse;
   i) Issue of Parents of Predeceased Spouse;
   j) State of California.

2. **Distribution (CPC § 240)**: How persons within a given class that take divide their shares by modern per stirpes:
   Step 1: Find the first generation with a living member (skip deceased generations).

Step 2: Divide the inheritance into shares equal to as many living members there are in that generation plus deceased members who are survived by living issue. Predeceased individuals who leave no living issue are dead-lines and do not count.

Step 3: Distribute shares to the living members of that first living generation and the predeceased members leaving issue. For predeceased members leaving issue, divide up and distribute their share to their issue by right of representation.

3. Collateral ancestors who are related to the decedent through great-grandparents or beyond are considered "next of kin," and their shares are distributed by:

Step 1: Determining how many degrees away each kin is from the decedent. To do this: a) Find the common ancestor; b) Count one degree "up" for each generation from decedent to the common ancestor; c) Count one degree "down" from the common ancestor to the kin; and d) Add up and down steps to get total degrees of relation.

Step 2: Determining who, among kin, takes priority: a) Kin of closer (lower) degree take to the exclusion of kin of further (higher) degree; b) If kin are of equal degree, the one related to the decedent through the closest ancestor (i.e., fewest degrees "up") takes to the exclusion of the other; and c) If kin are of equal degree *and* through equal "up" degrees, they share equally.

IX. MISCELLANEOUS

A. CONTRACTS RELATING TO WILLS (CPC § 21700)

1. A contract to make or revoke a will or other instrument or to die intestate is established only by one of the following:
   - **a)** Provisions of a will or instrument stating the material provisions of the contract;
   - **b)** Express reference in the will to a contract and extrinsic evidence proving the terms of contract;
   - **c)** The actual contract;
   - **d)** Clear and convincing evidence of an agreement by the decedent with the claimant; ***OR***
   - **e)** Clear and convincing evidence of an agreement by the decedent but for the benefit of a third party.

2. Joint or mutual wills do not create a presumption of a contract not to revoke a will/wills.
   - **a) Joint Wills:** Both people dispose of their property in one will.
   - **b) Mutual Wills:** Two separate documents that are mirror images of each other.

3. **Effect:** If a contract concerning a will is breached, an action for damages against the testator's estate or to impose a constructive trust on the testator's beneficiaries may exist, but any duly executed will must be probated. Remedies include:

   Suing in contract to recover the value of services rendered or for breach. However, spousal care is not valid consideration for a contract, as the spouse already had a duty to do it before the promise. Where there is a pre-existing duty, there is no consideration.

Primer Outlines

BUSINESS ASSOCIATIONS PRIMER

I. CORPORATIONS

A. Formation

1. **Statutory Requirements**

   a) **Effect of Defective Incorporation**

      (1) **Corporation Liability:** The shareholders of a validly formed corporation will not be subject to personal liability for the corporation's debts.

   b) **De Facto and De Jure Corporations**

      (1) **De Jure Corporations:** Compliance with all applicable statutory requirements, and the Articles of Incorporation have been filed with the state.

      (2) **De Facto Corporations:** The law may still recognize a business as a legal corporation where: (i) there is an incorporation statute under which the entity could have been validly incorporated; (ii) the corporation made a good-faith effort to comply; and (iii) the business is being conducted as a corporation.

   c) **Corporation by Estoppel:** Where a person operates a business as if it were a corporation, or a person who deals with a business as if it were a corporation, will be estopped from denying its existence.

2. **Actions by Promoter:** Promoters may enter into contracts for the corporation.

   a) **Fiduciary Duty:** A promoter owes a fiduciary duty to act in good faith and is accompanied by the obligations of confidence and trust.

      (1) **Breach Arising from Sales to the Corporation:** A promoter may make profits by selling property to the corporation as long as he provides a full disclosure of all material facts to an independent board, which approves the sale.

   b) **Pre-Incorporation Agreements**

      (1) **Promoter's Liability:** If a promoter enters into a contract on behalf of a planned, but not-yet-formed, corporation, the promoter will be held personally liable on the contract for its duration, or until there is an express release.

      (2) **Promoter's Right to Reimbursement:** If a promoter is held personally liable on a pre-incorporation contract, the corporation may have to reimburse him.

      (3) **Corporation's Liability:** Until the corporation expressly or impliedly adopts or ratifies the contract, it will not be bound by it, only the promoter will be bound.

   c) **Stock Subscriptions:** Under a strict definition, a "stock subscription" is a promise to purchase shares of stock in a yet-to-be formed corporation.

      (1) **Pre-Incorporation Subscriptions:** Subscribers cannot revoke their subscriptions for six (6) months without an express provision providing the right, or the unanimous consent of all subscribers.

      (2) **Post-Incorporation Subscriptions:** Post-incorporation subscriptions are revocable before acceptance, except in California.

      (3) **Enforcement of Subscriptions**

         (a) **Enforcement by Corporation:** An agreement can be enforced against a subscriber but not a bona fide purchaser transferee without notice.

(b) **Release of Subscription:** Subscriptions can be released only when shareholders and subscribers consent and there is no harm to creditors.

(4) **Valid Issuance of Stock Subscriptions**

(a) **Requirements for Valid Issuance**

i. **Proper Authorization and Issuance:** The Articles of Incorporation and the Board of Directors must authorize the issuance of stock.

ii. **Consideration:** Adequate consideration must be paid for the stock.

iii. **Effect:** The corporation can cancel the stock to the extent that the stock is not supported by valid consideration, but it cannot recover damages.

(b) **Preemptive Rights Issues:** Shareholders may have the right to purchase a proportionate number of shares of newly authorized stock before it is offered to outsiders, where provided for in the Articles of Incorporation.

(c) **Classification of Stock**

i. **Preferred Stock:** Stockholders receive dividends before common stockholders, and they may have priority as to liquidation/conversion.

ii. **Treasury Shares:** Such shares are issued and repurchased by the corporation.

3. **Amendment to Articles of Incorporation:** Most changes require shareholder approval. "Housekeeping" amendments can be made without shareholder approval.

4. **Merger and Share Exchange**

A merger is a blending of one or more corporations into another.

a) **Merger - Approval of Shareholder is Not Required When:**

(1) The Articles of Incorporation of the surviving corporation are the same as the Articles before the merger;

(2) The shareholders will retain the same number of shares with identical preferences, limitations, and rights;

(3) The voting power of the shares issued do not amount to more than 20% of the outstanding shares before the merger; and

(4) The parent company owns at least 90% of the outstanding shares of the subsidiary with which it is merging.

b) **Share Exchange:** Where one corporation purchases all of the outstanding shares of another corporation. Only the shareholders of the acquired corporation need to give approval, as it is a fundamental change.

B. Corporate Powers

1. **Share Re-Purchase:** Such occurs where a corporation agrees to buy back shares at a shareholder's option. This is enforceable where there are available funds.

a) **Redemption:** A corporation may acquire outstanding shares pursuant to its Articles of Incorporation, unless insolvency will result.

2. **Gifts and loans**

a) **Gifts:** Most states permit corporate gifts if they are reasonable, approved by directors, paid from profits and for charitable purposes.

b) **Loans:** Corporations may lend money and invest and reinvest funds.

3. **Asset Transfer:** The sale, lease, or exchange of all or substantially all, of a corporation's property, outside of the regular course of business, is considered a fundamental corporate change that requires approval (See Fundamental Changes, below).

4. **Ultra Vires Acts:** Activities beyond the scope of a corporation's enumerated powers are said to be ultra vires. Ultra vires acts are not automatically void, but are voidable.

C. Officers and Directors

1. Duties and Powers

a) **Duties:** Duties are determined by bylaws and the Board and its delegates.

b) **Powers:** Ordinary rules of agency apply regarding actual and apparent authority.

(1) The corporation is not liable for a contract made by an officer without authority.

(2) The corporation may become bound by ratification, adoption, or estoppel.

2. Indemnification

a) **Mandatory Indemnification:** A director or officer who prevails in defending a proceeding against himself is entitled to indemnification from the corporation.

b) **Discretionary Indemnification:** If the director or officer is unsuccessful, a corporation has the discretion to indemnify the officer where: (i) the director acted in good-faith; and (ii) acted in the best interests of the corporation (when within her official capacity), or it was not opposed to the best interests of the corporation (when not within official capacity).

c) **Exceptions:** There is no discretion to indemnify when an officer is found liable to the corporation, or when an officer received an improper benefit.

d) **Determination:** The decision to indemnify an officer is made by a disinterested majority of the Board, independent committee, shareholders, or legal counsel.

(1) **Officers:** Officers may be indemnified to the same extent as directors.

3. **Inspection Rights:** Directors have a right to inspect all books, records, documents, facilities, and premises. Some states limit a director's right to inspect to purposes reasonably related to the director's position as a director.

4. Meetings and Actions

a) **Meetings**

(1) **Annual:** Every corporation must hold an annual meeting.

(2) **Special:** Either a Board of Directors, or the holders of 10% of the shares entitled to vote may call a special meeting.

(3) **Written Notice:** Written notice is required at least 10 days before a meeting and not more than 60 days. Notice can be expressly waived.

(4) **Actions Taken at Meetings**

(a) Failure to comply with formalities makes any action taken void.

(b) Regular meetings do not require notice. Special meetings require reasonable written notice (at least two (2) days in advance, absent a waiver).

(c) A quorum of directors is required at meetings or as stated in the bylaws, but not less than one third of all directors.

(d) Unlike shareholder meetings, a withdrawing director can break a quorum.

(5) **Approval of Action:** A director has actual authority to bind corporation where a directors' meeting was held after proper notice was given, a quorum was present and a majority of the directors approved the action.

5. **Fiduciary Obligations**

a) **Conflicts of Interest**

(1) **Conflicting Interest Transactions:** A director's duty of loyalty may be implicated by a conflict of interest with respect to a transaction if the director knows that he, or a related person, is either:

(a) A party to the transaction;

(b) Someone with a financial interest in, or closely linked to, the transaction, making the director's judgment susceptible to influence; or

(c) A director, partner, agent, or employee of another entity with whom the corporation is transacting business and the transaction is one that would normally be brought before the Board.

(2) **Upholding the Transaction:** A transaction does not give rise to damages if:

(a) A majority of directors approved of the transaction after all material facts were disclosed;

(b) The shareholders, upon proper notice, approved of the transaction, through casting a majority of the votes entitled to be cast, after material facts have been disclosed to the shareholders; or

(c) The transaction was fair to the corporation and judged according to the circumstances present when the transaction was entered into.

(3) **Requirements:** A quorum must be present and comprised of disinterested directors or shareholders.

(4) **Fairness:** Courts will look at the consideration provided, corporate need to enter into transaction, corporate finances, available alternatives, and waste.

(5) **Remedies:** Remedies include enjoining the transaction, setting aside the transaction and awarding damages.

b) **Competition Against Corporation**

(1) **Competing Business:** Directors may engage in businesses unrelated to the corporation's business, but not a competing business.

c) **Transactions Involving Corporation**

(1) Directors' duty of due care requires directors to make decisions: (i) in good faith; (ii) with the care that a reasonably prudent person in their position would apply; and (iii) in a manner they reasonably believe is in the corporation's best interest.

d) **Delegation of Authority**

(1) **Powers:** (i) Unfettered discretion in making management decisions (with a quorum present unless the bylaws state otherwise); (ii) Select, remove, and compensate officers and agents, with or without cause; (iii) Incur debt; (iv) Declare dividends; (v) Fill vacancies on boards by a majority vote; (vi) Make and amend bylaws where a statute so provides, or where shareholders grant the power to do so; (vii) Delegate duties; (viii) Buy and sell corporation property and stock; and (ix) Delegate authority to officers or executive committees.

6. **Director Liability**

   a) **Limitation of Personal Liability:** The Articles may limit or eliminate a director's personal liability for money damages to the corporation or shareholders for a breach of fiduciary duty through an action or omission, except where: (i) he receives financial benefits to which he is not entitled; (ii) he intentionally inflicts harm on the corporation or its shareholders; (iii) he unlawfully makes corporate distributions; or (iv) he intentionally commits a crime.

7. **De Facto Officers and Directors:** A person who was not formally appointed as a director or officer, but performs the duties of the position, may be a de facto officer, or director with rights, obligations and liabilities of a director.

8. **Election, Resignation, and Removal**

   a) **Directors**

      (1) **Election:** There need only be one director, unless the Articles or bylaws require additional directors. Directors are elected at shareholder meetings.

      (2) **Removal:** The shareholders may remove the directors with or without cause, unless the Articles state otherwise. If the directors are elected by a cumulative vote, a director cannot be removed if the number of votes cast against removal would be enough to elect him. If a director was elected by a voting group of shareholders, only that group of shareholders vote.

   b) **Officers**

      (1) **Election:** The Board of Directors chooses officers to manage the corporation.

      (2) **Resignation and Removal:** An officer may resign at any time upon giving notice to the corporation and the corporation may remove an officer with or without cause, regardless of any term in the Articles, bylaws, or other contract.

9. **Business Judgment Rule**

   a) **Duty of Care:** The duty of due care requires decisions to be made: (i) in good faith; (ii) with the care that a reasonably prudent person in their position would; and (iii) in a manner they reasonably believe is in the best interests of the corporation.

   b) **Business Judgment Rule:** Directors will not be liable for corporate decisions made in accordance with these standards even if they later turn out to be wrong.

      (1) **Burden on Challenger:** The party challenging the decision must prove the standard was not met.

      (2) **Director May Rely on Reports, etc.:** When making decisions, a director may rely on information, opinions, reports, or statements, if prepared or presented by:

         (a) Corporate employees who are believed to be reliable and competent;

         (b) Legal counsel, accountants, or other persons, as to matters that are within the person's professional competence; or

         (c) A committee of which the director is not a member, if the director reasonably believes the committee merits confidence.

10. **Obligations with Respect to Corporate Opportunities**

   a) **Corporate Opportunity Doctrine:** A director's fiduciary duties prohibit him from taking advantage of a business opportunity that would benefit the corporation without first disclosing the opportunity to act.

(1) **Corporation Interest or Expectancy:** A director only violates his fiduciary duty if the opportunity is one in which the corporation would have an interest or expectancy.

(2) **Financial Ability:** The director cannot claim that the corporation could not have financially taken advantage of the opportunity in his defense.

(3) **Board Generally Decides:** Generally, the Board must decide whether to accept or reject an opportunity.

b) **Remedies:** Corporation can either recover the director's profits, or force the director to convey the opportunity for whatever consideration the director paid.

D. Shareholders

1. Rights

a) **Meetings and Elections**

(1) **Attendance:** A quorum is required for any vote to be taken. A quorum requires a majority of the outstanding shares that are entitled to vote, unless the Articles or bylaws require a greater number.

b) **Voting**

(1) The shareholders elect the directors and may remove them.

(2) Only the shareholders of record date can vote.

(3) **Proxy Votes:** A proxy is a power of attorney to vote shares.

(a) **Duration:** An appointment of a proxy is valid for eleven months unless the appointment provides otherwise. A shareholder may revoke an appointment of a proxy at any time. He cannot revoke a proxy if the appointment states that it is irrevocable and grants the proxy an interest.

(b) **Solicitation of Proxies:** Common law proxies obtained by fraud are void.

i. Section 14(a) applies only to corporations with more than $10 million in assets and at least 500 shareholders. Proxy statements must include all pertinent facts and be filed with the SEC and cannot contain material misstatements or omissions.

ii. Remedy for Violation: The SEC can get an injunction; a private plaintiff can enjoin voting of proxies, cancel election of directors, or receive money damages.

(c) **Close Corporation Shareholder Agreements:** Close corporation shareholder agreements are valid if they are for a proper purpose.

i. **Pooling Agreements:** Shareholders may enter into agreements providing for the manner in which they will vote their shares.

ii. **Voting Trust:** A voting trust is a written agreement among shareholders under which all the parties transfer their shares to a trustee, who then votes in accordance with the agreement.

iii. **Stock Transfer Agreements:** Reasonable restrictions to keep stock from being freely transferred will be enforced and bind a third-party purchaser if: (i) the restrictions are conspicuously noted on the certificate; and (ii) the third party knew of the restrictions at time of purchase.

(d) **Straight and Cumulative Voting for Directors**

i. **Straight Voting:** One vote per share.

ii. **Cumulative Voting:** The number of shareholder's shares multiplied by the number of directors to be elected.

iii. **Class Voting:** When an amendment to the Articles will affect only a particular class of stock, that class has the right to vote on the action even if the class otherwise does not have voting rights.

c) **Inspection**

(1) Shareholders have a right to inspect corporate books and records.

(2) Generally, any shareholder may inspect the annual reports, minutes of shareholder meetings, bylaws, charter, and list of the shareholders.

(3) A group of shareholders (usually 5-10% of outstanding stock) may inspect all books and records. Some states require a showing of good cause.

d) **Dividends:** A corporation may make distributions in the form of dividends, through the redemption or repurchase of shares, or by distributing assets upon liquidation.

(1) **Rights to Distributions:** Generally left to the discretion of the corporation, but at least one stock class must have the right to receive net assets on dissolution.

(a) **Board's Discretion:** Unless otherwise agreed, shareholders cannot compel a distribution. Even if the Articles authorize distributions in certain circumstances, the decision whether or not to declare a distribution is left solely to the directors, subject to solvency limitations.

i. **Solvency Requirements:** A corporation cannot make a distribution if: (i) the corporation could not pay debts as they become due; or (ii) the corporation's total assets would be less than its total liabilities plus the amount needed to satisfy the preferential rights of shareholders whose rights are superior to those receiving the distribution.

ii. **Restrictions in the Articles:** The Articles may limit a Board's discretion and restrict its right to declare dividends.

iii. **Share Dividends:** Shares of another class may not be issued as dividends unless otherwise agreed.

e) **Protection Against and Limitations on Fundamental Changes**

(1) **Dissenting Shareholders:** Dissenting shareholders may exercise their right to have the corporation purchase their shares.

(a) Dissenting Shareholders must: (i) have been entitled to vote on the merger; or (ii) be the shareholders of corporation being acquired; or (iii) be the shareholders entitled to vote on disposition of corporation property; or (iv) be the shareholders whose rights will be materially and adversely affected by an amendment of the Articles.

(b) **Procedure**

i. Corporation must give the shareholders notice of the meeting and notice of change and how to submit claims.

ii. Before voting, dissenting shareholder must give written notice of their intent to demand payment for shares.

iii. Shareholder must demand payment under terms of notice.

iv. The corporation must pay amount estimated at fair value.

v. A notice of dissatisfaction must be filed within 30 days with the shareholder's estimated value and a payment demand.

vi. If the corporation disagrees as to the amount, it must file a demand to determine the fair value of the shares within 60 days.

2. **Derivative Actions**

a) **Direct Actions:** A shareholder may bring a lawsuit, on her own behalf, against an officer or director for breach of fiduciary duty. Must look at:

(1) Who suffers the most immediate and direct damage; and

(2) To whom did the defendant's duty run? In a shareholder action, any recovery will benefit the individual shareholder.

b) **Derivative Actions:** A shareholder may bring a lawsuit against an officer or director on behalf of the corporation. Shareholder will still be named as defendant.

(1) The corporation generally receives a recovery in a derivative action.

c) **Standing:** Shareholder must have been a shareholder at the time of the act or omission, or have become a shareholder through a transfer from an individual who was a shareholder at that time.

d) **Demand:** Before filing an action, the shareholder must demand in writing that the corporation take suitable action.

(1) The shareholder must wait 90 days from the date of demand before filing the action unless the corporation rejects the demand; or the corporation would suffer irreparable injury if the shareholder waits for the 90 days to pass.

(2) **Corporation's Best Interests:** A majority of the directors with no personal interest in the controversy may petition the court to dismiss the action.

(a) **Burden of Proof:** Shareholder bringing the suit must show that the corporation's decision to petition the court was not made in good faith after reasonable inquiry.

(b) If a majority of the directors have a vested interest, the corporation must show good faith after reasonable inquiry.

(3) **Discontinuance or Settlement:** The parties may discontinue or settle a derivative proceeding only with the approval of the court.

(4) **Payment of Expenses:** A court may order the corporation to pay a shareholder's reasonable expenses upon finding that the corporation substantially benefited from the action; the shareholder may have to pay the corporation's reasonable expenses if suit brought for improper purpose or without reasonable cause.

3. **Fiduciary Obligation:** Shareholders only owe a duty of loyalty to the corporation and other shareholders when engaging in transactions with the corporation.

4. **Shareholder Liability:** Shareholder liability is generally limited to the liabilities for unpaid stock, a pierced corporate veil, or absence of a de facto corporation.

a) **Controlling Shareholder:** One exception is a controlling shareholder, who has a fiduciary duty, who cannot take any action to the detriment of other minority shareholders, or to the corporation.

(1) Controlling shareholder: (i) must investigate a buyer to prevent looting and corporate raiding; (ii) must share premiums with minority shareholders when

selling corporate assets; and (iii) may not use her power to exploit corporate assets.

5. **Restrictions on Share Transfer**

   a) **Preemptive Rights:** Shareholders do not have a preemptive right, or right of first refusal, to purchase new shares unless the Articles provide otherwise.

      (1) If shareholders do have a preemptive right, it will not apply to shares that were issued for consideration other than cash, within 6 months after incorporation, and those without voting rights regardless of a distribution preference.

   b) **Compulsory Buy-Out Provisions:** One shareholder may compel the company or other shareholders to purchase his shares in the event of certain triggering events.

   c) **"Shotgun" Clauses:** A dissatisfied shareholder can ask other shareholders to buy all their shares or to sell his shares.

E. Federal Securities Laws

1. **Rule 10(b)(5):** It is illegal for any person to engage in any practice that operates as a fraud in connection with the purchase or sale of any security. A plaintiff must prove:

   a) **Fraudulent Conduct:** The defendant engaged in some fraudulent conduct by making a material misstatement or omission of material fact.

   b) **Materiality:** A statement or omission is material if there is a substantial likelihood that a reasonable investor would have considered it important.

   c) **Scienter:** Defendant must have had intent to deceive, manipulate, or defraud.

   d) **In Connection with Purchase or Sale by Plaintiff:** If plaintiff is a private person, he must connect the fraudulent conduct to the actual sale or purchase.

   e) **In Interstate Commerce:** Defendant used some means of interstate commerce.

   f) **Reliance:** Plaintiff relied on the defendant's fraudulent representation.

   g) **Damages:** Defendant's fraud caused the plaintiff's damages.

2. **Insider Trading**

   a) Rule 10(b)(5) also prohibits most instances of insider trading where a person breaches a duty of trust and confidence owed to the issuer, shareholders of the issuer, or another person who is the source of the material nonpublic information.

   b) **Insider Liability:** If an insider gives a tip to someone who then trades on the basis of that information, the tipper is liable if the tip was made for any improper purpose, such as in exchange for money, kickbacks, and reputational benefits. The person receiving and using the information is liable only if the tipper breached a duty, of which the tipper knew.

   c) **Misappropriation:** The government can prosecute a person for trading on market information, thus breaching the duty of trust and confidence.

3. **Short Swing Profits**

   a) Section 16(b) requires a director, officer, or shareholder owning more than 10% of a class of stock to surrender any profit realized from the purchase and sale, or sale and purchase, of any equity security within a 6 month period.

      (1) The section applies to publicly held corporations:

         (a) With more than $10 million in assets and 500 or more shareholders; or

         (b) Whose shares are traded on the National Stock Exchange.

b) **Strict Liability:** The purpose is to prevent unfair use of inside information and internal manipulation of price. This is accomplished by strict liability.

c) **Essay Approach**

(1) Was the defendant an officer, director, or more than 10% shareholder?

(2) Did the defendant trade an equity security?

(3) Did a purchase and sale occur within a 6 month period?

(4) What was the profit realized? Can be either a gain or avoidance of loss.

4. **Sale of Controlling Interest**

a) **Tender Offers:** Widespread public offering to purchase a substantial percentage of the target's shares.

(1) **Regulation of Bidder:** Bidder must file a 14D schedule disclosing: (i) identities of the bidder and subject company; (ii) the source of funds used to finance the tender offer; (iii) past dealings with the target; (iv) its plans for the target; (v) the bidder's financial statements; and (vi) any arrangements made with target persons.

(2) **Regulation of the Offer:** A tender offer must be held open for at least 20 days and open to all members of the class. Shareholders must be permitted to withdraw.

(3) **Regulation of Target:** The target company's Board of Directors or management must make recommendations for acceptance or rejection of the tender offer or state why it cannot make a recommendation

(4) **Anti-Fraud:** Shareholders can sue for damages, or the SEC may seek an injunction blocking the transaction where there are false or misleading statements.

F. **Disregard of the Corporate Entity:** Courts can hold shareholders liable for corporate actions or debts.

1. **Grounds for Piercing the Veil**

a) **Fraud:** A court may pierce the corporate veil to prevent shareholders from using the corporation to commit fraud, or to avoid existing personal obligations.

b) **Undercapitalization:** A court may pierce the corporate veil when the corporation is inadequately capitalized.

c) **Alter Ego Theory:** If the corporation is merely an "alter ego" of the owner or another corporation, the corporate veil may be pierced.

(1) Evidence includes where shareholders: (i) utterly fail to observe formalities; (ii) treat the corporation's assets as their own; or (iii) operate the corporation solely on their own funds.

d) **Enterprise Liability Theory:** When the same shareholders own stock of two corporations engaged in the same enterprise, a creditor of one corporation can reach the assets of the other.

e) **Deep Rock Doctrine:** Loans to a corporation by controlling shareholders may be subordinated to claims by outside creditors when the corporation is undercapitalized, or where there is bad-faith, fraud, or gross mismanagement.

2. **Who is Liable?** The individuals who actively operated or managed the corporation will be jointly and severally liable as individuals.

3. **Types of Liability:** The corporate veil can be pierced in tort cases and in contract cases.

4. **Who May Pierce:** Creditors may pierce the corporate veil.

G. **Dissolution:** A corporation's existence can be terminated voluntarily or judicially.

1. **Effect**

a) A dissolved corporation still exists, but it cannot carry out any activities, other than those associated with winding up and liquidation.

b) After dissolution, the Board of Directors liquidates the assets and distributes the proceeds – first to creditors, then to the preferred shareholder, and finally to the common shareholders.

2. **Voluntary and Involuntary Methods**

a) **Voluntary:** To voluntarily dissolve a corporation, the Board of Directors adopts a resolution and provides written notice to shareholders; the shareholders approve changes by a majority of votes that are entitled to be cast; and the corporation files the changes with the state.

b) **Administrative:** The state may seek dissolution for failure to pay fees, fines, file annual reports, or failure to maintain a registered agent.

c) **Judicial**

(1) **Attorney General:** The Attorney General may seek dissolution on the basis that the corporation fraudulently obtained its Articles of Incorporation, or is exceeding or abusing its authority.

(2) **Action by Shareholders:** Grounds include:

(a) The Board of Directors are deadlocked and irreparable injury to the corporation is threatened because of the deadlock;

(b) The directors have committed or will commit fraud, illegal or oppressive acts; or

(c) The directors have failed to elect one or more directors for two consecutive annual meetings; corporation assets are being wasted or used for non-corporation purposes.

(3) **Creditors:** Where a creditor's claim has been reduced to a judgment and the corporation is insolvent.

H. **Close Corporations:** A close corporation is a corporation held by a few persons, usually family members. Most states limit the number of stockholders.

1. **Formation:** Formed in the same way as ordinary corporations, but the Articles must state that the corporation shall be considered a "close corporation."

a) May be operated like a partnership with no Board of Directors or officers.

2. **Rights and Liabilities:** Shareholders may manage the corporation and override the directors. Manager–shareholders may be liable for acts or omissions for which the corporate directors are usually liable.

3. **Creditors' Rights:** A creditor may get a charging order to satisfy a shareholder's personal debt liability.

4. **Dissolution:** A close corporation may be dissolved voluntarily or judicially.

I. **Professional Corporations:** A professional corporation is like a corporation, but is limited to certain professions. Each individual is still liable for her own malpractice.

1. **Formation:** Professional corporations are created by state-licensed professions.

   a) A professional corporation is organized under state laws and must get approval from the state licensing board that regulates the relevant profession.

2. **Operation**

   a) The shareholders must be actively engaged in the business.

   b) Many states require that the corporation be established only to provide professional services.

3. **Creditor rights:** Shareholder cannot be sued for the corporation's business debts, or for the careless acts of another shareholder.

4. **Dissolution:** Voluntarily or judicially. Most states require an agreement of dissolution to be filed with the Secretary of State.

II. PARTNERSHIPS AND UNINCORPORATED ASSOCIATIONS

A. Agency Principles:

Agency Principles: Agency is a legally binding relationship wherein the agent represents the principal in business dealings with third parties.

1. **Formation of the Agency:** Agency is a relationship created by the mutual consent of the principal and agent.

   a) **Capacity:** The principal must have the capacity to enter into a contract. An agent must have mental capacity, but not contract capacity.

   b) **Disqualification:** An agent risks disqualification for representing the principal as well as the third party, or for not having a required license.

   c) **Formalities**

      (1) **Consent:** The consent of both the principal and the agent is required.

      (2) **Consideration:** Consideration is not required to create an agency relationship.

      (3) **Writing:** Generally, no writing is required unless so required by a state.

   d) **Modes of Creation**

      (1) **Act of Parties:** By agreement between the principal and agent (actual authority); by the principal holding out the agent as its agent (apparent authority); or the principal's approval of an act of its agent (ratification).

      (2) **Operation of Law**

         (a) **Estoppel:** An agency may be created through estoppel, if the third party relies on the principal's communication.

         (b) **Statute:** State statutes may create agency relationships. This generally applies to real estate transactions.

2. **Powers of the Agent**

   a) An agent is authorized to act for the principal. The terms of the contract provide the powers for which the agent is authorized to exercise on behalf of the principal.

   b) When acting within her authority, the agent can bind the principal contractually.

3. **Principal's Liability for Contracts and Torts of the Agent**

   a) **Actual Authority:** Actual authority is that which the agent reasonably believed he possessed based on the principal's dealings with him.

(1) **Express Authority:** Express authority is that which is actually described within the agency agreement.

(2) **Implied Authority:** Implied authority is that which the agent reasonably believed he had as a result of the principal's actions. It includes authority:

(a) Incidental to the principal's given, express authority;
(b) In line with the principal's customs, of which the agent knows;
(c) Under a prior agreement;
(d) Necessary in an emergency;
(e) Necessary to delegate authority for ministerial acts when delegation is customary for the required performance;
(f) Necessary to pay for and accept delivery of goods where the agent has the authority to purchase and accept goods;
(g) Necessary to give general warranties as to fitness and quality, authorize covenants regarding land sales, collect payment, and deliver where the agent has the authority to sell; and
(h) Necessary to manage investments in accordance with the prudent investor standard.

(3) **Termination of Actual Authority:** Has the authority been terminated? Termination of actual authority may occur by:

(a) Lapse of specified or reasonable time;
(b) Occurrence of a specified event;
(c) Change in circumstances such as when the subject matter is destroyed, insolvency or a change in law or the business's status;
(d) The agent's breach of his fiduciary duty;
(e) One party terminating the authority;
(f) Operation of law such as the death of the principal.

(4) **Irrevocable Agencies:** An agency coupled with an interest, or a power given as security, may not be unilaterally terminated by the principal if the agency was given to protect the agent's (or a third party's) rights and the agency is supported by consideration, or by operation of law.

b) **Apparent Authority:** A principal directly or indirectly confers apparent authority on an agent when he holds another out as possessing certain authority, thereby inducing reasonable reliance by third parties.

(1) **Types of Apparent Authority**

(a) **Imposters:** Principal will be held liable for an imposter's actions when the principal negligently allows the person to appear to have authority.

(b) **Lingering Apparent Authority**

i. **Notice:** When the principal terminates the agent's actual authority, the agent will still have apparent authority with third parties with whom the principal knows the agent dealt, until the third parties receive actual or constructive notice of termination.

ii. **Writing:** When third parties rely on a written authority, the agent will still have apparent authority.

iii. **Death or Incompetency:** An agent's authority ends when the principal dies or becomes incompetent.

(2) **Exceeding Actual Authority:** In certain situations, the principal may still be bound by an agent's acts even when he has exceeded his authority.

(a) **Prior Act:** When the principal has previously permitted the agent to exceed his authority, of which the third party is aware.

(b) **Position:** Acts within the scope of the agent's customary responsibilities.

(3) **Inherent Authority (Inherent Agency Power):** A principal may be bound by an agent's act that is within the agent's inherent authority even though the agent had no actual authority to perform the particular acts.

(a) **Respondeat Superior:** The principal is liable for the torts that an employee commits within the scope of employment.

(b) **Conduct Similar to that Authorized:** Where an agent exceeds his actual authority, but the agent's conduct is similar to authorized conduct, the principal will be held liable for the agent's acts.

c) **Ratification:** When an agent purports to act on behalf of a principal and the principal subsequently validates the act, the principal is bound by the act.

(1) **Prerequisites:** To be bound by ratification, the principal must know (or should have known) all material facts, ratify the entire transaction, and have the capacity – competency, be of legal age – to ratify the act.

(2) **Methods:** Principal can expressly or impliedly ratify the conduct of the principal.

(3) **Effective:** Where performance is not illegal, a third party has not withdrawn, or there is no material change in the situation.

d) **Liabilities of the Parties**

(1) **Third Party v. Principal:** The principal is liable to a third party on a contract entered into by an agent with authority.

(2) **Third Party v. Agent:** The agent's liability depends on whether or not the principal was disclosed.

(a) **Disclosed Principal:** A disclosed principal is always liable. An agent is not liable unless otherwise agreed, or the agent misrepresents the principal's contractual capacity or agent's authority.

(b) **Partially Disclosed/Undisclosed Principals:** If the principal is partially disclosed or undisclosed, the principal and the agent are liable.

(3) **Third Party Liability to Principal and Agent**

(a) **Principal Disclosed:** Only the principal, not the agent, may enforce the contract where the principal is disclosed.

(b) **Partially or Undisclosed:** Either the principal or the agent may enforce the contract where the principal is undisclosed or partially disclosed.

(c) **Not Enforceable:** Contract is not enforceable where there is fraud.

e) **Tort Liability – Respondeat Superior:** The doctrine of Respondeat Superior imputes joint and several liability to the employer-principal for torts committed by the employee-agent within the scope of the employee's employment.

(1) **Employer-Employee Relationship**

(a) **Independent Contractor or Employee:** A principal is only liable for torts committed by agents who are employees, not independent contractors.

i. **Right to Control:** A principal cannot control the manner or method in which an independent contractor performs a job. A principal can exercise such control over an employee.

ii. **Factors to Consider:** (i) the parties; (ii) whether the business is distinct; (iii) local customs; (iv) the level of skill required for the job; (v) whether the contractor is using his own tools or the facility's tools; (vi) time; and (vii) the basis for compensation.

(b) **Estoppel:** If the principal creates the appearance of an employer-employee relationship and a third party relies on it, that principal will be estopped from denying the existence of such a relationship.

(c) **Borrowed Employee:** Any liability is determined by who has the primary right to control the employee's actions.

(d) **Liability for Acts by Independent Contractors:** The principal will be liable where: (i) the work is inherently dangerous; (ii) the independent contractor delegates non-delegable duties; (iii) the principal knowingly selected an incompetent independent contractor

(2) **Scope of Employment:** The employer will be liable for the employee's torts if they were committed within the scope of employment.

(a) **Same General Nature of Job:** If the nature of the conduct is similar or incidental to that which is authorized, the conduct is probably within the scope of employment. Criminal acts are never within the scope.

(b) **Frolic and Detour:** A detour or small deviation is within scope. When there is a major detour, proof of return is needed before liability resumes.

(c) **Intentional Torts:** Intentional torts are not within the scope of employment unless they are incidental to the employee's duties, such as where the use of force is authorized.

(d) **Ratification:** An employer may ratify the tortious acts of an employee if the employer has knowledge of all material facts.

4. **Fiduciary duties:** The agent owes all express contractual duties to the principal, as well as the fiduciary duties of loyalty, obedience to any reasonable directives given by the principal, reasonable care under the circumstances, and the duty to disclose.

B. General Partnerships: When two or more persons carry on as co-owners of a business venture for profit, they are engaged in a partnership.

1. **Formation**

a) **Agreement:** A writing is generally not required unless it falls within the purview of the Statute of Frauds. Intent – which can be implied – is sufficient.

(1) **Sharing of Profits:** Raises a presumption of an existing partnership, unless done as a payment of debt, services rendered, rent payment, as an annuity or other retirement benefit, interest on a loan, or goodwill of a business.

(2) **Evidence Indicative of Partnership:** A court will likely find that a partnership existed where parties hold title to property in joint tenancy or tenancy in common, have designated their relationship as a partnership, there is extensive activity among the parties, and they share gross returns or expenses.

b) **Capacity:** A partner may be anyone who is capable of entering into a contract.

c) **Legal Purpose:** Individuals may not form a partnership to achieve an illegal purpose.

d) **Consent:** No third party can become a partner without the express or implied consent of all existing partners.

2. **Partnership Assets**

a) **Titled Property:** Property is that of the partnership if: (i) the partnership holds title in its name; or (ii) one or more of the partners hold title in their name(s) and the instrument transferring title denotes the titleholder's capacity as a partner.

b) **Presumed Partnership Property:** Property that is purchased with partnership funds is presumed to be partnership property.

c) **Presumed Separate Property:** Property is presumed to be separate property if: (i) the property is held in the name of one or more of the partners; (ii) the instrument transferring title does not indicate the person's capacity as a partner or mention the existence of a partnership; and (iii) partnership funds were not used.

d) **Untitled Property:** Courts will look to: (i) source of funds; (ii) use of the property; (iii) whether it was entered into the partnership's books as an asset; (iv) relationship between the property and the business; and (v) whether partnership funds were used to maintain or improve the property.

e) **Rights of Partner:** If partner is not a co-owner, he will have no transferable interest in the property and can only use property for the benefit of the partnership.

3. **Powers of Partners to Bind the Partnership**

a) **Apparent Authority**: (i) The act of any partner; (ii) for apparently carrying on in the ordinary course of business; (iii) binds the partnership unless: (a) the partner had no authority to act for the partnership; and (b) the third party knew that the partner lacked authority.

(1) Partners have apparent authority to bind the partnership to any contract within the scope of the partnership business.

b) **Actual Authority:** If a partner has actual authority, a partnership will be bound by an act of the partner.

4. **Enforcement of Partnership Rights and Obligations**

a) **Partners' Rights**

(1) **Management:** All partners have an equal right to participate in the management of the partnership unless the partnership agreement provides otherwise.

(2) **Distributions:** Partners have whatever rights are granted in the partnership agreement as to distribution of profits. If the agreement is silent, the partners share equally in profits and losses.

(3) **Remuneration:** Except for the winding up of the partnership business, partners have no right to remuneration for their services to the partnership.

(4) **Indemnification:** A partner has the right to be indemnified by fellow partners for expenses incurred on behalf of the partnership.

(5) **Contribution:** A partner has a right to contribution from fellow partners where the partner has paid more than his share of partnership liability.

(6) **Inspection:** A partner has the right to inspect and copy financial records.

5. **Lawsuits:** Generally, a partner may sue his partnership and the partnership may sue a partner in an action at law or in equity.

a) **Obligations:** Unless the partners agree otherwise, generally each partner:

(1) Has the right and duty to help manage the partnership;
(2) Must contribute to the partnership fund;
(3) Must work only on behalf of the partnership;
(4) Must observe any limitations adopted by a majority of the partners;
(5) Has a duty to inform the partnership of all relevant matters;
(6) Has a duty to produce complete information on all aspects of partnership's business; and
(7) Has a duty to maintain the confidentiality of partnership information.

b) **Fiduciary Obligations**

(1) Each partner is an agent for the other partners. Therefore, he owes the others a fiduciary duty of care similar to that of a principal–agent relationship.
(2) Partner must act in good faith for the benefit of the corporation.

6. **Dissolution:** Dissolution generally requires that the partnership business be wound up.

a) **Events Causing Dissolution:** (i) The notification of the intent to withdraw; (ii) the expiration of a term; (iii) the consent of all the partners to dissolve; (iv) the happening of an agreed upon event; or (v) a judicial decree.

b) **Partner's Power to Bind Partnership After Dissolution:** A partnership can be bound by the act of any partner that is appropriate for winding up the partnership.

c) **Partnership Continues After Dissolution:** A partnership continues until the business is wound up, unless waived by a unanimous vote.

d) **Distribution of Assets:** The partnership's assets are liquidated and the partnership's liabilities are paid first to creditors and then to the other partners.

7. **Dissociation**: Dissociation of a partner is any partner ceasing to be associated with the carrying on of the partnership business.

a) **Events of Dissociation:** (i) Notice of the partner's express will to withdraw; (ii) the happening of an agreed upon event; (iii) a partner's expulsion by agreement, vote, or judicial decree; (iv) a partner's bankruptcy; (v) the death/incapacity of a partner; (vi) the appointment of a receiver; and/or (vii) the termination of a business entity that is a partner.

b) **Dissociated Partner's Power to Bind Partnership:** If within two (2) years an ex-partner performs an act that would have bound the partnership and the other party reasonably believes that he is still a partner and the other party did not have notice of dissociation, the partnership is bound.

c) **Dissociated Partner's Liability:** An ex-partner is liable for former partners' acts if the other party reasonably believed the person was still a partner.

8. **Personal Liability of Partners for Partnership Obligations**

a) **Purported Partners**

(1) **Liability of Person Held Out as Partner:** A person who represents herself as a partner, or consents to being represented by another as a partner, will be liable to third parties who extend credit in reliance on the representation.

(2) **Liability of Person Who Holds Another Out as Partner:** When a person holds another out as a partner, that person is an agent who is bound by third parties.

b) **Liability of Partnership**

(1) **Civil:** The partnership is liable for all contracts entered into by a partner within the scope of partnership business or outside of the scope, but with valid

authority. The partnership is liable for all torts committed by a partner or partnership employee within the ordinary course of partnership business.

(a) **Joint and Several Liability:** A partner is liable for all obligations of the partnership whether in tort or in contract.

(b) **Incoming Partner:** An incoming partner is not liable for obligations incurred by the partnership before the person became a partner.

(c) **Outgoing Partner**: An outgoing partner remains liable for obligations incurred while a partner, unless there has been a release or novation.

(2) **Criminal:** Partners will not be criminally liable for the crimes of other partners unless he participated in the commission of the crime.

C. **Limited Partnerships**: A limited partnership is comprised of one or more general partners and one or more limited partners.

1. **Formation**

a) **Certificate of Limited Partnership:** Must be signed by all partners and set forth the name of the partnership, identity and address of agent for service and each general partner, and the latest date upon which the partnership is to dissolve. Subsequently the documents must be filed with the Secretary of State.

b) **Records Office:** A limited partnership must maintain an office with records of the certificate, partnership agreements, tax returns for the last three (3) years, the amount of each partner's contribution and special rights.

c) **Agent:** A limited partnership must maintain – in the state – an agent for service of legal process.

d) **Name of Partnership:** The name of a partnership may not contain the name of a limited partner unless it is also the name of a general partner. It must contain the words "Limited Partnership" and cannot be deceptive or similar to another limited partnership.

e) **Addition of a Partner:** Adding a partner is governed by the partnership agreement. If it is silent, written consent of all partners is required.

f) **Nature of Contribution:** It can be cash, property, or services rendered.

2. **Partnership Assets**

a) Partnership assets are those assets that are owned by the partnership as such, as opposed to assets used by the partnership, but owned by one of the partners.

b) Even where one partner purchases an asset, it may be a partnership asset if all partners so intend.

c) Individual partners may not sell or assign partnership property without consent of all partners.

3. **General Partners' Rights and Liabilities**

a) **General partners have the right:** (i) to share in profits and losses pursuant to a partnership agreement or in proportion to contribution (cf. regular partnerships where the share is equal); (ii) to assign their interest, but the assignee is not entitled to exercise the rights of a partner; (iii) to transact business with the partnership (lend it money); (iv) to withdraw; and (v) to apply for dissolution.

b) General partners have all the rights that a partner in a regular partnership would have with regard to management.

c) General partners are subject to all of the liabilities of a partner in a regular partnership, including personal liability for partnership obligations.

4. **Limited Partners' Rights and Liabilities**

a) Limited partners have the right to: (i) share in profits and losses pursuant to the partnership agreement or in proportion to contribution (cf. regular partnerships where the share is equal); (ii) assign their interest, but the assignee is not entitled to exercise the rights of a partner; (iii) to transact business with the partnership (lend it money); (iv) to withdraw; and (v) to apply for dissolution.

b) Limited partners have the right to: (i) vote on specific matters, but not control the business; (ii) obtain partnership information (inspect books); (iii) bring a derivative action if the general partners refuse to do so or an attempt would be futile.

c) A limited partner is not liable for partnership obligations beyond her contributions. Exceptions: Where the limited partner: (i) is also a general partner; (ii) participates in control of the business and person dealing with partnership reasonably believes the limited partner is a general partner; and (iii) knowingly permits her name to be used improperly.

d) One who believes she is a limited partner, but is a general partner can avoid liability if she files with the Secretary of State a certificate of amendment, or withdraws from participation by filing a certificate of withdrawal.

5. **Fiduciary Obligations**

a) Because limited partners are not usually involved in managing the business, they typically do not owe fiduciary duties to the limited partnership.

b) General partners owe the same fiduciary duties to limited partners that partners owe to each other in a general partnership.

6. **Dissolution and Disassociation**

a) **Dissolution:** by: (i) occurrence of time stated in certificate of limited partnership; (ii) occurrence of event/time provided in partnership agreement; (iii) written consent of all parties; (iv) withdrawal of a general partner unless otherwise provided for in the agreement or by consent of all partners; or (v) judicial dissolution.

D. Joint Ventures

1. A joint venture is formed when two or more individuals or companies are engaged in a single business enterprise, but have not formed a partnership or corporation. A joint venture is based on a single business transaction, not an ongoing relationship.

2. A joint venture is formed by a contract or an agreement.

3. A joint venture terminates upon a time or event specified in the contract, accomplishment of purpose, death of a member, or court order.

III. LIMITED LIABILITY COMPANIES ("LLC")

A. Nature of the Entity: LLCs are hybrid organizations that offer pass-through taxation, offer their owners limited liability similar to that of the shareholders of a corporation, and can be run like a corporation or a partnership.

B. Formation: Must file the Articles of Organization with the Secretary of State.

1. **Contents:** A statement that the entity is an LLC, name of the LLC, address of the registered office, the name of the registered agent for service, and names of the members.

C. Management: Management is presumed to be by all members.

D. **Financial Rights and Obligations of Members**

1. **Internal Allocation of Financial Interests:** Members share profits and losses equally unless provided otherwise.

2. **Member Contributions:** Members must adequately fund the LLC so that it can meet its foreseeable expenses and liabilities.

3. **Liability of Members for LLC obligations:** The members are not personally liable for the LLC's obligations.

4. **Creditors' Rights:** A personal creditor of a member may get a court order requiring the LLC to pay the creditor from the LLC; foreclose on the owner's LLC ownership interest; or ask a court to dissolve the LLC.

E. **Management**

1. **Members and Managers**

   a) **Member-Managed LLC:** In most LLCs, the members manage the business.

   b) **Manager-Managed LLC:** May designate members or outsiders as managers.

2. **Liability of Managers and Officers**

   a) A member may be personally liable if she: (i) personally guarantees a loan or debt and the LLC defaults; (ii) intentionally does something fraudulent, illegal, or reckless that harms the LLC or another person; or (iii) fails to treat the LLC as a legal entity separate from her personal affairs.

3. **Indemnification:** LLCs can agree that an LLC reimburse and indemnify members and managers for payments and liabilities incurred in the ordinary course of business.

4. **Failure to Comply with Organization Formalities:** If managers and owners do not treat the LLC as a separate business, a court may decide they are personally liable.

F. **Fiduciary Obligations of Managers, Managing Members, and Members:** Members of a manager-managed LLC owe fiduciary duties of loyalty and care to the company and its other members. However, members may reasonably restrict or eliminate fiduciary duties.

G. **Dissolution:** Dissociation (death, incompetency, etc.) of an LLC member generally causes dissolution.

IV. LIMITED LIABILITY PARTNERSHIP ("LLP")

A. **Nature of the Entity:** An LLP provides pass-through taxation and personal liability protection from business debts and liabilities. LLP members are shielded from the liability created by other members.

B. **Formation Requirements**

1. **Voting:** The terms and conditions by which a partnership becomes an LLP must be approved by whatever vote is required to amend the partnership agreement. If the agreement is silent, all partners must approve the creation of the LLP.

2. **Filing:** To become an LLP, a statement of qualification must be filed with the Secretary of State. It must be executed by at least two (2) partners and contain such information as: (i) the name and address of the partnership; (ii) a statement that the partnership elects to become an LLP; and (iii) the preferred effective date.

3. **Name:** The name of the partnership must end with the words "Registered Limited Liability Partnership" or the letters "LLP."

C. **Financial Rights and Obligations of Partners**

1. **Agreements of Partner Compensation and Profit Shares:** The partners may freely negotiate compensation and profit-sharing, and it will be memorialized in the partnership agreement.

2. **Indemnification and Loss-Sharing Provisions:** Indemnification and loss-sharing provisions may provide for indemnification and contributions for a partner's negligent acts.

D. **Liability of Partners:** A partner in an LLP is not personally liable for the obligations of the partnership. However, a partner remains personally liable for his wrongful acts.

1. **Creditor Rights**

    a) Creditors can pierce the protection from a limited liability corporation to hold a partner individually liable.

    b) An individual's liability depends on the scope of the state's statute. Many states only provide protection for intentional torts and not negligence or incompetence. Some states extend protection for contractual claims.

2. **Extent of Liability:** Partners will not be personally liable for professional malpractice against another partner.

3. **Indemnification:** Some states hold that a negligent partner is not entitled to indemnification or contribution for his negligent acts.

E. **Fiduciary Obligations:** Partners owe fiduciary duties of loyalty and care to the LLP and other partners.

F. **Dissolution:** Like in a partnership, an LLP may be voluntarily or judicially dissolved. It must file Articles of Dissolution or a Certificate of Cancellation with the Secretary of State. It generally must notify creditors and anyone else who has an interest in the LLP first.

CIVIL PROCEDURE PRIMER

I. JURISDICTION OVER PERSONS AND PROPERTY

A. In Personam Jurisdiction: In personam jurisdiction refers to the ability of the court having subject matter jurisdiction to exercise power over a particular defendant or item of property. Under the Constitution, personal jurisdiction is valid if: (i) the party is personally served in state; (ii) the party is domiciled in the forum state; (iii) the party consents to jurisdiction; or (iv) the party's act falls within the state's long arm statute.

1. **Due Process Notice Requirements:** The defendant must be notified of the lawsuit by a reasonable method and given an opportunity to appear and be heard.

2. **Personal Service:** Occurs when the defendant is present in the forum state and is personally served with process.

3. **Consent to Jurisdiction**

   a) **Actual:** Actual consent occurs by making a general appearance so as to defend on the merits of the plaintiff's claim and accept the court's jurisdiction; or answering the complaint.

      (1) Special Appearance: The defendant may make a special appearance in court to challenge the jurisdiction by a motion to dismiss or motion to quash service for lack of jurisdiction.

   b) **Implied Consent:** The mere fact the defendant owns property in the state will not give the court personal jurisdiction over the defendant-owner unless the action is directly related to the piece of property.

4. **Long Arm Statutes (LAS):** Allow a state to exercise jurisdiction over an out-of-state defendant, provided the prospective defendant has sufficient minimum contact with the forum state (infra), in order to satisfy the Due Process Clause of the Constitution. A nonresident defendant whose activities within the state are substantial, continuous, and systematic is subject to "general jurisdiction" in the state, meaning jurisdiction is available on any cause of action. But, if the position is otherwise, that is the activities are not as pervasive in order to satisfy "general jurisdiction," the defendant is subject to "specific jurisdiction" only if:

   a) The defendant purposefully availed himself of the benefit of conducting activities in the forum state, thereby obtaining the benefit and protection of the state's laws;
   b) The dispute arises out of or has a substantial connection with the defendant's contacts with the state;
   c) The exercise of jurisdiction will be fair and reasonable.

   California's Long Arm Statute in short states that a court may exercise jurisdiction on any basis that is not inconsistent with the constitution of California or the USA and which therefore provides California courts with wide jurisdiction over non-residents (subject to any limiting constitutional factors).

5. **Minimum Contacts Doctrine:** The Fourteenth Amendment's Due Process Clause restricts a state's authority to bind a nonresident defendant to a judgment of its court and requires the nonresident to have "certain minimum contacts" with the forum state.

   a) **Contacts:** The contacts must show that the defendant: (i) Purposefully availed himself of the forum state's laws; and (ii) Knew or reasonably should have anticipated that his activities in the forum state made it foreseeable that he may be "haled into court" there.

b) **Fairness**

(1) If the claim is related to the defendant's contact with the forum state (specific personal jurisdiction), the court is more likely to find the exercise of jurisdiction to be fair and reasonable; or

(2) If the defendant engages in systematic and continuous activity in the forum state, the court is likely to find this activity to be a sufficient basis for exercising personal jurisdiction over any cause of action (general personal jurisdiction). The court, also, will consider other factors, including: (a) Whether the forum is "so gravely difficult and inconvenient" that the defendant is put at a severe disadvantage; (b) The forum state's legitimate interest in providing redress for its residents; (c) The plaintiff's interest in obtaining convenient and effective relief; (d) The interstate judicial system's interest in efficiency; and (e) The shared interest of the states in furthering social policies.

B. Quasi in Rem and In Rem Jurisdiction: If personal jurisdiction is not possible or the plaintiff's claim is limited to property interests within the jurisdiction, the court can hear the case under either of these doctrines.

1. **Location of the Property (i.e., Situs of the Res):** In rem jurisdiction exists when the court has the power to adjudicate the rights of all persons in the world with respect to a particular item over property located within the physical borders of the state.

2. **Subjecting the Property (Res) to Jurisdiction:** Where quasi in rem jurisdiction exists, the court can attach or garnish property in the state belonging to the defendant. The plaintiff's action against the defendant could be litigated but the judgment is limited to the property before the court.

   a) There must be a nexus between the defendant and the state, in addition to the mere presence of the property in order to impose jurisdiction.

   b) Quasi & in rem jurisdiction requires that the defendant receive notice reasonably calculated to reach the defendant and provide an opportunity to be heard.

3. **Effect of Adjudication of Jurisdictional Issue:** Parties may waive a jurisdictional issue related to venue. Waiver:

   a) Unless there is a timely objection to "venue," any issue relating thereto is deemed to be waived.

   b) Subject matter jurisdiction cannot be waived because it relates to the authority of the court to determine the issue in dispute.

4. **Lack of Jurisdiction**

   a) **Procedures for Raising Jurisdictional Defects**

   (1) A party pursuing a claim must bring proceedings in a court of competent jurisdiction. All legal and factual defenses to a claim must be set out in the response to the claim. The time for serving an answer is within 21 days after being served with the summons and complaint, or if time has been waived, within 60 days after the request for waiver was sent (or 90 days if sent to a defendant outside any judicial district of the United States) and the answer to a counterclaim or cross claim within 21 days after being served with a pleading stating a counterclaim or cross claim.

   (2) By Rule 12(b), every defense to a claim for relief in any pleading must be asserted in the responsive pleading if one is required, BUT a party may assert the following defenses by motion: (i) Lack of subject matter jurisdiction; (ii) Lack of personal jurisdiction; (iii) Improper venue; (iv) Insufficient process; (v) Insufficient service

of process; (vi) Failure to state a claim for which relief is available; and (vii) Failure to join a party under Rule 19.

b) **Note:** The following defenses are not waived by not including them in the answer: (i) failure to state a claim upon which relief can be granted; (ii) failure to join a party under Rule 19; and lack of subject matter jurisdiction.

c) **Special Appearances:** The defendant can appear to challenge the jurisdiction by a motion to dismiss or motion to quash service for lack of jurisdiction.

II. FEDERAL COURT SUBJECT MATTER JURISDICTION

A. Federal Courts: Federal courts are courts of limited jurisdiction and a civil action is commenced by filing a complaint with the court, and which must comply with the provisions of Rule 4, FRCP. To bring a suit in federal court, the court must have jurisdiction over the subject matter of the dispute, which can be based either on diversity of citizenship or federal question.

B. Federal Questions: The district courts have original jurisdiction over all civil actions arising under the Constitution, laws, or treaties of the United States.

C. Diversity Requirements

1. **Diversity of Citizenship:** Federal courts can hear a case: (i) between "citizens of different states"; and (ii) if the amount in controversy exceeds $75k, excluding costs and interest.

a) **Complete Diversity Rule:** There is no diversity of citizenship if any plaintiff is a citizen of the same state as any defendant.

(1) **Individual Citizenship:** Domicile is established by: (i) physical presence in the state; with (ii) the intent to make that state her permanent home.

(2) **Corporations:** Corporations are citizens of: (i) the state where they are incorporated; and (ii) the state where they have their principal place of business.

(a) **Place of Business:** (i) Nerve Center Test: The court will look at where the main decisions of the corporation are made.

(3) **Amount in Controversy:** Actions brought under the diversity statute must be in excess of $75,000, exclusive of interest and costs.

D. Removal and Remand: If the plaintiff files the case in state court, the defendant may move to have the case removed to federal court, or vice versa. If the court grants the defendant's motion, the plaintiff may move to remand the case back to state court.

1. **Removal:** An action can be removed from state court to federal court, if the action could have originally been brought in federal court to begin with. The defendant must remove within 30 days after service of the first document. All defendants must agree to remove.

2. **Remand:** The plaintiff may file a motion to remand within 30 days of removal if the plaintiff can show that the federal court does not have original subject matter jurisdiction.

E. Supplemental Jurisdiction: Under the doctrine of supplemental jurisdiction, a court may entertain claims that could not, by themselves, invoke federal question jurisdiction or diversity jurisdiction if the claims arise from the same common nucleus of operative fact as the claim that invoked federal subject matter jurisdiction.

III. CHOICE OF LAW

The California Code of Civil Procedure is the primary source of procedural law for California state courts and deals with matters relating to: jurisdictions, joinder of parties and claims, service of process, pleadings, motions, attachment, trials, appeals and enforcement of judgments.

A. **Erie Doctrine:** Under the Erie doctrine, a federal court sitting in diversity will apply federal procedural law but must apply the substantive law and conflict of laws rules of the state in which it is sitting.

B. **California Conflict Laws:** A federal court sitting in diversity must apply California's conflict of laws rules in determining the applicable substantive law.

1. **Tort Claims – Government Interest Approach**

   a) The court first determines whether the laws of the two or more states are identical. If they are not, the court evaluates whether each state has an interest in the application of its law and if they do, a true conflict arises.

   b) If there is a true conflict, the court must evaluate the impact on each state's interest, depending on the law applied for the purpose of determining the issue.

2. **Contract Claims – Choice of Law Clauses**

   a) If the choice of law clause in the contract encompasses all claims, the court must determine whether the clause is enforceable by examining whether the chosen state's law has a substantial relationship to the parties or their transaction or any other reasonable basis exists for the parties' choice of law.

   b) If the clause is enforceable, the court then assesses whether the chosen state's law conflicts with a fundamental California policy. If such a conflict exists, the court must decide whether California has a material interest greater than the chosen state in determination of the specific issue.

C. **Statute of Limitations:** An action against an attorney for a wrongful act or omission arising in the performance of professional services shall be commenced within 1 year after the plaintiff discovers the facts constituting the wrongful act or omission, or 4 years from the date of the wrongful act or omission, whichever occurs first.

An action for injury or death against a health care provider based upon such person's alleged professional negligence shall be commenced 3 years after the date of injury or 1 year after the plaintiff discovers, or through the use of reasonable diligence should have discovered, the injury, whichever occurs first.

1. **Relation Back Doctrine:** An amended complaint by adding a new party after the statute of limitations has expired will relate back to the filing of the original complaint, provided that the complaint and amended complaint involve the same transaction, and the added party knew they should have been added.

D. **Federal Law in State Courts:** A federal court has subject matter jurisdiction in a civil action arising under federal law or the parties are of diverse citizenship.

E. **Situs of an Action:**

1. **Local Actions:** Venue is proper in the county in which the land is situated, or where the act or omission giving rise to the action occurred.

2. **Transitory Actions:** For transitory actions, the general rule is that venue is proper in the county in which any defendant resides at the commencement of the action.

3. **Forum Non Conveniens:** A court may stay or dismiss a case because there is a court in another jurisdiction considered to be a far more convenient forum to deal with the case. Courts look to similar factors that would justify the transfer.

F. Venue

1. **Federal Venue:** Original jurisdiction of the federal court is established where there is subject matter jurisdiction over the dispute and personal jurisdiction over the defendant.

   a) Venue is proper in any district where: (i) any defendant resides if all defendants reside in the same state; (ii) a substantial part of the claim arose; or (iii) where a substantial part of the property that is the subject of the action is situated. If no district satisfies (i) or (ii), in diversity actions, a district where any defendant is subject to personal jurisdiction at the time the action is commenced, or for actions not based on diversity, any district in which any defendant may be found (improper venue can be waived).

2. **Removal Actions:** Venue is proper only in a district that includes the place in which the state action was pending.

3. **Transfer of Venue:** Courts can only transfer to a district that is a proper venue and that has personal jurisdiction over the defendant.

   a) Transfer may be based on: (i) the convenience of parties and witnesses; and (ii) in the interest of justice.

4. **State Venue**

   a) **Change of Venue:** The court has discretion to allow for a change of venue. In making such a determination, the court will consider: (i) the convenience of witnesses (not the parties); and (ii) the interests of justice in obtaining an impartial forum.

5. **Transfer of Cases:** If venue is improper, the court may transfer venue to the proper county. On the motion of either party, the court may transfer venue, even if the original venue is proper, when: (i) the court does not have a judge that is qualified to hear the case; (ii) there are reasonable grounds to believe that a fair trial would not take place in the original county; (iii) the interests of justice so require; or (iv) for the convenience of witnesses.

IV. PLEADINGS AND THEIR REQUIREMENTS

A. Complaints, Counterclaims and Cross-Complaints

1. **The Complaint:** The complaint is required to contain a statement of the facts constituting the cause of action in ordinary and concise language and a demand for judgment.

   a) **Procedural Challenges to the Complaint**

      (1) **Motion for Judgment on the Pleadings:** An action cannot be dismissed on the pleadings unless, taking everything in the complaint as true, no claim for relief has been stated by the defendant as a matter of law. Any party may move for summary judgment in any action or proceeding if it is contended that the action has no merit or that there is no defense to the action or the proceeding. The motion may be made at any time after 60 days have elapsed since the general appearance in the action or proceedings of each party against whom the motion is directed or at any earlier time after the general appearance that the court. The court shall grant summary judgment if the movant shows that there is no genuine dispute as to any material fact and the movant is entitled to judgment as a matter of law. The court is required to state on the record the reasons for granting or denying the motion. Further, unless a different time is set by local rule or the court orders otherwise, a party may file a motion for summary judgment at any time until 30 days after the close of all discovery.

b) **Cause of Action Issue:** To determine the pleading's sufficiency, consider whether it is a notice system or a code system of pleading.

(1) **Notice Pleading:** The plaintiff must merely allege sufficient facts to put the defendant on notice of what the cause of action is against him.

(2) **Code Pleading (State Court):** The complaint must allege all the elements of at least one cause of action or the complaint is subject to dismissal.

c) **Pleading Damages**

(1) **General Damages:** Those damages that necessarily flow from the defendant's wrongful act, the law will imply them.

(2) **Specific Damages:** Those damages which took place, but which are not a necessary consequence of the defendant's wrongful act.

B. Service of Process

1. Service Within California

a) **Personal service** upon a defendant in California (substituted service may be effected if personal service is not possible with reasonable diligence by leaving a copy of the summons at a person's dwelling house, usual place of abode, usual place of business, in the presence of a competent member of the household (at least 18) and who shall be informed of the contents).

b) **Service by mail:** by mailing copies of the complaint and summons, with two copies of the Notice of Acknowledgment and a prepaid self-addressed return envelope.

c) **Constructive service by publication:** only allowed where the court is satisfied that the party to be served cannot, with reasonable diligence, be served personally or by substituted service.

2. **Service on Defendant in Another State:** CCP §415.40 permits service on a defendant in another state in any manner provided by the jurisdiction and service of process act for interstate service, plus service by mail (which requires a return receipt).

3. **Service Outside the United States:** The United States has ratified two multilateral agreements which govern service of proceedings among signatory countries – the Hague Convention and the Inter American Convention.

4. **Time Limits on Service of Process:** The complaint and summons must be served on the defendant within three (3) years after the action is commenced.

A defendant must serve an answer within 21 days after being served with the summons and complaint, or within 60 days after the request for a waiver was sent or within 90 days after it was sent to the defendant outside any judicial district of the United States.

C. Answers, General Denials and Affirmative Defenses

1. **Answers:** An answer is a pleading that responds to the allegations in the complaint. If a defendant does nothing, he risks entry of default and default judgment. Alternatively, he can attack the complaint and seek a partial or complete dismissal through use of demurrer/other motion(s), or he can respond to the complaint.
A new matter constituting an affirmative defense must be stated in the answer, and a failure to plead an affirmative defense will be considered a waiver of that defense. A new matter is something relied upon by the defendant, which is put in issue by the defendant.

In short, the answer must admit, deny, or claim lack of knowledge of information sufficient to answer, and where the answer is defective, the court will grant the defendant leave to amend. Entry of default judgment is improper without granting leave to amend first.

2. **General Denial:** A simple statement denying the whole complaint; i.e., the defendant denies each and every allegation in the plaintiff's complaint.

3. **Special Denial:** The defendant admits allegations that are true and rejects only those allegations that are specifically untrue.

D. Methods of Challenging Pleadings

1. **Demurrer:** Demurrers are used in code-pleading states where the complaint fails to state a cause of action or the court lacks subject matter jurisdiction and presents an objection to a complaint, cross complaint or answer when the ground of objection appears on the face of the pleading, and may object to the complaint or cross complaint on one of a number of grounds. **See outline for list of grounds.*

2. **Motion to Dismiss:** Under FRCP Rule 12(b)(6), a motion to dismiss can be brought for the following reasons: (i) failure to state a claim upon which relief can be granted; (ii) lack of subject matter jurisdiction; and (iii) improper venue or insufficient service of process.

3. **Motion to Strike:** Motions to strike challenge irrelevant allegations and the moving party asks to have the irrelevant allegations stricken from the complaint.

4. **Motion for Judgment on the Pleadings:** If a defendant files an answer that does not respond to the complaint raised in the claim, the defendant will default and a claimant may move for judgment on the pleadings.

5. **Motion for Summary Judgment:** Any party may move for summary judgment in any action or proceeding if it is contended that the action has no merit or that there is no defense to the action or proceedings. A party may move for summary judgment, identifying each claim or defense or the part of each claim or defense on which summary judgment is sought. A motion of summary judgment must be granted if, from the pleadings, affidavits, and discovery materials on file, it appears that no genuine issue of material fact exists and that the moving party is entitled to a judgment as a matter of law.

   a) The defending party may move for summary judgment at any time, the plaintiff may not do so until 20 days after the commencement of the action or after an adverse party moves for summary judgment.

E. Amendment of Pleadings

1. **Federal Court:** Plaintiff can amend pleadings within 21 days of serving the pleading to be amended or 21 days after the responsive pleading.

   a) **New Claims – Statute of Limitations:** After the statute has run, an amendment to add new claims is only allowed if it relates back to the original complaint.

   b) **New Parties:** An amendment to add a new party only relates back if the defendant had actual knowledge of the suit before the statutory period ran and he knew he was the defendant who should have been sued.

2. **State Court:** Courts generally do not permit an amendment to add new parties after the statute has run. Such an amendment is seen as a new cause of action.

   a) **Supplemental Pleadings:** Supplemental pleadings set forth events or discoveries occurring after the initial pleadings and face no statute of limitation problems.

V. JOINDER

A. Parties

1. **Compulsory Joinder:** A party is needed for just adjudication if: (i) complete relief cannot be given to existing parties in his absence; (ii) disposition in his absence may impair his ability

to protect his interest in the controversy; or (iii) his absence would expose existing parties to a substantial risk of double or inconsistent adjudications.

a) **Where Joinder is Impossible:** The court must decide whether the action can proceed in the party's absence or it must be dismissed. The court must consider the following: (i) whether the judgment in the party's absence would prejudice him or the existing parties; (ii) whether the prejudice can be reduced by shaping the judgment; (iii) whether a judgment in the other party's absence would be adequate; and (iv) whether the plaintiff will be deprived of an adequate remedy if the action is dismissed.

2. **Permissive Joinder:** Parties may join as plaintiffs or defendants whenever: (i) there is a question of law or fact that is common to all parties; and (ii) a claim is made by each plaintiff against each defendant that stems out of the same occurrence or transaction.

3. **Interpleader:** Interpleader permits a person in the position of a stakeholder to require two or more claimants to litigate among themselves to determine which, if any, has the valid claim where separate actions might result in double liability on a single obligation.

a) **Grounds:** Interpleader requires: (i) complete diversity between the stakeholder and all adverse claimants, and in excess of $75,000 at issue; or (ii) a federal question claim.

4. **Impleader:** A defending party may implead a non-party who is or may be liable to him for any part of a judgment that the plaintiff may recover against him. Venue need not be proper for a third party-defendant. Additional claims may be asserted by the third party-defendant, but they need an independent jurisdiction basis. A third party can assert defenses to the plaintiff as well as the defendant. The court may sever claims and try separately for justice.

a) **California:** A defending party may implead a non-party who is or may be liable to him for any part of a judgment that the plaintiff may recover against him. Venue need not be proper for a third party-defendant. Additional claims may be asserted by the third party-defendant, but they need an independent jurisdiction basis. A third party can assert defenses to the plaintiff as well as the defendant. The court may sever claims and try separately for justice.

5. **Intervention:** Upon timely application, any person who has an interest in the matter in litigation, or in the success of either of the parties, or an interest against both, may intervene in the action or proceeding.

6. **Permissive Intervention:** A third party may intervene if the intervenor has common claims and rights with the main parties. The court has discretion to grant the intervention and will look to see if the intervenor's presence will unduly complicate the case.

B. **Claims:** A plaintiff can join multiple claims against a defendant. At least one of the claims must arise out of a transaction in which all were involved.

1. **Compulsory Joinder:** If the defendant's counterclaim arises out of the same transaction or occurrence, failure to raise it bars a subsequent suit. Supplemental jurisdiction is extended to mandatory counterclaims; thus no independent source of federal subject matter jurisdiction is necessary to support a counterclaim arising out of the same transaction as the plaintiff's original claim.

2. **Cause of Action v. Primary Rights Theory:** Since the federal rules are premised on the "same transaction or occurrence test," if the case is in federal court, discuss whether any claim arising out of the same transaction or occurrence should be barred if the facts give you a state court action as well.

a) **Primary Rights Jurisdiction:** California and a minority of other jurisdictions look at primary rights and thus separate suits are not barred by res judicata from being separately litigated in state court action.

3. **Permissive Joinder:** A defendant may bring counterclaims as long as they are supported by independent subject matter jurisdiction.

4. **Cross-Claim:** If arising out of the same transaction or occurrence, the defendant can sue a co-defendant, although she is not required to bring a claim. In addition, no independent jurisdictional basis is needed.

C. **Class Actions:** A party seeking certification as a class action representative must establish the existence of an ascertainable class and a well-defined community of interest involving: (i) common questions of law or fact; (ii) class representatives that have claims or defenses typical of the class; (iii)class representative that adequately represent the interests of the class.

1. **Federal Rule 23:** A representative will be permitted to sue on behalf of a class if the following criteria are met: (i) Numerosity; (ii) Commonality; (iii) Typicality; (iv) Fair and adequate representation; and (v) Action meets any of the requirements of Rule 23(b)(1) and (2).

2. **Notice Requirement:** In federal court, under Rule 23, notice to all members of the class is required in "common question suits" so that class members can opt out if they so choose.

3. **Effect of Judgment:** All members of a class are bound by the judgment rendered in a class action, except those individuals in a common question class action who opt out.

a) Members of 23(b)(1), (2) class action cannot opt out. Such cases involve injunctive relief or risk inconsistent results.

4. **Jurisdiction:** In class actions that are established on diversity, only the citizenship of the named representative is taken into consideration in establishing complete diversity.

a) **Amount of Controversy:** One class representative's claim generally must exceed $75,000. Claims can only be aggregated if members are attempting to enforce a single right. Class members with claims not exceeding $75,000 may invoke supplemental jurisdiction as long as complete diversity is not destroyed.

b) **Class Action Fairness Act of 2005:** Under the CAFA, subject matter jurisdiction is established where: (i) there is a minimum of 100 members in the proposed class; (ii) the aggregated amount in controversy is more than five million dollars; and (iii) any class member is different from any defendant.

c) **Excluded Actions:** No federal jurisdiction exists if primary defendants are states, state officials, or other government entities, or it is a claim regarding federal securities law that relates to internal affairs of a corporation and is based on the law of the state of incorporation.

VI. DISCOVERY

A. **Discovery California:** Any party may obtain discovery regarding any matter, not privileged, that is relevant to the subject matter involved in the pending action or to the determination of any motion made in that action.

The scope of discovery extends to any relevant matter that either is admissible in evidence or appears to be reasonably calculated to lead to the discovery of admissible evidence.

Absolute Privilege: If protected by absolute privilege, information is protected from disclosure, irrespective of relevance. Absolute privilege applies to, amongst other things: attorney–client privilege, physician–patient privilege, spousal privilege and privilege against self-incrimination.

Qualified Privilege: In some instances, sensitive information may be protected by qualified privilege unless contrary to the interests of justice, for example, relating to trade secrets, newsgatherers' immunity.

Initial disclosure must be made at or within 14 days after the parties' Rule 26(f) conference, unless a different time is set by stipulation or court order.

A party must also disclose the identity of any witness (expert testimony) it may use at trial to present evidence, at least 90 days before the date set for trial, or if solely contradictory or in rebuttal of another party's evidence, within 30 days of the other party's disclosure.

B. Types and Mechanics of Discovery Devices

1. **Interrogatories:** Discovery by written interrogatories must be answered under oath.
    a) Responses are required within 30 days. A respondent must answer by providing the information sought or his objection, and each answer shall be as complete and straightforward as possible, as the information available to him permits.
    b) No more than 25 interrogatories are permitted without court permission.

2. **Inspections:** A party may obtain discovery by inspecting documents or other relevant material in the possession, custody or control of the other, and this includes documents stored electronically.

3. **Medical Examinations:** If a party's mental or physical condition is in controversy, discovery by mental or physical examination is permitted. After examination, the person examined may demand in writing a copy of the detailed medical report.

4. **Expert Witness Disclosure:** CCP §2034.210 provides for the compulsory exchange of the identity of expert witnesses who will testify at trial and the nature of their testimony. If a party unreasonably fails to comply with this requirement, the trial court, after objection, is required to exclude the expert witnesses evidence.

5. **Depositions:** Testimony taken under oath and upon notice to all other parties. Unless the parties have agreed otherwise, the depositions must be recorded by a stenographer and transcribed.

6. **Limit:** A party cannot take more than 10 depositions or depose the same person more than once, unless by court order or stipulation.

7. **Requests for Admissions:** Prepared by one party to another party (not a non-party), to admit the truth of a factual matter, the genuineness of a document or opinions relating to fact. The other party is required to respond under oath, either with an answer or an objection within 30 days after service. Admissions are binding only in the present action, but constitute the conclusive establishment of the fact or matter admitted, and a party can only withdraw or amend such an admission with leave of the court.

8. **Duty to Supplement:** If a party learns that a response to a required disclosure, interrogatory, request for documents, or admission is incomplete or incorrect, it must supplement its response.

C. Limits on Discovery

1. **Work Product:** Work product consists of documents that reflect the pre-litigation investigation of or by a party or her attorney. In California, "work product" is protected absolutely and which include attorney's impressions, conclusions, opinions or legal research. Federal rules protect as "work product" any materials prepared in anticipation of litigation or trial by a party's attorney.

a) **Exception: Good-Cause:** Documents or other matters obtained in anticipation of litigation or preparation for trial are discoverable only upon a showing of substantial need and unavailability from other sources.

b) **Exception: Attorney's Handwritten Notes:** A party can never obtain an attorney's handwritten notes, because an attorney's mental impressions are absolutely protected.

D. Use of Discovery at Trial: A party who fails to comply with discovery obligations may be subject to sanctions, unless there is "substantial justification" for the failure.

E. Discovery Remedies and Sanctions

1. **Subpoena:** Used to compel production of a witness at deposition or trial.

2. **Subpoena Duces Tecum:** An SDT is a court summons ordering the recipient to appear before the court and produce documents and evidence for use at trial or hearing.

3. **Sanctions**
   a) Contempt for violating a court order;
   b) Default against non-complying person;
   c) Costs; and/or
   d) Strike pleadings of the non-complying party.

VII. PRE-TRIAL

A. Pre-Trial Conferences

1. **FRCP 26(F):** The parties must confer as soon as practicable, and in any event at least 21 days before a scheduling conference is to be held or a scheduling order is due under FRCP 16(b) to consider the nature and basis of their claims and defenses, including the possibility of settlement, initial disclosures, discuss any issues about preserving discoverable information and develop a discovery plan. The parties must submit a proposed discovery plan addressing the timing and form of required disclosures, the subjects on which discovery may be needed, the timing of and limitations on discovery, and relevant orders that may be required of the court.

2. **Additional Pre-Trial Conferences:** Additional conferences may be held to expedite trial and foster settlement. A final pretrial conference may be held to formulate a plan for the trial, including a program for the administration of evidence.

B. Pre-Trial Orders

1. **Scheduling Order:** The court must hold a scheduling conference and enter a scheduling order limiting the time for joinder, motions, and discovery.

VIII. DISPOSITION WITHOUT TRIAL

A. Voluntary Dismissal: A plaintiff may dismiss his action without prejudice as a matter of right only before the defendant files an answer or a summary judgment motion, or by stipulation of all parties. Otherwise, a dismissal without prejudice can be taken only with leave of court.

B. Involuntary Dismissal: A suit can be dismissed against a party for failure to pursue the action; failure to comply with the court orders; or as the result of a ruling on a motion by the opposing party. Dismissal is mandatory if there is: (i) A failure to serve the action within 3 years of the filing of the complaint; (ii) A failure to bring the case to trial within 5 years; or (iii) A failure to bring a case to a new trial within 3 years.

C. **Discretionary Dismissal:** Is permitted if there is a failure to serve a defendant within 2 years, there is a failure to bring the case to trial within 2 years, or there is a failure to bring a case to a new trial within 2 years.

D. **Summary Judgment**

1. Any party may move for summary judgment in any action or proceeding if it is contended that the action has no merit or that there is no defense to the action or proceeding.

2. The motion for summary judgment shall be granted if all the papers submitted show that there is no triable issue as to any material fact and that the moving party is entitled to a judgment as a matter of law.

The time for filing a motion for summary judgment is any time until 30 days after the close of all discovery, unless the court sets a different timetable.

E. **Default Judgment:** If a defendant who is properly served with a complaint and summons fails to file an appropriate response in time, the plaintiff may obtain a default judgment.

IX. RIGHT TO A JURY TRIAL

The right to a jury trial is constitutionally guaranteed to the extent that it existed at common law when the federal and state constitutions were adopted.

The right exists: (i) when legal and equitable issues are joined; (ii) in a state proceeding; or (iii) federal diversity cases.

A. Joined Issues of Law and Equity

1. Parties have a right to a jury trial when legal and equitable claims or defenses are joined in a single suit.

   a) Issues of fact common to both the legal and equitable claims are triable by the jury. Issues that are solely equitable are tried before a judge.

   b) If there are no common issues, a jury will hear legal claims. A judge will hear equitable claims.

2. **Diversity Cases:** The Seventh Amendment preserves the right to jury trial in federal courts in all suits at common law.

   a) **Waiver:** A timely demand for a jury trial must be made or the right is waived. The party who desires a jury trial must file a written demand with the court and serve it on the parties within 10 days after the filing of the pleading in which the jury triable issue arose. If the party fails to file the written demand, it is waived.

3. **State Court:** The Seventh Amendment right to trial by jury does not apply to the states. California grants the right to civil jury trials for questions of fact where the claim exceeds small claims limits.

X. JURY SELECTION

A. **Equal Protection Requirements**

1. **Jury Size:** A jury in a civil case must have at least 6 and not more than 12 jurors. A juror may be excused for good cause without causing a mistrial, so long as at least 6 jurors participate in reaching the verdict.

2. **Selection:** The selection procedure must meet due process and equal protection requirements of fairness and community representation.

B. Juror Qualifications: All persons are eligible for selection except: (i) persons who are not citizens of the United States; (ii) persons under 18; (iii) persons who are not domiciled in the state of California; (iv) persons not residents of the jurisdiction where they are summoned to serve; (v) persons convicted of malfeasance in office; (vi) persons who have insufficient knowledge of the English language; (vii) persons currently serving as jurors in another court of the state; or (viii) persons who are the subject of conservatorship.

C. Voir Dire: Voir dire is the process used to determine if any juror is biased or is unsuitable to deal with issues fairly. A trial judge initially examines prospective jurors in a civil trial for the purpose of selecting a fair and impartial jury, and attorneys for the parties have considerable freedom to voir dire prospective jurors.

D. Challenging Jurors

1. **Cause:** Each party can challenge an unlimited amount of prospective jurors for cause. Challenges for general disqualification arise on two grounds – lack of eligibility and implied bias. Challenge also arises for actual bias.

2. **Peremptory Challenge:** Each party is only granted 6 peremptory challenges. Although if there are more than 2 parties, the number of peremptory challenges is increased to 8. A race-neutral-reason is required in exercising peremptory challenges.

XI. ROLES OF JUDGE AND JURY

In trial courts a judge, and sometimes a jury, hears testimony and evidence relating to the issues to be determined in the case for the purpose of determining the outcome by applying the relevant applicable law to the facts found by the jury. The judge is the sole arbiter in relation to matters of law and will provide relevant direction as and when required. The judge's role is impartial, to ensure fairness, to interpret the law and to protect the rights and liberties of citizens guaranteed by the Constitutions of the United Sates and California for the purpose of ensuring legal disputes are resolved fairly and efficiently according to law.

XII. REMOVING A CASE FROM A JURY

A. Nonsuit: A defendant may move for a motion for nonsuit after the plaintiff's opening statement or the completion of the plaintiff's evidence in a jury trial. If granted, the judgment of nonsuit constitutes an adjudication on the merits of the case, but if denied the defendant still has the right to present his evidence. Further, after all the evidence, either party may move for an order directing a verdict in its favor.

B. Judgment as a Matter of Law: A motion for a judgment as a matter of law allows judgment to be granted for either party if the evidence is such that reasonable persons could not disagree. A motion for judgment as a matter of law is a prerequisite for the making of a renewed motion for judgment as a matter of law.

C. Renewed Motion for a Judgment as a Matter of Law: A party may file a renewed motion for a judgment as a matter of law no later than 28 days in federal court after entry of judgment.

XIII. POST-TRIAL MOTIONS

A. Setting Aside or Correcting Verdicts

1. **Errors Justifying Set Aside:** Someone other than a juror can move to have the verdict set aside if: (i) juror bias or prejudice was not disclosed on voir dire; (ii) jurors received unauthorized evidence; or (iii) the jury failed to reach its decision by a rational, group deliberation of the facts.

2. **Motion for New Trial:** A motion for a new trial must be filed no later than 28 days after judgment has been rendered. If granted, a new trial takes place and proceeds as though the first trial never took place

   Grounds for a new trial: (i) irregularity in proceedings of the court, jury or adverse party, or any order of the court or abuse of discretion, which prevented a party having a fair trial; (ii) misconduct of the jury; (iii) accident or surprise, which ordinary prudence could not have guarded against; (iv) newly discovered evidence which could not have been discovered and produced at trial; (v) excessive or inadequate damages; (vi) insufficiency of evidence to justify the verdict; or (vii) error of law at the trial.

   In California, such a motion must be filed no later than 15 days of the date of mailing of notice of entry of judgment, or within 180 days after entry of judgment, whichever is earliest.

3. **Remittitur:** If the verdict is excessive, the court may order a new trial or offer the plaintiff remittitur, which allows the plaintiff to choose between a lesser award or a new trial.

4. **Additur:** If the verdict is more favorable to the defendant than it ought to have been, the defendant must agree either to pay a larger amount than the jury verdict or submit to a new trial (California state courts only).

B. Variation and Modification of Judgment Without a New Trial

1. **Motion for Relief form Judgment:** Is a motion made in an independent action requesting relief from a prior judgment. The basic grounds for the motion are: (i) mistake; (ii) surprise; (iii) excusable neglect; (iv) newly-discovered evidence; (v) fraud or misconduct by the other party. The motion must be made within a reasonable time following the judgment.

XIV. EXTRAORDINARY RELIEF FROM JUDGMENT

A. Statutory Relief: Relief pursuant to statutory authority that has the effect of reversing an otherwise valid judgment.

B. Equitable Relief

1. **Injunctive Relief:** An injunction is a remedy used to require a person to take, or refrain from taking, a specified action. A court will issue an injunction when necessary to protect a legal right of an individual or group.

   a) **Classifications**

      (1) **Mandatory:** A mandatory injunction requires someone to engage in affirmative conduct.

      (2) **Prohibitory:** A prohibitory injunction prohibits an individual or group from engaging in certain behavior.

      (3) **Temporary Restraining Order:** A TRO may be issued to maintain the status quo pending a ruling by the court on an application for a preliminary injunction. They can be granted ex parte upon a showing of great or irreparable injury.

      (4) **Preliminary/Provisional Injunction:** Such injunctions cannot be granted without an evidentiary hearing where both parties are present. A preliminary injunction does not determine the ultimate rights of the parties, and a factual determination made at the hearing on the preliminary injunction does not bind the court at the trial.

(5) **Permanent/Final Injunction:** Permanent injunctions are issued following a trial and a final adjudication of the ultimate rights in controversy.

b) **Requirements:** An injunction can be granted upon a showing of: (i) An inadequate remedy at law; (ii) a serious risk of irreparable harm absent injunctive relief; (iii) a likelihood that the plaintiff will prevail on the merits of the underlying controversy; and (iv) a comparison of the harm to the defendant in issuing an injunction versus the harm to plaintiff in withholding it, which on balance favors the plaintiff.

c) **Duration:** An injunction may state its date of expiration or may be valid "until further order of the court." A temporary restraining order terminates automatically when the preliminary injunction is granted or denied.

d) **Modification:** A trial court may modify or dissolve a final injunction on a showing that there has been a material change in the facts on which the injunction was granted or that the ends of justice would be served by the modification or dissolution of the injunction.

XV. APPEAL

A. Appealable Orders

1. **Final Judgment Rule:** An appeal is to the court of appeal and may be taken from a number of judgments or orders.

   **Please see full outline for list of judgments or orders.*

   A notice of appeal must be filed on or before the earliest of: (i) 60 days after the superior court clerk serves the party filing the notice of appeal with a document entitled "Notice of Entry of Judgment" or a file stamped copy of the judgment showing the date either was served; (ii) 60 days after the party filing the notice of appeal serves or is served by a party with a document entitled "Notice of Entry of Judgment" or a file stamped copy of the judgment accompanied by proof of service; or (iii) 180 days after entry of judgment.

   Note that if a notice of appeal is filed late, the reviewing court must dismiss the appeal.

2. **Non-Appealable Orders:** Generally, non-final interlocutory orders cannot be appealed.

3. **Finality of Judgment:** On determination of the evidence and law, judgment is given which is final and binding subject to any right of appeal and which is exercised. The court is not limited to the relief sought in the pleadings and can give such relief as it considers appropriate. In California, the state court is restricted by any applicable jurisdictional issues and cannot issue a declaratory judgment.

4. **Limitations of Reviewing Court:** If lack of subject matter jurisdiction is not raised until after final judgment and any appeal is dealt with, the judgment may nevertheless be set aside in a subsequent case subject to consideration of: (a) lack of jurisdiction being clear; the issue of jurisdiction is one of law not fact; (b) the court has a limited not general jurisdiction; (c) the issue of jurisdiction did not arise in the proceedings; or (d) public policy is against the court acting in excess of jurisdiction.

XVI. FRCP 59 NEW TRIALS; ALTERING OR AMENDING A JUDGMENT

Generally, the court may on motion grant a new trial on all or some of the issues, to any party: (i) after a jury trial for any reason for which a new trial has before been granted in an action at law in federal court; or (ii) after a non jury trial for any reason for which a rehearing has before been granted in a suit in equity in federal court.

After a non jury trial the court may, on motion for a new trial, open the judgment if one has been entered, take additional testimony, amend findings of fact and conclusions of law, or make new ones and direct the entry of a new judgment.

A motion for a new trial must be filed no later than 28 days after the entry of judgment

Further, no later than 28 days after the entry of judgment, the court on its own motion may order a new trial for any reason that would justify granting one on a party's motion.

A motion to alter or amend a judgment must be filed no later than 28 days after the entry of judgment.

XVII. FRCP RELIEF FROM A JUDGMENT OR ORDER

The court may correct a clerical mistake or a mistake arising from oversight or omission whenever one is found in a judgment order or other part of the record. The court may do so on motion or on its own, with or without notice. But after an appeal has been docketed in the appellate court and while it is pending, such a mistake may be corrected only with the appellate court's leave.

XVIII. RES JUDICATA AND RELATED DOCTRINES

A. Claim Preclusion or Res Judicata: Requires that a party seeking relief in a proceeding must pursue all available claims or forms of relief and all available theories at the first proceeding.

1. **Res Judicata:** Applies only to final judgments or orders by a court of competent jurisdiction on the merits of the case and which is conclusive upon the parties in subsequent litigation involving the same cause of action. The California rule is that a judgment is not final for the purpose of res judicata if it is still open to direct attack by appeal. A judgment must not only be final but also rendered on the merits in order to have res judicata effect. Res judicata must be properly pleaded or proved at trial and, if not, it is deemed to have been waived.

2. **Requirements**

   a) **Final Judgment:** The prior judgment must be final; all appeals or time for appeal are over.

   b) **Competent Jurisdiction:** The court must have proper subject matter jurisdiction and personal jurisdiction.

   c) **Judgment on the Merits of the Case:** A default judgment is not a judgment on the merits.

   d) **Parties or Privies:** Parties in the present lawsuit, and the previous lawsuit upon which the claim is based, must be identical and identically aligned.

   e) **Same Cause of Action:** The claim itself has to be identical to the one brought in the former lawsuit.

   f) **Primary Rights Theory:** California and a minority of jurisdictions apply the primary rights theory, which allows parties to split their causes of action. Property rights are severable from personal injury rights.

   g) **Federal Rules:** The federal rules require that all causes of action, including personal injury and property rights arising from the same transaction or occurrence, must be brought at the same time or res judicata will bar subsequent re-litigation. Courts will dismiss the entire lawsuit if res judicata applies.

B. Issue Preclusion or Collateral Estoppel: A judgment for the plaintiff or the defendant is conclusive in a subsequent action between them or their privies, as to issues of fact essential to the judgment that were actually litigated and resolved in the first action. This conclusive effect of the first judgment is called collateral estoppel. "The doctrine of collateral estoppel precludes relitigation of an issue previously adjudicated if: (i) the issue necessarily decided in the previous suit is identical to the issue sought to be relitigated; (ii) there was a final judgment on the merits of the previous suit; and (iii) the party against whom the plea is asserted was a party or in privity with a party to the previous suit.

1. **Requirements**

   a) **Final judgment**

   b) **Same parties:** The use of CE by a stranger against a former party was permissible if: (a) the first party had a full and fair opportunity to litigate the issue; and (b) use of CE would not be unfair to the defendant under the circumstances.

      (1) Use of CE can be applied against a party to the first action by someone who was not a party to it, if the party had an opportunity and motive to litigate the issue in the first suit.

      (2) A former party can never use CE against a stranger who had no opportunity to litigate the issue in the previous suit.

   c) Identical issues and facts essential to the judgment: The determination of the issue must have been necessary to the prior lawsuit's result. CE applies only to issues that were necessary to the prior judgment.

   d) Actually litigated and resolved: Issues and facts must have been actually litigated and resolved in the first lawsuit.

2. **Result of a Finding of Collateral Estoppel:** Those issues to which collateral estoppel applies are deemed to have been conclusively determined. If those issues are crucial to the plaintiff's prima facie case, or those issues are critical to the defendant's defense, the case may be dismissed on a motion for judgment as a matter of law.

C. Parties Bound By A Judgment

1. **Mutuality of Estoppel:** Since a judgment cannot be used against a person who was not a party, that person has traditionally been barred from taking advantage of the judgment.

2. **Parties and Persons in Privity:** A judgment for the plaintiff or the defendant is conclusive in a subsequent action/cause of action between them or their privies.

D. Full Faith and Credit: The U.S. Constitution provides that states must recognize judicial decisions of other states and the full faith and credit provision ensures that judicial decisions of courts of one state are recognized and honored in every other state.

XIX. ARBITRATION

Arbitration is a form of alternative dispute resolution in which parties to a dispute agree to participate in.

A. Enforcement of Agreements to Arbitrate: A written contractual provision referring disputes to arbitration is valid and enforceable between the parties to the contract or other relevant agreement.

B. Enforcement of Arbitration Awards: After arbitration, a party can move to have the arbitrator's award confirmed by the court.

COMMUNITY PROPERTY PRIMER

See full outline for statutory cross-references

I. RELATIONSHIP OF THE PARTIES

A. Valid California Marriage: In California, a lawful marriage requires both legal capacity and performance of formal legal procedures. California does not recognize common law marriages.

B. Non-California Marriage: California courts test the validity of marriages according to the place of celebration.

C. Putative Marriage: A putative spouse is not lawfully married, but has a good faith belief that she is lawfully married. A putative spouse has the same property rights as a lawful spouse until she learns the marriage is invalid.

D. Meretricious/Non-Marital Relationships: California applies general contract principles. If there is no express contract, a party may prove a contract implied by the behavior of the parties and may employ the doctrine of quantum meruit and apply equitable remedies such as a constructive or resulting trust.

II. GENERAL PRESUMPTION

California is a community property state. All property acquired during the course of a marriage is presumed community property. All property acquired before marriage/after permanent separation is presumed to be separate property. In addition, any property acquired by gift or devise is presumed separate property. To determine the character of any asset, courts will trace back to the source of funds used to acquire the asset.

III. ALTERING THE CHARACTER OF PROPERTY

A. Premarital Agreement: A premarital agreement must be in writing and signed by both parties and is valid provided it does not promote divorce. Exception: An oral agreement may be enforced: (i) where it has been fully performed; or (ii) where there is estoppel based on detrimental reliance by one party.

1. **Defenses:** The agreement was not signed voluntarily (without independent legal counsel, or seven days to review it); or it was unconscionable when made because: (i) there was not a full disclosure of a spouse's financial situation; (ii) disclosure was not waived in writing; or (iii) a party had no adequate knowledge of the other party's financial situation.

IV. CHARACTER OF THE PROPERTY

A. When Were the Assets Acquired?

B. Source of the Funds

1. **Separate Property & Exchange Rule:** Property acquired during marriage that is received by: (i) gift, bequest, devise, or descent; (ii) rents and profits of separate property acquired before or during marriage; and (iii) property acquired in exchange for separate property, is consider separate property.

   a) **Out-of-State Realty** is included within the definition of community property. Proof that an asset was acquired during marriage only raises a presumption that the asset is community property. A spouse can rebut this presumption.

2. **Community Property:** California is a community property state. All property acquired during the course of a marriage is presumed community property. However, that presumption may be overcome, as certain rules apply to specific types of property.

3. **Quasi-Community Property:** Such property is acquired by either spouse that would have been community property had the spouse been domiciled in California at the time of acquisition. Quasi-community property retains its separate property nature when the parties become domiciled in California. The quasi-community property label only becomes significant at divorce or death.

4. **Quasi-Marital Property:** This is property acquired by putative spouses and treated like community property. However, once a putative spouse learns that her marriage is invalid, she no longer accrues putative spouse property rights.

5. **Assets Purchased with Community and Separate Funds:** When community property and separate property are used to purchase an asset, the community property and separate property acquire a pro rata ownership interest in the asset (including a proportionate increase in value). If the property was acquired on credit, either the community property or separate property will be given credit for the loan depending on what the lender relied upon when making the loan.

C. Conduct of the Parties

1. **Transmutation:** A transmutation is an agreement by the spouses during marriage to alter the character of property. Prior to 1985, oral transmutations were allowed. Since 1985, in order for a transmutation to be valid, it must be in writing and signed by the person whose interest is adversely affected. No writing is required for interspousal gifts of a personal nature, which are relatively insignificant in value considering community assets.

2. **Improvements**

   a) Community property to improve own separate property: The community has the right of reimbursement for the greater cost of improvements/increased value.

   b) Community property to improve other's separate property: There is split of authority – no reimbursement because there is presumption of a gift to spouse; or a community claim for reimbursement should be recognized.

   c) Separate property to improve community property: In divorce, reimbursement is without interest for separate property contribution. In death, there is no reimbursement unless there is a written agreement.

3. **Commingling:** The mere fact that separate property funds are commingled with community property funds does not transform or transmute the separate property into community property. However, the burden of proof is on the claiming spouse to prove each asset was acquired with separate property.

   a) **Direct Tracing:** At the time the asset was purchased, there were separate funds available and the separate property proponent intended to use those separate funds to purchase a separate property asset.

   b) **Exhaustion Method:** At the time the asset was purchased, community property funds in the account had already been exhausted by payment of family expenses; therefore, the asset must have been purchased with separate funds.

4. **Installment Purchase Before Marriage; Debt Paid with Community Property:** The community estate takes a pro rata portion of the property, measured by a percentage of principal debt reduction attributable to community funds.

5. **Title of Property:** Prior to 1984, when a couple took title to an asset in joint and equal form, any separate property used to purchase the property was presumed to be a gift. The

separate property was not entitled to a separate ownership interest in the property unless there was an oral or written agreement. In addition, the separate property was not entitled to reimbursement unless there was an oral or written agreement.

Post 1984: When a married couple took title to an asset in joint tenancy after 1984, the asset was presumed to be community property for purposes of divorce unless there was a writing to the contrary. Any separate property used as a down-payment, for improvement, or as principal payment is reimbursed to the separate property contributor without interest. Beginning in 1987, this rule was extended to all jointly titled assets, except bank accounts. The presumption can be rebutted by an express statement in a deed or written agreement of the parties.

6. **Separation:** Separation is established by permanent physical separation and at least one party has no intent to reconcile. After separation, all earnings/accumulations are separate property of each spouse thereafter.

V. RULES GOVERNING SPECIFIC PROPERTY

A. **Personal Injury Awards:** Personal injury awards and settlements are community property if the cause of action arose during marriage. If the cause of action arose before marriage or after permanent separation, the award or settlement is separate property. Personal injury awards against the other spouse are always the separate property of the injured spouse. Upon divorce, community property personal injury awards are assigned entirely to the injured spouse so long as they have not been commingled with the other community property funds, and so long as the interests of justice do not require otherwise (the other spouse can get up to one-half).

B. **Pension Benefits:** These are community property if earned during the course of the marriage. When pension benefits are earned before marriage and during marriage, courts use the time rule to determine how much of the pension is attributable to community labor and how much is attributable to separate labor. The community's share is calculated by determining the number of years the pension was earned while married and dividing that number by the total number of years the pension was earned. A court can make a spouse pay: (i) when and if received; (ii) by cashing the other spouse out; or (iii) the court can retain jurisdiction until the pension starts.

C. **Disability Pay and Workers' Compensation Benefits:** Disability benefits, including workers' compensation benefits, are characterized as community property or separate property depending on the wages they are designed to replace.

D. **Severance Pay:** There is no fixed rule. To the extent that the severance pay looks like a benefit, which was earned during the course of the marriage, courts are likely to treat it as community property. However, in a few cases, courts have treated severance pay as equivalent to post-separation earnings and have therefore characterized the pay as separate property.

E. **Bonuses:** They are treated as community property or separate property depending on the facts and circumstances of the case. Bonuses in many cases will be community property because they are a form of compensation for the spouse's labor during the marriage. In some cases, however, an employee's bonus is more analogous to a personal gift from the employer to employee.

F. **Stock Options:** To the extent stock options are earned during the course of the marriage, the community has the right to share in their value as community property. Use proration to establish the community interest: number of years as community property divided into total number of years.

G. **Education and Training:** Education and training received during a marriage are not community property assets subject to division. However, the community may be entitled to reimbursement when community funds were used to pay for the education/training of a spouse and that education or training substantially enhanced the earning capacity of the spouse.

Defenses: (i) more than 10 years have passed, thus the community was indirectly reimbursed; (ii) the other spouse received community property education; (iii) the spouse who was educated now wants spousal support.

H. **Life Insurance:** The community has an interest in a whole-life insurance policy to the extent that the community paid the premiums (percentage of premiums paid before marriage is separate property; after marriage, it is community property). For term-life insurance, courts look at who paid the premium for the latest term. If the community paid the premium, the community is entitled to the benefits of the policy. If the premium for that period was paid by separate property, then it is separate property.

I. **Growth in Separate Property Business Caused by Community Labor:** When community labor is used to enhance the value of a separate property business, the community is entitled to share in the increased value. Courts use one of two formulas for calculating the community's interest in the increased value of a separate property business.

1. Pereira is used when the increase in value of a separate property business is primarily the result of community labor. Using Pereira, you determine the value of the separate property at the beginning of the marriage and give it a fair rate of return over the course of the marriage. Normally this is the legal interest rate calculated annually. The remainder is community property.
2. Van Camp is used when the increase in value of a business is primarily the result of the unique nature of the separate property asset. Using Van Camp, you determine what a fair salary would be for the community labor. You multiply that by the years of the marriage. You subtract any amounts paid out for community expenses. The result is the community property share. The rest is separate property.
3. Supreme Court holds whichever formula will achieve substantial justice between the parties should be used.

J. **Growth in Community Property Business Caused by Post Separation Labor:** When labor after separation is used to enhance the value of community property business, the separate estate is entitled to share in the increased value. Courts use one of two formulas to determine the separate property's share: Reverse-Pereira and Reverse-Van Camp. Reverse-Pereira gives the community a fair rate of return for the period after separation; the remainder of the increase belongs to the separate estate. Reverse-Van Camp assigns a fair salary to the separate estate and deducts any salary already taken by the spouse after separation and any separate expenses paid out of the business. The remainder belongs to the community.

K. **Married Woman's Special Presumption:** This applies to property taken in the married woman's name prior to 1975. According to the presumption, where community property was used to acquire written title in the name of a married woman: (i) alone; (ii) with her husband (but not in joint tenancy form or as husband and wife); or (iii) with a third party; prior to 1975 it was presumed to be her separate property.

1. **Overcoming the Presumption:** The husband may rebut the presumption by showing that he did not put title in his wife's name (because she had control over community property at the time title was taken) OR he did not intend to make a gift to his wife when he put title in her name. A bona-fide purchaser is protected.

VI. POTENTIAL RIGHTS

A. **Creditors:** The debtor's separate property is liable for debts she incurred before or during marriage. The other spouse's separate property is not liable for this debt. A creditor may reach the entire community property of both spouses. However, community property earnings of the non-debtor spouse are not liable for the debtor's premarital obligations held in an account where the debtor spouse has access. Additionally, where one spouse incurs a debt for "necessities of life" during marriage, the other spouse will be held personally liable for the debt.

B. **Tort Liability**: A person is not liable for her spouse's torts except where the activity benefited the community. If so, liability is satisfied from community property and then separate property of the married person. If there is no community benefit, liability is satisfied from separate property of the married person, then community property.

C. **Divorce:** Each spouse is personally liable for all debts he/she incurred whether or not the court assigned the debt for payment by the other spouse. If a debt is assigned by the court to one spouse, that spouse is personally liable for the debt. If the debt was not personal and not assigned, there is no personal liability. Any of the spouse's property used to satisfy the debt is reimbursable plus interest.

VII. SPOUSES' MANAGEMENT/CONTROL

A. **Separate Property:** Each spouse has the exclusive management and control of his or her separate property (and quasi-community property).

B. **Community Property:** Generally, each spouse has equal management and control of community property. Either spouse acting alone may buy, sell, spend, or encumber all community property. A spouse's one-half interest in community property cannot be encumbered unless it is used to retain a family law attorney.

1. **Real Property:** Both spouses must join in executing any instrument by which community real property is sold, conveyed, or leased for more than one (1) year. If only one spouse's name is on the title, and that spouse misrepresents his or her marital status to an innocent transferee, the non-consenting spouse has one (1) year to bring an action to void the transfer.

2. **Personal Property:** One spouse cannot sell or encumber personal property used in a family dwelling or clothing without written consent of the other spouse. The transaction is voidable by the other spouse at any time; there is no statute of limitations.

3. **Business Exception:** A spouse who is operating a business or an interest in a business that is all or substantially community property has primary management and control of the business.

C. **Limitations on Power**

1. **Gifts:** A spouse may not make a gift of community property without the written consent of the other spouse. The non-donor spouse may ratify the gift in a separate writing or revoke the gift. If the donor dies, the non-donor can recover against the donor's estate.

2. **Fiduciary Duties:** Each spouse must act in the highest good faith and fair dealing in the management and control of community property.

   a) **Managing Spouse:** The managing spouse must give a full accounting to the non-manager when requested and must secure the consent of the non-manager before committing certain acts (such as transferring community property). Intentional grossly negligent or reckless conduct breaches a spouse's fiduciary duty.

   b) **Breach:** The non-managing spouse has a claim against the managing spouse if there is a breach of fiduciary duty that results in substantial impairment of the non-manager's interest. She can seek an order for accounting and reformation of title to reflect her interest. An action may be brought upon death or divorce or three (3) years from the date that the non-manager becomes aware of the breach.

VIII. DISTRIBUTION OF PROPERTY

A. Divorce: At dissolution, each community asset will be divided equally unless some special rule requires deviation therefrom.

B. Statutory Exceptions to 50:50 Division on Divorce Rule

1. **Misappropriation of Community Property:** If done by one spouse before/during pendency of divorce.

2. **Liabilities Exceed Assets:** The relative ability of spouses to pay the debt will be considered.

3. **Education Debts:** These are treated as the recipient's separate debt.

4. **Tort Liability:** Tort liability is excepted if incurred by one spouse not based on activity for benefit of the community.

5. **Separate Debt:** Debt incurred before marriage or after separation.

6. **Personal Injury Recovery:** Recovery is given to the injured spouse unless justice requires otherwise.

7. **Good Will:** The value of good will attributable to repeat patronage is divisible.

C. Out-of-State Community Property and Quasi-Community Property: A California divorce court has the power to distribute all community property and quasi-community out-of-state realty. If community property or quasi-community property to be divided at divorce includes real property situated in another state, the California court will:

1. Divide all community property and quasi-community property in such a manner that it is not necessary to alter the nature of the interests held in out-of-state realty; or

2. If that is not possible, either: (i) require the parties to execute whatever conveyances are necessary to divide the out-of-state realty; or (ii) award to the party who would have benefited from the conveyance the money value of her interest.

D. Death: A spouse may transfer one-half of community property and all separate property (including quasi-community property in decedent's name) by will. The surviving spouse owns the other half of community property. Unless she consents, her community property claims are not satisfied by 1/2 of the aggregate community property.

1. **Widow's Election:** A widow can elect to challenge the will to receive her share of the community property. However, in doing so, she must relinquish all testamentary gifts in her favor.

2. **Gift of Community Property by One Spouse:** Neither spouse can make a gift of community property without the other spouse's written consent. The other spouse can recover her 1/2 of community property from the estate/donee.

3. **Out-of-State Community Property and Quasi-Community Property Realty:** Out-of-state realty is normally probated in ancillary administration in the state in which the realty is located. When a spouse owning out-of-state realty that would be community property or quasi-community property if it were located in California exchanges that realty for personalty or California realty, the new property is community property or quasi-community property.

4. **Intestate:** All property not transferred by will passes by intestacy.

IX. PREEMPTION

Areas in which federal law preempts California community property law include: (i) federal homestead law; (ii) armed forces life insurance benefits; (iii) U.S. savings bonds (unless there is fraud/breach of trust on the part of the spouse managing the community property funds); (iv) Social Security benefits; and (v) supplemental railroad retirement benefits are subject to state community property distribution.

CONSTITUTIONAL LAW PRIMER

I. JUSTICIABLE CASE

Whether the case is justiciable depends on whether there is a case in controversy. In order for the court to hear the case, the plaintiff must show: (i) that he has standing to bring the claim; (ii) the claim is ripe; (iii) the claim has not become moot; and (iv) the claim does not pose a political question.

A. Standing: Standing is the issue of whether the plaintiff is the proper party to bring the matter before the court. The plaintiff must show that he has suffered or will suffer an injury caused by the defendant that is redressable by the court.

1. **Injury:** The plaintiff must prove that he has been injured or will be imminently injured (an injury personally suffered; or for injunctive or declaratory relief, the likelihood of future harm).

2. **Causation and Redressability:** The plaintiff must prove that the defendant caused the injury so that a favorable court decision is likely to remedy the injury.

   a) **No Third-Party Standing:** A plaintiff cannot assert claims of third parties who are not before the court. Exceptions:

      (1) **Close Relationship:** A close relationship exists between the plaintiff and the injured party.

      (2) **Unable to Assert Own Rights:** The plaintiff is unable to assert her own right because she cannot or will not.

      (3) **Organization:** An organization may sue on behalf of its members if: (i) the members would have standing to sue; (ii) the interests are germane to the organization's purpose; and (iii) neither the claim nor relief requires the participation of individual members.

      (4) **Ballot Initiative:** Those who lack injury have no standing to challenge the enforcement of ballot initiatives.

   b) **No Generalized Grievances:** A plaintiff must not solely be suing as a citizen or taxpayer interested in having the government follow the law. Exception: Taxpayers have standing to challenge government expenditures as violating the First Amendment's Establishment Clause.

B. Ripeness: Ripeness is the question of whether the federal court may grant pre-enforcement review of a statute or regulation. The court will look to: (i) the hardship that will be suffered without pre-enforcement review; and (ii) the fitness of the issues and the record for judicial review.

C. Mootness: If events and the filing of the lawsuit end a plaintiff's injury, the case must be dismissed as moot. Exceptions:

1. **Wrong Capable of Repetition:** A wrong that is capable of repetition is one where the injury is short in duration or there is a chance that the plaintiff will suffer injury again.

2. **Voluntary Cessation:** The defendant voluntarily stops the offending practice but is free to resume.

3. **Class Action Suits:** If the named plaintiff's claim becomes moot, it is still acceptable if one class member still has an injury.

D. Political Question Doctrine: The political question doctrine refers to constitutional violations that the federal courts will not adjudicate and will therefore dismiss as not justiciable: (i) the republican form of government; (ii) the President's foreign policy; (iii) the impeachment and removal process; and (iv) partisan gerrymandering.

E. **United States Supreme Court Review:** The U.S. Supreme Court may only hear cases after a final judgment of the highest state court, the U.S. Court of Appeals, or a three-judge federal district court. To review a state court decision, there must not be an independent and adequate state law ground for the decision. If a state court decision rests on two grounds, one state law and one federal law, and the U.S. Supreme Court's reversal of the federal law basis will not change the result in the case, the U.S. Supreme Court cannot hear it.

F. **Sovereign Immunity:** The 11th Amendment is a jurisdictional bar that prohibits a federal court from hearing a claim by a party against a state government (sovereign immunity bars suits against states in state court or federal agencies). Exceptions:

1. **Waiver:** An explicit waiver is an exception to sovereign immunity. Waivers that are considered constructive or implied do not apply.
2. **Laws to Enforce 14th Amendment:** States may be sued pursuant to a federal law adopted under §5 of the 14th Amendment. Congress cannot authorize suits against states under other constitutional provisions (e.g., the Commerce Clause).
3. **Federal Government:** The federal government may sue a state government.
4. **Suits Against Officials:** Suits against officials are allowed in the following circumstances: (i) state officers may be sued for injunctive relief (person named as the defendant, not the state); (ii) state officers may be sued for money damages to be paid out of their own pockets (they are held to be personally liable and thus sovereign immunity is not applicable); (iii) state officers may not be sued if it is the state treasury that will be paying retroactive damages.

G. **Abstention:** Federal courts may not enjoin pending state court proceedings.

II. FEDERAL EXECUTIVE POWER

A. Foreign Policy

1. **Treaties:** Treaties are agreements between the United States and a foreign country that are negotiated by the President and are effective when ratified by the Senate. Treaties prevail over conflicting state law. When in conflict with a statute, the law that was last adopted wins. The U.S. Constitution prevails over treaties.
2. **Executive Agreement:** An executive agreement is an agreement between the U.S. and a foreign country that is effective when signed by the President and a foreign nation. An executive agreement can be used for any purpose. Such an agreement prevails over state law, but it does not prevail over a federal statute or the U.S. Constitution.
3. **Commander-in-Chief:** The President has broad powers to use troops in foreign countries without declaring war. Cases brought to challenge the exercise of such powers are dismissed as political questions.

B. Domestic Affairs

1. **Appointment:** The President appoints ambassadors, federal judges, and officers of the U.S. Congress may bestow appointment of inferior officers in the President, heads of departments or lower federal courts. Congress may not give itself or its officers appointment power.
2. **Removal Power:** Unless limited by statute, the President may fire any executive branch officer. For Congress to limit removal, there must be an office where independence from the President is desirable and Congress cannot prohibit removal. Removal power is only limited where good cause is found.

3. **Impeachment:** The President, Vice President, federal judges, and officers of the U.S. may be impeached where any of the following are found: treason, bribery, high crimes, or misdemeanors. Impeachment does not remove a person from office. For impeachment to result in removal, there must be a majority vote in the house and conviction in the Senate with a 2/3 vote.

4. **Immunity:** The President is immune to civil actions for any acts while in office, but not for conduct engaged in prior to taking office.

5. **Executive Privilege:** Executive privilege exists in papers and conversations, unless the papers or conversations are important to a government interest (e.g., evidence in criminal trial).

6. **Pardon:** A person can be pardoned by the President for federal crimes only, not state crimes.

III. FEDERAL LEGISLATIVE POWER

A. **Congress' Authority:** In order for Congress to have authority over an issue, the authority must be express or implied. There is no general federal police power exception to Congress' authority.

B. **Tax and Spend for the General Welfare:** Congress may tax and spend for the general welfare and, in doing so, place "strings" or conditions on funding, provided such strings meet a rational basis standard.

C. **Commerce Clause:** Under the Commerce Clause, Congress may regulate: (i) the channels of interstate commerce; (ii) the instrumentalities of interstate commerce and persons or things in interstate commerce; and (iii) economic activities that have a substantial effect on interstate commerce.

D. **Tenth Amendment:** The 10th Amendment limits Congressional power. The 10th Amendment provides that all powers not expressly granted to the federal government, or prohibited to the states, are reserved to the states or the people. Congress cannot compel state regulatory or legislative action. However, Congress can induce state government action by putting strings on grants, so long as the conditions are expressly stated and related to the purpose of the spending program. Congress may also prohibit harmful commercial activity by state governments.

E. **14th Amendment §5:** Under §5 of the 14th Amendment, Congress may not create new rights or expand the scope of rights. Congress may act only to prevent or remedy violations of rights recognized by the courts and such laws must be proportionate and congruent to remedying constitutional violations.

F. **Necessary and Proper Clause:** Under the Necessary and Proper Clause, Congress can adopt all laws necessary and proper to carry out its authority that are not prohibited by the Constitution.

G. **Delegation**

1. **No Limits:** There are no existing limits on Congress' ability to delegate legislative power.

2. **Legislative Vetoes/Line Item Vetoes:** Legislative and line item vetoes are unconstitutional. For Congress to act, there must always be bicameralism (passage by House and Senate) and presentment (to the President). The President must sign or veto the bill in its entirety.

3. **Executive Powers:** Executive powers may not be delegated to Congress by Congress.

IV. STATE LEGISLATION

A. **Preemption:** The Supremacy Clause provides that federal law is the supreme law of the land. Therefore, a federal law may supersede or preempt local laws. If a federal law conflicts with a state law, the state law will be invalid.

1. **Express Preemption:** A federal statute specifically states that the federal law is exclusive.

2. **Implied Preemption:** If federal and state laws are mutually exclusive, the federal law preempts the state law. Where it is not possible to comply with both federal and state law at the same time, the federal law preempts the state law. If state law impedes achievement of an important federal objective, the federal law preempts state law. However, states may impose stricter limits on conduct than the federal government unless expressly prohibited by Congress (e.g., states may impose stricter environmental standards than those imposed by Congress).

3. **Intent:** If Congress evidences a clear intent to preempt state law, federal law preempts state law under the "occupy the field" doctrine.

4. **Inter-governmental Immunity:** States may not tax or regulate federal government activity.

B. **Dormant Commerce Clause:** Under the Commerce Clause, states may regulate those activities that are purely local and do not discriminate against out-of-state commerce or impose an unreasonable burden on interstate commerce.

1. **Discriminatory:** If a law discriminates against interstate commerce, it violates the Dormant Commerce Clause unless it is necessary to achieve an important government purpose. The burden is placed upon the state to show that there are no less restrictive methods available to further the important government interest.

2. **Burden:** If a non-discriminatory state law burdens interstate commerce, it will be valid unless the burden outweighs the promotion of a legitimate local interest. The court will consider whether less restrictive alternatives are available.

Exceptions: (i) Congressional approval; (ii) Market Participant Exception. Under the Market Participant Exception, a state or local government may prefer its own citizens in receiving benefits from government programs or in dealing with government-owned business.

C. **Privileges and Immunities Clause of Article IV:** If a law discriminates against out-of-state residents on the basis of a fundamental right or with regard to their ability to earn their livelihood or other civil liberties, it violates the Privileges and Immunities Clause of Article IV unless it is necessary to achieve an important government purpose. The burden is placed upon the state to show that there are no less restrictive methods available to further the important government interest (corporations and aliens cannot sue here).

D. **Contract Clause:** The Contract Clause prohibits states or local government from enacting laws that interfere with existing contracts. Laws that interfere with existing private contracts must pass intermediate scrutiny. Laws that interfere with existing government contracts must meet strict scrutiny.

1. **Not Applicable to the Federal Government:** The Contract Clause does not apply to the Federal Government but flagrant contract impairment would violate the 5th Amendment Due Process.

E. **Taxation of Interstate Commerce:** (i) States may not use their tax system to help in-state business; (ii) A state may only tax activities if there is a substantial nexus to the state; (iii) State taxation of interstate business must be fairly apportioned (i.e., only tax the money earned in the state).

V. PROTECTION OF INDIVIDUAL LIBERTIES

A. State Action: The Constitution only applies to government action. Private conduct need not comply with the Constitution. Exceptions:

1. **Public Function Exception:** Under the Public Function Exception, the Constitution applies if a private entity is performing a task traditionally and exclusively performed by the government.

2. **Entanglement Exception:** Under the Entanglement Exception, the Constitution applies if the government affirmatively authorizes, encourages, or facilitates unconstitutional activity (e.g., a court enforced racially restrictive covenant).

3. **No State Action:** No state action has been found where a government subsidy is involved, free books have been provided, a liquor license has been granted, or in the case of interstate athletics.

4. **Congressional Action:** Congress, by statute, may apply Constitutional norms to private conduct through: (i) the 13th Amendment to stop private racial discrimination; (ii) the Commerce Power (requiring those engaged in interstate commerce to comply with civil rights provisions).

B. Bill of Rights: The Bill of Rights applies only to the federal government. Select incorporation does not include: (i) the 2nd Amendment right to bear arms; (ii) the 3rd Amendment right not to have a soldier quartered; (iii) the 5th Amendment right to a grand jury; (iv) the 7th Amendment right to a civil jury trial; (v) the 8th Amendment right against excessive fines, not including bail.

C. Takings: The 5th Amendment provides that private property may not be taken for public use without just compensation. This rule is applicable to the states via the 14th Amendment. The Takings Clause is not a source of power for taking, but rather a limitation. "Taking" includes not only physical appropriations, but also some government action that damages property or impairs its use.

1. **Public Use:** If the government action is rationally related to a legitimate public purpose (i.e., for health, safety, economic, or aesthetic reasons), the public use requirement is satisfied. Authorized takings by private enterprises are included if they redound to the public advantage (e.g., to build railroads or public utilities).

   a) **Physical Taking or Regulation:** The crucial issue is whether the government action is a taking or merely a regulation that does not require compensation. There is no clear-cut formula for making this determination.

      (1) **Denial of All Economic Value:** If a government regulation denies a landowner of all economic use of his land, the regulation amounts to a taking unless the principles of nuisance or property law make the use prohibited.

      (2) **Decreasing Economic Value – Balancing Test:** Regulations that merely decrease the value of property do not amount to a taking if it leaves an economically viable use for the property. The court will consider: (i) The social goals sought to be promoted; (ii) the diminution in value to the owner; and (iii) the owner's reasonable expectations regarding the property.

   b) **Remedy:** If the regulation amounts to a taking, the government must: (i) pay the fair market value, or (ii) terminate the regulation and pay for the loss of use.

D. Due Process: The Due Process clause of the 5th and 14th Amendments provides that no person shall be denied life, liberty, or property without due process of law. The prevailing view is that the Due Process clause does not provide only procedural protections, but also limits what the government can do.

1. **Procedural Due Process:** A fair process (i.e., notice and a hearing) is required for a government agency to individually take a person's "life, liberty, or property."

   a) **Liberty:** A deprivation of liberty occurs if a person: (i) loses a significant freedom or action; or (ii) is denied a freedom provided by the Constitution or statute.

   b) **Property:** There must be a legitimate claim or entitlement to the benefit under state or federal law where loss of property is alleged.

   c) **What due process is due?** The type and extent of the required procedures are determined by a three-part balancing test that weighs the: (i) importance of the interest to the individual; (ii) the value of specific procedural safeguards to that interest; and (iii) the government interest in fiscal and administrative efficiency.

   d) **Waiver:** Due process rights are subject to waiver if the waiver is voluntary and made knowingly.

2. **Substantive Due Process:** Certain fundamental rights are protected under the Constitution. If they are denied to everyone, it is a substantive due process problem. If they are denied to some individuals, but not others, it is an equal protection problem.

   a) **Right to Privacy:** The right to privacy is a fundamental right that includes the right to: (i) Contraception; (ii) Marry; (iii) Procreate; (iv) Private education; (v) Relatives living together; (vi) Raise children; (vii) Possess illicit Materials; and (viii) Refuse medical treatment. Abortion is no longer protected by the federal Constitution.

   b) **Right to Vote:** The right to vote is a fundamental right. Thus, restrictions on that right, other than on the basis of residence, age, and citizenship, are invalid unless they can pass strict scrutiny.

      (1) **Restrictions on Right to Vote:** Reasonable time periods for residency are valid (e.g., 30 days of residence prior to being allowed to vote). Any requirement that a voter own property or pay as a prerequisite for voting is invalid.

      (2) **Dilution of Right to Vote:** Dilution of votes through gerrymandering is not permitted unless strict scrutiny is satisfied.

      (3) **Candidates and Campaigns:** A fee cannot be charged that would make it impossible for indigents to run for office. A ballot access regulation must be a reasonable, non-discriminatory means of promoting important state interests; the government may allocate more public funds to the two major parties than to minor parties for political campaigns.

   c) **Right to Travel:** An individual has a fundamental right to migrate from state to state and to be treated equally after moving into a new state.

   d) **Right to Associate/Speech/Religion:** See below.

   e) **Economic Rights:** When the government employs economic and social regulation, it is permissible provided that the legislation is rationally related to a legitimate governmental purpose.

E. Equal Protection: The Equal Protection clause of the 14th Amendment provides that no state shall make or enforce any law that shall deny to any person within its jurisdiction equal protection of the laws. It prohibits governmental regulations that discriminate on the basis of an arbitrary classification, as individuals similarly situated must be treated the same.

Step 1: Identify the Classification

a) **Fundamental Right:** Fundamental rights include the right to privacy; vote; travel; speech; association; and religion.

b) **Suspect:** Classifications are suspect if they are based on race, alienage, or national origin.

c) **Quasi-Suspect:** Classifications of legitimacy and gender, including sexual orientation.

d) **Other Classes**

Step 2: Determine Standard of Review: If a fundamental right or suspect classification is involved, the strict scrutiny standard is used to evaluate the regulation. If a quasi-suspect classification is involved, intermediate scrutiny is the applicable standard. If the classification does not affect a fundamental right or involve a suspect or quasi-suspect classification, the rational basis test applied.

a) **Strict Scrutiny:** The law is upheld if it is necessary to achieve a compelling government purpose. The government has the burden of proof.

b) **Intermediate Scrutiny:** The law is upheld if it is substantially related to an important government purpose. For intermediate scrutiny, the burden of proof typically rests with the government.

c) **Rational Basis:** The law is upheld if it is rationally related to a legitimate government purpose. The person challenging the law has the burden of proof. The law is usually valid unless it is arbitrary or irrational. Exception:

(1) **Facially Neutral Law:** Where a facially neutral law is being applied in a discriminatory manner or there is a discriminatory motive behind the law, the government is said to have the intent to discriminate, and strict or intermediate scrutiny will be applied depending on the classification of those targeted.

Step 3: Determine the Government's Interest in the Legislation

Step 4: Determine How the Classification Furthers That Interest

Step 5: Determine Whether There Are Less Burdensome Means Available

F. **First Amendment Speech:** The 1st Amendment prohibits Congress from abridging the freedoms of speech and press, or interfering with the right of assembly. These prohibitions are applicable to the states through the 14th Amendment.

1. **Facial Attack**

a) **Prior Restraints:** Prior restraints prevent speech before it occurs, rather than punishing it afterwards. Court orders suppressing speech are rarely allowed and must meet strict scrutiny. Procedurally proper orders must be complied with until vacated or overturned (violating a court order precludes the ability to challenge the order). Requiring a license for speech is permissible if there is an important reason for licensing and clear criteria, leaving almost no discretion to the licensing authority. Such schemes must contain procedural safeguards such as prompt review.

b) **Vague:** A law is unconstitutionally vague if a reasonable person cannot determine what speech is prohibited and what is allowed.

c) **Over-breadth:** A law is unconstitutionally overbroad if it regulates substantially more speech than the Constitution allows to be regulated.

d) **Unfettered Discretion:** A regulation cannot give officials broad discretion over speech issues. There must be defined standards for applying the law. If a statute gives licensing officials unbridled discretion, it is void on its face and the speakers need not even apply for a permit.

2. **Content-Based:** When a state regulates the content of speech, it is presumptively unconstitutional. The burden is on the state to prove that the regulation is necessary to serve a compelling government interest and that the means are narrowly tailored (i.e.,

balancing a person's interest, the government's interest, and evaluating less restrictive alternatives). However, the U.S. Supreme Court has previously determined that certain prohibitions on speech are valid despite the 1st Amendment. These unprotected categories of speech include:

a) **Defamation:** Defaming statements are those that serve to damage an individual's reputation.

b) **Fighting Words:** Speech can be burdened if it constitutes fighting words that are personally abusive and are likely to incite immediate physical retaliation in an average person.

c) **Advocacy of Imminent Lawless Action:** Speech can be burdened if it creates a clear and present danger of imminent lawless action. Under the Brandenburg Test, the government may prohibit speech if: (i) the speech advocates imminent lawless action; (ii) the threatened action poses serious risk of harm; (iii) the speaker specifically intends the unlawful activity to occur; and (iv) illegal action is likely to occur.

d) **Commercial Speech:** Commercial speech is afforded 1st Amendment protection if it is truthful. However, commercial speech that proposes unlawful activity or that is misleading or fraudulent may be burdened. Any other regulation of commercial speech will be upheld only if it is substantially related to an important governmental purpose.

e) **Obscenity:** Obscene speech is not protected. Under the Miller Test, speech is obscene if it describes or depicts sexual conduct that, if taken as whole by the average person: (i) appeals to the morbid interest in sex, using a community standard; (ii) is patently offensive by community standards; and (iii) lacks serious value (literary, artistic, political, or scientific), using a national standard.

   (1) **Minors:** A state can adopt a specific definition of obscenity that applies to materials sold to minors. However, the government cannot prohibit the sale of goods to adults that would be inappropriate to minors.

3. **Content-Neutral Regulation of Conduct:** The U.S. Supreme Court has allowed the government more leeway in regulating conduct-related speech, permitting it to adopt content-neutral time, place, and manner restrictions. The limitations depend on whether the speech involves a public forum or a nonpublic forum.

a) **Time, Place, or Manner Restrictions on Speech:** The government has the power to regulate the conduct associated with speech and assembly, although the breadth of this power depends on whether the forum involved is a public forum, a limited public forum, or a non-public forum.

   (1) **Public Forums and Limited Public Forums:** Public property that has historically been open to speech-related activities (e.g., streets, sidewalks, and public parks) is called a public forum. Public property that has not historically been open to speech-related activities, but which the government has opened for such activities on a permanent or limited basis, by practice or policy (e.g., schoolrooms that are open for after-school use by social, civic, or recreational groups), is called a limited public forum. The government may regulate speech in public and limited public forums with reasonable time, place, and manner regulations that: (i) Are content-neutral; (ii) Are substantially related to an important government purpose; and (iii) Leave open alternative channels of communication.

b) **Non-Public Forum:** Speech and assembly can be more broadly regulated in nonpublic forums (e.g., government-owned forums not historically linked with speech, military bases, schools in session, government workplaces). In such locations, regulations are valid if they are: (i) Viewpoint neutral; and (ii) Reasonably related to a legitimate government purpose.

G. **First Amendment Religion:** The 1st Amendment prohibition on passing laws respecting an establishment of religion and the protections of the free exercise of religion are applicable to the states through the 14th Amendment.

1. **Establishment Clause:** The Establishment Clause prohibits laws respecting the establishment of religion.

    a) **Sect Preference:** A sect preference in a law or regulation must pass strict scrutiny.

    b) **No Sect Preference:** If a government regulation contains no sect preference the court no longer employs the Lemon Test or endorsement test, but looks to "historical practices and understandings". Under this approach, traditional monuments and practices that have explicit references to religion (for example, "In God we trust") are likely acceptable even though they would not be permitted if created today.

2. **Free Exercise Clause:** The Free Exercise Clause cannot be used to challenge a law of general application that is neutral and not intended to discriminate against religious practice. However, a law designed to interfere with religion must meet strict scrutiny.

H. **First Amendment Association:** Laws that prohibit or punish group membership (even indirectly through disclosure of membership) must meet strict scrutiny. To punish membership in a group, it must be proven that the person: (i) is actively affiliated with the group; (ii) knows of its illegal activity; and (iii) has the specific intent of furthering those illegal activities.

1. **Exception:** Laws that prohibit a group from discriminating are constitutional unless they interfere with intimate association or expressive activity.

I. **First Amendment Symbolic Speech:** 1st Amendment Symbolic Speech laws must pass intermediate scrutiny.

VI. MISCELLANEOUS CONSIDERATIONS

A. **Privileges of National Citizenship:** Under the 14th Amendment, states may not deny their citizens the privileges or immunities of national citizenship (e.g., the right to petition Congress for redress of grievances, the right to vote for federal officers, and the right to interstate travel). Corporations are not protected by this clause.

B. **Full Faith and Credit:** If a judgment is entitled to full faith and credit, it must be recognized in sister states. This clause applies only if: (i) the court that rendered the judgment had jurisdiction over the parties and the subject matter; (ii) the judgment was on the merits; and (iii) the judgment is final.

C. **Ex Post Facto Laws:** Such laws apply to criminal cases only. The state or federal government may not pass an ex post facto law (i.e., a law that retroactively alters criminal offenses or punishment in a prejudicial manner for the purpose of punishing a person for some past activity). A statute retroactively alters a law in a substantially prejudicial manner if it: (i) makes criminal an act that was innocent when done; (ii) prescribes greater punishment for an act than was prescribed for the act when it was done; or (iii) reduces the evidence required to convict a person of a crime from what was required when the act was committed.

D. **Bills of Attainder:** Bills of Attainder are legislative acts that inflict punishment on individuals without a judicial trial. Both federal and state governments are prohibited from passing bills of attainder.

E. **Due Process Considerations:** If a retroactive law does not violate the Contracts, Ex Post Facto, or Bill of Attainder Clauses, it still must pass muster under the Due Process Clause. If the retroactive law does not relate to a fundamental right, it need only be rationally related to a legitimate government interest.

CONTRACTS & UCC PRIMER

See full outline for statutory cross-references

I. APPLICABLE LAW

A. **Contract Involving Sale of Goods - UCC**

B. **If Both Parties are Merchants - UCC**

C. **Contract Involving Services or Non-Sale of Goods - Common Law**

D. **Predominant Purpose Test**

II. IS THERE A VALID CONTRACT?

A. **Formation is not an Issue:** If the fact pattern states there is a valid contract, in your essay answer, provide an introductory paragraph stating how each element of the contract is satisfied.

B. **Where Formation is an Issue**

1. **Offer**

a) **Manifestation of Present Intent:** The offeror must intend to contract and not simply negotiate.

b) **Definite and Certain Terms:** Offer must include: (i) identification of the parties; (ii) subject matter; (iii) time for performance; and (iv) a price, that includes:

(1) **Requirement/Output Contract:** Offers that designate quantity by requirement or output are certain since these quantity terms can be objectively determined.

(2) **UCC Sale of Goods:** Agreements for the sale of goods controlled by the UCC will not fail due to the omission of an essential term if: (i) the parties make a contract; (ii) there is a reasonably certain basis for remedy in the event of breach; and (iii) the parties exercise good faith (honesty in fact in the conduct of the transaction). Exception: Quantity term will not be implied by the UCC.

c) **Communication Requirement:** The offer must be communicated to the offeree.

2. **Termination of Offer:** An offer may be accepted only as long as it has not been terminated. It may be terminated by: (i) an act of either party; or (ii) operation of law.

a) **Termination by Acts of Parties:** The offeror terminates an offer if he: (i) directly communicated the revocation; or (ii) acts inconsistently with continued willingness to maintain the offer, and the offeree receives correct information of this from a reliable source.

b) **Termination by the Offeree**

(1) **Rejection:** An offeree may reject an offer: (i) by express rejection; or (ii) by making a counteroffer which serves as a rejection of the original offer.

(2) **Lapse of Time:** An offer may be terminated by the offeree's failure to accept within the time specified by the offer or within a reasonable period if no deadline was specified.

c) **Termination by Operation of Law:** The following events will terminate an offer: (i) Death or insanity of either party; (ii) Destruction of the contract's proposed subject matter; or (iii) Illegality of the contract's subject matter.

3. **Acceptance:** A valid acceptance of a bilateral contract requires there to be: (i) an offeree with the power of acceptance; (ii) unequivocal terms of acceptance; and (iii) communication of acceptance.

a) **Acceptance Must Be Unequivocal**

(1) **Common Law:** Acceptance must mirror the offer's terms, neither omitting nor adding terms.

(2) **UCC:** Unless expressly prohibited, an acceptance will be effective even if additional or different terms are contained therein.

(3) **Additional Terms:** Such terms are typically construed as proposed additions to the contract and must be separately accepted to modify the original offer.

Between Merchants: If both parties to the contract qualify as merchants, the new terms do become part of the contract unless:

(a) **Prior Objection:** The original offeror objected in advance to the addition of terms.

(b) **Subsequent Objection:** If the original offeror objects to the new terms within a reasonable time after notice of them is received.

(c) **Material Alteration:** If the new terms would materially alter the original terms.

(4) **Different Terms:** An acceptance form that contains different terms than the offer is considered an acceptance, provided the acceptance does not insist upon the new terms being accepted, and a contract will be formed unless the offeror specifically limits the acceptance to the terms of the offer.

(5) **Open Terms:** The fact that one or more terms are left open (including price) does not prevent the formation of a contract if the parties intended such. The court can supply reasonable terms for those that are missing.

(6) **Performance:** If the parties have exchanged non-matching forms and begin to perform, a contract has been created. The contract will consist of the terms on which the parties agree, plus supplementary terms supplied by the UCC where the parties are silent.

b) **Communication of Acceptance:** Acceptance is judged by an objective reasonable person standard. The modern rule and the UCC permit acceptance by any reasonable means unless the offeror unambiguously limits acceptance to particular means.

(1) **Mailbox Rule:** Under the mailbox rule, if the acceptance is by mail or similar means and it is properly addressed and stamped, it is effective at the moment of dispatch. If it is improperly sent, it will be effective on receipt.

4. **Consideration:** Courts will enforce a bilateral or unilateral contract only if it is supported by consideration or a substitute for consideration.

a) **Insufficient Consideration:** Examples of insufficient consideration include: (i) gift; (ii) past consideration; (iii) moral consideration; (iv) economic adequacy; (v) pre-existing duty; and, (vi) an illusory promise.

b) **Substitute for Consideration**

(1) **Promissory Estoppel or Detrimental Reliance:** Promissory estoppel is a sufficient substitute for consideration.

(2) **Specific Circumstances:** An obligation discharged by law can be revived by a gratuitous promise made in writing.

C. Defenses to Formation: Although the requirements for the existence of a contractual relationship appear to be present, in some circumstances, the contract may be voidable due to mistake.

1. **Absence of Mutual Assent**

   a) **Mutual Mistake:** A mistake by both parties at the time the contract is made is a defense to a contract if: (i) the mistake concerns a basic assumption on which the contract was made; (ii) the mistake has a material adverse effect on the agreed-upon exchange of performance; and, (iii) the adversely affected party did not assume the risk of the mistake.

   b) **Unilateral Mistake:** A mistake by one party is generally insufficient to make a contract voidable. However, if the non-mistaken party knew or should have known of the mistake, the contract is voidable by the mistaken party if the effect of the mistake would be to make enforcement of the contract unconscionable or the other party knew of the mistake or she caused it.

   c) **Misrepresentation:** If a party induces another to enter into a contract using fraudulent misrepresentation or by using non-fraudulent material misrepresentation, the contract is voidable by the innocent party if she justifiably relied on the misrepresentation.

   d) **Illegality of Contract:** If the consideration or subject matter of the contract is illegal, the contract is void.

D. Defenses to Enforcement

1. **Statute of Frauds:** Types of agreements that fall under the statute of frauds: (i) in consideration of marriage; (ii) that by their terms cannot be performed within one year; (iii) creating an interest in land; (iv) by executors to pay an estates' debts out of their own pockets; (v) to pay the debts of another; and (vi) for the sale of goods for $500 or more.

   a) **Memorandum Requirements:** The statute is satisfied if the writing contains the following: (i) the identity of the parties; (ii) the contract's subject matter; (iii) the terms and conditions; (iv) a recital of consideration; and (v) the signature of the party to be charged.

   b) **Removing the Contract from the Statute of Frauds**

      (1) **Part Performance:** Such performance of an oral land sale contract will permit equitable enforcement of the contract.

      (2) **Detrimental Reliance:** An oral contract is enforceable if the promisor represented that a writing would be made, and the other party detrimentally relied on the representation.

      (3) **Full Performance:** Full performance by one party of a multi-year oral contract in less than one year makes the contract enforceable.

      (4) **Sale of Goods:** Oral contracts for the sale of goods will be enforced under the UCC when the merchant sends a written confirmation.

      (5) **Writing:** Is not required in the following situations: (i) Specially manufactured goods; (ii) Delivered goods; (iii) Full payment received; (iv) Admission; or (v) Estoppel.

2. **Unconscionability:** If a contract was unconscionable when made, the court may refuse to enforce it or limit enforcement to avoid unconscionable results. Contract is unconscionable if, at the time of execution, the contract (or a provision thereof) could result in unfair surprise and was oppressive to a disadvantaged party.

3. **Lack of Capacity:** Without legal capacity to enter into a contract, the "incapacity" of a party makes the contract voidable. Three types of "incapacity" are: (i) minors, (ii) mental incompetence, or (iii) intoxication.

III. MODIFICATION: CHANGING THE TERMS OF AN EXISTING CONTRACT

A. New Consideration: Whether new or additional consideration will be required in order for a contract modification to be valid depends upon the underlying subject matter of the contract.

1. **Common Law:** For modifications to be valid, they need to be supported by additional consideration.

2. **UCC:** Contract modifications sought in good faith are valid. An agreement modifying a contract within Article 2.209 UCC is binding without consideration. Contract modifications must meet the statute of frauds requirements if the contract, as modified, falls within the statute.

B. Oral Modifications

1. **Statute of Frauds**

   a) **Modification:** Modification of a written contract bringing the subject within the purview of the statute of frauds must be in writing. If goods are over $500, modification must be in writing. However, (i) Part-performance takes the contract out of the statute of frauds, and (ii) Full performance of an oral agreement by both parties need not be in writing.

   b) **Writing Prohibiting Oral Modification:** A provision that a written contract cannot be modified or rescinded except by a writing is valid and binding. Where a no-oral-modifications provision is provided by a merchant to a consumer, it must be signed by the consumer.

   c) **Waiver of the Writing Requirement:** An invalid oral modification may serve as a waiver of a party's rights to enforce the contract as written if one of the parties relied to her detriment on the modification.

   d) **Written Confirmations – UCC:** Where there is an oral modification that is then followed by a written confirmation, this will satisfy the statute of frauds.

   e) **Waiver of Condition:** A condition can be waived by words or conduct, and no considered is required.

C. By Operations of Law

1. **Destruction or Injury to Identified Goods:** If goods are destroyed without fault of either party, before the risk of loss passes to the buyer, the contract is avoided. For damaged goods, the buyer may elect to take goods with a reduction in price. If the goods are destroyed or damaged after the risk of loss has passed to the buyer, the buyer will bear the loss.

2. **Failure of Agreed-Upon Method of Transportation:** If the agreed-upon delivery facilities become unavailable or commercially impractical, any commercially reasonable transportation must be tendered and must be accepted.

IV. WHAT ARE THE TERMS OF THE CONTRACT?

A. Interpretation

1. Where the parties agree upon the meaning of a promise/agreement, the contract will be interpreted in accordance with that meaning. When the contract is made, if one party attaches a different meaning, that meaning will prevail if:

a) That party did not know of any different meaning and the other party was aware of this, and

b) That party had no reason to know of any different meaning.

2. **Interpreting the Terms/Conditions of the Contract:** Generally, an interpretation which gives a lawful reasonable and effective meaning will be applied:

a) **Specific Express Terms:** Will be given greater weight than terms/conditions implied by a course of dealing or usage in the trade.

b) **An Integrated Agreement:** an agreement in writing in which one or more of the terms/conditions is expressed, is construed as the final expression of the parties' intentions.

c) **Different Interpretations:** If the meaning of a term/condition is subject to different interpretations, the preferred meaning adopted is usually that which operates against the person who supplied the words.

B. **Parol Evidence Rule:** Evidence of prior or contemporaneous agreements are not admissible to contradict or modify a written agreement that was intended as a full and final expression of the parties' bargain.

1. **Is the writing intended as a final expression?** Intent is a question of fact determined by: (i) Face of the agreement; (ii) All relevant evidence; or (iii) Existence of a merger clause.

2. **Is the writing a complete or partial integration?** After establishing that the writing was "final," determine if the integration was complete or partial.

a) **Complete:** the terms may not be contradicted or supplemented.

b) **Partial:** the terms may be supplemented by proving consistent additional terms.

C. **Outside the Purview of the Parol Evidence Rule**

1. **Ambiguities:** Where terms of an agreement are uncertain, evidence to clarify the meaning of the terms may be introduced.

2. **Conditions Precedent:** Evidence that a stated event must take place prior to a contract becoming effective is not precluded by the parol evidence rule.

3. **Collateral Agreements:** Where the subject matter of an agreement is typically considered independent of the subject matter that is the subject of an agreement precluding parol evidence, such evidence can be admitted to show a collateral agreement exists.

V. WARRANTIES – UCC-SPECIFIC PROVISIONS

A. **Warranties:** Under the UCC, there are four types of warranties: (i) Warranty of title and against infringement; (ii) Implied warranty of merchantability; (iii) Implied warranty of fitness for a particular purpose; (iv) Express warranties; and, (v) Exclusion or modification of warranties.

1. **Warranty of Title:** In a contract of sale, the seller warrants that he is conveying good title that is free of liens, encumbrances or other security interest of which the buyer has no knowledge.

2. **Implied Warranty of Merchantability:** In every mercantile contract of sale where it is not expressly disclaimed, the law implies a warranty that the goods shall be of merchantable quality. Merchantability is defined as goods that would: (i) pass without objection in the trade; (ii) be of fair average quality; and (iii) be fit for the ordinary purpose for which goods are used.

3. **Implied Warranty of Fitness for a Particular Purpose:** If a seller has reason to know of any particular purpose for which the goods are required by the buyer and is also aware that the

buyer is relying on the seller's skill or judgment to select suitable goods, then an implied warranty of fitness for that particular purpose arises.

4. **Express Warranty:** An affirmation of fact or promise made by the seller to the buyer in the course of negotiations that relates to the goods and is part of the basis for the bargain creates an express warranty that the goods will conform to the affirmation or promise.

5. **Exclusion or Modification of Warranties**

   a) A purported written modification of the implied warranty of merchantability by way of exclusion or limitation must refer to merchantability and the writing must be conspicuous.

   b) An exclusion of the warranty of fitness for purpose must be in writing and conspicuous.

B. **Obligations to Remote Purchasers**

1. **Packaged with a Record:** A seller has an obligation to a remote purchaser that new goods sold or leased that are packaged with a record making an affirmation of fact or remedial promise relating to the goods will conform thereto.

2. **Communication to the Public:** If an advertisement to the public provides an affirmation of fact or promise relating to the goods, and the remote purchaser enters into a transaction with **knowledge** of and with the **expectation** that the goods will conform thereto, the seller has an obligation to make the goods conform unless a **reasonable person** would not believe the affirmation/remedial promise.

C. **Third Parties:** In most states, the seller's warranty extends to any natural person who is in the family or household of the buyer or who is a guest in her home if it is reasonable that such a person may use, consume, or be affected by the goods, and he suffers personal injury because of the breach of warranty.

D. **Vouching In:** If a reseller is sued, the reseller can give the initial seller or other party notice of the suit. If that party does not come and defend, the party will be bound by whatever determination of fact is made that is common to the litigants.

E. **Federal Consumer Product Warranties Law:** If a consumer product manufacturer issues a full warranty, implied warranties cannot be disclaimed. If a limited warranty is issued, implied warranties cannot be disclaimed or modified, but they can be limited in duration to the length of the limited warranty.

VI. BENEFICIARIES, ASSIGNMENT, DELEGATION, RIGHTS

A. **Intended Beneficiary:** A person other than the promisee and who will benefit from the performance of the promise, and the performance of the promise will satisfy an obligation of the promisee to pay money to the beneficiary.

B. **Incidental Beneficiary:** Someone who benefits from the performance of the contract but not as an intended beneficiary and in consequence no duty is owed to him.

C. **Third-Party Beneficiary**

1. **Step 1: Intended v. Incidental Beneficiary:** Intended beneficiaries have contractual rights, whereas incidental beneficiaries do not. To characterize the beneficiary, the court will look to whether the beneficiary: (i) is identified in the contract; (ii) receives performance directly; or (iii) has a relationship with the promisee that demonstrates the promisee's intent to benefit.

2. **Step 2: Creditor v. Donee Beneficiary:** Assuming the beneficiary is intended, the intended beneficiary will take one of two forms: (i) a creditor of the promise; or (ii) a donee who will benefit gratuitously.

3. **Step 3: When does the beneficiary acquire contract rights?** A contract is enforceable by a third party upon the vesting of contractual rights. Vesting occurs when the third party either: (i) assents to performance; (ii) seeks to enforce performance; or (iii) detrimentally relies on the promise.

4. **Step 4: Who can sue whom?**

    a) **Third-Party Beneficiary v. Promisor:** A third-party beneficiary has the same rights of enforcement and/or for breach against the promisor as does the promisee. The third-party beneficiary is subject to the same defenses the promisor has against the promisee.

    b) **Third-Party Beneficiary v. Promisee:** Creditors can sue the promisee or the promisor on the basis of any outstanding debt. However, double recovery is not permitted.

    c) **Promisee v. Promisor:** A promisee may seek specific performance where the promisor has failed to perform and remedies at law are insufficient.

D. Assignment of Contract Rights: Assignment is the transfer of a contractual right by the assignor to the assignee as a result of which the assignee stands in the place of the original contracting party. An assignment cannot take place if specifically excluded by the contract or is contrary to law.

1. **Is the assignment revocable?** An assignment for consideration is irrevocable. An assignment without consideration is generally revocable.

    a) **Revocation:** An assignment without consideration is irrevocable where: (i) delivery or performance has been rendered; (ii) there is a written agreement; or (iii) there is detrimental reliance on the part of the assignee.

    b) **Termination:** Revocable assignments may be terminated by: (i) death, incapacity or bankruptcy of the assignor; (ii) providing adequate notice of revocation to the assignee or the obligor; or (iii) the conduct of the assignor.

2. **Who can sue whom?**

    a) **Assignee v. Obligor:** The assignee may enforce the contract and be subject to the same defenses as the assignor.

    b) **Assignee v. Assignor:** Where an assignment is supported by consideration the assignee can sue the assignor: (i) if the assignor wrongfully revokes an irrevocable assignment; or (ii) if the obligor successfully asserts a defense against the assignor in an action brought by the assignee against the obligor to enforce the obligation.

3. **Successive Assignments:** If the first assignment is revocable, a subsequent assignment revokes it. If it is irrevocable, the first assignment will usually prevail over a subsequent assignment.

E. Delegation of Contract Duties: Delegation occurs when a party to a contract transfers her primary obligation under the contract to a third person.

1. **Requirements:** The delegor must manifest a present intention to make a delegation. There are no special formalities to be complied with to have a valid delegation.

2. **Rights and Liabilities:** The obligee must accept performance from the delegate if the duty can be delegated. The delegor is still liable on the contract and the obligee may sue the delegor if the delegate does not perform.

F. UCC Third-Party Rights

1. **Entrustment:** Entrusting includes any delivery and any acquiescence in retention of possession. Entrusting goods to a merchant who deals in goods of that kind gives him power to transfer all rights of the entruster to a buyer in the ordinary course of business.

2. **Voidable Title:** If a sale is induced by fraud, the title is voidable and the seller can rescind the sale and recover the goods. But the seller cannot recover goods from one who purchases in good faith for value even where: (i) the seller was deceived as to the identity of the buyer; (ii) the delivery was in exchange for a check later dishonored; (iii) the sale was a cash sale; or (iv) the buyer's fraudulent conduct is punishable as larcenous under the criminal law.

3. **Thief Cannot Pass Good Title:** If a thief sells goods that he stole from a true owner, the title is void and the thief cannot pass good title to a buyer. This means that even if the buyer has purchased in good faith for value, the true owner can recover the stolen goods from the buyer.

VII. HAVE THE TERMS OF THE CONTRACT BEEN PERFORMED?

A. Promise or Condition:

Promise or Condition: A promise is a commitment to do, or refrain from doing, something. Promises may be conditional or unconditional. A conditional promise is subject to an event, occurrence, or nonoccurrence, which will create, limit, or extinguish the duty to perform.

1. **Condition Precedent**
2. **Concurrent Condition**
3. **Subsequent Condition**
4. **Express Conditions**
5. **Implied In Fact Conditions**
6. **Constructive Conditions**

B. Have the conditions been satisfied or excused?

Have the conditions been satisfied or excused? A duty of performance becomes absolute when conditions are either performed or excused.

1. **Excusing of Conditions By:**

   a) **Failure to Cooperate:** A party who wrongfully prevents a condition from occurring cannot claim the benefit of the contract, and the condition is excused.

   b) **Actual Breach:** If one party materially breaches the contract, the other party is excused from performance. A minor breach suspends the duty, but will not excuse it.

   c) **Right to Demand Assurances:** If a party reasonably believes that the other party will not fulfill his duties, he may in writing demand adequate assurance of due performance.

   d) **Anticipatory Repudiation:** If, through a party's words, actions, or circumstances, it becomes clear that he is unwilling or unable to perform, the other party may: (i) ignore the repudiation and urge the other party perform; (ii) resort to any remedy for a breach; or (iii) suspend his own performance.

   e) **Substantial Performance:** If a party breaches the contract in a minor way but has almost completely performed his essential duties, he does not forfeit return performance.

f) **Divisibility of Contract:** When a party performs one part of a divisible contract, she is entitled to the agreed-to equivalent unit from the other party even if she fails to perform the other parts.

(1) **Requirements to Find a Contract Divisible:** (i) The performance of each party is divided into two or more individual matching parts; (ii) The failure to perform one part of the contract does not necessarily put the party in breach of the entire contract.

(2) **UCC – Installment Contracts:** An installment contract authorizes or requires delivery in separate lots. The buyer may declare a total breach only if defects in an installment substantially impair the value of the entire contract.

g) **Waiver or Estoppel**

(1) **Estoppel Waiver:** A party may waive a condition by indicating that he will not insist on the other party performing it.

(2) **Election Waiver:** If a condition is broken, the party who was to have its benefit may either terminate his liability or continue under the contract.

(3) **No Consideration:** A waiver is not enforceable if there is no consideration.

h) **Impossibility, Impracticability, or Frustration:** Infra.

C. **Has the duty to perform been discharged?** Once it has been established that there is an immediate duty to perform, that duty must be discharged by:

1. **Performance or Tender of Performance:** A party discharges his duty by complete performance or tender of performance as long as he has the present ability to perform.

2. **Condition Subsequent:** The duty to perform may be discharged by a condition subsequent.

3. **Illegality:** The duty to perform may be discharged if the subject matter is illegal.

4. **Impossibility/Impracticability/Frustration**

a) **Impossibility:** Measured by an objective standard where performance is rendered impracticable without the fault of either of the contracting parties.

b) **Impracticability:** Unanticipated extreme and unreasonable difficulty or expense in performing a promise.

c) **Frustration of Purpose:** Duty discharged if there is a supervening event that the parties could not reasonably know of or reasonably foresee at the time they entered the contract which completely or almost completely destroys the understood purpose of the contract.

5. **Mutual Rescission:** Both parties may expressly agree to a mutual rescission of the contract and a consequent to discharge of respective duties. A bilateral contract can be rescinded only where the contract has been partially performed. A unilateral contract cannot be rescinded if only one party is left to perform.

6. **Novation:** If a new contract substitutes a new party for one of the parties to the original contract, the original party's duty will be discharged.

7. **Release/Covenant not to sue:** The release must be in writing and supported by consideration or be detrimentally relied upon.

8. **Accord and Satisfaction**

a) **Accord:** An agreement in which one party to a contract agrees to accept an identified performance different from that originally promised in satisfaction of the original promise.

VIII. MISTAKE, MISREPRESENTATION, DURESS AND UNDUE INFLUENCE

A. Mistake

1. **Unilateral Mistake:** If the mistake is unilateral and has a material effect on the performance of the contract, the contract is voidable by him, if he does not bear the risk of the mistake and to enforce the contract would be unconscionable, or the other party knew of the mistake or it arose because of his fault.

2. **Risk of Mistake:** A party bears the risk of mistake if pursuant to the contract the risk is his, he was aware of it at the time the contract was made, or only had limited knowledge of the risk and relied upon that limited knowledge, or the court allocates the risk to him because it is reasonable to do so.

B. **Misrepresentation:** An assertion of an incorrect fact which induces a party to enter into a contractual relationship constitutes a misrepresentation. Misrepresentation will be fraudulent where the maker: (i) intends to induce a contract by the misrepresentation; (ii) he knows his assertion is not in accordance with the relevant facts; or (iii) he does not believe in the truth of the assertion and will be material if the misrepresentation would be likely to induce a reasonable person to enter into a contract.

C. **Duress:** Where a party is compelled by an improper threat to enter into a contractual relationship, the contract is voidable at his option. A threat is improper if: (i) it constitutes a crime or a tort; (ii) it threatens a criminal prosecution; (iii) it threatens civil proceedings; or (iv) it breaches good faith.

D. **Undue Influence:** Unfair persuasion of a party who is subject to the other party's dominance, and if such dominance induces a contract, it will be voidable at the option of the innocent party.

IX. BREACH AND REMEDIES

A. General

1. **Breach:** If the promisor has an absolute duty to perform and has not yet discharged his duty in accordance with the contractual terms, he may be in breach of contract.

   a) **Is the breach minor or material?** A minor breach may allow the aggrieved party to recover damages, but she still must perform under the contract. If the breach is material, the aggrieved party does not need to perform and may recover damages.

      (1) **Test:** Whether a breach is minor or material is a factual issue that courts resolve under a reasonable-person test. A party materially breaches a contract when he does not fully perform a promise that goes to the heart of the contract.

      (2) **Minor Breach:** If a breach is minor, the aggrieved party is entitled to an award of damages in an amount to compensate for the defective performance. The contract is still in force and enforceable and he must still perform.

      (3) **Material Breach:** If the breach is material, the party's duties are discharged, but he must still take affirmative actions. In order to mitigate his damages, he must seek a replacement contract and notify the obligor of the defective performance. If the aggrieved party does mitigate, the amount he is entitled to recover is reduced.

2. **Damages:** Damages compensate the injured party for the loss suffered arising from the breach of contract. Factors to be taken into account include: (i) whether compensation will provide an adequate remedy; (ii) the extent to which the injured party will be deprived of

the contractual benefit to which she was entitled; and (iii) the prospects of the party in breach actually performing her part of the bargain and thereby ending the breach.

a) **Compensatory:** Compensatory damages must be causal, foreseeable, certain, and unavoidable.

   (1) **Causal:** To recover compensatory damages, the plaintiff's harm must have been caused by the defendant's breach;

   (2) **Foreseeable:** The damages caused must have been foreseeable at the time the contract was entered into;

   (3) **Certain:** Future profits of a new business are difficult to recover because they are uncertain;

   (4) **Unavoidable:** The plaintiff cannot recover damages that he could have reasonably avoided.

b) **Liquidated Damages:** A liquidated damages clause in a contract limits the damages that the plaintiff may recover. They are valid if it would have been too difficult for the parties to determine actual damages when entering into the contract; they must also reasonably forecast the actual harm.

c) **Punitive Damages:** Intended to punish. Not available in contract actions.

d) **Interest and Attorney Fees:** Courts will only grant prejudgment interest awards as to liquidated sums. A party may recover attorney fees if a statute or contract provides for them.

3. **Restitution:** An innocent party, who in response to her contractual obligation has conferred benefit upon the party in breach, prior to the breach of contract arising, may be entitled to "restitution," i.e., to receive back the benefit conferred.

4. **Specific Performance/Injunction:** Specific performance is an order of the court requiring a contracting party to perform what he promised to perform in circumstances where damages will not provide an adequate remedy. The court may order specific performance where: (i) a contract exists; (ii) all of the conditions of the contract have been satisfied; (iii) the legal remedy is inadequate; (iv) the terms are definite and certain; (v) the decree must be feasible to enforce; and (vi) there must be mutuality of performance.

5. **Defenses**
   a) **Laches:** Laches is an unreasonable delay in pursuing a right. A plaintiff who waits an unreasonable amount of time in initiating his equitable claim to the prejudice of the defendant is barred from bringing the claim.
   b) **Unclean Hands:** The party seeking equitable damages must not have engaged in unfair conduct with respect to the transaction sued upon.
   c) **Hardship:** A court will not order specific performance if it would result in an undue hardship to the breaching party or public that greatly outweighs the harm that the plaintiff would suffer if the court did not grant specific performance.
   d) **Mistake and Misrepresentation:** A court will not order specific performance if one party or both parties were mistaken as to the terms of the contract, or if the contract was induced through misrepresentation.

6. **Rescission:** Where the agreement was induced by fraud, the aggrieved party can rescind the agreement and recover their consideration.

B. UCC Remedies

1. UCC Risk of Loss in the Absence of Breach

a) **Non-Carrier Cases:** If the seller is a merchant, risk of loss passes to the buyer only upon buyer taking physical possession of the goods. If the seller is not a merchant, risk of loss passes to the buyer upon tender of delivery.

b) **Carrier Cases:** In a shipment contract, risk of loss passes to the buyer when the goods are duly delivered to the carrier. In a destination contract, the risk of loss passes to the buyer when the goods are tendered to the buyer at the destination.

c) **Sale or Return and Sale on Approval Contracts:** Upon sale or return, the risk of loss is on the seller until acceptance. Upon sale on approval, risk of loss is on the buyer and the buyer must pay for return.

2. UCC Risk of Loss Upon Breach

a) **Buyer Has the Right of Rejection:** The seller bears the risk of loss until the buyer receives the goods.

b) **Buyer Rightfully Revokes Acceptance:** The seller bears the risk of loss, subject to the buyer's insurance.

c) **Buyer in Breach:** Where the seller is in possession of the goods, the buyer bears the risk of loss, subject to the seller's insurance.

3. Buyer's Remedies

a) **Acceptance:** The buyer accepts goods when: (i) the buyer, after reasonable opportunity to inspect them, indicates to the seller that they conform or that she will keep them in spite of their non-conformance; (ii) the buyer fails to reject the goods within a reasonable time after tender of delivery, or fails to reasonably notify the seller of her rejection; or (iii) the buyer does anything inconsistent with the seller's ownership.

b) **Rejection**

(1) **Single Delivery:** If the goods or the tender fails to conform to the contract, the buyer may: (i) reject all of them, (ii) accept all of them, or (iii) accept some units and reject the rest. The buyer cannot reject the goods just because the seller did not notify the buyer of the shipments, unless the buyer experiences material loss or there is a material delay.

(2) **Installment Contracts:** The buyer can reject an installment shipment only if the nonconformity substantially impairs the value of that installment and cannot be cured. The seller breaches the whole contract if the nonconformity substantially impairs the value of the entire contract.

c) **Revocation of Acceptance:** The buyer may revoke her previous acceptance of the goods if the defect substantially impairs their value to her. The buyer must revoke acceptance within a reasonable time after the buyer discovers or should have discovered the defect and before any substantial change occurs in the goods not caused by their own defects.

4. Buyers Damage

a) **For non-delivery or upon rejection or revocation of acceptance:** Buyer's remedy for undelivered or rejected goods is the difference between the contract price and either the market price or the cost of buying replacement goods, plus incidental and consequential damages, less expenses saved.

b) **For accepted goods:** Buyer may recover the difference between the value of goods delivered and the value they would have had if they had conformed to the contract, plus incidental and consequential damages. The buyer must notify the seller within a reasonable time after he discovers the breach.

c) **Specific Performance:** *Supra.*

5. **Seller's Remedies**

a) **Right to Withhold Goods:** If the buyer does not make a payment that is due on or before delivery, the seller may withhold delivery of goods.

b) **Seller's Right to Recover Goods**

(1) **From Buyer or Buyer's Insolvency:** If buyer has received delivery of goods on credit while insolvent, seller may demand to reclaim the goods within 10 days after buyer receives the goods.

(2) **From Bailee:** The seller may stop a carrier from delivering goods in its possession when he discovers the buyer is insolvent.

6. **Seller's Damages:** When the buyer wrongfully refuses to accept conforming goods, the seller can: (i) accept the goods and recover the difference between the market price and the contract price of the goods; (ii) resell the goods and recover the difference between the market price and the contract price; (iii) accept the goods and recover the difference between the list price and the cost to the seller; or (iv) recover incidental damages, including the expense of storing and reselling the goods.

7. **Liquidated Damages:** Either party may recover liquidated damages as provided by the contract if they are reasonable when measured in light of: (i) the anticipated or actual breach caused; (ii) the difficulties in proof of loss; or (iii) the inconvenience or non feasibility of otherwise obtaining an adequate remedy.

8. **Limitations on Damages:** Parties may limit or alter the measure of damages otherwise recoverable under the UCC by requiring a seller to repair and replace, or return and refund.

a) **Exclusive Remedy:** If the contract provides for its own remedies, a court does not have to resort to only those remedies unless the contract declares such remedies to be exclusive.

b) **Consequential Damages:** Parties may limit or exclude consequential damages as an award, unless it would be unconscionable.

9. **Statute of Limitations:** Accrual of SOL is four years; discovery SOL is one year; maximum total period of SOL is five years from accrual.

10. **When does accrual occur?**

a) **Breach of Warranty:** On delivery of goods.

b) **Repudiation:** When a party treats it as a repudiation.

c) **Warranty of Title:** When the aggrieved party discovers or should have discovered the breach.

d) **Remote Purchaser:** When the plaintiff remote purchaser receives the goods.

e) **"Explicitly Extends to the Future":** When a party discovers or should have discovered the breach.

f) **Remote Purchaser:** When the party receives the goods.

g) **Third-Party Beneficiaries:** Third-party beneficiaries are not treated as remote purchasers, rather, they step into the shoes of the dealer.

CRIMINAL LAW PRIMER

I. PROPERTY CRIMES

A. **Larceny:** (i) a taking; (ii) and carrying away; (iii) of tangible personal property; (iv) of another; (v) by trespass; (vi) with intent to permanently deprive that person of their property interest.

B. **Robbery:** Robbery is larceny achieved by force or the threat of force.

C. **Embezzlement:** (i) the fraudulent; (ii) conversion; (iii) of personal property; (iv) of another; (v) by a person in lawful possession.

D. **Larceny by False Pretenses:** (i) obtaining title; (ii) to personal property of another; (iii) by making an intentional false statement of fact; (iv) with the intent to defraud the other.

E. **Larceny by Trick:** This is proven with the same elements as Larceny by False Pretenses; however, possession is obtained rather than title.

F. **Larceny by Extortion:** (i) obtaining the property; (ii) from another; (iii) by means of oral or written threats.

G. **Receipt of Stolen Property:** (i) receiving possession and control; (ii) of stolen personal property; (iii) known to have been stolen; (iv) by another person; (v) with the intent to permanently deprive the owner.

H. **Forgery:** Forgery is defined as: the (i) making or altering; (ii) of a writing with apparent legal significance; (iii) so that it is false.

I. **Uttering or Passing a Forged Instrument:** (i) offering as genuine; (ii) an instrument that may be the subject of forgery and is false; (iii) with intent to defraud.

J. **Burglary:** The (i) breaking; (ii) and entry; (iii) of a dwelling; (iv) of another; (v) at nighttime; (vi) with the intent to commit a felony therein. Modernly, a dwelling includes all buildings. Further, the nighttime requirement is relaxed.

K. **Arson:** (i) the malicious; (ii) burning; (iii) of the dwelling; (iv) of another.

II. CRIMES OF PROCEDURE

A. **Perjury:** Making a false statement of a material fact under oath.

B. **Subornation of Perjury:** Inducing another to commit perjury.

C. **Bribery:** Payment exchange for official action.

D. **Obstruction of Justice:** Intentionally acting to interfere with the administration of justice.

E. **Compounding a Crime:** An individual accepts payment and agrees not to prosecute another for a felony, or to conceal the commission of a felony, or a felon. Modern law attaches liability for any crime.

F. **Misprision of a Felony:** Under common law, it was a crime not to disclose knowledge of felonious activity. Modernly, this is no longer a crime.

III. CRIMES AGAINST THE PERSON

A. **Battery:** The unlawful application of force to the person of another resulting in either bodily injury or an offensive touching.

B. **Assault:** The intentional creation of reasonable apprehension in the mind of the victim of imminent bodily harm. Words are insufficient to establish an assault, but can rise to the level of criminal threats.

C. **Mayhem:** The intentional dismemberment, disfigurement, or disablement of a body part.

D. **False Imprisonment:** The unlawful, unconsented confinement of another. Confinement is not present if reasonable alternative routes of exit or escape are available. If consent is provided, consider its validity, as consent that is the product of duress or incapacity is invalid.

E. **Kidnapping:** Unlawful confinement of a person involving either: (i) movement of the victim, or (ii) concealment in a secret place.

F. **Rape:** The unlawful carnal knowledge of a woman by a man, not her husband, without her consent.

G. **Statutory Rape:** The carnal knowledge of a female under the age of consent. Statutory rape is a strict liability crime; therefore, consent or a mistake as to age or consent is irrelevant.

H. **Incest:** Marriage or a sexual act between closely related persons.

I. **Seduction:** Inducing an unmarried woman to engage in intercourse by the promise of marriage. The Model Penal Code ("MPC") relaxes the unmarried requirement.

J. **Bigamy:** Bigamy is a strict liability offense that provides criminal liability for one who marries another while having a living spouse.

IV. HOMICIDE

Homicide is the unlawful killing of one human being by another. It is criminal when it is done without excuse or legal justification.

A. **Murder:** Murder is the killing of another human being with malice aforethought. Malice aforethought is defined as one of four states of mind: (i) Intent to kill; (ii) Intent to inflict great bodily injury; (iii) Reckless indifference to an unjustifiably high risk to human life; or (iv) The intent to commit an inherently dangerous felony.

B. **First-Degree Murder**

1. **Premeditation and Deliberation:** If the defendant made the decision to kill in a cool and dispassionate manner and actually reflected on the idea of killing, it is first degree murder.
2. **Felony Murder:** If a murder is committed during the commission of, or in an attempt to commit, an enumerated felony, it is first degree murder. The felonies most commonly listed include Burglary, Arson, Robbery, Rape, Kidnapping and Mayhem.

C. **Voluntary Manslaughter:** Voluntary manslaughter is a killing that would be murder but for the existence of adequate provocation.

1. **Provocation** is sufficient where:
    a) The victim's conduct would arouse intense passion in the mind of an ordinary person, causing the loss of self-control;
    b) The defendant was in fact provoked;
    c) There was insufficient time between the provocation and the killing for a reasonable person to cool off; and
    d) The defendant did not cool off between the provocation and the killing.

2. **Imperfect Self-Defense:** Murder may be reduced to manslaughter where the defendant unreasonably, but in good faith, believed that deadly force was necessary given the circumstances.

D. **Involuntary Manslaughter:** A killing committed with criminal negligence or during the commission of an unlawful act.

E. **Second-Degree Murder:** All murder that is not first degree or manslaughter. The prosecution must prove: (i) the defendant intentionally killed a human being; (ii) with malice aforethought; and (iii) actual and proximate causation.

V. INCHOATE OFFENSES

A. Accomplice Liability

1. **Accomplice:** One who aids and abets the commission of the crime, with the intent that the crime be committed by the principal, will be guilty to the same degree as the principal.

2. **Defense of Withdrawal:** If a co-conspirator (i) voluntarily withdraws; and (ii) communicates his withdrawal to all co-conspirators and attempts to neutralize his contribution, he will cut off liability for any subsequent crimes.

B. **Accessory After the Fact:** This is one who receives, relieves, comforts, or assists another, knowing that the other has committed a felony, in order to help the felon escape arrest, trial, or conviction.

C. **Solicitation (Specific Intent "SI" crime):** Inciting, counseling, advising, urging, or commanding another party to commit a crime, with the intent that the person solicited commit the crime.

1. **Defenses:** Impossibility of completion of the solicited crime is not a defense. Withdrawal is not a defense.

2. **Merger:** If the person commits (or attempts to commit) the solicited crime, both that person and the solicitor can be found guilty of that crime (or attempt).

D. **Conspiracy (SI crime):** Conspiracy is: (i) an agreement between two or more people to perform an illicit act; (ii) the intent to agree; and (iii) the intent to carry through the agreement. A majority of states require an overt act in furtherance, but mere preparation is sufficient. Common law required two guilty minds (a conspirator and an undercover officer would not suffice). Under the MPC, only one "guilty mind" is needed.

1. **Liability:** Liability for crimes committed by other conspirators attaches if the crimes: (i) were committed in furtherance of the objectives of the conspiracy; and (ii) were foreseeable.

2. **Defenses:**

    a) **Withdrawal:** Withdrawal is not a defense to the conspiracy, but it may be a defense to crimes committed in furtherance of the conspiracy after notifying members of the conspiracy of her withdrawal and reversing any assistance provided.

3. **No Defense:** Factual impossibility is no defense to conspiracy.

4. **No Merger:** Conspiracy is a separate offense.

E. **Attempt (SI crime):** An attempt is an overt act beyond mere preparation, committed with specific intent to commit a crime, which fails to complete the crime. Most states require a substantial step towards the commission of a crime to demonstrate criminal intent.

1. **Attempt Defenses**

   a) **Legal Impossibility:** That it is not a crime to do what the defendant intended to do is a defense.

2. **No Defense**

   a) **Factual Impossibility:** That it would have been impossible to complete the crime is not a defense.

   b) **Abandonment:** If the defendant had the requisite intent and committed an overt act, she is guilty of attempt.

VI. DEFENSES

A. **Insanity:** If a person is insane when he commits a criminal act, he is excused. The state must prove beyond a reasonable doubt that the defendant is sane. States may abolish this defense.

1. **M'Naghten Test:** A mental disease or defect that caused him to either: (i) not know that his act would be wrong; or (ii) not understand the nature or quality of his actions.

2. **Irresistible Impulse Test:** He was unable to control his actions or conform his conduct to the law.

3. **A.L.I. or Model Penal Code Test:** He lacked the substantial capacity to either: (i) appreciate the criminality of his actions; or (ii) conform his actions to the requirements of the law.

4. **Durham "Product" Test:** If the committed act was the product of mental illness, he must be acquitted.

   a) **Mental Illness:** If the defendant is so mentally ill that he is unable to comprehend the proceedings or to assist in his defense, he may not be tried, convicted or sentenced as long as the condition exists.

B. **Intoxication:** Intoxication can be raised as a defense to negate an element of a crime. Intoxication may take one of two forms: (i) voluntary; or (ii) involuntary.

1. **Voluntary:** Voluntary intoxication is the result of the intentional taking of a substance with knowledge of its intoxicating properties, without duress.

   a) **Defense to Specific Intent Crime:** A defendant may assert voluntary intoxication as a defense if the crime requires a purpose, intent, or knowledge (i.e., specific intent), and the intoxication prevented the defendant from formulating the requisite purpose. Voluntary intoxication is not a defense to general intent crimes.

2. **Involuntary:** Such results from the taking of a substance without knowledge of its intoxicating propensity, under duress, or in accordance with medical advice. Once established, you must apply the insanity tests.

C. **Infancy:** A child under 7 is not subject to criminal liability at common law. Children over the age of 7, but younger than 14, are presumed to understand the nature and quality of their conduct.

D. **Justified Conduct**

1. **Defense of Self**

   a) **Non-Deadly Force:** A person who is without fault may use such force as reasonably appears necessary to protect herself from the imminent application of unlawful force. There is no duty to retreat.

   b) **Deadly Force:** Such force may be used by one who is without fault and who is threatened with the immediate prospect of death or great bodily injury.

(1) **Retreat:** A majority of jurisdictions do not require retreat. A minority require retreat before using deadly force if the victim can do so safely.

c) **Aggressor's Use of Self-Defense:** An aggressor may use force if: (i) he communicates his withdrawal; or (ii) the initial victim escalates the level of violence and the initial aggressor does not have the opportunity to withdraw.

2. **Defense of Another:** A person has the right to defend another to the same degree that the other could have defended himself.

3. **Defense of Dwelling:** The use of non-deadly force against unlawful entry or attack is permitted. Deadly force is only permitted where there is a reasonable belief that a personal attack or other felonious conduct is forthcoming.

a) **Defense of Other Property**

(1) **Defending Possession:** The use of deadly force is unavailable in defense of property. Non-deadly force may be used following a demand upon the aggressor to cease his conduct.

(2) **Reclaiming Property:** Force may be used to reclaim property that has been unlawfully taken when the victim is in pursuit of a thief. Otherwise, force may not be used to recover property.

4. **Arrest:** Police officers may use reasonable force when necessary. Deadly force is permitted where the subject threatens serious bodily injury or death. A private party may use non-deadly force to make an arrest if she has reasonable grounds to believe that the person has committed a crime.

5. **Necessity:** The person reasonably believed that commission of the crime was necessary to avoid a greater injury than that involved in the crime.

a) **Application:** An objective test is applied.

b) **Limitation:** Killing another person is never justified.

c) **Exclusion:** A defendant must not be at fault.

d) **In Comparison to Duress:** Necessity involves natural/physical forces; duress involves human threat.

E. **Duress:** The defendant reasonably believed that another person would inflict great bodily injury or death to him or a family member. The threat must have been imminent. Not applicable to a murder charge.

F. **Other Defenses**

1. **Mistake of Fact:** This is a defense if it establishes the lack of the required state of mind. Therefore, it is not applicable to strict liability crimes. For specific intent, the mistake can be unreasonable, provided it was made in good faith. For general intent crimes, the mistake must be reasonable.

2. **Mistake of Law:** It is not a defense that the defendant believed that her activity would not be a crime.

3. **Consent:** Consent can serve as a defense to crimes where it was voluntarily given by one with the legal capacity to consent.

4. **Entrapment:** (i) the criminal design originated with law enforcement; and (ii) the defendant was not predisposed to commit the crime.

CRIMINAL PROCEDURE PRIMER

I. FOURTH AMENDMENT: SEARCH AND SEIZURE

A. Generally: The 4th Amendment establishes the right of people to be secure in their persons, houses, papers and effects. It protects against an unlawful governmental intrusion on a person's reasonable expectation of privacy.

B. Arrests: An arrest occurs when the police take a person into custody against her will for purposes of criminal prosecution or interrogation. An arrest must be based on probable cause.

1. **Probable Cause:** Probable cause exists when an officer knows of facts and circumstances that would warrant a person of reasonable caution to believe that an offense has been or is being committed or that the place to be searched contains the fruits or instrumentalities of a crime.

    a) **Warrant:** A warrant is required when there is a non-emergency arrest in one's own home.

C. Search and Seizure

1. **Does the Defendant Have a 4th Amendment Right?**

    a) **Reasonable Expectation of Privacy:** To have a 4th Amendment right, a person must have his own reasonable expectation of privacy with respect to the place searched or the item seized. The determination is made on the totality of the circumstances and must be an expectation that society is prepared to recognize.

    (1) **Automatic Standing:** An individual has automatic standing if: (i) he owns or has right of possession of the premises or property searched (including the contents and location of a cell phone and property tracked by GPS); (ii) he is an overnight guest; or (iii) the search is of his person.

    (2) **Sometimes Standing:** An individual sometimes has standing if: (i) he is present; or (ii) he has ownership of the property seized.

    (3) **No Standing:** An individual does not have standing if: (i) he is a passenger in the car (for a search other than that of his person or belongings); or (ii) he is briefly on the premises of a business.

    (4) **Exception – Things Held Out to Be Public:** (i) handwriting; (ii) voice; (iii) paint; (iv) account records; (v) property visible from the air; (vi) public street; and (vii) odors.

    b) **Government Conduct:** Government conduct is any conduct that involves: (i) the police (or the like); (ii) any private person acting at the direction of police; or (iii) privately paid police who have been deputized.

2. **Did the Government Have a Warrant?** A warrant will be issued only if there is probable cause to believe that seizable evidence will be found on the premises/person to be searched. Officers must submit to a neutral and detached magistrate an affidavit setting forth circumstances enabling the magistrate to make a determination of probable cause independent of police.

    a) **Probable Cause:** supra. Probable cause can include an informant's anonymous information, or information that is hearsay.

    b) **Invalidation of the Warrant:** A warrant is invalid if: (i) there is a false statement in the affidavit; (ii) that was intentionally or recklessly included; and (iii) the false statement was material to the finding of probable cause.

3. **If There is No Warrant, is There an Exception to the Warrant Requirement?** All warrantless searches are unconstitutional unless they fit into one of the recognized exceptions to the warrant requirement.

a) **Search Incident to Lawful Arrest:** Incident to lawful arrest, police may search the person and areas into which he might reach to obtain weapons or destroy evidence (wing-span – includes entire passenger compartment). A protective sweep of the area may be made if he believes there are accomplices present or there is a threat to those on scene. The search must be contemporaneous to the arrest. A search at the curtilage of the home does not provide the right to search the house.

b) **Automobile Exception:** If probable cause exists to believe that the vehicle contains fruits, instrumentalities, or evidence of a crime, they may search the whole vehicle and containers that might reasonably contain the item for which they had probable cause to search (a car can be towed and searched later). Passenger's belongings may be searched (not a cell phone absent exigent circumstances). A motor home is considered to be an automobile if it is still mobile. Police may not use this exception to enter private property and perform a search of a vehicle parked next to the owner's home.

c) **Plain View:** Under the plain view exception, a search is valid when police: (i) are legitimately on the premises; (ii) discover evidence or instrumentalities of crime; (iii) in plain view; and (iv) have probable cause to believe that it is contraband.

d) **Consent:** If one consents to a search, the consent given must be voluntary and intelligent.

(1) **Authority:** Those with the right to use and/or occupy can consent. However, the consent to search provided by a tenant will not be valid in the case of a non-consenting co-tenant who is physically present at the premises to be searched.

e) **Stop and Frisk:** The police may detain an individual for investigation if they have reasonable suspicion that criminal activity is afoot. The police may frisk or pat down the individual and retrieve any items that feel like weapons or contraband.

f) **Hot Pursuit, Evanescent Evidence:** In hot pursuit, the police can make a warrantless search, including entry into private homes, and seize items that impose an immediate threat to public safety. A warrantless search and seizure is allowed when someone is in danger. The police can keep searching even after detainment in case people are hiding. The police can also seize evidence likely to disappear before a warrant can be obtained. An individual suspected of DUI may be subjected to a blood draw without prior consent or a valid warrant, in exigent circumstances.

4. **Warrant Needed**

a) **Wiretapping:** Wiretapping and other forms of electronic surveillance constitute a search under the 4th Amendment. The government must: (i) demonstrate that it has probable cause; (ii) name the suspects; (iii) describe the conversations to be monitored; (iv) limit the duration thereof; (v) terminate after receipt of the information sought; and (vi) inform the court of all conversations recorded.

(1) **Exceptions:** A speaker assumes the risk that the person he is speaking to is an informant and is wired and thus no warrant would be required.

II. FIFTH AMENDMENT

A. Miranda Warnings: Anyone in the custody of the government and subject to interrogation must be given Miranda warnings prior to interrogation by the police. For an admission or confession to be admissible under the 5th Amendment privilege against self-incrimination, a person must, prior to interrogation, be informed that: (i) he has the right to remain silent; (ii) anything he says can be used against him in court; (iii) he has the right to the presence of an attorney; and (iv) if he cannot afford an attorney, one will be appointed for him if he so desires.

1. **Custody:** A person is in custody when he has been deprived of freedom of action in a significant way (i.e., a reasonable person would feel that he was not free to leave). Custody is not present during a traffic stop, probation interview, or where the suspect is incarcerated on other charges.

2. **Interrogation:** An interrogation consists of any direct questioning, words or actions which police should have known were reasonably likely to elicit an incriminating response. Interrogation does not include voluntary statements. Interrogation does not apply to an undercover officer unless the defendant knows that he is a police officer.

3. **Waiver:** Where a waiver is given, it must be knowingly and voluntarily made.

4. **Invocation of Right to Counsel:** If a suspect invokes his right to counsel, all interrogation must stop and the suspect may not be re-questioned.

5. **Invocation of Right to Remain Silent:** If a suspect invokes his right to remain silent, the police may resume questioning after passage of a significant period of time and the provision of fresh Miranda warnings.

6. **Scope:** Miranda only applies to testimonial evidence, not real or physical evidence.

B. Compelled Testimony: The 5th Amendment privilege against self-incrimination applies to compelled testimony in any kind of case or hearing where a person is asked under oath to provide a response that would tend to incriminate them. The right must be asserted the first time the person is questioned or else he will lose the right to refuse to answer in subsequent proceedings.

III. SIXTH AMENDMENT – RIGHT TO COUNSEL

A. Post-Charge: A suspect has a right to the presence of an attorney at any post-charge lineup. A suspect does not have a right to counsel at photo identifications or the taking of physical evidence.

1. **Remedy:** If a suspect's 6th Amendment right to counsel is violated, the remedy for such a violation is the exclusion of the identification, unless the identification is made by an independent source.

B. Due Process: The defendant can attack an identification as denying due process if the identification is unnecessarily suggestive and there is a substantial likelihood of misidentification.

C. Critical Stage: The 6th Amendment guarantees the right to assistance of counsel in all criminal proceedings, which include all critical stages of prosecution after formal charges have been filed. It prohibits the police from deliberately eliciting an incriminating statement from a defendant outside the presence of counsel after the defendant has been charged, unless he waived his right to counsel.

1. **Offense-Specific:** This right is offense-specific. Thus, after attachment, he may be questioned regarding unrelated, uncharged offenses.

2. **Informants:** Informants are paid and act under instructions of the government. The use of an informant at this stage violates the defendant's 6th Amendment rights unless the defendant's statements are voluntarily made and the informant took no action to elicit the statements.

IV. EXCLUSIONARY RULE

A. Exclusionary Rule: The exclusionary rule prohibits the introduction of evidence obtained in violation of a defendant's 4th, 5th and 6th Amendment rights. The exclusionary rule does not apply to grand juries, civil cases, or parole revocation hearings.

1. **Exceptions:** (i) violation of knock-and-announce warrant requirement; and (ii) the evidence can still be used for impeachment.

B. Fruit of Poisonous Tree: Under the fruit of the poisonous tree rule, illegally obtained evidence is inadmissible at trial, and all "fruits of the poisonous tree" – evidence obtained from the exploitation of the illegally obtained evidence – must also be excluded.

1. **Exceptions:**

   a) **Independent Source:** Evidence obtained from an independent source of the original illegality.

   b) **Attenuation:** Evidence sufficiently attenuated from the initial illegality, so as to purge the taint of the illegality, may be used.

   c) **Inevitable Discovery:** The prosecution can show that the police would have discovered the evidence, whether or not the police acted unconstitutionally.

   d) **Good faith:** The police relied on a warrant that was issued by a neutral magistrate that was later found to be defective. Exceptions: (i) affidavit lacks probable cause and it was obvious; (ii) affiant lied to magistrate; (iii) warrant did not state with particularity the place to search; or (iv) magistrate abandoned his judicial role.

V. PROCEDURAL CONSIDERATIONS

A. Bail: Bail denial is immediately appealable. It is constitutional to have preventative detention.

B. Grand Juries: A suspect has no right to be present, to confront witnesses, or to present evidence in his defense.

C. Trial

1. **Independent Judge:** A judge must have no bias or financial interest or malice against a defendant.

2. **Jury:** A defendant has the right to a trial by a jury, where he could be sentenced to more than 6 months in jail.

3. **Right to an Attorney:** This right exists where jail is possible, probation can be given, or a suspended sentence is possible upon conviction.

4. **Batson:** Under Batson, it is unconstitutional for the prosecution or the defense to exercise peremptory challenges based on race or gender. The Equal Protection Clause gives the defendant the right to have the jury pool reflect a cross-section of the community. The defendant does not have the right for the sworn jury itself to be a cross-section of the community.

D. Guilty Pleas: Guilty pleas must be knowingly and voluntarily made. A judge must advise the defendant of: (i) the nature of the charge; (ii) the maximum and minimum sentence that he may be given; (iii) the right not to plead guilty; and (iv) the fact that he is waiving a trial by pleading guilty.

1. **Setting Aside Plea:** The U.S. Supreme Court does not like to disturb pleas after sentencing unless: (i) the plea was involuntary; (ii) the court had no jurisdiction; (iii) there is a finding of ineffective assistance of counsel; or (iv) there is a failure to keep a plea bargain.

E. **Death Penalty:** Any death penalty statute that does not give the defendant a chance to present mitigating facts is unconstitutional. There can be no automatic category for imposing death. In a death penalty case, a state may not limit mitigating factors by statute; all relevant evidence must be admitted, and only a jury can determine whether aggravating factors justify imposition of the death penalty. Imposition of the death penalty, or life without the possibility of parole, is unconstitutional where the defendant was under the age of 18 when he committed the crime.

F. **Double Jeopardy:** A person may not be retried for the same offense once jeopardy has attached. Jeopardy attaches in a jury trial once the jury is sworn in or in a bench trial once the first witness is sworn.

1. **Exceptions Permitting Retrial:** A retrial is allowed when:
   a) There is a hung jury.
   b) A mistrial is declared on any ground not constituting grounds for acquittal on the merits.
   c) The defendant successfully appeals a conviction, unless the ground for reversal was insufficient evidence. On retrial, a defendant may not be tried for a greater offense than that for which he was convicted.
   d) Charges may be reinstated if the defendant breaches a plea bargain.

2. **Same Offense:** Two crimes are the same offense unless each crime requires proof of an additional element that the other does not.
   a) **Lesser Included Offenses:** Attachment of jeopardy for a greater offense bars retrial for lesser included offenses. However, retrial for murder is permitted where the victim dies after attachment of jeopardy for battery.
   b) **Exception – New Evidence:** New evidence is allowed to prove the greater offense if it: (i) had not occurred at the time of prosecution for the lesser offense; or (ii) had not been discovered despite due diligence.

3. **Separate Sovereigns:** Double jeopardy does not apply to trials by separate sovereigns. Thus, a person may be tried for the same conduct by both state and federal government or by two states, but not by a state and its municipalities.

EVIDENCE PRIMER

I. RELEVANCE

A. Logical Relevance: Logically relevant evidence has a tendency to make a fact that is of consequence to the determination of the case more or less probable [FRE 401; CEC 350]. **California** requires the fact to be in dispute [CEC 210].

B. Proposition 8: California's Truth-in-Evidence Amendment requires the admission of all relevant evidence. However, as the Supremacy Clause requires courts to enforce an individual's rights under the U.S. Constitution, Proposition 8 has little effect and does not apply to: (i) the exclusionary rule; (ii) hearsay (right to confront); (iii) limitations on character evidence concerning a victim in a rape case; (iv) the preclusion of offering bad character evidence of a defendant before he opens the door; (v) the Secondary Evidence Rule; and (vi) legal relevance.

II. FORM OF EVIDENCE

A. Documents

1. **Authentication:** A writing or any secondary evidence must be authenticated by proof that shows that it is what the proponent claims [FRE 901; CEC 1400].

   a) **Authentication by Stipulation:** Authentication may be stipulated.

   b) **Evidence of Authenticity**

      (1) **Admissions:** Authentication may be admitted [CEC 1414].

      (2) **Eyewitness Testimony:** Testimony can authenticate a document [FRE 901(b)(1); CEC 1413].

      (3) **Handwriting Verifications:** Evidence of a handwriting comparison is admissible [FRE 901(b)(1)-(3); CEC 1415-17].

      (4) **Ancient Documents:** A document that: (i) is at least 20 years old; (ii) is free from suspicion as to authenticity; and (iii) was found in a place where such a writing would likely be kept [FRE 901(b)(8)]. In California, the writing must be more than 30 years old [CEC 1419].

      (5) **Reply Letter Doctrine:** A writing may be authenticated by evidence that it was written in response to a communication [CEC 1420].

      (6) **Photographs:** Photographs are admissible only if identified by a witness as a correct representation [FRE 901(b)(1)].

      (7) **X-Ray Pictures, MRI, ECG, etc.:** Authentication is valid where the process used is accurate, the machine was working, the operator was qualified, and there is a valid chain of custody [FRE 901(b)(9)].

   c) **Self-Authenticating Documents:** Extrinsic evidence is not required for: (i) certified copies of public records; (ii) official publications; (iii) periodicals; (iv) trade inscriptions; (v) acknowledged documents; (vi) commercial paper; and (vii) certified business records [FRE 902; CEC 1450-54].

2. **Best Evidence Rule:** To prove the terms of a writing, the original writing (or duplicate) must be produced if the terms are material or the knowledge of a witness concerning a fact results from having read the document [FRE 1002-03].

   a) **Admissibility of Secondary Evidence of Contents:** Without the original, a proponent may offer secondary evidence of its contents if a satisfactory explanation is given for the non-production of the original [FRE 1004].

(1) **California:** (No Best Evidence Rule) Secondary Evidence Rule allows secondary evidence unless: (i) there is a genuine dispute as to the material terms; or (ii) admission would be unfair [CEC 1520-23].

3. **Parol Evidence Rule:** Prior or contemporaneous agreements are merged into the written agreement (if so intended), and they are inadmissible to vary the terms of the agreement.

a) **Exceptions**

(1) **Incomplete or Ambiguous Contract:** Parol evidence is admissible to complete an incomplete contract or explain ambiguous terms.

(2) **Reformation of Contract:** The rule does not apply where a party alleges facts entitling him to reformation (mistake).

(3) **Challenge to Validity of Contract:** Parol evidence is admissible to show that the contract is void or subject to condition precedent.

b) **Subsequent Modifications:** Parol evidence is admissible to show subsequent modification or discharge of the written contract.

B. Testimony

1. **Competency of the Witness:** The witness must: (i) have personal knowledge of the matter about which he is to testify; and (ii) declare he will testify truthfully [FRE 601-03; CEC 700-01].

a) **Infants:** Sufficient capacity and intelligence are required.

b) **Insanity:** The ability and understanding to tell the truth is required.

2. **Form of Examination of Witness**

a) **Leading Questions:** These are questions that suggest the answer and are permitted: (i) on cross-examination; (ii) to elicit a preliminary matter; (iii) to aid a witness because of loss of memory, immaturity, or mental weakness; or (iv) if the witness is hostile.

b) **Assumes Facts Not in Evidence:** The question contains facts relevant to the case that have not been previously introduced into evidence.

c) **Compound:** The single question seeks to elicit two separate answers.

d) **Non-Responsive Answers:** Here, the witness fails to answer the question.

e) **Argumentative:** A question that includes inferences or conclusions.

f) **Asked and Answered:** A question that has previously been asked.

III. CATEGORY OF EVIDENCE

A. Judicial Notice: Courts take notice of indisputable facts that are either matters of common knowledge or capable of verification [FRE 201; CEC 450-51].

B. Hearsay

1. **Definition:** Hearsay is an out-of-court statement offered for the truth of the matter asserted [FRE 801(c); CEC 1200].

2. **Out-of-Court Statements Not Offered for the Truth**

a) **Verbal Acts of Legally Operative Facts:** Evidence of such statements is not hearsay because the issue is simply whether the statement was made.

b) **Statements Offered to Show the Effect Upon Listener:** Statements may be admitted to show the effect on the hearer (notice; knowledge; motive).

c) **Statements Offered as Circumstantial Evidence of Declarant's State of Mind:** Such a statement is admissible to show knowledge or capacity.

3. **Not Considered Hearsay under Federal Rules of Evidence (FRE) [California Hearsay Exceptions]**

a) **Admission by Party Opponent:** Any statement by a party offered against that party [FRE 801(d); CEC 1204, 1220-28].

(1) **Adoptive Admission:** A party may expressly or impliedly adopt someone else's statement as his own.

(2) **Vicarious Admission:** A statement made by the party's employee within the scope of that relationship. **(No California provision).**

(3) **Co-Conspirators:** A statement made by a co-conspirator in furtherance of a conspiracy is admissible as a vicarious admission, provided the statement was made at a time when the declarant was participating in the conspiracy and the defendant has an opportunity to cross-examine the declarant.

(4) **Wrongful Death: California Only** – A statement of the deceased can be used against the family as though he were a party [CEC 1227].

b) **Prior Statements of a Witness:** Under the Federal Rules [FRE 801(d)] and California Evidence Code [CEC 1235-38], a prior statement by a witness is not hearsay if:

(1) **Prior Inconsistent Statement:** The prior statement is inconsistent with in-court testimony and was given under oath at a prior proceeding. **In California,** "under oath" is not required [CEC 1235].

(2) **Prior Consistent Statements:** The prior statement is consistent with in-court testimony and is offered to rebut a charge that the witness is lying and the statement was made before any motive to lie arose.

(3) **Prior Statements of Identification:** The statement of identification of a person made after perceiving him. The witness must be testifying.

4. **Hearsay Exceptions**

a) **Documentary**

(1) **Past Recollection Recorded:** After being unable to refresh her recollection, the writing may be read into evidence if a proper foundation is laid: (i) the witness had personal knowledge of the facts in the writing; (ii) the writing was made by the witness, at her direction, or was adopted by the witness; (iii) the writing was timely made when the matter was fresh in the witness's mind; (iv) the writing is accurate; and (v) the witness has insufficient recollection to testify accurately [FRE 803; CEC 1237].

(a) **Present Recollection Refreshed:** (Not a hearsay issue) Any writing may be used to refresh a witness's memory. However, they cannot read directly from it [FRE 612].

(2) **Business Records:** Business records are entries made in the regular course of business by a person who has a business duty to accurately record the information and who either has personal knowledge or receives the information from a person with personal knowledge and a business duty to accurately report. The entry has to have been made at or near the time of the transaction or event [FRE 803(6)]. **California** does not permit opinions or diagnoses to be admitted through business records, only acts and observations [CEC 1271]. The rule also includes the absence of a business record [CEC 1272].

(3) **Official Records:** Records and reports of a public agency or office are admissible if the record was made at or near the time of the occurrence by one with a duty to accurately record the information [FRE 803(8); CEC 1280]. **California** prohibits the admission of opinions within records without personal knowledge.

(a) **Police Reports:** Such reports cannot be used against a criminal defendant, but can be used by a criminal defendant. However, they can be used in civil cases.

(4) **Ancient Documents:** Statements made in documents, which are authenticated as being more than 20 years old, are admissible under the ancient documents exception to the hearsay rule [FRE 803(16)]. In **California**, the document must be more than 30 years old [CEC 1419].

(5) **Learned Treatises:** A learned treatise is admissible if the treatise is established as reliable and if it was utilized in examining or cross-examining an expert witness, or if the expert relied on the treatise during testimony [FRE 803(18); CEC 1341].

b) **Declarant's Availability is Irrelevant**

(1) **Excited Utterance:** A statement made in response to a startling or exciting event, which relates to the event and is made contemporaneously with the event [FRE 803(2)]. **In California**, they are known as spontaneous statements [CEC 1240].

(2) **Present Sense Impression:** A statement made while describing an event as it takes place or shortly thereafter [FRE 803(1)]. There is **no California parallel.**

(a) **Contemporaneous Statement – California Only:** Such a statement describes the conduct of the declarant while he is engaged in it and is offered to explain the conduct [CEC 1241].

(3) **Present State of Mental, Emotional, or Physical Condition:** A declarant's statement regarding his present state is an exception to the hearsay rule [FRE 803(3)]. Additionally, a declarant's statement of intent is also included [CEC 1250-51].

(4) **Statement of Physical Condition for Medical Diagnoses**

(a) **Past or Present Physical Condition:** Statements are admissible if made to medical personnel to assist in diagnosing or treating the condition [FRE 803(4)]. **California** requires that the declarant be unavailable, but also admits statements of the declarant's prior state, including statements of future intent [CEC 1253].

(b) **Statements in Contemplation of Litigation:** Courts will prevent statements of physical symptoms where the patient-declarant has consulted a physician for the purpose of preparing for litigation.

(c) **California:** There is no broad exception, the physical state must be at issue and the witnesses is unavailable/or victim is under 12 and action is for child abuse or neglect [CEC 1253].

c) **Declarant Must Be Unavailable**

(1) **Statements Against Interest:** A declarant's statement against his penal or pecuniary interest is an exception to the hearsay rule when the declarant is unavailable [FRE 804(b)(3); CEC 1230].

(2) **Dying Declaration:** A dying declaration is a statement made under fear of impending death, which relates to the cause or circumstances of that death. The declarant need not have died [FRE 804(b)(2)]. **California:** The declarant must be dead and the statement must concern cause of death [CEC 1242].

(3) **Former Testimony:** Such testimony is admissible if it was under oath and the declarant is unavailable. The declarant has to have been subject to cross-examination by one with a similar motive [FRE 804(b)(1); CEC 1290].

(4) **Statements of Personal Family History:** Statements of an unavailable declarant's personal family history, or another related person, are admissible [FRE 804(b)(4); CEC 1310-11].

(5) **Statements Offered Against a Party that Caused the Declarant's Unavailability:** Such statements are admissible, provided the party engaged in, or allowed, wrongdoing, resulting in the declarant's unavailability [FRE 804(b)(6)]. **California** requires a prosecution for a "serious felony" [CEC 1350].

d) **Catch-All Exception**: A statement may be admitted where:

(1) It is offered as evidence of a material fact;

(2) It is more probative than other evidence which can be procured through reasonable efforts; and,

(3) The interests of justice will be served by its admission [FRE 807].

5. **Sixth Amendment Right to Confrontation:** Prior testimonial evidence is inadmissible against a criminal defendant unless the hearsay declarant is unavailable and the defendant had the opportunity to cross-examine the hearsay declarant at the time the statement was made.

C. Character

1. Substantive Purposes

a) **Criminal Case:** Evidence of a person's character or a trait of his character is not admissible for the purpose of proving that he acted in conformity therewith on a particular occasion [FRE 404; CEC 1101-02].

(1) **Exception – Mercy Rule:** The mercy rule allows a defendant to offer evidence of his good character to establish his innocence in the form of opinion and reputation testimony. No specific instances are permitted.

Once the defendant opens the door, the prosecution can put on evidence of the defendant's bad character by: (i) opinion and reputation testimony, and (ii) cross-examination of witnesses about defendant's specific instances of misconduct [FRE 404(a)(2), 405].

(2) **Exception – Specific Acts:** Evidence of misconduct is admissible where relevant to some issue other than the defendant's character or disposition [FRE 404(b)(2); CEC 1101(b)].

(a) Motive; identity; mistake; intent;

(b) Common plan/scheme; knowledge; notice.

(3) **Exception – Sexual Assault/Child Molestation Cases:** Specific instances of the defendant's prior acts of sexual assault or molestation are admissible [FRE 413, 414]. **California** expands this exception to also include prior possession of child pornography, exploitation of children, and prior domestic violence [CEC 1108-09].

(4) **Exception – Character of Victim:** Except in rape cases, the defendant may introduce reputation or opinion evidence of a bad character trait of the alleged crime victim when it is relevant to show the defendant's innocence [FRE 404(a)(2)(B)]. In addition, **California** allows the introduction of specific instances of the victim's conduct [CEC 1103]. Once the defendant has introduced evidence of a bad character trait of the victim, the prosecution may counter with reputation or opinion evidence of: (i) the victim's good character; or (ii) defendant's bad character for the same trait. **California** allows the prosecution to rebut with specific instances.

(a) **Sexual Assault Exceptions:** In any civil or criminal proceeding involving alleged sexual misconduct, evidence offered to prove the sexual behavior or sexual disposition of the victim is generally inadmissible [FRE 412; CEC 1106]. Exceptions: (i) prior consensual conduct with the defendant; and (ii) conduct with others offered to show an alternative source of physical evidence.

b) **Civil Cases:** Unless character is directly in issue, evidence of character being offered by either party to prove the conduct of a person in the litigated event is generally not admissible in a civil case. Where it is admissible, reputation and opinion testimony may be offered, with inquiry into specific instances of conduct on cross-examination allowed [FRE 404]. Where character is essential to the cause of action or defense, specific instances of conduct are allowed [FRE 405]. **California** permits all three forms of character evidence when admissible [CEC 1100 et seq.].

(1) **Character in Issue:** (i) child custody; (ii) defamation; (iii) negligent entrustment.

(2) **Sexual Assault Cases:** If not placed in issue, the same rule as for criminal proceedings applies. If placed in issue, evidence of the alleged victim's sexual behavior is admissible if it is not excluded by any other rule and its probative value substantially outweighs the danger of harm to the victim and of unfair prejudice to any party [FRE 412(b)(2); CEC 1106].

D. Habit/Custom: Evidence of the habit of a person or of the routine practice of an organization is relevant to prove that the conduct of the person or organization on a particular occasion acted in conformity [FRE 406; CEC 1105].

E. Opinion

1. **Lay:** A lay opinion is allowed where: (i) the opinion would be helpful to the trier of fact; (ii) the opinion is based on the perception of the witness; and (iii) the subject is a proper subject for lay opinion [FRE 701; CEC 800].

2. **Expert Opinion:** An expert opinion is allowed where: (i) the opinion would be helpful to the trier of fact; (ii) the opinion is based upon matter upon which an expert might reasonably rely; (iii) the expert is properly qualified based on education, training or experience [FRE 702]. In federal courts, the expert theory need not have been generally accepted within the scientific community [FRE 703].

a) **California General Test:** The proponent of the scientific evidence must prove that the underlying scientific theory has been generally accepted as valid and reliable in the relevant scientific field [CEC 801].

F. Impeachment

1. **Convictions:** A witness can be impeached with evidence that the witness has been convicted of a felony or of any crime involving perjury or false statements [FRE 609(a)]. If more than 10 years have passed from the date of the conviction, the conviction is not admissible [FRE 609(b)]. In **California**, any witness may be impeached with any prior felony

conviction or the facts of any misdemeanor where the adjudicated elements necessarily involve moral turpitude.

2. **Bad Reputation for Truth or Veracity:** A witness can be impeached by the introduction of other witnesses who can testify to the reputation of the witness for untruthfulness [FRE 608(a)]. Specific instances can be inquired into on cross-examination, but extrinsic evidence is not permissible [FRE 608(b)]. In civil cases, **California** precludes such cross-examination unless a conviction resulted [CEC 780]. Prop 8 allows cross-examination as to prior specific instances in criminal cases.

3. **Bias and Prejudice:** Extrinsic evidence that a witness is biased against one of the parties is admissible for impeachment purposes [FRE 608; CEC 780].

4. **Prior Bad Acts Involving Dishonesty:** Under the FRE, a witness can be cross-examined regarding prior bad acts involving dishonesty so long as the questioning is conducted in good faith. Extrinsic evidence is not admissible [FRE 608]. In **California,** such questioning is precluded in civil cases [CEC 780]. **California** permits cross-examination in criminal cases and the use of extrinsic evidence under Prop 8.

5. **Prior Inconsistent Statements:** Under the FRE, if the statements were made under oath, they are admissible for impeachment purposes and as substantive proof. Extrinsic evidence is only admissible where the witness is given an opportunity to explain or deny the statement [FRE 613].

   a) California: Such statements can be used for the truth regardless of whether they were made under oath [CEC 1235].

6. **Evidence of Poor Memory/Poor Sight:** Such evidence is admissible to impeach.

IV. PRIVILEGE & WAIVER

FRE: Privileges are governed by common law [FRE 501].

A. **Attorney-Client:** Communications between an attorney and a client, made during professional consultation, are privileged from disclosure [CEC 950-62].

1. **Corporate Clients:** Statements made by employees to an attorney are protected if the employees were authorized to make such statements.

2. **Holder of the Privilege:** The client holds the privilege and he alone may waive it.

3. **Exceptions:** There is no privilege:

   a) If the attorney's services were sought to aid a crime or fraud;
   b) Regarding a communication relevant to an issue between parties claiming through the same deceased client; and
   c) For communications relevant to an attorney/client dispute.

B. **Doctor-Patient:** Confidential communications between a patient and his physician are privileged, provided that: (i) a professional relationship exists; (ii) the information was acquired in the course of treatment; and (iii) the information was necessary for treatment [CEC 990-95]. **Not recognized in federal court.**

1. **Exceptions:** The privilege does not apply or is waived if:

   a) The patient has put his physical condition in issue;
   b) The physician's assistance was sought to aid wrongdoing;
   c) For communications relevant to a doctor/patient dispute; or
   d) The patient agreed by contract.

C. **Psychiatrist/Psychotherapist/Social Worker-Client Privilege:** The Supreme Court recognizes a federal privilege for communications between a therapist and his client, as does **California** [CEC 1010-38].

D. **Clergy-Penitent:** A privilege exists for statements made to a member of the clergy, the elements of which are the same as the attorney-client privilege [CEC 1038].

E. **Husband-Wife Privilege**

1. **Spousal Immunity:** A married person may not be compelled to testify against his spouse in any criminal proceeding. There must be a valid marriage for the privilege to apply, and the privilege lasts only during marriage.

    a) **Holder of the Privilege:** In federal court and **California,** the privilege belongs to the witness-spouse [CEC 970-71].

2. **Privilege for Confidential Marital Communications:** In any civil or criminal case, confidential communications between a husband and wife during a valid marriage are privileged [CEC 980]. Here, either spouse can invoke the privilege.

3. **When Neither Marital Privilege Applies:** No privilege applies in cases between the spouses or in cases involving crimes against the spouse or their children.

F. **Self-Incrimination:** Under the Fifth Amendment, a witness cannot be compelled to testify against himself [CEC 930].

G. **Work Product:** Privilege protects material prepared by an attorney in preparation of litigation [CEC 915].

1. **Absolute Privilege:** Documents containing the attorney's impressions, conclusions, opinions, or research are never discoverable.

2. **Qualified Privilege:** Documents not protected by the absolute privilege will be discoverable unless the opposing party can show substantial hardship and that unfair prejudice would result from the inability to pursue a claim or defense.

3. **Not Privileged:** The locations of witnesses and evidence are not privileged.

4. **Expert Reports:** If the report was made based upon privileged communications, it will be protected. If the report was not made based upon privileged communications, the privilege will not apply.

    a) **Testifying Expert:** Where an expert will testify at trial, the privilege is deemed waived.

H. **Waiver:** Any privilege is waived by: (i) failure to claim the privilege; (ii) voluntary disclosure of the privileged matter; or (iii) a contractual provision waiving the privilege.

V. POLICY EXCLUSIONS

A. **Subsequent Remedial Measures:** Such are inadmissible to prove liability or fault. They are admissible to show ownership or control if it is in dispute, or to show the feasibility of repair [FRE 407; CEC 1151].

B. **Proof of Insurance:** Such is inadmissible to show fault or to show the ability to pay. Proof of insurance is admissible to show ownership or control if in dispute [FRE 411; CEC 1155].

C. **Offers to Settle/Withdrawn Guilty Pleas:** Any statement made in conjunction with the offer to settle is also inadmissible [FRE 408; CEC 1152-53].

D. **Offers to Pay Medical Expenses:** Such offers are inadmissible [FRE 409]. In **California,** all statements surrounding negotiations are inadmissible, including admissions [CEC 1152].

E. **Doctrine of Completeness:** When part of a statement is introduced, an adverse party may require the admission of any other part in the interests of fairness.

F. **Doctrine of Limited Admissibility:** When evidence is admitted only as to one party or for one purpose, the court should restrict the evidence to its proper scope and instruct the jury accordingly.

VI. LEGAL RELEVANCE

A. **Legal Relevance:** Although relevant, evidence may be excluded if its probative value is substantially outweighed by the danger of unfair prejudice, confusion of the issues, or misleading the jury, or by considerations of undue delay, waste of time, or the needless presentation of cumulative evidence [FRE 403; CEC 352].

PROFESSIONAL RESPONSIBILITY PRIMER

New California Rules of Professional Conduct became effective on November 1, 2018. The numbering in this outline follows the new California rule numbering system, except where noted that the rule is an American Bar Association (ABA) Model Rule. Please review the full outline for additional information.

Function of the Rules of Professional Conduct

(a) A willful violation of the rules of Professional Conduct is a basis for discipline but does not establish a civil cause of action or a basis for civil liability alone.

Terminology

(a) **"Informed consent":** an agreement after the lawyer has communicated and explained (i) the relevant circumstances and (ii) the material risks, including any actual and reasonably foreseeable adverse consequences.

(b) **"Informed written consent":** the disclosures and the consent required by must be in writing.

(c) **"Reasonable" or "reasonably":** the conduct of a reasonably prudent and competent lawyer.

(d) **"Reasonable belief" or "reasonably believes":** the lawyer believes the matter and that the circumstances are such that the belief is reasonable.

(e) **"Reasonably should know":** a lawyer of reasonable prudence and competence would ascertain the matter in question.

1 LAWYER-CLIENT RELATIONSHIP

1.1 COMPETENCE

(a) A lawyer shall not intentionally, recklessly, with gross negligence, or repeatedly fail to perform legal services with competence. "Competence" requires the lawyer to have the requisite (i) learning and skill, and (ii) mental, emotional, and physical ability necessary for the performance of such service.

(b) **Exceptions**: (i) the lawyer associates or consults with a competent lawyer; (ii) the lawyer acquires sufficient competence through learning before performing; (iii) the lawyer refers the client to a competent lawyer.

(c) **Emergencies:** The lawyer may provide assistance in an area in which the lawyer is not competent provided representation is appropriately limited

1.2 SCOPE OF REPRESENTATION AND ALLOCATION OF AUTHORITY

(a) A lawyer shall abide by a client's decisions concerning the objectives of representation and shall reasonably consult with the client as to the means by which they are to be pursued, provided that such decisions do not constitute a violation of law, as discussed below. A lawyer may take such action on behalf of the client as is impliedly authorized to carry out the representation. If a client wishes to settle a civil case, or plead guilty in a criminal case, or testify in a criminal case, a lawyer must defer to the client's wishes after fully advising the client.

(b) **Limited Scope:** Such agreements are permissible provided they are reasonable under the circumstances with following informed client consent.

1.2.1 ADVISING OR ASSISTING THE VIOLATION OF LAW

A lawyer shall not counsel a client to engage, or assist, a client in conduct known to be criminal, fraudulent, or a violation of any law, rule, or ruling of a tribunal. However, a lawyer can discuss the consequences of any proposed conduct, and help the client make a good faith effort to determine the validity, scope, or application of a law, rule, or ruling.

1.3 Diligence

A lawyer shall not intentionally, repeatedly, recklessly or with gross negligence fail to act with reasonable diligence in representing a client.

1.4 Communication with Clients

(a) Where not otherwise prohibited by law, a lawyer shall:

(1) Explain issues to a client so that informed decisions can be made;

(2) Promptly inform of any circumstance where informed consent is required;

(3) Reasonably consult with the client about the means used to accomplish the client's objectives;

(4) Keep the client reasonably informed of significant developments, including providing copies of documents when necessary;

(5) Advise the client whenever representation is limited in some way.

(b) A lawyer may delay communicating information to a client if there is a reasonable basis to believe that the client may cause harm.

1.4.1 Communication of Settlement Offers

A lawyer shall promptly communicate all terms of a proposed settlement or plea agreement in all cases.

1.4.2 Disclosure of Professional Liability Insurance

(a) A lawyer must disclose in writing that the lawyer does not have liability insurance at the time of hiring. If it is later learned that the lawyer no longer has insurance or learns that it was not disclosed previously, it must be disclosed within thirty days of learning of the deficiency.

(b) **Exceptions:**

(1) a lawyer previously provided written notification to the client that the lawyer does not have insurance;

(2) a lawyer knows or reasonably should know that the lawyer's legal representation of the client in the matter will not exceed four hours. If the representation exceeds four hours, disclosure is required;

(3) a government lawyer or in-house counsel need not comply provided the advice is being given to the government agency or company;

(4) a lawyer who is providing emergency legal services.

1.5 Fees for Legal Services

(a) A lawyer shall not agree to, charge, or collect an unconscionable fee. Unconscionability is determined by the facts and circumstances. Consider: whether the lawyer overreached or engaged in fraud; whether material facts were withheld; the sophistication of the client; the value of the services relative to the labor; the skill, experience, and reputation needed to execute the representation; the nature, scope, and length of the representation.

(b) **Contingent Fees:** They are not permissible in criminal cases or in family law cases where fees are contingent upon dissolution of a marriage, or upon the amount of spousal or child support, or value of property obtained.

(c) **Earned on Receipt:** Fees considered to be "earned on receipt" or "non-refundable" are permissible where a client agrees in writing after disclosure that the client will not be entitled to a refund of all or part of the fee charged.

(d) **Flat Fee:** Such fees are permissible. A flat fee is a fixed amount that constitutes complete payment for the stated representation regardless of the amount of work ultimately involved.

1.5.1 Fee Divisions Among Lawyers

(a) Lawyers who are members of the same firm may divide fees earned. Lawyers from different firms may do so provided:

(1) the total fee charged is not increased because of the fee splitting;

(2) the fee splitting agreement is in writing;

(3) the client provides written consent after disclosure of terms of the division, including the identity of the lawyers or firms involved.

(b) The ABA requires the division to be proportional to the services performed, or each lawyer assumes joint responsibility for the case.

1.6 Confidential Information of a Client

(a) **California:** A lawyer shall not reveal confidential information unless the client gives informed consent, or the lawyer reasonably believes the disclosure is necessary to prevent a criminal act likely to result in death or substantial bodily harm. Prior to revealing confidential information to thwart a criminal act, the lawyer must attempt to persuade the client not to commit the act, or to prevent the potential harm. The lawyer must not disclose more than necessary and must reasonably inform the client of the disclosure.

(b) **ABA Model Rule:** The ABA rule expands upon California's exception to also include: preventing the client from committing a crime or fraud that is reasonably certain to result in substantial injury to the financial interests or property of another and in furtherance of which the client has used or is using the lawyer's services; and to prevent, mitigate or rectify substantial injury to the financial interests or property of another that is reasonably certain to result or has resulted from the client's commission of a crime or fraud in furtherance of which the client has used the lawyer's services.

(c) **Self-Defense:** The ABA rules provide that an attorney may reveal confidential information to defend him or herself against a civil or criminal action involving the client. The California rules do not explicitly provide such an exception. However, California Evidence Code § 958 provides that "there is no privilege ... relevant to an issue of breach, by the lawyer or by the client, of a duty arising out of the lawyer-client relationship."

1.7 Conflict of Interest: Current Clients

(a) A lawyer shall not, without informed written consent from each client represent a client if the representation is directly adverse to another client.

(b) A lawyer shall not, without informed written consent from each affected client, represent a client if there is a significant risk the lawyer's representation will be materially limited by the lawyer's responsibilities to another or former client.

(c) A lawyer shall not represent a client without written disclosure of the relationship to the client, where the lawyer or firm has a relationship with a party in the same matter.

(d) Representation is permitted under this rule only if the lawyer complies with paragraphs (a), (b), and (c), and:

(1) the lawyer reasonably believes that they can provide competent and diligent representation to each affected client;

(2) the representation is not prohibited by law; and

(3) the representation does not involve the assertion of a claim by one client against another client represented by the lawyer in any proceeding before a tribunal.

1.8 Conflicts of Interest (California & ABA Rule Comparison)

(a) **ABA Model Rule 1.8** lists specific conflicts of interest. California articulates such conflicts as Rules 1.8.1 *et seq.* As a reminder, the rule numbering herein tracks California's number system.

(b) **Media Rights:** Under the ABA rules, prior to the conclusion of representation of a client, a lawyer shall not make or negotiate an agreement giving the lawyer literary or media rights relating to the representation. There is no California corollary.

(c) **Interest In The Case Subject Matter:** A lawyer shall not acquire a proprietary interest in the subject matter of litigation, except that the lawyer may: (i) acquire a lien authorized by law to secure the lawyer's fee or expenses; and (ii) contract with a client for a reasonable contingent fee in a civil case. There is no California corollary, however see CA Rule 1.8.9.

1.8.1 Business Transactions with a Client and Pecuniary Interests

A lawyer shall not enter into a business transaction, or knowingly acquire an interest adverse to a client, unless (i) the terms are fair, reasonable, and fully disclosed in writing; (ii) the client has been advised or has independent counsel; and (iii) informed written consent is provided.

1.8.2 Use of Current Client's Information

A lawyer shall not use a client's confidential information to the disadvantage of the client unless the client gives informed consent, except as permitted by these rules or the State Bar Act.

1.8.3 Gifts from Clients

A lawyer shall not: (i) solicit a client for a substantial gift unless the lawyer or recipient is related to the client; or (ii) prepare an instrument giving the lawyer or person related any substantial gift unless they are related to the client or the client has been advised by independent counsel.

1.8.4 [Rule Reserved for Future Use By The California Bar]

1.8.5 Payment of A Client's Personal or Business Expenses

A lawyer shall not pay or agree to pay the expenses of a prospective or existing client. However, a lawyer may: (i) pay expenses to third persons, with consent, from funds collected for the client; (ii) after the lawyer is retained, agree to lend money to the client based provided no material conflict is present; (iii) advance the costs of litigation in contingent fee cases; and (iv) pay the costs of representing the interests of an indigent person.

1.8.6 Compensation from One Other than Client

A lawyer shall not accept compensation for representing a client from someone other than the client unless:

(a) there is no interference with the lawyer's independent professional judgment or with the lawyer-client relationship;

(b) confidential information is protected; and

(c) the lawyer obtains the client's informed written consent, unless:

(1) nondisclosure or the compensation is otherwise authorized by law or a court order; or

(2) the lawyer provides legal services on behalf of any public agency or nonprofit organization that provides legal services to the public.

1.8.7 Aggregate Settlements

A lawyer who represents two or more clients shall not enter into an aggregate settlement of the claims in a civil or criminal matter unless each client gives informed written consent. This rule does not apply to class action settlements subject to court approval.

1.8.8 Limiting Liability to Client

A lawyer shall not contract with a client to limit liability for malpractice or settle a malpractice claim, unless the client is: (i) represented by independent counsel; or (ii) advised in writing to seek the advice of independent counsel and given a reasonable opportunity to seek advice.

1.8.9 Purchasing Property at a Foreclosure or a Sale Subject to Judicial Review (No ABA Counterpart)

A lawyer shall not purchase property in an action when they or their affiliates represent a party or as executor, trustee, administrator, or conservator from that action. Nor shall a lawyer represent the seller at a probate, foreclosure, receiver, trustee, or judicial sale in an action where the purchaser is a relative of the lawyer or their affiliates.

1.8.10 Sexual Relations with Current Client

A lawyer shall not have sexual relations with a client who is not their spouse unless the relationship existed before the representation.

1.8.11 Imputation of Prohibitions Under Rules 1.8.1 to 1.8.9

While lawyers are associated in a law firm, a prohibition in rules 1.8.1 through 1.8.9 that applies to any one of them shall apply to all of them.

1.9 Duties to Former Clients

(a) A lawyer who has formerly represented a client shall not represent another person in the same or substantially related matter where interests are adverse without informed written consent from the former client.

(b) A lawyer shall not knowingly represent a person in the same or a substantially related matter if their prior firm previously represented a client who has adverse interests, and whom the lawyer has material confidential information about, without informed written consent from the former client.

(c) A lawyer or prior firm formerly represented a client shall not thereafter use or reveal confidential information gained from that former representation unless allowed to by law or the information has become generally known.

1.10 IMPUTATION OF CONFLICTS OF INTEREST: GENERAL RULE

(a) Lawyers associated in a firm cannot knowingly represent a client when any of them would be prohibited from doing so by rules 1.7 or 1.9, unless:

(1) it is based on a personal interest of a lawyer and there is not a significant risk of limiting the representation of the client; or

(2) the prohibition is based upon rule 1.9(a) or (b) and arises out of the prohibited lawyer's association with a prior firm, and the prohibited lawyer did not substantially participate in the matter, is timely screened, and written notice is given to any affected former client.

(b) When a lawyer is not with a firm anymore, that firm can later represent a person with adverse interests to a former client of that lawyer, unless the matter is the same or related to a prior matter and the firm has material or confidential information of the former client.

(c) A prohibition under this rule may be waived by each affected client under the conditions stated in rule 1.7.

(d) The imputation of a conflict of interest to lawyers associated in a firm with former or current government lawyers is governed by rule 1.11.

1.11 SPECIAL CONFLICTS OF INTEREST FOR FORMER/CURRENT GOVERNMENT OFFICIALS & EMPLOYEES

(a) Except as law may otherwise expressly permit, a lawyer who has formerly served as a public official or employee of the government:

(1) cannot use or reveal confidential information; and

(2) shall not represent a client connected to any matter the lawyer participated in as a government employee, without informed written consent from the government. This paragraph shall not apply to matters governed by rule 1.12(a).

(b) A lawyer's prohibition under (a) also prohibits their firm unless that lawyer is timely screened and written notice from the government.

(c) A lawyer who was a public official or employee and received confidential government information about a person may not represent a client whose interests are adverse in a matter to that person. That lawyer's firm may continue representation in the matter if there is timely screening and no fee sharing.

(d) A lawyer currently serving as a public official or employee:

(1) is subject to rules 1.7 and 1.9; and

(2) shall not: (i) participate in a matter where the lawyer personally participated while in nongovernment employment without informed written consent from the government; or (ii) negotiate for private employment with any person involved, except if a law clerk to a judge as permitted by rule 1.12(b) and subject to the conditions of rule 1.12(b).

1.12 FORMER JUDGE, ARBITRATOR, MEDIATOR, OR NEUTRAL

(a) A lawyer shall not represent anyone connected to a matter where they participated as a judge, arbitrator, or other third-party neutral without informed written consent from all parties.

(b) A lawyer shall not seek employment from any person involved in a matter where they participated as a judge, arbitrator, or other third party neutral, except if that lawyer was a staff attorney or law clerk.

(c) If a lawyer is prohibited from representation by paragraph (a), their firm may continue representation if the lawyer was not a settlement judge, that lawyer is timely screened, and written notice is given.

(d) An arbitrator selected as a partisan of a party in a multimember arbitration panel is not prohibited from subsequently representing that party.

1.13 ORGANIZATION AS CLIENT

(a) A lawyer employed or retained by an organization shall recognize that the client is the organization itself.

(b) If a lawyer representing an organization knows that a constituent has, or intends to, act in a way that violates the law with respect to the organization which will likely result in substantial injury to the organization, the lawyer shall act as reasonably necessary in the best interest of the organization including referring the matter to a higher authority in the organization.

(c) If, despite the lawyer's actions, the highest authority continues in unlawful action, the lawyer shall maintain the best interest of the organization and may withdraw or resign if necessary.

(d) A lawyer may represent constituents of the organization with consent, provided the lawyer's representation of the organization is disclosed.

1.14 CLIENT WITH DIMINISHED CAPACITY (ABA ONLY)

An attorney must maintain a normal attorney-client relationship to the extent possible. If the attorney believes the client is at risk of substantial physical or financial harm, he may take reasonable protective action, including the appointment of a guardian, if necessary. There is no California corollary.

1.15 SAFEKEEPING FUNDS AND PROPERTY OF CLIENTS AND OTHER PERSONS

(a) All funds received or held by a lawyer shall be deposited in a "Trust Account" in the California, or with written consent of the client in another jurisdiction.

(b) Notwithstanding paragraph (a), a flat fee paid in advance may be deposited in an operating account if disclosed in writing to the client that they may require a Trust Account and that the client gets a refund if services are terminated. For fees over $1000, the disclosure must be signed by the client.

(c) Funds belonging to the lawyer cannot be commingled with the Trust Account unless funds are needed to pay bank charges. However, if there are funds belonging to both client and lawyer, the lawyer's funds must be withdrawn whenever the lawyer's interest in the money becomes fixed.

(d) A lawyer shall:

(1) promptly tell a client when they receive funds for the client;

(2) place in safekeeping any securities received for the client;

(3) maintain records of client interests received by the lawyer;

(4) promptly account in writing to the client;

(5) preserve these records for no less than five years after final distribution;

(6) comply with any order for an audit of such records issued pursuant to the Rules of Procedure of the State Bar; and

(7) promptly distribute, as requested, any undisputed interests in the lawyer's possession that the client is entitled to receive.

1.16 Declining or Terminating Representation

(a) A lawyer shall not represent a client, or shall withdraw from representation, if (i) they know the action is without probable cause and is malicious; (ii) they know it will violate the rules of conduct; (iii) their mental or physical condition affects the representation; or (iv) the client discharges the lawyer.

(b) A lawyer may withdraw from representing a client if (i) the client insists on unwarranted or bad faith litigation; (ii) the representation pursues crime or fraud; (iii) the client's behavior causes unreasonable or ineffective representation; (iv) there is a material breach of the client agreement; (v) the client agrees to termination; (vi) it serves the best interest of the client; (vii) the lawyer's mental or physical condition requires it; (viii) a violation of State Bar rules will occur; or (ix) the tribunal will find good cause to withdraw.

(c) A lawyer shall not terminate representation until they have taken reasonable steps to avoid prejudice to the client. Upon termination, the lawyer shall promptly release all client materials and property to the client and shall refund any fees not earned.

1.17 Sale of a Law Practice

All, or substantially all, of the law practice of a lawyer, living or deceased, including goodwill, may be sold to subject to all the following conditions:

(a) Fees charged to clients do not increase by the sale only;

(b) If the sale includes transfer of unfinished work or confidential client information, then written notice must be given to each client included in the sale, and the purchaser shall obtain written consent of the client. If after 90 days there is no response, consent by the client is presumed;

(c) If substitution is required by the rules of a tribunal in which a matter is pending, all steps necessary to substitute a lawyer shall be taken;

(d) The purchaser shall comply with all conflict rules of current/former clients;

(e) Confidential information shall not be disclosed to a nonlawyer;

(f) This rule does not apply to the admission to or retirement from a law firm.

1.18 Duties to Prospective Clients

A prospective client is a person who consults a lawyer for securing legal service or advice from the lawyer. Even when no relationship ensues, a lawyer who communicated with the prospective client shall not use or reveal confidential information. A lawyer or firm shall not represent a client who is adverse to that prospective client unless there is informed written consent from both parties, or the lawyer is timely screened and written notice given to the prospective client.

2 COUNSELOR

2.1 Advisor

Lawyers shall exercise independent professional judgment and render candid advice.

2.2 [Rule Reserved for Future Use By The California Bar]

2.3 Evaluation for Use by Third Persons (ABA Only)

Under the ABA rules only, a lawyer may provide an evaluation affecting a client if the lawyer believes that the evaluation is in keeping with the attorney-client relationship. An evaluation that is likely to materially and adversely affect the client's interest shall not be provided without the client's informed consent. There is no California corollary to this rule.

2.4 Lawyer as Third-Party Neutral

A lawyer is a third-party neutral when they assist two or more persons who are not clients to resolve a dispute. They shall inform unrepresented parties that they are not representing them.

3 ADVOCATE

3.1 Meritorious Claims and Contentions

A lawyer shall not bring or continue an action or a position without probable cause, that is malicious, or that is not warranted by law. A lawyer for a criminal defendant may defend the charge by requiring every element be established.

3.2 Delay of Litigation

A lawyer shall not use means that have no substantial purpose other than to delay the proceeding or to cause needless expense.

3.3 Candor Toward the Tribunal

(a) A lawyer shall not:

(1) knowingly make or fail to correct a false statement to a tribunal;

(2) fail to disclose adverse legal authority;

(3) knowingly offer false evidence. If the lawyer knows a witness has given false evidence, reasonable measures to remedy the situation must be taken, unless the information is privileged and cannot be disclosed;

(4) offer evidence in a criminal matter that is believed to be false, other than the testimony of the defendant.

(b) In an ex parte proceeding, the lawyer shall inform the tribunal of all material facts whether adverse or not to the client.

3.4 Fairness to Opposing Party and Counsel

(a) A lawyer shall not:

(1) unlawfully obstruct access to, alter, suppress, or destroy evidence;

(2) falsify evidence, counsel or assist a witness to testify falsely;

(3) pay a witness contingent on the content of their testimony or the outcome of the case;

(4) advise or direct a witness to leave the jurisdiction to become unavailable;

(5) knowingly disobey an order of the court unless not valid; or

(6) in trial, assert personal knowledge of facts unless testifying, or state a personal opinion as to guilt or innocence.

3.5 Contact with Judges, Officials, Employees, and Jurors

(a) A lawyer shall not give anything of value to a judge or official unless permitted by statute. This rule does not apply to campaign contributions.

(b) A lawyer shall not communicate with a judicial officer about a contested matter, except: (i) in open court; (ii) with consent from all counsel; (iii) in the presence of all counsel; (iv) in writing to all parties; or (v) in ex parte matters.

(c) A lawyer connected with a case shall not knowingly communicate with or investigate any juror (or juror's family member) during the proceeding, nor after the proceeding if the juror does not consent or is coerced.

3.6 Trial Publicity

(a) A lawyer, or member of the firm or agency, involved in litigation shall not make an extrajudicial public statement that will likely prejudice proceedings.

(b) **Exceptions:** A lawyer may state the claim/offense involved, identity, public records, scheduling, or reasonable warnings to the public if necessary. In a criminal case, this can also include arrest and officer information. In addition, a lawyer may make a statement reasonably necessary to protect a client from undue prejudice of recent publicity.

3.7 Lawyer as Witness

(a) A lawyer shall not act as an advocate in a trial in which the lawyer is likely to be a witness unless:

(1) the lawyer's testimony relates to an uncontested issue or matter;

(2) the lawyer's testimony relates to the nature and value of legal services rendered in the case; or

(3) the lawyer has obtained informed written consent.

(b) A lawyer may act as advocate in a trial in which another lawyer in the lawyer's firm is likely to be called as a witness unless precluded from doing so by law.

3.8 Special Responsibilities of a Prosecutor

The prosecutor in a criminal case shall:

(a) not prosecute without probable cause;

(b) make reasonable efforts to assure the rights of the accused to counsel;

(c) timely disclose all evidence negating guilt including any new evidence;

(d) prevent extrajudicial statements;

(e) make efforts to remedy any wrong convictions.

3.9 Advocate in Non-adjudicative Proceedings

A lawyer shall disclose an appearance before a legislative body when appearing as a representative in connection with a pending non-adjudicative matter.

3.10 Threatening Criminal, Administrative, or Disciplinary Charges (No ABA Counterpart)

A lawyer shall not threaten charges to gain an advantage in a dispute.

4 TRANSACTIONS WITH PERSONS OTHER THAN CLIENT

4.1 Truthfulness in Statements to Others

A lawyer shall not knowingly make a false statement of material fact or law or fail to disclose such fact to avoid crime or fraud unless it would violate confidentiality.

4.2 Communication with a Represented Person

(a) In representing a client, a lawyer shall not communicate about the representation with a person they know to be represented by another lawyer, without consent from the other lawyer. In the case of a represented organization, a lawyer cannot communicate with current officers, directors, or employees, who are the subject of the matter.

(b) **Exceptions:** (i) communications with a public official, board, committee, or body; or (ii)communications otherwise authorized by law or a court order.

4.3 Communicating with an Unrepresented Person

In communicating for a client with a person who is not represented, a lawyer shall not state or imply that the lawyer is disinterested and should remedy any confusion. A lawyer cannot seek privileged information they are not entitled to.

4.4 Duties Concerning Inadvertently Transmitted Writing

Where it is reasonably apparent to a lawyer who receives a writing relating to a lawyer's representation of a client that the writing was inadvertently sent and is work product, the lawyer shall not read it and must promptly notify the sender.

5 LAW FIRMS AND ASSOCIATIONS

5.1 Responsibilities of Managerial and Supervisory Lawyers

A lawyer with managerial authority in a firm shall make reasonable efforts to ensure that all lawyers comply with State Bar rules. A lawyer shall be responsible for another lawyer's violation of these rules and the State Bar Act if: (i) the lawyer orders or, with knowledge, ratifies the conduct involved; or (ii) the lawyer with authority in the firm knows of the conduct and fails to take remedial action.

5.2 Responsibilities of a Subordinate Lawyer

A lawyer shall comply with these rules regardless if acting at the direction of another lawyer, however, a lawyer does not violate these rules if acting in accordance with a supervisor's reasonable acts.

5.3 Responsibilities Regarding Nonlawyer Assistants

With respect to a nonlawyer employed or retained by or associated with a lawyer:

(a) A lawyer with managerial authority in a firm shall make reasonable efforts to assure the nonlawyer's conduct is compatible with the professional obligations of the lawyer; and

(b) A lawyer is responsible for another person's violation of these rules if: (i) the lawyer orders or, with knowledge of the relevant facts and of the specific conduct, ratifies the conduct involved; or (ii) the lawyer with authority in the firm knows of the conduct and fails to take remedial action.

5.3.1 Employment of Disbarred, Suspended, Resigned, or Involuntarily Inactive Lawyer (No ABA Counterpart)

(a) A lawyer shall not in a legal capacity employ, associate in practice with, or assist a person the lawyer knows or reasonably should know is an ineligible person to practice law per the State Bar.

(b) A lawyer may employ, associate with, or assist an ineligible person to perform certain tasks, including but not limited to: legal preparation, research, drafting, billing, or clerical work.

(c) Prior to or at the time of employing, associating in practice with, or assisting an ineligible person, the lawyer shall provide written notice to the State Bar and to affected clients.

5.4 Financial and Similar Arrangements with Nonlawyers

(a) A lawyer shall not share legal fees with a nonlawyer except to: (i) pay to a deceased lawyer's estate; (ii) pay to employees for retirement / compensation; (iii) as part of a lawful lawyer referral service; or (iv) in sharing a court-awarded legal fee with a nonprofit organization.

(b) A lawyer shall not start a legal practice law with a nonlawyer.

(c) A lawyer shall not allow a person paying for the legal services of another to interfere with independent professional judgment.

5.5 Unauthorized Practice of Law; Multijurisdictional Practice

A lawyer admitted to practice law in California shall not practice or assist in another jurisdiction if that would violate the rules of the jurisdiction. Nor shall a lawyer who is not admitted to practice law in California shall not maintain a legal practice presence, nor represent that they can practice in, California.

5.6 Restrictions on a Lawyer's Right to Practice

Unless authorized by law, a lawyer shall not attempt to restrict another lawyer's right to practice after the termination of a relationship, unless upon retirement.

6 PUBLIC SERVICE

6.1 Pro Bono Service (ABA Only)

Lawyers should provide at least 50 hours of pro bono services a year and provide further assistance (reduced fees) to individuals and organizations in need.

6.2 Accepting Appointments (ABA Only)

A lawyer shall not avoid being appointed without good cause. For example, representation would violate a rule of conduct, pose an unreasonable financial burden, or the attorney-client relationship is compromised because the attorney finds the client repugnant.

6.3 Membership in Legal Services Organization

A lawyer may serve as a director, officer or member of a legal services organization, apart from their law firm even if that organization has adverse interests to a client. However, they cannot knowingly participate in a decision if it would violate confidentiality or have a material adverse effect on the client.

6.4 Law Reform Activities Affecting Client Interests (ABA Only)

A lawyer may serve as a director, officer or member of an organization involved in reform of the law or its administration notwithstanding that the reform may affect the interests of a client of the lawyer. When the lawyer knows that the interests of a client may be materially benefitted by a decision in which the lawyer participates, the lawyer shall disclose that fact but need not identify the client.

6.5 Limited Legal Services Programs

A lawyer who works as part of a program sponsored by a court, government agency, bar association, law school, or nonprofit organization, and provides short-term limited legal services is subject to conflict rules only if they know of it. Any disqualification under this section is not imputed to the firm.

7 INFORMATION ABOUT LEGAL SERVICES

7.1 Communications Concerning a Lawyer's Services

A lawyer shall not make a false or misleading communication about the lawyer or the lawyer's services that includes any material misrepresentation.

7.2 Advertising

(a) A lawyer shall not pay compensation for recommending or securing a client, except a lawyer may: (i) pay for lawful advertisements; (ii) pay for a lawful lawyer referral service; or (iii) offer a gift for a past recommendation if there is no future agreement. Advertisements shall include the name and address of at least one lawyer or law firm responsible for its content.

(1) A lawyer may refer clients to another lawyer or professional if it is not an exclusive arrangement and the client is informed.

7.3 Solicitation of Clients

(a) A lawyer shall not by in-person, live telephone or real-time electronic means, contact, solicit services for pecuniary gain unless that person is another lawyer, a relative, or has a prior relationship with the lawyer.

(b) A lawyer shall not solicit employment from a person who is known to not desire solicitation, or in a manner that is coercive or harassing in nature.

(c) Any solicitation to a person known to be in need of legal services shall include the word "Advertisement" or similar on the outside envelope, and at the beginning/end of a recording, unless it is apparent that it is an advertisement.

(d) A lawyer may participate in a prepaid legal service plan that uses live contact to solicit clients if it is not operated by the lawyer and it is sent to persons not known to need services.

7.4 Communication of Fields of Practice and Specialization

A lawyer shall not state that the lawyer is a certified specialist in a particular field of law, unless they are currently certified by that Board or the State Bar.

7.5 Firm Names and Trade Names

No firm name may be fraudulent, misleading, or imply a government relationship.

7.6 Political Contributions to Obtain Appointments (ABA Only)

A lawyer or law firm shall not accept a government legal engagement, or an appointment by a judge, if the lawyer or law firm makes a political contribution or solicits political contributions for the purpose of obtaining or being considered for that type of legal engagement or appointment.

8 MAINTAINING THE INTEGRITY OF THE PROFESSION

8.1 False Statement Regarding Application for Admission to Practice Law (No ABA Model Rule Counterpart)

An applicant for practice shall not make a false statement on that application. Nor shall a lawyer make a false statement on another person's application.

8.2 Judicial Officials

A lawyer shall not knowingly make a false statement about a judicial officer or candidate. Candidates for office shall comply with the Canons of Judicial Ethics.

8.3 Reporting Professional Misconduct (ABA Only)

A lawyer who knows that another lawyer or Judge has violated the relevant rules of conduct, or a substantial question as to the person's honesty, trustworthiness, or fitness for practice, shall inform the relevant professional governing body.

8.4 Misconduct

It is misconduct to: (i) violate the Rules of Professional Conduct or State Bar Act; (ii) commit a criminal act or engage in conduct regarding honesty or fitness as a lawyer; (iii) knowingly assist or induce a judicial officer to violate the law.

8.4.1 Prohibited Discrimination, Harassment, and Retaliation

(a) A lawyer shall not unlawfully harass, discriminate, or retaliate on the basis of any protected characteristic in representation or termination of a client, employee, or volunteer.

(b) A lawyer subject to a State Bar investigation shall notify of any criminal, civil, or administrative action based on the same conduct.

8.5 Disciplinary Authority; Choice of Law

Disciplinary Authority: A lawyer admitted in California is subject to discipline regardless of where the conduct occurs. A lawyer not admitted in California is subject to the discipline of California if they provide services in California.

REAL PROPERTY PRIMER

I. LANDLORD AND TENANT

A. Nature of Leasehold: A leasehold is an estate in land under which the tenant has a present long-term possessory interest in the premises. The landlord has a reversion.

1. **Tenancy for Years:** A fixed-term lease may also be defined by weeks or months (e.g., A rents to B for 2 years).

   a) **Creation:** Usually created by written leases. If the lease is for more than one year, it must be in writing under the Statue of Frauds.

   b) **Termination:** Ends automatically on its termination date; in most leases, the landlord reserves the right of entry, which allows him to terminate the lease if the tenant breaches any of the covenants.

   c) **Surrender:** Tenant may surrender the tenancy in writing.

2. **Periodic Tenancy:** A periodic tenancy continues for successive periods (month to month) until one party terminates it by giving proper notice.

   a) **Creation:** (i) *Express agreement* – the landlord to the tenant from month to month; (ii) *Implied agreement* – the landlord to the tenant at a monthly rental rate of $100; (iii) *Operation of Law* – the tenant remains in possession after the lease expires, or lease is invalid.

   b) **Termination:** The tenancy continues until one party gives proper notice, generally one full period in advance, or six months for yearly lease.

3. **Tenancies at Will:** Either the landlord, or the tenant may terminate the tenancy at his or her will.

   a) **Creation:** A tenancy at will often arises when there is a defect in the original lease, but it can also be created by an express agreement. The courts will also treat periodic rent payments as a periodic tenancy.

   b) **Termination:** The landlord and tenant must have the same rights to termination. Either party may terminate without notice.

4. **Tenancies at Sufferance**

   a) **Creation:** A tenancy at sufferance arises when a tenant continues to occupy the premises after the expiration of a lawful tenancy without the landlord's consent.

   b) **Termination:** A tenancy at sufferance lasts only until the landlord takes steps to evict the tenant, which he may do at any time without notice.

5. **Hold-Over Doctrine:** If a tenant does not vacate the premises after his right to possession has ended, the landlord may: (i) evict him; or (ii) bind him to a new periodic tenancy. Generally, the terms and conditions that governed the expired tenancy will govern the new tenancy, unless the landlord notifies the tenant otherwise and the tenant remains in possession.

   Exceptions: The hold-over doctrine does not apply where: (i) the tenant remains in possession for only a few hours, or only leaves a few pieces of property; (ii) the delay is not the tenant's fault (severe illness); or (iii) the lease is seasonal. In these situations, the landlord can only evict the tenant, not bind the tenant to a new tenancy.

B. Tenant's Duties and Landlord's Remedies

1. **Tenant's Duty to Repair (Doctrine of Waste):** The tenant cannot damage (commit waste on) the leased premises. There are three types of waste:

   a) **Voluntary (Affirmative) Waste:** The tenant intentionally, or negligently damages the premises, or exploits minerals on the property;

   b) **Permissive Waste:** The tenant fails to take reasonable steps to protect the premises from damage. The tenant is liable for all ordinary repairs, but not ordinary wear and tear;

   c) **Ameliorative Waste:** The tenant alters the leased property, increasing its value. Generally, the tenant is liable for restoration;

   d) **Tenant's Liability for Covenants to Repair:** The tenant has a duty to repair ordinary wear and tear unless expressly excluded, but has no duty to repair structural failures, or damage from fire or other casualty unless expressly included.

2. **Duty to Not Use Premises for Illegal Purpose:** The landlord may terminate the lease if the tenant regularly uses the premises for an illegal purpose.

3. **Duty to Pay Rent:** If the lease ends before the end of a rental period, the tenant must pay a proportional amount of rent.

4. **Landlord Remedies**

   a) **Tenant on Premises, but Fails to Pay Rent – Evict or Sue for Rent:** Most modern leases give the landlord the right to terminate under the unlawful-detainer statute and the tenant cannot raise counterclaims.

   b) **Tenant Abandons – Do Nothing or Repossess:** If the tenant unjustifiably abandons the property, the landlord is entitled to damages, but must mitigate damages by seeking to relet the premises.

C. Landlord Duties and Tenant Remedies: The general rule is that a landlord does not have to repair or maintain the premises.

1. **Duty to Deliver Possession of Premises:** Most states require the landlord to give the tenant actual possession of the premises at the beginning of the leasehold.

2. **Quiet Enjoyment:** Every lease has an implied covenant that neither the landlord nor a paramount titleholder will interfere with the tenant's quiet enjoyment and possession of the premises. This covenant may be breached by:

   a) **Actual Eviction:** The landlord, or a paramount titleholder, excludes the tenant from the premises. The tenant has no obligation to pay rent.

   b) **Partial Eviction:** The tenant is physically excluded from part of the premises. The tenant pays a portion based on the reasonable rental value of the portion she continues to possess.

   c) **Constructive Eviction:** If the landlord breaches a duty to provide that renders the property uninhabitable, the tenant may vacate the premises, terminate the lease and seek damages.

3. **Implied Warranty of Habitability:** Most jurisdictions imply a non-waivable covenant of habitability into residential leases, in which the premises must meet local housing codes. If the premises are uninhabitable, the tenant may: (i) terminate the lease; (ii) make repairs and offset the cost against future rent; (iii) abate the rent to an amount equal to the fair rental value in view of the defects; or (iv) remain in possession, pay full rent, and sue for damages.

4. **Retaliatory Eviction:** A landlord may not terminate a lease or penalize a tenant for exercising a legal right, including reporting housing or building code violations.

D. Assignments and Subleases: A tenant may freely transfer her leasehold interest unless the lease states otherwise. An assignment is a complete transfer of the entire remaining term. If the tenant retains any part of the remaining term (other than a right to renter upon breach), the transfer is a sublease.

1. **Consequences of Assignment:** The landlord and assignee are in privity of estate and both are bound to all covenants that "run with the land." There is no longer privity between the landlord and the original tenant.

   a) **Covenants that Run with the Land:** Covenants that run with the land are those that are tied to the land, not the owner, and are transferred as the land is transferred.

   b) **Rent Covenants:** A covenant to pay rent runs with the land so the assignee must pay rent to the landlord. After assignment, the original tenant and the landlord are in privity of contract and the original tenant remains liable on the original contract obligation to pay rent.

2. **Consequences of Sublease – Sublessee Not in Privity with Landlord:** Sublessee is not personally liable to the landlord for rent, or for the performance of any of the covenants in the original lease.

   a) **Landlord's Remedies:** Landlord may terminate the lease, and the sublease automatically ends. A number of jurisdictions allow a landlord who does not receive rent to assert a lien on personal property found on the premises.

   b) **Rights of Sublessee:** A sublessee cannot enforce any of the landlord's obligations in the lease, except for the implied warranty of inhabitability in a residential sublease.

3. **Covenants Against Assignment of Sublease:** Courts will strictly construe lease restrictions on assignment and sublease against the landlord. Thus, a prohibition against assignment does not preclude a sublease and vice versa.

   a) **Waiver:** A landlord waives a covenant against assignment if he accepts rent without an objection and knows of the assignment.

   b) **Transfer in Violation of Lease:** An assignment or sublease that violates a lease provision is not void, but the landlord may generally terminate the lease, or sue for damages.

4. **Assignments by Landlords:** A landlord may assign rents and his reversion without the tenant's consent.

   a) **Rights of Assignee Against Tenants – Attornment:** The beneficial covenants that run with the land are transferred to the new owner.

   b) **Liabilities of Assignee to Tenants:** Burdens and liabilities of the landlord's covenants that run with the land are transferred to the assignee.

E. Condemnation of Leaseholds: If the entire leasehold is taken by eminent domain, the tenant is entitled to compensation and no longer has to pay rent, as there is no longer a leasehold estate when the leasehold and reversion have merged in the condemnor.

F. Tort Liability of Landlord and Tenant

1. **Landlord's Liability:** Under common law, the landlord does not have a duty to make the premises safe. Today there are several exceptions:

   a) **Concealed Dangerous Condition (Latent Defect):** A landlord who fails to disclose a dangerous condition will be liable for any resulting injuries. If the tenant accepts the premises after disclosure, she assumes the risk for herself and others, relieving the landlord of any liability.

b) **Public Use:** The landlord is liable for injuries to the public if he: (i) knows (or should know) of a dangerous condition; (ii) has reason to believe the tenant may admit the public; and (iii) fails to repair.

c) **Repairs:** If the landlord undertakes such repairs, he owes a duty of reasonable care. The landlord also has a duty of reasonable care in maintaining common areas (halls, elevators). If the landlord covenants to repair, or has a statutory duty to repair, he is liable for injuries resulting from failure to repair, or negligent repair.

d) **Furnished Short-Term Residence:** A landlord who rents a fully furnished premises for a short period is liable for injuries resulting from any defect, whether or not he knew of the defect, or disclosed it.

e) **Modern Trend – General Duty of Reasonable Care:** Courts have found that a landlord owes a general duty of reasonable care to residential tenants, under which he is liable for injuries resulting from ordinary negligence if he had notice of a defect and an opportunity to repair it.

2. **Tenant's Liability:** For a tenant's duty of care as an occupier of land, see Torts.

II. COOPERATIVES, CONDOMINIUMS, AND ZONING

A. **Cooperative:** In a cooperative, a corporation holds title to the land and buildings, and leases individual apartments to shareholders.

B. **Condominiums:** In a condominium, each owner owns the interior of his individual unit, plus an undivided interest in the exterior and common areas.

C. **Zoning:** The state may enact statutes to reasonably control the use of land for the protection of the health, safety, morals and welfare of its citizens. Remember these terms:

1. **Nonconforming Use:** A use that exists when the state passes a zoning act that does not conform to the statute cannot be eliminated at once.

2. **Special Use Permit:** A special use permit is one that must be obtained even though the zoning is proper for the intended use. It is often required for hospitals, funeral homes, drive-through businesses, etc.

3. **Variance:** A variance is a departure from the literal restrictions of a zoning ordinance, granted by administrative action.

4. **Zoning Ordinances:** These are generally invalid if they have no reasonable relation to public welfare, are too restrictive, are discriminatory as to a particular parcel, are beyond the grant of authority, violate due process, or are racially discriminatory.

D. **Unconstitutional Takings and Exactions:** See Constitutional Law.

III. FIXTURES

A fixture is a chattel that has been so affixed to land that it is no longer personal property, but a part of the realty. A fixture passes with the land.

A. **Chattels Incorporated Into Structure:** Fixtures include Items that are incorporated into the realty so that they lose their identity (e.g. bricks, concrete) and items that, if removed, would cause damage (e.g. plumbing, heating ducts).

B. **Common Ownership Cases:** A common ownership case is one in which the person who brings the chattel to the land owns both the chattel and the land (X installs a furnace in his home).

These become "fixtures" if owner intended to make the item part of the realty. Intention is inferred from: (i) the nature of the article; (ii) the manner of attachment; (iii) the amount of damage that would be caused by its removal; and (iv) the adaptation of the item to the use of the realty.

1. **Constructive Annexation:** An article of personal property that is so uniquely adapted to the real estate that it makes no sense to separate it (keys to doors, custom curtain rods). It may be a fixture even if it is not physically attached to the property.

C. **Divided Ownership Cases:** The chattel is owned and brought to the realty by someone other than the landowner, such as a tenant or licensee.

1. **Landlord-Tenant:** Whether an annexed chattel is a fixture depends on whether there is a relevant agreement between the landlord and tenant. Absent an agreement, a tenant may remove his annexed chattels if removal would not damage the premises, or destroy the chattel.

2. **Life Tenant and Remainderman:** The same rules apply for life tenants except that the life tenant must remove annexations before the end of his tenancy.

3. **Licensee or Trespasser and Landlord:** Licensees are treated as tenants; however, trespassers normally lose their annexations. Thus, absent a statute, an adverse possessor or good faith trespasser cannot remove fixtures.

D. **Third-Party Cases**

1. **Third-Party Lien on Land to Which Chattel Affixed:** Generally, the mortgagee has no greater rights than the mortgagor. Thus, chattels annexed by the mortgagor's tenant are generally not within the lien of the mortgagee except where the mortgage is made after the lease and the mortgagee is without notice of the tenant's rights.

2. **Third-Party Lien on Chattel Affixed to Land:** If a landowner affixes a chattel, of which the seller retains a security interest, to mortgaged land and defaults on both the chattel and mortgage payments, the general rule is that the first to record his interest wins possession of the chattel.

IV. RIGHTS IN THE LAND OF ANOTHER

A. **Easements:** An easement is a non-possessory interest in land that creates a right to use land possessed by someone else.

1. **Creation**

a) **Express Grant:** Any easement expressly granted must be in writing to satisfy the Statute of Frauds.

b) **Express Reservation:** A grantor creates an easement by reservation when she conveys title to land, but reserves the right to continue to use a tract for a special purpose.

c) **Implication:** An easement by implication is created by operation of law as a result of surrounding circumstances that indicate they must have intended for an easement.

(1) **Implied from Existing Use:** An easement may be implied from existing use if: (i) the single tract was owned by the same person; (ii) who continuously and actively used it at the time of the conveyance; (iii) for a purpose that is reasonably necessary for the enjoyment of the property; and (iv) the court determines that the parties intended the use to continue after the transfer of the property.

(2) **Implication Without Existing Use**

(a) **Subdivision Plat**: Buyers of the lots that refer to a recorded plat, or map with streets leading to the lot have implied easements to use the streets to access their lots.

(b) **Profit a Prendre:** The holder of a profit a prendre has an implied easement to pass over the surface of the land to use it as is reasonably necessary to exercise his right to take something off the land, or extract it.

(3) **Necessity:** An easement by necessity arises when a landowner divides his property in a way that deprives one of the subdivisions access to something that is necessary for the use and enjoyment of the property.

d) **Prescription:** A person can acquire an easement by prescription in the same way a person can acquire property by adverse possession. The use must be: (i) open and notorious; (ii) adverse; (iii) continuous and uninterrupted; (iv) for the statutory period of time.

2. **Characteristics**

a) **Affirmative or Negative**

(1) **Affirmative:** The holder is entitled to make affirmative use of the servient tenement.

(2) **Negative:** The holder can forbid the possessor of the servient tenement to refrain from engaging in an activity on the servient estate. Negative easements are generally limited to: (i) light; (ii) air; (iii) lateral and subjacent support; and (iv) flow of an artificial stream.

b) **Appurtenant or In Gross**

(1) **Appurtenant:** An easement is appurtenant when it benefits the holder in his physical use, or enjoyment of another tract of land. The owner of the easement holds it in his capacity as the owner of another tract of property. Thus, there are two tracts: the dominant tenement and the servient tenement.

(2) **In Gross:** The holder of an easement in gross has a right to use the servient tenement independent of his possession of another tract of land.

3. **Scope:** Unless the grant provides otherwise, courts assume the easement was intended to meet both present and future needs of the dominant tenement. If, however, the dominant parcel is subdivided, the lot owners will not succeed to the easement if to do so would unreasonably overburden the servient estate.

4. **Termination**

a) **Stated Conditions:** The original grant may specify when, or under what conditions the easement will end.

b) **Unity of Ownership (Merger):** The easement is destroyed when the same person acquires ownership of both the easement and the servient estate, thus merging the two.

c) **Release:** The owner of the easement can terminate the easement, even an easement in gross, by executing a deed of release.

d) **Abandonment:** An easement owner who abandons an easement through physical action extinguishes the easement.

e) **Estoppel:** While oral expressions of intent to abandon do not terminate an easement unless they are put in writing, or accompanied by an action, if the owner of the servient estate changes his position in reasonable reliance on the oral representations, the easement ends through estoppel.

f) **Prescription:** An easement by prescription ends when the owner of the servient tenement excludes the easement holder for a prescribed statutory period, typically 20 years.

g) **Necessity:** Easements created by necessity end once the necessity ends.

h) **Condemnation and Destruction:** All easements end if the servient estate is condemned. If the easement is destroyed involuntarily, the easement ends; if it is destroyed voluntarily, the easement is not destroyed.

i) **A failed attempt to create an easement results in a license.**

B. **Licenses:** A holder of a license has the privilege to go upon the land of another. It is merely a privilege, not an interest in the land, revocable at the will of the licensor. A license is personal to the licensee and thus inalienable.

1. **Irrevocable Licenses:** A license cannot be revoked in the following situations:

   a) **Estoppel:** If a licensee relies on the license and invests substantial amounts of money or labor, the licensor is estopped to revoke the license.

   b) **License Coupled with an Interest:** A license, coupled with an interest, is irrevocable as long as the interest lasts.

2. **Profits:** A profit entitles the holder to take identified resources from the servient estate. Implied in every profit is an easement entitling the benefit holder to enter the servient estate to remove the resources. A profit may be extinguished by trough surcharge.

C. **Covenants Running with the Land at Law (Real Covenants):** A real covenant running with the land is a written promise to do something on the land, or a promise not to do something on the land.

1. **Requirements for Burden to Run:** If the following elements are present, any successor in interest to the burdened estate will be bound by the covenant:

   a) **Intent:** The parties to the covenant intended that successors be bound by its terms.

   b) **Notice:** Under modern recording acts, a subsequent purchaser for value must have had actual, inquiry, or record notice at the time of purchase.

   c) **Horizontal Privity:** When entering into the covenant, the parties must have shared some interest in the land independent of the covenant.

   d) **Vertical Privity:** The successor in interest to the covenanting party must hold the entire durational interest that the covenantor held at the time he made the covenant.

   e) **Touch and Concern:** Negative covenants touch and concern the land if they restrict the servient estate holder's use of the parcel. Affirmative covenants touch and concern the land if they require the servient estate holder to do something that increases his obligations.

2. **Requirements for Benefit to Run:** The promisor's successor in interest may enforce the covenant if the following elements are present:

   a) **Intent:** The covenanting parties intended that the successors in interest to the covenantee would be able to enforce the covenant.

   b) **Vertical Privity:** The benefits run to the assignees of the original estate, or any lesser estate.

c) **Horizontal Privity:** While the parties do not have to be in horizontal privity, if they are not, the promisee's successors can only enforce the covenant against the promisor, not the promisor's successors.

d) **Touch and Concern:** The benefit of a covenant touches and concerns the land if the promised performance benefits the covenantee.

3. **Specific Situations Involving Real Covenants:** Generally, promises to pay money to be used in connection with the land (homeowner association fees) and covenants not to compete run with the land.

4. **Remedy – Damages Only:** A non-breaching party to a real covenant may receive money damages.

5. **Termination:** As with all other non-possessory interests, a party may terminate a covenant by a written release; or it may end where there is a merger of the benefited and burdened estates, or the burdened property is condemned.

D. Equitable Servitudes: An equitable servitude is a covenant that can be enforced against assignees that have notice of the covenant, regardless of whether it runs with the land at law. The usual remedy for enforcement is an injunction – this is the crucial difference between real covenants and equitable servitudes.

1. **Creation:** By covenants contained in a writing that complies with the Statute of Frauds, or implied from a common scheme for the development of a subdivision.

   a) **Common Scheme:** Reciprocal negative servitudes will be implied only where the developer planned that all parcels would be subject to the same restriction when sales began.

   b) **Notice:** To be bound by an implied covenant not in her deed, a grantee must have had notice of the covenants in the deeds of others in the subdivision.

2. **Requirements for the Burden to Run**

   a) **Intent:** The covenanting parties intended that the servitude be enforceable by and against assignees;

   b) **Notice:** The successor of the promisor has actual, inquiry, or record notice of the servitude; and

   c) **Touch and Concern:** The covenant touches and concerns the land (i.e., it restricts the holder of the servient estate in his use of that parcel).

3. **Requirements for the Benefit to Run:** The benefit of an equitable servitude runs with the land and is enforceable by the promisee's successors as long as: (i) the original parties so intended; and (ii) the servitude touches and concerns the benefited property. No privity of estate is required.

4. **Equitable Defenses to Enforcement:** A court will not enforce if:

   a) **Unclean Hands:** The person seeking enforcement violates a similar restriction;

   b) **Consent:** A benefited party acquiesced in a violation;

   c) **Estoppel:** A benefited party acted in a way that a reasonable person would believe he was abandoning the covenant;

   d) **Laches:** The benefited party failed to bring a lawsuit against the violator within a reasonable time; or

   e) **Inequitable:** The neighborhood has changed so significantly that enforcing the covenant would be inequitable.

5. **Termination:** Like other non-possessory interests, an equitable servitude ends when: (i) the benefit holder executes a written release; (ii) the benefited and burdened estates are merged; or (iii) the burdened property is condemned.

6. **Party Walls and Common Driveways:** A wall erected partly on property of two adjoining landowners generally belongs to each owner to the extent it rests upon her land.

   a) **Creation:** Implication, prescription, or written agreement.

   b) **Running of Covenants:** By agreement, the rights of common wall and driveway owners will run to the successive owners of each parcel.

7. **Adverse Possession:** In order to take title by adverse possession, the possession must be: (i) hostile; (ii) open and notorious; (iii) actual and exclusive; and (iv) continuous.

   a) **Hostile:** Possession is hostile if the possessor enters without the owner's permission.

   b) **Open and Notorious:** Possession is open and notorious when it is the kind of use the owner would make of the land and is sufficiently apparent to put the true owner on notice.

   c) **Actual and Exclusive:** An adverse possessor will gain title only to land she actually occupies and does not share with the true owner, or the public.

   d) **Continuous Possession:** Possession must be continuous throughout the statutory period, unless intermittent possession is of a type that an owner would make.

      (1) **Tacking:** An adverse possessor can tack her own possession onto the periods of adverse possession of her predecessors, but privity is required.

      (2) **Disability:** The statutory period does not begin to run if the true owner was under some disability to sue when the cause of action first accrued.

      (3) **Future Interests:** The statutory period does not begin to run against a holder of a future interest until the interest becomes possessory.

      (4) **Restrictive Covenants:** If an adverse possessor violates a restrictive covenant in the owner's deed for the limitations period, she takes title free of that restriction. If the possession is consistent with the covenant, her title remains subject to the restriction.

V. ESTATES IN LAND

A. Present Possessory Interests

1. **Fee Simple Absolute:** A fee simple represents absolute ownership. The owner has the exclusive right to use it, sell it, divide it, or devise it.

2. **Defeasible Fee:** A defeasible fee is an estate in land that can be terminated upon the occurrence of an event stated in the granting document.

3. **Fee Simple Determinable ("FSD") – Possibility of Reverter:** A fee simple determinable automatically terminates upon the happening of the stated event.

   a) **Possibility of Reverter:** When a grantor conveys an FSD, he automatically retains future estate of a possibility of reverter.

4. **Fee Simple Subject to Condition Subsequent (Right of Entry):** The grantor reserves the right to terminate the estate upon the happening of a certain stated event.

   a) Right of Entry: The grantor has a right of entry if the triggering event occurs.

5. **Fee Simple Subject to Executory Interest:** This estate automatically terminates upon the happening of a stated event and then passes to a third party, not the grantor. The third party then has an executory interest.

6. **Fee Tail:** A fee tail is a restriction on the sale or inheritance of the property in which it can only be sold, devised, or inherited by lineal heirs.

7. **Life Estate:** A life estate gives the holder the use of the estate for the duration of a life. It is usually for the life of tenant, but it could be for the life of a third party.

   a) **Duration**

      (1) **Life of Grantee:** Generally measured by the life of the grantee.

      (2) **Life Estate Pur Autre Vie:** Generally measured by the life of a third party. May result when the life tenant conveys his life estate to another.

      (3) **Condition Subsequent/Executory Interest:** Can be characterized as subject to a condition subsequent, or executory interest.

   b) **Rights and Duties of Life Tenant – Doctrine of Waste:** A life tenant has the right to live on the property until death and enjoy any ordinary use and profits of the land, as long as it does not injure the interests of a remainderman or reversioner.

      (1) **Affirmative (Voluntary) Waste:** A life tenant can consume or exploit natural resources on the land where: (i) it is necessary to repair or maintain the land; (ii) the land is suitable only for such use; or (iii) it is expressly or impliedly permitted by the grantor.

      (2) **Permissive Waste:** Permissive waste occurs when a life tenant fails to protect or preserve the land.

      (3) **Ameliorative Waste:** Even if an improvement increases the property's value, if it changes the property's character, it is waste.

         (a) **Cf – Leasehold Tenant:** Remains liable for ameliorative waste if market value was increased.

         (b) **Cf – Worthless Property:** The life tenant may seek a partition and put the proceeds in trust with the income paid to the life tenant.

   c) **Renunciation of Life Estate:** If a life tenant renounces his interest in a life estate, the future interest immediately goes to the remaindermen.

B. Future Interests: A future interest gives the holder the right, or possibility of future possession of an estate. It is a present legally protected right in property.

1. **Reversionary Interests**

   a) **Possibilities of Reverter and Rights of Entry:** supra.

   b) **Reversion:** If a grantor conveys less than she owns, the remaining is a reversion. Its holder can sue for waste and for tortious damage to the reversionary interest (e.g. "to B for life"; A has a reversion). They are not subject to the Rule Against Perpetuities ("RAP").

2. **Remainder:** A remainder is a future interest that becomes possessory on the natural expiration of the preceding estate created by the same instrument – not before and not after a gap in time.

   a) **Indefeasibly Vested Remainder:** An indefeasibly vested remainder must be given to an existing and ascertained person, and cannot be subject to a condition precedent, nor can the remainder be taken away.

b) **Vested Remainder Subject to Open:** This is created in a class of persons, of which at least one member is known, but others may be added to the class.

c) **Vested Remainder Subject to Total Divestment:** A vested remainder subject to total divestment is a vested remainder subject to a condition subsequent and can thus be taken away.

d) **Contingent Remainder:** This is when the identity of the person to take possession is uncertain, or the fact the person will actually take possession is uncertain.

   (1) **Subject to Condition Precedent:** A condition precedent is an event or state of affairs that must be present or satisfied before the remainderman has a right to possession.

   (2) **Unborn or Unascertained Persons:** A remainder given to an unborn or unascertained person, is contingent because no one can take possession if the preceding estate ends until the remainderman is ascertained.

   (3) **Destructibility of Contingent Remainders:** Under common law, if a contingent remainder does not vest by the time the preceding estate is terminated, it is destroyed.

      (a) **Modern Jurisdictions:** Modern jurisdictions have abolished the destruction rule. C's interest would be converted to an executory interest upon B's death because it will divest A's reversionary estate when C turns 21.

      (b) **Doctrine of Merger:** Under common law, a contingent remainder is destroyed when one person acquires all of the present and future interests in land, except a contingent remainder.

   (4) **Rule in Shelley's Case:** If an instrument created a life estate in A and gave the remainder to A's heirs, common law did not recognize the remainder. A took the life estate and remainder.

   (5) **Doctrine of Worthier Title:** Any remainder in the grantor's heirs becomes a reversion in the grantor.

e) **Executory Interests:** Executory interests are future interests in a third party that will be triggered on the happening of a specified event. They can be "shifting" – previous interest was held by the grantor – or "springing" – the previous interest was held by someone other than the grantor.

   (1) **Springing:** A to B and his heirs when B marries C. B has a springing executory interest because it divests the grantor's estate.

   (2) **Shifting:** A to B for life, then to C, but if C predeceases B, then to D and his heirs. D has a shifting executory interest because it divests a transferee's preceding estate.

f) **Transferability of Remainders and Executory Interests:** Vested remainders are fully transferable, descendible and devisable. Contingent remainders and executory interests are descendible and devisable.

g) **Class Gifts:** A "class" is a group of persons having a common characteristic.

   (1) **When the Class Closes:** The class closes when any member of the class is entitled to her share of the class gift.

   (2) **Survivorship:** Generally, descendants of a deceased class member do not share in the gift unless it references descendants or heirs.

C. **Rule Against Perpetuities:** This limits an owner's power to control future dispositions of the property by stating that any present or future interest in property is invalid if it does not vest within 21 years after some life in being at the creation of the interest.

1. **When the Period Begins to Run:** In a will, the period begins to run at the time of death. In a deed, the period begins to run upon delivery. In an irrevocable trust, the period begins to run at the time of creation.

2. **Must Vest:** An interest vests when it becomes possessory or an indefeasibly vested remainder, or a vested remainder subject to total divestment. If there is any possibility that it could vest beyond the period, it is void.

3. **Lives in Being:** Unless other measuring lives are specified, any life of an identifiable person alive at the time the interest was created can be used.

4. **Exemptions from the Rule:** The rule applies to contingent remainders, executory interests, vested remainders subject to open (class gifts), options to purchase (not attached to a leasehold), rights of first refusal and powers of appointment. It does not apply to grantor's interests (reversion, possibility of reverter, rights of entry).

5. **Applications of the Rule**

   a) **Age Contingency Beyond 21 in Open Class:** A gift to an open class conditioned on members surviving beyond age 21 violates the RAP (e.g. To X for life, then to his children who attain 25).

   b) **Unborn Widow or Widower:** A gift to an unborn widow or widower violates RAP because a person's widow is not determined until his death and the widow may not be in existence at the time of the gift.

   c) **Administrative Contingency:** "To my issue surviving at the time my estate is distributed" is invalid, as the estate might not be distributed within 21 years.

   d) **Options and Rights of First Refusal:** An option to purchase, or right of first refusal that may be exercised after life plus 21 years is void. Exception: RAP does not apply to options to purchase held by the current lessee.

   e) **Class Gifts**

      (1) **Bad-as-to-One, Bad-as-to-All:** If the interest of any class member may vest after the perpetuities period, the whole class gift fails.

      (2) **Gift to Subclass Exception**: Each gift to a subclass is treated as a separate gift under RAP.

      (3) **Per Capita Gift Exception:** A fixed-amount gift to each member of class is judged as a separate gift, not a class gift.

D. **The Rule Against Alienation:** Generally, any restriction on the sale or transferability of property forever, or for an extremely long period of time, is void. There are three types of restraints of alienation: (i) disability restraints, where the grant states that a transfer by the grantee is ineffective; (ii) forfeiture restraints, under which a grantee forfeits his interest if he attempts to transfer it; and (iii) promissory restraints, under which an attempted transfer is a breach of the covenant.

1. **Disabling Restraints on Legal Interests are Void:** A disability restraint on any type of legal interest (fee simple, life estate) is void.

2. **Absolute Restraints on Fee Simple are Void:** All absolute restraints on the alienation of fee simple estates are void.

3. **Valid Restraints on Alienation:** (i) forfeiture and promissory restraints on life estates; (ii) forfeiture restraints on transferability on future interests; (iii) reasonable restrictions on

commercial transactions; (iv) rights of first refusal; and (v) restrictions on assignment and sublets of leaseholds.

E. **Concurrent Estates:** More than one person may hold an estate in land at the same time. All persons have the right to the enjoyment and possession of the land.

1. **Joint Tenancy:** In a joint tenancy, each individual shares equal ownership of the property and has the equal, undivided right to keep or dispose of the property.
    a) **Creation:** The interests of joint tenants must be equal in every way.
    b) **Severance of the Right of Survivorship**
        (1) **Inter Vivos Conveyance:** A joint tenancy is destroyed if a joint tenant conveys his or her interest; the transferee holds a tenancy in common.
            (a) **Judgment Liens:** Judgment liens do not sever the joint tenancy until sold at foreclosure.
            (b) **Mortgages:** A mortgage is a lien on title and will not sever a joint tenancy. The joint tenancy turns into a tenancy in common if the mortgage is foreclosed upon and the property is sold.
            (c) **Leases:** There is a split among states as to whether a lease will sever a joint tenancy.
            (d) **Testamentary Disposition:** A testamentary disposition has no effect because the testator's interest vanishes at her death and the interest passes to the other joint tenants.
            (e) **Murder:** Some state statutes provide for a constructive trust on one joint tenant's interest when she murders the other.
2. **Tenancy by the Entirety:** A tenancy by the entirety is a marital estate with the right of survivorship. Under common law, it arises presumptively in any conveyance to a husband or wife.
3. **Tenancy in Common:** A tenancy in common is a concurrent estate where the tenants are each entitled to possession and enjoyment of the whole, but there is no right of survivorship and tenants can hold different interests in the property.
4. **Rights and Duties of Co-Tenants**
    a) **Possession:** Each co-tenant has the right to possess all portions of the property but no co-tenant has the right to exclusively possess any portion.
    b) **Rents and Profits:** A co-tenant can keep profits from her own use of the property absent an agreement to the contrary. She must share any net rents from third parties and net profits from exploitations of the land, such as mining, with the other co-tenants.
    c) **Effect of One Concurrent Owner's Encumbering the Property:** A joint-tenant or tenant in common may only encumber her own interests.
    d) **Remedy of Partition:** Any co-tenant has a right to demand that the property be partitioned and split among the tenants.
5. **Expenses for Preservation of Property – Contribution:**
    a) **Repairs:** A co-tenant who pays more than her pro rata share of necessary repairs is entitled to contribution.
    b) **Improvements:** No co-tenant has a duty to improve the property and there is no right of contribution for improvements.

c) **Taxes and Mortgages:** A co-tenant is entitled to contribution for taxes, or mortgage payments paid on the entire property.

6. **Duty of Fair Dealing:** Co-tenants enjoy a confidential relationship. Acts by one co-tenant are presumed to be on behalf of other co-tenants.

VI. CONVEYANCING

A. Land Sale Contracts

1. **Statute of Frauds:** A contract for the sale of land must be in writing and contain the signature of the party to be charged and the essential terms.

2. **Doctrine of Equitable Conversion:** Once both parties sign a contract, the buyer is the owner of the property. The seller's interest is considered personal property. Legal title to the property, which remains with the seller, is considered to be held in trust for the buyer.

   a) **Risk of Loss:** If the property is destroyed (without fault) before closing, the majority rule places the risk on the buyer.

   b) **Passage of Title on Death:** If one party dies before the contract is completed, seller's interest passes as personal property and buyer's interest passes as real property.

3. **Marketable Title:** Every contract contains an implied warranty that the seller will provide marketable title (title reasonably free from doubt) at closing.

   a) **Defects in Record Chain of Title:** Title may be unmarketable if there is a defect in the chain of title.

   b) **Encumbrances:** Encumbrances such as mortgages, liens, and restrictive covenants generally render title unmarketable.

   c) **Zoning Restrictions:** Zoning restrictions do not affect marketability; existing violations of a zoning ordinance do.

   d) **Time of Marketability:** If the seller has agreed to furnish marketable title on the date of closing, the buyer cannot rescind before then on grounds that the seller's title is not marketable. **Remedy If Title Not Marketable:** If title is unmarketable, the buyer must notify the seller and give him a reasonable amount of time to cure the defect. If the seller fails to do so, the buyer may rescind the contract, seek damages, specific performance with abatement, or file a lawsuit to quiet title.

4. **Time of Performance:** A closing date is not binding as courts will presume that time is not "of the essence" unless the parties agreed otherwise.

   a) **Liability:** If time is of the essence, a party who does not tender performance on the closing date breaches the contract and may not enforce it. Regardless of whether time is of the essence or not, a party who tenders late is liable for incidental losses.

5. **Tender of Performance:** The buyer's obligation to pay and the seller's obligation to convey are concurrent conditions. Thus, neither party is in breach until the other tenders performance even if after the closing date.

6. **Remedies for Breach of Sales Contract:** The non-breaching party is entitled to damages or specific performance.

   a) **Liquidated Damages:** If the buyer does not perform, the seller may keep a deposit of earnest money as liquidated damages.

7. **Seller's Liabilities for Defective Property**

   a) **Warranty of Fitness or Quality--New Construction Only:** Contracts for the sale of real property carry no implied warranty of quality, or fitness for purpose.

b) **Sale of Existing Land and Buildings--Liability for Defects:** The seller of an existing building may be liable to a purchaser for some defects.

(1) **Misrepresentation (Fraud):** The seller is liable for defects about which he knowingly or negligently made a false statement of fact to the buyer.

(2) **Active Concealment:** The seller is liable for defects if he takes steps to conceal the defects.

(3) **Failure to Disclose:** Most states will hold a seller liable for not disclosing defects if: (i) he knows or has reason to know of the defect; (ii) the defect is not apparent to the buyer upon ordinary inspection; and (iii) the defect is of a serious nature so that the buyer would likely reconsider if known. If the property is a personal residence, the defect is dangerous, or the seller created the defect, or made a failed attempt to repair it, a court is more likely to hold the seller liable.

(4) **Negligence:** A person may sue a builder for negligence in performing a building contract. Some courts permit the ultimate vendee to sue the builder despite lack of privity.

c) **Disclaimers of Liability:** A general disclaimer in the sales contract will not relieve a seller from liability for fraud, concealment, or failure to disclose.

8. **Real Estate Brokers:** While a real estate broker is an agent of the seller, she should disclose material information if she has actual knowledge.

B. Deeds – Form and Content: Deeds transfer title to an interest in real property.

1. **Formalities:** Must be in writing, signed by the grantor, and identify parties and land.

2. **Defective Deeds:** A void deed will be set aside even if the property has passed to a bona fide purchaser. A voidable deed will be set aside only if the property has not passed to a bona fide purchaser.

a) **Void Deeds:** A deed is void if forged, never delivered, or obtained by fraud.

b) **Voidable Deeds:** A deed is voidable if executed by minors or incapacitated persons, or obtained through fraud in the inducement, duress, undue influence, mistake, or breach of fiduciary duty.

3. **Fraudulent Conveyances:** Even if a deed complies with the required formalities, the grantor's creditors may set it aside if it was made: (i) with an actual intent to hinder, delay, or defraud a creditor; or (ii) without receiving a reasonably equivalent value in exchange for the transfer and the debtor was insolvent.

4. **Description of Land Conveyed:** A description of the land only has to provide a good lead to the identity of the property. If a court finds the description is too indefinite, the grantor keeps title, but the court may order that the deed be reformed.

5. **Boundary Cases:** If there is a right-of-way or water boundary, the title to land presumptively passes in the center. A slow and imperceptible change will change the legal boundary; an accretion (slow deposit of soil on land abutting water) belongs to the abutting owner. Avulsion (sudden change of water-course) will not change ownership rights. Fixed boundaries are also not changed by the encroachment of water.

6. **Reformation of Deeds:** A court will reform a deed if it does not represent the parties' agreement due to: (i) a mutual mistake; (ii) a scrivener's error; or (iii) a unilateral mistake.

C. Delivery and Acceptance: A deed is ineffective until it is delivered and accepted. A deed to a dead person is void even if the grantor did not know the grantee had died. The grantee retains title.

1. **Delivery:** Delivery may be satisfied by manual delivery, notarized acknowledgment by the grantor, recording, or anything else showing the grantor's intent to deliver.

   a) **Title Passes Upon Delivery:** Delivery cannot be canceled or taken back.

2. **Retention of Interest by Grantor or Conditional Delivery:** If the grantor retains control or interest (right to revoke), the grantor shows a lack of intent to pass title.

   a) **Express Condition of Grantor's Death:** A properly executed and delivered deed that provides that title will not pass until the grantor's death is valid and gives the grantee a future interest.

   b) **Conditions Not Contained in Deed:** If a deed is complete on its face when delivered, any oral condition is disregarded and delivery is absolute.

   c) **Where Grantor Gives Deed to Third Party:** A grantor may make delivery conditional when giving the deed to a third party.

   d) **Transfer to Third Party with No Conditions:** A grantor who gives a deed to a third party with instructions to give it to the grantee makes a valid delivery.

   e) **Transfer to Third Party with Conditions (Commercial Transaction):** When a grantor gives a deed to a third party with instructions to give it to the grantee when a certain condition occurs, he has made a valid conditional delivery.

      (1) **Grantor's Right to Recover Deed:** A grantor can revoke a deed only if: (i) the condition has not yet occurred, and (ii) there is no enforceable written contract to deliver the deed.

      (2) **Breach of Escrow Conditions:** If a grantee wrongfully acquires the deed from the escrow holder before the condition occurs, title does not pass to the grantee.

      (3) **Relation Back Doctrine:** Title generally passes when the condition occurs. It may relate back to the time the grantor gave the deed to the third party when justice requires and there is an enforceable contract to convey.

   f) **Transfer to Third Party with Conditions (Donative Transaction):** When a grantor gives a deed to a third party to give to a donee upon the occurrence of a specified condition, the deed is not revocable unless the condition is the grantor's death, which gives the donee a springing executory interest and is revocable unless there is an enforceable contract to convey.

3. **Acceptance:** Once the grantee accepts the deed, delivery is complete.

   a) **Dedication:** A dedication must be accepted for such use by a formal resolution, approval of map or plat, or actual assumption of maintenance or improvements.

D. **Covenants for Title and Estoppel by Deed:** There are three types of deeds: a general warranty deed, a special warranty deed and a quitclaim deed.

1. **Covenants in General Warranty Deed**

   a) **Covenant of Seisin**: The grantor covenants that she has both title and possession of the estate she purports to convey.

   b) **Covenant of Right to Convey:** The grantor covenants that she has the authority to make the grant, which is satisfied by title alone.

   c) **Covenant Against Encumbrances:** The grantor covenants there are no physical (encroachment) or title (mortgage) encumbrances.

   d) **Covenant for Quiet Enjoyment:** The grantor covenants that no third party will disturb the grantee's possession by a lawful claim of title.

e) **Covenant of Warranty:** The grantor covenants to defend against a third party's reasonable claims of title and compensate the grantee for any loss sustained by a claim of superior title.

f) **Covenant for Further Assurances:** The grantor covenants to perform acts reasonably necessary to perfect the title.

(1) **Breach of the Covenants:** The covenants of seisin, right to convey, or encumbrances are breached, if at all, when the property is conveyed. Quiet enjoyment, warranty and further assurances are future covenants that are breached when the grantee's possession is disturbed.

(2) **Damages and Remote Grantees:** If the last grantee in a line of successive conveyances by general warranty deed is evicted by lawful claim of title, he may sue anyone up the line. Some states allow him to recover to the extent of consideration received by a defendant-covenantor. Other states limit recovery to the lesser of what he paid, or what the defendant-covenantor received.

2. **Statutory Special Warranty Deed:** The word "grant" in a deed implies that the grantor has not conveyed the same estate, or any interest therein to anyone other than the grantee, and that the estate is free from encumbrances.

3. **Quitclaim Deeds:** When a grantor transfers property by a quitclaim deed, he releases whatever interest he has and quits any right to claim the property.

4. **Estoppel by Deed:** If the grantor purports to convey an estate in property that she does not own, her subsequent acquisition of the estate will inure to the benefit of the grantee. This doctrine does not usually apply to quitclaim deeds.

a) **Rights of Subsequent Purchasers:** If the grantor transfers her after-acquired title to a bona fide purchaser ("BFP") for value, the BFP will prevail over original grantee.

b) **Remedies of Grantee:** The original grantee can either accept title or sue for damages for breach of covenant.

E. **Recording Acts:** Recording acts protect all bona fide purchasers from secret interests.

Notice Statutes: A subsequent BFP with no actual or constructive knowledge prevails over a prior grantee who failed to record his interest.

Race-Notice Statutes: A subsequent BFP is protected only if she records before the earlier grantee and lacks notice of prior unrecorded claims.

Race Statutes: Whoever records first wins, regardless of notice.

1. **Without Notice:** The purchaser had no actual, constructive (record), or inquiry notice of a prior conveyance when she paid consideration and received the interest.

2. **Actual Notice:** A grantee may obtain notice from any source.

3. **Record Notice--Chain of Title:** Recordation gives prospective subsequent grantees constructive notice of recorded instruments. A subsequent purchaser is charged with notice of only those conveyances that are recorded and appear in the chain of title.

a) **Wild Deeds:** A "wild deed" is a recorded deed that is not connected to the chain of title. A subsequent purchaser cannot have constructive notice.

b) **Deed in Chain Referring to Instrument Outside Chain:** A reference to another instrument, regardless of whether it is recorded, or in the chain of title, in a recorded document that is in the chain of title may impart constructive notice.

c) **Restrictive Covenants--Deeds from Common Grantor:** Courts are split on whether deeds are in the chain of title of a subject lot if they are for adjacent lots or lots in the same subdivision, executed by the same grantor, and contain restrictions and easements involving the subject lot.

4. **Inquiry Notice:** In certain circumstances, a purchaser must make reasonable inquiries and will be charged with whatever an inquiry would have revealed.

5. **Valuable Consideration:** To be protected by a recording statute, the subsequent grantee must have paid consideration of some pecuniary value.

6. **Those Protected by Recording Acts:** Only BFPs are protected from the claims of a prior transferee under "notice" and "race-notice" statutes.

   a) **Purchasers:** All statutes protect purchasers. Mortgagees for value are purchasers. Donees, heirs and devisees are not protected.

   b) **Judgment Creditors:** A judgment creditor generally is not protected by the recording statute against a prior unrecorded conveyance by the defendant.

   c) **Purchaser from Heir:** A purchaser from an heir, or devisee of the record owner is protected against prior unrecorded conveyances of the record owner.

   d) **Transferees from Bona Fide Purchaser--Shelter Rule:** A person who takes from a BFP will prevail against any interest the transferor-BFP would have prevailed against.

   e) **Recorder's Mistakes:** An instrument is recorded when the purchaser files it with the recorder's office, regardless of whether it is thereafter properly indexed. A subsequent purchaser is charged with notice of a mis-indexed instrument, but has a cause of action against the recorder's office.

   f) **Effect of Recording Unacknowledged Instrument:** An unacknowledged instrument is not entitled to recordation and it does not give a subsequent purchaser constructive notice.

F. **Crops (Emblements):** Generally, the conveyance of land includes the conveyance of all crops growing on it. There are exceptions for: (i) crops that have already been harvested or severed; and (ii) crops planted by a tenant during the tenancy.

VII. RIGHTS INCIDENTAL TO OWNERSHIP OF LAND (NATURAL RIGHTS)

A. **Generally:** An owner of real property has the exclusive right to use and possess the property's surface, airspace and soil.

B. **Rights to Lateral and Subjacent Support of Land**

1. **Lateral Support:** Ownership of land comes with the right to lateral support in the land's natural state by adjoining land.

2. **Subjacent Support:** An underground occupant of land, such as a mining company, must support the surface and buildings that existed when the subjacent estate was created.

C. **Water Rights:** Courts apply different rules to watercourses, ground water, and surface waters.

1. **Watercourses (Streams, Rivers, and Lakes):** The two doctrines courts use when determining allocation of water in watercourses are the riparian doctrine and the prior appropriation doctrine:

   a) **Riparian Doctrine:** Those who own the land bordering the watercourse own the water. Riparian rights attach to all contiguous tracts held by the same owner as long as the land abuts the water. Riparian owners can use the water only in connection with the riparian parcel.

(1) **Natural Flow Theory:** A riparian owner can be enjoined from using the water in a way that substantially, or materially decreases the quantity, quality, or velocity.

(2) **Reasonable Use Theory:** All riparians have a right of "reasonable use" of the water and one owner cannot be enjoined from use unless that use substantially interferes with the use of other riparian owners.

(3) **Natural Flow Theory vs. Artificial Use:** Natural uses prevail over artificial uses.

b) **Prior Appropriation Doctrine:** Individuals acquire rights by actual use. Appropriative rights are determined by priority of beneficial use. The first person to use, or divert, water for beneficial use can acquire rights to the water. He can lose it by abandoning it.

2. **Ground Water (Percolating Water):** Courts use four doctrines when determining rights in diffuse underground water recovered through wells:

a) **Absolute Ownership Doctrine:** The owner of overlying land owns the water and can take all the water she wishes for any purpose, including export.

b) **Reasonable Use Doctrine:** The overlying landowner owns the water but may only take it for export if doing so does not harm other owners who have rights in the same aquifer.

c) **Correlative Rights Doctrine:** Owners of overlying land own the underground water basin as joint tenants and each can take a reasonable amount for his own use.

d) **Appropriative Rights Doctrine:** The rights to the ground water are determined by priority.

3. **Surface Waters:** A landowner can use surface water within her boundaries for any purpose she desires. Questions on surface water usually concern liability for changing natural flow by dikes, drains, etc. Whether the landowner is liable depends on the theory the state follows:

a) **Natural Flow (Civil Law) Theory:** Owners cannot alter natural drainage patterns.

b) **Common Enemy Theory:** Owner can take protective measures to get rid of the water.

c) **Reasonable Use Theory:** Court balances utility of the use against gravity of harm.

d) The above theories apply to redirecting surface water. A landowner can capture (by a dam, or in barrels) as much surface water as he wishes and divert it for any purpose on or off the land. Owners below have no cause of action unless the landowner maliciously diverted the water.

D. Right in Airspace: A landowner does not have an exclusive right to airspace above a parcel, but she is entitled to freedom from excessive noise.

E. Right to Exclude: The possessor of real property has the right to exclude others. His remedies for invasions include actions for:

1. Trespass (land invaded by tangible physical object);
2. Private nuisance (land invaded by intangibles such as odors or noise);
3. Continuing trespass (land repeatedly invaded by trespasser); and
4. Ejectment or unlawful detainer to remove a trespasser or tenant.

VIII. SECURITY INTERESTS IN LAND

A. Types of Interest

1. **Mortgage:** On default, the lender can realize on the mortgaged real estate only by having a judicial foreclosure sale.
2. **Deed of Trust:** Trustor transfers a deed of trust to a third-party trustee, who is usually closely connected to the lender (the beneficiary).
3. **Installment Land Contract:** An installment purchaser obtains legal title only when he pays the contract price in full.
4. **Absolute Deed:** An absolute deed conveys an unrestricted title to a property.
5. **Sale-Leaseback:** A landowner may sell a property and then lease it back from the purchaser for a period of time with the proceeds.

B. Transfers By Mortgagee and Mortgagor

1. **Transfer by Mortgagee**

   a) **Transfer of Mortgage Without Note:** Some states hold that a note is automatically transferred with the mortgage, unless the mortgagee-transferor expressly reserves the rights to the note. In these states, the transferee can file an equitable action to compel a transfer of the note. In others, a mortgage without note is void.

   b) **Transfer of Note Without Mortgage:** The mortgage will automatically follow with a separate assignment unless the mortgagee-transferee expressly reserves the rights to the mortgage.

   c) **Methods of Transferring the Note:** The mortgagor-transferor may transfer the note by endorsing it and delivering it to the transferee, or a separate document.

2. **Transfer by Mortgagor--Grantee Takes Subject to Mortgage:** A grantee of mortgaged property takes the property subject to the mortgage.

   a) **Assumption:** A grantee who signs an assumption agreement becomes primarily liable to the lender; the original mortgagor is secondarily liable as a surety. Once a grantee has assumed a mortgage, any modification of the obligation by the grantee and mortgagee discharges the original mortgagor of all liability.

   b) **Due-on-Sale Clauses:** Due-on-sale clauses stipulate that the lender may demand full payment of the loan if the mortgagor transfers any interest in the property without the lender's consent.

3. **Possession Before Foreclosure:** Upon default, the mortgagee may be able take possession, or begin receiving the rents before foreclosing.

   a) **Theories of Title:** Whether the mortgagee can take possession before foreclosing depends on the state. Most states follow either the title, or the lien theory:

      (1) **The Lien Theory:** The mortgagee is the holder of a security interest and the mortgagor is the owner of the land until foreclosure. Thus, the mortgagee may not take possession before foreclosure.

      (2) **The Title Theory:** The mortgagee has legal title until the mortgage has been satisfied or foreclosed and the mortgagee is entitled to possession upon demand at any time.

      (3) **The Intermediate Theory:** The mortgagor has legal title until default. Upon default, the mortgagee has legal title and may demand possession when the mortgagor defaults.

b) **Mortgagor Consent and Abandonment:** The mortgagee may take possession if the mortgagor consents or abandons the property.

c) **Risks of Mortgagee in Possession:** Most mortgagees do not take possession because there are liability risks involving the duty to account for rents, the duty to manage the property in a prudent manner and potential tort liability for those injured on the property.

d) **Receiverships:** Most mortgagees attempt to intercept rents before foreclosure by asking the court to appoint a receiver to manage the property, which courts will generally do upon a showing: (i) that waste is occurring; (ii) that the value of the property is inadequate to secure the debt; and (iii) that the mortgagor is insolvent.

4. **Foreclosure:** Almost all states require foreclosure by sale.

a) **Redemption in Equity:** The mortgagor may redeem the property by paying the amount due any time before the foreclosure sale. This right cannot be waived.

b) **Statutory Redemption:** About half of the states allow the mortgagor to redeem the property for some fixed period (e.g. six months) after a foreclosure sale.

5. **Priorities:** Priority is usually determined by reference to the time it was placed on the property. Foreclosure generally destroys all junior interests.

a) **Modification of Priority:** Priority among mortgages generally follows the order in which they were placed on the property. This priority may be changed by: (i) the operation of a recording statute if a prior mortgagee fails to record; (ii) a subordination agreement between a senior and junior mortgagee; (iii) a purchase money mortgage; (iv) the modification of a senior mortgage; or (v) the granting of optional future advances by a mortgagee with notice of a junior lien.

b) **Purchase Money Mortgages:** A purchase money mortgage ("PMM") is a mortgage given by the seller in exchange for funds used to purchase the property. PMMs have priority over non-PMMs executed around the same time. A seller's PMM has priority over a third-party's PMM. If there are two third-party PMMs, priority is determined by whichever came first.

6. **Proceeds of Sale:** Proceeds of a sale are first applied to the expenses of the sale, attorney fees, and court costs; then applied to the principal and accrued interest on the foreclosed loan next to any other junior interests in the order of their priority.

7. **Deficiency Judgments:** If the sale proceeds do not satisfy the mortgage debt, the mortgagee retains a personal cause of action against the mortgagor.

C. **Installment Land Contracts:** Most installment contracts provide that the vendor's remedy for default is forfeiture rather than foreclosure. To avoid such a harsh result, courts will use the following theories:

1. **Equity of Redemption:** Purchaser has a grace period in which to pay the accelerated full balance of the contract and keep the land.

2. **Restitution:** A number of courts grant a forfeiture, but require the vendor to refund to the purchaser any amount by which his payments exceed the vendor's damages.

3. **Treat as a Mortgage:** A few courts treat installment contracts as mortgages and require a judicial foreclosure sale.

4. **Waiver:** A vendor's pattern of accepting late payments may waive the right of strict performance.

5. **Election of Remedies:** The vendor can choose only one remedy.

REMEDIES PRIMER

Full discussions of these topics can be found in the respective comprehensive substantive law outlines.

I. OVERVIEW

A. Determine the area of *substantive law* (may be more than one, normally torts, property or contracts).

B. Make sure the plaintiff has a case and *relief* is needed.

C. Determine *appropriate* remedies (based on available remedies for that substantive area of law).

1. Discuss **legal** remedies first;
2. Discuss **restitutionary** remedies second;
3. Discuss **pure equitable** remedies last.

II. TORT REMEDIES

A. General Tort Approach

1. Has the **plaintiff** been/is currently being **injured**?
Answer: Main issue is likely to be compensatory damages.

2. Has the **defendant** derived an **unjust enrichment**?
Answer: Main issue is likely to be restitutionary damages.

3. Does the **plaintiff** want the **property back**?
Answer: Main issues are likely to be replevin, ejectment, specific performance.

4. Does the **plaintiff** need an **injunction**?
Answer: Main issues are likely to be preliminary, temporary, and permanent injunctive relief.

B. Damages and Equitable Remedies

1. **Compensatory Damages:** The plaintiff is entitled to compensatory damages to put her in the position she would have been had the wrong not occurred. The plaintiff must show:

   a) *Causation:* the injury must have been caused by the tortious act (**"but for…" test**, i.e., "but for the tortious action, the injury would not have happened");

   b) *Foreseeability:* the injury must have been foreseeable at the time of the tortious act ("proximate cause"); and

   c) *Certainty:* the damages cannot be too speculative.

      (1) **Non-economic damages**: (general pain and suffering, disfigurement) – certainty requirement does not apply. Only required for economic losses (special damages).
      (2) **Future damages:** *"all or nothing rule"*- for **future** damages, the plaintiff must show that the damages "are more likely to happen than not." Failure to demonstrate this will result in no award.
      (3) Discuss probability of future event's occurrence
      (4) Lost profits
      (5) Historical records help – i.e., proves lost future business
      (6) Medical expenses
      (7) **Unavoidability:** The plaintiff must take **reasonable** steps to mitigate the damage. Damages limited to those that could not reasonably have been avoided.

2. **Nominal damages:** Where the plaintiff has no actual injury, the court may award nominal damages to serve to establish or to vindicate the plaintiff's rights (necessary if the plaintiff is seeking punitive damages but she has not incurred compensatory damages).

3. **Punitive damages:** Where the plaintiff's injury results from *"willful, wanton, or malicious conduct"* on the part of the defendant, the court may award punitive damages to punish the defendant.

   a) The plaintiff must first have been awarded compensatory, nominal, or restitutionary damages.

   b) *Calculation:* must be relatively proportional to actual damages. U.S. Supreme Court holding: *single digit multiple* of actual damages unless the defendant's conduct is extreme.

4. **Restitution:** Where the defendant has been **unjustly enriched**, the court may award damages based on the benefit to the defendant.

   a) *Calculation:* The amount is calculated based on the value of the benefit. However, where both compensatory and restitutionary damages are available, the plaintiff cannot get both. Instead, she must make an election of the two. Generally, the plaintiff should be awarded the larger sum of the two.

   b) No restitution for **encroachment or nuisance.**

5. **Replevin:** Action to recover possession of specific personal property.

   a) *Must show:* (i) The plaintiff has a right to possession; and (ii) There is wrongful withholding by the defendant.

   b) *Timing:* As long as the defendant is still in possession, the plaintiff can recover the chattel before trial. To do so the plaintiff will have to post a bond. However, the defendant may defeat an immediate recovery by posting a re-delivery bond, through which the defendant can keep the chattel until after the trial.

   c) *Loss of use:* Almost always **coupled with damages** for lost use. Or for benefit to the defendant during time of wrongful withholding.

   d) *Bona fide sale:* No recovery if sale to a bona fide purchaser.

6. **Ejectment:** Action to recover possession of real property (land).

   a) *Must show:* (i) The plaintiff has a *right to possession*; and (ii) There is a *wrongful withholding* by the defendant. This is only available against the defendant who has possession of the property.

   b) Usually coupled with damages for *lost use of the benefit* during the wrongful withholding. Note, ejectment does not give rise to punitive damages.

7. **Constructive Trust:** Equitable remedy imposed by the courts when the retention of property by the defendant (wrongdoer) would result in **unjust enrichment**. The defendant serves as "trustee" and must return the property to the plaintiff.

   a) *Legal remedies* must be inadequate (e.g., the defendant is insolvent or the property is unique).

   b) *Note:* ***Land*** *is always unique.* Personal property is typically not unique unless it: (i) Is one of a kind or very rare; or (ii) Has personal significance to buyer.

   c) *Tracing:* The plaintiff can follow the property to whatever form it takes, as long as the trust res can be identified.

   d) *Bona fide purchasers* prevail over the plaintiff.

   e) The plaintiff prevails over *unsecured creditors.*

8. **Equitable Liens:** Where the defendant has improperly acquired title to a property, an equitable lien allows the court to order an immediate sale of the property, and the monies received will go to the plaintiff.

   a) Must show: (i) The defendant misappropriated the plaintiff's property, creating a debt or obligation to pay; (ii) The plaintiff's property can be **traced** to property held by the defendant; and, (iii) Retention by the defendant would result in **unjust enrichment**.

   b) Sale price and damages: If the proceeds from the sale are less than the **fair market value** of the property when it was taken, a **deficiency judgment** will issue for the difference and can be used against the defendant's other assets.

   c) Where misappropriated money is used to *improve property* (e.g., house remodel), only an equitable lien is available.

   d) Same rules as constructive trusts: Tracing allowed. *Bona fide* purchaser prevails.

9. **Injunctive relief**

   a) **Temporary Injunctive Relief:** To recover temporary injunctive relief, the plaintiff must meet a two-part test:

      (1) **Irreparable Injury:** The plaintiff must show that without the injunction, she will incur irreparable injury while waiting for a full trial on the merits.

         (a) **Balancing Test:** Harm to the plaintiff if injunction is denied v. harm to the defendant if injunction is granted.

         (b) Where the defendant created the hardship – even if substantial – balance likely to weigh in the plaintiff's favor.

      (2) **Likelihood of Success:** The plaintiff must show that she has a strong likelihood of success on the merits. The court will look to the probability of this success.

         (a) This is not an inquiry on success of obtaining a permanent injunction.

         (b) The court should also impose a bond requirement on the plaintiff to reimburse the defendant if the injunction injured him/her and the plaintiff does not succeed.

   b) **Permanent Injunctive Relief:** The plaintiff must meet a five-part test:

      [**I** **P**ut **F**ive **B**ucks **D**own]

      (1) **Inadequate Legal Remedy:** Money damages may be too speculative; the defendant may be insolvent; the sheriff may be unable or unwilling to enforce a replevin or ejectment action.

      (2) **Property Interest/Protectable Interest of the Plaintiff:**

         (a) Traditional view: equity will grant relief only where there is a protectable property right involved.

         (b) Modern view: any protectable interest will suffice.

      (3) **Feasibility of Enforcement:** Only an issue with mandatory injunction. Enforcement problems may stem from: (i) the difficulty of supervision; or (ii) concern with effectively ensuring compliance.

      (4) **Balancing of Hardships:** The plaintiff's benefit v. the defendant's hardship + the public's hardship. However, if the defendant's conduct was willful, there is no balancing.

(5) **Defenses**

(a) **Laches:** Where there has been an unreasonable lapse of time between when the plaintiff learned of the injury and when the plaintiff filed the lawsuit, and that lapse of time is prejudicial to the defendant, laches will cut off the right to injunctive relief (but not monetary damages).

(b) **Unclean hands:** The person seeking equitable relief must not be guilty of any improper conduct that is related to the lawsuit.

(c) **Impossibility:** It would be impossible for the defendant to carry out the terms of the injunction.

(d) **Free speech:** Injunction may be denied on free speech grounds.

c) **Injunctive Relief Issues**

(1) **Crimes:** Equity will not enjoin crimes.

(a) Recharacterize as a tort.

(b) Exception for nuisance/public nuisance and partial exception for crime that is also a tort.

(2) **Who is Bound?** Parties, agent/employees, and others acting in concert with prior notice.

(3) **Erroneous Injunctions**: Injunctions must be complied with until modified or dissolved.

(4) **Contempt**: For noncompliance with an injunction:

(a) Civil contempt – to coerce.

i. Fines (money) to coerce;
ii. Imprisonment (the defendant holds keys to the jailhouse door).

(b) Criminal – to punish.

i. Fines (money) to punish;
ii. Imprisonment – remain in jail for set amount of time. Note: constitutional safeguards apply.

(c) No contempt for failing to comply with a monetary judgment, unless it concerns child support.

(5) **Encroachment:** Restitution is not allowed. Injunctions allowed.

(6) **Nuisance:** Consider traditional damages, permanent damages, and past damages. Restitution is not allowed.

III. CONTRACT REMEDIES

A. Overall Contract Approach

1. Has the **plaintiff** been/is currently being **injured**?
Answer: Main issue is expectation damages.

2. Has the **defendant** derived an **unjust enrichment**?
Answer: Main issue is restitution.

3. Does the **plaintiff** want the **property back**?
Answer: Main issues are replevin, ejectment, constructive trust, equitable lien.

4. Does the **plaintiff** want the contract **performed**?
Answer: Main issue is specific performance.

5. Does the **plaintiff** want the contract **ripped up**?
   Answer: Main issue is rescission.

6. Does the **plaintiff** want the contract **re-written**?
   Answer: Main issue is reformation.

B. Damages and Equitable Remedies

1. **Compensatory Damages (Compensation):** Based on injury to the plaintiff: Requires: (i) causation; (ii) foreseeability (tested at the time of formation); (iii) certainty; (iv) unavoidability (mitigation).

   a) **Consequential Damages:** available for related damages that were foreseeable at the time of formation (e.g., damage to reputation).

   b) **Incidental Damages**: available for "hassle" involved in dealing with breach.

   c) **Seller Breaches a Land Sale Contract:** compensatory damages = out-of-pocket loss or benefit-of-the-bargain.

   d) **Nominal Damages** are also allowed. But, **punitive damages** are not allowed. Note, if the defendant's conduct is willful, characterize as a tort as well, so you can get punitive damages.

   e) **Liquidated Damage** clauses are permissible, if they are **valid.** Must show:

      (1) Damages are difficult to ascertain at the time of contract formation.

      (2) Estimate was a reasonable forecast of what the damages would be. (If liquidated damages are too high, they will be viewed as a penalty.)

      (3) **Result:** if valid → only liquidated damage amount. If invalid → dismiss liquidated damages clause and determine actual damages. However, you cannot recover both compensatory and liquidated damages. But you can get other remedies outside of actual damages, such as specific performance.

2. **Restitution**

   a) **Unenforceable Contract**

      (1) If a contract is **unenforceable** after the plaintiff has performed (e.g., mistake, capacity, illegality), the plaintiff can get restitutionary damages for property/money given to the defendant, or for services rendered for the defendant for the value of the benefit.

      (2) Not necessary to find that the defendant actually benefited, only that the defendant received a benefit. If the value of the services is greater than the contract rate, the plaintiff can still recover that value.

      (3) The plaintiff can get specific property back if it is unique, or the defendant is insolvent.

   b) **Quasi-Contract:** The plaintiff awarded the reasonable value of the defendant's ill-gotten gain, or the difference between the present value of the good, less the value before the benefit conferred by the plaintiff.

   c) **Breach of Contract**

      (1) Where the plaintiff is the non-breaching party:

         (a) The plaintiff may recover restitutionary damages for property/money given to, or services rendered for the defendant for the value of the benefit.

(b) The plaintiff can get the property back if it is unique or the defendant is insolvent.

(2) Where the plaintiff is the breaching party:

(a) Traditional view – **no recovery** allowed.

(b) Modern view – **recovery allowed,** but **limited to contract price** and must be **offset to reflect the defendant's damages.** Cannot be greater than contract rate.

3. **Replevin** - see above, same principles available in contract disputes.

4. **Ejectment** - see above, same principles available in contract disputes.

5. **Constructive Trust** - see above, same principles available in contract disputes.

6. **Equitable Lien** - see above, same principles available in contract disputes.

7. **Specific Performance**

a) Five-part checklist:

(1) **Inadequacy of Legal Remedies:** Damages may be inadequate because: (i) they are speculative, (ii) the defendant is insolvent; (iii) multiple suits are necessary; and (iv) the thing bargained for is unique (tested at the time of litigation, not during contract formation). Where a liquidated damages clause is provided, the legal remedy will be adequate.

(2) **Definite and Certain Terms:** Terms of the contract must be sufficiently certain to constitute a valid contract.

(3) **Feasibility of Enforcement**: Is this possible? Too much court supervision needed?

(4) **Mutuality of Remedy**: Must show the other side can also secure performance. Only an issue where the plaintiff lacks capacity. Court will reject mutuality if it feels secure that the plaintiff can and will perform.

(5) **Lack of Defenses:** Unclean hands; laches; unconscionability; mistake; misrepresentation; equitable conversion (sale to a bona fide purchaser); Statute of Frauds (satisfied if: (i) part performance; (ii) in reliance on contract).

b) Special problems

(1) **Deficiencies Fact Pattern**

(a) Seller as the plaintiff: can enforce contract if the defect is minor. Cannot enforce contract if the defect is major unless the seller can cure the contract before closing.

(b) Buyer as the plaintiff: can enforce the contract even if the defect is major (abatement – court will lower the purchase price to take into account this defect). Cannot enforce the contract if the defect is very major.

(2) **"Time of the Essence" Clause**

(a) Includes forfeiture provision. Equity abhors forfeiture. Avoid forfeiture (and award specific performance), where: (i) loss to the seller is small; (ii) tardiness is de minimus; (iii) waiver – seller has accepted late payments in the past; and (iv) buyer would suffer undue hardship.

(b) Modern trend: courts will give a plaintiff restitutionary relief if specific performance is not granted. But, if buyer has not made even an initial payment – the forfeiture clause will be strictly enforced.

(3) **Equitable Conversion**

(a) Real property interest of the buyer and seller are switched upon execution of the land contract.
(b) Thus, the buyer will be regarded as having the real property interest (the specifically enforceable right to the land).
(c) Seller will be regarded as having the personal property interest (the specifically enforceable right to the money).

(4) **Covenants Not to Compete** (employment contracts/personal services contracts)
(a) Poses enforcement problems.
(b) Can be viewed as involuntary servitude.
(c) Two-part test for validity:
i. The covenant must protect a legitimate interest.
ii. The covenant must be reasonable in both geographical and durational scope.

8. **Rescission**

a) **Equitable Remedy:** Whereby one who is fraudulently induced into entering a contract may rescind the contract.

(1) Two-step analysis: Determine if there are **grounds** for the rescission (improper formation of contract):

(a) Mistake;
(b) Misrepresentation;
(c) Coercion/undue Influence;
(d) Lack of capacity;
(e) Failure of consideration;
(f) Illegality.

(2) What is the mistake?

(a) Mutual mistake of material fact = grounds for rescission;
(b) Mutual mistake of collateral fact ≠ grounds for rescission;
(c) Unilateral mistake ≠ grounds for rescission unless the non-mistaken party knows or should have known of the mistake.

b) **Defenses:** determine if there are **valid defenses:** unclean hands, laches (negligence is not a valid defense).

c) **Special Problems:**

(1) **Timing and Election of Remedies:**

(a) If the plaintiff sues for damages first, rescission is not allowed.
(b) If the plaintiff sues for rescission first, damages are allowed.

(2) **Availability of Restitution:** If a plaintiff, who is entitled to rescission, has previously rendered performance on the contract, she can get compensated for it or get the property back via restitution.

(3) **Legal Rescission:** The plaintiff accomplishes this by her own actions. The plaintiff gives notice and tenders back any consideration received. The plaintiff then sues for restitution for anything given to the defendant.

9. **Reformation**

a) **Generally:** The court may modify a written agreement to conform with the parties' original understanding.

b) **Process:** Three steps are employed:

(1) Determine if there is a **valid contract.**

(2) Determine if there are **grounds** for reformation:

   (a) Mutual mistake;

   (b) Unilateral mistake if the non-mistaken party knows of mistake; or

   (c) Misrepresentation.

(3) Determine if there are **valid defenses**: unclean hands; laches.

TORTS PRIMER

I. INTENTIONAL TORTS TO THE PERSON AND PROPERTY

A. Battery: A battery is: (i) a harmful/offensive contact; (ii) to the plaintiff's person; (iii) intent; and (iv) causation.

1. **Harmful/Offensive Contact:** The reasonable person standard is used in determining whether the contact is harmful or offensive. Socially acceptable contact (i.e., contact that is normally permitted) is not offensive. Non-consensual contact is always considered offensive.
2. **The Plaintiff's Person:** This includes anything connected to the plaintiff and travels through objects (e.g., a rock that has been thrown, a bullet fired from a gun, or poison left for the plaintiff to consume).
3. **Intent:** Intent is established where the defendant desires to produce the forbidden conduct or is substantially certain of the result.
   a) **Transferred Intent:** Where the defendant intends one tort against one person but injures another victim or commits a different tort (e.g., battery becomes assault when the defendant misses).
4. **Causation:** Causation is established using the "but for" approach.

B. Assault: An assault is defined as: (i) creating a reasonable apprehension in the plaintiff; (ii) of imminent harmful or offensive contact to the plaintiff's person; (iii) intent; and (iv) causation.

1. **Reasonable Apprehension:** A plaintiff has reasonable apprehension when he knows that he could be touched. If a plaintiff knows that he cannot be touched (e.g., an unloaded gun), he cannot recover.
2. **Imminent Contact:** The plaintiff must have an apprehension of a battery. Words alone lack eminence.
3. **Intent & Causation:** As defined above.

C. False Imprisonment: False imprisonment is defined as: (i) an act or omission by the defendant that confines and/or restrains the plaintiff; (ii) to a bounded area; (iii) intent; and (iv) causation.

1. **Confinement**: The confinement can be: (i) physical; (ii) a show of force; (iii) threats; (iv) invalid use of legal authority; or (v) the failure to act or get aid, when a duty to help exists. Note: Exclusion from an area is not false imprisonment, unless the plaintiff suffers an injury.
2. **Bounded Area:** The plaintiff is confined to a bounded area if: (i) her movement is limited in all directions; and (ii) no reasonable means of escape are known to the plaintiff.

D. Intentional Infliction of Emotional Distress: Intentional infliction of emotional distress is defined as: (i) an act by the defendant that amounts to extreme and/or outrageous conduct; (ii) intent/recklessness; (iii) causation; and (iv) damages.

1. **Extreme/Outrageous:** Conduct is considered extreme and/or outrageous if it transcends all bounds of decency tolerated in a civilized society. Normal conduct becomes extreme and/or outrageous if: (i) repetitive; (ii) the plaintiff is part of a fragile class; or (iii) committed by common carrier or innkeeper.
2. **Intent or Recklessness:** As defined above, or recklessness as to effect of the defendant's conduct.
3. **Causation:** As defined above. A third party may recover damages if she is: (i) present; (ii) a close relative; and (iii) the defendant had knowledge of both.

4. **Damages:** Actual damages are required; nominal damages are not available.

E. **Trespass:** A trespass requires: (i) an act of physical invasion of the plaintiff's real property; (ii) intent; and (iii) causation.

1. **Physical Invasion:** A physical invasion may be achieved by a person or object. A flying object must be unreasonably low to the ground. An intangible trespass may be achieved by noise in the case of nuisance.

2. **Intent:** There must be a deliberate or intentional act.

3. **Causation:** As defined above.

F. **Trespass to Chattel:** Trespass to chattel is defined as: (i) an act by the defendant that interferes with the plaintiff's right to possession of the chattel; (ii) intent; (iii) causation; and (iv) damages.

1. **Interference:** Interference is established by damage or dispossession.

2. **Damages:** The damages incurred must be actual. This includes loss of use.

G. **Conversion:** Conversion is defined as trespass to chattels that is so serious it warrants requiring the defendant to pay the chattel's full value.

1. **Acts of Conversion:** (i) theft; (ii) wrongful transfer or detention; (iii) substantial change in the property's character; or (iv) severe damage to the property.

2. **Serious Interference:** The longer the period of interference, the more likely that it is conversion.

3. **Damages:** The defendant will be required to pay the fair market value at time of conversion.

II. AFFIRMATIVE DEFENSES TO INTENTIONAL TORTS

A. **Consent:** The plaintiff must have had legal capacity and it cannot exceed scope of consent.

1. **Express:** Express consent is ignored where fraud or duress obtained such consent.

2. **Implied:** An objective standard is applied. It can be implied where a reasonable person would infer from custom or usage. Consent can be implied in law for a rescue.

B. **Arrest:** A person may perform an arrest using reasonable force for a misdemeanor committed in front of that person; however, deadly force may never be used. Similarly, for a felony, there needs to be a reasonable belief that the felony has been committed, a reasonable belief that the person committed it, and the use of reasonable force. No deadly force may be used unless there is a threat of death or serious bodily injury.

C. **Necessity:** The defendant may interfere with the real or personal property of another when it is reasonably necessary to avoid threatened injury that would be substantially more serious than steps taken to avert it.

1. **Public Necessity:** Where the tort is committed for the public good, there is no obligation to pay for damage.

2. **Private Necessity:** Where the tort is committed for a private good, the defendant pays for the actual damages, but not nominal or punitive damages.

D. **Defense of Self, Others, and Property**

1. **Of Self:** Conduct is excused where there is a reasonable belief of attack (or an actual attack). Only reasonable force is permitted. Deadly force may be used where there is an imminent threat of death or serious bodily Injury.

2. **Of Others:** If the defendant has a reasonable belief that another person could use force, then he is allowed to use reasonable force.

a) **Mistake:** A reasonable mistake of threat allowed.

3. **Property:** A demand to desist and/or leave is first required before using reasonable force in defense of property. Deadly force is forbidden.

   a) **Mistake:** A reasonable mistake is allowed.

4. **Recapture:** Recapture is defined as the privilege to enter the land of another to reclaim a chattel. In such cases, the defendant is not liable for reasonable damages.

   a) **Peaceable Means:** Peaceable means must be used to recapture when possession began peacefully. The defendant must demand the return of the chattel before entering the other's land.

   b) **No Mistake:** The defendant must not be mistaken; the chattel must actually be his.

5. **Shopkeepers:** The shopkeeper's defense applies when the defendant: (i) has the reasonable belief of theft; (ii) detains the other in a reasonable manner; (iii) for a reasonable period of time for purpose of investigation.

6. **Discipline:** The defense of discipline applies when reasonable force is used by a teacher or parent.

III. ECONOMIC HARM AND DIGNITARY INTERESTS

A. Defamation: Defamation is defined as: (i) defamatory language concerning the plaintiff; (ii) publication of the language; and (iii) damage to the plaintiff's reputation.

1. **Defamatory Language:** An assertion or allegation of fact that negatively affects the plaintiff's reputation. The statement must specifically identify the plaintiff.

2. **Publication:** The intentional or negligent communication of defamatory language to at least one other person than the plaintiff is required. Resellers will also be liable only if the defamation is known.

3. **Damages for Libel (Written Defamation):** In cases of libel, damages are presumed. A plaintiff does not have to prove damages for libel.

4. **Damages for Slander (Spoken Defamation):** In cases of slander, the plaintiff must prove up damages (i.e., economic loss).

5. **Damages for Slander Per Se:** In cases of slander per se, the plaintiff is not required to prove damages. Slander per se includes adverse statements regarding a person's business or profession, that he has a loathsome disease, or committed a crime of moral turpitude.

6. **First Amendment:** Where statements are regarding a matter of public concern, the plaintiff must prove: (i) that the statement is false; and (ii) fault on the part of the defendant.

   a) **Public Figures:** Under *NY Times v. Sullivan*, malice or reckless disregard for truth must be proven when brought by public officials or figures.

   b) **Private Persons:** Where the plaintiff is a private individual, only negligence regarding the falsity must be proven where there is public concern. Where malice is proven, punitive damages are available.

7. **Defenses to Defamation:** (i) *Truth* – the statements are factually accurate; (ii) *Consent* – by the defamed party; (iii) *Qualified Privilege* – between spouses, officers of the government in an official capacity; (iv) *Absolute Privilege* – Public interest in encouraging candor including references, credit reports, police statements, judicial proceedings.

8. **Vicarious Liability:** There is vicarious liability in report-publisher situations.

B. **Invasion of Privacy**

1. **Appropriation:** Appropriation is defined as the use of the plaintiff's name or picture by the defendant for the defendant's commercial advantage. In such cases, nominal damages are available.

   a) **Exception:** Appropriation associated with a news story is not actionable.

2. **Intrusion into Seclusion:** Intrusion into seclusion is defined as an act of spying or intruding into an area where the plaintiff has a reasonable expectation of privacy by means objectionable to a reasonable person.

3. **False Light:** False light is defined as attributing views or acts to the plaintiff that he didn't hold or take. False light is the: (i) publication of information (to more than one person); (ii) placing the plaintiff in a false light; (iii) that is offensive to a reasonable person.

4. **Disclosure:** Disclosure is: (i) publication (widespread) of; (ii) the plaintiff's private facts; (iii) that are highly objectionable to a reasonable person. The First Amendment requires that malice and fault need to be proven if the matter is of public concern.

5. **Defenses:** A defense to the invasion of privacy is consent. Truth and good-faith are not valid defenses unless it is a personal cause of action.

C. **Fraud:** Fraud is defined as: (i) misrepresentation; (ii) scienter (knowledge of falsity or the reckless disregard for the truth); (iii) intent; (iv) causation; (v) justifiable reliance; and (vi) damages (pecuniary).

D. **Negligent Misrepresentation:** Negligent misrepresentation is defined as: (i) misrepresentation by the defendant in a business capacity; (ii) breach of duty toward the plaintiff; (iii) causation; (iv) justifiable reliance; and (v) damages (pecuniary).

E. **Malicious Prosecution:** Malicious prosecution is defined as: (i) the institution of criminal and/or civil proceedings against the plaintiff; (ii) the termination in the plaintiff's favor; (iii) the absence of probable cause for liability and/or guilt; (iv) an improper purpose or malice; and (v) damages.

F. **Abuse of Process:** Abuse of process is defined as: (i) the wrongful use of the legal process for an ulterior purpose; and (ii) a definite act/threat against the plaintiff in order to accomplish that purpose.

G. **Interference with Business Expectancy:** Interference with a business expectancy is found when: (i) there is a valid contract between the plaintiff and a third party; (ii) the defendant has knowledge of the relationship; (iii) intentional interference by the defendant inducing breach or termination of the contract; and (iv) damages.

IV. NEGLIGENCE

Negligence is found when: (i) there is a duty on the part of the defendant to conform to a specific standard of care for protection of the plaintiff against unreasonable risk of injury; (ii) breach of duty by the defendant; (iii) the breach is the actual/proximate cause of the plaintiff's injury; and (iv) damages.

A. **Duty of Care:** A duty of care is owed to all foreseeable victims. The extent of that duty is determined by the applicable standard of care.

1. **Foreseeable Plaintiff:** A duty of care is only owed to foreseeable plaintiffs. Under the Cardozo view, a plaintiff can recover if she was located within the zone of danger created by the negligent conduct. Under the Andrew's view, every victim is foreseeable.

   a) **Rescuers:** Rescuers are foreseeable plaintiffs when the defendant negligently puts himself or a third person in peril.

2. **Standards of Care:** Where no specific duty is owed to the plaintiff, the applicable standard of care is that of a reasonably prudent person acting under similar circumstances.

   a) **Exceptions:** (i) **Superior Knowledge**: Where the defendant has special knowledge, the defendant is held to a standard of care of one with special knowledge; (ii) **Defendant's Characteristics**: A defendant's characteristics will be considered if relevant to the reasonable prudent person.

   b) **Specific Standards**

      (1) **Professionals:** Professionals are expected to provide the care of an average member of that profession who practices in a similar community. In professional malpractice cases, the custom sets the standard.

      (2) **Children:** A standard of care consistent with children of similar age, intelligence, and experience is employed. If the child is engaged in adult activity (e.g., driving), he is held to an adult standard of care. If the child is under the age of 4, he has no duty of care.

      (3) **Bailor:** A bailor must inform others of all known defects.

      (4) **Owners/Occupiers of Land**

         (a) **Undiscovered Trespasser:** An owner/occupier of land owes no duty to undiscovered trespassers.

         (b) **Discovered or Anticipated Trespassers:** An owner/occupier of land owes no duty to inspect the land to discovered or anticipated trespassers. **Conditions:** An owner/occupier of land must warn and make safe all known, man-made, concealed, dangerous conditions.

         (c) **Licensees:** Licensees are guests. An owner/occupier of land owes licensees no duty to inspect. **Conditions:** An owner/occupier of land must warn and make safe of all known or concealed traps existing on the land.

         (d) **Invitees:** Invitees are those individuals that come to engage in business activities or enter land that is held open to the public. An owner/occupier of land owes invitees the duty to inspect. **Conditions:** An owner/occupier of land must warn and make safe concealed conditions that he knows of (or should have known of) after reasonable inspection.

         (e) **Exceeding the Scope:** The applicable standard of care may fail where an invitee or licensee exceeds the scope of their permission to enter.

         (f) **Exceptions:** Fire and police officers (licensees) can never recover for an injury due to the inherent risks of their job. For child trespassers, a reasonably prudent person standard is employed regarding artificial conditions existing on the land when: (i) the land owner knows (or should have known) about artificial conditions; (ii) the land owner knows (or should have known) children frequent area; (iii) the condition is likely to cause injury; and (iv) the expense of fixing it is small when compared to the risk.

   c) **Negligence Per Se:** A statute's specific duty may replace the common law duty where: (i) there is a criminal statute that clearly defines the standard of care; (ii) the plaintiff is within class of protected people; or (iii) the statute was designed to prevent type of harm suffered. It conclusively establishes a duty owed and a breach of that duty.

   d) **Negligent Infliction of Emotional Distress (NIED):** Where the plaintiff suffered no physical injury, the plaintiff may recover for NIED where: (i) the defendant breached a duty owed to the plaintiff; (ii) although the plaintiff is not physically injured, the plaintiff was in the zone of danger; and (iii) the plaintiff suffered a subsequent physical manifestation of stress (this is not required for false death reports or the mishandling of a corpse).

(1) **Bystander:** A bystander may recover when: (i) present; and (ii) he is a close family member.

e) **Affirmative Duties to Act:** Generally, there are no affirmative duties to act.

(1) **Assumption:** One may assume a duty by acting to aid another. At that time, a reasonably prudent person standard is applicable.

(2) **Defendant's Fault:** Where the defendant caused peril (negligently or intentionally), he has the duty to act.

(3) **Preexisting Relationship:** (i) family, (ii) common carriers and inn keepers; and (iii) land occupiers to rescue invitee. The rescue must be reasonable under the circumstances, but one must not risk his own life.

B. Breach of Duty: A breach of duty is found when the defendant's conduct falls short of level required by applicable standard of care. On the exam, identify the specific wrongful conduct and explain why the conduct is unreasonable (i.e., there is another way to behave – employ a cost/benefit analysis).

1. **Res Ipsa Loquitur:** The very occurrence of the event establishes a breach where: (i) there is an accident causing the injury is a type that would not normally occur unless someone was negligent; (ii) the instrument that caused the injury was within the exclusive control of the defendant; and (iii) the plaintiff was not at fault.

C. Causation: Once negligent conduct is shown, the plaintiff must show that the breach was the cause of his injury.

1. **Actual Cause:** But for the conduct of the defendant, the plaintiff would not have suffered harm.

a) **Substantial Factor Test:** Where there are several causes that bring about the plaintiff's injury and any one of the causes alone would have been sufficient, the defendant's conduct is the cause in fact if it was a substantial factor in causing the harm.

b) **Alternative Causes:** Where there are alternative causes of injury and either could have caused the injury, the burden shifts to the defendant to prove that he is not the actual cause.

2. **Proximate Cause:** The defendant's conduct must also be the proximate legal cause of the plaintiff's injury. The defendant is generally liable for all harmful results that are foreseeable consequences of his act.

a) **Direct:** An uninterrupted chain of events from the defendant's conduct to the plaintiff's harm. The defendant is liable for the foreseeable harm and results.

b) **Indirect:** An affirmative intervening force comes into motion after the defendant's act and combines with it to cause the plaintiff's injury. The defendant is liable where the intervening act is foreseeable. Subsequent negligence is foreseeable, whereas intentional torts are not.

(1) **Always Foreseeable:** (i) subsequent medical malpractice; (ii) negligence of rescuers; (iii) defense of self, others, or property; and (iv) subsequent disease. An unforeseeable event will be considered superseding and will break the causal chain.

D. **Damages:** Damages are essential to recovery in negligence cases. Damages are never presumed, and nominal damages are not available. Punitive damages are not available absent wanton, willful, reckless, or malicious conduct. A plaintiff has a duty to mitigate damages after the fact.

E. **Defenses**

1. **Assumption of Risk:** The plaintiff assumes the risk if he: (i) knows of the risk; and (ii) voluntarily proceeded in the face of the risk. Assumption of risk is not applicable where there is no alternative or there is an emergency.

2. **Contributory Negligence:** Contributory negligence is found if the plaintiff is at fault and contributes to his own harm by failing to adhere to the same standard of care as the defendant. Even the slightest amount of fault (1%) will bar the plaintiff's recovery if the jurisdiction accepts this defense (only four states in the US do). However, the plaintiff can recover despite his contributory negligence if the defendant had the last clear chance to avoid injury. Contributory negligence is not imputed to another person unless there is an employer/employee relationship.

3. **Comparative Negligence**

   a) **Partial or Modified Comparative Negligence:** If the plaintiff's fault is less than 50% of the total fault, his recovery is reduced accordingly. If the plaintiff's fault is over 50% of the total fault, his recovery is barred.

   b) **Pure Comparative Negligence:** The plaintiff may recover regardless of how great his fault is.

V. STRICT LIABILITY

A. **Animals**

1. **Trespassing:** The defendant is strictly liable for foreseeable trespasses and foreseeable harm.

2. **Wild:** The defendant is strictly liable to licensees and invitees for personal injury, provided the plaintiff did not act to bring about harm. There is no strict liability in favor of undisclosed trespassers.

3. **Domestic:** The defendant is not strictly liable for his domestic animal's conduct unless he has knowledge of the particular animal's propensity that is not common to species (i.e., knowledge that the animal bites). The negligence standard is to be applied to the defendant for the animal's first bite. Thereafter, strict liability is applied to subsequent bites.

4. **Trespassers:** The defendant is not strictly liable to trespassers for his animal's actions. However, the defendant may be found to be negligent.

B. **Abnormally Dangerous Activities**: An activity is considered to be abnormally dangerous when: (i) the activity involves serious risk of harm; (ii) it cannot be performed without such risk regardless of care; and (iii) the activity is not common to community. Liability arises only if the harm results from an anticipated danger (i.e., chemicals spill from a chemical factory).

VI. PRODUCT LIABILITY

There are five theories of recovery in product liability: (i) strict liability; (ii) intentional conduct; (iii) negligence; (iv) implied warranties; and (v) representation.

A. **Strict Liability:** (i) the defendant is a commercial supplier; (ii) the product reached the consumer without substantial alteration; (iii) the product is defective and unreasonably dangerous; (iv) there is actual and proximate cause; and (v) damages.

1. **Commercial Supplier:** When a commercial supplier is involved, everyone up the chain of distribution is liable.

2. **Without Alteration:** Such is presumed if the product moved through the ordinary channels of distribution. For a used product, the plaintiff must show that there were no alterations to its original state.

3. **Defects**

    a) **Manufacturing:** A manufacturing defect arises when the product emerges different from and more dangerous than the correctly made products.

    b) **Design:** There is a design defect when every unit is defective. Here, apply the consumer expectation test (what would a reasonable consumer expect?) and the feasible alternative test (could a safer product be made?).

    c) **Failure to Warn:** Where the risk is not apparent, a manufacturer has a duty to warn customers of dangerous propensities.

4. **Damages:** For the plaintiff to recover, there must be personal injury or property damage. A plaintiff cannot claim damages for solely economic losses.

B. **Intentional Conduct:** A manufacturer will be liable for intentional torts if it knew that the injuries were substantially certain to occur. Any injured plaintiff can sue. Compensatory and punitive damages are available. The defenses of intentional torts apply here.

C. **Negligence**

1. **Duty:** The duty imposed is that of a reasonably prudent person in similar circumstances and it is owed to foreseeable persons. All users can sue.

2. **Breach:** A breach is shown by: (i) negligent conduct of the defendant leading to; (ii) supplying a defective product.

    a) **Retailer/Wholesalers:** Retailers and wholesalers are difficult to sue, as they only have cursory inspection duty.

3. **Causation:** Actual and proximate cause, defined above.

4. **Damages:** Personal injury or property damage is required. Solely economic loss is insufficient.

D. **Implied Warranties**

1. **Merchantability:** Under the implied warranty of merchantability, goods must be fit for ordinary purposes and be of average quality. Liability arises where: (i) the defendant is the merchant of goods of that kind; (ii) the product is not safe; (iii) actual proximate cause is present; and (iv) damages have been sustained.

2. **Fitness:** Under the implied warranty of fitness: (i) where the seller knows (or should have known) the plaintiff's particular purpose; (ii) that the plaintiff is relying on seller's skill or judgment; (iii) the product is not fit for that purpose; (iv) actual and proximate cause is present; and (v) damages have been sustained.

E. **Representation**

1. **Express Warranty:** An express warranty is: (i) an affirmation of fact or promise; (ii) regarding goods; (iii) during negotiations; (iv) that forms the basis of the bargain; (v) creating a warranty; (vi) a breach of warranty occurs; (vii) actual and proximate cause is present; and (viii) damages have been sustained.

2. **Misrepresentation:** A seller is liable for misrepresentation of facts concerning a product where: (i) the statement was of a material fact concerning quality or use of goods; and (ii) the seller intended to induce reliance by the buyer.

F. Defenses

1. **Failure to Mitigate:** A plaintiff's recovery may be reduced or precluded where there is a failure to mitigate (limit) damages.
2. **Contributory Negligence:** As defined above. However, contributory negligence is not a defense where the defendant failed to discover and/or protect against the defect, or where the misuse of the product was foreseeable.
3. **Assumption of Risk:** Voluntarily proceeding in the face of a known risk is a valid defense.
4. **Comparative Negligence:** As defined above, is an applicable defense.
5. **Multiple Parties:** A plaintiff is only allowed one satisfaction of her judgment. Consider the issues of contribution and indemnity.
6. **Disclaimers:** Disclaimers are not relevant unless they serve to establish an assumption of risk.

VII. NUISANCE

A. **Private:** Private nuisance is defined as: (i) the substantial, unreasonable (i.e., it outweighs the utility) interference; (ii) with another private individual's use or enjoyment of property; and (iii) he possesses or has the right to possess.

B. **Public:** Public nuisance is defined as an act that unreasonably interferes with health, safety, or property rights of the community.

C. **Remedies:** A plaintiff may receive damages and/or an injunction.

D. **Defenses:** Acting pursuant to legislative authority and coming to the nuisance (in essence assuming the risk) are valid defenses.

VIII. VICARIOUS LIABILITY

A. **Doctrine of Respondeat Superior:** An employer will be vicariously liable for the tortious acts committed by an employee, provided they occur within the scope of employment. Note: intentional torts are not within the scope of employment unless they are authorized as part of the employment. Remember to consider the extent of the employee's detour in assessing vicarious liability.

B. **Independent Contractors:** Vicarious liability does not apply to independent contractors. An employer can be liable for his own negligence in selecting or supervising the independent contractor. A land occupier is liable if an independent contractor hurts an invitee.

C. **Automobile Owner for Driver:** Vicarious liability does not apply to automobile owners for the actions of another driver. However, there may be negligent entrustment for the automobile owner's own negligence in entrusting a car to an unfit driver. An automobile owner can become vicariously liable if he sends someone on an errand as he becomes an agent.

D. **Parent-Child:** At common law, there was no parent-child vicarious liability. However, negligence on the part of parents may be found if the parents knew of their child's propensity for a particular act or course of conduct.

E. **Tavern Keepers:** Under common law, there was no liability for tavern keepers. Under modern law, ordinary negligence principals apply.

IX. MULTIPLE DEFENDANTS

A. **Joint and Several Liability:** Where two or more acts combine to proximately cause indivisible injury, both tortfeasors will be liable for the entire loss. If their acts are divisible, they will be liable for their own conduct.

B. **Satisfaction:** Recovery of full payment (or the agreement to accept a lower amount) is satisfaction.

C. **Release:** Under common law, release of one tortfeasor from an obligation or liability was a release of all. Under modern law, each tortfeasor must be individually released and the plaintiff can proceed against non-released parties.

D. **Contribution:** The concept of contribution allows a defendant who pays more than his fair share to have a claim against jointly liable parties for his excess payment.

E. **Indemnity:** Indemnity is full reimbursement from a co-tortfeasor.

F. **Government Immunity:** Government immunity is generally waived, though not for intentional torts where an employee was not acting within the scope of his employment.

G. **Survival:** Under common law, a victim's right to sue dies with the victim. Under modern law, states have survival statutes that allow others to sue on behalf of the deceased victim.

TRUSTS PRIMER

I. CREATION OF A VALID TRUST

A trust is a fiduciary relationship concerning property where one person, the trustee, holds a legal title to the trust property, the res, subject to the enforceable equitable rights of the beneficiary who holds equitable title. A trust is essentially a device whereby one or more persons manage property for the benefit of another.

For a valid trust, the creator of the trust (the settlor) must manifest the intent to create a trust for a valid trust purpose. The trust must contain identifiable property to be delivered to a trustee for the benefit of ascertainable beneficiaries.

A. Intent: There must be a present manifestation of trust intent made by settlor, demonstrated by written or spoken words. Precatory words (wish/hope) are not sufficient, unless they are accompanied by parol evidence. Oral trusts are valid unless the Statute of Frauds applies.

B. Valid Trust Purpose: Trusts can be established for any legal purpose, but are not valid if it is illegal, or contrary to public policy. If a single condition is illegal, try severance to avoid the failure of the trust. If the trust becomes illegal after creation, a resulting trust will result.

C. Trust Property (Res): Settlor must have a present existing property interest that is certain and identifiable. If the property interest comes into existence in the future, settlor must renew his intention to create a trust.

D. Trustee: A trust must have a trustee, but a court will not allow the trust to fail because there is not one and the court will appoint a trustee.

E. Beneficiaries: Any ascertainable person or group can be the beneficiary of a private express trust, including a corporation. They must be ascertainable at the time the trust comes into effect; otherwise, there is no one to enforce the trust. **Watch for Rule Against Perpetuity**

F. Method of Creation

1. **Testamentary Trust:** A testamentary trust is a trust that is created in a will.
2. **Pour-Over Trust:** Statutorily allowed in California, a pour-over trust is a trust where the property disposed of by the will is placed into a pre-existing trust. The pour-over clause must be validated either under incorporation by reference by identifying the previously existing trust, which the property will be poured into, or under the doctrine of acts of independent significance by referring to some act that has significance apart from disposing of probate assets, namely the revocable inter vivos trust, or under UTATA.
3. **Inter Vivos:** A trust can be created either by a person declaring himself trustee for another, or by the transfer of property to another as trustee. The present intent required must be manifested by conduct (delivery), or words (declaring oneself trustee). Delivery means placing the trust property out of the settlor's control (unless the settlor serves as the trustee).

II. TYPES OF TRUSTS

A. Mandatory Trust: A mandatory trust is a trust where the trustee lacks discretion and must pay in accordance with the terms of the trust. If the trustee fails to perform, the beneficiary can sue the trustee. **Example:** "Trustee shall distribute $1,000 per year to Beneficiary."

B. Discretionary Trust: A discretionary trust is a trust where the trustee is given sole and absolute discretion whether to apply or withhold payments to beneficiary to meet the intent of settlor.

The interest is alienable because assignors can receive payments whenever beneficiary would receive them.

1. **Duty to Inquire:** A trustee of a support trust has a duty to inquire as to the financial situation of the beneficiaries, regardless of absolute discretion; a trustee with absolute discretion does not actually have absolute discretion. Even those with absolute discretion must act with prudence and within reason. Inclusion of an exculpatory clause in an instrument in which the drafter is the trustee is not per se invalid. There must be some evidence of undue influence or overreaching.

C. **Revocable Trust:** A revocable trust is a trust where the settlor retains the right to amend, or revoke during the settlor's lifetime.

D. **Spendthrift Trust:** A spendthrift trust is a trust that is created for the benefit of a person, that gives an independent trustee full authority to make decisions as to how the trust funds may be spent for the benefit of the beneficiary. Creditors of beneficiary cannot reach the funds in the trust as payments are immune from voluntary/involuntary alienation. Therefore, a beneficiary's creditors cannot reach his interest until it has been paid to beneficiary.

1. **Exceptions:** Creditors have a right to the distributions for: (i) Suppliers of necessities (food, medical care); (ii) Alimony & child support obligations; (iii) Tort claims; (iv) Claims by government entities and taxes; and (v) Whenever a surplus exists over the standard of living. A trust that provides for voluntary, not involuntary, alienation is invalid for public policy reasons.

E. **Support Trust:** A support trust is a trust where the trustee is required to pay or apply only so much of the income or principal as is necessary for the support of the beneficiary. Even without a spendthrift clause, the interest is not alienable (voluntary/involuntary), as that would defeat the purpose of the trust.

F. **Honorary Trust:** An honorary trust exists where there is no ascertainable beneficiary and there is no substantial benefit on society. Since there is no named beneficiary, the implementation of the trust depends on the honor of the trustee. If the person does not execute the trust duties, he holds the property for the settlor or settlor's heirs on the theory of a resulting trust. **Rule Against Perpetuity issue**

G. **Secret Trust:** A secret trust exists where the will makes an absolute gift, on its face, to a named beneficiary. However, the gift was made in reliance upon the beneficiary's promise to hold the gift in trust for another. To prevent unjust enrichment, the court will hear extrinsic evidence of the agreement and, if proven by clear and convincing evidence, a constructive trust will be placed on the gift. **Always consider a semi-secret trust in this instance also.**

H. **Semi-Secret Trust:** A semi-secret trust exists where the will makes a gift to a person in trust, but does not name the beneficiary. As no beneficiary is named, the trust is unenforceable and a resulting trust results. **Always consider a secret trust in this instance also.**

I. **Charitable Trust:** A charitable trust is any trust that confers a substantial benefit upon society. The rules governing charitable trusts differ from those applicable to private trusts in three important ways: (i) A charitable trust must have indefinite beneficiaries; (ii) It may be perpetual; and (iii) The Cy Pres doctrine applies. The Rule Against Perpetuity does not apply.

1. **Cy Pres:** When a charitable purpose selected by the settlor is impractical, the court will select an alternative under the doctrine of Cy Pres, which means "as near as possible." The court must find general charitable intent by settlor and ascertain her primary purpose.

G. **Totten Trust:** A totten trust is a bank account for the benefit of a third party. It is not a true trust because the beneficiary simply takes whatever property is left when the trustee dies.

H. Resulting Trust: A resulting trust is a trust where a trust fails for want of a beneficiary, or other reason, such as the trust purpose has been completed. By operation of law, the trustee will hold a resulting trust in favor of the settlor's heirs.

I. Constructive Trust: A constructive trust is not really a trust, but rather a flexible equitable remedy to prevent unjust enrichment. The constructive trustee's only duty is to convey the property to the person who would have owned it, but for the wrongful conduct or failure of the trust/will.

III. MODIFICATION AND TERMINATION OF TRUSTS

A. Modification by Settlor: The modification of a trust is allowed if the settlor expressly reserves the right to modify, or has power to revoke.

B. Modification by Court: *See also Cy Pres.*

1. **Doctrine of Changed Circumstances:** Under the doctrine of changed circumstances, a court may, upon unforeseen circumstances, authorize a deviation from the administrative terms where it is necessary to achieve the trust purpose. Beneficiaries cannot be changed.

C. Termination of Revocable Trusts: In order to terminate a revocable trust, the settlor must expressly reserve this power in the trust instrument. A minority of jurisdictions do not require this.

D. Termination of Irrevocable Trusts: The settlor and all beneficiaries may agree to terminate the trust. All beneficiaries may agree to termination when the trust purpose has been accomplished. Or by operation of law (e.g., a passive trust [holding title]). The remaining res goes to the beneficiaries.

E. Reformation: Reformation is an equitable remedy that conforms the instrument to reflect what the settlor actually intended at the time of the trust execution.

IV. RIGHTS OF CREDITORS

A. Voluntary Alienation: Absent restrictions by statute, or by the trust instrument, a beneficiary may freely transfer his interest in the trust. The assigned interest remains subject to all previous conditions and limitations.

B. Involuntary Alienation: Absent restrictions by statute, or by the trust instrument (a spendthrift trust), an insolvent trust beneficiary's creditors may levy on his beneficial interest.

V. TRUST ADMINISTRATION AND DUTIES

A. Powers of the Trustee: A trustee has those powers expressly conferred by the trust instrument, state law and court decree, plus all powers implied as are necessary or appropriate to accomplish the trust purposes (sell property/spend/lease/borrow).

B. Fiduciary Duty: A trustee owes a fiduciary duty to administer the trust solely in the interest of the beneficiaries. A breach of duty can mean personal liability for the trustee.

C. Duty of Loyalty: The duty of loyalty requires that the trustee administer the trust for the benefit of the beneficiaries, having no other consideration in mind.

1. **Self-Dealing:** A trustee cannot enter into any transaction in which she is dealing with the trust in her individual capacity. A trustee owes a duty of undivided loyalty to the trust and its beneficiaries. Where court finds self-dealing, it applies the "no further inquiry rule," which says trustee will be liable, no matter how fair or reasonable the transaction. The trustee is personally liable for losses and will have profits disgorged.

a) **Trustee Options:** Obtain settlor authorization, court approval, or authorization from the beneficiaries. However, there must be full disclosure to all beneficiaries and the transaction must be objectively reasonable.

2. **Conflict of Interest:** If the trustee breaches the duty of loyalty by not acting in the best interest of the beneficiaries, available remedies include ratification by the beneficiaries, or surcharge of the trustee (including a suit for any loss).

D. Duty to Invest (Diversify): There are three alternate rules of the duty to invest:

1. **State Lists:** A trustee must follow state lists in absence of directions: (i) federal bonds; (ii) CDs; (iii) first deeds of trust only; and (iv) stocks.

2. **Common Law:** State list plus: (i) blue chip stocks; and (ii) mutual funds – never a second deed of trust.

3. **Uniform Prudent Investor Act:** Under the Uniform Prudent Investor Act, a trustee must act like a prudent investor based on an entire portfolio, not on an individual investment.

E. Duty to Earmark Trust Property: A trustee has a duty to earmark trust property. The trustee must label property as trust property. Under common law, failure to do so results in personal liability. Modernly, liability attaches only if there is a loss.

F. Duty to Segregate: A trustee has a duty to segregate, under which the trustee cannot commingle personal funds with trust funds or other trust funds. The trustee is liable for any loss.

G. Duty Not to Delegate: A trustee has the duty not to delegate, under which he can rely on professional advisors in reaching a decision, but cannot delegate decision-making authority. Modernly, he can delegate the duty to invest to a professional money manager.

H. Duty to Account: The duty to account requires the trustee, on a regular basis, to give beneficiaries a statement of trust income and expenses. A breach results in an action for accounting.

I. Duty of Care: A trustee has a duty of care. The trustee must act as a reasonable prudent person dealing with his own affairs.

J. Duty of Impartiality Between Beneficiaries: A trustee has a duty of impartiality between beneficiaries. If the beneficiaries are income beneficiaries, the trustee owes them the duty to maximize profits. If the beneficiaries are remainder beneficiaries, the trustee owes them the duty to protect the principal so money remains for them.

K. Remedies: Damages, constructive trust, tracing and equitable liens are available (until bona-fide purchaser is encountered). Ratification can occur if the breach was beneficial to the beneficiaries. Beneficiaries can void a prohibited transaction or remove a trustee.

VI. LIABILITY OF TRUSTEE TO THIRD PARTIES

A. Contract: Under common law, personal liability attaches unless sued as a trustee (indemnification from the trust can be sought). Modernly, if acting in representative capacity, there is no personal liability for the trustee.

B. Torts: Under common law, personal liability is present even if the trustee acted without fault, or where strict liability applies (indemnification from trust is available). Modernly, personal liability attaches only where the trustee is at fault; otherwise, trust vicarious liability attaches because the trustee acted in a representative capacity.

VII. INCOME AND PRINCIPAL

A. **To Life Tenant:** A life tenant receives cash dividends, interest income and net income. A life tenant pays interest on loans, taxes and minor repairs.

B. **To Remainderman:** A remainderman receives stock dividends, splits and proceeds on sale of trust assets. A remainderman pays loan principal, for major repairs and improvements.

C. **Adjustment Power of Trustee:** The trustee can disregard the above rules to administer the trust fairly (e.g., to provide for a life tenant).

WILLS PRIMER

See full outline for statutory cross-references

I. IS THERE A VALID WILL?

A. Formal Attested Will:

A. Formal Attested Will: A formal attested will requires: (i) a writing; (ii) a signature by the testator anywhere on the will (or by another person in the testator's presence at his or her direction); (iii) execution in the joint presence of at least two witnesses (who, alternatively, can witness the testator's acknowledgement); and (iv) who understand that the instrument being witnessed is the testator's will.

1. **Witnesses:** Witnesses need not sign in the presence of the testator, or each other; they can sign before testator dies. Also, the witness can sign first, and no attestation clause is needed.

2. **Conscious Presence Test:** The testator signs, or acknowledges the will within the witness's hearing, and the witness knows what is being done.

3. **Dates:** The date of execution is not required, but if it is inconsistent, the dated will controls. If there is no date and there is a lack of capacity, it must be proven that the testator had capacity.

B. Holographic Wills: The signature and material provisions are in the testator's own handwriting. Commercial preprinted wills are valid.

C. Falling Short of Compliance

1. **Dispensing Doctrine:** If there exists clear and convincing evidence that the testator intended the document to be his will, the court will ignore the lack of formality and probate the will.

2. **Substantial Compliance:** If the testator substantially complies with the requirements and there is clear and convincing evidence that the testator intended the document to be her will, it will be probated.

D. Testamentary Capacity

1. **Mental Capacity:** The testator must: (i) be 18 years old; (ii) be able to communicate wishes; and (iii) understand the nature of the disposition and its effects. If the testator is significantly impaired (unable to understand or appreciate the consequences of his or her actions with respect to the will), the will is set aside.

2. **Insane Delusion:** Insane delusion exists where: (i) the testator has a false belief; (ii) that is the product of a sick mind; (iii) there is no evidence to support the delusion; and (iv) the false belief affected the will. In such cases the gift is void.

3. **Mistake:** Mistake in the execution of the will, results in failure of the will due to the absence of testamentary intent. A court will not rewrite a will to remedy an omission by mistake. For a mistaken addition, the court can strike the applicable provision. When a gift is induced by an erroneous belief, there is no relief unless the mistake is on the face of the will (for example: "I would have given the property to X, but X is dead.").

4. **Undue Influence:** Undue influence is mental/physical coercion that deprives the testator of free will. Prima facie: (i) the testator is susceptible to influence; (ii) another's opportunity and disposition to influence occurs; (iii) provisions are unnatural. Undue influence is presumed where: confidential relationship (attorney/client, etc.) exists, or where there is a trust relationship. Statutory presumptions include: drafter of the document or one related

to her, employed by her, or is a fiduciary of her, or in a relationship with testator. This is not applicable if she is related to the testator who has an independent attorney, or where the court says there is clear and convincing evidence of no undue influence. As a result, the will can fail in whole or in part.

5. **Fraud:** Fraud is: (i) representation; (ii) of material fact; (iii) known to be false; (iv) for the purpose of inducing action/inaction; (v) that results in action/inaction. Fraud in the Execution: fraud regarding nature/contents of instrument; Fraud in Inducement: influences contents. Remedies include revocation of the applicable section and/or a constructive trust.

II. HAS THE WILL BEEN REVOKED?

A. By Written Instrument

1. **Express Revocation:** This can be made by a later will or codicil executed with the formalities required for a valid attested/holographic will.
2. **Implied Revocation:** This can be ascertained from the terms of a subsequent instrument. To the extent the second will makes an inconsistent disposition of property, the terms of the prior will are nullified. Where there is only a partial inconsistency, both are probated.

B. Physical Act: The instrument may be torn, burned, canceled, obliterated, or destroyed with simultaneous intent to revoke by the testator (revocation can also occur at the testator's direction).

C. Interlineation: In California, a will can be revoked in part as well as in whole by physical act. Interlineation of a holographic will is both a revocation of an altered provision and new disposition. Prior signature of a holographic will is adopted when the interlineation is made. Interlineation of a formal will must be accompanied by the testator's signature and be witnessed.

D. Codicil/Will: A revoked codicil does not revoke a will; a revoked will revokes a codicil and papers incorporated by reference. Revocation of a duplicate will is treated as revocation of the original.

E. Dependent Relative Revocation (DRR): DRR applies when the testator revokes a will, or provision upon the mistaken belief that another disposition of the property is effective and, but for this mistake, he/she would not have revoked the will. In California, DRR applies to revocation by physical act and subsequent instrument. If the other disposition fails, the revocation is set aside and the original will remain in force.

F. Revival: California has adopted the substance of the Uniform Probate Code. If will #2 is revoked by physical act, extrinsic evidence can prove the testator's intent to revive will #1. If will #2 was revoked by later will (will #3), will #1 is not revived unless will #3 so states.

G. Missing Will: A will is considered missing if it was last in the testator's possession, the testator was competent until death, and neither the original nor duplicate original of the will can be found after testator's death. The missing will is presumed destroyed with intent to revoke. If the presumption is rebutted, photocopies can be used to prove contents.

H. Revocation by Operation of Law:

1. Divorce: Unless the will provides otherwise, if testator divorces (or domestic partnership is dissolved), any disposition of property made to former spouse or domestic partner, or power of appointment, will be revoked. Remarriage to the spouse revives the disposition.

III. COMPONENTS OF THE WILL

A. Integration: All papers intended to be part of the will and are actually present at execution are integrated into the will if the testator so intended.

B. Republication by Codicil:

1. **Codicil:** A codicil is a testamentary instrument modifying an earlier will and must be executed with the same formalities as a will.

2. **Republication by Codicil:** Such republishes a will (re-executed at the time of codicil; consider omitted child issues and curing a defective will).

C. Incorporation by Reference: A separate document may be incorporated into a will by reference if: (i) it is in existence at the date of the will; (ii) it is clearly described in the will; (iii) it is proven to be the document described; and (iv) the testator intended to incorporate it by reference. Holographic wills can incorporate printed material.

Exam Tip: Republication by codicil can incorporate a writing not in existence when the will was executed.

D. Facts of Independent Significance: Blanks in a will can be filled in by referring to facts or documents executed during the testator's life. The critical issue is whether the fact/document has a sufficient significance apart from the will. In California, the acts may occur before/after execution of the will or before/after testator's death. Extrinsic evidence regarding identity of "X" will be admitted as an act of independent significance because people do not do "X" just to validate a devise in a will; they do "X" for reasons independent of the will.

E. Uniform Testamentary Additions to Trusts Act (UTATA): This is a pour-over provision. If there is a valid trust, which was in existence before a will is executed, a pour-over provision is valid by statute, even where the trust is amended after the will.

IV. INTERPRETATION OF THE WILL

A. Admission of Extrinsic Evidence

1. **Ambiguity:** In California, extrinsic evidence is admissible to explain any ambiguity or circumstances of a will execution. Such evidence will not be admitted to contradict a will.

V. RIGHTS OF OMITTED SPOUSES AND CHILDREN

A. Omitted Spouse: If a testator fails to provide in a will for the surviving spouse who married the testator after the execution of the will/codicil, the law presumes that he forgot to include the omitted spouse and she shall receive one-half of the testator's community property/quasi-community property; separate property = intestate share, up to one-half (including trusts).

1. **Exceptions:** (i) the failure to provide was intentional and it appears in instrument; (ii) Testator provided for spouse outside of the will and evidence shows the testator's intent that the transfer be in lieu of a testamentary gift; or (iii) spousal waiver (signed writing following disclosure with the advice of an independent attorney or objective fairness).

B. Omitted Children: If a testator fails to provide in a testamentary instrument for a child born/adopted after executing the will, the omitted child shall receive a share in the decedent's estate equal in value to that which the child would have received intestate (including trusts).

1. **Exceptions:** (i) the failure was intentional and it appears in will; (ii) Testator directed the disposition of substantial part of the estate to a parent; or (iii) Testator provided for the child by transfer outside of the will and evidence shows intent that the transfer be in lieu of testamentary gift.

2. **Decedent's Erroneous Belief:** If, at time of execution, the testator believed the child was dead, or he/she is unaware of the birth, the child gets the intestate share.

VI. BARS TO SUCCESSION

A. Interested Witnesses: If a will is signed by an interested party (not executrix or relative of beneficiary), it does not invalidate the will or any provision. However, unless there are at least two other signing disinterested witnesses, a presumption arises that the devise was procured by duress, fraud, or undue influence. Rebuttable Presumption: With a failure to rebut, a witness loses their share above intestate succession.

B. Prohibited Transferees: California holds invalid any will provision making a donative transfer to: (i) the drafter of the will; (ii) a relative living with or employed by drafter; (iii) a partner/shareholder/employee of a law partnership where drafter has an ownership interest; or (iv) a person who has a fiduciary relationship with the testator (or his/her relative, lives with, employed by) who transcribes the will or causes it to be transcribed.

1. **Exceptions:** Provision is valid if testator is related to, or lives with, the domestic partner of the drafter, or the will is reviewed by an independent attorney.

2. **Rebuttable Presumption:** Transferee may establish by clear and convincing evidence transfer was not the product of fraud, duress, or undue influence. If there is a failure to rebut, the transferee loses share above intestate succession.

C. Slayer Statute: One who intentionally kills the testator is not entitled to: (i) any benefit under a will or trust; (ii) the testator's property by intestate succession; or (iii) any of the testator's quasi-community property. The determination is made by conviction or by a preponderance of the evidence. The burden is on the challenger.

D. Elder Abuse: The beneficiary is deemed to have predeceased the testator where all of the following apply: (i) there is clear and convincing evidence the person abused is an elder/dependent adult; (ii) the beneficiary acted in bad-faith; (iii) the beneficiary acted recklessly, fraudulently, or maliciously; and (iv) the testator was unable to manage her finances, resist fraud, or undue influence.

E. No Contest Clause: A no contest clause is enforceable against a beneficiary who brings a contest within the terms of the clause.

1. **Not a contest** unless identified in the will: (i) a creditor's claim; (ii) an action regarding ownership of property; and (iii) the validity of the document containing the clause.
2. **Not a contest for public policy:** Action regarding: (i) the interpretation of the instrument containing the no contest clause; or (ii) reformation of the instrument to carry out testator's intent.

3. **Unenforceable no-contest clause:** Not enforceable where the beneficiary with:

   a) **Reasonable cause** brings a contest due to: Forgery, revocation, or to establish if someone is a prohibited transferee. Reasonable cause causes a reasonable person to believe that the allegations filed with the court may be, or are likely to be, proven.

   b) **Probable cause** contests a provision that benefits: (i) the drafter; (ii) a person who gave directions to the drafter; or (iii) a person who acted as a witness.

VII. DEVISES UNDER THE WILL

A. Lapse: Under common law, when a beneficiary dies after the testator executes his will but before the testator dies, the gift to the beneficiary fails.

B. Anti-Lapse: California has an anti-lapse statute providing a substitute beneficiary for a devisee who predeceased the testator. The statute applies only if the devisee who predeceased the testator was kindred of testator, or testator's surviving, deceased, or former spouse and left issue to take in his place. The anti-lapse statute applies to class gifts, but does not apply if the will expresses a contrary intention or substitute disposition.

C. Ademption by Extinction: If a gift made in the will is not there upon death, it is presumed the testator did not want the person to receive it. Only specific gifts adeem.

Exceptions:

1. **Money Owed Testator:** (i) balance owed to the testator for the sale of property; (ii) Eminent domain proceeds; (iii) insurance proceeds; or (iv) property acquired by foreclosure.
2. **Gifts Sold by Conservator:** Will gift recipient receives the sale price of the property, eminent domain award, or the proceeds of insurance.
3. **Exoneration of Liens:** Recipient takes the property subject to any deed of trust or lien, without right of exoneration, even where there is a directive to pay debts.
4. **Securities:** Securities owned by testator, includes stock acquired as a result of a merger, consolidation, purchase, or stock split.

D. Ademption by Satisfaction: Property given by the testator during his or her lifetime is a satisfaction of an at-death transfer if: (i) the will provides for the deduction of the lifetime gift from an at-death transfer; (ii) the testator declares in a contemporaneous writing that the gift is in satisfaction; (iii) the transferee acknowledges in writing that the gift is in satisfaction; or (iv) the property given is the same as the specific gift to that person.

E. Abatement: Gifts are reduced (abated) when the estate is not sufficient to pay debts or legacies. If the testator indicates an order of abatement, her wishes control. Otherwise the following order is observed: (i) intestate property; (ii) residuary gifts; (iii) general gifts to non-relatives; (iv) general gifts to testator's relatives; (v) specific gifts to non-relatives; (vi) specific gifts to testator's relatives. Gifts are abated pro-rata within a class.

1. **Abatement to Satisfy Omitted Spouse/Child:** (i) if gifts not passing under intestate/inter vivos trust; then (ii) all beneficiaries pro rata.

F. Advancements (intestate only): A gift is an advancement against an heir's intestate share if: (i) the testator states in a contemporaneous writing a gift is an advancement; and (ii) the heir acknowledges same.

G. Conditional Will: Such is one whose validity is made conditional by its own terms. It is not to be probated unless the condition is satisfied.

H. Cancellation: Cancellation to increase a gift is prohibited (e.g., B gives to C and D. If D cannot take the gift, D's one-half goes to the residuary/intestate; it does not go to C).

I. Survival: Clear and convincing evidence of survival is required to take under a will; but 120 hours of survival is required for intestate succession.

VIII. TOTAL OR PARTIAL FAILURE OF THE WILL: INTESTATE SUCCESSION

A. Who are the Decedent's Heirs?

1. **Adoption:** Adoption severs familial relationship with the natural family and establishes familial relationship with the adoptive family.

a) **Exceptions:** An adoptive child still inherits from natural parent if: (i) natural parent lived with the adopted child as a parent (or would have, but for death); AND (ii) adoption follows death of natural parent OR step-parent adoption.

b) **True Whole Blooded Siblings (WBS)** of the adopted child inherit from him whenever he would have inherited from the natural parent (i+ii).

2. **Equitable Adoption:** Under common law, if a natural parent gives up custody to a third party with the understanding that the third party will adopt and treat the child as a natural heir when the third party dies, courts will equitably enforce a child's right to claim as though he or she had been formally adopted.
3. **Foster or Step-Parent:** Intestate succession from or through a foster parent or stepparent if: (i) the relationship began in minority and continued through their joint lifetimes, and (ii) clear and convincing evidence establishes that the parent would have adopted, but for a legal barrier (e.g., the natural parent would not consent).
4. **Children Born Out of Wedlock:** Neither a natural parent nor relative of that parent inherits from/through child unless the parent acknowledged the child and the parent contributed to the support or the care of the child.
5. **Half-bloods:** Relatives of the half-blood inherit as if they were of the whole blood. Exception: Not through an adopted sibling.
6. **Unborn Relatives of the Decedent:** They inherit as though they were born in the lifetime of the decedent. However, if he/she is born more than 300 days after the testator's death, there is a rebuttable presumption the person is not the testator's child.

B. Did the Heirs/Beneficiaries Survive the Decedent?

1. **General Intestate:** If devolution of property depends upon priority of death and it cannot be established by clear and convincing evidence that one person survived the other by 120 hours, the property of each person shall be distributed as if that person had survived the other.

C. Is Succession Barred? Supra.

D. Share of Surviving Spouse: In California, the surviving spouse always gets the deceased spouse's community property and quasi-community property where the deceased left no will. As the surviving spouse already owned the other one-half of the community property and quasi-community property, the decedent's spouse owns 100% of the community property and quasi-community property. However, the surviving spouse's share of the deceased spouse's separate property depends on which other heir(s) survive:

1. Separate property: **Spouse 100% - Heirs 0%:** No issue, parents, or issue of parents (siblings, nieces/nephews, etc.)
2. Separate property: **Spouse 50% - Heirs 50%:** One issue, OR no issue but 1+ parent or issue of parent.
3. Separate property: **Spouse 33.3% - Heirs 66.6%:** Two or more issue; i.e., 2+ children, 1 child & 1+ grandchild, etc.

E. Share Not Passing to Surviving Spouse: Each category takes to the exclusion of all others: (1) Issue (children, grandchildren, great-grandchildren, etc.); (2) Parents; (3) Issue of parents; (4) Grandparents; (5) Issue of grandparents; (6) Issue of a predeceased spouse; (7) Next of kin (blood relatives, no matter how remote); (8) Parents of predeceased spouse; (9) Issue of parents of predeceased spouse; (10) California.

1. **Distribution:** Distribution within a given class that takes is determined by modern per stirpes:

   Step 1: Find the first generation with a living member (skip dead generations).

Step 2: Divide shares into as many lines that have living member, plus deceased lines leaving living issue.

Step 3: Distribute shares to the living members of that first living generation plus deceased lines leaving issue. For predeceased members leaving issue, divide up and distribute their share to their issue by right of representation.

2. **Strict Per Stirpes:** Distribute to first living generation.

IX. MISCELLANEOUS

A. Contracts Relating to Wills: Contract to make/revoke a will or die intestate is established only by one of the following: (i) provisions of a will/instrument stating the material provisions of the contract; (ii) express reference in will to a contract and extrinsic evidence proving the terms of the contract; (iii) the actual contract; or (iv) clear and convincing evidence of an agreement.

1. **Joint/Mutual Wills:** These do not create a presumption of a contract not to revoke will(s); joint will = one will; mutual wills = two wills that mirror each other.

2. **Effect:** If a contract concerning a will is broken, an action for damages against the testator's estate/constructive trust on the testator's beneficiaries may exist, but any duly executed will must be probated. A suit in contract to recover the value of services, or for whatever breach, is appropriate. Spousal care is not valid consideration for a contract as a pre-existing duty is not consideration.

B. Non-Probate: Specific California Probate Code Provisions: Technically not intestate succession

1. **Joint Tenants:** Without clear and convincing evidence that one survived the other, property shall be administered one-half as if one tenant had survived and one-half as if the other tenant had survived. The slayer statute applies and the perpetrator is treated as predeceased with no survivorship right.

2. **Life/Accident Insurance:** Without clear and convincing evidence that the beneficiary survived the insured, proceeds shall be administered as if the insured had survived the beneficiary, unless provided otherwise. The slayer statute also applies.

C. Choice of Law: A will can be probated in California if it complies with laws of California, the jurisdiction wherein it was executed, or the jurisdiction where the testator was domiciled.

Issue Spotter Outlines

Agency & Partnerships Issue Spotter

Agent-Principal Relationship

Independent Contractors

Tort Liability

Contract Liability
- Actual Express
- Actual Implied
- Apparent Authority
  - Lingering
- Ratification
- Termination
- Liability

Duties of Agent
- Care
- Obey Reasonable Instructions
- Loyalty

Liabilities to 3rd Parties:
- Agents for usual partnership business
- Torts
- Contracts
- Estoppel

Duties of Partners
- Loyalty

Rights
- Property Transfer
- Profit / Loss Sharing
- Equal Vote

Dissolution/Winding Up/Termination
- Liability Remaining
- Priority: Outside, inside creditors; partner capital
- Contributions

Civil Procedure Issue Spotter

Subject Matter Jurisdiction
Diversity: Total $ amount, domicile = subjective intent + presence
$75k+ (agg 1p, 1d)
Fed Questions
Supplemental: Common nucleus/same transaction or occurrence
Removal: Within 30 days if the federal court has jurisdiction
Venue: Where all Ds reside, where any D resides if all in same state, or cause of action arose
Transfer: Court needs personal jurisdiction
Interest of Justice: Public – law; private – evidence
Non-Conveniens: Public/private

Personal Jurisdiction
Traditional: Serve / domicile / consent
Long Arm
Contact: Personally availed & foreseeable
Fairness: Relatedness, convenience, state interest

Choice of Law: Erie in diversity

Joinder of Parties
Permissive: Same transaction / occurrence; common questions of law / fact
Compulsory: Incomplete relief without it/interests harm

Joiner of Claims
Compulsory: Same transaction/occurrence
Impleader: Third party defendant owes indemnity/contribution
Interpleader: All claimants into one suit
Intervention: Interest harmed if not joined

Class Actions
Prejudice: To class member
Injunction: Treated the class the same
Damages: Common questions = superior method no clog

Summary Judgment: No genuine issues

Judgment as a Matter of Law: After side heard, reasonable people could not disagree on result. Viewed in favor of non-moving party.

Claim Preclusion: Same parties / final judgment / same cause of action
Issue Preclusion: Final judgment on the merits/ issue actually litigated/essential/ against party to prior suit
Traditional: mutuality
Modern: non-mutual defensive: fair chance to litigation
Non-mutual offensive: (i) identical issue; (ii) final judgment; (iii) fair opportunity to litigate; and (iv) fair to use collateral estoppel (foreseeable)

Community Property Issue Spotter

Step 1: Basic Presumption
Step 2: Threshold Questions
a) Relationship of Parties

Valid CA Marriage / Non-CA Marriage
Putative Marriage
Meretricious Relationships/Non-Marital
Domestic Partnerships

b) Character of Property

Quasi-CP; Quasi-Marital
Spousal Support K; Child Support
Premarital Contract

c) Creditor's Rights

Premarital; Martial; Post Separation
Child/Spousal Support
Tort Liability

Step 3: Divide Up the Property
Step 4: Characterize the Property
a) Source of Funds

(i) PI Awards
(ii) Pension
(iii) Disability
(iv) Severance
(v) Bonus
(vi) Stock
(vii) Education / Training
(viii) Life Ins
(ix) Preemption
(x) Married Woman's Presumption

b) Action

(i) Transmutation
(ii) Improvements: CP own SP/other SP; SP to CP
(iii) Commingling
(iv) SP / CP funds for Debt
(v) Title of Property
(vi) Growth in SP business by Comm. Labor: Pereira / Van Camp / Cal. Supreme Court
(vii) Growth in CP by Post Sep. Labor

c) Presumption Overcome?
Step 5: Management and Control

CP; Limitations; Fiduciary Duty

Step 6: Distribution: 50/50

Statutory Exceptions
Death-Widow's Election
Out of State Property

Constitutional Law Issue Spotter

Justicability
- Ripeness
- Abstention
- Mootness
- Political Question
- Standing
- 11th Amendment

Federal Executive Power
Federal Legislative Power
- Tax and Spend
- Commerce Clause

State Legislation
- Preemption
- Dormant Commerce Clause
- Privileges and Immunities
- Contracts Clause
- State Tax of Interstate Commerce

Individual Rights
- State Action
- Procedural Due Process
- Substantive Due Process
- Equal Protection
- Takings

Speech
- Facial Attack: Prior Restraint, Vagueness, Overbroad, Unfettered Discretion
- Content Based
  - Defamation
  - Fighting Words
  - Commercial
  - Obscenity
- Content Neutral
  - Public / Limited Public Forum
  - Non-Public Forum

Religion
- Free Exercise Clause
- Establishment Clause

Association

Symbolic Speech

Contracts Issue Spotter

Applicable Law / Predominant Purpose

Valid Contract
- Offer
- Acceptance
- Consideration
- Defenses

Statute of Frauds

Modification

Terms

Warranties
- Title
- Express
- Implied Warranty of Merchantability
- Implied Warranty of Fitness

Third Party Right
- 3rd Party Beneficiaries
- Assignment
- Delegation

Conditions
- Excuse
- Impossibility / Impracticability / Frustration

Breach
- Material
- Minor

Remedies
- Rejection; Accept; Revoke Acceptance; Withhold Goods

Damages
- Compensatory; Reliance; Restitution; Incidental & Consequential
- Liquidated
- Specific Performance: Conditions Satisfied, Inadequate Legal Remedy, Mutuality, Feasibility

Defenses
- Laches/Unclean Hands/Hardship/Misrepresentation
- Quasi-Contract: Restitution for Unenforceable Contract

Corporations Issue Spotter

Formation Issues

Was the corporation validly created?
Can the corporate veil be pierced?
Who is liable? What are the types of liability?
Who may pierce?

Stock Issuance

Stock Subscriptions
Valid Issuance
Classification of Stock
Dividends
Repurchase/Redemption

Stock Transfer Liability

Common Law
Rule 10b-5; Insider Trading
Section 16(b)
Section 11
Sarbanes-Oxley Act

Duties/Rights of Promoters, Shareholders, Directors and Officers

Promoters

Fiduciary Duty
Pre-incorporation Agreements

Shareholders

Meetings
Voting Rights
Proxy Votes
Preemptive Rights
Shareholder Suits
Distributions
Shareholder Liabilities

Directors

Qualifications
Election
Powers
Removal
Meetings
Duties and Liabilities
Limitation of Personal Liability
Duty of Care
Duty of Loyalty

Officers

Duties / Powers
Standard of Conduct
Resignation and Removal
Indemnification

Terminating/Changing the Corporate Structure

Criminal Law & Procedure Issue Spotter

Accomplice Liability
Accessory after the Fact
Solicitation
Conspiracy
Attempt

Property Crimes
False Pretenses
Robbery
Embezzlement
Larceny / Trick

Personal Crimes
Kidnapping
Rape
Assault - Battery

Murder
1st: Pre Med / Felony Murder
Voluntary Manslaughter
2nd Degree
Involuntary Manslaughter
General Intent: Arson, Battery, Rape, Kidnapping

Defenses
Complete: Insanity; Involuntary Intoxication; Infancy
Partial: Vol. Intoxication / Withdrawal
Justifications: Self-defense, of others, of property
Mistake of Fact
Impossibility of Law
Entrapment

Arrest: P/C - reasonable caution person committed offense
R/S - criminal activity is afoot
4th Amendment
Right: REP + government conduct
Warrant? Exceptions
5th Am: custody + interrogation
6th Am: post charge + offense specific
14th Am: due process – coercion
Exclusionary Rule - Poisonous Tree; Exceptions:
Attenuation
Good-faith
Independent Source
Inevitable Discovery

Evidence Issue Spotter

Step 1: Question Form and Prop 8

Step 2: Logical Relevance & Legal Relevance

Step 3: Form
- **Documents:** Authentication; Best Evidence Rule
- **Testimony:** Competency; Personal Knowledge

Step 4: Category
- **Notice**
- **Opinion**
- **Character**
- **Habit**

- **Hearsay**
  - Not for the Truth
  - Not HS
  - Documents
  - Availability Irrelevant
  - Unavailable Declarants
  - Catch All & 6th Amendment

Step 5: Impeachment
- **Extrinsic Evidence OK**
  - Convictions
  - Bias and Prejudice
  - Bad Reputation for Truth
  - Inconsistent Statements
- **No Extrinsic Evidence**
  - Prior Bad Acts (lying): CA Extrinsic Evidence OK

Step 6: Privilege

Step 7: Policy Exclusions
- **Subsequent Remedial Measures**
- **Medical Expenses**
- **Offers to Settle**

Professional Responsibility Issue Spotter

I. The Duties to the Client

a) Duty of Loyalty

- (1) Client With Diminished Capacity
- (2) Concurrent Conflicts of Interest
- (3) Special Kinds of Conflicts
  - (a) Adverse Financial Interests
  - (b) Improper Use of Information Adverse to Client
  - (c) Designating Oneself as a Beneficiary
  - (d) Media Rights
  - (e) Financial Assistance to Client
  - (f) Fees Paid by Other Party
  - (g) Multiple Party Representation
  - (h) Limiting Liability for Malpractice
  - (i) Settling Malpractice Claim with Unrepresented or Former Client
  - (j) Lawyers w/ a Relationship
  - (k) Sexual Relations
  - (l) Liability Insurance
- (4) Former Clients
- (5) Organizations
- (6) Attorney as Witness
- (7) Conflicts When an Attorney Leaves a Firm
- (8) Former Government Employees

(b) Duty to Preserve Client's Confidential Information
(c) Duty of Confidentiality
(d) Duty of Competence
(e) Duty to Protect Clients Property
(f) Duty of Financial Integrity

II. Duties To Third Parties
(a) Duty of Fairness to Opposing Parties
(b) Duty to Accept Representation

III. To the Court
(a) The Duty of Candor
(b) The Duty of Honesty
(c) The Duty to Witnesses and Jurors

IV. To the Profession
(a) Unauthorized Practice of Law
(b) Avoid False and Misleading Advertisements
(c) Presumed False/Misleading
(d) Not Improperly Solicit Clients
(e) Personal Contacts with Family, Clients, Former Clients, and other Lawyers
(f) Direct Mailings
(g) Harassment
(h) Group and Prepaid Legal Service Plans

Real Property Issue Spotter

Landlord Tenant
- **Leasehold**
- **Rights: Implied Covenant of Quiet Enjoyment**
  - **Implied Covenant of Habitability**
- **Duties: Waste**
  - **Not Illegal Purpose**
- **Assignment**
- **Fixtures**

Rights in Land of Another
- **Easement**
  - **Creation:** P I N G
    - Prescription
    - Implication
    - Necessity
    - Grant
  - **Characteristics**
    - Affirmative / Negative
    - Appurtenant / In Gross
  - **Scope**
  - **Termination**

License

Profits

- **Covenant Running w/ Land at Law**
  - **Burden**
  - **Benefit**
  - **Remedy**
  - **Termination**
- **Equitable Servitude**
  - **Creation**
  - **Burden**
  - **Benefit**
  - **Defenses**

- **Adverse Possession:** HOAC

Conveyancing
- **Land Sale Contract**
- **Equitable Conversion**
- **Deed**
  - Conditional delivery ok
  - Covenants: Seisin, Right to Convey, Encumbrances,

Torts Issue Spotter

Intentional Torts
- Battery / Assault
- False Imprisonment
- Intentional Infliction of Emotional Distress
- Trespass to Chattles / Land, Conversion
- Defenses

Intentional Interference with Business Expectancy

Defamation

Invasion of Privacy

Fraud

Negligent Misrepresentation

Malicious Prosecution

Abuse of Process

Negligence

Strict Liability

Products
- Strict Liability
- Negligence
- Warranties
- Defenses

Nuisance

Vicarious Liability

Joint and Several Liability, Survival

Survival Statutes

Damages + Injunction

Trusts Issue Spotter

Valid Trust
- Intent
- Valid Trust Purpose
- Trust Property (Res)
- Trustee
- Beneficiaries
- How: Testamentary / Pour-Over / Inter Vivos

Characterization
- Mandatory
- Discretionary Trust
- Revocable Trust
- Spendthrift Trust
- Support Trust
- Honorary Trust
- Secret Trust
- Semi-Secret Trust
- Charitable Trust
- Totten Trust
- Resulting Trust
- Constructive Trust

Modification and Termination of Trusts
- Modification by Settlor
- Modification by Court: Doctrine of Changed Circumstances
- Termination of Revocable Trusts
- Termination of Irrevocable Trusts
- Reformation

Rights of Creditors
- Voluntary & Involuntary Alienation

Trust Administration and Duties
- Powers of the Trustee
- Duty of Loyalty: Self-Dealing; Conflict of Interest
  - Invest (diversify)
  - Earmark Trust Property
  - Segregate
  - Not to Delegate
  - Account
  - Care
  - Impartiality Between Beneficiaries
  - Remedies

Liability of Trustee to Third Parties

Income and Principal

Wills Issue Spotter

Valid Will
- Formal Attested Will / Holographic
- Dispensing Doctrine / Substantial Compliance
- Capacity / insane delusion
- Undue Influence
- Fraud: Execution / Inducement
- Mistake

Revocation
- Instrument: Express / Implied
- Physical Act
- Dependent Relative Revocation & Revival
- Missing Will
- Revocation by Operation of Law

Components
- Integration
- Incorporation by Reference
- Facts of Independent Significance
- Republication by Codicil

Interpretation: Ambiguity / Extrinsic Evidence

Bars to Succession
- Interested Witnesses & Prohibited Transferees
- Slayer Statute & Elder Abuse
- No Contest Clause

Distribution
- Changes to Property
  - Ademption
  - Satisfaction
  - Advancements
- Changes to People
  - Omitted Children / Spouse
  - Lapse & Anti-Lapse
  - Ademption & Mitigation

Intestate
- Decedent's Heirs?
- Survival: 120 hrs
- Succession Barred?
- Surviving Spouse / Rest of estate

Miscellaneous
- Contracts Relating to Wills
- Non-Probate: Joint Tenants / Insurance

Notes

Notes

Notes

Made in the USA
Las Vegas, NV
17 October 2024